Design and Analysis of ALGORITHMS

Design and Analysis of ALGORITHMS

Hitesh Singh
B.Tech., M.Tech. (CDAC, Noida)
Executive MBA IIT Mumbai
Assistant Professor, HMRITM, Delhi

Dr. Nidhi Arora
Ph.D. (CSE), MCA, BCA, MBA
Associate Professor, HMRITM, Delhi

KHANNA BOOK PUBLISHING CO. (P) LTD.
::: ***Publisher of Engineering and Computer Books*** :::

Head Office : 4C/4344, Ansari Road, Darya Ganj, New Delhi-110002
Phone: 011-23244447/48 Fax: 011-23244447
Regd. Office : 1694-95, Nai Sarak, Delhi-110006
Phone: 011-23283211 Fax: 011-23256658
E-Mail : contact@khannabooks.com
Website : www.khannabooks.com, www.khannapublishers.com

DESIGN AND ANALYSIS OF ALGORITHMS
Hitesh Singh & Nidhi Arora

First Edition 2013

Published by:
Khanna Book Publishing Co. (P) Ltd.
4C/4344, Ansari Road, Darya Ganj, New Delhi-110 002
Phone: 011-23244448 Telefax: 011-23244447
E-mail: contact@khannabooks.com
Website: www.khannabooks.com

Regd. Off: 1694-95, 1st Floor, Nai Sarak, Delhi-110006 (India)
Phone: 011-23283211 Telefax: 011-23256658

Cover Design & Layout by
Ajay Arts, New Delhi

Printed in India by:
S.P.S. Printers & Binders, Delhi

CONTENTS

CHAPTER 17: GRAPH TRAVERSAL 194

CHAPTER 18: DIRECTED ACYCLIC GRAPHS 210

CHAPTER 19: UNDIRECTED GRAPHS 226

CHAPTER 27: APPROXIMATE ALGORITHMS 339

CHAPTER 28: NP-COMPLETENESS 346

CHAPTER

1

ALGORITHM

1.1 INTRODUCTION

An algorithm is an effective method for solving a problem expressed as a finite sequence of steps. Algorithms are used for calculation, data processing and many other field. In more advanced or obstruct setting the instruction do not necessarily constitute a finite sequence, and even not necessarily a sequence. Each algorithm is a list of well-defined instruction for completing a task. Starting from in initial state, the instruction describe a computation that process through or well-defined series of successive states, eventually terminated in a final ending not necessarily deterministic, some algorithms are known as randomized algorithms, incorporate randomness.

Therefore an algorithm is a well-defined computational procedure that takes some values an input and procedure that takes some values an input an produces a value or set of values, as output. An algorithm is thus a sequence of computational steps that train storm the input into output. An algorithm is thus a sequence of computational steps that transform that input into an output.

"An algorithm is a well-ordered collection of unambiguous and effectively computable operations that when executed produces a result and halts in a finite amount of time.

1.2 CHARACTERISTICS OF ALGORITHMS

With the definition, we can identify the important characteristics of algorithms.

1. Algorithms are well ordered.
2. Algorithms have unambiguous operations.
3. Algorithms have effectively computable operations.
4. Algorithms produce a result.
5. Algorithms halt in finite amount of time.

These characteristics need a little more explanation, So we will look at each one in detail. Algorithms are well ordered.

Since an algorithm is a collection of operation or instructions, we must known the correct ordered in which to execute the instructions. If the order is unclear, we may perform the wrong instruction or we may be uncertain which instruction should be performed next. This characteristic is especially important for computers. A computers can only execute an algorithm if it knows the exact order of steps to perform-

Algorithms have unambiguous operations:

Each operation in an algorithm must be sufficiently clear so that it does not need not to be simplified.

Given a list of numbers, you can easily order them from largest to smallest with the simple instruction" sort these numbers". A computer, however, needs more detail to sort number. It must be tole to search for the smallest number, how to find the smallest number, how to compare numbers together, etc. The operation "Sort these number" is ambiguous to a computers because the computers has no basic operation for sorting. Basic operations used for writing algorithms are known as primitive operations or primitives. When an algorithm is written in computer primitives, then the algorithm is unambiguous and the computer can be execute t

Algorithms produce a result

In our simple definition of an algorithm, we stated that an algorithm is a set of instructions for solving a problem. Unless an algorithm produces some result, we can never be certain whether our solution is correct. Have you ever given a command to a computer and discovered that nothing changed? What was your response? You probably thought that the computer was malfunctioning because your command did not produce any type of result. Without some visible change, you have no way of determining the effect of your command. The same is true with algorithms. Only algorithms which produce results can be verified as either right or wrong.

Algorithms halt in a finite amount of time

Algorithms should be composed of a finite number of operation and they should complete their execution in a finite amount of time. Suppose we want to write an algorithm to print all integers greater than 1. Our steps might look something like this.

1. Print the number 2
2. Print the numbers 3
3. Print the number 4

   :

   :

   Print the number n

while our algorithm seems to be pretty clear, we have two problems. First, the algorithm must have an infinite number of steps because there are an infinite number of integers greatest than one. Second, the algorithm will seem forever trying to count to infinity. These problems violate our definition that an algorithm must halt in a finite amount of time. Every algorithm must reach some operation that tells it to stop.

1.3 HOW TO WRITE ALGORITHMS?

When writing algorithms, we have several choice of how we will specify the operations in our algorithm One options is to write the algorithm using plain English. Although plain English may seen like a good way to write an algorithm, it has some problems that make it a poor choice, First, plain English is too wordy when we write in plain English, we must include many words, that contribute to correct grammar or style but do nothing to help communicate the algorithm. Second, plain English is too ambiguous. Often an English sentence can be interpreted in many different ways Remember that our definition of an algorithm required that each operations be unambiguous

Another opinion for writing algorithm is using programming language. These language are collection of primilines (basic operations) that a computer understands. While programming language avoid the problems of being wordy and ambiguous. They have some other disadvantages that make them undesirable for writing algorithms consider the following lines of code from the programming language C++.

```
    a = 1;
    b = 0;
  white (a < 10)
    {
    b = b + a;
       a ++ ;
    }
    cout << b;
```

This algorithm sums the numbers from 1 to 10 and displays the answer on the computer screen. However, without some special knowledge of the C++ programming language, it would be difficult for you to know what this algorithm does using a programming language to specify algorithms mean learning special syntax and symbols that are not part of standard English. for example, in the code above, it is not very obvious what the symbol "++" or the symbol "<<" does. When we write algorithms, we would rather not worry about the details of a particular programming language.

Example 1: Let try to present the Scenario of a man brushing his own teeth as an algorithm as follows:

Steps 1: Take the brush

Steps 2: Apply the paste

Steps 3: Start brushing

Steps 4: Rinse

Steps 5: Wash

Steps 6 : Stop

If one goes through these 6 steps without being aware of the statement of the problem, he could possibly feel that this is the algorithm for cleaning a toilet. This is because of several ambiguities while comprehending ever step. The step 1 may imply tooth brush, paint brush, toilet brush etc. such an ambiguity doesn't an instruction an algorithm step thus every step should be made unambiguous an unambigious step is called definite instruction even if the step 2 is rewritten as apply the tooth past, to eliminate ambiguities yet the conflicts such as, where to apply the tooth paste and where is the source of the tooth paste, need to be resolved. Hence, the act of applying the tooth paste is not mentioned. Although unambiguous, such unrealized steps can't be included as algorithmic instruction as they are not effective. The definiteness and effectiveness of an instruction implies the successful termination of the algorithm. Therefore, while designing an algorithm are should be taken to provide a proper termination for algorithm.

Thus every algorithm should have the following fine main features:

1. Input
2. Output
3. Definiteness
4. Effectiveness
5. Termination

Therefore an algorithm can be defined and effective instruction, which terminates with the production of correct output from the given input. In other words, viewed little more formally, an algorithm is a step by step by step formalization of a mapping function map input set onto an output set. The problem of writing down the correct algorithm for the above problem of brushing the teeth is left reader. For the purpose of clarity in unde.standing let us consider the following examples:

Example 2:

Problem: Finding the largest value among n > = 1 numbers.

Input: The value of n and n numbers.

Output: the largest value

Steps

1. Let the value of the first be the largest value denoted by BIG
2. Let R denote the number of the remaining number
   R = n –1
3. If R! = 0 then it is implied that the list in still not exhausted. Therefore look the next number called NEW.
4. Now R becomes R – 1
5. If NEW is greater, then BIG then replace BIG by the value of NEW.
6. Repeat steps 3 to 5 until R becomes zero
7. Print BIG
8. Stop.

1.4 ALGORITHMIC EFFICIENCY

The two most frequently encountered and measurable metrics of an algorithm are:

1. Speed or running time: The time taken by an algorithm to be complete.
2. Space: The memory or non volatile storage used by the algorithm during its opeation.

Other metrics of an algorithm are:

- Transmission size, such as required band width during normal operation.
- Size of external memory, such as temporary disk space used to accomplish its task.
- The size of required long-term disk space required after its operation to record its output or maintain its required function during its required useful lifetime.
- The performance per watt and the total energy, consumed by the chosen hardware implementation (with its system requirements, necessary auxiliary support systems including interfaces, enabling switching, cooling and security), during its required lifetime.

The process of making code more efficient in known as optimization and in the case of automatic optimization, usually focus or space at the cost of speed or vice versa. There are also quite simple programming techniques and avoidance strategies, that can actually improve both at the same time, usually irrespective of hardware, software or language. Even the recording or rested conditional statements, to put the least frequently occurring condition first, can reduce actual instruction path length something an optimizing compiler would almost certainly note be aware of, but which a programmer can research relatively easily even without specialist medical knowledge.

1.4.1 Speed

The absolute speed of an algorithm for a given input can simply be measured as the duration of execution and the results can be averaged over several executions to eliminate possible random effects. Most modern processor, operate in a multi-processing and multi-programing environment so consideration must be made for parallel process occurring on the same physical machine, eliminating these as for as possible. For superscalar processors, the speed of a given algorithm can sometimes be improved through instruction-level parallelism within a single processor (but, for optimal results, the algorithm may require some adaptation to this environment to gain significant advantage ('Speedup'), becoming, in effect, an entirely different algorithm.) A relative measure of an algorithms performance can sometimes be gained from the total instruction path length which can be determined by a run time instruction set simulator.

An estimate of the speed of an algorithm can be determined in various ways. The most common method uses time complexity to determine the Big–O of an algorithm. See Run-time analysis for estimating how fast a particular algorithm may be according to its type (example: lookup unsorted list, lookup sorted list etc.) and in terms of scalability its dependance on 'size of input', processor power and other factors.

1.4.2 Space

Although, it is possible to make an algorithm faster at the expense of memory. This might be the case whenever the result of an 'expensive' calculation is cached rather than recalculating it afresh each time. The additional memory requirement would, in this case, be considered additional overhead although, in many situation, the stored result occupies very little extra space and can often be held in precompiled static storage, reducing not just processing time but also allocation & deallocation of working memory. This is a very common method of improving speed, so much so that some programming languages often add special features to support it, such as C++'s 'mutable' keyword.

The memory requirement of an algorithm is actually two separate but related things:-

(1) The memory taken up by the compiled executable code (the object code on binary file) itself/on disk or equivalent, depending on the hardware and language). This can often be reduced by preferring run-time decision making mechanisms (such as virtual functions and run-time type information) over certain compile-time decision making mechanism (such as macro substitution and templates). This, however, comes at the cost of speed.

(2) Amount of temporary "dynamic memory" allocated during processing for example, dynamically pre-caching results, improves speed at the cost of this attribute even the depth of sub-routine calls can impact heavily on this cost and once increase path length too, especially if there are 'heavy dynamic memory requirement for the particular functions invoked. The use of copied function parameters (rather than simply using pointers to earlier, already defined, and sometimes static values) actually doubles the memory requirement for this particular memory metric. This can be particularly relevant for quite 'lengthy parameters such as html script, Javascript source programs or extensive freeform text such as letters or emails.

1. What is an algorithm.

Sol. An algorithm is a procedure used to solve a well defined computational problem.

1. What is an algorithm? What are the criteria to be satisfied by an algorithm? [Osmania University]
2. Briefly explain how to analyze algorithms. [OU]
3. Write an algorithm to add an element to a circular queue. [OU]
4. What are five criteria that an algorithm must satisfy? [OU]

5. What are the factors on which the execution time of a program depends? [OU]
6. What do you understand by Analysis of Algorithms? Justify its nees. [MDU]

Example 1: Write an algorithm to find the smallest of 3 numbers?

Smallest (p, q ,r,)

P : first number

q: Second number

r: Third number

1. Set p ← {Enters first number}
2. Set q ← {Enter third number}
3. Set r ← {Enter third number}
4. If (p > q & p < r) then
5. print "A is smallest "& Exit
6. If (q < r & q < p) then
7. Print "q is smallest "& Exit
8. If (r < p & r < q) then
9. print "r is smallest "& Exit.

Example 2: Write an algorithm to swap two numbers using third variable?

swap (x, y)

x : First number

y: Second number

1. set x ← {Enter first number}
2. Set y ← {Snter second number}
3. set z ← x
4. set x ← y
5. Set y ← z
6. Exit

Example 3: Write an algorithm to swap two numbers without using third variable?

Swap (A, B)

A: First number

B: Second number

1. Set A ← {First number}
2. Set B ← {Second number}
3. Set A ← A + B
4. Set B ← A – B
6. Exit.

Example 4: Write an algorithm that reads a list of 50 integer values and prints the total of the list.

Val: list in a variable

SUM: accumulator

C: Counter

1. SUM = O
2. C = O
3. Read a number in Val
4. C = C + 1;
5. SUM = SUM + Val;
6. Compare C and 50;
7. If C is less than 50 repeat step 3 to 6
8. Print SUM
9. Exit

CHAPTER

2

ANALYSING AND DESIGN OF ALGORITHMS

2.1 INSERTION SORT

Insertion sort is an efficient algorithm for sorting a small number of elements. Insertion sort works the way many people sort a hand of playing cards. We start with an empty left hand and the cards face down on the table. We then remove one card at a time from the table and insert it into the correct position in the left hand. To find the correct position of the card, we compare it from each of the card already in the hand, from right to left as shown in the Fig. 2.1.

Fig.2.1 Playing Cards

In insertion sort we have:

Input: A sequence of n numbers al, a2, a3 an

Output: A permutation of input sequence a' l, a' 2, a' 3 a' n such that a' 1 < a' 2 < < a' n.

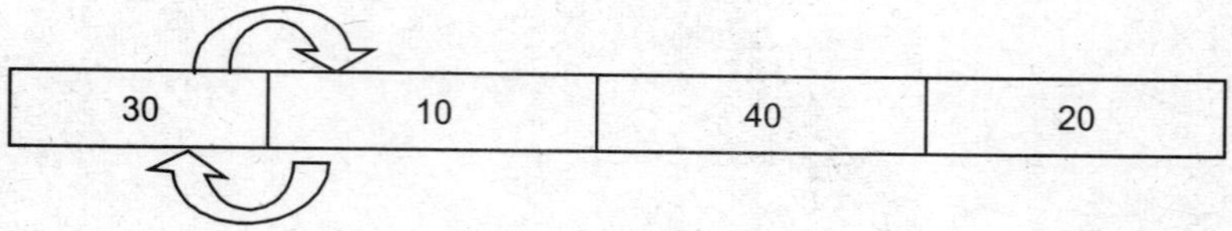

Fig. 2.2a

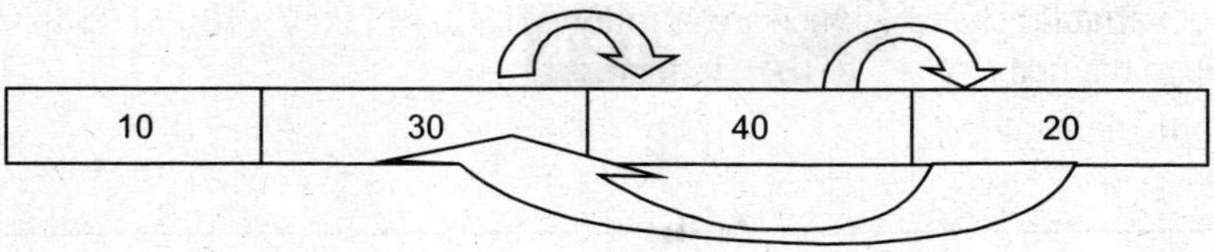

Fig. 2.2b

10	30	40	20

Fig. 2.2c

Suppose that we have an array of four numbers as shown in Fig. 2.2a. in that we choose second element as a key and compare it with first one. As 10 is less than 30 so we swap it. After swapping we get array as shown in Fig. 2.2.b. Now we compare second element with third in which 30 is less than 40, so there is no problem. Now when we compare third element with fourth one then we have a problem. As 40 is greater than 20. So we start finding the position right from the beginning of the array in order to fix that element. So we put fourth element in second position and shift rest of the elements toward the right side, as shown in the Fig. 2.2b. After that we have got a sorted array as shown in Fig. 2.2c.

The algorithm for insertion sort is as follows:

```
insertion Sort (A, n)
{
For I = 2 to n {
Key = A[i]
J = I – 1
While (j>0) and (A[ j ] > key)
{
A [j + l] = A[j]
J = j –1
}
A [ j + 1] = key
}
}
```

This is the algorithm for insertion sort. Let us see how this algorithm actually works line by line. In first line: Insertion Sort (A, n) { For I = 2 to n { Key = A[i] J = I – 1; we have an array

30	10	40	20
1	1	3	4

In this the value of different variables are as follows: I = 0, j= 0, key = 0, A[j] = 0, A[j+1] = 0. Now when we move to the line While (j > 0) and (A [j] > key) we have got the same array.

30	10	40	20
1	1	3	4

But the value of variables change, which are as follows: I = 2, j= 1, key = 10, j 30, A j+1 = 10. After that when we move to the line A j 1 A j then

we have got following values:

30	30	40	20
1	2	3	4

= 2, = 1, key = 10, = 30, +1 = 30. Then when line J j 1 is implemented we have got following result.

30	30	40	20
1	2	3	4

I = 2, j= 1, key = 10, A j = 30, A j+1 = 30. Now after while loop is implemented we have got

30	30	40	20
1	2	3	4

1 = 2, = 0, key = 10, = 0, +1 = 30. Now following line will be implemented: A j 1 e In that we have got following result.

30	30	40	20
1	2	3	4

= 2, = 0, key = 10, = 0, +1 = 10, and the algorithm will proceed in following manner. This is the actual working of insertion sort algorithm.

2.2 ANALYSE OF INSERTION SORT

The time taken by insertion sort depends on the input we have taken. Suppose we have taken thousanc items so it will take lot of time as compare to these items taken for sorting. In general, the time taken by ar algorithm grows with the size of the input, so it is traditional to describe the running time of a program as a unction o t e si e o its input. The input size depends on the problem being studied. For example in sor: algorithm, the input size depends on total number of items to be sorted. In multiplying two integers it wil depend on the total number of bits needed to represent the input in ordinary binary notation. In graphs the input size can be described by the numbers of vertices and edges in the graph.

The running time of an algorithm on a particular input is the number of primitive operations or "steps" executed. A constant amount of time is required to execute each line of our pseudo-code. One line may take a different amount of time than another line, but we shall assume that each execution of the ith line takes time ci, where ci is a constant.

We start by presenting the INSERTION-SORT procedure with the time "cost" of each statement and the number of times each statement is executed. For each = 2, 3 ... n, where n = length , we let i be the number of times the while loop test in line 5 is executed for that value of . When a for or while loop exits in the usual way (i.e., due to the test in the loop header), the test is executed one time more than the loop body. We assume that comments are not executable statements, and so they take no time.

	INSERTION-SORT (A)	cost times
1	for ← 2 to length	c_1 n
2	do key ← A	c_2 n–l
3	▷ insert Aft into the sorted sequence l... -1 .	0 n–l
4	i← – l	c_4 n–l
5	while i > 0 and i > key c_5	$c_5 \sum_{=2}^{n} t$
6	do i + l ← i	$c_6 \sum_{=2}^{n} (t\ -1)$
7	i ← i – 1	$c_7 \sum_{=2}^{n} (t\ -1)$
8	i + l ← key	c_8 n –1

Fig. 2.3 Insertion sort analysis

The running time of the algorithm is the sum of running times for each statement executed; a statement that takes ci steps to execute and is executed n times will contribute c_{in} to the total running time. To compute (n), the running time of INSERTIONSORT, we sum the products of the cost and times columns, obtaining

$$(n) = c_1 n + c_2 (n - l) + c_4 (n{-}l) + c_5 \sum_{=2}^{n} t + c_6 \sum_{=2}^{n} (t\ -1) + c_7 \sum_{=2}^{n} (t\ -1) + c_8 (n-1)$$

For the INSERTION-SORT, the best case occurs if the array is already sorted. For each j = 2, 3, .., n, we then find that i > key in line 5 when i has its initial value of –1 us t_j l for = 2, 3, .., n, and the best-case running time is: t_j is t e number o time t e ile loop is executed or t at alue o j

$$(n) = c_1 n + c_2 (n - 1) + c_4 (n - 1) + c_5 (n - 1) + c_8 (n - 1)$$
$$= (c_1 + c_2 + c_4 + c_5 + c_8)\ n - (c_2 + c_4 + c_5 + c_8)$$

This running time can be expressed as an b for constants a and b that depend on the statement costs ci it is thus a linear function of n.

If the array is in re erse sorted order-that is, in decreasing order-the orst case results. We must compare each element with each element in the entire sorted sub-array l... –l , and so t_j j for = 2, 3,..., n. Noting that:

$$\sum_{=2}^{n} \quad = \frac{n(n+1)}{2}, \text{and} \sum_{=2}^{n} (\ \ -1) = \frac{n(n+1)}{2}$$

This will result

$$(n) = c_1 n + c_2(n - l) + c_4(n - l) + c_5\left(\frac{n(n+1)}{2} - 1\right) + c_6\left(\frac{n(n-1)}{2}\right) + c_7\left(\frac{n(n-1)}{2}\right) + c_8(n-1)$$

$$= \left(\frac{c_5 + c_6 + c_7}{2}\right) n^2 + \left(c_1 + c_2 + c_4 \frac{c_5 - c_6 - c_7}{2} + c_8\right) n - 1(c_2 + c_4 + c_5 + c_8)$$

This worst-case running time can be expressed as $an^2 + bn + c$ for constants a, b, and c, that again depend on the statement costs c_i; it is thus a uadratic unction o n.

2.2.1 Worst-case and average-case analysis

The worst-case running timeof an algorithm is an upper bound on the running time for any input. Knowing it gives us a guarantee that the algorithm will never take any longer. The "average case" is often roughly as bad as the worst case. Suppose that we randomly choose n numbers and apply insertion sort. How long does it take to determine where in sub-array A[l.. .j – 1] to insert element A[j], On average, half the elements in A [l ...j – 1] are less than A[j], and half the elements are greater. On average, therefore, we check half of the sub-array A [l ...j – 1], so tj = j/2. If we work out the resulting average-case running time, it turns out to be a quadratic function of the input size, just like the worst-case running time. This worst-case running time can be expressed as $an^2 + bn + c$ for constants a, b, and c. To find the order of growth we consider only the leading term of a formula (e.g, an^2 since the lower-order terms are relatively insignificant for large n. We also ignore the leading term's constant coefficient, since constant factors are less significant than the rate of growth in determining computational efficiency for large inputs.

Thus,we write that insertion sort for example, has a worst-case running time of $\theta\ n^2$ (pronounced "theta of n-squared"). We usually consider one algorithm to be more efficient than another if its worst-case running time has a lower order of growth. Due to constant factors and lower-order terms, this evaluation may be in error for small inputs. But not for large enough inputs. We will discuss order of growth in next chapter.

2.3 MATHEMATICAL INDUCTION

Mathematical induction is a method of mathematical proof typically used to establish that a given statement is true of all natural numbers, or otherwise is true of all members of an infinite sequence. A somewhat more general form of argument used in mathematical logic and computer science shows that expressions that can be evaluated are equivalent; this is known as structural induction.

The simplest and most common form of mathematical induction proves that a statement holds for all natural numbers n and consists of two steps:

1. The basis: showing that the statement holds when n = 0.
2. The inductive step: showing that if the statement holds for n = m, then the same statement also holds for n = m + 1. (The proposition following the word "if is called the induction hypothesis. Do not call step 2 as a whole the induction hypothesis.)

This method works by first proving the statement is true for a starting value, and then proving that the process used to go from one value to the next is valid. If these are both proven, then any value can be obtained by performing the process repeatedly. It may be helpful to think of the domino effect; if you have a long row of dominos standing on end and you can be sure that:

1. The first domino will fall.
2. Whenever a domino falls, its next neighbour will also fall.

Example: Mathematical induction can be used to prove that the following statement

$$0 + 1 + 2 + ... + n = \frac{n(n+1)}{2}$$

holds for all natural numbers n. It gives a formula for the sum of the natural numbers less than or equal to number n. The proof that the statement is true for all natural numbers n proceeds as follows. Call this statement P(n). Basis: Show that the statement holds for n = 0.

P(0) amounts to the statement:

$$0 = \frac{0\ (0+1)}{2}.$$

In the left-hand side of the equation, the only term is 0, and so the left-hand side is simply equal to 0. In the right-hand side of the equation, 0 (0 + l)/2 = 0. The two sides are equal, so the statement is true for n = 0. Thus it has been shown that P(0) holds.

Inductive step: Show that if P(n) holds, then also P(n + 1) holds. This can be done as follows. Assume P(n) holds (for some unspecified value of n). It must then be shown that P (n + 1) holds, that is:

$$(0 + l + 2 + \dots + n) + (n + l) = \frac{(n+1)(n+1)+1}{2}$$

Using the induction hypothesis that P(n) holds, the left-hand side can be rewritten to:

$$\frac{n(n+1)}{2} + (n+1).$$

Algebraically:

$$\frac{n(n+1)}{2} + (n+1) = \frac{n(n+1)+2(n+1)}{2}$$

$$= \frac{(n+1)(n+2)}{2}$$

$$= \frac{(n+1)(n+1)+1)}{2}$$

Thereby showing that indeed P (n + 1) holds.

Since both the basis and the inductive step have been proved, it has now been proved by mathematical induction that P(n) holds for all natural n.

2.3.1 Generalizations

This type of proof can be generalized in several ways. For instance, if we want to prove a statement not for all natural numbers but only for all numbers greater than or equal to a certain number b then the following steps are sufficient:

1. Showing that the statement holds when n = b.
2. Showing that if the statement holds for n = b then the same statement also holds for n = b + l.

This can be used, for example, to show that $n^2 > 2n$ for $n \geq 3$. Note that this form of mathematical induction is actually a special case of the previous form because if the statement that we intend to prove is P(n) then proving it with these two rules is equivalent with proving P(n + b) for all natural numbers n with the first two steps.

Assume true for all lesser values

Another generalization, called complete induction, allows that in the second step we assume not only that the statement holds for n = m but also that it is true for n smaller than or equal to m. This leads to the following two steps

1. Showing that the statement holds when n = 0.
2. Showing that if the statement holds for all m d $\leq$ b then the same statement also holds for n = m + 1.

This can be used, for example, to show that $\text{fib}(n) = [\Phi^n - (-1/\Phi)^n] / 5^{1/2}$ where fib(n) is the nth Fibonacci number and $\Phi = (1 + 5^{1/2}) / 2$ (the so-called golden mean). Since fib(m + 1) = fib(m) + fib(m – 1) it is straightforward to prove that the statement holds for m + 1 if we can assume that it already holds for both m and m – 1.

Also this generalization is just a special case of the first form:

let (n) be the statement that we intend to prove, then proving it with these rules is equivalent to proving the statement ' (m) for all m ≤ n' for all natural numbers n with the first two steps.

2.3.2 Transfinite induction

The last two steps can be reformulated as one step:

1. Showing that if the statement holds for all n < m then the same statement also holds for n m.

This is in fact the most general form of mathematical induction and it can be shown that it is not only valid for statements about natural numbers, but for statements about elements of any well-founded set, that is, a set with a partial order that contains no infinite descending chains (where < is defined such that a < b iff a ≤ b and a ≠ b).

This form of induction, when applied to ordinals (which form a well-ordered and hence well-founded class), is called transfinite induction. It is an important proof technique in set theory, topology and other fields.

Proofs by transfinite induction typically need to distinguish three cases:

1. m is a minimal element, i.e. there is no element smaller than m
2. m has a direct predecessor, i.e. the set of elements which are smaller than m has a largest element
3. m has no direct predecessor, i.e. m is a so-called limit-ordinal

2.4 DIVIDE-AND-CONQUER ALGORITHM

i ide and con uer is an important algorithm design paradigm. It works by recursively breaking down a problem into two or more sub-problems of the same (or related) type, until these become simple enough to be solved directly. The solutions to the sub-problems are then combined to give a solution to the original problem. This technique is the basis of efficient algorithms for all kinds of problems, such as sorting (quicksort, merge sort) and Fourier transform (FFT).

2.4.1 Implementation

Divide-and-conquer algorithms are naturally implemented as recursive procedures. In that case, the partial sub-problems leading to the one currently being solved in implicitly stored in the procedure call stack. However, D&C solutions can also be implemented by a non-recursive algorithm that stores the partial sub-problems in some explicit data structure, such as a stack, queue, or priority queue. This approach allows more freedom in the choice of the sub-problem that is to be solved next, a feature that is important in some applications e g. in breadth-first recursion and the branch and bound method for function optimization.

2.4.2 Advantages

a. Solving difficult problems

Divide and conquer is a powerful tool for solving conceptually difficult problems, such as the classic Tower of Hanoi puzzle: all it requires is a way of breaking the problem into sub-problems, of solving the trivial cases and of combining sub-problems to to the original problem. Dividing the problem into sub-problems so that the sub-problems can be combined again is often the major difficulty in designing a new algorithm. Indeed, for many such problems the paradigm offers the only simple solution.

b. Algorithm efficiency

Moreover, divide and conquer often provides a natural way to design efficient algorithms. For example, if the work of splitting the problem and combining the partial solutions is proportional to the problem's size n, there are a bounded number p of subproblems of size n/p at each stage, and the base cases require O(1) (constant-bounded) time, then the divide-and-conquer algorithm will have O (n log n) complexity. This is used for problems such as sorting and FFTs to reduce the complexity from $O(n^2)$, although in general there may also be other approaches to designing efficient algorithms.

c. Parallelism

Divide and conquer algorithms are naturally adapted for execution in multi-processor machines, especially shared-memory systems where the communication of data between processors does not need to be planned in advance, because distinct sub-problems can be executed on different processors.

d. Memory access

Divide-and-conquer algorithms naturally tend to make efficient use of memory caches The reason is that once a sub-problem is small enough, it and all its sub-problems can, in principle, be solved within the cache, without accessing the slower main memory. An algorithm designed to exploit the cache in this way is called cache oblivious, because it does not contain the cache size(s) as an explicit parameter.

Moreover, D&C algorithms can be designed for many important algorithms, such as sorting, FFTs, and matrix multiplication, in such a way as to be optimal cache oblivious algorithms they use the cache in a provably optimal way, in an asymptotic sense, regardless of the cache size. In contrast, the traditional approach to exploiting the cache is blocking, where the problem is explicitly divided into chunks of the appropriate size this can also use the cache optimally, but only when the algorithm is tuned for the specific cache size(s) of a particular machine.

The same advantage exists with regards to other hierarchical storage systems, such as NUMA or virtual memory, as well as for multiple levels of cache: once a sub-problem is small enough, it can be solved within a given level of the hierarchy, without accessing the higher (slower) levels.

However, the kind of asymptotic optimality described here, analogous to big O notation, ignores constant factors, and additional machine/cache-specific tuning is in general required to achieve optimality in an absolute sense.

2.4.3 Disadvantages

One commonly argued disadvantage of a divide-and-conquer approach is that recursion is slow: the overhead of the repeated subroutine calls, along with that of storing the call stack (the state at each point in the recursion), can outweigh any advantages of the approach. This, however, depends upon the implementation style:' with large enough recursive base cases, the overhead of recursion can become negligible for many problems.

Another problem of a divide-and-conquer approach is that, for simple problems, it may be more complicated than a iterative approach, especially if large base cases are to be implemented for performance reasons. For example, to add N numbers, a simple loop to add them up in sequence is much easier to code than a divide-and- conquer approach that breaks the set of numbers into two halves, adds them recursively, and then adds the sums. (On the other hand, the latter approach turns out to be much more accurate in finite-precision floating-point arithmetic.)

Merge sort

Merge sort in an O (n log n) comparison based sorting algorithm. In most implementation it is stable, meaning.

That it presences the input order of equal elements in the sorted output. It is an example of the divide and conquer algorithmic paradigm.

Sorting by merging is a recursion, divide-and conquer strategy-In the base case, we have a sequence with exactly one element in it. Since such a sequence is already sorted, there is nothing to be done. To sort a sequence of element (n > 1)

(i) Divide the sequence into two sequences of length $\lceil n/2 \rceil$ and $\lfloor n/2 \rfloor$
(ii) Recursively sort each of the two subsequences; and then
(iii) Merge the sorted subsequences to obtain the final result.

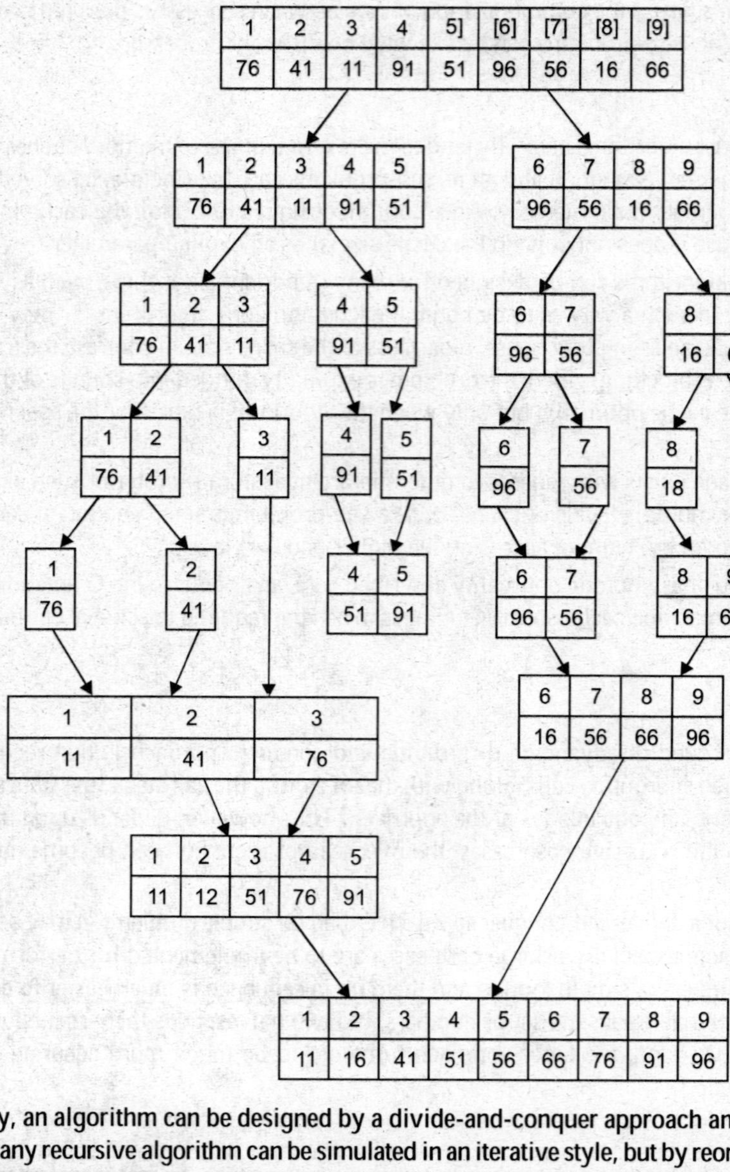

Alternatively, an algorithm can be designed by a divide-and-conquer approach and then implemented in an iterative style; any recursive algorithm can be simulated in an iterative style, but by reordering the computation it is sometimes possible to avoid simulating a recursive call stack altogether. The Cooley-Tukey FFT algorithm is a prime example of this: it was initially derived in a divide-and-conquer style, but implementations were traditionally implemented iteratively in a re-ordered fashion that avoided call-stack-like storage (although some recent implementations have returned to a recursive style).

2.5 MERGE SORT

One technique that often works for developing efficient algorithms is the divide-and-conquer approach. Suppose a friend and I were working together and trying to put our deck of cards in order. We could divide the problem up by splitting the deck of cards in half with one of us sorting each of the halves. Then we just need to figure out a way of combining the two sorted stacks. The process of combining two sorted lists into a single sorted result is called merging. The basic outline of our divide and conquer algorithm, called merge-Sort looks like this:

```
Algorithm: mergeSort nums
split nums into two halves
sort the first half.
sort the second half
merge the two sorted halves back into nums
MERGE –SORT (A, p, r)
1. if p < r
2. then
   q → ⌊(p+r)/2⌋
3. MERGE – SORT (A, p, q)
4. MERGE – SORT (A, q + 1r),
5. MERGE (A, P, q, r)
MERGE (A, P, q, r)
```

The first step in the algorithm is simple, we can just use list slicing to handle that. The last step is to merge the lists together. If you think about it, merging is pretty simple. Let' s go back to our card stack example to flesh out the details. Since our two stacks are sorted, each has its smallest value on top. Whichever of the top values is the smallest will be the first item in the merged list. Once the smaller value is removed, we can look at the tops of the stacks again, and whichever top card is smaller will be the next item in the list. We just continue this process of placing the smaller of the two top values into the big list until one of the stacks runs out. At that point, we finish out the list with the cards from the remaining stack.

Here is a C implementation of the merge process.

Merge Sort

1. $n_1 \leftarrow q - p + 1$
2. $n_2 \leftarrow r - q$
3. Create arrays L [1... n_1 +1] and R [1... n_2 + 1]
4. for $i \leftarrow 1$ to n_1
5. do $L[i] \leftarrow A[P+i-1]$
6. for $j \leftarrow 1$ to n_2
7. do $R[j] \leftarrow A[q+j]$
8. $L[n_1+1] \leftarrow \infty$

```
R[n1 +1] ← ∞
i ← 1
j ← 1
for K ← p to r
do if L[i] ≤ R [j]
then A[K] ← L[i]
i ← i+1
else A[K] ← R[j]
j ← j+1
```

Now we can slice a test into two, and if those lists are sorted, we know how to merge them back into a single list But how are we going to sort the smaller lists? Well, let's think about it. We are trying to sort two smaller list. This sound like a perfect place to use recursion. May be we can use merge sort itself to sort the two lists Let's go back to our recursion guidelines to develop a proper recursive algorithm. In order for recursion to work, we need to find at least one base case that does not require a recursion call, and we also name to make sure that reclusive calls are always made on smaller version of the original problem. The recursion in our merge sort will always occur. On a list that is half as large as the original, so the latter property is automatically met. Eventually, our lists will be very small, containing only a single item. Fortunately, a list with just one item is already sorted! Voil'a, we have a base case. When the length of the list is less than 2, we do nothing, leaving the list unchanged. Given our analysis, we can update the mergeSort algorithm to make it properly recursive.

```
if len(nums) > 1:
split nums into two halves
mergeSort the first half
mergeSort the second halfl
merge the two sorted halves back into nums
```

You might try tracing this algorithm with a small list (say eight elements), just to convince yourself that it really works. In general, though, tracing through recursive algorithms can be tedious and often not very enlightening. Recursion is closely related to mathematical induction, and it requires practice before it becomes comfortable. As long as you follow the rules and make sure that every recursive chain of calls eventually reaches a base case, your algorithms will work. You just have to trust and let go of the grungy details.

Comparing Sorts

Now that we have developed two sorting algorithms, which one should we use? Before we actually try them out, let's do some analysis. As in the searching problem, the difficulty of sorting a list depends on the size of the list. We need to figure out how many steps each of our sorting algorithms requires as a function of the size of the list to be sorted. Take a look back at the algorithm for selection sort. Remember, this algorithm works by first finding the smallest item, then finding the smallest of the remaining items, and so on. Suppose we start with a list of size n. In order to find the smallest value, the algorithm has to inspect each of the n items. The next time around the outer loop, it has to find the smallest of the remaining n – 1 items. The third time around, there are n – 2 items of interest. This process continues until there is only one item left to place. Thus, the total number of iterations of the inner loop for the selection sort can be computed as the sum of a decreasing sequence.

$$n + (n-1) + (n-2) + (n-3) + \ldots + 1$$

In other words, the time required by selection sort to sort a list of n items is proportional to the sum of the first n whole numbers. There is a well-known formula for this sum, but even if you do not know the formula, it is easy to derive. If you add the first and last numbers in the series you get n + 1. Adding the second and second to last values gives (n – l) + 2 = n +l. If you keep pairing. up the values working from the outside in, all of the pairs add to n + 1. Since there are n numbers, there must be n/2 pairs. That means the sum of all the pairs is n (n + 1) /2.

You can see that the final formula contains an n2 term. That means that the number of steps in the algorithm is proportional to the square of the size of the list.

If the size of the list doubles, the number of steps quadruples. If the size triples, it will take nine times as long to finish. Computer scientists call this a quadratic or n2 algorithm.

Let' s see how that compares to the merge sort algorithm. In the case of merge sort, we divided a list into two pieces and sorted the individual pieces before merging them together. The real work is done during the merge process when the values in the sub lists are copied back into the original list. Fig.2.4 depicts the merging process to sort the list [3, 1, 4, 1, 5, 9, 2, 6]. The dashed lines show how the original list is continually halved until each item is its own list with the values shown at the bottom. The single-item lists are then merged back up into the two item lists to produce the values shown in the second level. The merging process continues up the diagram to produce the final sorted version of the list shown at the top. The diagram makes analysis of the merge sort easy. Starting at the bottom level, we have to copy the n values into the second level. From the second to third level, the n values need to be copied again. Each level of merging involves copying n values. The only question left to answer is how many levels are there? This boils down to how many times a list of size n can be split in half. You already know from the analysis of binary search that this is just log 2n. Therefore, the total work required to sort n items is n log 2n. Computer scientists call this an n log n algorithm. So which is going to be better, the n2 selection sort or the n log n merge sort?

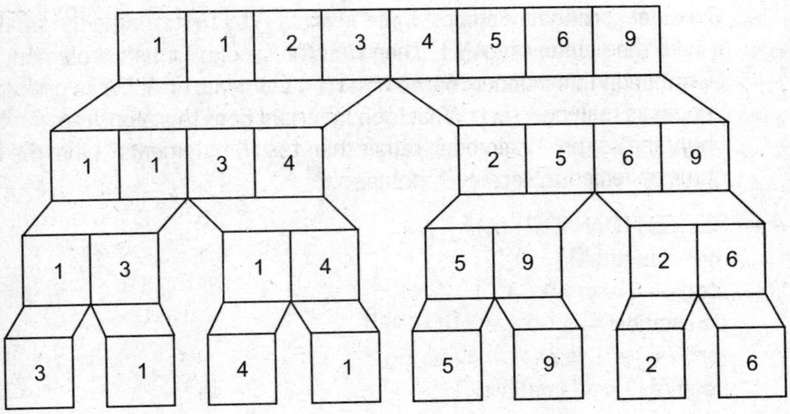

Fig. 2.4

If the input size is small, the selection sort might be a little faster because the code is simpler and there is less overhead. What happens, though as n gets larger? We saw in the analysis of binary search that the log function grows very slowly (log2 16; 000; 000 – 24) so n(log2 n) will grow much slower than n(n).

Solved Exercises

1. Suppose we comparing implementations of insertion sort and merge sort on the same machine. For input of size n, insertion sort runs in $8n^2$ steps. while merge sort runs of 64nlg n steps. For which value

of n does insertion sort beat merge sort?

Ans. Insertion sort beats merge when 8n2 < 64n log n,) n < 8 log n_1) 2n = 8 < n. This is true for 2 6 n 6 43 or less in order to improve the running time.

2. Express the function n_3 = 1000 – 100 n^2 – 100 n + 3 in terms of Q rotation.

Ans. n_3 = 1000 – 100 n^2 – 100 n + 3 = θ (n_3)

3. Discuss the best case and worst case running time of insertion sort.

Ans. The best case input is an array that is already sorted. In this case insertion sort has a linear running time (i.e., Θ(n)). During each iteration, the first remaining element of the input is only compared with the right-most element of the sorted subsection of the array.

The worst case input is an array sorted in reverse order. In this case every iteration of the inner loop will scan and shift the entire sorted subsection of the array before inserting the next element. For this case insertion sort has a quadratic running time (i.e., $O(n^2)$).

4. Explain Merge Sort

Sol. The merge sort is a divide and conquer sort as well. It works by considering the data to be sorted as a sequence of already-sorted lists (in the worst case, each list is one element long). Adjacent sorted lists are merged into larger sorted lists until there is a single sorted list containing all the elements. The merge sort is good at sorting lists and other data structures that are not in arrays, and it can be used to sort things that don't fit into memory. It also can be implemented as a stable sort.

5. Consider sorting n numbers stored in array A by first finding the smallest element of A and exchanging it with the element in A[1]. Then find the second smallest element of A, and exchange it with A[2]. Continue in this manner for the first n - 1 elements of A. Write pseudocode for this algorithm, which is known as selection sort. What loop invariant does this algorithm maintain? Why does it need to run for only the first n - 1 elements, rather than for all n lements? Give the best-case and worst-case running times of selection sort in Θ- notation.

Ans. SELECTION-SORT(A)

```
n ← length[A]
for j ← 1 to n – 1
do smallest ← j
for i ← j + 1 to n
do if A[i ] < A[smallest]
then smallest ← i
exchange A[ j ] ↔ A[smallest]
```

The algorithm maintains the loop invariant that at the start of each iteration of the outer for loop, the subarray A[1 . . j –1] consists of the j –1 smallest elements in the array A[1 . . n], and this subarray is in sorted order. After the first n –1 elements, the subarray A[1 . . n –1] contains the smallest n –1 elements, sorted, and therefore element A[n] must be the largest element. The running time of the algorithm is _(n2) for all cases.

6. Use mathematical induction to show that when n is an exact power of 2, the solution of the recurrence

$$T(n)\begin{cases}2 & \text{if } n = 2,\\ 2T(n/2)+n & \text{if } n = 2^k, \text{ for } k > 1\end{cases} \qquad \text{is } T(n) = n \lg n.$$

Ans. The base case is when n = 2, and we have n lg n = 2 lg 2 = 2 1 = 2.

For the inductive step, our inductive hypothesis is that T (n/2) = (n/2) lg(n/2).

Then

T (n) = 2T (n/2) + n

= 2(n/2) lg(n/2) + n

= n(lg n –1) + n

= n lg n – n + n

= n lg n ,

which completes the inductive proof for exact powers of 2.

7. Insertion sort can be expressed as a recursive procedure as follows. In order to sort A[1 _ n], we recursively sort A[1 _ n -1] and then insert A[n] into the sorted array A[1 _ n - 1]. Write a recurrence for the running time of this recursive version of insertion sort.

Ans. Since it takes _(n) time in the worst case to insert A[n] into the sorted array A[1 . . n –1], we get the recurrence

T (n) = O(1) if n = 1 ,

T (n –1) + O(n) if n > 1 .

The solution to this recurrence is T (n) = O(n2).

8. Write pseudocode, either iterative or recursive, for binary search. Argue that the worst-case running Θ(lg n).

Ans. Procedure BINARY-SEARCH takes a sorted array A, a value v, and a range [low . . high] of the array, in which we search for the value v. The procedure compares v to the array entry at the midpoint of the range and decides to eliminate half the range from further consideration. We give both iterative and recursive versions, each of which returns either an index i such that A[i] = v, or NIL if no entry of A[low . . high] contains the value v. The initial call to either version should have the parameters A, v, 1, n.

```
ITERATIVE-BINARY-SEARCH(A, v, low, high)
while low ≤ high
do mid ←                    (low+high)/2
if v = A[mid]
then return mid
if v > A[mid]
then low ← mid +1
else high ← mid –1
return NIL
RECURSIVE-BINARY-SEARCH(A, v, low, high)
if low > high
then return NIL
mid ← (low+high)/2
if v = A[mid]
then return mid\
if v > A[mid]
then return RECURSIVE-BINARY-SEARCH (A, v, mid +1, high)
else return RECURSIVE-BINARY-SEARCH (A, v, low, mid "1)
```

Both procedures terminate the search unsuccessfully when the range is empty (i.e., low > high) and terminate it successfully if the value v has been found. Based on the comparison of v to the middle element in the searched range, the search continues with the range halved. The recurrence for these procedures is therefore

T (n) = T (n/2) + _(1), whose solution is T (n) = _(lg n).

9. Describe a Θ(n lg n)-time algorithm that, given a set S of n integers and another integer x, determines whether or not there exist two elements in S whose sum is exactly x.

Ans. The following algorithm solves the problem:

1. Sort the elements in S.
2. Form the set S_ = {z : z = x – y for some y " S}.
3. Sort the elements in S.
4. If any value in S appears more than once, remove all but one instance. Do the same for S
5. Merge the two sorted sets S and S.
6. There exist two elements in S whose sum is exactly x if and only if the same value appears in consecutive positions in the merged output.

To justify the claim in step 4, Þrst observe that if any value appears twice in the merged output, it must appear in consecutive positions. Thus, we can restate the condition in step 5 as there exist two elements in S whose sum is exactly x if and only if the same value appears twice in the merged output. Suppose that some value w appears twice. Then w appeared once in S and once in S. Because w appeared in S, there exists some y " S such that w = x – y, or x = w + y. Since w " S, the elements w and y are in S and sum to x. Conversely, suppose that there are values w, y " S such that w + y = x. Then, since x – y = w, the value w appears in S_. Thus, w is in both S and S, and so it will appear twice in the merged output. Steps 1 and 3 require O(n lg n) steps. Steps 2, 4, 5, and 6 require O(n) steps. Thus the overall running time is O(n lg n).

10. Although merge sort runs in Θ(n lg n) worst-case time and insertion sort runs in Θ(n2) worstcase time, the constant factors in insertion sort make it faster for small n. Thus, it makes sense to use insertion sort within merge sort when subproblems become sufficiently small. Consider a modification to merge sort in which n/k sublists of length k are sorted using insertion sort and then merged using the standard merging mechanism, where k is a value to be determined.

a. Show that the n/k sublists, each of length k, can be sorted by insertion sort in Θ(nk) worst-case time.

b. Show that the sublists can be merged in Θ(n lg (n/k) worst-case time.

c. Given that the modified algorithm runs in Θ(nk + n lg (n/k)) worst-case time, what is the largest asymptotic (notation) value of k as a function of n for which the modified algorithm has the same asymptotic running time as standard merge sort?

d. How should k be chosen in practice?

Ans. a. Insertion sort takes Θ(k2) time per k-element list in the worst case. Therefore, sorting n/k lists of k elements each takes Θ(k2n/k) = Θ(nk) worst-case time.

b. Just extending the 2-list merge to merge all the lists at once would take Θ (n (n/k)) = Θ(n2/k) t me (n from copying each element once into the result list, n/k from examining n/k lists at each step to select next item for result list). To achieve Θ(n lg(n/k))- time merging, we merge the lists pair wise, then merge the resulting lists pairwise, and so on, until there just one list. The pair wise merging requires Θ (n) work at each level, since we are still working on n elements, even if they are partitioned among sublists. The number of levels, starting with n/k lists (with k elements each) and finishing with 1 list (with n elements), is Θ lg(n/k) Θ. Therefore, the total running time for the merging is Θ (n lg(n/k)).

c. The modified algorithm has the same asymptotic running time as standard merge sort when Θ (nk +n lg(n/k)) = Θ (n lg n). The largest asymptotic value of k as a function of n that satisfies this condition is k = Θ (lg n).

To see why, first observe that k cannot be more than Θ(lg n) (i.e., it can't have a higher-order term than lg n), for otherwise the left-hand expression wouldnot be Θ (n lg n) (because it would have a higher-order term than n lg n). So all we need to do is verify that k = Θ (lg n) works, which we can do by plugging

k = lg n into Θ (nk + n lg(n/k)) = Θ (nk + n lg n –n lg k) to get

Θ (n lg n + n lg n –n lg lg n) = Θ (2n lg n –n lg lg n) ,

which, by taking just the high-order term and ignoring the constant coefficient,

Equals Θ (n lg n).

d. In practice, k should be the largest list length on which insertion sort is faster than merge sort.

11. Let A[1 _ n] be an array of n distinct numbers. If i < j and A[i] > A[j], then the pair (i, j) is called an inversion of A.

a. List the five inversions of the array 2, 3, 8, 6, 1.

b. What array with elements from the set {1, 2, . . . , n} has the most inversions? How many does it have?

c. Give an algorithm that determines the number of inversions in any permutation on n elements in Θ(n lg n) worst-case time. (Hint: Modify merge sort.)

Ans. a. The inversions are (1, 5), (2, 5), (3, 4), (3, 5), (4, 5). (Remember that inversions are speciÞed by indices rather than by the values in the array.)

b. The array with elements from {1, 2, . . . , n} with the most inversions is n, n –1, n – 2, . . . , 2, 1. For all $1 \leq i < j \leq n$, there is an inversion (i, j). The number of such inversions is (n_2) = n(n –1)/2.

c. We follow the hint and modify merge sort to count the number of inversions in Θ(n lg n) time. To start, let us deÞne a merge-inversion as a situation within the execution of merge sort in which the MERGE procedure, after copying A[p . . q] to L and A[q + 1 . . r] to R, has values x in L and y in R such that x > y. Consider an inversion (i, j), and let x = A[i] and y = A[j], so that i < j and x > y. We claim that if we were to run merge sort, there would be exactly one merge inversion involving x and y. To see why, observe that the only way in which array elements change their positions is within the MERGE procedure. Moreover, since MERGE keeps elements within L in the same relative order to each other, and correspondingly for R, the only way in which two elements can change their ordering relative to each other is for the greater one to appear in L and the lesser one to appear in R. Thus, there is at least one merge-inversion involving x and y. To see that there is exactly one such merge-inversion, observe that after any call of MERGE that involves both x and y, they are in the same sorted sub array and will therefore both appear in L or both appear in R in any given call thereafter. Thus, we have proven the claim. We have shown that every inversion implies one merge-inversion. In fact, the correspondence between inversions and merge-inversions is one-to-one. Suppose we have a merge-inversion involving values x and y, where x originally was A[i] and y was originally A[j]. Since we have a merge-inversion, x > y. And since x is in L and y is in R, x must be within a subarray preceding the subarray containing y. Therefore x started out in a position i preceding y. S original position j , and so (i, j) is an inversion. Having shown a one-to-one correspondence between inversions and merge inversions, it surfaces for us to count merge-inversions. Consider a merge-inversion involving y in R. Let z be the smallest value in L that is greater than y. At some point during the merging process, z and y will be the .exposed. values in L and R, i.e., we will have z = L[i] and y = R[j] in line 13 of MERGE. At that time, there will be merge-inversions involving y and L[i], L[i +1], L[i +2], . . . , L[n1], and these n1 "i +1 merge-inversions will be the only ones involving y. Therefore, we need to detect the best time that z and y become exposed during the MERGE procedure and add the value of n1 – i + 1 at that time to our total count of merge-inversions. The following pseudocode, modeled on merge sort, works as we have just described. It also sorts the array A.

```
COUNT-INVERSIONS(A, p, r )
inversions ← 0
if p < r
then q ← (p + r)/2
inversions ← inversions +COUNT-INVERSIONS(A, p, q)
inversions ← inversions +COUNT-INVERSIONS(A, q + 1, r )
inversions ← inversions +MERGE-INVERSIONS(A, p, q, r )
return inversions
MERGE-INVERSIONS(A, p, q, r )
n1 ← q – p + 1
n2 ← r – q
create arrays L[1 . . n1 + 1] and R[1 . . n2 + 1]
for i ← 1 to n1
do L[i ] ← A[p + i –1]
for j ← 1 to n2
do R[ j ] ← A[q + j ]
L[n1 + 1]←∞
R[n2 + 1]←∞
i ← 1
j ← 1
inversions ← 0
counted ← FALSE
for k ← p to r
do if counted = FALSE and R[ j ] < L[i ]
then inversions ← inversions +n1 – i + 1
counted ← TRUE
if L[i ] ≤ R[ j ]
then A[k] ← L[i ]
i ← i + 1
else A[k] ← R[ j ] j ← j + 1
counted ← FALSE
return inversions
```

The initial call is COUNT-INVERSIONS(A, 1, n).

In MERGE-INVERSIONS, the boolean variable counted indicates whether we have counted the merge-inversions involving R[j]. We count them the first time that both R[j] is exposed and a value greater than R[j] becomes exposed in the L array. We set counted to FALSE upon each time that a new value becomes exposed in R. We donot have to worry about merge-inversions involving the sentinel "in R, since no value in L will be greater than ". Since we have added only a constant amount of additional work to each procedure call and to each iteration of the last for loop of the merging procedure, the total running time of the above pseudocode is the same as for merge sort: $\Theta(n \lg n)$.

12. **Discuss the best case and worst case running time of insertion sort.**

Ans. The best case input is an array that is already sorted. In this case insertion sort has a linear running time (i.e., $\Theta(n)$). During each iteration, the first remaining element of the input is only compared with the right-most element of the sorted subsection of the array.

The worst case input is an array sorted in reverse order. In this case every iteration of the inner loop will scan and shift the entire sorted subsection of the array before inserting the next element. For this case insertion sort has a quadratic running time (i.e., $O(n^2)$).

13. Explain Merge Sort

Ans. The merge sort is a divide and conquer sort as well. It works by considering the data to be sorted as a sequence of already-sorted lists (in the worst case, each list is one element long). Adjacent sorted lists are merged into larger sorted lists until there is a single sorted list containing all the elements. The merge sort is good at sorting lists and other data structures that are not in arrays, and it can be used to sort things that don't fit into memory. It also can be implemented as a stable sort.

Previous Year University Question

1. Differentiate between quick sort and mergesort algorithms. [GGSIPU]
2. Write the quick sort algorithm using divide and conquer strategy. [OU]
3. Write an algorithm for merge sort. Also, find its time complexity. [OU]
4. Explain the meaning of deterministic algorithms and infinite algorithms. [Madrass University]
5. Determine the product of 5678 and 349 using divide and conquer technique. [Madrass University]
6. Arrange the following numbers in ascending order using three way merge-sort: 26, 15, 47, 05, 99, 47, 90, 50, 70, 47, 98, 26. [Madrass University]
7. Differentiate between space and time complexity of an algorithm. [MDU]
8. Explain Merge sort with an example. Also analyse it in best, average and worst case. [MDU]
9. What is Divide and Conquer strategy? Design Merge sort algorithm using Divide and Conquer strategy. Also give its recurrence relation. [MDU]

Exercise

1. Express an algorithm for factorial to a number?
2. What are the methodologies for the design of an algorithm?
3. What are the advantages and disadvantages of algorithm?
4. What is the difference between algorithm and Pseudo-codes.
5. Describe the factors affecting the running time of an algorithm.
6. Write down the algorithm for merge sort and final act its complexity.

CHAPTER

3

ASYMPTOTIC GROWTH OF FUNCTION

The asymptotic notation are used to compare the performance and efficiency of algorithm. The asymptotic run time of an algorithm given a simple, and machine independent, characterization of its complexity.

The running time of an algorithm as input size approaches infinity is called the asymptotic running time.

In any algorithm we have three types of case, which are require to analiyse the algorithm.

1. Best Case. [Ω] omega notation
2. Worst Case [O] Big Oh. notation
3. Average case. [θ] Theta notation.

In the best case the algorithm will run in minimum time. Suppose in the case of insertion sort the best case is when array was already sorted.

The worst case running time of an algorithm is on upper bound an the running time for any input. In this algorithm will take maximum time to run Example is again in case of insertion sort. when array is reverse sorted.

The average case in between best and worst. If is also called asymptotic tight bound

3.1 θ NOTATION

The θ (theta) notation describe the asymptotic tight bound on the growth rate of an algorithm.

Definition

For a given function g (n), which is denoted by θ (g (n))

The set of function

$$\theta(g(n)) = \{ f(n): \text{there exists positive constants } C_1, C_2 \text{ and } n_o \text{ such that } 0 \le C_1 g(n) \le f(n) \le C_2 (g(n)) \text{ for all } n \ge (n_o)\}$$

This can be explained is such a way that a function f(n) belongs to the set θ (g (n)) if there exists a positive constant C_1 and C_2 such that it can be sandwiched between C_1 g (n) and C_2 g(n). for sufficient large n.

Note: • $f(n) \varepsilon \theta (g(n))$
which means f(n)) is a member of $\theta (g(n))$
• The every function used within θ notation is asymptotically nonnegative.

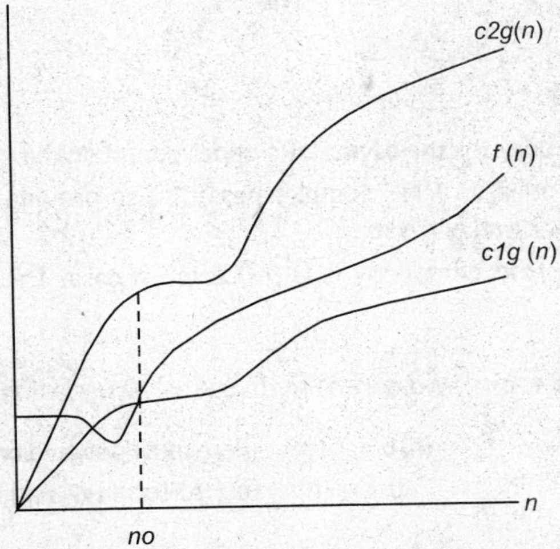

$f(n) = \theta(g(n))$

EXAMPLES

Example 3.1: $f(n) = n^2 - 3n$, find θ notation.

Solution We have $f(n) = n^2 - 3n$

Let $g(n) = n^2$

Now

$$C_1n^2 \leq n^2 - 3n \leq C_2n^2$$

$$C_1 \leq 1 - \frac{3}{n} \leq C_2 \quad \text{[divide by } n_2\text{]}$$

$$C_2 \geq 1 - \frac{3}{n}$$

Since C_2 is +ve constant, C_2 can have maximum value 1 as –ve term is substracted

so $C_2 \geq 1$

$$C_1 \leq 1 - \frac{3}{n}$$

for n = 4 C_1 is +ve. $C_1 = 1 - \frac{3}{4} = \frac{1}{4}$

$$C_1 \le \frac{1}{4}$$

Hence lowest value of n for which f(n) lies between C_1 g(n) and C_2 g (n) is $n_0 = 4$.

∴ Order of θ (n^2).

3.2 O-NOTATION

The big "Oh" notation 'O' describe the asymptotic upper bound on the growth of an algorithm.

The O notation is used in theory of NP completeness. If also provide information on the maximum number of operation that an algorithm perform.

For example in insertion sort its complexly is O (n^2) is worst case. This mens that in the worst case it perform at most Cn^2 operation

Definition: For a given function g(n), we denote by O (g (n)) the set of function.

$$O(g(n)) = \{ f(n) : \text{there exist positive constants } C \text{ and } n_0 \text{ such that } 0 \le f(n) \le \{cg(n) \text{ for all } n \ge n_0 \}$$

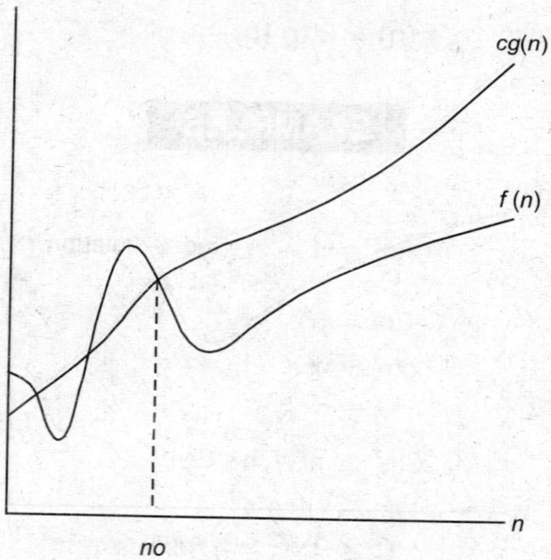

f (n) = O (g (n))

3.3 Ω -ROTATION

The omega notation describe the asymptotic lower bound on the growth of an algorithm or a problem. We use Ω notation when we have to provide information on the minimum number of operation that an algorithm perform. For example best case complexity of insertion sort is Ω (n).

Definition: For a given function g(n) we denote by Ω(g (n)) the set function.

$$\Omega(g(n)) = \{ f(n) : \text{there exist positive constants } C \text{ and } n_0 \text{ such that } 0 \le cg(n) \le f(n) \text{ for all } n \ge n_0 \}$$

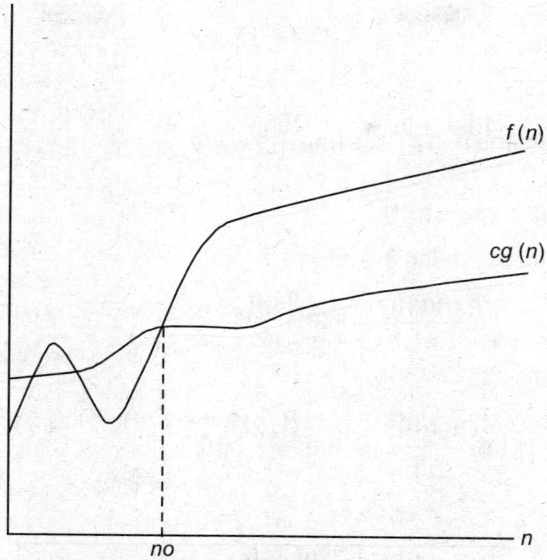

$f(n) = \Omega(g(n))$

Example 3.2: Suppose f(n) and g(n) are given then tell weather they are in which relation θ, Ω or O)

(a)	$f(n) = \log n^2$	$g(n) = \log n + 5$
(b)	$f(n) = n$	$g(n) = \log n^2$
(c)	$f(n) = \log \log n$	$g(n) = \log n$
(d)	$f(n) = n$	$g(n) = \log^2 n$
(e)	$f(n) = n \log n$	$g(n) = \log n$
(f)	$f(n) = 10$	$g(n) = \log 10$
(g)	$f(n) = 2^n$	$g(n) = 10n^2$
(h)	$f(n) = 2^n$	$g(n) = 3^n$

Solution:

(b) As $f(n) = n$ and $g(n) = \log n^2$

n	$\log n^2$	
1	0	[put n = 1]
2	0.6	
3	0.9.5	
4	1.20	
5	1.80	
6	1.56	

So f(n) > g (n) so, it is in [Ω]

Solve rest of the problems yourself.

We can also determine order by using limits.

$$\text{If } \lim_{n\to\infty} \frac{f(n)}{g(n)} = \begin{cases} C & \text{then } f(n) = \theta(g(n)[c > 0] \\ O & \text{then } f(n) = O(g(n) \text{ or } C < \infty \\ \infty & \text{then } f(n) = \Omega(g(n) \text{ or } > 0 \end{cases}$$

Example 3.3:

(a) $10n^3 - 3n = \theta(n^3)$

if $$\lim_{n\to\infty}\frac{10n^3-3n}{n^3} = \lim_{n\to\infty}\frac{10n^3}{n^3} - \lim_{n\to\infty}\frac{3n}{n^3} = 10$$

So $10n^3 - 3n \in \theta(n^3)$

(b) $n \log n \in O(n^2)$

$$\lim_{n\to\infty}\frac{n\log n}{n^2} = \lim_{n\to\infty}\frac{\log n}{n}$$

by using L' Hospital 's Rule

$$\lim_{n\to\infty}\frac{(\log n)'}{(n)} = \lim_{n\to\infty}\frac{(1/2)}{1} = 0$$

So $n \log n \in O(n^2)$

(c)
$$f(n) = 27n^2 + 16$$
$$g(n) = n$$

$$\lim_{n\to\infty}\frac{(27n^2+16n)}{n} = \infty$$

so $f(n) = \Omega(n)$

Lemma: $f(n) = O(g(n))$ if and only

if $g(n) = \Omega(f(n))$

Proof: If $f(n) = O\,g(n)$ then there exists positive number C_1, n_1 such that $0 \le f(n) \le C_1 g(n)$ for all $n \ge n_1$ Let $C_2 = 1/C_1$ and $n_2 = n_1$. Then $0 \le C_2 f(n) \le gn$ for all $n \ge n_2$, proving $g(n) = \Omega(f(n))$

Lemma: If $f(n) \le h(n)$ for all sufficiently large n, and if $h(n) = O(g(n))$, then $f(n) = O(g(n))$

Proof: The above hypothesis say that there exist positive numbers C and $n_1$such that $h(n) \le Cg(n)$ for all $n \ge n_1$. Also there exists n_2 such that $0 \le f(n) \le h(n)$ for all $n \ge n_2$. Define $n_0 = \max(n_1, n_2)$, so that if $n \ge n_0$ we have both $n \ge n_1$ and $n \ge n_2$. Then $n \ge n_0$ implies $0 \le f(n) \le Cg(n)$, and therefore $f(n) = O(g(n))$.

Example 3.4: Prove $n! = w(2^n)$

Solution: We have $\lim_{n\to\infty}\frac{f(n)}{g(n)} = \infty$ for $f(n) = w(g/n)$

We can write.

$$\lim_{n\to\infty}\frac{n!}{2^n} = \frac{n^n\left(1-\frac{1}{n}\right)\left(1-\frac{2}{n}\right)\ldots\frac{3}{n}.\frac{2}{m}\ldots\frac{1}{n}}{2^n}$$

$$= \frac{\infty}{2^\infty} = \infty$$

Hence it holds

Example 3.5: Let f(n) and g(n) be asymptotically non-negative function. Using the basic definition of θ-rotation, prove that max (f (n), g (n)) = θ (f (n) + g(n)).

Solution: Let f(n) and g(n) be asymptotically nonnegative. Show that max f(n), g(n) = θ (f(n + g(n)), This mean that there exists positive constants C_1, C_2 and n_0 such that.

$$0 \leq C_1 (f(n) + g(n)) \leq \max (f(n)), g(n)) \leq C_2 (f(n) + g(n)).$$

for all $n \geq n_0$

Selecting $C_2 = 1$ Clearly shows that third inequality inequality since the maximum must be smaller than the sum. C_1 should be selected as 1/2 since the maximum is always greater than the weighted average of f(n) and g(n). Note the significance of the "asymptotically nonnegative" assumption. The first inequality could not be satisfied otherwise.

Example 3.6 : Is $2^{n+1} = 0 (2^n)$? $2^{2n} = 0 (2^n)$?

Solution $2^{n+1} = 0 (2^n)$ since $2^{n+1} = 2.2^{2n} \leq 2.2^n$! However 2^{2n} is not $0(2^n)$; by definition we have $2^{2n} = (2^n)^2$; which for the constant C asymptotically may be less than or equal to $C.2^n$.

Example: 3.7 : Is f(n) = O(g (n)) implies g(n) = 0 (f (n))

Solution No, f(n) = O (g (n)) does not imply g(n) = 0 (f (n)) clearly, $n = O(n^2)$ but $n^2 \neq 0 (n)$

Example: 3.8 : f(n) + g(n) = θ(min (f(n), g(n))

Solution No, f(n) + g(n) is not θ (min (f(n), g(n)). As an example notice that n + 1 ≠ θ (min (n, 1)) = θ (1).

Example 3.9 : Prove that f(n) = O (g (n)) implies 1g (f (n)) = O (1g (g (n)), where 1g (g (n) ≥ 1 for all sufficiently large n.

Solution If f(n) = 0 (g (n)) then 1g (f(n)) = O (1g (g (n))) proved that f(n) ≥ 1 and 1g (g (n)) ≥ 1 are greater then or equal 1. We have that: f(n) ≤ cg (n) ⇒ 1g f(n) ≤ 1g ((g (n)) = 1g C + 1g g(n)

To show that this is smaller then b1g g(n) for some constant b we set 1g c + 1g g (n) = b/g g (n). Dividing by 1g g (n) yields.

$$b = \frac{1g(c) + 1g\ g(n)}{1g\ g(n)} = \frac{1g\,c}{1g\ g(n)} + 1 \leq 1g\,c + 1$$

That last inequality holds since 1g g(n) ≥ 1.

Example 3.10 : Weather f(n) = O (g (n) implies $2^{f(n)} = O(2^{g(n)})$

Solution No f(n) = 0 (g (n)) does not imply $2^{f(n)} = O(2^{g(n)})$. If f(n) = 2n and g(n) = n we have that 2n ≤ 2.n but not $2^{2n} \leq C.2$ for any constant C by example 3.6

Example 3.11 : Is f(n) = O (g (n)) implies g(n) = Ω (f (n))

Solution Yes. f(n) = O (g(n)) implies g (n) = Ω f(n). We have f(n) ≤ cg (n) for positive C and thus 1/C. f(n) ≤ g(n).

Solved Exercise

1. Give the complexity in terms of Big O notation for the following algorithmic equations ?
   (a) 5.n^2 – 6n + 2 (b) 6.2^n + 6

Sol. (a) O(n^2) (b) O(2^n)

2. Arrange the following in increasing order of time complexity ?
   O(1), O(2^n), O(n^2), O(nlogn), O(n^3), O(n), O(logn)

Sol. O(1) < O(logn) < O(n) < O(nlogn) < O(n^2) < O(n^3) < O(2^n)

3. What do you understand by term O in Big O notation ?

Sol. O(g(n)) = {f(n) : there exists positive constants c, n_0 such that 0 <= f(n) <= cg(n) for all n}

4. Let f(n) and g(n) be asymptotically nonnegative functions. Using the basic definition of Θ- notation, prove that max(f(n), g(n)) = Θ(f(n) + g(n)).

Ans. First, let.s clarify what the function max(f (n), g(n)) is. Let.s deÞne the function

h(n) = max(f (n), g(n)).

Then h(n) = f (n) if f (n) ≤ g(n) ,

g(n) if f (n) < g(n) .

Since f (n) and g(n) are asymptotically nonnegative, there exists n0 such thatf (n) ≥ 0 and g(n) ≥ 0 for all n ≥ n0. Thus for n ≥ n0, f (n) + g(n) ≥ f (n) ≥ 0 and f (n)+g(n) ≥ g(n) ≥ 0. Since for any particular n, h(n) is either f (n) or g(n), we have f (n) + g(n) ≥ h(n) ≥ 0, which shows that h(n) = max(f (n), g(n)) ≤ c2(f (n) + g(n)) for all n ≥ n0 (with c2 = 1 in the definition of Θ).

Similarly, since for any particular n, h(n) is the larger of f (n) and g(n), we have for all n ≥ n0, 0 ≤ f (n) ≤ h(n) and 0 ≤ g(n) ≤ h(n). Adding these two inequalities yields 0 ≤ f (n) + g(n) ≤ 2h(n), or equivalently 0 ≤ (f (n) + g(n))/2 ≤ h(n),

which shows that h(n) = max(f (n), g(n)) ≥ c1(f (n)+g(n)) for all n ≥ n0 (with c1 = 1/2 in the definition of Θ).

5. Show that for any real constants a and b, where b > 0,

(3.2) $(n+a)^b = \Theta(n^b)$.

Ans. To show that (n + a)b = _(nb), we want to find constants c1, c2, n0 > 0 such that

0 ≤ c1nb ≤ (n + a)b ≤ c2nb for all n ≥ n0.

Note that

n + a ≤ n + |a|

≤ 2n when |a| ≤ n ,

And n + a ≥ n – |a| ≥ 1

2n when |a| ≤ 12 n .

Thus, when n ≥ 2 |a|,

0 ≥ 1

2n ≤ n + a ≤ 2n .

6. Give the complexity in terms of Big O notation for the following algorithmic equations ?
   (a) n^2 – 6n + 2 (b) 6.2^n + 6

Ans. (a) O(n^2) (b) O(2^n)

7. Arrange the following in increasing order of time complexity ?
   O(1) , O(2^n) , O(n^2), O(nlogn), O(n^3), O(n), O(logn)

Ans. O(1)< O(logn)< O(n)< O(nlogn)< O(n^2)< O(n^3)< O(2^n)

8. What do you understand by term O in Big O notation ?

Ans. O(g(n)) = {f(n) : there exists positive constants c , n_0 such that 0 <= f(n)<= cg(n) for all n}

Previous Year University Question

1. Define the following notations [OU]
   (i) BigOh (ii) Omega (iii) Theta
2. Explain the big-o notation and its significance. [OU]
3. Find the maximum and minimum element in an array with minimum complexity. [GGSIPU]
4. Differentiate between Divide and Conquer and Dynamic programming. [GGSIPU]
5. Determine the asymptotic order of following expressions:
   (i) $F(n) = 6.2^n + n^2$ (ii) $F(n) = 7$ [GBTU]
6. Show that for any real constant a and b, where b > 0, $(n + a)^b = q(n)^b$. [GBTU]
7. Explain how can we modify almost any algorithm to have a good best case running time? [GBTU]
8. Show that if ¦1 (n) = 0 [¦2 (n)], then ¦2 (n) = 0 [¦1 (n)]. [Madras University]
9. Write short note on asymptotic notations. [MDU]
10. Write and explain different types of asymptotic notations with suitable example. [MDU]

Exercise

1. Let x and y be real number such that 0 < x < y Show that n^x is in $O(n^4)$ but n^y is not in $O(n^x)$
2. Prove that running time of an algorithm is $\theta(g(n))$.
3. What is the significance of asymptotic rotations in study of algorithm? Describe various asymptotic rotation.
4. Show that $\log^3 n$ is $0(n^{1/3})$.
5. Prove $\sum_{i=2}^{n}\left(\frac{1}{2}i+0(1)\right)=O(n^2)$
6. Prove that following:

   (a) $20n^2 + 10 = O(n)$ (b) $\frac{n^2}{\log n} = \theta(n^2)$

   (c) $n^3 2^n + 7n^2 + 3^n = O(n^3 2^n)$ (d) $2^{n+1} = 00(2^n)$

   (e) $O(2^{\log_b n}) = O(2^{\log_a n})$

CHAPTER

4

RECURSION

Recursion is an important concept in computer field. Many algorithm can be best defined in terms of recursion.

Suppose X is a procedure containing either a call statement to itself or a cell statement to a second procedure that may result in a call statement back to the original procedure X. Then X is called recursive procedure.

A function f(n) is said to be recursively defined if the function definition refers to itself. Again in order for definition not to be circular, it must have the following two properties.

(a) There must be certain arguments called base values, for which the function does no refers to itself.

(b) Each time the function does refer to itself, the argument of the function must be closer to a base value.

A recursive function f(n) with there two values properties is also said to be well-defined.

A recurrence in an equation or inequality that describes a function in terms of its value in smaller inputs.

Example: Worst case running time of mere-sort is described by the recurrence

$$T(n) = \begin{cases} \theta(1) & \text{if } n = 1 \\ 2T(n/2) + \theta(n) & \text{if } n > 1 \end{cases}$$

whose solution is $T(n) = \theta(n\log n)$.

In this chapter we discuss four methods for solving recurrence, there are.

1. Substitution method
2. Iteration method
3. Recursion tree method
4. Master method

4.1 SUBSTITUTION METHOD

There are two steps for solving recursion by substitution method.

1. Guess the form of solution.
2. Use mathematical induction to find the constants and show that the solution works.

The substitution method can be used to establish either upper or lower bounds or a recurrence

Example :1 : Solve the following recurrence with substitution method.

$$T(n) = 4T(n/2) + n$$

Solution: Suppose we are given the recurrence

$$T(n) = 4T(n/2) + n$$

Let us given that our solution is $O(n^2)$. To prove this inductively let use $T(n) < cn^2$ and assume that it is true for T(n/2m). That is assume that $T(n/2) \le c(n/2)^2 - 6(n/2)$ true.

$$\begin{aligned} T(n) &\le 4(C(n/2)^2 - b(n/2)) + n \\ &= 4C(n/2)^2 - 4b(n/2) + n \\ &= cn^2 - 2bn + n \\ &= cn^2 - n(2b-1) \\ &\le cn^2 - n\theta(1) \end{aligned}$$

where the last inequality holds so long that $b > 1/2$

Example 2: Solve the recurrence by substitution method.

$$T(n) = 2T(\lfloor n/2 \rfloor) + n$$

Solution. Suppose we are given the recurrence

$$T(n) = 2T(\lfloor n/2 \rfloor) + n \qquad \text{... (1)}$$

We must first given a solution for (1). Let us guess that T(n) = O (nlgn).

The substitution method now requires us to show that $T(n) \le cn/gn$ for some constants $c > 0$.

The proof will be inductive. That is we assume that $T(\lfloor n/2 \rfloor) \le c\lfloor n/2 \rfloor \lg(\lfloor ns$ holds, and our goal is to use this to show that this yields our claim that $T(n) \le (nlgn)$

$$\begin{aligned} T(n) &\le 2(c\lfloor n/2 \rfloor \lg(\lfloor n/2 \rfloor)) + n \\ &\le cn\lg(n/2) + n \\ &= cn\lg n - cn\lg 2 + n \\ &= cn\lg n - cn + n \\ &\le cn\lg n \end{aligned}$$

Example3: Solve $T(n) = T(\lfloor n/2 \rfloor) + T(\lceil n/2 \rceil) + 1$

Solution. Suppose that we are given the recurs

$$T(n) = T(\lfloor n/2 \rfloor) + T(\lceil n/2 \rceil) + 1$$

We guess that T(n) = O(n), and want to show $T(n) \le cn$;

$$\begin{aligned} T(n) &\le c\lfloor n/2 \rfloor + c\lceil n/2 \rceil + 1 \\ &= cn + 1 \end{aligned}$$

However, this is incorrect since it does not imply T(n) $\leq$ cn for all values of c. instead, we should given T(n) $\leq$ cn – b. for some constant b $\geq$ 0, giving us;

$$\begin{aligned} T(n) &\leq (c\lfloor n/2 \rfloor - b) + (c\lceil n/2 \rceil - b) + 1 \\ &= cn - 2b + 1 \\ &\leq cn - b \end{aligned}$$

where the final inequality holds if our constant b $\geq$ 1. The arithmetic for the last inequality seems a bit off. However, what is important is that the form of the conclusion matches that of inductive hypothesis. Now, since that result of our induction matches our hypothesis, we can cn terms dominates the term b, yielding our result: T(n) = O (n).

Example 4: Solve

$$T(n) = T(\lceil n/2 \rceil) + 1 = O(1g\,n).$$

Solution. We guess that T(n) $\leq$ clg (n–b) for some b > 0, and assume that T (n/2) $\leq$ clg $(\lceil n/2 \rceil - b)$ holds,

Next is the induction:

$$\begin{aligned} T(n) &\leq c\lg(\lceil n/2 \rceil - b) + 1 \\ &\leq c\lg\ (n+1-2b/2) + 1 \\ &= c\lg(n+1-2b) - \log 2 + 1 \\ &= c\lg(n+1-2b) \\ &= 1g(n - \theta(1)) \end{aligned}$$

where it must be that b > 1/2.

4.2 ITERATION METHOD

In this method recurrences is expanded as summation of terms, then summation provides the solution.

Example 5: Given the recurrence T (n) = 3T (n/2) + n use the iteration method to get a big O estimate for T(n).

Solution. The iteration proceeds as follows:

$$\begin{aligned} T(n) &= n + 3T\left(\frac{n}{2}\right) \\ &= n + 3\left(\frac{n}{2}\right) + 3T\left(\frac{n}{4}\right) \\ &= n + \frac{3n}{2} + \frac{9n}{4} + 27T\left(\frac{n}{8}\right) = \ldots \end{aligned}$$

The coefficients form the term of the geometric series $\sum_{i=0}^{\infty}(r^i)$ where r =3/2 Since |r| > 1, the infinite series diverges. However, there are only finitely many terms in the sum. The sum terminates for the smallest integer K where 2^K > n (the number of times we divide n by 2 is $\log_2 n$), i.e when k $\approx$ $\log_2 n$.

Since $\left[\frac{n}{2}\right] \le \frac{n}{2}$ we have

$$T(n) \le n + \frac{3n}{2} + \frac{9n}{4} + \ldots + \left(\frac{3^{\log_2 n-1}}{2^{\log_2 n-1}}\right).n$$

$$= n \cdot \sum_{i=0}^{\log_2 n-1}\left(\frac{3}{2}\right)^i = n.\frac{\left(\left(\frac{3}{2}\right)^{\log_2 n} - 1\right)}{\left(\frac{3}{2} - 1\right)}$$

$$= 2n\left(\left(\frac{3}{2}\right)^{\log_2 n} - 1\right)$$

$$= 2n\left(\frac{3}{2}\right)^{\log_2 n} - 2n$$

$$= 2n\left(\frac{3^{\log_2 n}}{2^{\log_2 n}}\right) - 2n$$

$$= 2.3^{\log_2 n} - 2n \qquad [\text{Using } 2^{\log_2 n} = n]$$

$$= 2.n^{\log_2 3} - 2.n \qquad [a^{\log_b n} = n^{\log_b a}]$$

Since $\log_2 3 > 1$ we know that term $n^{\log_2 3}$ dominates n. So we can say that

$$T(n) = O(n^{\log_2 3})$$

Example 6: Given recurrence $T(n) = 3T\ (\lfloor n/4 \rfloor) + n$ show by on iteration method that $T(n) = \theta\ (n)$

Solution. For simplicity, we shall use m for $(\lfloor m \rfloor)$ since the occurrence is in terms at floor function.

The iteration proceeds as follows:

$$T(n) \le n + 3T\left(\frac{n}{4}\right)$$

$$= n + 3\left(\left(\frac{n}{4}\right) + 3T\left(\frac{n}{16}\right)\right)$$

$$= n + \frac{3n}{4} + \frac{9n}{16} + 27T\left(\frac{n}{64}\right)$$

$$\le n\sum_{i=0}^{\infty}\left(\frac{3}{4}\right)^i = 4n$$

from the formula $\sum_{i=0}^{\infty}(r^i) = \frac{1}{1-r}$

when $|r| < 1 \left(\text{here } r = \frac{3}{4}\right)$

The formula for T(n) involves a decreasing geometric series with ratio r = 3/4.
Therefore, T(n) = 0 (n)
(use C = 4 and $X_0 = N_0 = 1$ in the definition of O)

also $T(n) \geq n \text{since } 3T\left(\frac{n}{4}\right) > 0.$

So $T(n) = \Omega(n)$
(use C = 1 and $X_0 = N_0 = 1$ in definition of Ω)
By the definition of θ, we have T(n) = θ (n).

4.3 CHANGE VARIABLES.

Sometimes one can do algebraic manipulation to write an unknown recurrence in terms of a familiar one. Then one solves the familiar one and writes the solution in terms of the original variable.

Example 7: Solve $T(n) = 2T(\sqrt{n}) + \log_2 n.$

Solution. Let m = $\log_2$ n. Then thin recurrence becomes $T(2^m) = 2T(2^{m/2}) + m$. Let $S(m) = T(2^m)$, i.e S(m) = T (g (m)) where $g(m) = 2^m$.

So S (m/2) = T $(2^{m/2})$ and the new recurrence
S(m) = S (m/2) + m is produced.
Therefore it has the solution
S(m) = θ (m log $_2$ m), By the substitution $n = 2^m$, we get

$$T(n) = T(2^m)$$
$$S(m) = \theta(m \log_2 m)$$
$$= \theta(\log_2 m).\log_2(\log_2 n))$$

4.4 THE RECURSION TREE METHOD

The recursion free method can be used generate a good quess for an asymptotic bound on a recurrence. This guess can then be verified by substitution method. Since our guess will be verified, we can take same liberation in our calculation, sum as dropping floors and ceilings or restricting the value of n.

Example 8: Solve recurrence with free method.

$$T(n) = \begin{cases} \theta(1) & 1 \leq n < 3 \\ 2T(\lfloor n/3 \rfloor) + \theta(n) & n \geq 3 \end{cases}$$

Solution. We simplify the recurrence by dropping the floor and replacing θ(n) by n to get T(n) = 2T (n/3) +3. Each rode in a recursion of 1 (n) obtained by recursively substituting the expression for T into itself. We construct a recurrence of such. trees of increasing depth.

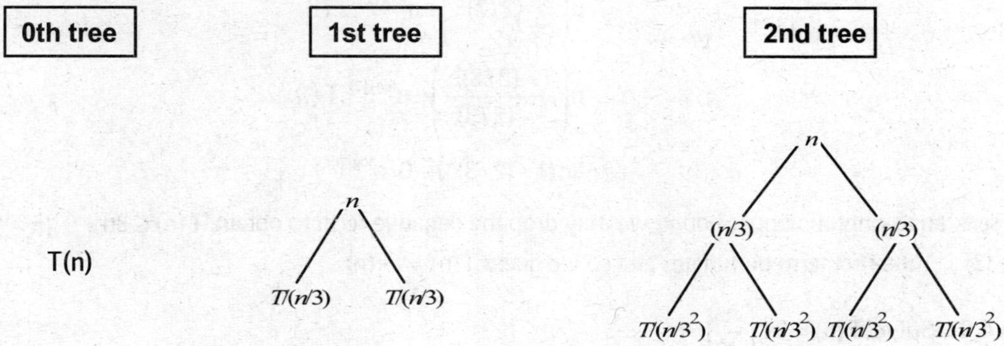

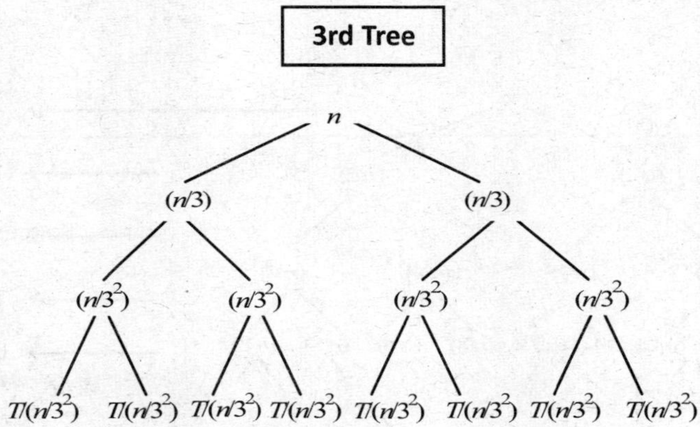

By summing the modes in any one of there, we obtain an expression for T(n). After to iteration of this process we reach a tree in which all bottom level nodes are $T(n/3^k)$

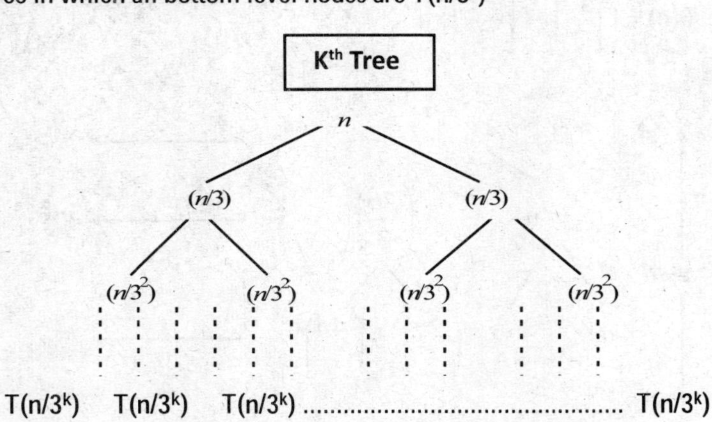

Note that there are 2^i nodes at depth i, each of which has value $n/3^i$ (for $0 \leq k - 1$). The sequence of trees termination when all bottom level nodes are T(1), i.e when $n/3^k = 1$, which implies implies $k = \log_3(n)$. The number of nodes at this bottom level is therefore $2k = 2\log_3 (n) = n \log_3 (2)$. Summing all nodes in the final recursion trees gives us the following expression for T(n)

$$T(n) = \sum_{i=0}^{n=1} 2^i + (n/3^i) + n^{\log_3(2)}\ T(1)$$

$$= n\left(\sum_{i=0}^{k-1} (2/3)^i\right) + n^{\log_3(2)}.T(1)$$

$$= n\left(\frac{1-(2/3)^k}{1-(2/3)}\right) + n^{\log_3(2)}.T(1)$$

$$= 3n(1-(2/3)^k) + \theta(n^{\log_3(2)})$$

If we seek an asymptotic upper bound we may drop the negative term to obtain $T(n) \le 3n + \theta\ (n^{\log_3(2)})$. Since $\log_3(2) < 1$ the first term dominates and so we guess $T(n) = O(n)$.

Example 4.9: Solve $T(n) = 2T\left(\frac{n}{2}\right) + n^2$

Solution:

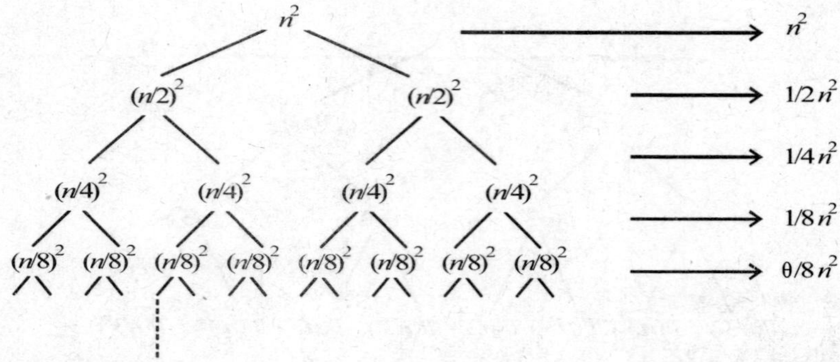

Hence Solution is $\theta(n^2)$

Example 4.10 Solve $T(n) = T\left(\frac{n}{3}\right) + T\left(\frac{2n}{3}\right) + n$

Solution:

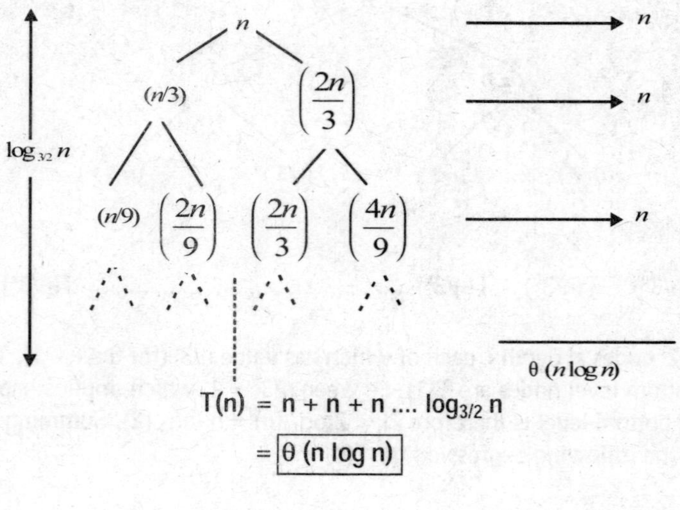

$$T(n) = n + n + n \ldots \log_{3/2} n$$

$$= \boxed{\theta\ (n \log n)}$$

Example 4.11 Solve $T(n) = 4T(\lfloor n/2 \rfloor) + n$

Solution:

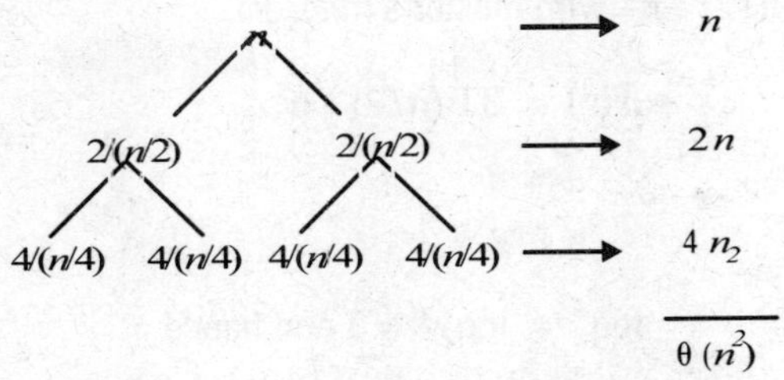

$$= n + 2n + 4n .... + n \log n$$

$$= n(1 + 2 + 4 .... \log n)$$

$$= n \cdot \frac{(2^{\log_2 n} - 1)}{(2-1)}$$

$$= n^2 - n$$

$$= \theta(n^2)$$

$$\boxed{T(n) = \theta(n^2)}$$

4.5 THE MASTER METHOD

This is a method for finding (asymptotic) solution to recurrence of the form

$$T(n) = at(n/b) + f(n) \quad \boxed{T(n) = aT(n/b) + f(n)}$$

where $a \geq 1$, $b > 1$, and the function f(n) is asymptotically positive. Here T (n/b) denotes either $T(\lfloor n/b \rfloor)$ or $T(\lceil n/b \rceil)$, and it is understood that $T(n) = \theta(1)$ for some finite set of initial terms. Such a recurrence describes the run time of a divide and conquer algorithm which divides a problem of size n into a subproblems, each of size n/b. In this context f(n) represents the cost of doing the dividing and re-combining.

MASTER'S THEOREM

Let $a \geq 1$, $b > 1$, f(n) be asymptotically positive, and let T(n) be defined by

$$T(n) = aT(n/b) + f(n)$$

Then we have 3 cases:

(1) If $f(n) = O(n^{\log_b(a) - \varepsilon})$ for same $\varepsilon > 0$ then

$$T(n) = \theta(n^{\log_b(a)})$$

(2) If $f(n) = \theta(n^{\log_b(a)})$ then $T(n) = \theta(n^{\log_b^a} \log n)$

(3) If $f(n) = \Omega(n^{\log_b^{(a)+\varepsilon}})$ for some $\varepsilon > 0$ and if $af(n/b) \le cf(n)$ for some $0 < 0 < 1$ and for all sufficiently large n, then $T(n) = \theta(f(n))$.

Example 12: Solve $T(n) = 8T(n/2) + n^3$ with master's theorem.

Solution

$$T(n) = 8T(n/2) + n^3$$

Then

$$a = 8$$
$$b = 2$$
$$\log_b^a = \log_2 8 = 3 \text{ and hance}$$

$f(n) = n^3 = \theta(n^{\log_b^a})$ so we are in case 2.

Therefore $T(n) = \theta(n^3 \log(n))$.

Example 13: Solve $T(n) = 5T(n/4) + 5$

Solution.

$$T(n) = 5T(n/4) + 5$$
$$a = 5, b = 4, \log_b^{(a)} = 1.609 > 1$$

Let $\varepsilon = \log_4(5) - 1$ so that $\varepsilon > 0$.

$$f(n) = n = O(n^{\log_4^{(5)-\varepsilon}})$$

Therefore we are in case 1. So .

$$T(n) = \theta(n^{\log_4^5})$$

Example 14: Solve $T(n) = 5T(n/4) + n^2$.

Solution. $a = 5, b = 4$ so

$\log_b^{(a)} = \log_4^5 = 1.609 < 2$

Let $\varepsilon = 2 - \log_4^{(5)}$,

So $\varepsilon = 0$, and $f(n) = n^2 = \Omega(n^{\log_4^{5+\varepsilon}})$

and therefore case 3. seems to apply

To check reqularity condition:

$5f(n/4) \le cf(n)$ for some $0 < C < 1$ and all sufficiently large n. This inequality say $5(n/4)^2 \le Cn^2$ i.e. $(5/16)n^2 \le cn^2$. Then we may choose any C satisfying $5/16 \le C < 1$.

Since the reqularity condition in satisfied we have $T(n) = \theta(n^2)$.

Solved Exercise

1. Show that the solution of $T(n)=T(n/2) + 1$ is $O(\lg n)$.

Sol. Using the iteration method, we substitute the function recursively till we arrive at T(1).

i.e $T(n) = T(n/2) + 1 = T(n/4) + 1 + 1 = ...$

We get a total of lg(n) iterations

i.e T(n) = T(1) +lg(n)
Thus the complexity is O(lg n).

2. Show that the solution to T(n)=2*T((n/2)+17) is O(n*(lg n)).

Sol. Using the iteration method, it takes lg(n) iterations to reach T(1).After final iteration:
T(n) = (2^lg(n))*(T(1) + lg(n)*17)
Thus the complexity is (2^lg(n))*(lg n) = O(n*lg(n))

3. Solve the recurrence T(n)=2*T(sqrt(n)) + 1.

Sol. Let n=2^m,then T(2^m)=2*T(2^m/2) + 1
Now let S(m)=T(2^m).
$\Rightarrow$ S(m) = 2*S(m/2) +1
This is the same as 2nd problem.Thus the complexity is O(m*lg(m)),but m=lg(n)
Thus the final complexity is O(lg(n)*lg(lg(n)))

4. Show that the solution of T(n)=T(n/2) + 1 is O(lg n).

Ans. Using the iteration method, we substitute the function recursively till we arrive at T(1). i.e T(n)=T(n/2)+1=T(n/4)+1+ 1=....
we get a total of lg(n) iterations
i.e T(n)=T(1) +lg(n)
Thus the complexity is O(lg n).

5. Show that the solution to T(n)=2*T((n/2)+17) is O(n*(lg n)).

Ans. Using the iteration method, it takes lg(n) iterations to reach T(1).After final iteration:
T(n)=(2^lg(n))*(T(1) + lg(n)*17)
Thus the complexity is (2^lg(n))*(lg n) = O(n*lg(n))

6. Solve the recurrence T(n)=2*T(sqrt(n)) + 1.

Ans. Let n=2^m,then T(2^m)=2*T(2^m/2) + 1
Now let S(m)=T(2^m).
=>S(m)=2*S(m/2) +1
This is the same as 2nd problem.
Thus the complexity is O(m*lg(m)),but m=lg(n)
Thus the final complexity is O(lg(n)*lg(lg(n)))

Previous Year University Question

1. Solve the recurrence relation [GBTU]

   T(n) = 2T("n) +1 whenever the n is perfect square grater then 1 and T(2) = 3

2. Solve the recurrence relation using master theorem. [GBTU]

   $T(n) = 7T(n/2) + 18n^2$ where n >2 and power of 2.

3. You are given an array of n integers a1,a2,.....an. given an O(log n) algorithm that finds index I where a_i is I or prove that I does not exist. [GBTU]

4. Explain how you will determine the total number of partitions of a positive integer using a recursive algorithm. [Madrass University]

5. Solve the recurrence relation by iteration: $T(n) = T(n+1) + n^4$ [GBTU]
6. Can the Masters Method be applied to solve recurrence $T(n) = 4T(n/2) + n^2 \log n$? Why or why not? [GBTU]
7. What is the recurrence relation? Solve the following recursive method $T(n) = 2T(n/2 + 17) + n$. [MDU]

Exercise

1. Solve the recurrence exactly for n a power if 2

$$T(n) = \begin{cases} 1 & \text{if } n=1 \\ 7T(n/2) + (n1gn)^2 & \text{otherwise} \end{cases}$$

2. Solve the following recurrence for n of the form 2^{2^k}

$$T(n) = \begin{cases} 1 & \text{if } n=1 \\ 3T(\sqrt{n}) + 1gn & \text{otherwise} \end{cases}$$

3. Show that the recursion solution to the Towers, of Hanol problem requires $f(n) = 2^n - 1$ moves for n disks. Show that no other solution uses fever than f(n) move
4. Use iteration to solve

$$T(n) = T(n-x) + T(x) + n \text{ whose } x \geq 1 \text{ is a constant.}$$

5. Solve the recurrence
   (a) $T(n) = 24\,T(n/4 + 8) + n/4$
   (b) $T(n) = T(n-1) + 1g\,n$

CHAPTER 5

HASHING

5.1 INTRODUCTION

Hashing is the transformation of a string of characters into a usually shorter fixed-length value or key that represents the original string. Hashing is used to index and retrieve items in a database because it is faster to find the item using the shorter hashed key than to find it using the original value. It is also used in many encryption algorithms.

As a simple example of the using of hashing in databases, a group of people could be arranged in a database like this:

Amit, Sita, Ram, imal, eepak (and many more sorted into alphabetical order)

Each of these names would be the key in the database for that person s data. A database search mechanism would first have to start looking character-by-character across the name for matches until it found the match (or ruled the other entries out). But if each of the names were hashed, it might be possible (depending on the number of names in the database) to generate a unique four-digit key for each name.

A search for any name would first consist of computing the hash value (using the same hash function used to store the item) and then comparing for a match using that value. It would, in general, be much faster to find a match across four digits, each having only 10 possibilities, than across an unpredictable value length w

The hashing algorithm is called the hash function (and probably the term is derived from the idea that the resulting hash value can be thought of as a "mixed up version of the represented value). In addition to faster data retrieval, hashing is also used to encrypt and decrypt digital signatures (used to authenticate message senders and receivers). The digital signature is transformed with the hash function and then both the hashed value (known as a message-digest) and the signature are sent in separate transmissions to the receiver. Using the same hash function as the sender, the receiver derives a message-digest from the signature and compares it with the message-digest it also received. They should be the same.

5.2 HASH FUNCTION

A hash function is any well defined procedure or mathematical function that converts a large, possibly variable-sized amount of data into a small datum, usually a single integer that may serve as an index to an array. The values returned by a hash function are called hash values, hash codes, hash sums, checksums or simply hashes.

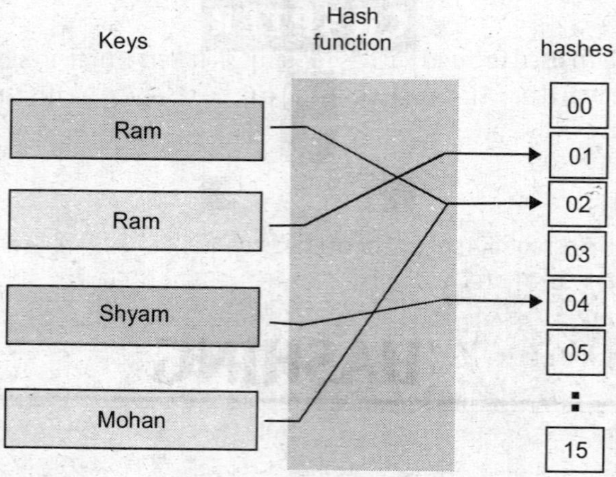

Fig. 5.1

Therefore, Hash functions are mostly used to speed up table lookup or data comparison tasks such as finding items in a database detecting duplicated or similar records in a large file finding similar stretches in DN sequences, and so on.

A hash function may map two or more keys to the same hash value. In many applications, it is desirable to minimize the occurrence of such collisions which means that the hash function must map the keys to the hash values as evenly as possible., epending on the application, other properties may be required as well. Although the idea was conceived in the 1950s, the design of good hash functions is still a topic of active research.

5.3 APPLICATIONS OF HASH FUNCTION

1. Hash tables
2. Caches
3. Bloom filters
4. Finding duplicate records
5. Finding similar records
6. Finding similar substrings
7. Geometric hashing.

Hash tables

Hash functions are primarily used in hash tables to quickly locate a data record (for example, a dictionary definition) given its search key (the headword). So the hash function is used to map the search key to the hash. The index gives the place where the corresponding record should be stored. Hash tables, in turn, are used to implement associative arrays and dynamic sets.

In general, a hashing function may map several different keys to the same index. Therefore, each slot of a hash table is associated with (implicitly or explicitly) a set of records, rather than a single record. For this reason, each slot of a hash table is often called a bucket and hash values are also called bucket indices.

Thus, the hash function only hints at the record s location it tells where one should start looking for it Still, in a half-full table, a good hash function will typically narrow the search down to only one or two entries.

Caches

Hash functions are also used to build caches for large data sets stored in slow media. A cache is generally simpler than a hashed search table, since any collision can be resolved by discarding or writing back the older of the two colliding items.

Bloom filters

Hash functions are an essential ingredient of the Bloom filter a compact data structure that provides an enclosing approximation to a set of keys.

Finding duplicate records

When storing records in a large unsorted file, one may use a hash function to map each record to an index into a table T, and collect in each bucket T[i] a list of the numbers of all records with the same hash value i. Therefore Once the table is complete, any two duplicate records will end up in the same bucket. The duplicates can then be found by scanning every bucket T[i] which contains two or more members, fetching those records, and comparing them. With a table of appropriate size, this method is likely to be much faster than any alternative approach (such as sorting the file and comparing all consecutive pairs).

Finding similar records

Hash functions can also be used to locate table records whose key is similar, but not identical, to a given key or pairs of records in a large file which have similar keys. Although for that purpose, one needs a hash function that maps similar keys to hash values that differ by at most m, where m is a small integer (say, 1 or 2). If one builds a table of T of all record numbers, using such a hash function, then similar records will end up in the same bucket, or in nearby buckets. Then one need only check the records in each bucket T [i] against those in buckets T [i + k] where k ranges between - m and m.

This class includes the so-called acoustic fingerprint algorithms, that are used to locate similar-sounding entries in large collection of audio files (as in the Music Brain song labeling service). For this application, the hash function must be as insensitive as possible to data capture or transmission errors, and to "trivial changes such as timing and volume changes, compression, etc.

Finding similar substrings

The same techniques can be used to find equal or similar stretches in a large collection of strings, such as a document repository or a genomic database. In this case, the input strings are broken into many small pieces, and a hash function is used to detect potentially equal pieces,

Geometric hashing

This principle is widely used in computer graphics computational geometry and many other disciplines, to solve many proximity problems in the plane or in three-dimensional space, such as finding closest pairs in a set of points, similar shapes in a list of shapes, similar images in an image database and so on. In these applications, the set of all inputs is some sort of metric space and the hashing function can be interpreted as a partition of that space into a grid of cells. The table is often an array with two or more indices (called a grid file grid index bucket grid and similar names), and the hash function returns an index tuple. This special case of hashing is known as geometric hashing or the grid method. Geometric hashing is also used in telecommunications (usually under the name vector uanti ation) to encode and compress multi-dimensional signals.

5.4 PROPERTIES OF HASH FUNCTION

Good hash functions, in the original sense of the term, are usually required to satisfy certain properties listed below. Different requirements apply to the other related concepts.

Low cost

The cost of computing a hash function must be small enough to make a hashing-based solution more efficient than alternative approaches. For instance, a self-balancing binary tree can locate an item in a sorted table of n items with O (log n) key comparisons. Therefore, a hash table solution will be more efficient than a self-balancing binary tree if the number of items is large and the hash function produces few collisions and less efficient if the number of items is small and the hash function is complex.

Determinism

A hash procedure must be deterministic—meaning that for a given input value it must always generate the same hash value. In other words, it must be a function of the hashed data, in the mathematical sense of the term. Bas cally this requirement excludes hash functions that depend on external variable parameters, such as, pseudo-random number generators or the time of day. It is also excludes functions that depend on the memory address of the object being hashed, if that address may change during processing (as may happen in systems that use certain methods of garbage collection), although sometimes rehashing of the item can be done.

Uniformity

A good hash function should map the expected inputs as evenly as possible over its output range. That is every hash value in the output range should be generated with roughly the same probability. The reason for this last requirement is that the cost of hashing-based methods goes up sharply as the number of collisions pairs of inputs that are mapped to the same hash value — increases. Basically, if some hash values are more likely to occur than others, a larger fraction of the lookup operations will have to search through a larger set of colliding table entries. Note that this criterion only requires the value to be uniformly distributed, not random in any sense. A good randomizing function is (barring computational efficiency concerns) generally a good choice as a hash function, but the converse need not be true.

Hash tables often contain only a small subset of the valid inputs. For instance, a club membership list may contain only a hundred or so member names, out of the very large set of all possible names. Mostly In this cases, the uniformity criterion should hold for almost all typical subsets of entries that may be found in the table, not just for the global set of all possible entries.

In other words, if a typical set of m records is hashed to n table slots, the probability of a bucket receiving many more than m/n records should be vanishingly small. In particular, if m is less than n, very few buckets should have more than one or two records. (In an ideal "perfect hash function", no bucket should have more than one record; but a small number of collisions is virtually inevitable, even if n is much larger than m — see the birthday paradox).

When testing a hash function, the uniformity of the distribution of hash values can be evaluated by the chi-square test.

Variable range

In many applications, the range of hash values may be different for each run of the program, or may change along the same run (for instance, when a hash table needs to be expanded). In those situations, one needs a hash function which takes two parameters — the input data z, and the number n of allowed hash values.

A common solution is to compute a fixed hash function with a very large range (say, 0 to $2^{32} - 1$), divide the result by n, and use the division's remainder. If n is itself a power of 2, this can be done by bit masking and bit shifting. Thus when this approach is used, the hash function must be chosen so that the result has fairly uniform distribution between 0 and n – 1, for any n that may occur in the application. Depending on the function, the remainder may be uniform only for certain n, e.g. odd or prime numbers.

It is possible to relax the restriction of the table size being a power of 2 and not having to perform any modulo, remainder or division operation - as these operation are considered computational costly in some contexts. When n is much lesser than 2^b take a pseudo random number generator (PRNG) function P (key), uniform on the interval $[0, 2^b - 1]$. Consider the ratio $q = 2^b / n$. Now the hash function can be seen as the value of P(key) / q. Rearranging the calculation and replacing the 2^b – division by bit shifting right (>>) b times you end up with hash function n * P (key) >> b.

Variable range with minimal movement (dynamic hash function)

When the hash function is used to store values in a hash table that outlives the run of the program, and the hash table needs to be expanded or shrunk, the hash table is referred to as a dynamic hash table.

A hash function that will relocate the minimum number of records when the table is resized is desirable. What is needed is a hash function H (z, n,) where z is the key being hashed and n is the number of allowed hash values such that H (z, n + 1) = H(z, n) with probability close to n / (n + 1).

Linear hashing and spiral storage are examples of dynamic hash functions that execute in constant time but relax the property of uniformity to achieve the minimal movement property.

Extendible hashing uses a dynamic hash function that requires space proportional to n to compute the hash function, and it becomes a function of the previous keys that have been inserted.

Several algorithms that preserve the uniformity property but require time proportional to n to compute the value of H(z,n) have been invented.

Data normalization

In some applications, the input data may contain features that are irrelevant for comparison purposes. For example, when looking up a personal name, it may be desirable to ignore the distinction between upper and lower case letters. For such data, one must use a hash function that is compatible with the data equivalence criterion being used that is, any two inputs that are considered equivalent must yield the same hash value. This can be accomplished by normalizing the input before hashing it, as by upper-casing all letters.

Continuity

A hash function that is used to search for similar (as opposed to equivalent) data must be as continuous as possible: two inputs that differ by a little should be mapped to equal or nearly equal hash values.

Note that continuity is usually considered a fatal flaw for checksums, cryptographic hash functions, and other related concepts. Continuity is desirable for hash functions only in some applications, such as hash tables that use linear search.

5.5 VARIOUS FORMS OF HASHING

Hashing as a tool to associate one set or bulk of data with an identifier has many different forms of application in the real-world. Below are some of the more common uses of hash functions.

- **String Hashing**

Used in the area of data storage access. Mainly within indexing of data and as a structural back end to associative containers (i.e. hash tables)

- **Cryptographic Hashing**

Used for data/user verification and authentication. A strong cryptographic hash function has the property of being very difficult to reverse the result of the hash and hence reproduce the original piece of data. Cryptographic hash functions are used to hash user's passwords and have the hash of the passwords stored on a system rather than having the password itself stored. Cryptographic hash functions are also seen as irreversible compression functions, being able to represent large quantities of data with a signal ID, they are useful in seeing whether or not the data has been tampered with, and can also be used as data one signes in order to prove authenticity of a document via other cryptographic means.

- **Geometric Hashing**

This form of hashing is used in the field of computer vision for the detection of classified objects in arbitrary scenes.

The process involves initially selecting a region or object of interest. From there using affine invariant feature detection algorithms such as the Harris corner detector (HCD), Scale-Invariant Feature Transform (SIFT) or Speeded-Up Robust Features (SURF), a set of affine features are extracted which are deemed to represent said object or region. This set is sometimes called a macro-feature or a constellation of features. Depending on the nature of the features detected and the type of object or region being classified it may still be possible to match two constellations of features even though there may be minor disparities (such as missing or outlier features) between the two sets. The constellations are then said to be the classified set of features.

Therefore a hash value is computed from the constellation of features. This is typically done by initially defining a space where the hash values are intended to reside - the hash value in this case is a multidimensional value normalized for the defined space. Coupled with the process for computing the hash value another process that determines the distance between two hash values is needed - A distance measure is required rather than a deterministic equality operator due to the issue of possible disparities of the constellations that went into calculating the hash value. Also owing to the non-linear nature of such spaces the simple Euclidean distance metric is essentially ineffective, as a result the process of automatically determining a distance metric for a particular space has become an active field of research in academia.

Typical examples of geometric hashing include the classification of various kinds of automobiles, for the purpose of re-detection in arbitrary scenes. Hence the level of detection can be varied from just detecting a vehicle, to a particular model of vehicle, to a specific vehicle.

- **Bloom Filters**

A Bloom filter allows for the "state of existence" of a large set of possible values to be represented with a much smaller piece of memory than the sum size of the values. In computer science this is known as a membership query and is core concept in associative containers. The Bloom filter achieves this through the use of multiple distinct hash functions and also by allowing the result of a membership query for the existence of a particular value to have a certain probability of error. The guarantee a Bloom filter provides is that for any membership query there will never be any false negatives, however there may be false positives. The false positive probability can be controlled by varying the size of the table used for the Bloom filter and also by varying the number of hash functions. Subsequent research done in the area of hash functions and tables and bloom filters by Mitzenmacher et al. suggest that for most practical uses of such constructs, the entropy in the data being hashed contributes to the entropy of the hash functions, this further leads onto theoretical results that conclude an optimal bloom filter (one which provides the lowest false positive probability for a given table size or vice versa) providing a user defined false positive probability can be constructed with at most two distinct hash functions also known as pairwise independent hash functions, greatly increasing the efficiency of membership queries. Bloom filters are commonly found in applications such as spell-checkers, string matching algorithms, network packet analysis tools and network/ internet caches.

5.6 HASH FUNCTION ALGORITHMS

For most types of hashing functions the choice of the function depends strongly on the nature of the input data, and their probability distribution in the intended application.

Trivial hash function

If the datum to be hashed is small enough, one can use the datum itself (reinterpreted as an integer in binary notation) as the hashed value. The cost of computing this "trivial" (identity) hash function is effectively zero.

The meaning of "small enough" depends on how much memory is available for the hash table. A typical PC (as of 2008) might have a gigabyte of available memory, meaning that hash values of up to 30 bits could be accommodated. However, there are many applications that can get by with much less. For example, when mapping character strings between upper and lower case, one can use the binary encoding of each character, interpreted as an integer, to index a table that gives the alternative form of that character ("A" for "a", "8" for "8", etc.). If each character is stored in 8 bits (as in ASCII or ISO Latin 1), the table has only $2^8 = 256$ entries; in the case of Unicode characters, the table would have $17 \times 2^{16} = 1114112$ entries.

The same technique can be used to map two-letter country codes like "us" or "za" to country names ($26^2 = 676$ table entries), 5-digit zip codes like 13083 to city names (100000 entries), etc. Invalid data values (such as the country code "xx" or the zip code 00000) may be left undefined in the table, or mapped to some appropriate "null" value.

Perfect hashing

A hash function that is injective that is, maps each valid input to a different hash value — is said to be perfect. With such a function one can directly locate the desired entry in a hash table, without any additional searching.

Unfortunately, perfect hash functions are effective only in situations where the inputs are fixed and entirely known in advance, such as mapping month names to the integers 0 to 11, or the cases of a switch statement. A perfect function for a given set of n keys, suitable for use in a hash table, can be found in time proportional to n, can be represented in less than 3*n bits, and can be evaluated in a constant number of operations. There are generators that produce optimized executable code to evaluate a perfect hash for a given input set.

Minimal perfect hashing

A perfect hash function for n keys is said to be minimal if its range consists of nconsecutive integers, usually from 0 to n - 1. Besides providing single-step lookup, a minimal perfect hash function also yields a compact hash table, without any vacant slots. Minimal perfect hash functions are much harder to find than perfect ones with a wider range.

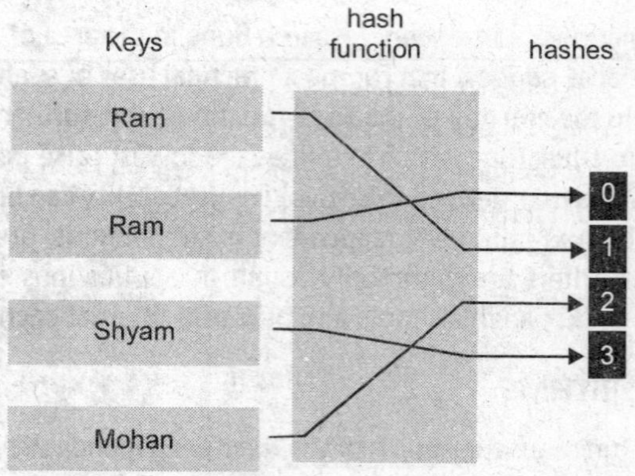

Fig. 5.2 A minimal perfect hash function for the four names shown

Hashing uniformly distributed data

If the inputs are bounded-length strings (such as telephone numbers, car license plates, invoice numbers, etc.), and each input may independently occur with uniform probability, then a hash function need only map roughly the same number of inputs to each hash value. For instance, suppose that each input is an integer z in the range 0 to N – 1, and the output must be an integer h in the range 0 to n – 1, where N is much larger than n. Then the hash function could be h = z mod n (the remainder of z divided by n), or h = (z × n) N (the value z scaled down by n / N and truncated to an integer), or many other formulas.

Warning: h = z mod n was used in many of the original random number generators, but was found to have a number of issues. One of which is that as n approaches N, this function becomes less and less uniform.

Hashing data with other distributions

These simple formulas will not do if the input values are not equally likely, or are not independent. For instance, most patrons of a supermarket will live in the same geographic area, so their telephone numbers are likely to begin with the same 3 to 4 digits. In that case, if n is 10000 or so, the division formula (z × n) * N, which depends mainly on the leading digits, will generate a lot of collisions; whereas the remainder formula z mod n, which is quite sensitive to the trailing digits, may still yield a fairly even distribution of hash values.

Hashing variable-length data

When the data values are long (or variable-length) character strings—such as personal names, web page addresses, or mail messages — their distribution is usually very uneven, with complicated dependencies. For example, text in any natural language has highly non-uniform distributions of characters, and character pairs, very characteristic of the language. For such data, it is prudent to use a hash function that depends on all characters of the string — and depends on each character in a different way.

In cryptographic hash functions, a Merkle-Damgdrd construction is usually used. In general, the scheme for hashing such data is to break the input into a sequence of small units (bits, bytes, words, etc.) and combine all the units b[1], b [2], ..., b [m] sequentially, as follows.

```
S ← S0;                      // Initialize the state.
for kin 1, 2, ..., m do      // Scan the input data units:
    S ← F (S, b [k]);        // Combine data unit k into the state.
return G (S, n)              // Extract the hash value from the state.
```

This schema is also used in many text checksum and fingerprint algorithms. The state variable S may be a 32 – or 64-bit unsigned integer; in that case, S0 can be 0, and G (S, n) can be just S mod n. The best choice of F is a complex issue and depends on the nature of the data. If the units b [k] are single bits, then F (S,b) could be, for instance.

```
ifhighbit(S)= 0 then
return 2* S + b
else
return (2 * S + b) ^ P
```

Here highbit (S) denotes the most significant bit of S; the '*' operator denotes unsigned integer multiplication with lost overflow; '^t' is the bitwise exclusive or operation applied to words; and P is a suitable fixed word.

Special-purpose hash functions

In many cases, one can design a special-purpose (heuristic) hash function that yields many fewer collisions than a good general-purpose hash function. For example, suppose that the input data are file names such as FILE0000.CHK, FILE0001.CHK, FILE0002.CHK, etc., with mostly sequential numbers. For such data, a function that extracts the numeric part k of the file name and returns k mod n would be nearly optimal. Needless to say, a function that is exceptionally good for a specific kind of data may have dismal performance on data with different distribution.

Rolling hash

In some applications, such as substring search, one must compute a hash function h for every k-character substring of a given n-character string t; where k is a fixed integer, and n is much larger than k. The straightforward solution, which is to extract every such substring s of t and compute h (s) separately, requires a number of operations proportional to k n. However, with the proper choice of h, one can use the technique of rolling hash to compute all those hashes with an effort proportional to k + n.

Universal hashing

A universal hashing scheme is a randomized algorithm that selects a hashing function h among a family of such functions, in such a way that the probability of a collision of any two distinct keys is 1/n, where n is the number of distinct hash values desired —independently of the two keys. Universal hashing ensures (in a probabilistic sense) that the hash function application will behave as well as if it were using a random function, for any distribution of the input data. It will however have more collisions than perfect hashing, and may require more operations than a special-purpose hash function.

Hashing with checksum functions

One can adapt certain checksum or fingerprinting algorithms for use as hash functions. Some of those algorithms will map arbitrary long string data z, with any typical real-world distribution — no matter how non-uniform and dependent — to a 32-bit or 64-bit string, from which one can extract a hash value in 0 through n –1.

This method may produce a sufficiently uniform distribution of hash values, as long as the hash range size n is small compared to the range of the checksum or fingerprint function. However, some checksums fare poorly in the avalanche test, which may be a concern in some applications. In particular, the popular CRC32 checksum provides only 16 bits (the higher half of the result) that are usable for hashing. Moreover, each bit of the input has a deterministic effect on each bit of the CRC32, that is one can tell without looking at the rest of the input, which bits of the output will flip if the input bit is flipped; so care must be taken to use all 32 bits when computing the hash from the checksum.

Hashing with cryptographic hash functions

Some cryptographic hash functions, such as SHA-1, have even stronger uniformity guarantees than checksums or fingerprints, and thus can provide very good general-purpose hashing functions.

In ordinary applications, this advantage may be too small to offset their much higher costi However, this method can provide uniformly distributed hashes even when the keys are chosen by a malicious agent. This feature may help protect services against denial of service attacks.

5.7 HASH TABLE

In computer science, a hash table or hash map is a data structure that uses a hash function to map identifying values, known as keys (e.g., a person's name), to their associated values (e.g., their telephone number). The hash function is used to transform the key into the index (the hash) of an array element (the slot or bucket) where the corresponding value is to be sought.

Ideally, the hash function should map each possible key to a unique slot index, but this ideal is rarely achievable in practice (unless the hash keys are fixed; i.e. new entries are never added to the table after creation). Most hash table designs assume that hash collisions the situation where different keys happen to have the same hash value — are normal occurrences and must be accommodated in some way.

In a well-dimensioned hash table, the average cost (number of instructions) for each lookup is independent of the number of elements stored in the table. Many hash table designs also allow arbitrary insertions and deletions of key-value pairs, at constant average (indeed, amortized) cost per operation.

In many situations, hash tables turn out to be more efficient than search trees or any other table lookup structure. For this reason, they are widely used in many kinds of computer software, particularly for associative arrays, database indexing, caches, and sets.

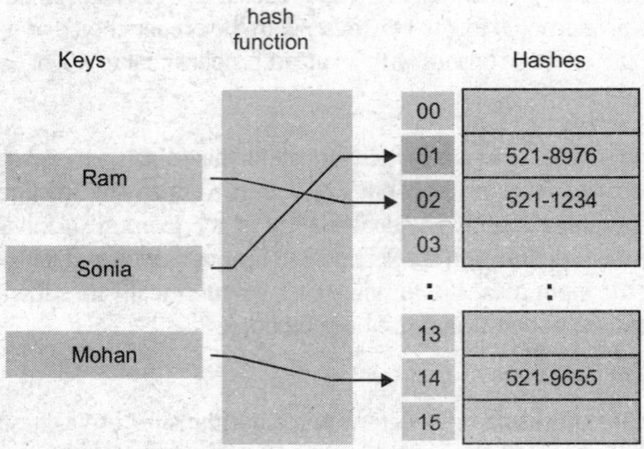

Fig.5.3 A small phone book as a hash table

5.8 COLLISION

In computer science, a collision or clash is a situation that occurs when two distinct pieces of data have the same hash value, checksum, fingerprint, or cryptographic digest.

Collisions are unavoidable whenever members of a very large set (such as all possible person names, or all possible computer files) are mapped to a relatively short bit string. This is merely an instance of the pigeonhole principle.

The impact of collisions depends on the application. When hash functions and fingerprints are used to identify similar data, such as homologous DNA sequences or similar audio files, the functions are designed so as to maximize the probability of collision between distinct but similar data. Checksums, on the other hand, are designed to minimize the probability of collisions between similar inputs, without regard for collisions between very different inputs.

In most other applications, however, collisions of any kind are equally undesirable. Any collision in a hash table increases the average cost of lookup operations. When fingerprints are used to avoid unnecessary file storage or transfer, e.g. in a proxy server or backup system, a collision may cause incorrect operation and even permanent data loss. A successful collision attack on a cryptographic hash function may compromise the security of computer and communication systems. Therefore, much effort is devoted to the design of algorithms that minimize the occurrence of collisions for various applications.

In the context of cryptographic hash functions, the inability of an adversary to compute collisions efficiently is often essential to the security of the protocol. A collision-free hash function is a type of one-way function that formalizes this property: it is not possible for a randomized polynomial-time algorithm to locate a collision of a collision-free hash function with non-negligible probability. It is unknown whether such a function exists.

5.9 COLLISION RESOLUTION

Hash collisions are practically unavoidable when hashing a random subset of a large set of possible keys. For example, if 2500 keys are hashed into a million buckets, even with a perfectly uniform random distribution, according to the birthday paradox there is a 95% chance of at least two of the keys being hashed to the same slot.

Therefore, most hash table implementations have some collision resolution strategy to handle such events. Some common strategies are described below. All these methods require that the keys (or pointers to them) be stored in the table, together with the associated values.

5.9.1 Load factor

The performance of most collision resolution methods does not depend directly on the number n of stored entries, but depends strongly on the table's load factor, the ratio n/s between n and the size s of its bucket array. With a good hash function, the average lookup cost is nearly constant as the load factor increases from 0 up to 0.7 or soBeyond that point, the probability of collisions and the cost of handling them increases.

On the other hand, as the load factor approaches zero, the size of the hash table increases with little improvement in the search cost, and memory is wasted.

Separate chaining

In the strategy known as separate chaining, direct chaining, or simply chaining, each slot of the bucket array is a pointer to a linked list that contains the key-value pairs that hashed to the same location. Lookup requires scanning the list for an entry with the given key. Insertion requires adding a new entry record to either end of the list belonging to the hashed slot. Deletion requires searching the list and removing the element.

(The technique is also called open hashing or closed addressing, which should not be confused with 'open addressing' or 'closed hashing'.)

Chained hash tables with linked lists are popular because they require only basic data structures with simple algorithms, and can use simple hash functions that are unsuitable for other methods.

The cost of a table operation is that of scanning the entries of the selected bucket for the desired key. If the distribution of keys is sufficiently uniform, the average cost of a lookup depends only on the average number of keys per bucket — that is, on the load factor.

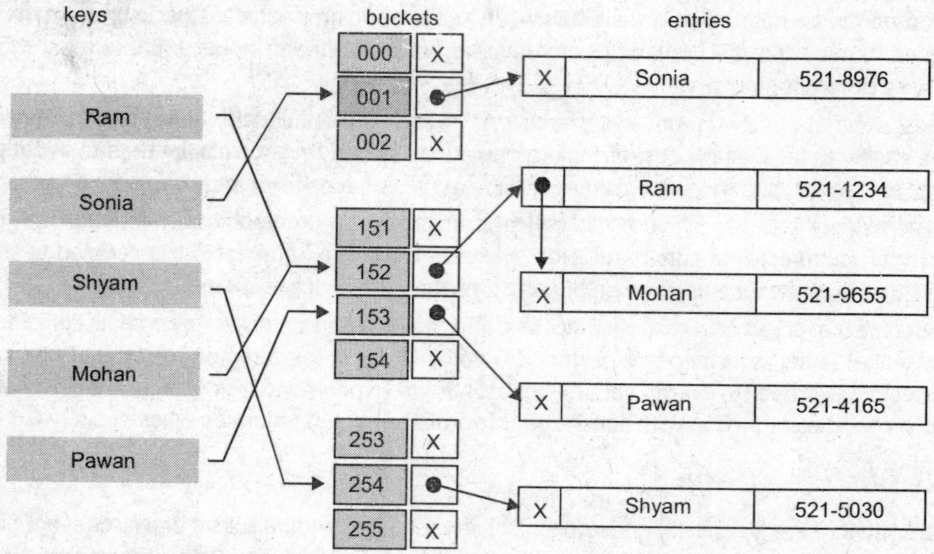

Fig. 5.4 Hash collision resolved by separate chaining

Chained hash tables remain effective even when the number of entries n is much higher than the number of slots. Their performance degrades more gracefully (linearly) with the load factor. For example, a chained hash table with 1000 slots and 10,000 stored keys (load factor 10) is five to ten times slower than a 10,000-slot table (load factor l); but still 1000 times faster than a plain sequential list, and possibly even faster than a balanced search tree.

For separate-chaining, the worst-case scenario is when all entries were inserted into the same bucket, in which case the hash table is ineffective and the cost is that of searching the bucket data structure. If the latter is a linear list, the lookup procedure may have to scan all its entries; so the worst-case cost is proportional to the number n of entries in the table.

The bucket chains are often implemented as ordered lists, sorted by the key field; this choice approximately halves the average cost of unsuccessful lookups, compared to an unordered list. However, if some keys are much more likely to come up than others, an unordered list with move-to-front heuristic may be more effective. More sophisticated data structures, such as balanced search trees, are worth considering only if the load factor is large (about 10 or more), or if the hash distribution is likely to be very non-uniform, or if one must guarantee good performance even in the worst-case. However, using a larger table and/or a better hash function may be even more effective in those cases.

Chained hash tables also inherit the disadvantages of linked lists. When storing small keys and values, the space overhead of the next pointer in each entry record can be significant. An additional disadvantage is that traversing a linked list has poor cache performance, making the processor cache ineffective.

Separate chaining with list heads

Some chaining implementations store the first record of each chain in the slot array itself. The purpose is to increase cache efficiency of hash table access. To save memory space, such hash tables often have about as many slots as stored entries, meaning that many slots have two or more entries.

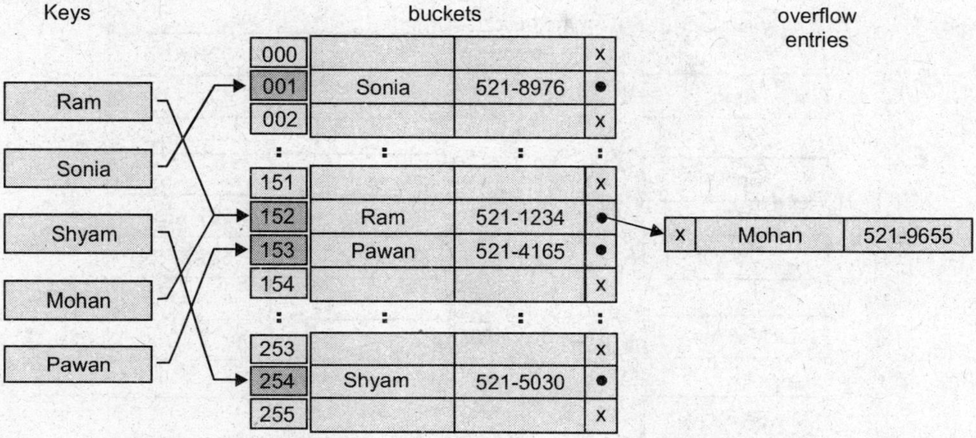

Fig. 5.5 Hash collision by separate chaining with head records in the bucket array.

Separate chaining with other structures

Instead of a list, one can use any other data structure that supports the required operations. By using a self-balancing tree, for example, the theoretical worst-case time of a hash table can be brought down to O (log n) rather than O (n). However, this approach is only worth the trouble and extra memory cost if long delays must be avoided at all costs (e.g. in a real-time application), or if one expects to have many entries hashed to the same slot (e.g. if one expects extremely non-uniform or even malicious key distributions).

The variant called array hash table uses a dynamic array to store all the entries that hash to the same slot. Each newly inserted entry gets appended to the end of the dynamic array that is assigned to the slot 50.The dynamic array is resized in an exact-fit manner, meaning it is grown only by as many bytes as needed. Alternative techniques such as growing the array by block sizes or pages were found to improve insertion performance, but at a cost in space. This variation makes more efficient use of CPU caching and the TLB (Translation lookaside buffer), since slot entries are stored in sequential memory positions. It also dispenses with the next pointers that are required by linked lists, which saves space and despite frequent array resizing, space overheads incurred by operating system such as memory fragmentation, were found to be small.

An elaboration on this approach is the so-called dynamic perfect hashing, where a bucket that contains k entries is organized as a perfect hash table with k^2 slots. While it uses more memory (n^2 slots for n entries, in the worst case), this variant has guaranteed constant worst-case lookup time, and low amortized time for insertion.

Open addressing

In another strategy, called open addressing, all entry records are stored in the bucket array itself. When a new entry has to be inserted, the buckets are examined, starting with the hashed-to slot and proceeding in some probe sequence, until an unoccupied slot is found. When searching for an entry, the buckets are scanned in the same sequence, until either the target record is found, or an unused array slot is found, which indicates that there is no such key in the table he name "open addressing" refers to the fact that the location ("address") of the item is not determined by its hash value. (This method is also called closed hashing; it should not be confused with "open hashing" or "closed addressing" which usually mean separate chaining).

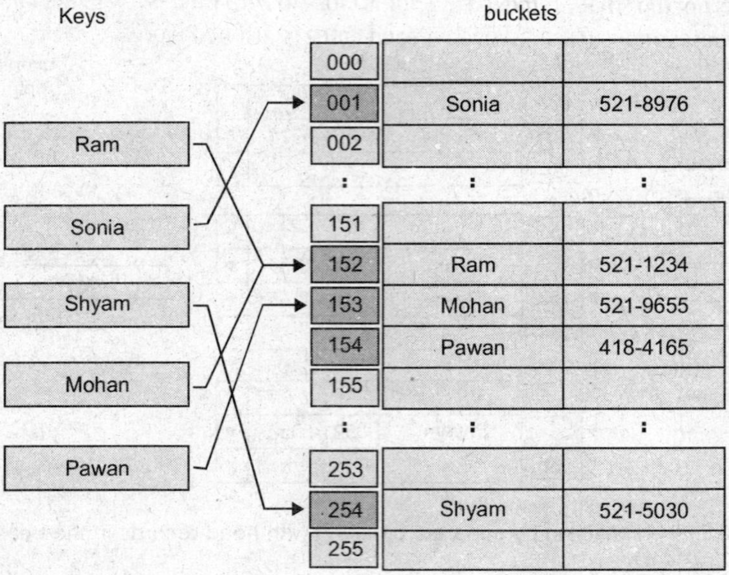

Fig. 5.6 Hash collision resolved by open addressing with linear probing (interval = 1). Note that "Ted Baker" has a unique hash, but nevertheless collided with "Sandra Dee" which had previously collided with "John Smith".

Well-known probe sequences include

- Linear probing, in which the interval between probes is fixed (usually 1)
- Quadratic probing, in which the interval between probes is increased by adding the successive outputs of a quadratic polynomial to the starting value given by the original hash computation
- Double hashing, in which the interval between probes is computed by another hash function.

A drawback of all these open addressing schemes is that the number of stored entries cannot exceed the number of slots in the bucket array. In fact, even with good hash functions, their performance seriously degrades when the load factor grows beyond 0.7 or so. For many applications, these restrictions mandate the use of dynamic resizing, with its attendant costs.

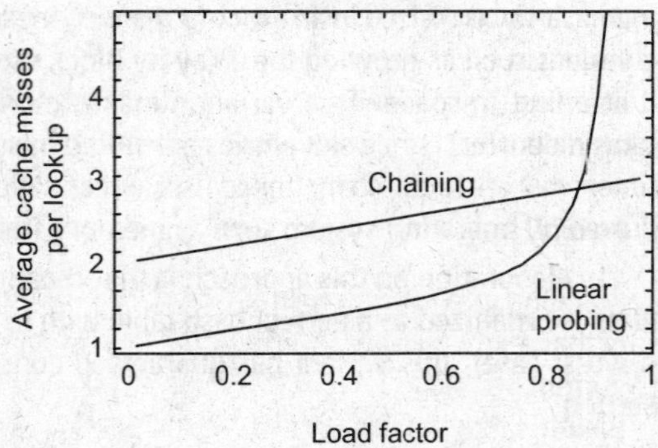

Fig. 5.7 This graph compares the average number of cache misses required to lookup elements in tables with chaining and linear probing. As the table passes the 80%-full mark, linear probing's performance drastically degrades.

Open addressing schemes also put more stringent requirements on the hash function: besides distributing the keys more uniformly over the buckets, the function must also minimize the clustering of hash values that are consecutive in the probe order. Even experienced programmers may find such clustering hard to avoid.

Open addressing only saves memory if the entries are small (less than 4 times the size of a pointer) and the load factor is not too small. If the load factor is close to zero (that is, there are far more buckets than stored entries), open addressing is wasteful even if each entry is just two words.

Open addressing avoids the time overhead of allocating each new entry record, and can be implemented even in the absence of a memory allocator. It also avoids the extra indirection required to access the first entry of each bucket (which is usually the only one). It also has better locality of reference, particularly with linear probing. With small record sizes, these factors can yield better performance than chaining, particularly for lookups.

Hash tables with open addressing are also easier to serialize, because they don't use pointers.

On the other hand, normal open addressing is a poor choice for large elements, since these elements fill entire cache lines (negating the cache advantage), and a large amount of space is wasted on large empty table slots. If the open addressing table only stores references to elements (external storage), it uses space comparable to chaining even for large records but loses its speed advantage.

Generally speaking, open addressing is better used for hash tables with small records that can be stored within the table (internal storage) and fit in a cache line. They are particularly suitable for elements of one word or less. In cases where the tables are expected to have high load factors, the records are large, or the data is variable-sized, chained hash tables often perform as well or better.

Ultimately, used sensibly, any kind of hash table algorithm is usually fast enough and the percentage of a calculation spent in hash table code is low. Memory usage is rarely considered excessive. Therefore, in most cases the differences between these algorithms are marginal, and other considerations typically come into play.

Coalesced hashing

A hybrid of chaining and open addressing,coalesced hashing links together chains of nodes within the table itself. Like open addressing, it achieves space usage and (somewhat diminished) cache advantages over chaining. Like chaining, it does not exhibit clustering effects; in fact, the table can be efficiently filled to a high density. Unlike chaining, it cannot have more elements than table slots.

Robin Hood hashing

One interesting variation on double-hashing collision resolution is that of Robin Hood hashing. The idea is that a key already inserted may be displaced by a new key if its probe count is larger than the key at the current position. The net effect of this is that it reduces worst case search times in the table. This is similar to Knuth's ordered hash tables except that the criterion for bumping a key does not depend on a direct relationship between the keys. Since both the worst case and the variation in the number of probes is reduced dramatically, an interesting variation is to probe the table starting at the expectecLsuccessful probe value and then expand from that position in both directions. External Robin Hashing is an extension of this algorithm where the table is stored in an external file and each table position corresponds to a fixed sized page or bucket with Brecords.

Cuckoo hashing

Another alternative open-addressing solution is cuckoo hashing, which ensures constant lookup time in the worst case, and constant amortized time for insertions and deletions. It uses two or more hash functions, which means any key/value pair could be in two or more locations. For lookup, the first hash function is used. if the key/value is not found, then the second hash function is used, and so on. If a collision happens during insertion, then the key is re-hashed with the second hash function to map it to another bucket. If all hash functions are used and there is still a collision, then the key it collided with is removed to make space for the new key, and the old key is re-hashed with one of the other hash functions, which maps it to another bucket. If that location also results in a collision, then the process repeats until there is no collision or the process traverses all the buckets, at which point the table is resized. By combining multiple hash functions with multiple cells per bucket, very high space utilisation can be achieved.

Hopscotch hashing

Another alternative open-addressing solution is hopscotch hashing, which combines the approaches of cuckoo hashing and linear probing, yet seems in general to avoid their limitations. In particular it works well even when the load factor grows beyond 0.9. The algorithm is well suited for implementing a resizable concurrent hash table.

The hopscotch hashing algorithm works by defining a neighborhood of buckets near the original hashed bucket, where a given entry is always found. Thus, search is limited to the number of entries in this neighborhood, which is logarithmic in the worst case, constant on average, and with proper alignment of the neighborhood typically requires one cache miss. When inserting an entry, one first attempts to add it to a bucket in the neighborhood. However, if all buckets in this neighborhood are occupied, the algorithm traverses buckets in sequence until an open slot (an unoccupied bucket) is found (as in linear probing). At that point, since the empty bucket is outside the neighborhood, items are repeatedly displaced in a sequence of hops (in a manner reminiscent of cuckoo hashing, but with the difference that in this case the empty slot is being moved into the neighborhood, instead of items being moved out with the hope of eventually finding an empty slot). Each hop brings the open slot closer to the original neighborhood, without invalidating the neighborhood property of any of the buckets along the way. In the end the open slot has been moved into the neighborhood, and the entry being inserted can be added to it.

Dynamic resizing

To keep the load factor under a certain limit e.g., under 3/4, many table implementations expand the table when items are inserted. In Java'sHashMap class, for example, the default load factor threshold for table expansion is 0.75. Since buckets are usually implemented on top of a dynamic array and any constant proportion for resizing greater than one will keep the load factor under the desired limit, the exact choice of the constant is determined by the same space-time tradeoff as for dynamic arrays.

Resizing is accompanied by a full or incremental table rehash whereby existing items are mapped to new bucket locations.

To limit the proportion of memory wasted due to empty buckets, some implementations also shrink the size of the table -followed by a rehash -when items are deleted. From the point of space-time tradeoffs, this operation is similar to the deallocation in dynamic arrays.

Resizing by copying all entries

A common approach is to automatically trigger a complete resizing when the load factor exceeds some threshold r_{max}. Then a new larger table is allocated, all the entries of the old table are removed and inserted into this new table, and the old table is returned to the free storage pool. Symmetrically, when the load factor falls below a second threshold r_{min}, all entries are moved to a new smaller table.

If the table size increases or decreases by a fixed percentage at each expansion, the total cost of these resizings, amortized over all insert and delete operations, is still a constant, independent of the number of entries n and of the number m of operations performed.

For example, consider a table that was created with the minimum possible size and is doubled each time the load ratio exceeds some threshold. If m elements are inserted into that table, the total number of extra re-insertions that occur in all dynamic resizings of the table is at most m - 1. In other words, dynamic resizing roughly doubles the cost of each insert or delete operation.

Incremental resizing

Some hash table implementations, notably in real-time systems, cannot pay the price of enlarging the hash table all at once, because it may interrupt time-critical operations. If one cannot avoid dynamic resizing, a solution is to perform the resizing gradually:

- During the resize, allocate the new hash table, but keep the old table unchanged.
- In each look up or delete operation, check both tables.
- Perform insertion operations only in the new table.
- At each insertion also move r elements from the old table to the new table.
- When all elements are removed from the old table, deallocate it.

To ensure that the old table is completely copied over before the new table itself needs to be enlarged, it is necessary to increase the size of the table by a factor of at least (r + l)/r during resizing.

Other solutions

Linear hashing is a hash table algorithm that permits incremental hash table expansion. It is implemented using a single hash table, but with two possible lookup functions.

Another way to decrease the cost of table resizing is to choose a hash function in such a way that the hashes of most values do not change when the table is resized. This approach, called consistent hashing, is prevalent in disk-based and distributed hashes, where rehashing is prohibitively costly.

Solved Questions

1. What is hashing ?

Ans. Hashing is a way retrieving records from memory in faster way. Record is inserted into memory by using hash function (division, midsqure, folding, digit analysis) and also records are retrieved using same hash function.

2. Classify the Hashing Functions based on the various methods by which the key value is found?

Ans. Direct method, Subtraction method, Modulo-Division method, Digit-Extraction method, Mid-Square method, Folding method, Pseudo-random method.

3. We wish to implement a dictionary by using direct addressing on a huge array. At the start, the array entries may contain garbage, and initializing the entire array is impractical because of its size. Describe a scheme for implementing a direct-address dictionary on a hugc array. Each stored object should use

O(1) space; the operations SEARCH, INSERT, and DELETE should take O(1) time each; and the initialization of the data structure should take O(1) time. (Hint: Use an additional stack, whose size is the number of keys actually stored in the dictionary, to help determine whether a given entry in the huge array is valid or not.)

Ans: We denote the huge array by T and, taking the hint from the book, we also have a stack implemented by an array S. The size of S equals the number of keys actually stored, so that S should be allocated at the dictionary maximum size. The stack has an attribute top[S], so that only entries S[1 . . top[S]] are valid. The idea of this scheme is that entries of T and S validate each other. If key k is actually stored in T, then T [k] contains the index, say j , of a valid entry in S, and S[j] contains the value k. Let us call this situation, in which $1 \le T[k] \le top[S]$, S[T [k]] = k, and T [S[j]] = j, a validating cycle. Assuming that we also need to store pointers to objects in our direct-address table, we can store them in an array that is parallel to either T or S. Since S is smaller than T , we use an array S O, allocated to be the same size as S, for these pointers. Thus, if the dictionary contains an object x with key k, then there is a validating cycle and S_[T [k]] points to x.

The operations on the dictionary work as follows:

- Initialization: Simply set top[S] = 0, so that there are no valid entries in the stack.
- SEARCH: Given key k, we check whether we have a validating cycle, i.e.,
  whether $1 \le T[k] \le top[S]$ and S[T [k]] = k. If so, we return S_[T [k]], and otherwise we return NIL.
- INSERT: To insert object x with key k, assuming that this object is not already in the dictionary, we increment top[S], set S[top[S]] $\leftarrow$ k, set S_[top[S]] $\leftarrow$ x, and set T [k] $\leftarrow$ top[S].
- DELETE: To delete object x with key k, assuming that this object is in the dictionary, we need to break the validating cycle. The trick is to also ensure that we don.t leave a .hole. in the stack, and we solve this problem by moving the top entry of the stack into the position that we are vacating and then fixing up that entry validating cycle. That is, we execute the following sequence of assignments:

S[T [k]] $\leftarrow$ S[top[S]]
S_[T [k]] $\leftarrow$ S_[top[S]]
T [S[T [k]]] $\leftarrow$ T [k]
T [k] $\leftarrow$ 0
top[S] $\leftarrow$ top[S] – 1

Each of these operations initialization, SEARCH, INSERT, and DELETE takes O(1) time.

4. Suppose we use a hash function h to hash n distinct keys into an array T of length m. Assuming simple uniform hashing, what is the expected number of collisions? More precisely, what is the expected cardinality of {{k, l} : k '≠ l and h(k) = h(l)}?

Ans. For each pair of keys k, l, where k = l, define the indicator random variable
Xkl = I {h(k) = h(l)}. Since we assume simple uniform hashing, Pr{Xkl = 1} = Pr {h(k) = h(l)} = 1/m, and so E[Xkl] = 1/m.
Now define the random variable Y to be the total number of collisions, so that Y = k_=l Xkl . The expected number of collisions is

$$E[Y] = E\left[\sum_{k \neq l} X_{kl}\right]$$

$$= \sum_{k \neq l} E\,[X_{kl}] \qquad \text{(linearity of expection)}$$

$$= \binom{n}{2}\frac{1}{m}$$

$$= \frac{n(n-1)}{2}\cdot\frac{1}{m}$$

$$= \frac{n(n-1)}{2m}$$

5. Suggest how storage for elements can be allocated and deallocated within the hash table itself by linking all unused slots into a free list. Assume that one slot can store a flag and either one element plus a pointer or two pointers. All dictionary and free-list operations should run in O(1) expected time. Does the free list need to be doubly linked, or does a singly linked free list suffice?

Ans. The flag in each slot will indicate whether the slot is free.
A free slot is in the free list, a doubly linked list of all free slots in the table.
The slot thus contains two pointers. A used slot contains an element and a pointer (possibly NIL) to the next element that hashes to this slot. (Of course, that pointer points to another slot in the table)
OPERATIONS

- Insertion: If the element hashes to a free slot, just remove the slot from the free list and store the element there (with a NIL pointer). The free list must be doubly linked in order for this deletion to run in O(1) time. If the element hashes to a used slot j, check whether the element x already there belongs there (its key also hashes to slot j).
If so, add the new element to the chain of elements in this slot. To do so, allocate a free slot (e.g., take the head of the free list) for the new element and put this new slot at the head of the list pointed to by the hashed-to slot (j).
If not, E is part of another slot chain. Move it to a new slot by allocating one from the free list, copying the old slot (j .s) contents (element x and pointer) to the new slot, and updating the pointer in the slot that pointed to j to point to the new slot. Then insert the new element in the now-empty slot as usual. To update the pointer to j, it is necessary to find it by searching the chain of elements starting in the slot x hashes to.
- Deletion: Let j be the slot the element x to be deleted hashes to.

  If x is the only element in j (j doesn.t point to any other entries), just free the slot, returning it to the head of the free list. If x is in j but there.s a pointer to a chain of other elements, move the first pointed-to entry to slot j and free the slot it was in. If x is found by following a pointer from j, just free x.s slot and splice it out of the chain (i.e., update the slot that pointed to x to point to x.s successor).
- Searching: Check the slot the key hashes to, and if that is not the desired element, follow the chain of pointers from the slot. All the operations take expected O(1) times for the same reason they do with the version in the book: The expected time to search the chains is $O(1 + \alpha)$ regardless of where the chains are stored, and the fact that all the elements are stored in the table means that $\alpha \leq 1$. If the free list were singly linked, then operations that involved removing an arbitrary slot from the free list would not run in O(1) time.

6. Consider a version of the division method in which h(k) = k mod m, where m = 2p - 1 and k is a character string interpreted in radix 2p. Show that if string x can be derived from string y by permuting its characters, then x and y hash to the same value. Give an example of an application in which this property would be undesirable in a hash function.

Ans. [hint] First, we observe that we can generate any permutation by a sequence of interchanges of pairs of characters. One can prove this property formally, but informally, consider that both heapsort and quicksort work by interchanging pairs of elements and that they have to be able to produce any permutation of their input array. Thus, it sufÞces to show that if string x can be derived from string y by interchanging a single pair of characters, then x and y hash to the same value.

Let us denote the i th character in x by xi , and similarly for y.

Exercise

1. Draw a hash table with open addressing and a size of 9. Use the hash function "k%9". Insert the keys: 5, 29, 20, 0, 27 and 18 into your table (in that order).
2. Draw a hash table with chaining and a size of 9. Use the hash function "k%9" to insert the keys 5, 29, 20, 0, and 18 into your table.
3. Draw a hash table with chaining and a size of 9. Use the hash function "k%9" to insert the keys 5, 29, 20, 0, and 18 into your table.
4. I plan to put 1000 items in a hash table, and I want the average number of accesses in a successful search to be about 2.0. A. About how big should the array be if I use open addressing with linear probing? NOTE: For a load factor of A, the average number of accesses is generally '/i (1 + 1/(1- A)). B. About how big should the array be if I use chained hashing? NOTE: For a load factor of A, the average number of accesses is generally (1 + A / 2).
5. Suppose that I have the following record _type definition for a record in a hash table:

```
structrecord_type
  { int key;
          ... other stuff may also appear here ...
  };
```

The hash table uses open addressing with linear probing. The table size is a global constant called CAPACITY. Locations of the table that have NEVER been used will contain the key -1. Locations of the table that were once used but are now vacant will contain the key -2. All valid keys will be non-negative, and the hash function is:

```
size_t hash(int key)
  {
return (key % CAPACITY);
  }
```

Complete the implementation of the following function. There is no need to check the precondition, but your code must be as efficient as possible.

```
boolkey_occurs(constrecord_type data[ ], intsearch_key)
// Precondition: data[0]...data[CAPACITY-I] is an open address hash table
// as described above.
// Postcondition: If search_key occurs as a key of a record in the table, then
// the function returns true; otherwise the function returns false.
```

CHAPTER

6

QUICKSORT

6.1 INTRODUCTION

Quicksort is a sorting algorithm developed by C. A. R. Hoare that, on average, makes O(nlogn) (big O notation) comparisons to sort n items. In the worst case, it makes O(n^2) comparisons, though if implemented correctly this behaviour is rare. Typically, quicksort is significantly faster in practice than other O(nlogn) algorithms, because its inner loop can be efficiently implemented on most architectures, and in most real-world data, it is possible to make design choices that minimize the probability of requiring quadratic time.

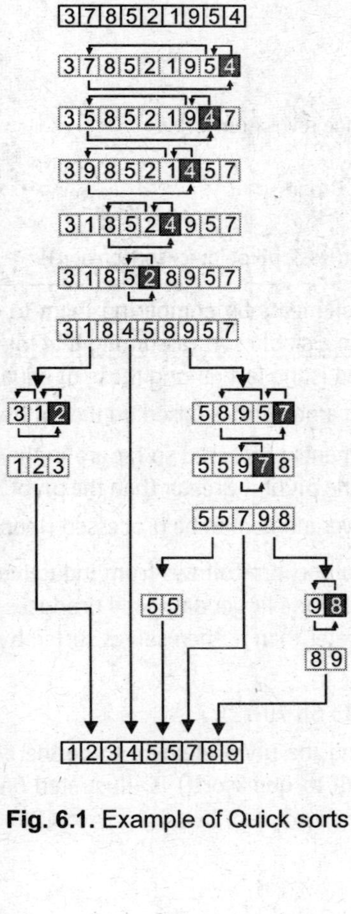

Fig. 6.1. Example of Quick sorts

Additionally, quicksort tends to make excellent usage of the memory hierarchy, taking perfect advantage of virtual memory and available caches. Although quicksort is usually not implemented as an in-place sort, it is possible to create such an implementation.

Quicksort (also known as "partition-exchange sort") is a comparison sort and, in efficient implementations, is not a stable sort.

Full example of quicksort on a random set of numbers. The shaded element is the pivot. It is always chosen as the last element of the partition. However, always choosing the last element in the partition as the pivot in this way results in poor performance ($O(n^2)$) on already sorted lists, or lists of identical elements. Since sub-lists of sorted / identical elements crop up a lot towards the end of a sorting procedure on a large set, versions of the quicksort algorithm which choose the pivot as the middle element run much more quickly than the algorithm described in this diagram on large sets of numbers.

Quicksort sorts by employing a divide and conquer strategy to divide a list into two sub-lists.

The steps are:

1. Pick an element, called a pivot, from the list.
2. Reorder the list so that all elements with values less than the pivot come before the pivot, while all elements with values greater than the pivot come after it (equal values can go either way). After this partitioning, the pivot is in its final position. This is called the partition operation.
3. Recursively sort the sub-list of lesser elements and the sub-list of greater elements.

The base case of the recursion are lists of size zero or one, which never need to be sorted.

```
function quicksort(array)
    var list less, greater
    if length(array) ≤ 1
        return array
    select and remove a pivot value pivot from array
    for each x  in array
        if x ≤ pivot then append x to less
        else append x to greater
    return concatenate(quicksort(less), pivot, quicksort(greater))
```

Notice that we only examine elements by comparing them to other elements. This makes quicksort a comparison sort. This version is also a stable sort (assuming that the "for each" method retrieves elements in original order, and the pivot selected is the last among those of equal value).

The correctness of the partition algorithm is based on the following two arguments:

- At each iteration, all the elements processed so far are in the desired position: before the pivot if less than the pivot's value, after the pivot if greater than the pivot's value (loop invariant).
- Each iteration leaves one fewer element to be processed (loop variancy)

The correctness of the overall algorithm follows from inductive reasoning: for zero or one element, the algorithm leaves the data unchanged; for a larger data set it produces the concatenation of two parts, elements less than the pivot and elements greater than it, themselves sorted by the recursive hypothesis.

We sort the array

A = (38 81 22 48 13 69 93 14 45 58 79 72)

with quicksort, always choosing the pivot element to be the element in position $\lfloor(\text{left}+\text{right})/2\rfloor$. The partitioning during the top-level call to quicksort() is illustrated on the next page. During the partitioning process,

(i) Elements strictly to the left of position lo are less than or equivalent to the pivot element (69).

(ii) Elements strictly to the right of position hi are greater than the pivot element.

When lo and hi cross, we are done. The final value of hi is the position in which the partitioning element ends up. An asterisk indicates an element compared to the pivot element at that step.

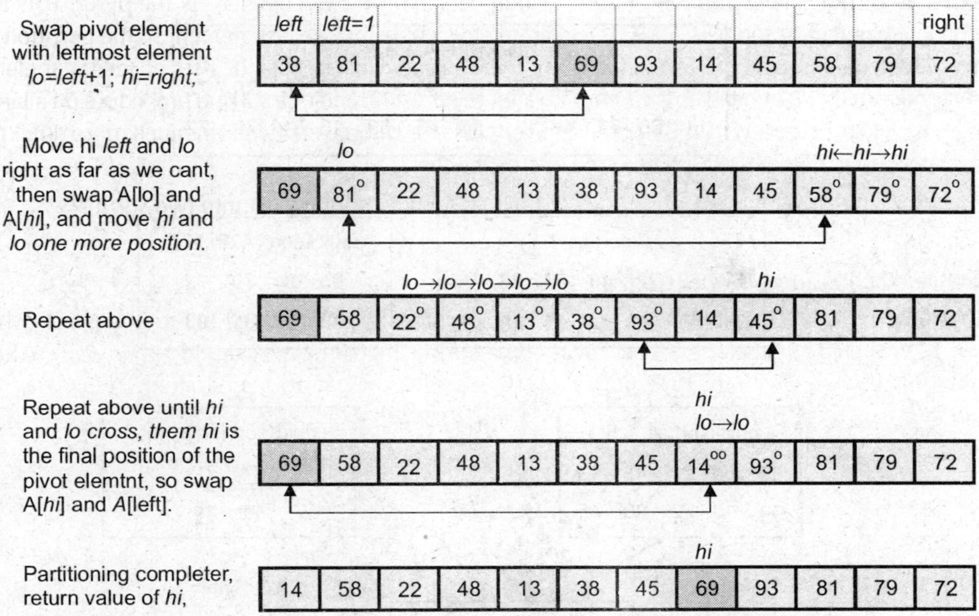

Fig.6.2: Quick sort example

Number of comparisons performed by partition():

(a) No comparison for leftmost column.

(b) One comparison for each remaining column, except two for the columns where hi and lo end up. (lo = hi+1 at the end.) C(n) = n + 1, where n is the size of the array (right—left+1). Expected number of exchanges performed by partition(), for a randomly ordered array, and a pivot element chosen from a designated position (and hence a random element of the array). Say the pivot element turns out to be the kth largest element of the n elements, so it ends up in the kth position.

Each exchange of A[lo] and A[lo] moves one element initially to the right of kth position, but less than (or equivalent but not equal to) the pivot element, to a position not right of the kth position.

Of the k–1 elements in the array less than the pivot element, we would expect ((n–k)l(n–1) (k–1) of these to lie initially right of the kth position. Thus we expect (k-l)(n-k)/(n–1) ~ k(n–k)/n exchanges. Since all values of k, 1 < k < n, are equally likely, the expected number of exchanges would be approximately

$$E_{ave}(n) \approx \sum_{k=1}^{n} k(n-k)/n$$

$$\approx (1/n^2)\left(\sum_{k=1}^{n} kn - \sum_{k=1}^{n} k^2\right)$$

$$\approx (1/n^2)\,(n^3/2 - n^3/3)$$

$$E_{ave}(n) \approx n/6$$

In other words, partition() performs only about 1 exchange for every 6 comparisons. An alternate version, designed specifically to work with moves, performs about one move for each 3 comparisons.

partition() does an extremely good job of minimizing the movement of elements. This is probably why quicksort tends to be faster than mergesort in the expected case, even though it performs move comparisons Here is the tree of recursive calls to quicksort. Calls to sort subarrays of size 0 or 1 are not shown. (They could be omitted.)

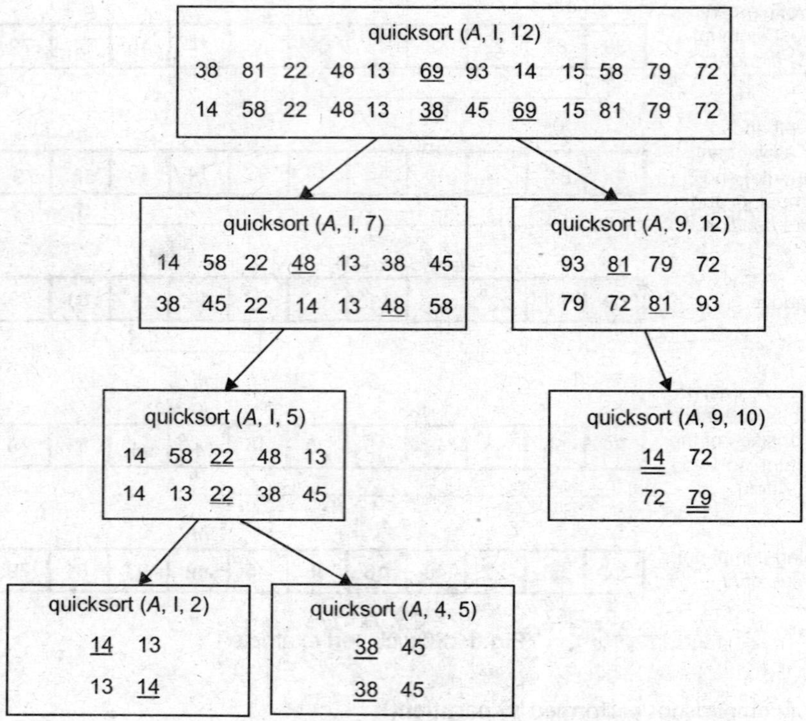

Fig. 6.3: Partitioning

partition(A, left, right) rarranges A[left..right] and finds and returns an integer q, such that A[left], ..., A[q–l] < pivot, A[q] = pivot, A[q+1], ..., A[right] > pivot, where pivot is the middle element of a[left..right], before partitioning. (To choose the pivot element differently, simply modify the assignment to m.)

```
Integer partition( T[] A. Integer left. Integer right)
m = ⌊.left + right⌋ / 2;
swap( A [left], A [m]);
pivot = A [left]; lo = left+1; hi = right:
while ( lo < hi)
    while (A[hi] >pivot)
        hi = hi – 1:
    while ( lo < hi and A[lo] <pivot)
         lo = lo+ 1;
    if (lo<hi)
        swap(A[lo], A [hi]) ;
        lo= lo+ 1; hi = hi— 1;
swap(A [left]. A[fa]):
return hi
```

quicksort(A, left, right) sorts A[left.. right] by using partition() to partition v4[/e/L right], and then calling itself recursively twice to sort the two subarrays.

```
void quicksort( T[] A Integer left. Integer right)
    if (left < right)
        q = partition(A. left right):
        quicksort(A. left g–1);
        quicksort (A. q+1. right):
```

Later we will show that quicksort runs in Θ(n2) time in the worst case, but that it runs in Θ(nlg(n)) time in the expected case, assuming the input is randomly ordered. At the moment, let us consider the extra space (in addition to the array being sorted) used by quicksort. The function partition() uses only constant extra space. At first, it might appear that quicksort() also uses only constant extra space. But this can never be the case for a recursive function (unless the maximum depth of recursion is bounded by a constant). Each time a function is called (recursively or otherwise), we get a new activation of the function. The activation continues to exist until the function returns to its caller. Each activation has its own activation record, or stack frame, on the run-time stack. The activation record may contain space for automatic local variables and paraméters, a return address, and an area to save the current status. For a recursive function, the memory requirements are determined by the maximum number of activations existing at any one time, that is, by the maximum depth of recursion. For quicksort() as we have implemented it, the maximum depth of recursion will be n in the worst case. This would occur if every call to partition() produced as uneven a split as possible (sublist sizes n–1 and 0). It would make the extra space requirements Θ(n) — possibly with a fairly large constant multiplying n. With a little effort, we can limit the maximum depth of recursion to approximately lg(n), even in the worst case. Then the extra space required will be 0(lg(n)) — insignificant compared to the Θ(n) space for the array being sorted. Note, however, the worst case running time remains Θ(n2).

quicksort2(A, left, right) performs the same function as quicksort(A, left, right), but the depth of recursion is limited to lg(n), and the extra space is only (lg(n)) even in the worst case.

```
void quicksort 2( T[] A, Integer left, Integer right)
    while (left < right)
    q= partitkm( A, left, right);
    if ( q – left < right – q )
        quicksort 2 ( A, left, q–1);      // Recursive call sorts smaller sublist
        left = q + 1;                     // Loop back to sort larger sublist
else
        quicksort2 ( A. q+1, right);      // Recursive call sorts smaller sublist
        right = q — 1;                    // Loop back to sort larger sublist
```

Each time quicksort 2() calls itself recursively, it does so only for the smaller of the two sublists. This means that each time the depth of recursion rises by one, the size of the input to quicksort2() is cut at least in half. Thus the depth of recursion cannot exceed lg(n). Note the larger sublist is sorted by repeating the while-loop with the value of left or right adjusted to correspond to the larger sublist, rather than the original list. This requires no additional space.

6.2 PERFORMANCE OF QUICKSORT

We will count the number C(n) of comparisons performed by quicksort in sorting an array of size n. We have seen that partition() performs n comparisons (possibly n–1 or n+1, depending on the implementation). In fact, n–1 is the lower bound on the number of comparisons that any partitioning algorithm can perform. The reason is that every element other than the pivot must be compared to the pivot; otherwise we have no way of knowing whether it goes left or right of the pivot. So our recurrence for C(n) is:

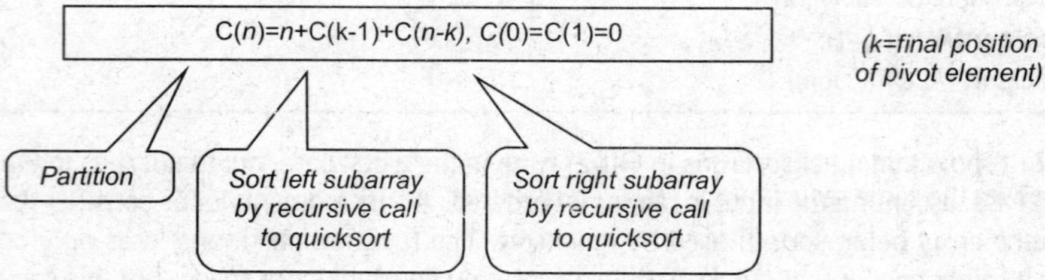

A bad case (actually the worst case): At every step, partition() splits the array as unequally as possible (k = 1 or k = n). Then our recurrence becomes $C(n) = n + C(n-l)$, $C(0) = C(l) = 0$ This is easy to solve.

$$\begin{aligned} c(n) &= n + c(n-1) \\ &= n + n-1 + C(n-2) \\ &= n + n-1 + n-2 + C(n-3) \\ &= n + n-1 + n-2 + \ldots + 3 + 2 \\ &= (n + n-1 + n-2 + \ldots + 3 + 2 + 1) - 1 \\ &= n(n+1)/2 - 1 \\ &\approx n^2/2 \end{aligned}$$

It is no better than simple quadratic time algorithms like straight insertion sort.

A good case (actually the best case): At every step, partition() splits the array as equally as possible (k = (n+l)/2; the left and right subarrays each have size (n-l)/2)).

This is possible at every step only if n = 2k –1 for some k. However, it is always possible to split nearly equally. The recurrence becomes $C(n) = n + 2C((n-1)/2)$, $C(0) = C(l) = 0$, which we approximate by $C(n) = n + 2C(n/2)$, $C(l) = 0$ This is the same as the recurrence for mergesort, except that the right side has n in place of n–1. The solution is essentially the same as for mergesort: $C(n) = n\lg(n)$. This is excellent — essentially as good mergesort, and essentially as good as any comparison sorting algorithm can be.

The expected case: Here we assume either (i) the array to be partitioned is randomly ordered, or (ii) the pivot element is selected from a random position in the array. In either case, the pivot element will be a random element of the array to be partitioned. That is, for k = 1, 2, ..., n, the probability that the pivot element is the kth largest element of the array is 1/n, (Recall that, if the pivot element is the kth largest element of the array, it ends up after partitioning in position k.)

In the recurrence

$$C(n) = n + C(k-l) + C(n-k). \; C(0) = C(l) = 0,$$

all values of k are equally likely. We must average over all k.

$$\begin{aligned} C(n) &= (1/n) \sum_{k=1}^{n} n + C(k-1) + C(n-k)), C(0) = C(1) = 0, \\ &= n + (1/n)\sum_{k=1}^{n} C(k-1) + (1/n)\sum_{k=1}^{n} C(n-k) \end{aligned}$$

Note: $\sum_{k=1}^{n} C(k-1) = \sum_{i=0}^{n-1} C(i)$, by substituting i = k–1.

$\sum_{k=1}^{n} C(n-k) = \sum_{i=0}^{n-1} C(i)$, by substituting i = n – k.

So our recurence becomes

$$C(n) = n + (2/n) \sum_{i=0}^{n-1} C(i), \text{ or}$$

$$nC(n) = n^2 + 2 \sum_{i=0}^{n-1} C(i)$$

Writing down the same recurrence with n–1 replacing n, we get

$$(n-l)C(n-l) = (n-1)^2 + 2\sum_{i=0}^{n-2} C(i).$$

Subtracting this recurrence from the one above it gives

$$nC(n) - (n-1)\,C(n-l) = n^2 - (n-l)^2 + 2C(n-1), \text{ or}$$

$$nC(n) = (n+l)\,C(n-l) + 2n-l$$

Dividing by n(n+1) gives

$$C(n)/(n+1) = C(n-1)/n + (2n-1)/(n(n+1)).$$

To a very good approximation. $C(n)/(n+l) = C(n-l)/n + 2/n$.

Now if let $D(n) = C(n)/(n+l)$ then the recurrence becomes

$$D(n) = D(n-l) + 2/n \quad D(l) = 0.$$

This is easy to solve:

$$\begin{aligned} D(n) &= D(n-l) + 2/n \\ &= D(n-2) + 2/(n-l) + 2/n \\ &= D(n-3) + 2/(n-2) + 2/(n-1) + 2/n \\ &= D(1) + 2/2 + 2/3 + \ldots + 2/(n-2) + 2/(n-l) + 2/n = 2\ln(n) - 2 \\ &\approx 21n(n) - 2 \\ &\approx 2\ln(2)\,\lg(n) \\ &= 1.39\,\lg(n) \end{aligned}$$

So $C(n) = (n+l)D(n) \approx 1.39\,(n+1)\,\lg(n)$. or $C(n) \approx 1.39n\,\lg(n)$

The expected case for quicksort is fairly close to the best case (only 39% more comparisons) and nothing like the worst case.

In most (not all) tests, quicksort turns out to be a bit faster than mergesort. Quicksort performs 39% more comparisons than mergesort, but much less movement (copying) of array elements.

We saw that, in the expected case, quicksort performs one exchange for every six comparisons, or about 1.39 n lg(n) / 6 ≈ 0.23 n lg(n) exchanges. A slightly different partitioning algorithm performs one move (copy) for each three comparisons, or about 0.46 n lg(n) moves. By contrast, the version of mergesort given in class performs 2nlg(n) moves, although this can be reduced to nlg(n) moves — still more than twice as many as quicksort is likely to perform.

With a randomized version of quicksort (pivot element chosen randomly), the standard deviation in the number of comparisons is also small. The probability of performing substantially more than 1.39 n lg(n) comparisons is extremely low. Quicksort is not stable, since it exchanges nonadjacent elements. If stability is not required, quicksort provides a very attractive alternative to mergesort. Quicksort is likely to run a bit faster than mergesort — perhaps 1.2 to 1.4 times as fast. Quicksort requires less memory than mergesort. A good implementation of quicksort is probably easier to code than a good implementation of mergesort.

Solved Exercise

1. Explain Quick Sort

Sol. The quick sort algorithm is of the divide and conquer type. That means it works by reducing a sorting problem into several easier sorting problems and solving each of them. A dividing value is chosen from the input data, and the data is partitioned into three sets: elements that belong before the dividing value, the value itself, and elements that come after the dividing value. The partitioning is performed by exchanging elements that are in the first set but belong in the third with elements that are in the third set but belong in the first Elements that are equal to the dividing element can be put in any of the three sets the algorithm will still work properly.

2. Sort the given values using Quick Sort?

65	70	75	80	85	60	55	50	45

Sol. Sorting takes place from the pivot value, which is the first value of the given elements, this is marked bold. The values at the left pointer and right pointer are indicated using L and R respectively.

65	70^L	75	80	85	60	55	50	45^R

Since pivot is not yet changed the same process is continued after interchanging the values at L and R positions

65	**45**	**75^L**	**80**	**85**	**60**	**55**	**50^R**	**70**

65	45	50	80^L	85	60	55^R	75	70

65	45	50	55	85^L	60^R	80	75	70

65	45	50	55	60^R	85^L	80	75	70

When the L and R pointers cross each other the pivot value is interchanged with the value at right pointer. If the pivot is changed it means that the pivot has occupied its original position in the sorted order (shown in bold italics) and hence two different arrays are formed, one from start of the original array to the pivot position-1 and the other from pivot position+1 to end.

60^L	45	50	55^R	65	85^L	80	75	70^R

55^L5	45	50^R	60	65	70^R	80^L	75	85

50^L	45^R	55	60	65	70	80^L	75^R	85

In the next pass we get the sorted form of the array.

50^L	45^R	55	60	65	70	80^L	75^R	85

3. What is difference between Bubble Sort and Quick sort?

Ans. Bubble Sort: The simplest sorting algorithm. It involves the sorting the list in a repetitive fashion. It compares two adjacent elements in the list, and swaps them if they are not in the designated order. It continues until there are no swaps needed. This is the signal for the list that is sorted. It is also called as comparison sort as it uses comparisons.

Quick Sort: The best sorting algorithm which implements the 'divide and conquer' concept. It first divides the list into two parts by picking an element a 'pivot'. It then arranges the elements those are smaller than pivot into one sub list and the elements those are greater than pivot into one sub list by keeping the pivot in its original place.

4. What is the difference between quick sort and randomized quick sort?

Sol. In quick sort the first element in the array is chosen as the pivot but in randomized quick sort any number in the array is chosen as the pivot.

Previous Year University Question

1. Write quick sort algorithm. Also prive that run time average complexity of quick sort is O(n log n). [GBTU]
2. How can you adapt Quicksort algorithm to find the mth order statistic in a given list of size n? [GBTU]
3. Discuss Merge sort and quick sort Algorithms. Merge sort is good choice instead of quick sort. Do you agree wit statement? Justify your answer. [MDU]
4. Explain the procedure Quick sort with an example. Also analyse it in best, average and worst case. [MDU]

Exercise

1. $\theta\ (n^2)$ when the array A to sorted in decreasing order.
2. Prove that beat care running time for quick sort is $\Omega\ (nl\ gn)$.
3. Draw the recursion tree for 33, 26, 18, 35, 24, 12, using quick sort partitioning method.
4. Show that $q^2 + (n - q2)$ achieves a maximum over $q = 1, 2, ..., n - 1$ where $q = 1$or $q = n = 1$.
5. Compare the insertion sot with quick with the help of example.

CHAPTER 7

HEAP SORT

7.1 HEAP

The binary heap data structures is an array that can be viewed as a complete binary tree. Each noce of the binary tree corresponds to an element of the array. The array is completely filled on all levels except possibly lowest.

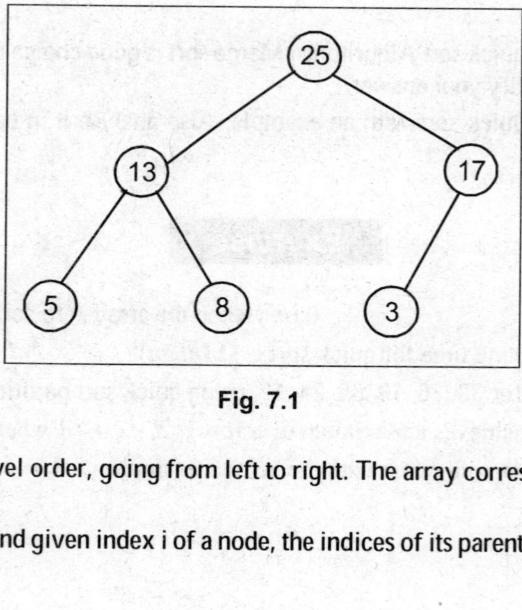

Fig. 7.1

We represent heaps in level order, going from left to right. The array corresponding to the heap above is [25, 13, 17, 5, 8, 3].

The root of the tree A[I] and given index i of a node, the indices of its parent, left child and right child can be computed

```
PARENT (i)
    return floor(i/2)
LEFT (i)
    return 2i
RI  HT (i)
    return 2i + 1
```

Let's try these out on a heap to make sure we believe they are correct. Take this heap

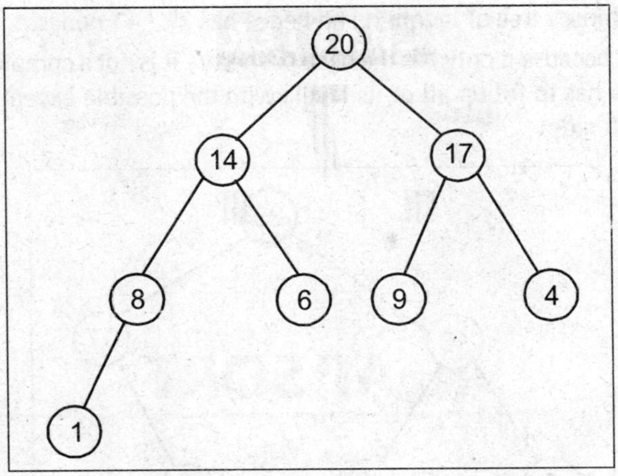

Fig 7.2

which is represented by the array [20, 14, 17, 8, 6, 9, 4, 1].

We'll go from the 20 to the 6 first. The index of the 20 is 1. To find the index of the left child, we calculate 1   2 = 2. This takes us (correctly) to the 14. Now, we go right, so we calculate 2   2 + 1 = 5. This takes us (again, correctly) to the 6.

Now let's try going from the 4 to the 20. 4's index is 7. We want to go to the parent, so we calculate 7/2 = 3, which takes us to the 17. Now, to get 17's parent, we calculate 3/2 = 1, which takes us to the 20.

7.2 HEAP PROPERTY

In a heap, for every node i other than the root, the value of a node is greater than or equal (at most) to the value of its parent.

$$A[PARENT (i)] \geq A[i]$$

Thus, the largest element in a heap is stored at the root.

Following is an example of Heap:

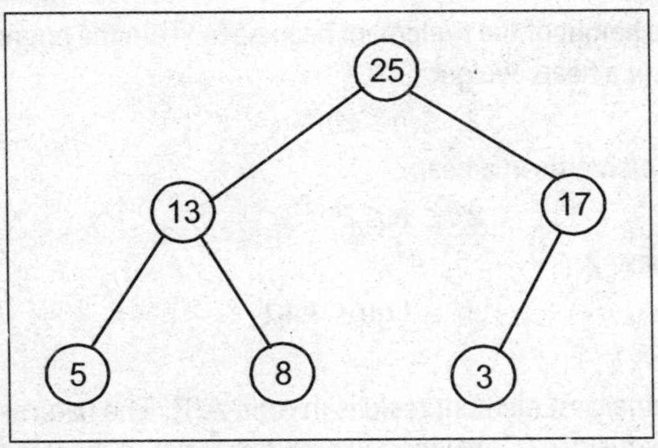

Fig 7.3

By the definition of a heap, all the tree levels are completely filled except possibly for the lowest level, which is filled from the left up to a point. Clearly a heap of height h has the minimum number of elements when it has just one node at the lowest level. The levels above the lowest level form a complete binary tree of height h –1 and 2 –1 nodes. Hence the minimum number of nodes possible in a heap of height h is 2. Clearly a heap of height h, has the maximum number of elements when its lowest level is completely filled. In this case the heap is a complete binary tree of height h and hence has $2^{h+1}-1$ nodes.

Following is not a heap, because it only has the heap property - it is not a complete binary tree. Recall that to be complete, a binary tree has to fill up all of its levels with the possible exception of the last one, which must be filled in from the left side

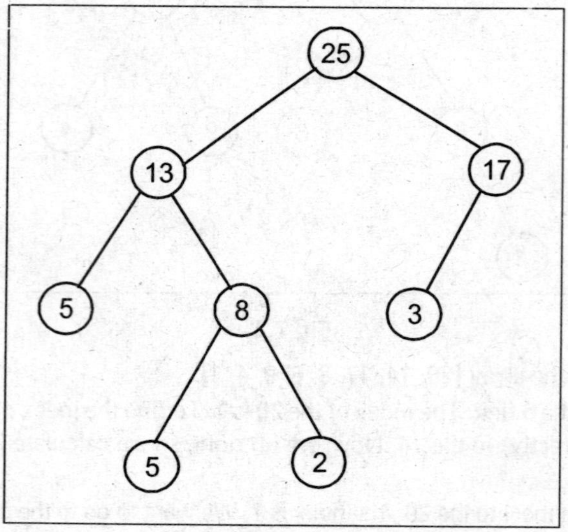

Fig. 7.4

7.3 HEIGHT OF A NODE

We define the height of a node in a tree to be a number of edges on the longest simple downward path from a node to a leaf.

7.4 HEIGHT OF A TREE

The number of edges on a simple downward path from a root to a leaf. Note that the height of a tree with n node is $\lfloor \lg n \rfloor$ which is Θ (lgn). Is implies that an n-element heap has height $\lfloor \lg n \rfloor$

In order to show this let the height of the n-element heap be h. From the bounds obtained on maximum and minimum number of elements in a heap, we get

$$2^h \leq n \leq 2^{h+1}-1$$

Where n is the number of elements in a heap.

$$2^h \leq n \leq 2^{h+1}$$

Taking logarithms to the base 2

$$h \leq \lg n \leq h+1$$

It follows that $h = \lfloor \lg n \rfloor$

We known from above that largest element resides in root, A[l]. The natural question to ask is where in a heap might the smallest element resides? Consider any path from root of the tree to a leaf. Because of the heap property, as we follow that path, the elements are either decreasing or staying the same. If it happens to be the case that all elements in the heap are distinct, then the above implies that the smallest is in a leaf of the tree. It could also be that an entire subtree of the heap is the smallest element or indeed that there is only one element in the heap, which in the smallest element, so the smallest element is everywhere. Note that anything below the smallest element must equal the smallest element, so in general, only entire subtrees of the heap can contain the smallest element.

7.5 INSERTING ELEMENT IN THE HEAP

Suppose we have a heap as follows:

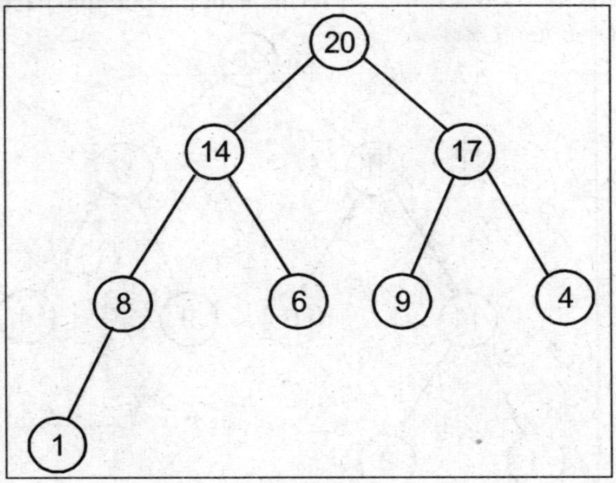

Fig 7.5

Let's suppose we want to add a node with key 15 to the heap. First, we add the node to the tree at the next spot available at the lowest level of the tree. This is to ensure that the tree remains complete.

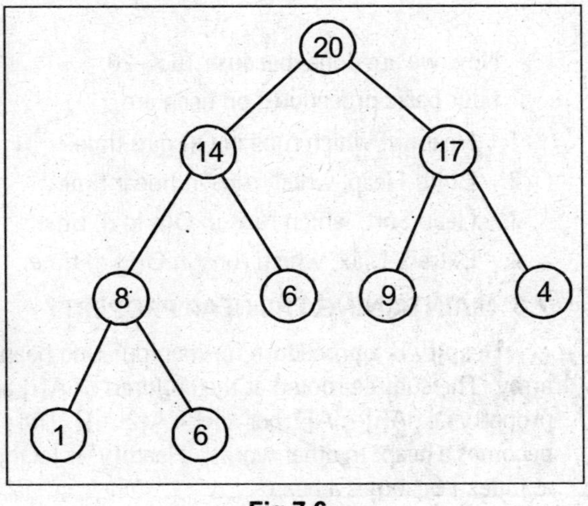

Fig 7.6

Let's suppose we want to add a node with key 15 to the heap. First, we add the node to the tree at the next spot available at the lowest level of the tree. This is to ensure that the tree remains complete.

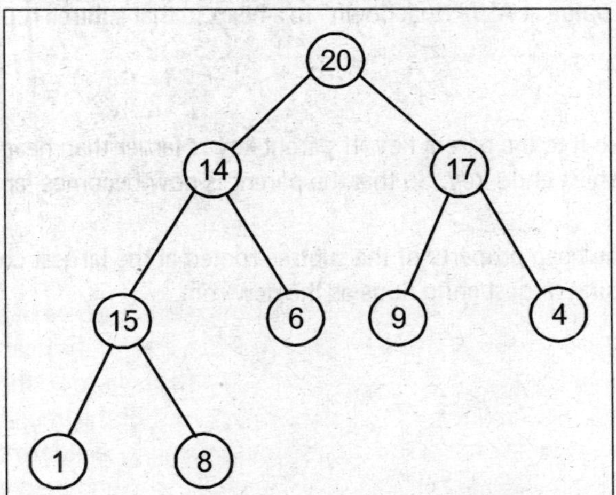

Fig. 7.7

Now we do the same thing again, comparing the new node to its parent. Since 14 < 15, we have to do another swap:

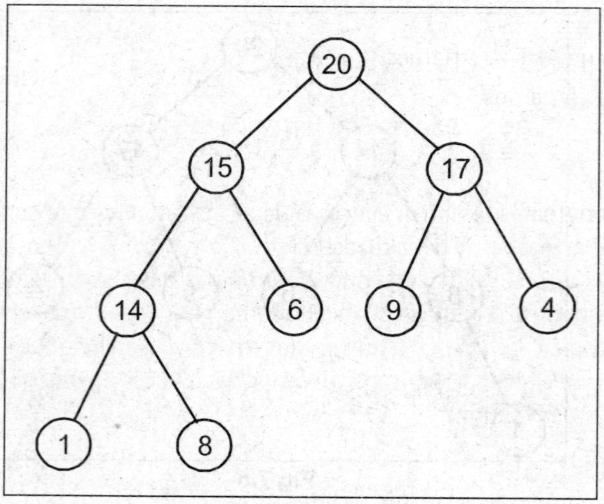

Fig. 7.8

Now we are done, because 15 ≤ 20.

Four basic procedures on heap are

1. Heapify, which runs in O(l g n) time.
2. Build-Heap, which runs in linear time.
3. Heap Sort, which runs in O(n lg n) time.
4. Extract-Max, which runs in O(lg n) time.

7.6 MAINTAINING THE HEAP PROPERTY

Heapify is a procedure for manipulating heap data structures. It is given an array A and index i into the array. The subtree rooted at the children of A[i] are heap but node A[i] itself may possibly violate the heap property i.e., A[i] < A[2i] or A[i] < A[2i +1]. The procedure 'Heapify' manipulates the tree rooted at A[i] so it becomes a heap. In other words, 'Heapify' is let the value at A[i] "float down" in a heap so that subtree rooted at index i becomes a heap.

7.7 OUTLINE OF PROCEDURE HEAPIFY

Heapify picks the largest child key and compare it to the parent key. If parent key is larger than heapify quits, otherwise it swaps the parent key with the largest child key. So that the parent is now becomes larger than its children.

It is important to note that swap may destroy the heap property of the subtree rooted at the largest child node. If this is the case, Heapify calls itself again using largest child node as the new root.

eapify (A, i)

1. l ← left [i]
2. r ← right [i]
3. if l ≤ heap-size [A] and A[l] > A[i]
4. then largest ← l
5. else largest ← i

```
if r ≤ heap-size [A] and A[i] > A[largest]
    then largest ← r
if largest ≠ i
    then exchange A[i] ↔ A[largest]
        Heapify (A, largest)
```

7.8 ANALYSIS

If we put a value at root that is less than every value in the left and right subtree, then 'Heapify' will be called recursively until leaf is reached. To make recursive calls traverse the longest path to a leaf, choose value that make 'Heapify' always recurse on the left child. It follows the left branch when left child is greater than or equal to the right child, so putting 0 at the root and 1 at all other nodes, for example, will accomplished this task. With such values 'Heapify' will called h times, where h is the heap height so its running time will be $\theta(h)$ (since each call does $\Theta(1)$ work), which is $\Theta(\lg n)$. Since we have a case in which Heapify's running time $\Theta(\lg n)$, its worst-case running time is $\Omega(\lg n)$.

7.9 EXAMPLE OF HEAPIFY

Suppose we have a complete binary tree somewhere whose subtrees are heaps. In the following complete binary tree, the subtrees of 6 are heaps:

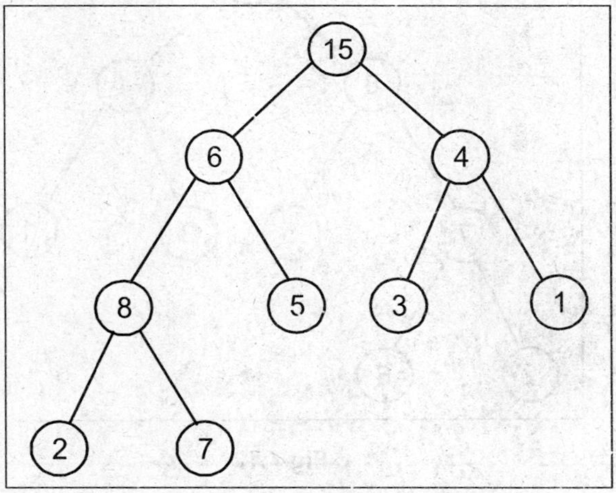

Fig 7.9

The Heapify procedure alters the heap so that the tree rooted at 6's position is a heap. Here's how it works. First, we look at the root of our tree and its two children.

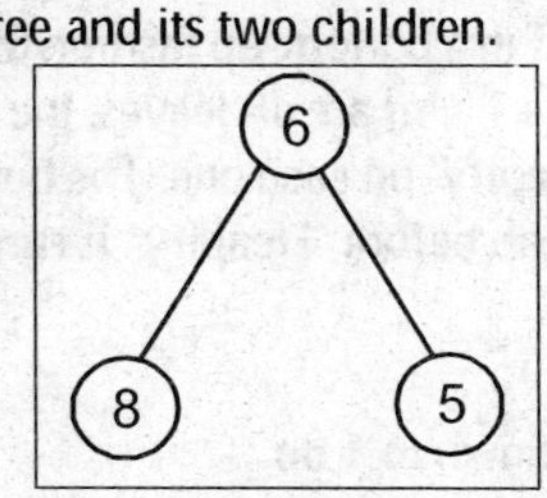

Fig 7.10

We then determine which of the three nodes is the greatest. If it is the root, we are done, because we have a heap. If not, we exchange the appropriate child with the root, and continue recursively down the tree. In this case, we exchange 6 and 8, and continue.

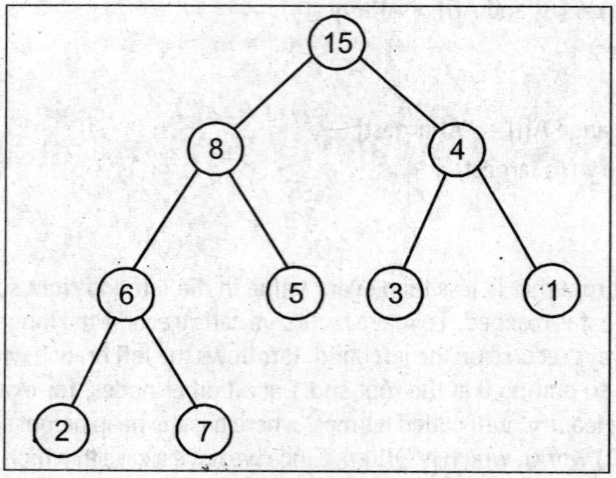

Fig 7.11

Now, 7 is greater than 6, so we exchange them.

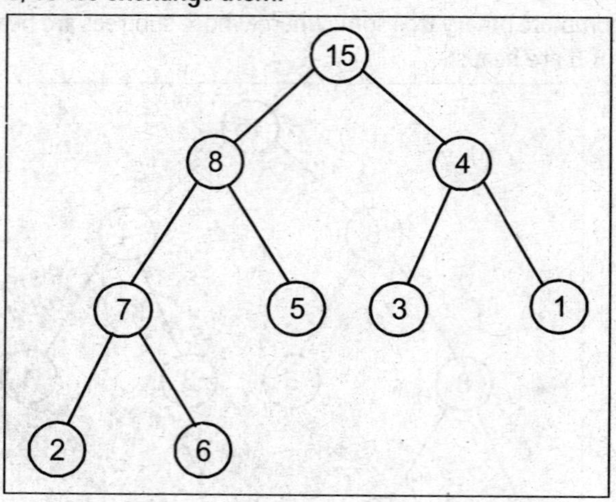

Fig 7.12

We are at the bottom of the tree, and can't continue, so we terminate.

7.10 BUILDING A HEAP

We can use the procedure 'Heapify' in a bottom-up fashion to convert an array A[l . . n] into a heap. Since the elements in the subarray A[⌊n/2⌋ +1 . . n] are all leaves, the procedure BUILD_HEAP goes through the remaining nodes of the tree and runs 'Heapify' on each one. The bottom-up order of processing node guarantees that the subtree rooted at children are heap before 'Heapify' is run at their parent.

BUILD_HEAP (A)

1. heap-size (A) ← length [A]
2. For i ← floor(length[A]/2) down to 1 do
3. Heapify (A, i)

We can build a heap from an unordered array in linear time.

7.11 HEAP SORT ALGORITHM

The heap sort combines the best of both merge sort and insertion sort. Like merge sort, the worst case time of heap sort is O(n log n) and like insertion sort, heap sort sorts in-place. The heap sort algorithm starts by using procedure BUILD-HEAP to build a heap on the input array A[l . . n]. Since the maximum element of the array stored at the root A[1], it can be put into its correct final position by exchanging it with A[n] (the last element in A). If we now discard node n from the heap than the remaining elements can be made into heap. Note that the new element at the root may violate the heap property. All that is needed to restore the heap property.

HEAPSORT

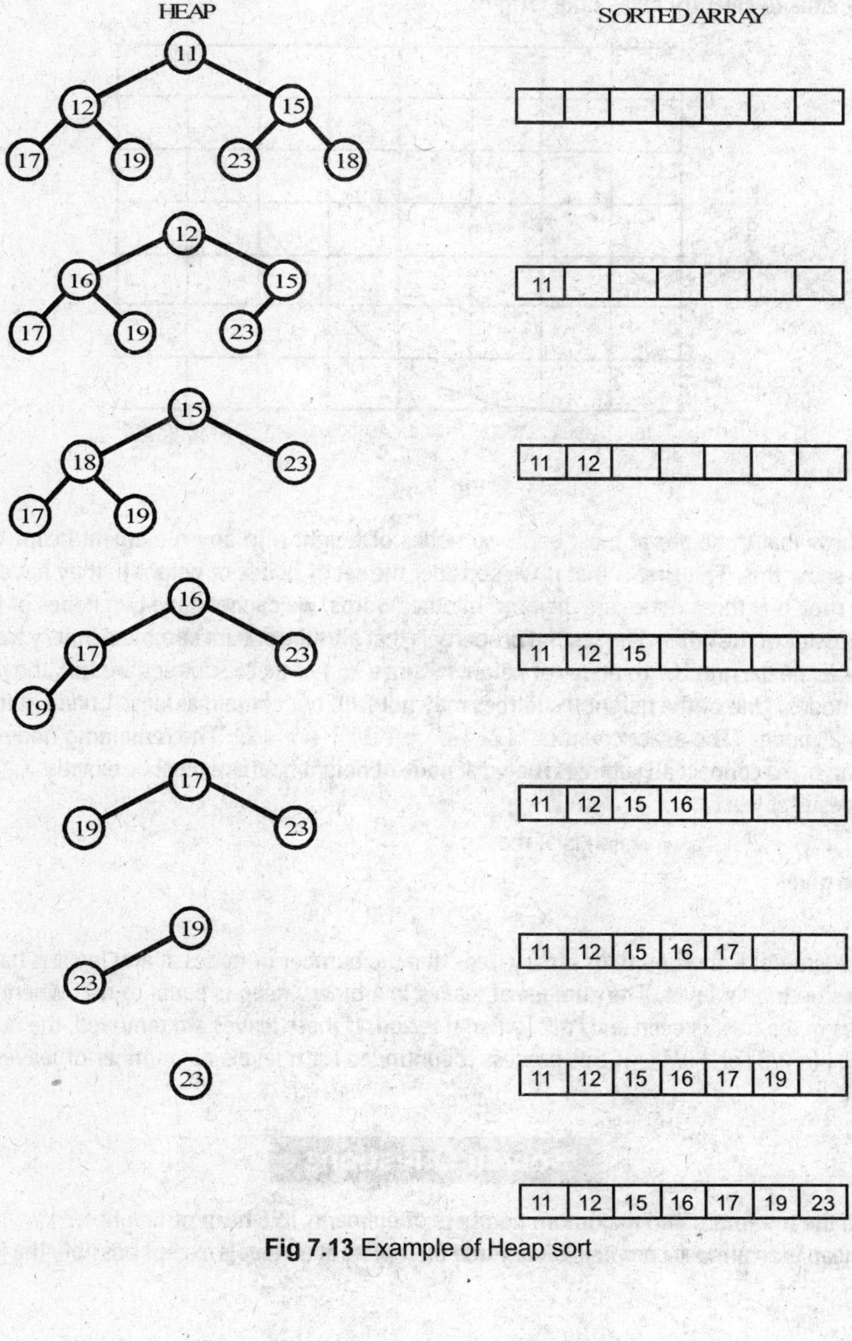

Fig 7.13 Example of Heap sort

HEAPSORT (A)

1. BUILD_HEAP (A)
2. for i ← length (A) down to 2 do
   exchange A[1] ↔ A[i]
   heap-size [A] ← heap-size [A] – 1
   Heapify (A, 1)

The HEAPSORT procedure takes time O(n lg n), since the call to BUILD_HEAP takes time O(n) and each of the n –1 calls to Heapify takes time O(lg n).

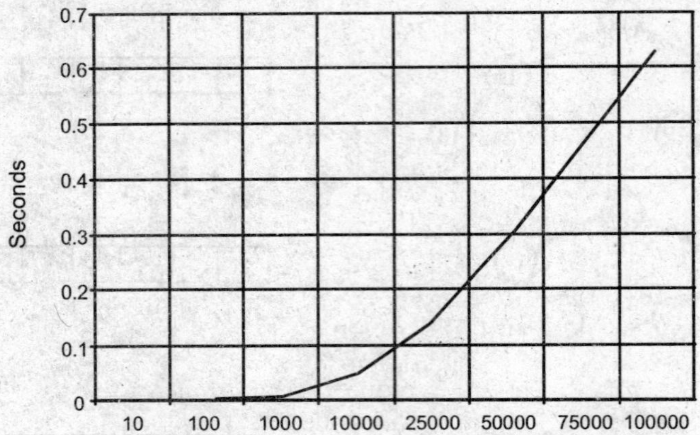

Fig. 7.14

Now we show that there are at most en/2^{h+l} u nodes of height h in any n-element heap. We need two observations to show this. The first is that if we consider the set of nodes of height h, they have the property that the subtree rooted at these nodes are disjoint. In other words, we cannot have two nodes of height h with one being an ancestor of the other. The second property is that all subtrees are complete binary trees except for one subtree. Let X_h be the number of nodes of height h. Since X_{h-1} of these subtrees are full, they each contain exactly 2^{h+l} –1 nodes. One of the height h subtrees may not full, but contain at least 1 node at its lower level and has at least 2^h nodes. The exact count is 1+2+4+ . . . + 2^{h+1} + 1 = 2^h. The remaining nodes have height strictly more than h. To connect all subtrees rooted at node of height h., there must be exactly X_{h-1} such nodes. The total of nodes is at least

$(X_h–l)(2^{h+1} + 1) + 2^h + X_h–1$ which is at most n.

Simplifying gives

$$X_h \leq n/2^{h+l} + 1/2$$

In the conclusion, it is a property of binary trees that the number of nodes at any level is half of the total number of nodes up to that level. The number of leaves in a binary heap is equal to n/2, where n is the total number of nodes in the tree, is even and $\lceil nl2 \rceil$ when n is odd. If these leaves are removed, the number of new leaves will be lg $\lceil (n/2/2 \rceil$ or $\lceil n/4 \rceil$. If this process is continued for h levels the number of leaves at that level will be $\lceil n/2^{h+1} \rceil$.

Solved Questions

1. What are the minimum and maximum numbers of elements in a heap of height h?

Ans. Since a heap is an almost-complete binary tree (complete at all levels except possibly the lowest), it has at most 2h+1 –1 elements (if it is complete) and at least 2h "1+1 = 2h elements (if the lowest level has just 1 element and the other levels are complete).

2. Show that an n-element heap has height lg n.

Ans. Given an n-element heap of height h, that 2h ≤ n ≤ 2h+1 – 1 < 2h+1 .
Thus, h ≤ lg n < h + 1. Since h is an integer, h =lg n (by definition of).

3. Show that in any subtree of a max-heap, the root of the subtree contains the largest value occurring anywhere in that subtree.

Ans. Assume the claim is false.i.e., that there is a subtree whose root is not the largest element in the subtree. Then the maximum element is somewhere else in the subtree, possibly even at more than one location. Let m be the index at which the maximum appears (the lowest such index if the maximum appears more than once). Since the maximum is not at the root of the subtree, node m has a parent. Since the parent of a node has a lower index than the node, and m was chosen to be the smallest index of the maximum value, A[PARENT(m)] < A[m]. But by the maxheap property, we must have A[PARENT(m)] ≥ A[m]. So our assumption is false, and the claim is true.

4. Show that the worst-case running time of MAX-HEAPIFY on a heap of size n is Ω(lg n). (Hint: For a heap with n nodes, give node values that cause MAX-HEAPIFY to be called recursively at every node on a path from the root down to a leaf.)

Ans. If you put a value at the root that is less than every value in the left and right subtrees, then MAX-HEAPIFY will be called recursively until a leaf is reached. To make the recursive calls traverse the longest path to a leaf, choose values that make MAX-HEAPIFY always recurse on the left child. It follows the left branch when the left child is ≥ the right child, so putting 0 at the root and 1 at all the other nodes, for example, will accomplish that. With such values, MAX-HEAPIFY will be called h times (where h is the heap height, which is the number of edges in the longest path from the root to a leaf), so its running time will be Ω (h) (since each call does Ω (1) work), which is Ω (lg n). Since we have a case in which MAX-HEAPIFY.S running time is Ω (lg n), its worst-case running time is _(lg n).

Previous Year University Question

1. What is Heap? How to delete an element from the Heap? [OS 08]
2. Describe heap sort algorithm. [GBTU 11]
3. Write the pseudo code for heapify algorithm. [GBTU]
4. Write an algorithm HEAP_DELETE (A,i), which deletes the items in node I from heap A. [GBTU]
5. What is heap sort? Write an algorithm to sort elements using heapsort.Show the steps for the following list:(40,80,35,90,45,50,70)
   Analyse its time complexity and compare it with quick sort. [KU]
6. Explain the algorithm of Quick Sort and compare time complexity with Heap Sort. [MDU]
7. Explain heap sort with its complexity? What is running time of heap sort when list is already sorted? Sort the following list using heap sort:
   14, 8, 15, 6, 3, 20,22, 28, 10, 40. [MDU]
8. Explain the implementation of Priority queue using max-heap. Give the procedure for HEAP, INSERT and HEAP_EXTRACT_MAX for implementation of Priority Queue? Give the time complexity also. [MDU]

Exercise

1. Show that array using heap sort.
   (a) (16, 10, 14, 20, 18, 9, 2)
   (b) (3, 1, 8, 6, 4, 9)
   (c) (19, 25, 16, 75, 90, 95, 10)
   (d) (85, 9, 2, 30, 45, 60)
2. The reverse sorted array is heap or not? Justify
3. Show that hight of of a tree in heap is $\lfloor 1g\ n \rfloor$.
4. What are the maximum and minimum no of elements in a heap of height l.
5. Explain how heap can be created in linear time.
6. What are the average care and worst are complexity of heap sort. Explain.
7. Let A = [7, 2, 4, 17, 11, 6, 8, 15, 10, 20]
   (a) Draw a binomial heap whose keys are elementry of A.
   (b) Insert of a new element with the key 5 into this heap.
   (c) To a binomial heap obtained this way, apply the operation of extracting the node minimum key two times. After each change in the structre of the heap draw its current diagram.

CHAPTER

8

SORTING IN LINEAR TIME

8.1 LOWER BOUNDS FOR SORTING

The preceding sections present three O(nlogn) sorting algorithms — quicksort, heapsort, and the two-way merge sort. But is O(nlogn) the best we can do? In this section we answer the question by showing that any sorting algorithm that sorts using only binary comparisons must make Ω (nlogn) such comparisons. If each binary comparison takes a constant amount of time, then running time for any such sorting algorithm is also Ω(nlog n).

Consider the problem of sorting the sequence S = {a, b, c} comprised of three distinct items. i.e., $a \neq b$ ^ $a \neq c$ ^ $b \neq c$. Figure 8.1 illustrates a possible sorting algorithm in the form of a decision tree . Each node of the decision tree represents one binary comparison. I.e., in each node of the tree, exactly two elements of the sequence are compared. Since there are exactly two possible outcomes for each comparison, each non-leaf node of the binary tree has degree two.

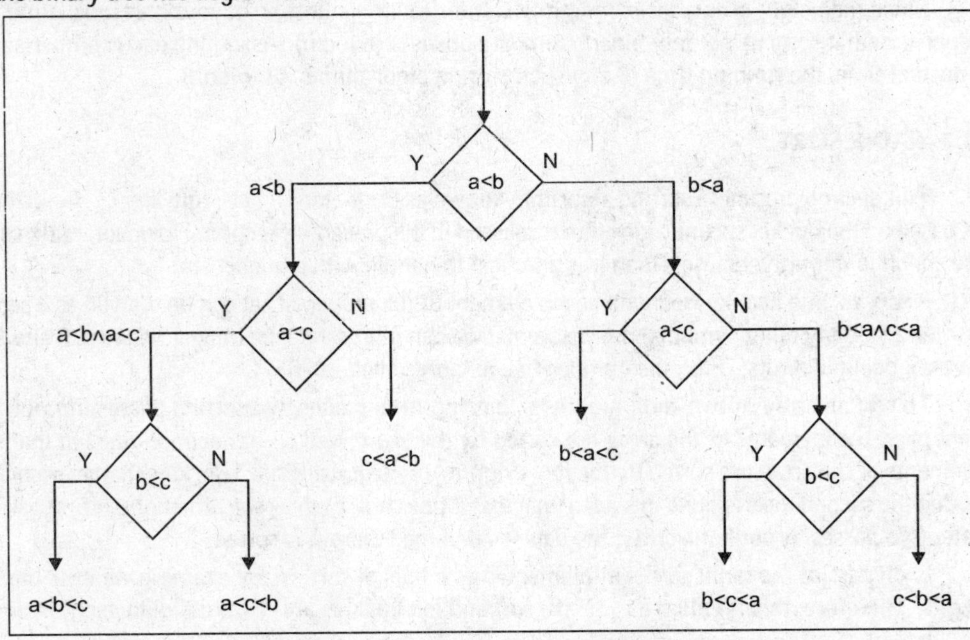

Fig. 8.1 A Decision Tree for Comparison Sorting

For example, suppose that $a < b < c$. Consider how the algorithm shown in Fig 8.1 discovers this. The first comparison compares and which reveals that < . The second comparison compares and to find that < . At this point it has been determined that < and < the relative order of and is not yet known. Therefore, one more comparison is required to determine that < . Notice that the algorithm shown in Fig 8.1 works correctly in all cases because every possible permutation of the sequence S appears as a leaf node in the decision tree. Furthermore, the number of comparisons required in the worst case is equal to the height of the decision tree

Any sorting algorithm that uses only binary comparisons can be represented by a binary decision tree. Furthermore, it is the height of the binary decision tree that determines the worst-case running time of the algorithm. In general, the size and shape of the decision tree is a function of the sorting algorithm and the number of items to be sorted.

Given an input sequence of n items to be sorted, every binary decision tree that correctly sorts the input sequence must have t l t n leaves one for each permutation of the input. Therefore, the height of the binary decision tree is t l t $\log_2$ n :

$$\lceil f\log_2 n \rceil \geq \log_2 n$$

$$\geq \sum_{i=1}^{n} \log_2 n$$

$$\geq \sum_{i=1}^{n} \log_2 n/2$$

$$\geq n/2 \log_2 n/2$$

$$\geq \Omega(n \log n)$$

Since the height of the decision tree is Ω(nlogn), the number of comparisons done by any sorting algorithm that sorts using only binary comparisons isΩ (n log n). Assuming each comparison can be done in constant time, the running time of any such sorting algorithm is Ω (nlogn).

8.2 RADIX SORT

This section presents a sorting algorithm known as l t- igni i nt- igit- ir t r i orting. Radix sorting is based on the bucket sorting algorithm discussed in the preceding section. However, radix sorting is practical for much larger universal sets than it is practical to handle with a bucket sort.

Radix sorting can be used when each element of the universal set can be viewed as a sequences of digits (or letters or any other symbols). For example, we can represent each integer between 0 and 99 as a sequence of two, decimal digits. (E.g., the number five is represented as "05").

To sort an array of two-digit numbers, the algorithm makes two sorting passes through the array. In the first pass, the elements of the array are sorted by the l t igni i nt decimal digit. In the second pass, the elements of the array are sorted by the mo t igni i nt decimal digit. The key characteristic of the radix sort is that the second pass is done in such a way that it does not destroy the effect of the first pass. Consequently, after two passes through the array, the data is contained therein is sorted.

Each pass of the radix sort is implemented as a bucket sort. In the example we base the sort on im l digits. Therefore, this is called a r i -10 sort and ten buckets are required to do each sorting pass.

Fig. 8.2 illustrates the operation of the radix-10 sort. The first radix sorting pass considers the least significant digits. As in the bucket sort, a single pass is made through the unsorted data, counting the number of times each decimal digit appears as the least-significant digit. E.g., there are no elements that have a 0 as the least-significant digit there are two elements that have a 1 as the least-significant digit and so on.

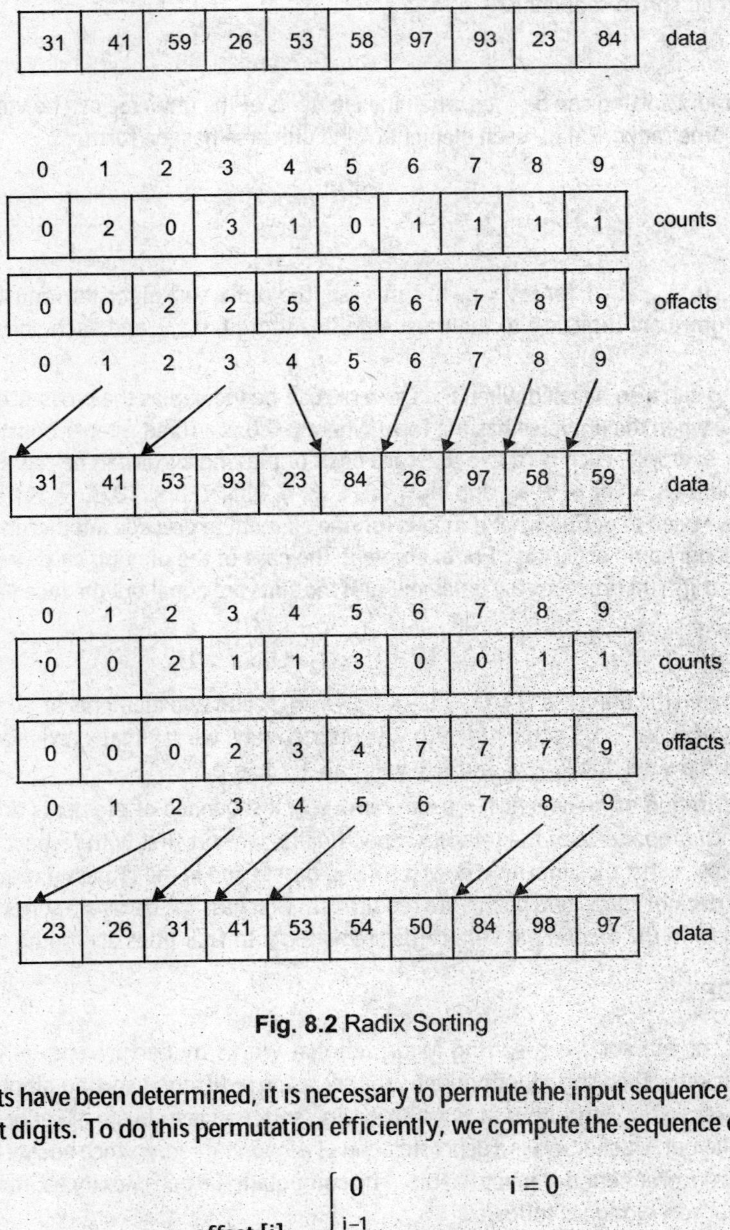

Fig. 8.2 Radix Sorting

After the counts have been determined, it is necessary to permute the input sequence so that it is sorted by the least-significant digits. To do this permutation efficiently, we compute the sequence of o t given by

$$\text{offset}[i] = \begin{cases} 0 & i = 0 \\ \sum_{=0}^{i-1} \text{count}[i] & 0 < i < \ , \end{cases}$$

where is the sorting radix. Note that offset [i] is the position in the permuted sequence of the first occurrence of an element whose least significant digit is i. By making use of the offsets, it is possible to permute the input sequence by making a single pass through the sequence.

The second radix sorting pass considers the most significant digits. As above a single pass is made through the permuted data sequence counting the number of times each decimal digit appears as the most-significant digit. Then the sequence of offsets is computed as above. The sequence is permuted again using the offsets producing the final, sorted sequence.

In general, radix sorting can be used when the elements of the universe can be viewed as p-digit numbers with respect to some radix, R. i.e., each element of the universe has the form

$$\sum_{i=0}^{p-1} d_1 R^i$$

where $d_i \in$ {0,1,..., R –1 for $\in i < p$. In this case, the radix sort algorithm must make p sorting passes from the least significant digit, d_0, to the most significant digit, d_{p-1}, and each sorting pass uses exactly R counters.

Radix sorting can also be used when the universe can be viewed as the cross-product of a finite number of finite sets. i.e., when the universe has the form where $p > 0$ is a fixed integer constant and U_i is a finite set for $1 \le i \le p$. For example, each card in a 52-card deck of playing cards can be represented as an element of $U = U_1 \times U_2$, where U_1 = {♣,♦,♥,♠} and U_2 = {A, 2, 3, 4, 5, 6, 7, 8,9, 10, J, Q, K} Before we can sort over the universe U, we need to define what it means for one element to precede another in U. The usual way to do this is called lexicographic ordering . For example in the case of the playing cards we may say that one card precedes another if its suit precedes the other suit or if the suits are equal but the face value precedes that of the other.

$$U = U_1 \times U_2 \times U_2 \times \ldots \times U_P,$$

In general, given the universe $U = U_1 \times U_2 \times U_2 \times \ldots \times U_p$ and two elements of U, say x and y, represented by the p-tuples $x = (x_1, x_2, \ldots, x_p)$ and $y = (y_1, y_1 \ldots y_p)$, respectively, we say that x lexicographically precedes y if there exists $1 \le k \le p$ such that $x_k < y_k$ and $x_i = y_i$ for all $1 \le k, \le p_k$.

With this definition of precedence, we can radix sort a sequence of elements drawn from U by sorting with respect to the components of the p-tuples. Specifically, we sort first with respect to U_p, then U_{p-1}, and so on down to U_1. Notice that the algorithm does p sorting passes and in the ith pass it requires $| U_1 |$ counters. For example to sort a deck of cards, two passes are required. In first pass the cards are sorted into 13 piles according to their face values. In the second pass the cards are sorted into four piles according to their suits.

8.4 BUCKET SORT

Bucket sort, or bin sort, is a sorting algorithm that works by partitioning an array into a number of buckets. Each bucket is then sorted individually, either using a different sorting algorithm, or by recursively applying the bucket sorting algorithm. It is a distribution sort, and is a cousin of radix sort in the most to least significant digit flavour. Bucket sort is a generalization of pigeonhole sort. Since bucket sort is not a comparison sort, the O (n log n) lower bound is inapplicable. The computational complexity estimates involve the number of buckets. Bucket sort works as follows:

1. Set up an array of initially empty "buckets."
2. Scatter: Go over the original array, putting each object in its bucket.
3. Sort each non-empty bucket.
4. Gather: Visit the buckets in order and put all elements back into the original array.

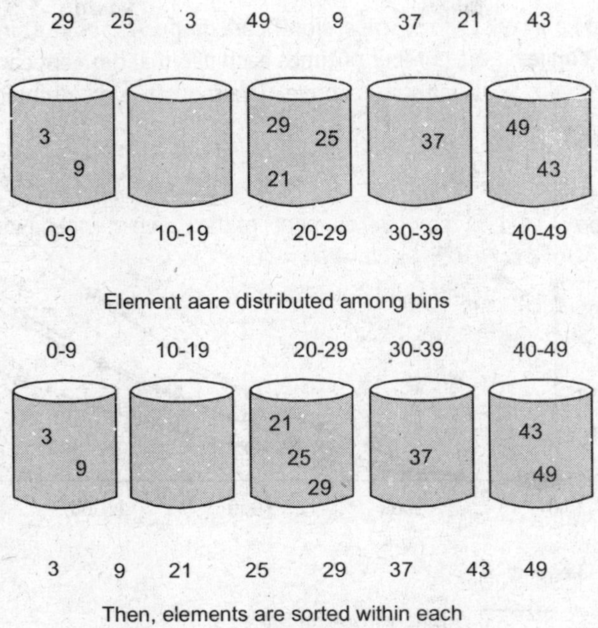

Fig. 8.3.

Pseudocode

```
function bucket-sort(array, n) is
buckets ← new array of n empty lists
for i = 0 to (length(array)-1) do
  insert array[i] into buckets[msbits(array[i], k)]
for i = 0 to n - 1 do
  next-sort(buckets[i])
return the concatenation of buckets[0], ..., buckets[n-l]
```

Here array is the array to be sorted and n is the number of buckets to use. The function msbits (x, k) returns the k most significant bits of x (floor (x / 2 ^ (size (x) – k))); different functions can be used to translate the range of elements in array to n buckets, such as translating the letters A – Z to 0 – 25 or returning the first character (0 – 255) for sorting strings. The function next-sort is a sorting function; using bucket-sort itself as next-sort produces a relative of radix sort; in particular, the case n = 2 corresponds to quicksort (although potentially with poor pivot choices).

8.5 PERFORMANCE DATA

In order to better understand the actual performance of the various sorting algorithms presented in this chapter, it is necessary to conduct some experiments. Only by conducting experiments is it possible to determine the relative performance of algorithms with the same asymptotic running time.

To measure the performance of a sorting algorithm, we need to provide it with some data to sort. To obtain/he results presented here, random sequences of unsigned integers were sorted. i.e., for each value of n, the Random Number Generator class is defined was used to create a sequence of n integers. In all cases (except for bucket sort) the random numbers are uniformly distributed in the interval (I, $2^{31}-1$). For the bucket sort the numbers are uniformly distributed in [0, $2^{10}-1$]

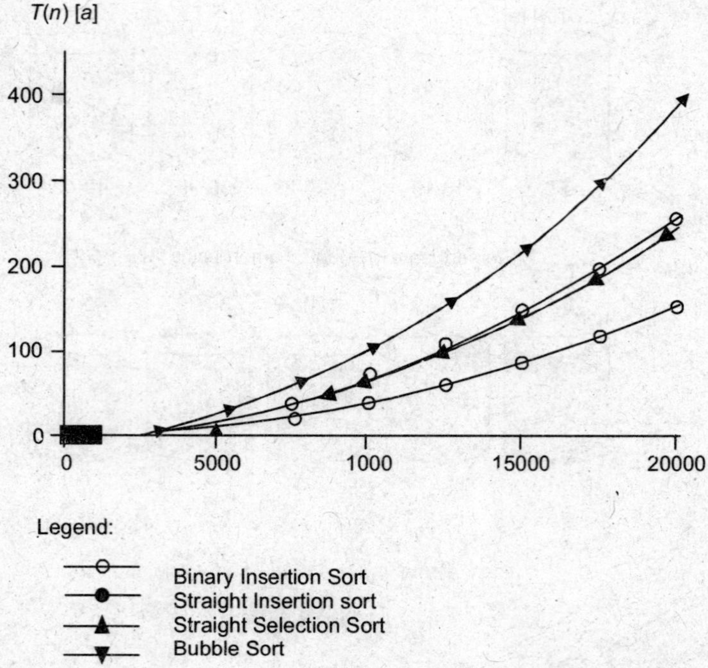

Fig. 8.4 Actual Running Times of the $O(n^2)$ Sorts

Fig. 8.4, 8.5 and 8.6 show the actual running times of the sorting algorithms presented in this chapter. These running times were measured on a Sun SPARCstation 5, Model 85, which has an 85 MHz clock, and 32MB RAM. The programs were compiled using the SPARCompiler C++ 4.1 compiler, and run under the Solaris 2.3 operating system. The times shown are user CPU times, measured in seconds. Fig. 8.4 shows the running times of the $O(n^2)$ sorts for sequences of length n, $100 \le n \le 20000$. Notice that the bubble sort has the worst performance and that the binary insertion sort has the best performance. Fig. 8.4 clearly shows that, as predicted, binary insertion is better than straight insertion. Notice too that all of the $O(n^2)$ sorts require in excess of two minutes of execution time to sort an array of 20000 integers.

The performance of the O(nlog n) sorts is shown in Fig. 8.5. In this case, the length of the sequence varies between n = 100 and n = 100000. The graph clearly shows that the O(nlogn) algorithms are significantly faster that the $O(n^2)$ ones.

All three algorithms sort 100000 integers in under 6 seconds. Clearly, quick sort is the best of the three, whereas the two-way merge sort and heap sort have similar running times.

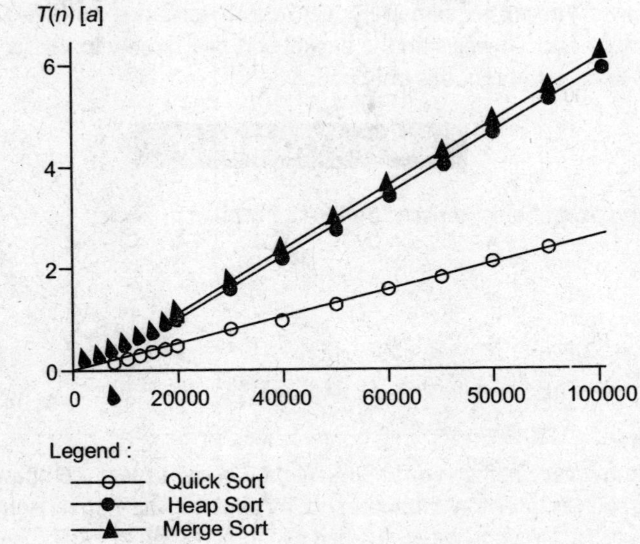

Fig. 8.5 Actual Running Times of the *O* (n log *n*) Sorts

Fig. 8.6 shows the actual running times for the bucket sort and radix sort algorithms. Both these algorithms were shown to be O(n) sorts. The graph shows results for n between 100 and 1000000. The universe used to test bucket sort was 0, 1, ... 1023 . i.e., a total of m = 1024 counters (buckets) were used. For the radix sort, 32-bit integers were sorted by using the radix R = 256 and doing p = 4 sorting passes.

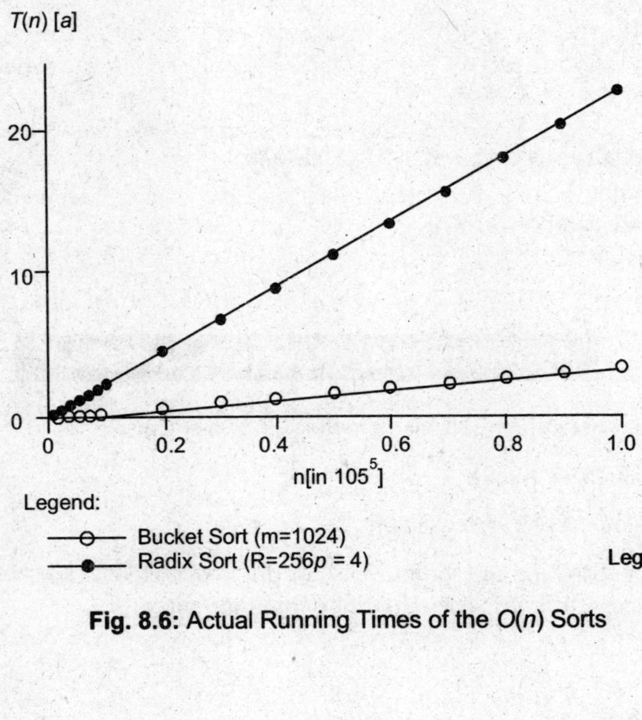

Fig. 8.6: Actual Running Times of the *O*(*n*) Sorts

Clearly, the bucket sort has the best running time. For example, it sorts one million 10-bit integers in about 5 seconds. Radix sort performs extremely well too. It sorts one-million 32-bit integers in about 20 seconds. This is a factor of four slower than the bucket sort due largely to the fact that radix sort does four sorting passes whereas bucket sort requires only one.

Solved Questions

1. Sort the following using Selection sort: 64 25 12 22 11

Ans. 64 25 12 22 11
11 25 12 22 64
11 12 25 22 64
11 12 22 25 64
11 12 22 25 64

2. What is shell sort?

Ans. Shell sort, also known as Shell sort or Shell's method is an in-place comparison sort. It generalizes an exchanging sort, such as insertion or bubble sort, by allowing the comparison and exchange of elements that lie far apart. Its first version was published by Donald Shell in 1959. The running time of Shell sort is heavily dependent on the gap sequence it uses. For many practical variants, determining their time complexity remains an open problem. Shell sort is a multi-pass algorithm. Each pass is an insertion sort of the sequences consisting of every h-th element for a fixed gap h (also known as the increment). This is referred to as h-sorting.

3. Write the algorithm for counting sort.

Ans.
```
"allocate an array Count[0..k] ; initialize each array cell to zero ; THEN "'
for each input item x:
Count[key(x)] = Count[key(x)] + 1
total = 0
for i = 0, 1, ... k:
c = Count[i]
Count[i] = total
total = total + c
"' allocate an output array Output[0..n-1] ; THEN "'
for each input item x:
store x in Output[Count[key(x)]]
Count[key(x)] = Count[key(x)] + 1
return Output
```

Previous Year University Question

1. Using selection sort algorithm sort the following set of elements.

   {30,25,15,10,12,20} [OU]

2. Explain the topological sort with example. [KU]

3. What is meant by searching and sorting? Discuss different methods (any two) used for searching and sorting. Also discuss their efficiency in terms of time and space. [MDU]

Exercises

1. Consider the sequence of integers

$$S = \{8,9, 7,9,3, 23,8, 4, 6\}$$

For each of the following sorting algorithms, draw a sequence of diagrams that traces the execution of the algorithm as it sorts the sequence S: straight insertion sort, binary insertion sort, bubble sort, quick sort, straight selection sort, heapsort, merge sort, and bucket sort.

2. Draw a sequence of diagrams that traces the execution of a radix-10 sort of the sequence

$$S = \{89,79, 32,38,46,26,43,38,32, 70\}.$$

3. For each of the sorting algorithms prove that whether the sorting algorithm is stable or not"?
4. Consider a sequence of three distinct keys [a, b, c]. Draw the binary decision tree that represents each of the following sorting algorithms: straight insertion sort, straight selection sort, and bubble sort.
5. Devise an algorithm to sort a sequence of exactly three elements. Make your algorithm as efficient as possible.
6. Prove that the swapping of a pair of adjacent elements removes at most one inversion from a sequence.
7. Consider the sequence of elements $\{s_1,s_2,..., s_n\}$. What is the maximum number of inversions that can be removed by the swapping of a pair of distinct elements S_i and S_j ? Express the result in terms of the distance between s_i and s_j. $d(s_1, s_j) = j - i + 1$
8. Devise a sequence of keys such that exactly eleven inversions are removed by the swapping of one pair of elements.
9. Prove that binary insertion sort requires O (n log n) comparisons.
10. Consider an arbitrary sequence $\{s_1, s_2,..., s_n\}$. To sort the sequgnce, we determine the permutation $\{p_1, p_2..., p_n\}$ such that

$$S_{p_1} \le S_{p_2} \le ... \le s_{pn}.$$

Prove that bubble sort requires at least p passes where

$$P = \max (1- pi)$$
$$1 \le n$$

11. Modify the bubble sort algorithm so that it terminates the outer loop when it detects that the array is sorted. What is the running time of the modified algorithm?
12. A variant of the bubble sorting algorithm is the so-called odd-even transposition sort. Like bubble sort, this algorithm a total of n–1 passes through the array. Each pass consists of two phases: The first phase compares array[i] with array [i +1] and swaps them if necessary for all the odd values of of i. The second phase does the same for the even values of i.
    - Show that the array is guaranteed to be sorted after n –1 passes.
    - What is the running time of this algorithm?
13. Another variant of the bubble sorting algorithm is the so-called cocktail"shaker sort. Like bubble sort, this algorithm a total of n –1 passes through"the array. However, alternating passes go in opposite directions. e.g., during"the first pass the largest item bubbles to the end of the array and during the"second pass the smallest item bubbles to the beginning of the array.
    - Show that the array is guaranteed to be sorted after n --1 passes.
    - What i s the running time of this algorithm?

14. Consider the following algorithm for selecting the th largest element from an"unsorted sequence of of n elements, S = 1, 2,..., n .
    - If n ≤ 5, sort S and select directly the th largest element.
    1. Otherwise n > 5: Partition the sequence S into subsequences of length five. In general, there will b e [n/5] subsequences of length five and one of length n mod 5.
    2. Sort by any means each of the subsequences of length five.
    3. Form the sequence M= m_1, m_2, ..., $m_{[n/5]}$ containing the [n/5] median values of each of the subsequences of length five.
    4. Apply the selection procedure recursively to find the median element of M. Let m be the median of the medians.
    5. Partition S into three subsequences, S = L, E, G such that all the elements in are less than m, all the elements in are equal to m, and all the elements of G are greater than m.
    6. If ≤ L then apply the procedure recursively to select the th largest element of if < < L + , the result is m otherwise apply the procedure recursively to select the (– (+))th largest element of G.
    7. What is the running time of this algorithm?
    8. Show that if we use this algorithm to select the pivot the worst-case running time of i ort is O (n log n).
15. Show that the sum of the heights of the nodes in a complete binary tree with n nodes altogether is n – (n), where (n) is the number of ones in the binary representation of n.

CHAPTER

9

RANDOMIZED ALGORITHMS

9.1 INTRODUCTION

A randomized algorithm or probabilistic algorithm is an algorithm which employs a degree of randomness as part of its logic. The algorithm typically uses uniformly random bits as an auxiliary input to guide its behaviour, in the hope of achieving good performance in the "average case" over all possible choices of random bits. Formally, the algorithm's performance will be a random variable determined by the random bits; thus either the running time, or the output (or both) are random variables.

In both cases, random performance and random output, the term "algorithm" for a procedure is somewhat questionable. In the case of random output, it is no longer formally effective. However, in some cases, probabilistic algorithms are the only practical means of solving a problem.

In common practice, randomized algorithms are approximated using a pseudorandom number generator in place of a true source of random bits; such an implementation may deviate from the expected theoretical behaviour.

For an example, consider the problem of finding an 'a' in an array of n elements.

Input: An array of n elements, in which half are 'a' s and the other half are 'b' s.

Output: Find an 'a' in the array.

There are two versions of the algorithm, one Las Vegas algorithm and one Monte Carlo algorithm.

Las Vegas algorithm

```
findingA_LV (array A, n)
begin
    repeat
        Randomly select one element out of n elements.
    until 'a' is found
end
```

This algorithm succeeds with probability 1, but the running time is random and its expectation is upper-bounded by O(1).

Monte Carlo algorithm

```
findingA_MC(array A, n)
begin
    i=l
    repeat
        Randomly select one element out of n elements.
        i = i + 1
    until i=k
end
```

If an 'a' is found, the algorithm succeeds, else the algorithm fails. After k times execution, the probability of finding an 'a' is:

$$Pr[\text{find } a] \quad 1 - (1/2)^k$$

This algorithm does not guarantee success, but the run time is fixed. The selection is executed exactly k times, therefore the runtime is O(k).

Randomized algorithms are particularly useful when faced with a malicious "adversary" or attacker who deliberately tries to feed a bad input to the algorithm (see worst-case complexity and competitive analysis (online algorithm)) such as in the Prisoner's dilemma. It is for this reason that randomness is ubiquitous in cryptography. In cryptographic applications, pseudorandom numbers cannot be used, since the adversary can predict them, making the algorithm effectively deterministic. Therefore either a source of truly random numbers or a cryptographically secure pseudo-random number generator is required. Another area in which randomness is inherent is quantum computing.

In the example above, the Las Vegas algorithm always outputs the correct answer, but its running time is a random variable. The Monte Carlo algorithm(related to the Monte Carlo method for simulation) completes in a fixed amount of time (as a function of the input size), but allow a small probability of error. Observe that any Las Vegas algorithm can be converted into a Monte Carlo algorithm (via Markov's inequality), by having it output an arbitrary, possibly incorrect answer if it fails to complete within a specified time. Conversely, if an efficient verification procedure exists to check whether an answer is correct, then a Monte Carlo algorithm can be converted into a Las Vegas algorithm by running the Monte Carlo algorithm repeatedly till a correct answer is obtained.

9.2 COMPUTATIONAL COMPLEXITY

Computational complexity theory models randomized algorithms as probabilistic uring machines. Both Las Vegas and Monte Carlo algorithms are considered, and several complexity classes are studied. The most basic randomized complexity class is RP, which is the class of decision problems for which there is an efficient (polynomial time) randomized algorithm (or probabilistic Turing machine) which recognizes NO-instances with absolute certainty and recognizes ES-instances with a probability of at least 1/2. The complement class for RP is co-RP. Problem classes having (possibly nonterminating) algorithms with polynomial time average case running time whose output is always correct are said to be in ZPP.

The class of problems for which both ES and NO-instances are allowed to be identified with some error is called BPP. This class acts as the randomized equivalent of P, i.e BPP represents the class of efficient randomized algorithms.

9.3 APPLICATIONS

9.3.1 Quicksort

Quicksort is a familiar, commonly-used algorithm in which randomness can be useful. Any deterministic version of this algorithm requires O n time to sort n numbers for some well-defined class of degenerate inputs (such as an already sorted array), with the specific class of inputs that generate this behavior defined by the protocol for pivot selection. However, if the algorithm selects pivot elements uniformly at random, it has a provably high probability of finishing in O(n log n) time regardless of the characteristics of the input.

9.3.2 Randomized incremental constructions in geometry

In computational geometry, a standard technique to build a structure like a convex hull or Delaunay Triangulation is to randomly permute the input points and then insert them one by one into the existing structure. The randomization ensures that the expected number of changes to the structure caused by an insertion is small, and so the expected running time of the algorithm can be upper bounded. This technique is known as randomized incremental construction.

9.3.3 Verifying matrix multiplication

Input: Matrix $A \in R^{m \times p}$, $B \in R^{p \times n}$, and $C \in R^{m \times n}$.

Output: True if C = A B; false if $C \neq A\ B$

We give a Monte Carlo algorithm to solve the problem.[4]

```
begin
    i = l
    repeat
        Choose r= (r1,... , rn) ∈ {0,1}^n at random.
        Compute C  r and A  (B . r)
        if C  r ≠ A  (B  r)
            return FALSE
        end if
        i = i + 1
    until i = k
    return TRUE
end
```

The running time of the algorithm is $O(kn^2)$.

Theorem: The algorithm is correct with probability at least $1-\left(\frac{1}{2}\right)^k$

We will prove that if $A\ B \neq C$ then $\Pr[A\ B\ r = C . r] \leq 1/2$

If $A . B \neq C$, definition we have $D = A\ B - C \neq 0$. Without loss of generality, we assume that $d_{11} \neq 0$

On the other hand,

$$\Pr[A . B . r = C . r] = \Pr[(A B - C)\ r = 0] = \Pr[D\ r = 0].$$

If $D\ r = 0$, then the first entry of D. r is 0, that is

$$\sum_{j=1}^{n} d_{ij} r_j = 0$$

Since $D_{11} \neq 0$, we can solve for r_1:

$$r_1 = \frac{\sum_{j=2}^{n} d_1 j r_j}{d_{11}}$$

If we fix all r_j except r_1, the equality holds for at most one of the two choices for $r_1 \in \{0.1\}$. Therefore, Pr [ABr = Cr] ≤ 1/2.

We run the loop for k times. If C = A .B, the algorithm is always correct; if $C \neq A . B$, the probability of getting the correct answer is at least $1-\left(\frac{1}{2}\right)^k$

9.3.4 MIN CUT

Input: A graph G (V, E)

Output: A cut partitioning the vertices into L and R, with the minimum number of edges between L and R.

Recall that the contraction of two nodes, u and v, in a (multi-)graph yields a new node u ' with edges that are the union of the edges incident on either u or v, except from any edge(s) connecting u and v. Figure 1 gives an example of contraction of vertex A and B. After contraction, the resulting graph may have parallel edges, but contains no self loops.

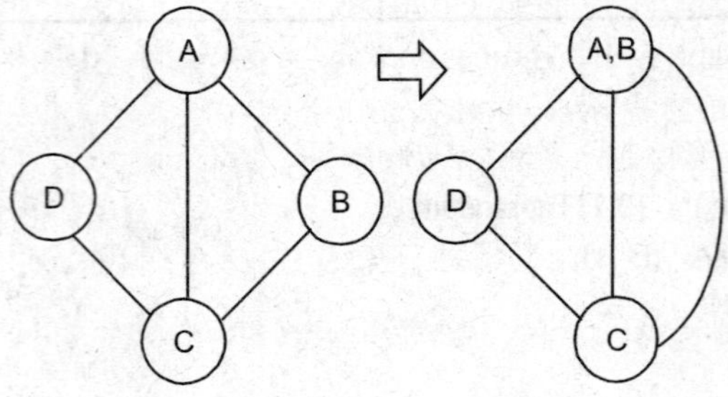

Fig. 9.1: Contraction of vertex A and B

Karger' s basic algorithm:

```
begin
i =1
repeat
   repeat
        Take a random edge (u,v) ∈ E in G
        replace u and v with the contraction u'
     until only 2 nodes remain
  obtain the corresponding cut result C_i
   i=i + l'
until i=m
output the minimum cut among C_1, C_2, ...,C_m.
end
```

In each execution of the outer loop, the algorithm repeats the inner loop until only 2 nodes remain, the corresponding cut is obtained. The run time of one execution is O(n), and n denotes the number of vertices. After m times executions of the outer loop, we output the minimum cut among all the results. The figure 9.2 gives an example of one execution of the algorithm. After execution, we get a cut of size 1.

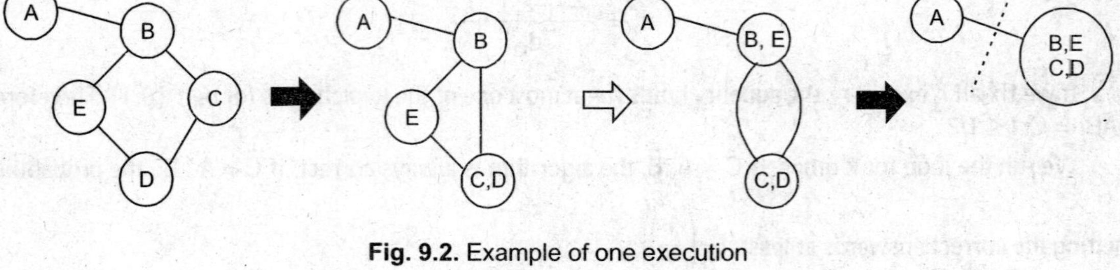

Fig. 9.2. Example of one execution

Lemma 1: Let k be the min cut size, and let $C=\{e_1,e_2,..,e_k\}$ be the min cut. If, during iteration i', no edge $e \in C$ is selected for contraction, then $C_i = C$.

Proof: If G is not connected, then G can be partitioned into L and R without any edge between them. So the min cut in a disconnected graph is 0. Now, assume G is connected. Let $V=L \cup R$ be the partition of V induced by $C : C=\{ \{u,v\} \in E : u \in L, v \in R\}$ (well-defined since G is connected). Consider an edge {u,v} of C. Initially, u,v are distinct vertices. As long as we pick an edge $f \neq e$, u and v do not get merged. Thus, at the end of the algorithm, we have two compound nodes covering the entire graph, one consisting of the vertices of L and the other consisting of the vertices of R. As in figure 9.2, the size of min cut is 1, and C={(A,B)}. If we don't select (A,B) for contraction, we can get the min cut.

Lemma 2: If G is a muitigraph with p vertices and whose min cut has size k, then G has at least pk/2 edges.

Proof: Because the min cut is k, every vertex v must satisfy degree (v)> k. Therefore, the sum of the degree is at least pk. But it is well known that the sum of vertex degrees equals 2|E|. The lemma follows.

9.3.5 Analysis of algorithm

The probability that the algorithm succeeds is 1- the probability that all attempts fail. By independence, the probability that all attempts fail is

$$\prod_{i=1}^{m} \Pr(C_i \neq C) = \prod_{i=1}^{m} (1 - \Pr(C_i = C)$$

By lemma 1, the probability that $C_i=C$ is the probability that no edge of C is selected during iteration i. Consider the inner loop and let G_j denote the graph after j edge contractions, where $j \in \{0,l,...,n-3\}$. Gj has n – j vertices. We use the chain rule of conditional possibilities. The probability that the edge chosen at iteration j is not in C, given that no edge of C has been chosen before, is $1-\frac{k}{|E(G_j)|}$. Note that G_j still has min cut of size k, so by Lemma 2, it still has at least $\frac{(n-j)k}{2}$ edges.

Thus, $1-\frac{k}{|E(Gj)|} \geq 1-\frac{2}{n-j} = \frac{n-j-2}{n-j}$

So by the chain rule, the probability of finding the min cut C is

$$\Pr[C_i = C] \geq \left(\frac{n-2}{n}\right)\left(\frac{n-3}{n-1}\right)\left(\frac{n-4}{n-2}\right)...\left(\frac{3}{5}\right)\left(\frac{2}{4}\right)\left(\frac{1}{3}\right)$$

Cancellation gives $\Pr[C_i = C] \geq \frac{2}{n(n-1)}$. Thus the probability that the algorithm succeeds is at least $1-\left(1-\frac{2}{n(n-1)}\right)m$. For $m=\frac{n(n-1)}{2}$ In n, this is equivalent to $1-\frac{1}{n}$. The algorithm finds the min cut with probability $1-\frac{1}{n}$, in time O (mn) = O(n^3 log n).

9.4 DERANDOMIZATION

Randomness can be viewed as a resource, like space and time. Derandomization is then the process of removing randomness (or using as little of it as possible). From the viewpoint of computational complexity, derandomizing an efficient randomized algorithm is the question, Is P = BPP ?

There are also specific methods that can be employed to deraridomize particular randomized algorithms

- The method of conditional expectation, and its generalization, pessimistic estimators
- Discrepancy theory (which is used to derandomize geometric algorithms)
- The exploitation of limited independence in the random variables used by the algorithm, such as the pairwise independence used in universal hashing
- The use of expander graphs (or dispersers in general) to amplify a limited amount of initial randomness (this last approach is also referred to as generating pseudorandom bits from a random source, and leads to the related topic of pseudorandomness)

Solved Questions

1. Write the algorithm for Topological Sort.

Ans.
```
int topologicalOrderTraversal(){
int numVisitedVertices = 0;
while(there are more vertices to be visited){
if(there is no vertex with in-degree 0)
break;
else{
select a vertex v that has in-degree 0;
visit v;
numVisitedVertices++;
delete v and all its emanating edges;
}
}
return numVisitedVertices;
}
```

2. Suppose that you want to output 0 with probability 1/2 and 1 with probability 1/2. At your disposal is a procedure BIASED-RANDOM, that outputs either 0 or 1. It outputs 1 with some probability p and 0 with probability 1 - p, where 0 < p < 1, but you do not know what p is. Give an algorithm that uses BIASED-RANDOM as a subroutine, and returns an unbiased answer, returning 0 with probability 1/2 and 1 with probability 1/2. What is the expected running time of your algorithm as a function of p?

Ans. To get an unbiased random bit, given only calls to BIASED-RANDOM, call BIASED-RANDOM twice. Repeatedly do so until the two calls return different values, and when this occurs, return the first of the two bits:

```
UNBIASED-RANDOM
while TRUE
do
x ← BIASED-RANDOM
y ← BIASED-RANDOM
if x _= y
then return x
```

To see that UNBIASED-RANDOM returns 0 and 1 each with probability 1/2, observe that the probability that a given iteration returns 0 is

$$\Pr\{x = 0 \text{ and } y = 1\} = (1 - p)p,$$

and the probability that a given iteration returns 1 is

$$\Pr\{x = 1 \text{ and } y = 0\} = p(1 - p).$$

(We rely on the bits returned by BIASED-RANDOM being independent.) Thus, the probability that a given iteration returns 0 equals the probability that it returns 1. Since there is no other way for UNBIASED-RANDOM to return a value, it returns 0 and 1 each with probability 1/2.

Assuming that each iteration takes O(1) time, the expected running time of UNBIASED-RANDOM is linear in the expected number of iterations. We can view each iteration as a Bernoulli trial, where .success. means that the iteration returns a value. The probability of success equals the probability that 0 is returned plus the probability that 1 is returned, or $2p(1 - p)$. The number of trials until a success occurs is given by the geometric distribution, and the expected number of trials for this scenario is $1/(2p(1 - p))$. Thus, the expected running time of UNBIASED-RANDOM is $(1/(2p(1 - p))$.

3. In HIRE-ASSISTANT, assuming that the candidates are presented in a random order, what is the probability that you will hire exactly one time? What is the probability that you will hire exactly n times?

Ans. Since HIRE-ASSISTANT always hires candidate 1, it hires exactly once if and only if no candidates other than candidate 1 are hired. This event occurs when candidate 1 is the best candidate of the n, which occurs with probability 1/n.
HIRE-ASSISTANT hires n times if each candidate is better than all those who were interviewed (and hired) before. This event occurs precisely when the list of ranks given to the algorithm is 1, 2, . . . , n, which occurs with probability 1/n!

4. Professor Kelp decides to write a procedure that will produce at random any permutation besides the identity permutation. He proposes the following procedure:

```
PERMUTE-WITHOUT-IDENTITY(A)
n ← length[A]
for i ← 1 to n
do swap A[i] ← [RANDOM(i + 1, n)]
```

Does this code do what Professor Kelp intends?

Ans. Although PERMUTE-WITHOUT-IDENTITY will not produce the identity permutation, there are other permutations that it fails to produce. For example, consider its operation when n = 3, when it should be able to produce the n! – 1 = 5 nonidentity permutations. The for loop iterates for i = 1 and i = 2. When i = 1, the call to RANDOM returns one of two possible values (either 2 or 3), and when i = 2, the call to RANDOM returns just one value (3). Thus, there are only 2 1 = 2 possible permutations that PERMUTE-WITHOUT-IDENTITY can produce, rather than the 5 that are required.

5. Suppose that instead of swapping element A[i] with a random element from the subarray A[i ..n], we swapped it with a random element from anywhere in the array:

```
PERMUTE-WITH-ALL(A)
n ← length[A]
for i ← 1 to n
do swap A[i] ← A[RANDOM(1, n)]
```

Does this code produce a uniform random permutation? Why or why not?

Ans. The PERMUTE-WITH-ALL procedure does not produce a uniform random permutation. Consider the permutations it produces when n = 3. There are 3 calls to RANDOM, each of which returns one of 3 values, and so there are 27 possible outcomes of calling PERMUTE-WITH-ALL. Since there are 3! = 6 permutations, if PERMUTE-WITH-ALL did produce a uniform random permutation, then each permutation would occur 1/6 of the time. That would mean that each permutation would have to occur an integer number m times, where m/27 = 1/6. No integer m satisfies this condition. In fact, if we were to work out the possible permutations of 1, 2, 3 and how often they occur with PERMUTE-WITH-ALL, we would get the following probabilities:

permutation	probability
<1, 2, 3>	4/27
<1, 3, 2>	5/27
<2, 1, 3>	5/27
<2, 3, 1>	5/27
<3, 1, 2>	4/27
<3, 2, 1>	4/27

Although these probabilities add to 1, none are equal to 1/6.

Previous Year University Question

1. What are randomized algorithms? Explain with the help of an example. [OU]
2. Give the randomized version of quicksort. Analyse it for finding the expected running time. [GBTU]

Exercise

1. Explain different types of randomize algorithm:
2. If a coin is tossed 2000 times. What is the probability that the no. of head is $\geq$ 6000?
3. Explain advantages and disadvantages of randomized algorithm.
4. Explain Baye's Theorem for computing conditional probabilities.
5. Discuss Median of 3 partition method used to improve the RANDOMIZED-QUICK SORT procedure to partition around an element x.

CHAPTER

10

ELEMENTRY DATA STRUCTURES

10.1 STACKS

Defination

A stack is an ordered list where insertion and deletion take place at one end called top of the stack (stack pointer)

A stack is a basic data structure that is used all throughout programming. The idea is to think of your data as a stack of plates or books where you can only take the top item off the stack in order to remove things from it.

A stack is also called a LIFO (Last In First Out) to demonstrate the way it accesses data.

Stack<item-type>

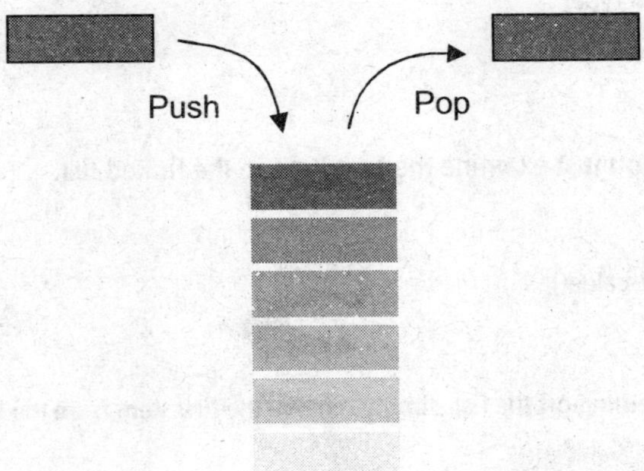

Fig. 10.1 Simple representation of a stack

10.1.1 Operations

push (new-item:item-type)

Adds an item onto the stack.

top () :item-type

Returns the last item pushed onto the stack.

pop

Removes the most-recently-pushed item from the stack.

is-empty():Boolean

True if no more items can be popped and there is no top item.

is-full():Boolean

True if no more items can be pushed.

get-size():Integer

Returns the number of elements on the stack.

All operations except get-size () can be performed in O(1) time, get-size () runs in at worst O(N).

10.1.2 Linked List Implementation

The basic linked list implementation is one of the easiest linked list implementations you can do. Structurally it is a linked list.

```
type Stack<item_type>
    data list:Singly Linked List<item_type>

constructor ()
    list := new Singly-Linked-List {()
end constructor
```

Most operations are implemented by passing them through to the underlying linked list. When you want to push something onto the list, you simply add it to the front of the linked list. The previous top is then "next" from the item being added and the list's front pointer points to the new item.

```
method push(new_item:item_type)
    list.prepend(new_item)
end method
```

To look at the top item, you just examine the first item in the linked list.

```
method top () : item__type
    return list.get-begin().get-value()
end method
```

When you want to pop something off the list, simply remove the first item from the linked list.

```
method pop()
    list.remove-first ()
end method
```

A check for emptiness is easy. Just check if the list is empty.

```
method is-empty():Boolean
    return list.is-empty()
end method
```

A check for full is simple. Linked lists are considered to be limitless in size.

```
method is-full():Boolean
    return False
end method
```

A check for the size is again passed through to the list.

```
method get-size():Integer
    return list.get-size()
  end method
end type
```

A real Stack implementation in a published library would probably re-implement the linked list in order to squeeze the last bit of performance out of the implementation by leaving out unneeded functionality. The above implementation gives you the ideas involved, and any optimization you need can be accomplished by inlining the linked list code.

10.1.3 Performance Analysis

In a linked list, accessing the first element is an O(1) operation because the list contains a pointer checks for empty/fullness as done here are also O(1). depending on what time/space tradeoff is made. Most of the time, users of a Stack do not use the getsize () operation, and so a bit of space can be saved by not optimizing it.

Since all operations are at the top of the stack, the array implementation is now much, much better.

```
public class StackArray implements Stack
{
    protected int top;
    protected Object[] data;
    ...
}
```

The array implementation keeps the bottom of the stack at the beginning of the array. It grows toward the end of the array. The only problem is if you attempt to push an element when the array is full. If so

```
Assert.pre(! is Full(), "Stack is not full.");
```

will fail, raising an exception. Thus it makes more sense to implement with Vector (see StackVector) to allow unbounded growth (at cost of occasional O(n) delays).

10.1.4 Complexity

All operations are O(1) with exception of occasional push and clear, which should replace all entries by null in order to let them be garbage-collected. Array implementation does not replace null entries. The Vector implementation does.

A queue is a basic data structure that is used throughout programming. You can think of it as a line in a grocery store. The first one in the line is the first one to be served. Just like a queue.

A queue is also called a FIFO (First In First Out) to demonstrate the way it accesses data.

10.2 QUEUES

A queue is a basic data structure that is used throughout programming. You can think of it as a line in a ticket counter. The first one in the line is the first one to be served. ust like a queue.

A queue is also called a FIFO (First In First Out) to demonstrate the way it accesses data.

ueue item t pe

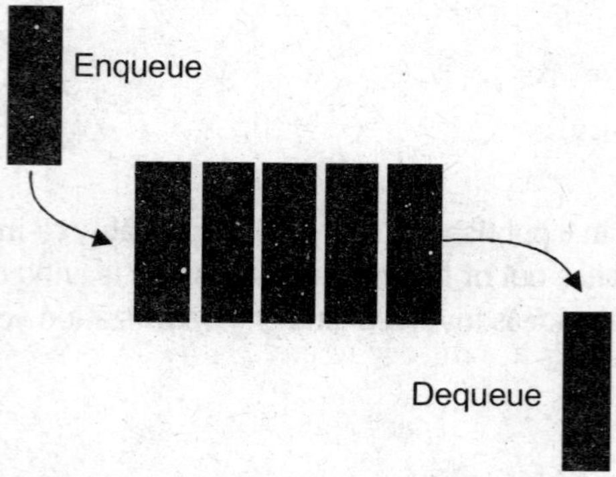

Fig. 10.2 Representation of a FIFO Queue

10.2.1 Operations

en ueue(new-item:item-type)

Adds an item onto the end of the queue.

front ():item-type

Returns the item at the front of the queue.

dequeue()

Removes the item from the front of the queue.

is-empty():Boolean

True if no more items can be dequeued and there is no front item.

is-full.() : Boolean

True if no more items can be enqueued.

get-size():Integer

Returns the number of elements in the queue.

All operations except get-size () can be performed in O(1) time, get-size () runs in at worst O(N).

10.2.2 Linked List Implementation

The basic linked list implementation uses a singly-linked list with a tail pointer to keep track of the back of the queue.

```
type Queue<item_type>
   data list:Singly Linked List<item_type>
   data tail:List Iterator<item_type>

constructor ()
  list := new Singly-Linked-List ()
  tail := list.get-begin() # null
end constructor
```

When you want to enqueue something, you simply add it to the back of the item pointed to by the tail pointer. So the previous tail is considered next compared to the item being added and the tail pointer points to the new item. If the list was empty, this doesn't work, since the tail iterator doesn't refer to anything

```
method enqueue(new_item:item_type)
    if is-empty()
      list.prepend(new_item)
      tail := list.get-begin ()
  else
    list.insert_after(new_item, tail)
    tail.move-next()
  end if
end method
```

The front item on the queue is just the one referred to by the linked list's head pointer

```
method front():item_type
   return list.get-begin().get-value()
end method
```

When you want to dequeue something off the list, simply point the head pointer to the previous from head item. The old head item is the one you removed of the list. If the list is now empty, we have to fix the tail iterator.

```
method dequeue()
   list.remove-first ()
   if is-empty()
     tail := list.get-begin()
   end if
  end method
```

A check for emptiness is easy. Just check if the list is empty.

```
method is-empty():Boolean
  return list.is-empty()
end method
```

A check for full is simple. Linked lists are considered to be limitless in size.

```
method is-full():Boolean
   return False
end method
```

A check for the size is again passed through to the list.

```
method get-size():Integer
   return list.get-size ()
 end method
end type
```

10.2.3 Performance Analysis

In a linked list, accessing the first element is an O(1) operation because the list contains a pointer directly to it. Therefore, enqueue, front, and dequeue are a quick O(1) operations.

The checks for empty/fullness as done here are also O(1).

The performance of getsize () depends on the performance of the corresponding operation in the linked list implementation. It could be either O(n), or O(1), depending on what time/space tradeoff is made. Most of the time, users of a Queue do not use the getsize () operation, and so a bit of space can be saved by not optimizing it.

10.3 LINKED LISTS

A linked list is a data structure that consists of a sequence of data records such that in each record there is a field that contains a reference (i.e., a link) to the next record in the sequence.

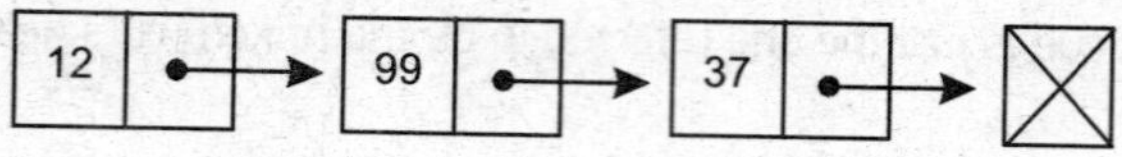

Fig. 10.3 A linked list whose nodes contain two fields: an integer value and a link to the next node

Linked lists are among the simplest and most common data structures; they provide an easy implementation for several important abstract data structures, including stacks, queues, associative arrays, and symbolic expressions.

The principal benefit of a linked list over a conventional array is that the order of the linked items may be different from the order that the data items are stored in memory or on disk. For that reason, linked lists allow insertion and removal of nodes at any point in the list, with a constant number of operations.

On the other hand, linked lists by themselves do not allow random access to the data, or any form of efficient indexing. Thus, many basic operations — such as obtaining the last node of the list, or finding a node that contains a given datum, or locating the place where a new node should be inserted — may require scanning most of the list elements.

10.3.1 Linear and circular lists

In the last node of a list, the link field often contains a null reference, a special value that is interpreted by programs as meaning "there is no such node". A less common convention is to make it point to the first node of the list; in that case the list is said to be circular or circularly linked; otherwise it is said to be open or linear.

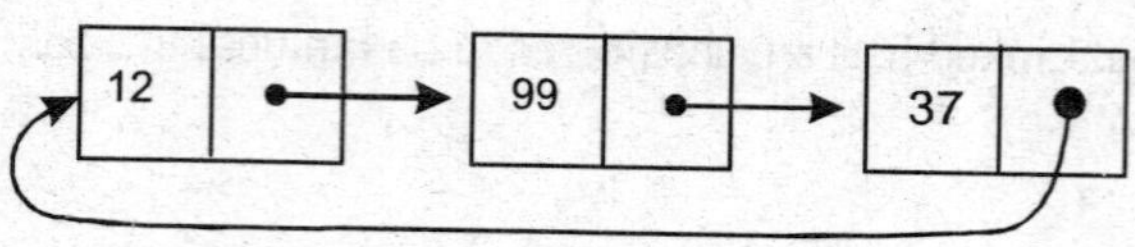

Fig .10.4. A circular linked list

10.3.2 Singly-, doubly-, and multiply-linked lists

Singly-linked lists contain nodes which have a data field as well as a next field, which points to the next node in the linked list.

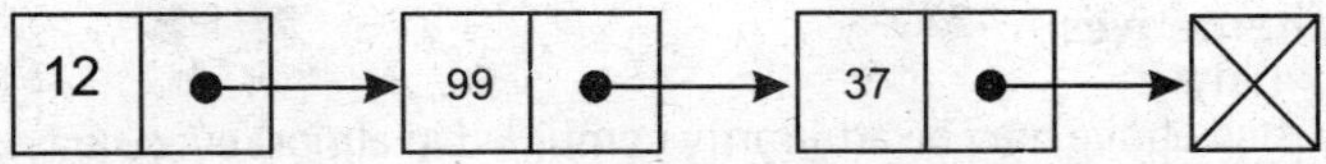

Fig 10.5 A singly-linked list whose nodes contain two fields: an integer value and a link to the next node

In a doublv-linked list, each node contains, besides the next-node link, a second link field pointing to the previous node in the sequence. The two links may be called forward(s) and backwards, or next and prev(ious).

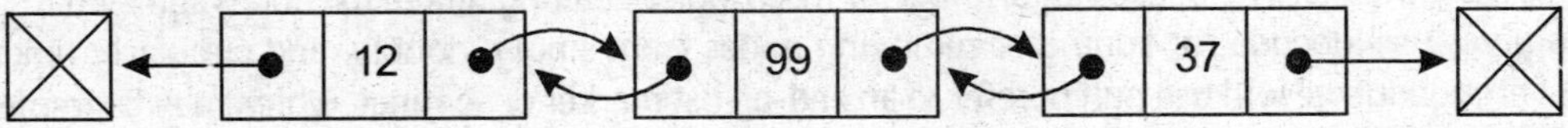

Fig 10.6 A doubly-linked list whose nodes contain three fields: an integer value, the link forward to the next node, and the link backward to the previous node

The technique known as XOR-linking allows a doubly-linked list to be implemented using a single link field in each node. However, this technique requires the ability to do bit operations on addresses, and therefore may not be available in some high-level languages.

In a multiply-linked list, each node contains two or more link fields, each field being used to connect the same set of data records in a different order (e.g., by name, by department, by date of birth, etc.). (While doubly-linked lists can be seen as special cases of multiply-linked list, the fact that the two orders are opposite to each other leads to simpler and more efficient algorithms, so they are usually treated as a separate case.)

In the case of a doubly circular linked list, the only change that occurs is the end, or "tail" of the said list is linked back to the front, "head", of the list and vice versa.

10.3.3 Sentinel nodes

In some implementations, an extra sentinel or dummy node may be added before the first data record and/or after the last one. This convention simplifies and accelerates some list-handling algorithms, by ensuring that all links can be safely dereferenced and that every list (even one that contains no data elements) always has a "first" and "last" node.

10.3.4 Empty lists

An empty list is a list that contains no data records. This is usually the same as saying that it has zero nodes. If sentinel nodes are being used, the list is usually said to be empty when it has only sentinel nodes.

10.3.5 Hash linking

The link fields need not be physically part of the nodes. If the data records are stored in an array and referenced by their indices, the link field may be stored in a separate array with the same indices as the data records.

10.3.6 List handles

Since a reference to the first node gives access to the whole list, that reference is often called the address, pointer, or handle of the latter. Algorithms that manipulate linked lists usually get such handles to the input lists and return the handles to the resulting lists. In fact, in the context of such algorithms, the word "list" often means "list handle". In some situations, however, it may be convenient to refer to a list by a handle that consists of two links, pointing to its first and last nodes.

10.3.7 Combining alternatives

The alternatives listed above may be arbitrarily combined in almost every way, so one may have circular doubly-linked lists without sentinels, circular singly-linked lists with sentinels, etc.

10.3.8 Linked list operations

When manipulating linked lists in-place, care must be taken to not use values that you have invalidated in previous assignments. This makes algorithms for inserting or deleting linked list nodes somewhat subtle. This section gives pseudocode for adding or removing nodes from singly, doubly, and circularly linked lists in-prace. Throughout we will use null to refer to an end-of-list marker or sentinel, which may be implemented in a number of ways.

Singly-linked lists

Our node data structure will have two fields. We also keep a variable firstNode which always points to the first node in the list, or is null for an empty list.

```
record Node {
    data // The data being stored in the node
    next // A reference to the next node, null for last node
}
record List {
    Node firstNode    // points to first node of list; null for empty list}
```

Traversal of a singly-linked list is simple, beginning at the first node and following each next link until we come to the end:

```
node := list.firstNode
while node not null {
    (do something with node.data)
    node = node.next
}
```

The following code inserts a node after an existing node in a singly linked list. The diagram shows how it works. Inserting a node before an existing one cannot be done directly; instead, you have to keep track of the previous node and insert a node after it.

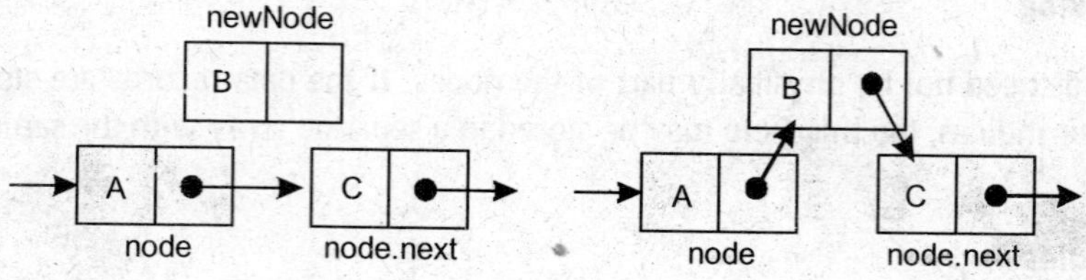


```
function insertAfter[Node node, Node newNode) { // insert newNode after node
    newNode.next := node.next
    node.next := newNode
}
```

Inserting at the beginning of the list requires a separate function. This requires updating firstNode.

```
function insertBeginning(List list, Node newNode) { // insert node before current first node
    newNode.next   := list.firstNode
    list.firstNode := newNode
}
```

Similarly, we have functions for removing the node after a given node, and for removing a node from the beginning of the list. The diagram demonstrates the former. To find and remove a particular node, one must again keep track of the previous element.

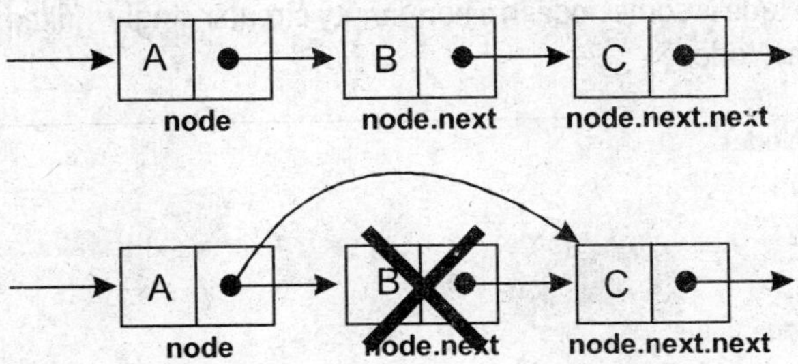


```
function removeAfter (node node) { // remove node past this one
  obsoleteNode := node.next
  node.next := node.next.next
  destroy obsoleteNode
}
function removeBeginning(List list) { // remove first node
    obsoleteNode := list.firstNode
    list.firstNode := list.firstNode.next // point past delete node
    destroy obsoleteNode
}
```

Notice that removeBeginning() sets list.firstNode to null when removing the last node in the list.

Since we can't iterate backwards, efficient "insertBefore" or "removeBeforc" operations are not possible.

Appending one linked list to another can be inefficient unless a reference to the tail is kept as part of the List structure, because we must traverse the entire first list in order to find the tail, and then append the second list to this. Thus, if two linearly-linked lists are each of length n, list appending has asvmntotic time complexity of O(n). In the Lisp family of languages, list appending is provided by the append procedure.

Many of the special cases of linked list operations can be eliminated by including a dummy element at the front of the list. This ensures that there are no special cases for the beginning of the list and renders both insertBeginning() and removeBeginning() unnecessary. In this case, the first useful data in the list will be found at list.firstNode.next.

10.3.9 Circularly-linked list

In a circularly linked list, all nodes are linked in a continuous circle, without using null. For lists with a front and a back (such as a queue), one stores a reference to the last node in the list. The next node after the last node is the first node. Elements can be added to the back of the list and removed from the front in constant time.

Circularly-linked lists can be either singly or doubly linked.

Both types of circularly-linked lists benefit from the ability to traverse the full list beginning at any given node. This often allows us to avoid storing firstNode and lastNode, although if the list may be empty we need a special representation for the empty list, such as a lastNode variable which points to some node in the list or is null if it's empty; we use such a lastNode here. This representation significantly simplifies adding and removing nodes with a nonempty list, but empty lists are then a special case.

Algorithms

Assuming that someNode is some node in a non-empty circular singly-linked list, this code iterates through that list starting with someNode:

```
function iterate(someNode)
  if someNode ≠ null
    node := someNode
do
  do something with node.value
  node := node.next
while node ≠ someNode
```

Notice that the test "while node ≠ someNode" must be at the end of the loop. If it were replaced by the test"" at the beginning of the loop, the procedure would fail whenever the list had only one node.

This function inserts a node "newNode" into a circular linked list after a given node "node". If "node" is null, it assumes that the list is empty.

```
function insertAfter(Node node, Node newNode)
    if node = null
      newNode.next := newNode
    else
      newNode.next := node.next
       node.next := newNode
```

Suppose that "L" is a variable pointing to the last node of a circular linked list (or null if the list is empty). To append "newNode" to the end of the list, one may do

```
insertAfter(L, newNode)
L := newNode
```

To insert "newNode" at the beginning of the list, one may do

```
insertAfter(L, newNode)
if L = null
  L := newNode
```

10.3.10 Linked lists using arrays of nodes

Languages that do not support any type of reference can still create links by replacing pointers with array indices. The approach is to keep an arrav of records, where each record has integer fields indicating the index of the next (and possibly previous) node in the array. Not all nodes in the array need be used. If records are also not supported, parallel arrays can often be used instead.

As an example, consider the following linked list record that uses arrays instead of pointers:

```
record Entry {

    integer next // index of next entry in array
    integer prev // previous entry (if double-linked)
    string name
    real balance
}
```

By creating an array of these structures, and an integer variable to store the index of the first element, a linked list can be built:

```
integer listHead
Entry Records[1000]
```

Links between elements are formed by placing the array index of the next (or previous) cell into the Next or Prev field within a given element. For example:

Index	Next	Prev	Name	Balance
0	1	4	Ram Shaym	123.45
1	–1	0	Amit Ankit	234.56
2 (list Head)	4	–1	Rani anju	0.00
3			Mamta Sita	999.99
4	0	2	Gravav, Anita	876.54
5				
6				
7				

In the above example, ListHead would be set to 2, the location of the first entry in the list. Notice that entry 3 and 5 through 7 are not part of the list. These cells are available for any additions to the list. By creating a ListFree integer variable, a free list could be created to keep track of what cells are available. If all entries are in use, the size of the array would have to be increased or some elements would have to be deleted before new entries could be stored in the list.

The following code would traverse the list and display names and account balance:

```
i := listHead
while  i >= 0 { '// loop through the list
       print i, Records[i].name, Records[i].balance // print entry
       i := Records[i].next }
```

When faced with a choice, the advantages of this approach include:

- The linked list is relocatable, meaning it can be moved about in memory at will, and it can also be quickly and directly serialized storage on disk or transfer over a network.
- Especially for a small list, array indexes can occupy significantly less space than a full pointer on many

architectures.

- Locality of reference can be improved by keeping the nodes together in memory and by periodically rearranging them although this can also be done in a general store.
- Naive dynamic memory allocators can produce an excessive amount of overhead storage for each node allocated, almost no allocation overhead is incurred per node in this approach.
- Seizing an entry from a pre-allocated array is faster than using dynamic memory allocation for each node, since dynamic memory allocation typically requires a search for a free memory block of the desired size.

This approach has one main disadvantage, however: it creates and manages a private memory space for its nodes. This leads to the following issues:

- It increase complexity of the implementation.
- Growing a large array when it is full may be difficult or impossible, whereas finding space for a new linked list node in a large, general memory pool may be easier.
- Adding elements to a dynamic array will occasionally (when it is full) unexpectedly take linear (O(n)) instead of constant time (although it's still an amortized constant).
- Using a general memory pool leaves more memory for other data if the list is smaller than expected or if many nodes are freed.

For these reasons, this approach is mainly used for languages that do not support dynamic memory allocation. These disadvantages are also mitigated if the maximum size of the list is known at the lime the array is created.

Solved Questions

1. Clarify whether Linked List is linear or Non-linear data structure ?

Ans. Link list is always linear data structure because every element (NODE) having unique position and also every element has its unique successor and predecessor. Also,linear collection of data items called nodes and the linear order is given by means of pointers. Each node is divided into two parts. First part contains information of the element and another part contains the address of the next node in the list.

2. What is the main difference between ARRAY and STACK?

Ans. Stack follows LIFO. Thus the item that is first entered would be the last removed. In array the items can be entered or removed in any order. Basically each member access is done using index and no strict order is to be followed here to remove a particular element .Array may be multi dimensional or one dimensional but stack should be one-dimensional. Size of array is fixed, while stack can be grow or shrink. We can say stack is dynamic data structure.

3. What is mean by d-queue?

Ans. D-queue stands for double ended queue. It is a abstract data structure that implements a queue for which elements can be added to front or rear and the elements can be removed from the rear or front. It is also called head-tail linked list

Previous Year University Question

1. What is a "priority queue"? Explain with the help of an example. [OU]
2. Augment a linked list data structure, where each node maintains the number of preceding nodes. [GBTU]

EXERCISE

1. Write an algorithm to implement stacks and queues using linked list.
2. Write an algorithm for ascending and descending priority queue.
3. Implement the input and output resuicted queue.
4. Implement doubly linked list using multiple array representation.
5. Write an algorithm of quicksort using stack.
6. Write an algorithm of circuular link list and calculate its complexity.
7. Write an algorithm to swap two numbers in a singly linked list.

CHAPTER

11

INTRODUCTION TO TREE

11.1 INTRODUCTION

A tree is a widely-used data structure that emulates a hierarchical tree structure with a set of linked nodes. Mathematically, it is a tree, more specifically: an acyclic connected graph where each node has zero or more children nodes and at most one parent node. Furthermore, the children of each node have a specific order.

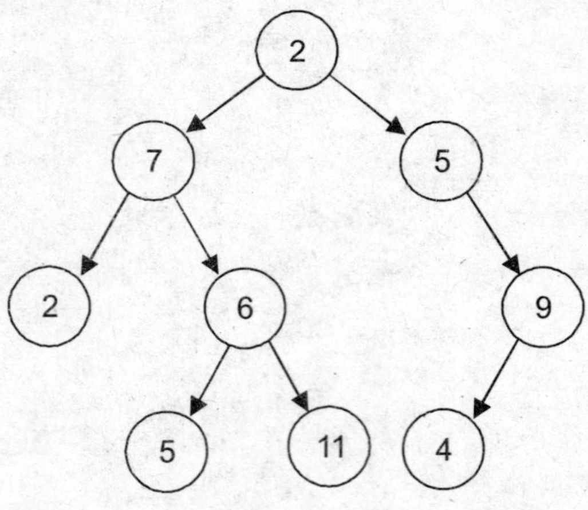

Fig. 11.1. Example of Tree

In fig. 11.1, the node labelled 7 has two children, labelled 2 and 6, and one parent, labelled 2. The root node, at the top, has no parent. A node is a structure which may contain a value, a condition, or represent a separate data structure (which could be a tree of its own). Each node in a tree has zero or more child nodes, which are below it in the tree (by convention, trees are drawn growing downwards). A node that has a child is called the child's parent node (or ancestor node, or superior). A node has at most one parent. Nodes that do not have any children are called leaf nodes. They are also referred to as terminal nodes.

A free tree is a tree that is not rooted.

The height of a node is the length of the longest downward path to a leaf from that node. The height of the root is the height of the tree. The depth of a node is the length of the path to its root (i.e., its root path). This is commonly needed in the manipulation of the various self balancing trees, AVL Trees in particular.

Conventionally, the value -1 corresponds to a subtree with no nodes, whereas zero corresponds to a subtree with one node.

The topmost node in a tree is called the root node. Being the topmost node, the root node will not have parents. It is the node at which operations on the tree commonly begin (although some algorithms begin with the leaf nodes and work up ending at the root). All other nodes can be reached from it by following edges or links. (In the formal definition, each such path is also unique). In diagrams, it is typically drawn at the top. In some trees, such as heaps, the root node has special properties. Every node in a tree can be seen as the root node of the subtree rooted at that node.An internal node or inner node is any node of a tree that has child nodes and is thus not a leaf node. Similarly, an external node or outer node is any node that does not have child nodes and is thus a leaf.

A subtree of a tree T is a tree consisting of a node in T and all of its descendants in T. The subtree corresponding to the root node is the entire tree; the subtree corresponding to any other node is called a proper subtree (in analogy to the term proper subset).

11.2 TYPES OF TREES

Binary: Each node has zero, one, or two children. This assertion makes many tree operations simple and efficient.

Binary Search: A binary tree where any left child node has a value less than its parent node and any right child node has a value greater than or equal to that of its parent node.

AVL: A balanced binary search tree according to the following specification: the heights of the two child subtrees of any node differ by at most one.

Red-Black Tree: A balanced binary search tree using a balancing algorithm based on colors assigned to a node, and the colors of nearby nodes.

AA Tree: A balanced tree, in fact a more restrictive variation of a red-black tree.

11.3 TRAVERSAL

Many problems require we visit* the nodes of a tree in a systematic way: tasks such as counting how many nodes exist or finding the maximum element. Three different methods are possible for binary trees: preorder, postorder, and in-order, which all do the same three things: recursively traverse both the left and rights subtrees and visit the current node. The difference is when the algorithm visits the current node:

preorder: Current node, left subtree, right subtree(DLR)

postorder: Left subtree, right subtree, current node(LRD)

in-order: Left subtree, current node, right subtree.(LDR)

levelorder: Level by level, from left to right, starting from the root node.

- Visit means performing some operation involving the current node of a tree, like incrementing a counter or checking if the value of the current node is greater than any other recorded.

Examples of Tree Traversals

preorder: 50, 30, 20, 40, 90, 100

inorder: 20, 30, 40, 50, 90, 100

postorder: 20, 40, 30, 100, 90, 50

levelorder 50, 30, 90, 20, 40, 100

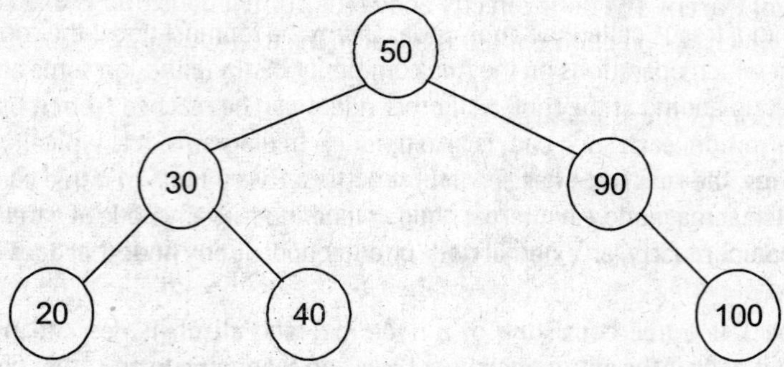

Fig. 11.2. Tree Traversal

11.4 BALANCING

When entries that are already sorted are stored in a tree, all new records will go the same route, and the tree will look more like a list (such a tree is called a degenerate tree). Therefore the tree needs balancing routines, making sure that under all branches are an equal number of records. This will keep searching in the tree at optimal speed. Specifically, if a tree with n nodes is a degenerate tree, the longest path through the tree will be n nodes; if it is a balanced tree, the longest path will be log n nodes.

11.5 BINARY SEARCH TREE

Binary Search tree is a binary tree in which each internal node x stores an element such that the element stored in the left subtree of x are less than or equal to x and elements stored in the right subtree of x are greater than or equal to x. This is called binary-search-tree property.

The basic operations on a binary search tree take time proportional to the height of the tree. For a complete binary tree with node n, such operations runs in $\Theta(\lg n)$ worst-case time. If the tree is a linear chain of n nodes however, the same operations takes Θ (n) worst-case time.

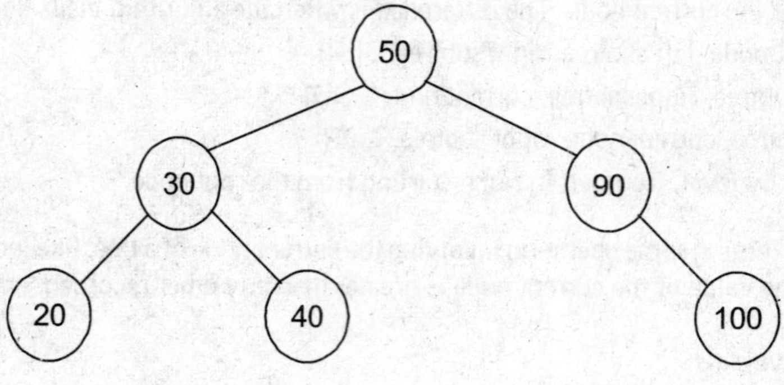

Fig. 11.3. Binary search tree

A typical example of binary search tree is given in fig. 11.3. Node Any item that is stored in the tree. oot The top item in the tree. (50 in the tree above) hild Node(s) under the current node. (20 and 40 are children of 30 in the tree above) Parent The node directly above the current node. (90 is the parent of 100 in the tree above) eaf A node which has no children. (20 is a leaf in the tree above).

11.5.1 Implementation of Binary Search Tree

Binary Search Tree can be implemented as a linked data structure in which each node is an object with three pointer fields. The three pointer fields left, right and p point to the nodes corresponding to the left child, right child and the parent respectively NIL in any pointer field signifies that there exists no corresponding child or parent. The root node is the only node in the BST structure with NIL in its p field.

11.5.2 Binary-Search-Tree property Vs. Heap Property

In a heap, a nodes key is greater than equal to both of its children's keys. In binary search tree, a node's key is greater than or equal to its child's key but less than or equal to right child's key. Furthermore, this applies to entire subtree in the binary search tree case. It is very important to note that the heap property does not help print the nodes in sorted order because this property does not tell us in which subtree the next item is. If the heap property could used to print the keys (as we have shown above) in sorted order in O(n) time, this would contradict our known lower bound on comparison sorting.

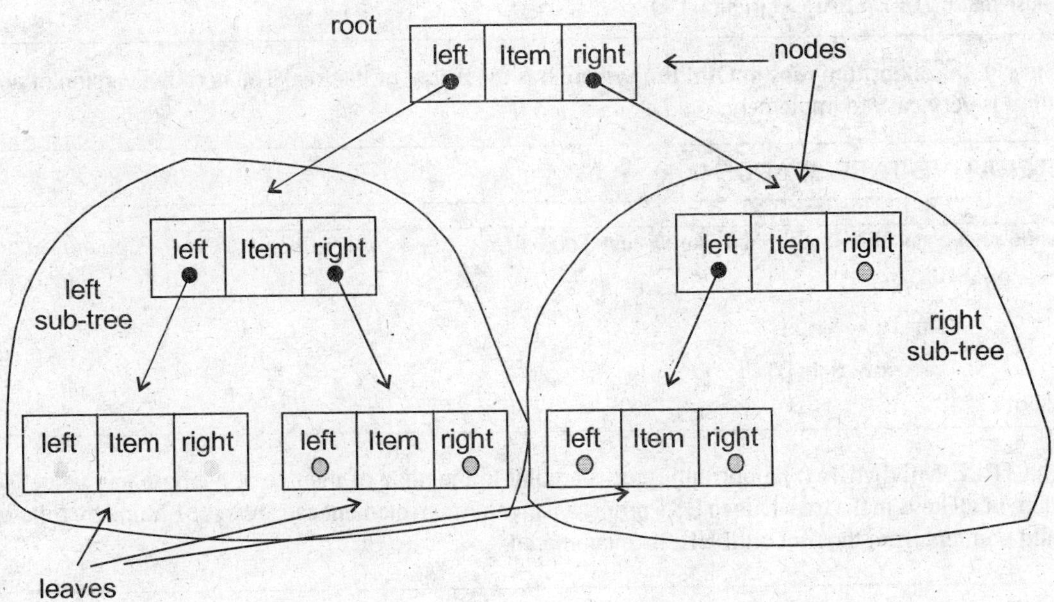

Fig.l 1.4. Implementation of BST

The last statement implies that since sorting n elements takes $\Omega(n \lg n)$ time in the worst case in the comparison model, any comparison-based algorithm for constructing a Binary Search Tree from arbitrary list n elements takes $\Omega(n \lg n)$ time in the worst case.

We can show the validity of this argument (in case you are thinking of beating Ω(n lg n) bound) as follows: let c(n) be the worst-case running time for constructing a binary tree of a set of n elements. Given an n-node BST, the inorder walk in the tree outputs the keys in sorted order (shown above). Since the worst-case running time of any computation based sorting algorithm is Ω(n lg n), we have

$$c(n) + O(n) = \Omega(n \lg n)$$

Therefore, $$c(n)=\Omega(n \lg n).$$

11.5.3 Querying a Binary Search Tree

The most common operations performed on a BST is searching for a key stored in the tree. Other operations are MINIMUM, MAXIMUM, SUCCESSOR and PREDESESSOR. These operations run in O(h) time where h is the height of the tree i.e., h is the number of links root node to the deepest node. The TREE-SEARCH (x, k) algorithm searches the tree root at x for a node whose key value equals k. It returns a pointer to the node if it exists otherwise NIL.

```
TREE-SEARCH (x, k)

if x = NIL  OR   k = key[x]
    then return x
if k < key [x]
  then return TREE-SEARCH (left[x], k)
  else return TREE-SEARCH (right [x], k)
```

Clearly, this algorithm runs in O(h) time where h is the height of the tree. The iterative version of above algorithm is very easy to implement.

```
ITERATIVE-TREE-SEARCH (x, k)

while x not equal NIL          .AND. key ≠ key[x] do
        if k < key [x]
                then x ← left[x]
                else x ← right [x]
return x
```

The TREE-MINIMUN (x) algorithm returns a point to the node of the tree at x whose key value is the minimum of all keys in the tree. Due to BST property, an minimum element can always be found by following left child pointers from the root until NIL is uncountered.

```
TREE-MINIMUM (x)

while left [x] ≠ NIL do
    x ← left [x]
return x
```

Clearly, it runs in O(h) time where h is the height of the tree. Again thanks to BST property, an element in a binary search tree whose key is a maximum can always be found by following right child pointers from root until a NIL is encountered.

```
TREE-MAXIMUM (x)

while right [x] ≠ NIL do
    x ← right [x]
return x
```

Clearly, it runs in O(h) time where h is the height of the tree. The TREE-SUCCESSOR (x) algorithm returns a pointer to the node in the tree whose key value is next higher than key [x].

```
TREE-SUCCESSOR (x)
if  right [x] ≠ NIL
  then return TREE-MINIMUM (right[x])
  else y ← p [x]
     while y ≠ NIL   .AND.   x = right [y] do
          x ← y
          y ← p[y]
     return y
```

Note that algorithm TREE-MINIMUM, TRE-MAXIMUM, TREE-SUCCESSOR, and TREE-PREDESSOR never look at the keys.

An inorder tree walk of an n-node BST can be implemented in Θ(n)-time by finding the minimum element in the tree with TREE-MINIMUM (x) algorithm and then making n-1 calls to TREE-SUCCESSOR (x).

11.5.4 Another way of Implementing Inorder walk on Binary Search Tree

Algorithm

- find the minimum element in the tree with TREE-MINIMUM
- Make n–1 calls to TREE-SUCCESSOR

Let us show that this algorithm runs in (Θ(n) time. For a tree T, let m_T be the number of edges that are traversed by the above algorithm. The running time of the algorithm for T is $\Theta(m_T)$. We make following claim:

m_T is zero if T has at most one node and 2e – r otherwise, where e is the number of edges in the tree and r is the length of the path from root to the node holding the maximum key.

Note that e = n – 1 for any tree with at least one node. This allows us to prove the claim by induction on e (and therefore, on n).

Base case Suppose that e = 0. Then, either the tree is empty or consists only of a single node. So, e = r = 0. Therefore, the claim holds.

Inductive step Suppose e > 0 and assume that the claim holds for all e′< e. Let T be a binary search tree with e edges. Let x be the root, and Tl and T2 respectively be the left and right subtree of x. Since T has at least one edge, either Tl or T2 respectively is nonempty. For each i = 1, 2, let e_i be the number of edges in Ti, p_i the node holding the maximum key in T_i, and r_i the distance from p_i to the root of Ti. Similarly, let e,p and r be the correspounding values for T. First assume that both Tl and T2 are nonempty. Then $e = e_1 \quad e_2 \quad 2$, $p = p_2$, and $r = r_2 \quad 1$. The action of the enumeration is as follows:

- Upon being called, the minimum-tree(x) traverses the left branch of x and enters Tl.
- Once the root of Tl is visited, the edges of Tl are traversed as if Tl is the input tree. This situation will last until p_1 is visisted.
- When the Tree-Successor is called form p_1. The upward path from p_1 and x is traversed and x is discoverec to hold the successor.
- When the tree-Successor called from x, the right branch of x is taken.
- Once the root of T2 is visited, the edges of T2 are traversed as if T2 is the input tree. This situation will last until p_2 is reached, whereby the algorithm halts.

By the above analysis, the number of edges that are traversed by the above algorithm, m_T, is

$$\begin{aligned} m_T &= 1 \quad (2e_1 - r_1) \quad (r_1 \quad 1) \quad 1 \quad (2e_2 - r_2) \\ &= 2(e_1 \quad e_2 \quad 2) - (r_2 \quad 1) \\ &= 2e - r \end{aligned}$$

Therefore, the claim clearly holds for this case.

Next suppose that T2 is emply. Since $e > 0$, Tl is nonempty. Then $e = e_1 \quad 1$. Since x does not have a right child, x holds the maximum. Therefore, $p = x$ and $r = 0$. The action of the enumeration algorithm is the first two steps. Therefore, the number of edges that are traversed by the algorithm in question is

$$\begin{aligned} m_T &= l \quad (2e_1 - r_1) \quad (r_1 \quad l) \\ &= 2(e_1 \quad 1) - 0 \\ &= 2e - r \end{aligned}$$

Therefore, the claim holds for this case.

Finally, assume that T1 is empty. Then T2 is nonempty. It holds that $e = e_2 \quad 1$, $p \quad p_2$, and $r \quad r_2 \quad 1$. This time x holds the minimum key and the action of the enumeration algorithm is the last two steps. Therefore, the number of edges that are traversed by the algorithm is

$$\begin{aligned} m_T &= 1 \quad (2e_2 - r_2) \\ &= 2(e_2 \quad l) - (r_2 \quad l) \\ &= 2e - r \end{aligned}$$

Therefore, the claim holds for this case.

The claim is proven since $e = n \quad 1$, $m_T \leq \; n$. On the other hand, at least one edge has to be traversed when going from on node to another, so $m_T \geq n \quad 1$. Therefore, the running time of the above algorithm is $\Theta(n)$.

Consider any binary search tree T and let y be the parent of a leaf . Our goal is to show that key[y] is

either the smallest key in T larger than key [x]

or the largest key in the T smaller than key[x].

Proof Suppose that x is a left child of y. Since key [y] ≥ key [x], only we have to show that there is no node with key[y] > key[z] > key[x]. Assume, to the contrary, that there is such a z.

Choose so that it holds the smallest key among such nodes. Note for every node u ≠ , x, key [ ] ≤ key [u] if and only if key[x] ≤ key [u]. If we search key [ ], then the search path is identical to that of key [x] until the path rearches or x. Since x is a leaf (meaning it has no children), the search path never reaches x.

Therefore, is an ancestor of x. Since y is the parent of x (it is given, in case you've forgotton!) and is not , has to be an ancestor of y. So, key [y] > dey[ ] > dey[x]. However, we are assuming key[y] > key[ ] > key[x], so this is clearly impossible. Therefore, there is no such .

The case when x is a right child of y is easy.

11.5.5 An Example of searching through a binary search tree

To search for an item in a binary tree:

1. Start at the root node
2. If the item that you are searching for is less than the root node, move to the left child of the root node, if the item that you are searching for is more than the root node, move to the right child of the root node and if it is equal to the root node, then you have found the item that you are looking for.
3. Now check to see if the item that you are searching for is equal to, less than or more than the new node that you are on. Again if the item that you are searching for is less than the current node, move to the left child, and if the item that you are searching for is greater than the current node, move to the right child.
4. Repeat this process until you find the item that you are looking for or until the node doesn't have a child on the correct branch, in which case the tree doesn't contain the item which you are looking for.

Example:

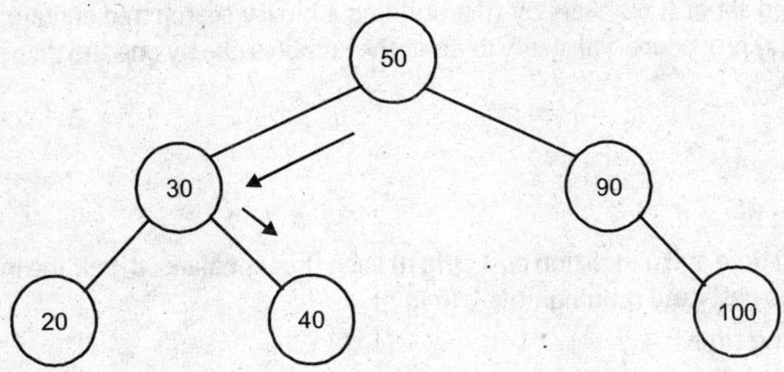

Fig.11.5 Example of tree traversal

For example, to find the node 40...

1. The root node is 50, which is greaterthan 40, so you go to 50's left child.
2. 50's left child is 30, which is less than 40, so you next go to 30's right child.
3. 30's right child is 40, so you have found the item that you are looking for.

11.5.6 Insertion

To insert a node into a BST

1. find a leaf st the appropriate place and
2. connect the node to the parent of the leaf

```
TREE-INSERT (T, z)

y ←NIL
x ← root [T]
while x ≠ NIL do
    y ← x
    if key [z] < key[x]
      then x ← left [x]
      else x ← right [x]
p[z] ← y
if y = NIL
   then root [T ] ← z
   else if key [z] < key [y]
       then left [y]← z
       else right [y] ← z
```

Like other primitive operations on search trees, this algorithm begins at the root of the tree and traces a path downward. Clearly, it runs in O(h) time on a tree of height h.

11.5.7 Sorting

We can sort a given set of n numbers by first building a binary search tree containing these number by using TREE-INSERT (x) procedure repeatedly to insert the numbers one by one and then printing the numbers by an inorder tree walk.

Analysis

Best-case running time

Printing takes O(n) time and n insertion cost O(lg n) each (tree is balanced, half the insertions are at depth lg(n) –1). This gives the best-case running time O(n lg n).

Worst-case running time

Printing still takes O(n) time and n insertion costing O(n) each (tree is a single chain of nodes) is $O(n^2)$. The n insertion cost 1, 2, 3,... n, which is arithmetic sequence so it is $n^2/2$.

Adding an item to a binary search tree

1. To add an item, you first must search through the tree to find the position that you should put it in. You do this following the steps above.
2. When you reach a node which doesn't contain a child on the correct branch, add the new node there.

For example, to add the node 25...

1. The root node is 50, which is greater than 25, so you go to 50's left child.
2. 50's left child is 30, which is greater than 25, so you go to 30's left child.
3. 30's left child is 20, which is less than 25, so you go to 20's right child.
4. 20's right child doesn't exist, so you add 25 there 0.

11.5.8 Deletion

Removing a node from a BST is a bit more complex, since we do not want to create any "holes" in the tree. If the node has one child then the child is spliced to the parent of the node. If the node has two children then its successor has nc left child; copy the successor into the node and delete the successor instead TREE-DELETE (T, z) removes the node pointed to by z from the tree T. IT returns a pointer to the node removed so that the node can be put on a free-node list, etc.

```
TREE-DELETE (T, z)
```

```
ifleft[z] = NIL .OR. right[z] = NIL
then y ← z
else y ←TREE-SUCCESSOR (z)
ifleft[y]≠NIL
then x ← left[y]
else x ← right [y]
if x ≠ NIL
then p[x] ← p[y]
ifp[y]=NIL
then root [T]← x
else if y = left [p[y]]
then left [p[y]]← x
else right [p[y]] ← x
if y ≠ z
then key [z] ← key [y]
if y has other field, copy them, too
return y
```

The procedure runs in 0(h) time on a tree of height h.

Deleting an item from a binary search tree

It is assumed that you have already found the node that you want to delete, using the search technique described above.

Case 1: The node you want to delete is a leaf

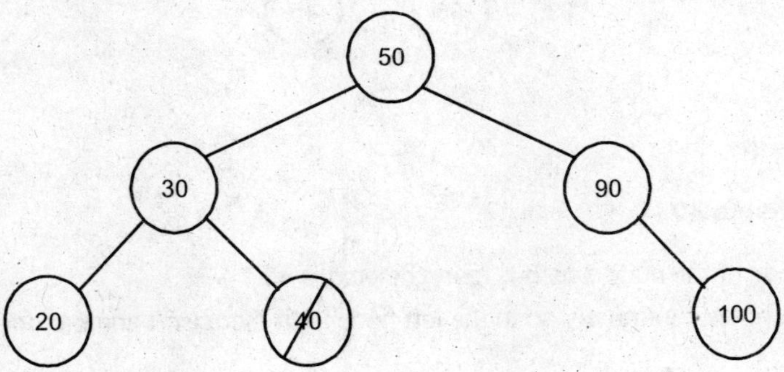

For example, do delete 40...

- Simply delete the node!

Case 2: The node you want to delete has one child

1. Directly connect the child of the node that you want to delete, to the parent of the node that you want to delete.

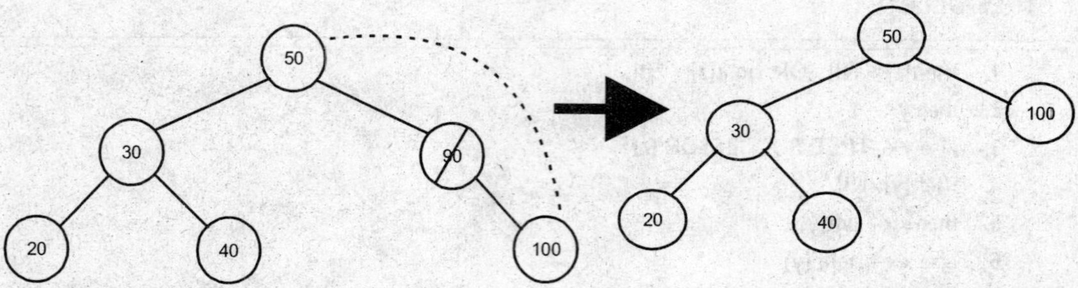

For example, to delete 90...

- Delete 90, then make 100 the child node of 50.

Case 3: The node you want to delete has two children

1. Find the left-most node in the right subtree of the node being deleted. (After you have found the node you want to delete, go to its right node, then for every node under that, go to its left node until the node has no left node) From now on, this node will be known as the successor.

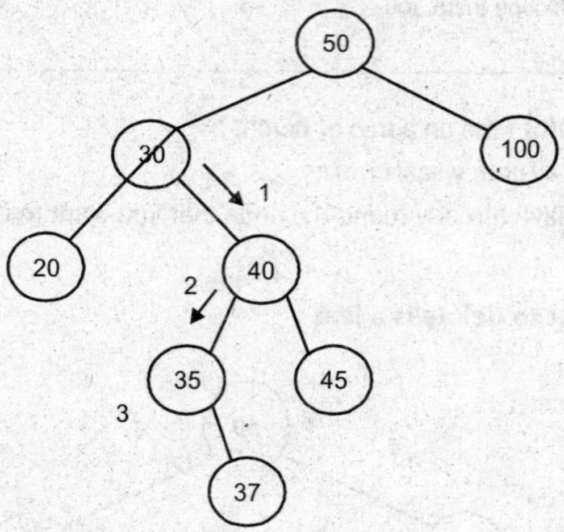

For example, to delete 30

1. The right node of the node which is being deleted is 40.
2. (From now on, we continually go to the left node until there isn't another one...) The first left node of 40, is 35.

3. 35 has no left node, therefore 35 is the successor!

Case 1: The successor is the right child of the node being deleted

1. Directly move the child to the right of the node being deleted into the position of the node being deleted.
2. As the new node has no left children, you can connect the deleted node's left subtree's root as it's left child.

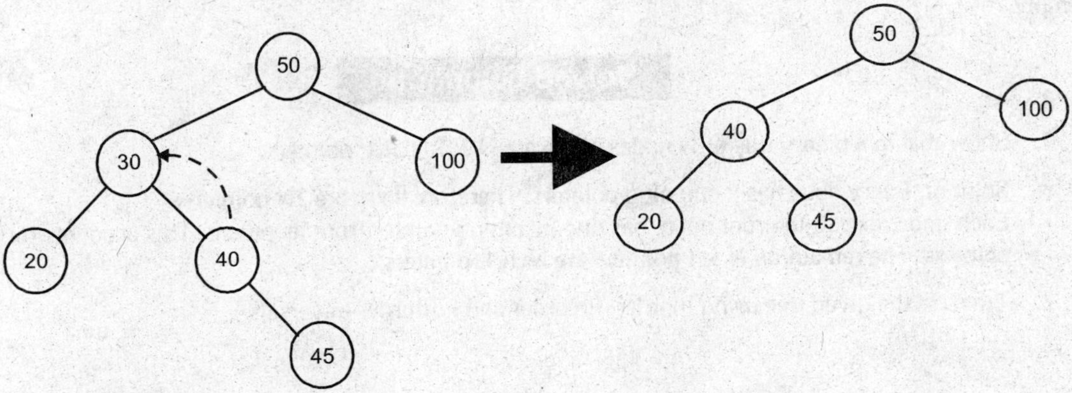

For example, to delete 30

1. Move 40 up to where 30 was.
2. 20 now becomes 40's left child.

Case 2: The successor isn't the right child of the node being deleted

This is best shown with an example

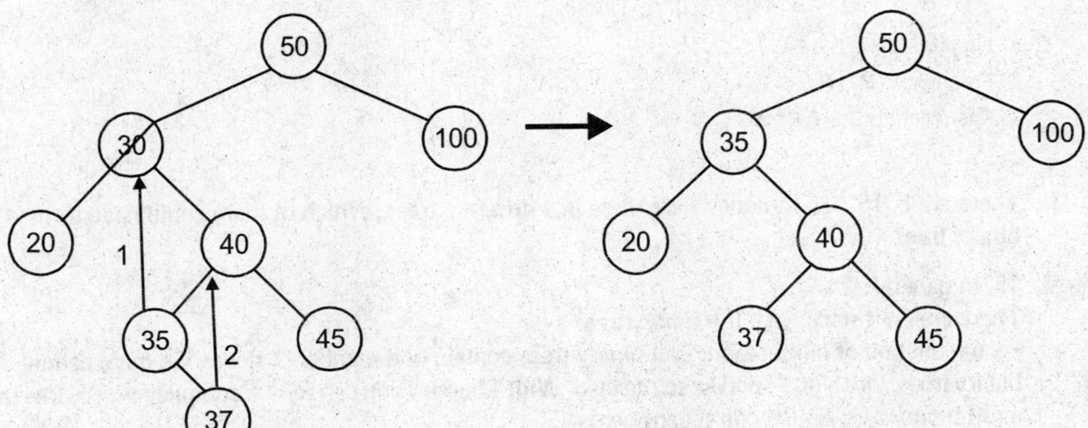

To delete 30...

1. Move the successor into the place where the deleted node was and make it inherit both of its children. So 35 moves to where 30 was and 20 and 40 become its children.
2. Move the successor's (35s) right subtree to where the successor was. So 37 becomes a child of 40.

In general, remember that a node's left subtree's rightmost node is the closest node on the left , and the right subtree's leftmost node is the closest node on the right, and either one of these can be chosen to replace the deleted node, and the only complication is when the replacing node has a child subtree on the same side to that node as the replacing node's side of the deleting node, and the easiest thing to do is to always return the same side subtree of the replacing node as the child of the parent of the replacing node, even if the subtree is empty.

Solved Questions

1. Show that in a binary tree of N nodes, there are N + 1 NULL pointers.

Ans. Solution Every node has 2 outgoing pointers. Therefore there are 2N pointers.
Each node, except the root node, has one incoming pointer from its parent. This accounts for N Û 1 pointers. The remaining N + 1 pointers are NULL pointers.

2. Traverse the given tree using Inorder, Preorder and Postorder traversals.

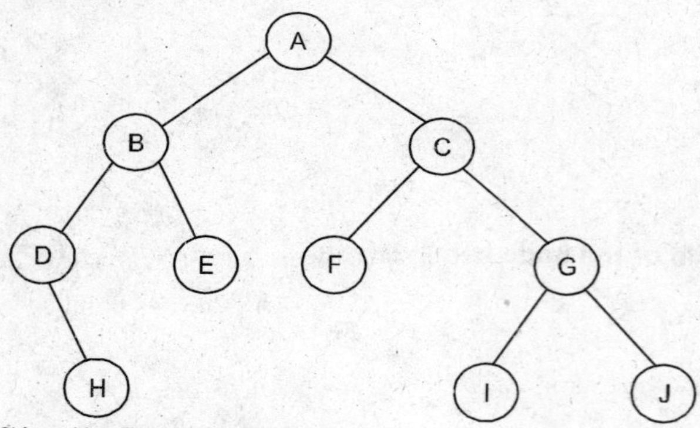

Ans.

∅ Inorder : D H B E A F C I G J

∅ Preorder : A B D H E C F G I J

∅ Postorder : H D E B F I J G C A

3. There are 8, 15, 13, 14 nodes were there in 4 different trees. Which of them could have formed a full binary tree?

Ans. 15. In general:
There are 2n-1 nodes in a full binary tree.
By the method of elimination: Full binary trees contain odd number of nodes. So there cannot be full binary trees with 8 or 14 nodes, so rejected. With 13 nodes you can form a complete binary tree but not a full binary tree. So the correct answer is 15.
(Full and Complete binary trees are different. All full binary trees are complete binary trees but not vice versa.)

4. What is optimal binary search tree?

Ans. OBST is one special kind of advanced tree. It focus on how to reduce the cost of the search of the BST. It needs 3 tables to record probabilities, cost, and root.

It has n keys (representation k1,k2, ,kn) in sorted order (so that k1<k2< <kn), and we wish to build a binary search tree from these keys. For each ki ,we have a probability pi that a search will be for ki.

In contrast of, some searches may be for values not in ki, and so we also have n 1 "dummy keys" d0,d1, ,dn representating not in ki.

In particular, d0 represents all values less than k1, and dn represents all values greater than kn, and for i=1,2, ,n-1, the dummy key di represents all values between ki and ki 1.

5. What is the difference between binary searching and Fibonacci search?

Ans. Binary Search: Binary search is the process of locating an element in a sorted list. The search starts by dividing the list into two parts. The algorithm compares the median value. If the search element is less than the median value, the top list only will be searched, after finding the middle element of that list. The process continues until the element is found or the search in the top list is completed. The same process is continued for the bottom list, until the element is found or the search in the bottom list is completed. If an element is found that must be the median value.

Fibonacci Search: Fibonacci search is a process of searching a sorted array by utilizing divide and conquer algorithm. Fibonacci search examines locations whose addresses have lower dispersion. When the search element has non-uniform access memory storage, the Fibonacci search algorithm reduces the average time needed for accessing a storage location.

Previous Year University Question

1. Show that if a tree has n vertices, then it has (n-1) edges. [Madrass University]
2. Write an iterative algorithm to created Binary search tree. [OU]
3. What is binary search? Write an algorithm to search an element using binary search with suitable example.Analyse its time complexity and compare it with linear search. [KU]
4. Explain binary search tree with suitable example and find its comlaxity in best, average and worst cases. [MDU]
5. How can we insert the element in binary search tree? Write an algorithm and give suitable example. [MDU]

Exercise

1. Diffrientiate between binary search tree and heap?
2. Write an algorithm for TREE-PREDECESSOR.
3. Prove that the deletion of two nodes p and q in binary search tree is commutative.
4. Implement an algorithm for radix tree. and give its running time.
5. Insert items with the following pigs into an initianlly empty binary search tree: 30,41, 23, 58, 48, 26, 11, 13, Draw the tree.

CHAPTER

12

RED-BLACK TREE

12.1 INTRODUCTION

A red-black tree is a type of self-balancing binary search tree, a data structure used in computing science, typically used to implement associative arrays. The original structure was invented in 1972 by Rudolf Bayer[1] and named "symmetric binary B-tree", but acquired its modern name in a paper in 1978 by Leonidas Guibas and Robert Sedgewick.[2] It is complex, but has good worst-case running time for its operations and is efficient in practice: it can search, insert, and delete in O(log n) time, where n is total number of elements in the tree. Put very simply, a red-black tree is a binary search tree which inserts and removes intelligently, to ensure the tree is reasonably balanced.

12.2 TERMINOLOGY

A red-black tree is a special type of binary tree, used in computer science to organize pieces of comparable data, such as text fragments or numbers.

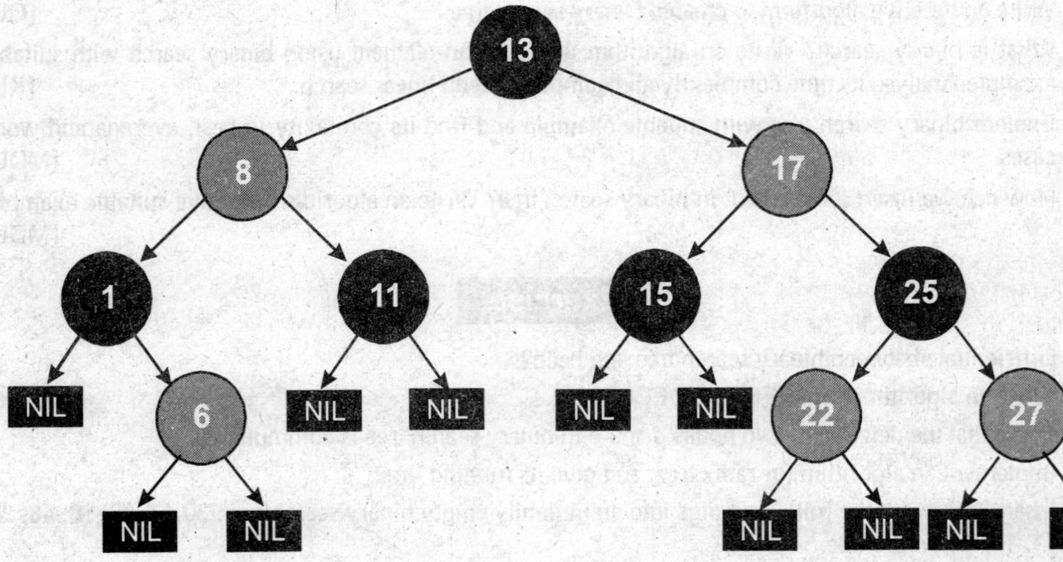

Fig.12.1. An example of a red-black tree

The leaf nodes of red-black trees do not contain data. These leaves need not be explicit in computer memory a null child pointer can encode the fact that this child is a leaf but it simplifies some algorithms for operating on red-black trees if the leaves really are explicit nodes. To save memory, sometimes a single sentinel node performs the role of all leaf nodes; all references from internal nodes to leaf nodes then point to the sentinel node.

Red-black trees, like ail binary search trees, allow efficient in-order traversal in the fashion, Left-Root-Right, of their elements. The search-time results from the traversal from root to leaf, and therefore a balanced tree, having the least possible tree height, results in O(log n) search time.

12.3 PROPERTIES

A red-black tree is a binary search tree where each node has a color attribute, the value of which is either red or black. In addition to the ordinary requirements imposed on binary search trees, the following requirements apply to red-black trees:

1. A node is either red or black.
2. The root is black. (This rule is sometimes omitted from other definitions. Since the root can always be changed from red to black but not necessarily vice-versa this rule has little effect on analysis.)
3. All leaves are black.
4. Both children of every red node are black.
5. Every simple path from a given node to any of its descendant leaves contains the same number of black nodes.

These constraints enforce a critical property of red-black trees: that the longest path from the root to any leaf is no more than twice as long as the shortest path from the root to any other leaf in that tree. The result is that the tree is roughly balanced. Since operations such as inserting, deleting, and finding values require worst-case time proportional to the height of the tree, this theoretical upper bound on the height allows red-black trees to be efficient in the worst-case, unlike ordinary binary search trees.

To see why these properties guarantee this, it suffices to note that no path can have two red nodes in a row, due to property 4. The shortest possible path has all black nodes, and the longest possible path alternates between red and black nodes. Since all maximal paths have the same number of black nodes, by property 5, this shows that no path is more than twice as long as any other path.

In many of the presentations of tree data structures, it is possible for a node to have only one child, and leaf nodes contain data. It is possible to present red-black trees in this paradigm, but it changes several of the properties and complicates the algorithms. For this reason, this article uses "null leaves", which contain no data and merely serve to indicate where the tree ends, as shown above. These nodes are often omitted in drawings, resulting in a tree that seems to contradict the above principles, but in fact does not. A consequence of this is that all internal (non-leaf) nodes have two children, although one or both of those children may be null leaves. Property 5 ensures that a red node must have either two black null leaves or two black non-leaves as children. For a black node with one null leaf child and one non-null-leaf child, properties 3, 4 and 5 ensure that the non-null-leaf child must be a red node with two black null leaves as children.

Some explain a red-black tree as a binary search tree whose edges, instead of nodes, are colored in red or black, but this does not make any difference. The color of a node in this article's terminology corresponds to the color of the edge connecting the node to its parent, except that the root node is always black (property 2) whereas the corresponding edge does not exist.

12.4 ANALOGY TO B-TREES OF ORDER 4

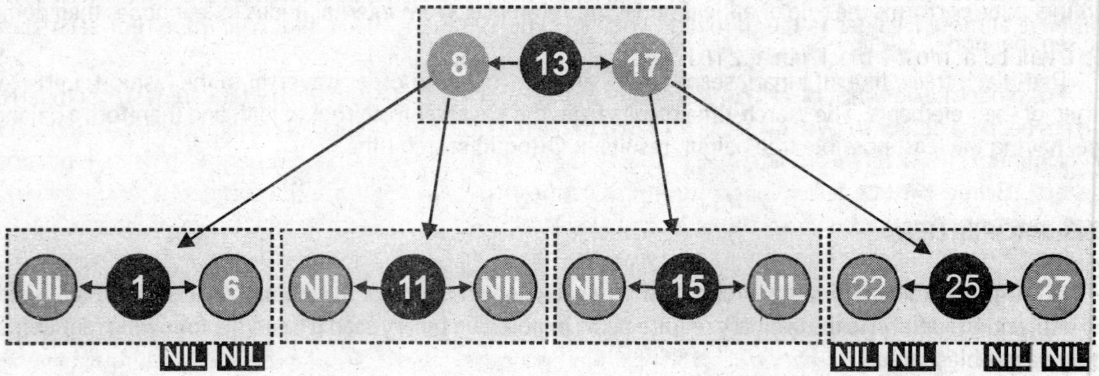

Fig.12.2. The same red-black tree as in the example above, seen as a B-tree.

A red-black tree is similar in structure to a B-tree of order 4, where each node can contain between 1 to 3 values and (accordingly) between 2 to 4 child pointers. In such B-tree, each node will contain only one value matching the value in a black node of the red-black tree, with an optional value before and or after it in the same node, both matching an equivalent red node of the red-black tree.

One way to see this equivalence is to "move up" the red nodes in a graphical representation of the red-black tree, so that they align horizontally with their parent black node, by creating together a horizontal cluster. In the B-tree, or in the modified graphical representation of the red-black tree, all leaf nodes are at the same depth.

The red-black tree is then structurally equivalent to a B-tree of order 4, with a minimum fill factor of 33 of values per cluster with a maximum capacity of 3 values.

This B-tree type is still more general than a red-black tree though, as it allows ambiguity in a red-black tree conversion multiple red-black trees can be produced from an equivalent B-tree of order 4. If a B-tree cluster contains only 1 value, it is the minimum, black, and has two child pointers. If a cluster contains 3 values, then the central value will be black and each value stored on its sides will be red. If the cluster contains two values, however, either one can become the black node in the red-black tree (and the other one will be red).

So the order-4 B-tree does not maintain which of the values contained in each cluster is the root black tree for the whole cluster and the parent of the other values in the same cluster. Despite this, the operation s on red-black trees are more economical in time because you don't have to maintain the vector of values. It may be costly if values are stored directly in each node rather than being stored by reference. B-tree nodes, however, are more economical in space because you don't need to store the color attribute for each node. Instead, you have to know which slot in the cluster vector is used. If values are stored by reference, e.g. objects, null references can be used and, so the cluster can be represented by a vector containing 3 slots for value pointers plus 4 slots for child references in the tree. In that case, the B-tree can be more compact in memory, improving data locality.

The same analogy can be made with B-trees with larger orders that can be structurally equivalent to a colored binary tree: you just need more colors. Suppose that you add blue, then the blue-red-black tree defined like red-black trees but with the additional constraint that no two successive nodes in the hierarchy will be blue and all blue nodes will be children of a red node, then it becomes equivalent to a B-tree whose clusters will have at most 7 values in the following colours: blue, red, blue, black, blue, red, blue (For each cluster, there will be at most 1 black node, 2 red nodes, and 4 blue nodes).

For moderate volumes of values, insertions and deletions in a colored binary tree are faster compared to B-trees because colour trees don't attempt to maximize the fill factor of each horizontal cluster of nodes (only the minimum fill factor is guaranteed in colored binary trees, limiting the number of splits or junctions of clusters). B-trees will be faster for performing rotations (because rotations will frequently occur within the same cluster rather than with multiple separate nodes in a colour binary tree). However for storing large volumes, B-trees will be much faster as they will be more compact by grouping several children in the same cluster where they can be accessed locally.

All optimizations possible in B-trees to increase the average fill factors of clusters are possible in the equivalent multi-coloured binary tree. Notably, maximizing the average fill factor in a structurally equivalent B-tree is the same as reducing the total height of the multicoloured tree, by increasing the number of non-black nodes. The worst case occurs when all nodes in a colour binary tree are black, the best case occurs when only a third of them are black (and the other two thirds are red nodes).

12.5 APPLICATIONS AND RELATED DATA STRUCTURES

Red-black trees offer worst-case guarantees for insertion time, deletion time, and search time. Not only does this make them valuable in time-sensitive applications such as real-time applications, but it makes them valuable building blocks in other data structures which provide worst-case guarantees; for example, many data structures used in computational geometry can be based on red-black trees, and the Completely Fair Scheduler used in current Linux kernels uses red-black trees.

The AVL tree is another structure supporting O(log n) search, insertion, and removal. It is more rigidly balanced than red-black trees, leading to slower insertion and removal but faster retrieval. This makes it attractive for data structures that may be built once and loaded without reconstruction, such as language dictionaries (or program dictionaries, such as the opcodes of an assembler or interpreter).

Red-black trees are also particularly valuable in functional programming, where they are one of the most common persistent data structures, used to construct associative arrays and sets which can retain previous versions after mutations. The persistent version of red-black trees requires O(log n) space for each insertion or deletion, in addition to time.

For every 2-4 tree, there are corresponding red-black trees with data elements in the same order. The insertion and deletion operations on 2-4 trees are also equivalent to color-flipping and rotations in red-black trees. This makes 2-4 trees an important tool for understanding the logic behind red-black trees, and this is why many introductory algorithm texts introduce 2-4 trees just before red-black trees, even though 2-4 trees are not often used in practice.

In 2008, Sedgewick introduced a simpler version of red-black trees called Left-Leaning Red-Black Trees by eliminating a previously unspecified degree of freedom in the implementation. The LLRB maintains an additional invariant that all red links must lean left except during inserts and deletes. Red-black trees can be made isometric to either 2-3 trees, or 2-4 trees, for any sequence of operations. The 2-4 tree isometry was described in 1978 by Sedgewick. With 2-4 trees, the isometry is resolved by a "colour flip," corresponding to a split, in which the red colour of two children nodes leaves the children and moves to the parent node.

12.6 OPERATIONS

Read-only operations on a red-black tree require no modification from those used for binary search trees, because every red-black tree is a special case of a simple binary search tree. However, the immediate result of an insertion or removal may violate the properties of a red-black tree. Restoring the red-black properties requires a small number (O(log n) or amortized O(1)) of colour changes (which are very quick in practice) and no more than three tree rotations (two for insertion). Although insert and delete operations are complicated, their times remain O(log n).

12.7 INSERTION

Insertion begins by adding the node much as binary search tree insertion does and by coloring it red. Whereas in the binary search tree, we always add a leaf, in the red-black tree leaves contain no information, so instead we add a red interior node, with two black leaves, in place of an existing black leaf.

What happens next depends on the color of other nearby nodes. The term uncle node will be used to refer to the sibling of a node's parent, as in human family trees. Note that:

- Property 3 (All leaves are black) always holds.
- Property 4 (Both children of every red node are black) is threatened only by adding a red node, repainting a black node red, or a rotation.
- Property 5 (All paths from any given node to its leaf nodes contain the same number of black nodes) is threatened only by adding a black node, repainting a red node black (or vice versa), or a rotation.

Note: The label N will be used to denote the current node (colored red). At the beginning, this is the new node being inserted, but the entire procedure may also be applied recursively to other nodes (see case 3). P will denote N's parent node, G will denote N's grandparent, and U will denote N's uncle. Note that in between some cases, the roles and labels of the nodes are exchanged, but in each case, every label continues to represent the same node it represented at the beginning of the case. Any color shown in the diagram is either assumed in its case or implied by those assumptions.

The uncle and grandparent nodes can be found by these algorithms:

```
grandparent(n)
{
    if ((n != NULL)      (n->parent != NULL))
            return n->parent->parent;
    else
            return NULL;
```

```
uncle(n, g)

        if (g == NULL) [g = grandparent(n)]
                return NULL;    No grandparent means no uncle
        if (n->parent == g->left)
                return g->right;
        else
                return g->left;
```

Case 1: The current node N is at the root of the tree. In this case, it is repainted black to satisfy Property 2 (The root is black). Since this adds one black node to every path at once, Property 5 (All paths from any given node to its leaf nodes contain the same number of black nodes) is not violated.

```
insert_casel(n)

    if (n->parent == NULL)
        n->color = BLAC  ;
    else
        insert case2(n);
```

Case 2: The current node's parent P is black, so Property 4 (Both children of every red node are black) is not invalidated. In this case, the tree is still valid. Property 5 (All paths from any given node to its leaf nodes contain the same number of black nodes) is not threatened, because the current node N has two black leaf children, but because N is red, the paths through each of its children have the same number of black nodes as the path through the leaf it replaced, which was black, and so this property remains satisfied.

```
insert_case2(n)

    if (n->parent->color == BLAC  )
        return;  * Tree is still valid *
    else
        insert case3(n);
}
```

Note: In the following cases it can be assumed that N has a grandparent node G, because its parent P is red, and if it were the root, it would be black. Thus, N also has an uncle node U, although it may be a leaf in cases 4 and 5.

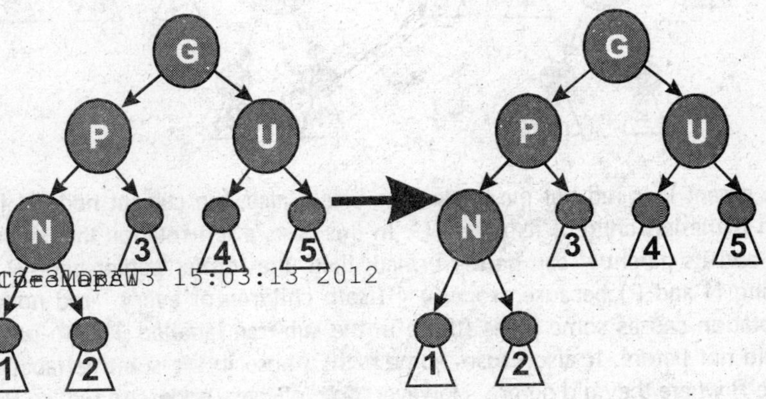

Case 3: If both the parent P and the uncle U are red, then both of them can be repainted black and the grandparent G becomes red (to maintain Property 5 (All paths from any given node to its leaf

nodes contain the same number of black nodes)). Now, the current red node N has a black parent. Since any path through the parent or uncle must pass through the grandparent, the number of black nodes on these paths has not changed. However, the grandparent G may now violate properties 2 (The root is black) or 4 (Both children of every red node are black) (property 4 possibly being violated since G may have a red parent). To fix this, the entire procedure is recursively performed on G from case 1. Note that this is a tail-recursive call, so it could be rewritten as a loop; since this is the only loop, and any rotations occur after this loop, this proves that a constant number of rotations occur.

```
insert_case3(n)

    if ((u != NULL)      (u->color == RED))
        n->parent->color = BLAC  ;
        u->color = BLAC  ;
        g = grandparent(n);
        g->color = RED; insert  casel(g);
    else
        insert  case4(n);

  }
```

Note: In the remaining cases, it is assumed that the parent node P is the left child of its parent. If it is the right child, left and right should be reversed throughout cases 4 and 5. The code samples take care of this.

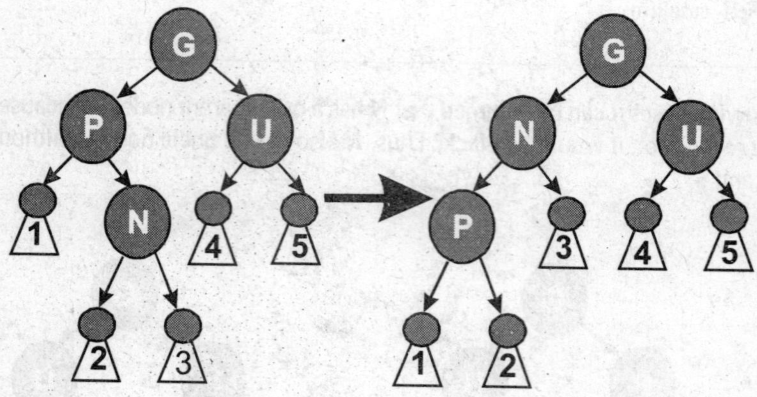

Case 4: The parent P is red but the uncle U is black; also, the current node N is the right child of P, and P in turn is the left child of its parent G. In this case, a left rotation that switchesjhe roles of the current node N and its parent P can be performed; then, the former parent node P is dealt with using Case 5 (relabeling N and P) because property 4 (Both children of every red node are black) is still violated. The rotation causes some paths (those in the sub-tree labelled "1") to pass through the node N where they did not before. It also causes some paths (those in the sub-tree labelled "3") not to pass through the node P where they did before. However, both of these nodes are red, so Property 5 (All paths from any given node to its leaf nodes contain the same number of black nodes) is not violated by the rotation.

```
insert_case4(n)

    if ((n == n->parent->right)      (n->parent == g->left))
            rotate  left(n->parent);
            n = n->left;
      else if ((n == n->parent->left)      (n->parent == g->right))
            rotate  right(n->parent); n = n->right;

    insert  case5(n) ;
```

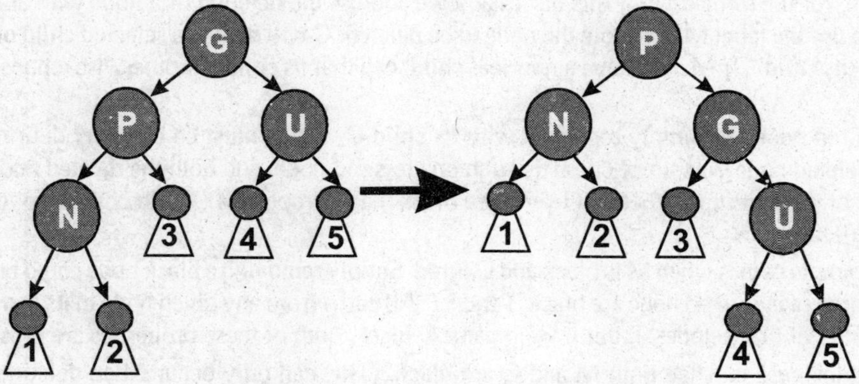

Case 5: The parent P is red but the uncle U is black, the current node N is the left child of P, and P is the left child of its parent G. In this case, a right rotation on G is performed; the result is a tree where the former parent P is now the parent of both the current node N and the former grandparent G. G is known to be black, since its former child P could not have been red otherwise (without violating Property 4). Then, the colors of P and G are switched, and the resulting tree satisfies Property 4 (Both children of every red node are black). Property 5 (All paths from any given node to its leaf nodes contain the same number of black nodes) also remains satisfied, since all paths that went through any of these three nodes went through G before, and now they all go through P. In each case, this is the only black node of the three.

```
insert_case5(n)

    n->parent->color = BLAC  ;
    g->color = RED;
    if ((n == n->parent->left)      (n->parent == g->left))
          rotate  right(g);
      else    * (n == n->parent->right) and (n->parent == g->right) *
          rotate  left (g);
```

Note that inserting is actually in-place, since all the calls above use tail recursion.

12.8 REMOVAL

In a regular binary search tree, when deleting a node with two non-leaf children, we find either the maximum element in its left subtree (which is the in-order predecessor) or the minimum element in its right subtree (which is the in-order successor) and move its value into the node being deleted. We then delete the node we copied the value from, which must have less than two non-leaf children. (Non-leaf children, rather than all children, are specified here because unlike normal binary search trees, red-black trees have leaf nodes anywhere they can have them, so that all nodes are either internal nodes with two children or leaf nodes with, by definition, zero children. In effect, internal nodes having two leaf children in a red-black tree are like the leaf nodes in a regular binary search tree.) Because merely copying a value does not violate any red-black properties, this reduces to the problem of deleting a node with at most one non-leaf child. Once we have solved that problem, the solution applies equally to the case where the node we originally want to delete has at most one non-leaf child as to the case just considered where it has two non-leaf children.

Therefore, for the remainder of this discussion we address the deletion of a node with at most one non-leaf child. We use the label M to denote the node to be deleted; C will denote a selected child of M, which we will also call "its child". If M does have a non-leaf child, call that its child, C; otherwise, choose either leaf as its child, C.

If M is a red node, we simply replace it with its child C, which must be black by definition. All paths through the deleted node will simply pass through one less red node, and both the deleted node's parent and child must be black, so Property 3 ("All leaves are black") and Property 4 ("Both children of every red node are black") still hold.

Another simple case is when M is black and C is red. Simply removing a black node could break Properties 4 ("Both children of every red node are black") and 5 ("All paths from any given node to its leaf nodes contain the same number of black nodes"), but if we repaint C black, both of these properties are preserved.

The complex case is when both M and C are black. (This can only occur when deleting a black node which has two leaf children, because if the black node M had a black non-leaf child on one side but just a leaf child on the other side, then the count of black nodes on both sides would be different, thus the tree would had been an invalid red-black tree by violation of Property 5.) We begin by replacing M with its child C. We will call (or label—that is, relabel) this child (in its new position) N, and its sibling (its new parent's other child) S. (S was previously the sibling of M.) In the diagrams below, we will also use P for N's new parent (M's old parent), S_L for S's left child, and S_R for S's right child (S cannot be a leaf because if N is black, which we presumed, then P's one subtree which includes N counts two black-height and thus P's other subtree which includes S must also count two black-height, which cannot be the case if S is a leaf node).

Note: In between some cases, we exchange the roles and labels of the nodes, but in each case, every label continues to represent the same node it represented at the beginning of the case. Any color shown in the diagram is either assumed in its case or implied by those assumptions. White represents an unknown color (either red or black).

We will find the sibling using this function:

```
sibling(n)
{
    if    (n == n->parent->left)
              return n->parent->right;
    else
              return n->parent->left;
}
```

Note: In order that the tree remains well-defined, we need that every null leaf remains a leaf after all transformations (that it will not have any children). If the node we are deleting has a non-leaf (non-null) child N, it is easy to see that the property is satisfied. If, on the other hand, N would be a null leaf, it can be verified from the diagrams (or code) for all the cases that the property is satisfied as well.

We can perform the steps outlined above with the following code, where the function replace_node substitutes child into n's place in the tree. For convenience, code in this section will assume that null leaves are represented by actual node objects rather than NULL (the code in the Insertion section works with either representation).

```
delete_one_child (n)
{
    /*
     * Precondition: n has at most one non-null child.
     */
    struct node *child = is_leaf(n->right) ? n->left : n->right;
    replace_node(n, child);
    if (n->color == BLACK) {
        if (child->color == RED)
            child->color = BLACK;
        else
            delete_casel(child);
    }
    free(n);
}
```

Note: If N is a null leaf and we do not want to represent null leaves as actual node objects, we can modify the algorithm by first calling delete_casel() on its parent (the node that we delete, n in the code above) and deleting it afterwards. We can do this because the parent is black, so it behaves in the same way as a null leaf (and is sometimes called a 'phantom' leaf). And we can safely delete it at the end as n will remain a leaf after all operations, as shown above.

If both N and its original parent are black, then deleting this original parent causes paths which proceed through N to have one fewer black node than paths that do not. As this violates Property 5 (All paths from any given node to its leaf nodes contain the same number of black nodes), the tree must be rebalanced. There are several cases to consider:

Case 1:N is the new root. In this case, we are done. We removed one black node from every path, and the new root is black, so the properties are preserved.

```
delete_casel(n)
{
    if (n->parent != NULL)
        delete_case2(n);
}
```

Note: In cases 2, 5, and 6, we assume N is the left child of its parent P. If it is the right child, left and right should be reversed throughout these three cases. Again, the code examples take both cases into account.

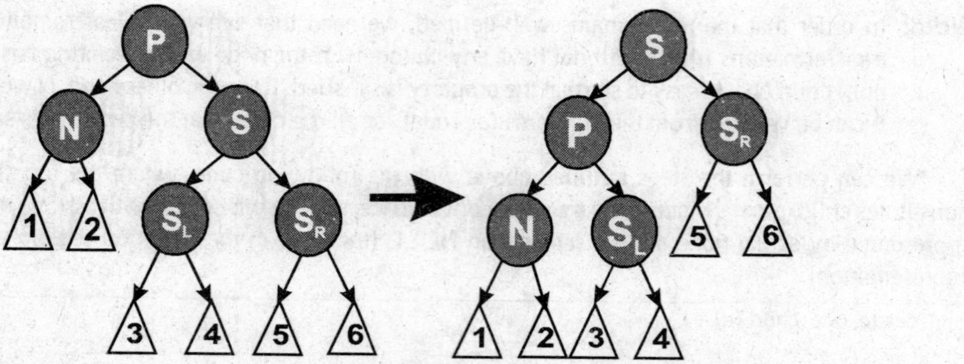

Case 2: S is red. In this case we reverse the colors of P and S, and then rotate left at P, turning S into N's grandparent. Note that P has to be black as it had a red child. Although all paths still have the same number of black nodes, now N has a black sibling and a red parent, so we can proceed to step 4, 5, or 6. (Its new sibling is black because it was once the child of the red S.) In later cases, we will relabel N's new sibling as S.

```
delete__case2 (n)

    if (s->color == RED)
        n->parent->color = RED;
        s->color = BLAC  ;
        if (n == n->parent->left)
            rotate left(n->parent);
        else
            rotate right(n->parent);

    delete case3(n);
```

Case 3:P, S, and S's children are black. In this case, we simply repaint S red. The result is that all paths passing through S, which are precisely those paths not passing through N, have one less black node. Because deleting N's original parent made all paths passing through N have one less black node, this evens things up. However, all paths through P now have one fewer black node than paths that do not pass through P, so Property 5 (All paths from any given node to its leaf nodes contain the same number of black nodes) is still violated. To correct' this, we perform the rebalancing procedure on P, starting at case 1.

```
delete_case3(n)
{
    if    ((n->parent->color == BLAC  )
          (s->color == BLAC  )
          (s->left->color == BLAC  )
          (s->right->color == BLAC  ))
             s->color = RED;
          delete casel(n->parent);
      else
          delete case4(n) ;
```

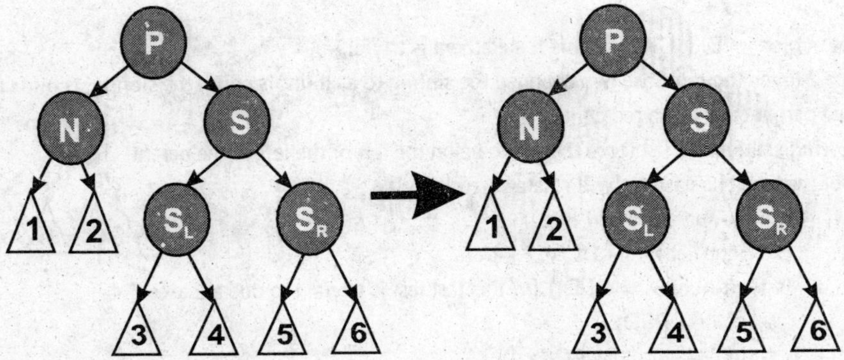

Case 4: S and S's children are black, but P is red. In this case, we simply exchange the colors of S and P. This does not affect the number of black nodes on paths going through S, but it does add one to the number of black nodes on paths going through N, making up for the deleted black node on those paths.

```
delete_case4(n)
{
      if ( (n->parent->color == RED)
          (s->color == BLAC  )
          (s->left->color == BLAC  )
          (s->right->color == BLAC  ))
             s->color = RED;
             n->parent->color = BLAC  ;
      else
             delete  case5(n);
```

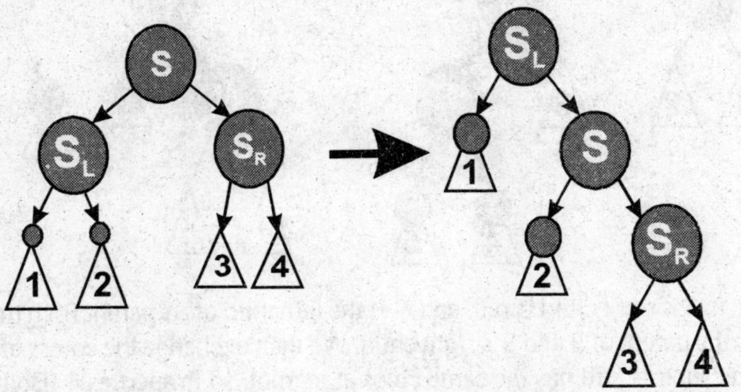

Case 5: S is black, S's left child is red, S's right child is black, and N is the left child of its parent. In this case we rotate right at S, so that S's left child becomes S's parent and N's new sibling. We then exchange the colors of S and its new parent. All paths still have the same number of black nodes, but now N has a black sibling whose right child is red, so we fall into case 6. Neither N nor its parent are affected by this transformation. (Again, for case 6, we relabel N's new sibling as S.)

```
delete_bcase5(n)
{
        if (s->color == BLACK) { /* this if statement is trivial,
due to Case 2 (even though Case two changed the sibling to a sibling's child, the sibling's child can't be red,
since no red parent can have a red child). */
// the following statements just force the red to be on the left of the left of the parent,
// or right of the right, so case six will rotate correctly.
            if  ((n == n->parent->left) &&
                (s->right->color == BLACK) &&
                (s->left->color == RED)) { // this last test is trivial too due to cases 2-4.
                 s->color = RED;
                 s->left->color = BLACK;
                 rotate_right(s);
            }  else if ((n == n->parent->right) &&
                      (s->left->color == BLACK) &&
                      (s->right->color == RED)) {// this last test is trivial too due to cases 2-4.
                      s->color = RED;
                      s->right->color = BLACK;
                      rotate_left (s);
            }
        }
        delete_case6(n);
}
```

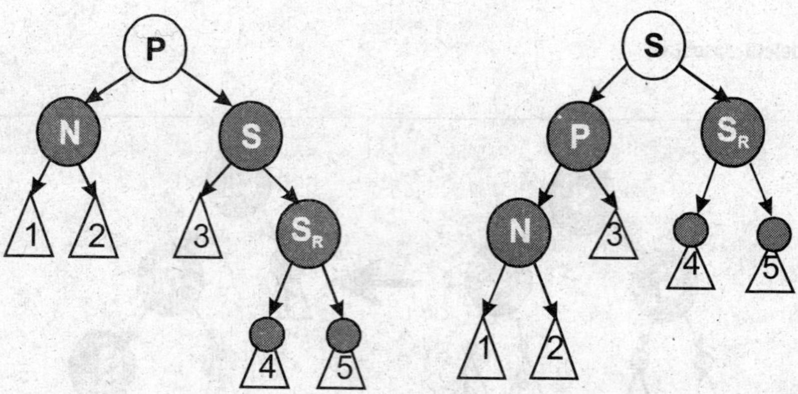

Case 6: S is black, S's right child is red, and N is the left child of its parent P. In this case we rotate left at P, so that S becomes the parent of P and S's right child. We then exchange the colors of P and S, and make S's right child black. The subtree still has the same color at its root, so Properties 4 (Both children of every red node are black) and 5 (All paths from any given node to its leaf nodes contain the same number of black nodes) are not violated. However, N now has one additional black ancestor: either P has become black, or it was black and S was added as a black grandparent. Thus, the paths passing through N pass through one additional black node.

Meanwhile, if a path does not go through N, then there are two possibilities:

- It goes through N's new sibling. Then, it must go through S and P, both formerly and currently, as they have only exchanged colors and places. Thus the path contains the same number of black nodes.
- It goes through N's new uncle, S's right child. Then, it formerly went through S, S's parent, and S's right child (which was red), but now only goes through S, which has assumed the color of its former parent, and S's right child, which has changed from red to black (assuming S's color: black). The net effect is that this path goes through the same number of black nodes.

Either way, the number of black nodes on these paths does not change. Thus, we have restored Properties 4 (Both children of every red node are black) and 5 (All paths from any given node to its leaf nodes contain the same number of black nodes). The white node in the diagram can be either red or black, but must refer to the same color both before and after the transformation.

```
delete_case6(n)
{
        struct node *s = sibling(n);
        s->color = n->parent->color;
          n->parent->color = BLACK;

        if  (n == n->parent->left) {
                    s->right->color = BLACK;
                rotate_left(n->parent) ;
        }  else  {
                s-> left->color = BLACK;
                rotate_right(n~>parent);
        }
}
```

Again, the function calls all use tail recursion, so the algorithm is in-place. In the algorithm above, all cases are chained in order, except in delete case 3 where it can recurse to case 1 back to the parent node: this is the only case where an in-place implementation will effectively loop (after only one rotation in case 3).

Additionally, no tail recursion ever occurs on a child node, so the tail recursion loop can only move from a child back to its successive ancestors. No more than O(log n) loops back to case 1 will occur (where n is the total number of nodes in the tree before deletion). If a rotation occurs in case 2 (which is the only possibility of rotation within the loop of cases 1-3), then the parent of the node N becomes red after the rotation and we will exit the loop. Therefore at most one rotation will occur within this loop. Since no more than two additional rotations will occur after exiting the loop, at most three rotations occur in total.

12.9 PROOF OF ASYMPTOTIC BOUNDS

A red black tree which contains n internal nodes has a height of O(log(n)).

Definitions:

- h(v) = height of subtree rooted at node v
- bh(v) = the number of black nodes (not counting v if it is black) from v to any leaf in the subtree (called the black-height).

Lemma: A subtree rooted at node v has at least $2^{bh(v)} - 1$ internal nodes.

Proof of Lemma (by induction height):

Basis: h(v) = 0

If v has a height of zero then it must be null, therefore bh(v) = 0. So:

$$2^{bh(v)} - 1 = 2^0 - 1 = 1-1 = 0$$

Inductive Step: v such that h (v) = k, has at least $2^{bh(v)}$ 1 internal nodes implies that v′ such that h(v′) = k+1 has at least $2^{bh(v')} - 1$ internal nodes.

Since v′ has h(v′) > 0 it is an internal node. As such it has two children both of which have a black-height of either bh(v′) or bh(v′)–l (depending on whether v′ is red or black). By the inductive hypothesis each child has at least $2^{bh(v')-1} - 1$ internal nodes, so v′ has at least:

$$2^{bh}(v')-1 \quad 1 + 2^{bh(v)-1} - 1 + 1 = 2^{bh(v)} - 1$$

internal nodes.

Using this lemma we can now show that the height of the tree is logarithmic. Since at least half of the nodes on any path from the root to a leaf are black (property 4 of a red black tree) the black-height of the root is at least h(root) 2. By the lemma we get:

$$n \geq 2\frac{h(root)}{2} - 1 \leftrightarrow \log_2(n+1) \geq \frac{h(root)}{2} \leftrightarrow h(root) \leq 2\log_2(n+1)$$

Therefore the height of the root is O(log(n)).

12.10 COMPLEXITY

In the tree code there is only one loop where the node of the root of the red-black property that we wish to restore, x, can be moved up the tree by one level at each iteration.

Since the original height of the tree is O(log n), there are O(log n) iterations. So overall the insert routine has O(log n) complexity.

Solved Questions

1. Let us define a relaxed red-black tree as a binary search tree that satisfies red- black properties 1, 3, 4 and 5. In other words, the root may be either red or black. Consider a relaxed red-black tree T whose root is red. If we color the root of T black but make no other changes to T, is the resulting tree a red-black tree?

Ans. If we color the root of a relaxed red-black tree black but make no other changes, the resulting tree is a red-black tree. Not even any black-heights change.

2. Suppose that we "absorb" every red node in a red-black tree into its black parent, so that the children of the red node become children of the black parent. (Ignore what happens to the keys.) What are the possible degrees of a black node after all its red children are absorbed? What can you say about the depths of the leaves of the resulting tree?

Ans. After absorbing each red node into its black parent, the degree of each node black node is

2, if both children were already black,

3, if one child was black and one was red, or

4, if both children were red.

All leaves of the resulting tree have the same depth.

3. Show that the longest simple path from a node x in a red-black tree to a descendant leaf has length at most twice that of the shortest simple path from node x to a descendant leaf.

Ans. In the longest path, at least every other node is black. In the shortest path, at most every node is black. Since the two paths contain equal numbers of black nodes, the length of the longest path is at most twice the length of the shortest path. We can say this more precisely, as follows: Since every path contains bh(x) black nodes, even the shortest path from x to a descendant leaf has length at least bh(x). By definition, the longest path from x to a descendant leaf has length height(x). Since the longest path has bh(x) black nodes and at least half the nodes on the longest path are black (by property 4), bh(x) $\geq$ height(x)/2, so length of longest path = height(x) $\leq$ 2 bh(x) $\leq$ twice length of shortest path .

4. Show that any arbitrary n-node binary search tree can be transformed into any other arbitrary n-node binary search tree using O(n) rotations. (Hint: First show that at most n - 1 right rotations suffice to transform the tree into a right-going chain.)

Ans. Since the exercise asks about binary search trees rather than the more specific redblack trees, we assume here that leaves are full-edged nodes, and we ignore the sentinels. Taking the books hint, we start by showing that with at most n "1 right rotations, we can convert any binary search tree into one that is just a right-going chain. The idea is simple. Let us define the right spine as the root and all descendants of the root that are reachable by following only right pointers from the root. A binary search tree that is just a right-going chain has all n nodes in the right spine. As long as the tree is not just a right spine, repeatedly and some node y on the right spine that has a non-leaf left child x and then perform a right rotation on y:

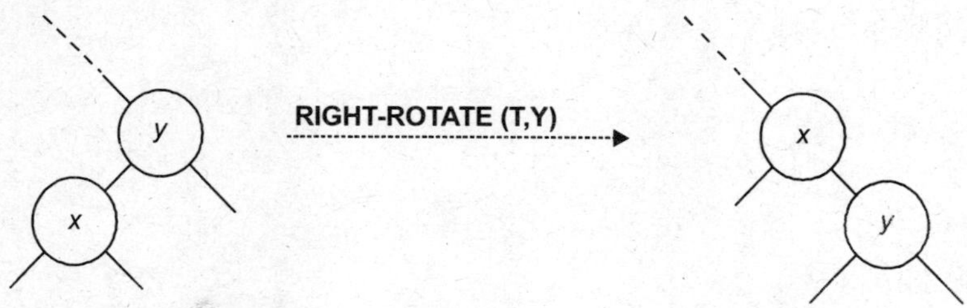

(In the above figure, note that any of α, β, and γ can be an empty subtree.) Observe that this right rotation adds x to the right spine, and no other nodes leave the right spine. Thus, this right rotation increases the number of nodes in the right spine by 1. Any binary search tree starts out with at least one node the root in the right spine. Moreover, if there are any nodes not on the right spine, then at least one such node has a parent on the right spine. Thus, at most n – 1 right rotations are needed to put all nodes in the right spine, so that the tree consists of a single right-going chain. If we knew the sequence of right rotations that transforms an arbitrary binary search tree T to a single right-going chain T , then we could perform this sequence in reverse. Turning each right rotation into its inverse left rotation. To transform T Therefore, here is how we can transform any binary search tree T1 into any other binary search tree T2. Let T be the unique right-going chain consisting of the nodes of T1 (which is the same as the nodes of T2).

Previous Year University Question

1. Show the Red Black tree that is to be resulted after successively inserting the keys 41, 38, 31, 12,19,8 into an initiall red black tree. [GBTU]
2. Give the properties of red black tree. Show that the longest simple path from a node x in a RB tree to a

descendent leaf has length at most twice that of the shortest simple path from node x to a descendant leaf. [GBTU]

3. Give an efficient algorithm to determine whether or not a graph can be painted with just two colours. [Madrass University]

EXERCISE

1. Define Red Black Tree
2. Define the black height of a node, x.
3. What is the "big-OH" performance (in terms of the number of nodes in the tree) for the operations find, insert and remove for a red black tree in the best, worst and average cases?
4. What property of red-black tree is most significant in explaining their "big-oh" behaviour for-the operations find, insert and remove?
5. Prove that in any red-black tree with root X, there are at least n = 2bh (x)_1 internal nodes where bh(x) is the black-height of x.
6. Prove that if a black node has just one child, that child be red.

CHAPTER

13

AVL TREE

13.1 INTRODUCTION

In computer science, an AVL tree is a self-balancing binary search tree, and it was the first such data structure to be invented. In an AVL tree, the heights of the two child subtrees of any node differ by at most one. Lookup, insertion, and deletion all take O(log n) time in both the average and worst cases, where n is the number of nodes in the tree prior to the operation. Insertions and deletions may require the tree to be rebalanced by one or more tree rotations.

The AVL tree is named after its two Soviet inventors, G.M. Adelson-Velskii and E.M. Landis, who published it in their 1962 paper "An algorithm for the organization of information."

The balance factor of a node is the height of its left subtree minus the height of its right subtree (sometimes opposite) and a node with balance factor 1, 0, or –1 is considered balanced. A node with any other balance factor is considered unbalanced and requires rebalancing the tree. The balance factor is either stored directly at each node or computed from the heights of the subtrees.

AVL trees are often compared with red-black trees because they support the same set of operations and because red-black trees also take O(log n) time for the basic operations. Because AVL trees are more rigidly balanced, they are faster than red-black trees for lookup intensive applications. A red-black tree, however, is not as rigidly balanced as an AVL tree and has faster insertion and removal times. The AVL tree balancing algorithm appears in many computer science curricula.

13.2 OPERATIONS

The basic operations of an AVL tree involve carrying out the same actions as would be carried out on an unbalanced binary search tree, but modifications are preceded or followed by one or more operations called tree rotations, which help to restore the height balance of the subtrees.

13.2.1 Lookup

Lookup in an AVL tree is performed exactly as in an unbalanced binary search tree. Because of the height-balancing of the tree, a lookup takes O(log n) time. No special actions need to be taken, and the tree's structure is not modified by lookups. (This is in contrast to splay tree lookups, which do modify their tree's structure.)

If each node additionally records the size of its subtree (including itself and its descendants), then the nodes can be retrieved by index in O(log n) time as well.

Once a node has been found in a balanced tree, the next or previous nodes can be explored in amortized constant time. A few cases require traversing up to 2×log(n) links. However exploring all n nodes in the tree in this manner would use each link exactly twice, and there are n–1 links, so the amortized cost is 2 × (n–1)/n, approximately 2.

13.2.2 Insertion

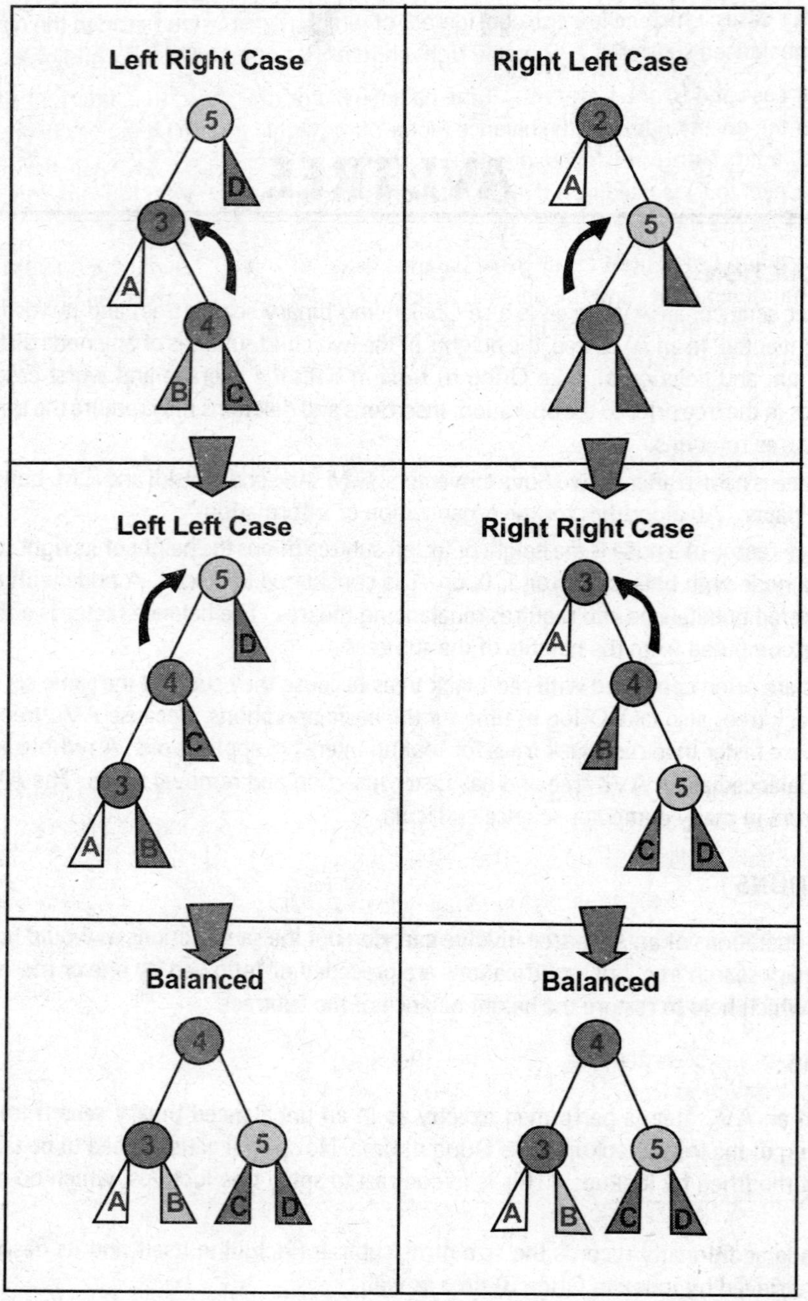

Fig. 13.1 Pictorial description of how rotations cause rebalancing tree, and then retracing one's steps toward the root updating the balance factor of the nodes .

After inserting a node, it is necessary to check each of the node's ancestors for consistency with the rules of AVL. For each node checked, if the balance factor remains –1, 0, or +1 then no rotations are necessary. However, if the balance factor becomes ±2 then the subtree rooted at this node is unbalanced. If insertions are performed serially, after each insertion, at most two tree rotations are needed to restore the entire tree to the rules of AVL.

There are four cases which need to be considered, of which two are symmetric to the other two. Let P be the root of the unbalanced subtree. Let R be the right child of P. Let L be the left child of P.

Right-Right case and Right-Left case: If the balance factor of P is +2, then the right subtree outweighs the left subtree of the given node, and the balance factor of the right child (R) must be checked. If the balance factor of R is ≤ 0, a left rotation is needed with P as the root. If the balance factor of R is +1, a double left rotation (with respect to P) is needed. The first rotation is a right rotation with R as the root. The second is a left rotation with P as the root.

Left-Left case and Left-Right case: If the balance factor of P is +2, then the left subtree outweighs the right subtree of the given node, and the balance factor of the left child (L) must be checked. If the balance factor of L is ≥ 0, a right rotation is needed with P as the root. If the balance factor of L is –1, a double right rotation (with respect to P) is needed. The first rotation is a left rotation with L as the root. The second is a right rotation with P as the root.

Rotation Algorithms for putting an out-of-balance AVL-tree back in balance

Note: After the insertion of each node the tree should be checked for balance. The only nodes that need checked are the ones along the insertion path of the newly inserted node. Once the tree is found to be out-of-balance then re-balance it using the appropriate algorithm. If the out-of-balance is detected as soon as it happens and the proper algorithm is used then the tree will be back in balance after one rotation.

Step 1: Set up the pointers:

A – points to the node that is out of balance. If more than one node is out of balance then select the one that is furthest from the root. If there is a tie then you missed a previous out-of-balance.

B – points to the child of A in the direction of the out-of-balance

C – points to the child of B in the direction of the out-=of-balance

F – points to the parent of A. This is the only pointer of these 4 that is allowed to be NULL.

Step 2: Determine the appropriate algorithm:

The first letter of the algorithm represents the direction from A to B (either Right or Left). The second letter represents the direction from B to C (either Right or Left).

Step 3: Follow the algorithm:

RR:	LL:
A.Right = B.Left	A.Left = B.Right
B.Left = A	B.Right = A
If F = NULL	If F = NULL
B is new Root of tree	B is new Root of tree

```
Else
    If F.Right = A
        F.Right = B
    Else
        F.Left = B
    End If
End If

RL:
    B.Left = C.Right
    A.Right = C.Left
    C.Right = B
    C.Left = A
    If F = NULL
        C is new Root of tree
    Else
        If F.Right = A
            F.Right = C
        Else
            F.Left = C
        End If
    End If
```

```
Else
    If F.Right = A
        F.Right = B
    Else
        F.Left = B
    End If
End If

LR:
    A.Left = C.Right
    B.Right = C.Left
    C.Left = B
    C.Right = A
    If F = NULL
        C is new Root of tree
    Else
        If F.Right = A
            F.Right = C
        Else
            F.Left = C
        End If
    End If
```

13.3 INSERTION INTO OF AVL TREE

To balance the tree we undertake what are called rotations. Rotations are mechanisms which shift some of the subtrees of the unbalanced tree to obtain a balanced tree.

There are 4 different type of rotation in case of innertion.

(1) LL rotation – node is in inserted is the left subtree (L) of left subtree (L) of A

(2) LR rotation – node in is inserted is the right subtree of left subtree (L) of A.

(3) RR rotation – node in is inserted is the right subtree of right subtree of A

(4) RL rotation – node is in inserteds the left subtree if right subtree of A.

LL rotation

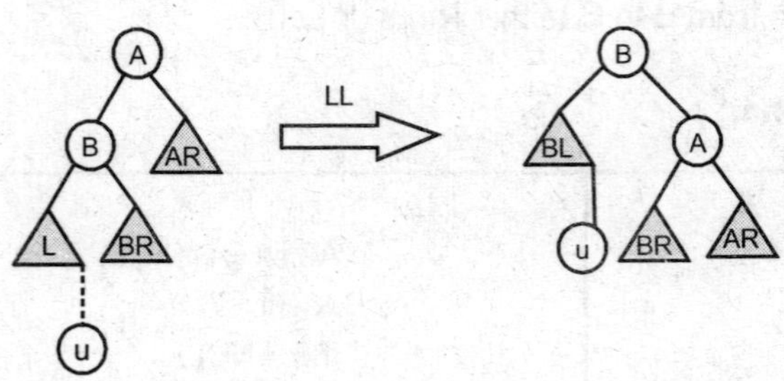

Example:

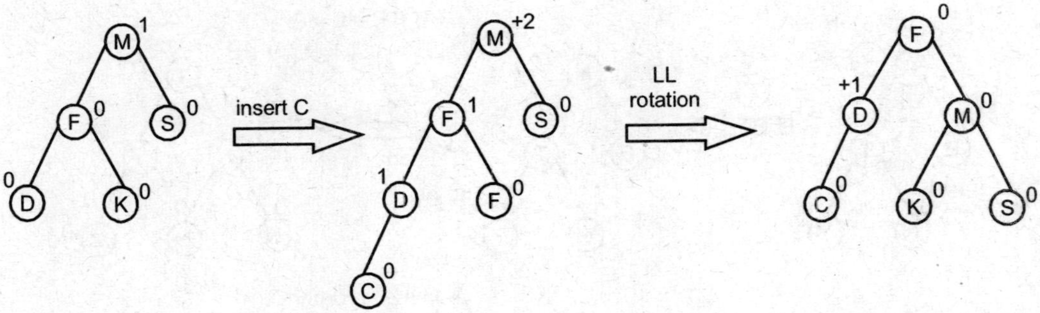

LR rotation

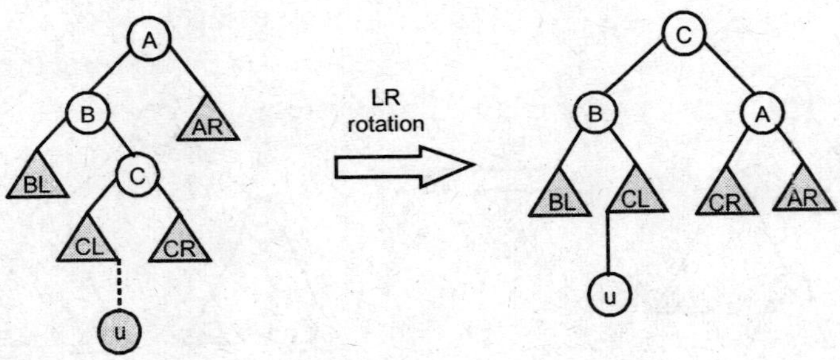

Example:

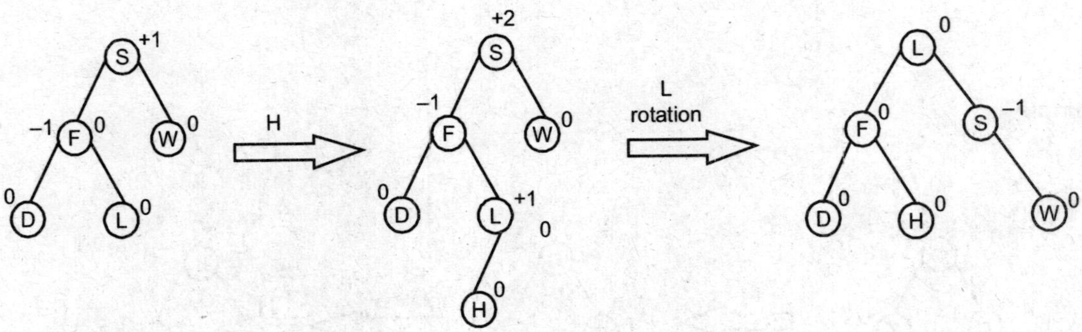

RR rotation

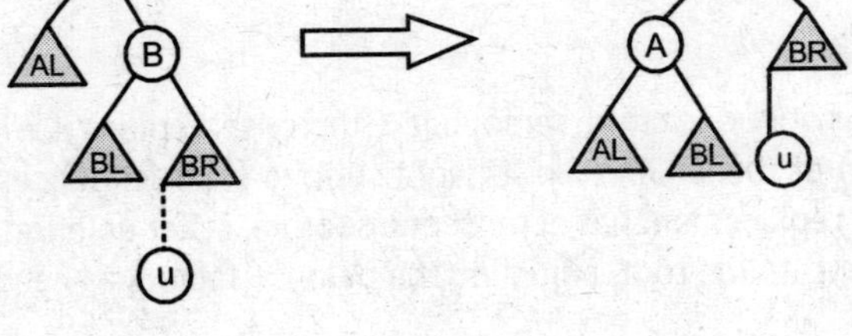

Example of RR rotation

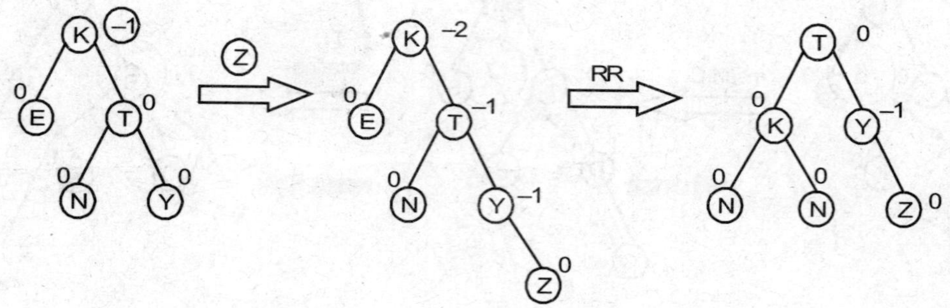

RL Rotation

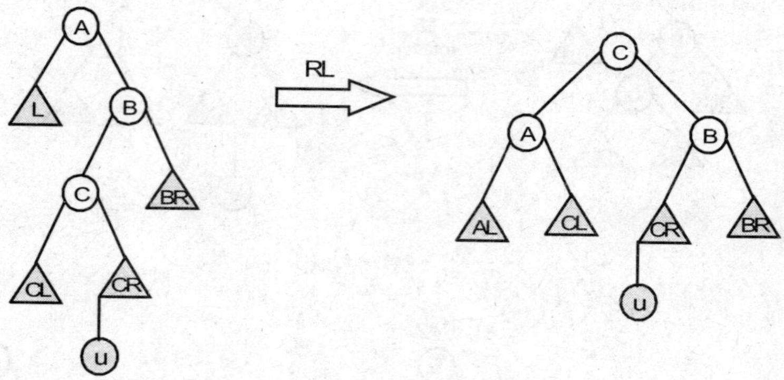

Example

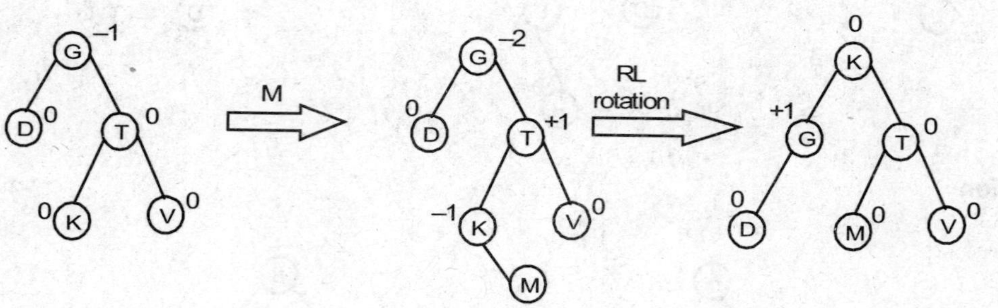

Deletion

If the node is a leaf or has only one child, remove it. Otherwise, replace it with either the largest in its left subtree (inorder predecessor) or the smallest in its right subtree (inorder successor), and remove that node. The node that was found as a replacement has at most one subtree. After deletion, retrace the path back up the tree (parent of the replacement) to the root, adjusting the balance factors as needed.

As with all binary trees, a node's in-order successor is the left-most child of its right subtree, and a node's in-order predecessor is the right-most child of its left subtree. In either case, this node will have zero or one children. Delete it according to one of the two simpler cases above.

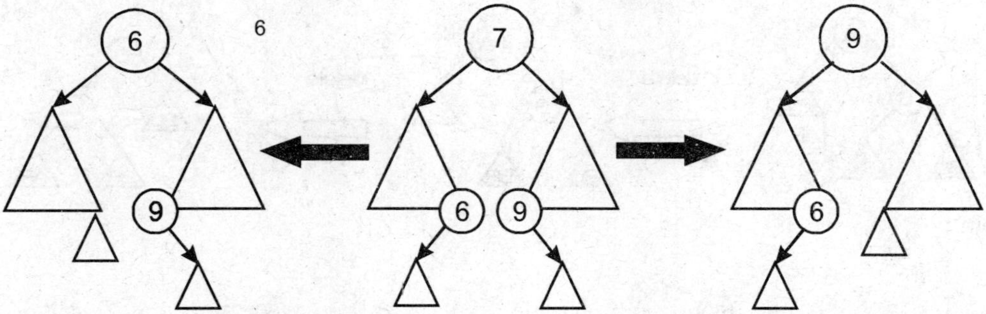

In addition to the balancing described above for insertions, if the balance factor for the tree is 2 and that of the left subtree is 0, a right rotation must be performed on P. The mirror of this case is also necessary.

The retracing can stop if the balance factor becomes -1 or +1 indicating that the height of that subtree has remained unchanged. If the balance factor becomes 0 then the height of the subtree has decreased by one and the retracing needs to continue. If the balance factor becomes –2 or +2 then the subtree is unbalanced and needs to be rotated to fix it. If the rotation leaves the subtree's balance factor at 0 then the retracing towards the root must continue since the height of this subtree has decreased by one. This is in contrast to an insertion where a rotation resulting in a balance factor of 0 indicated that the subtree's height has remained unchanged.

The time required is O(log n) for lookup, plus a maximum of O(log n) rotations on the way back to the root, so the operation can be completed in O(log n) time.

Deletion of AVL search tree:

Rotation free

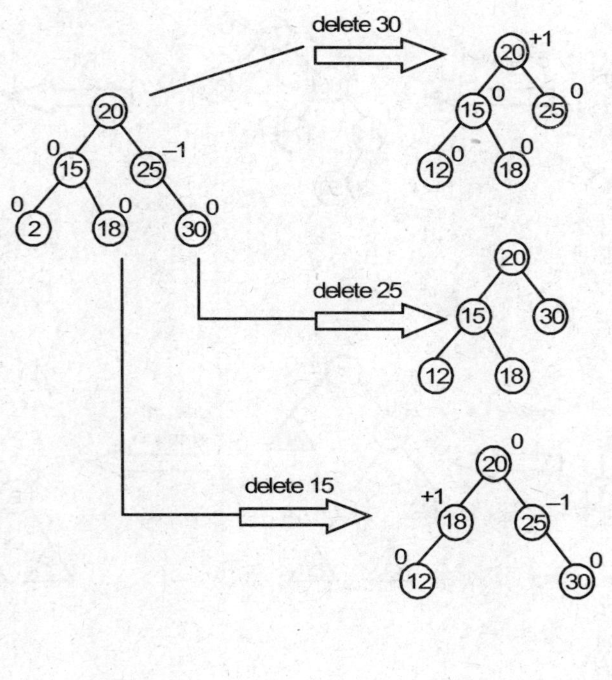

R category rotation associated with the delete operation

RO Rotation:

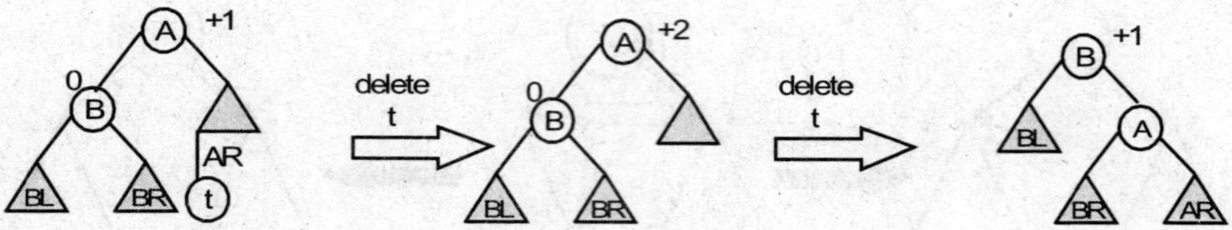

Example :

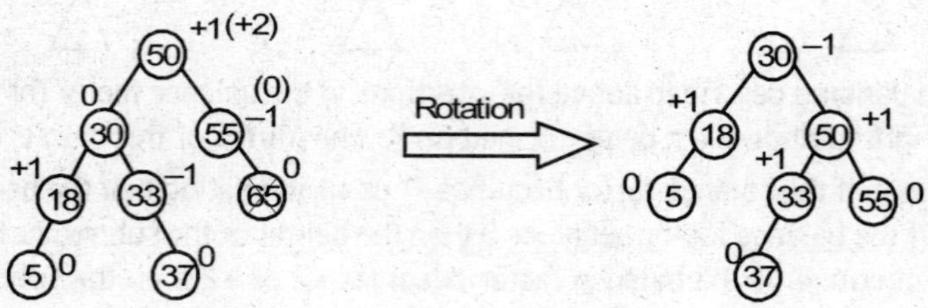

R1 Rotation:

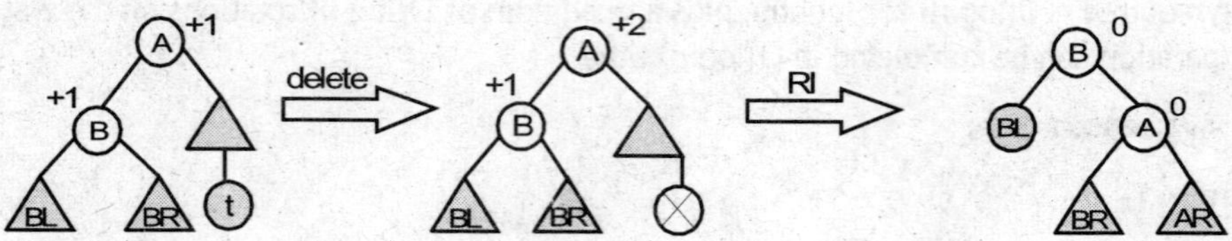

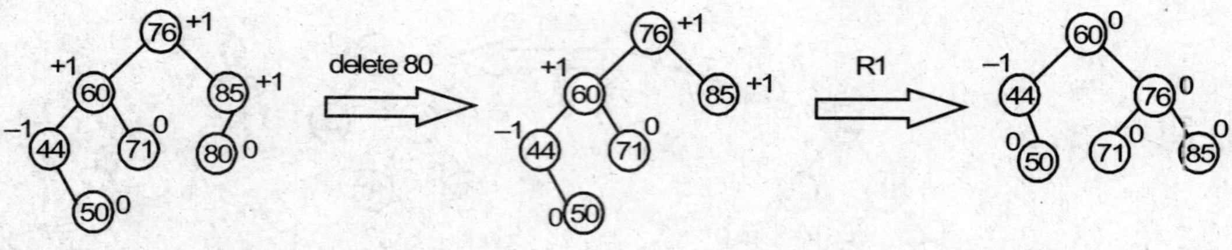

R–1 Rotation:

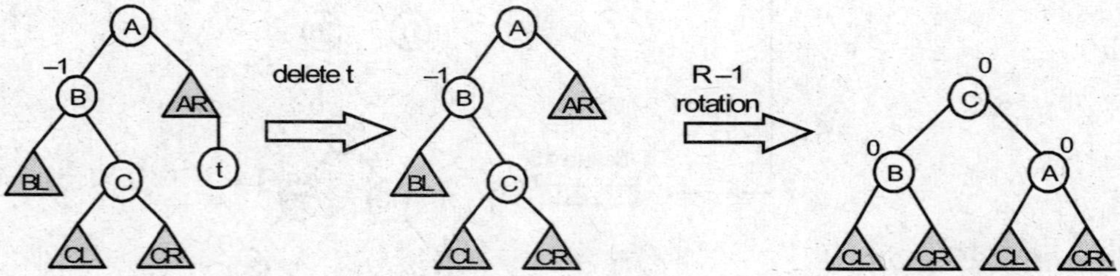

Example:

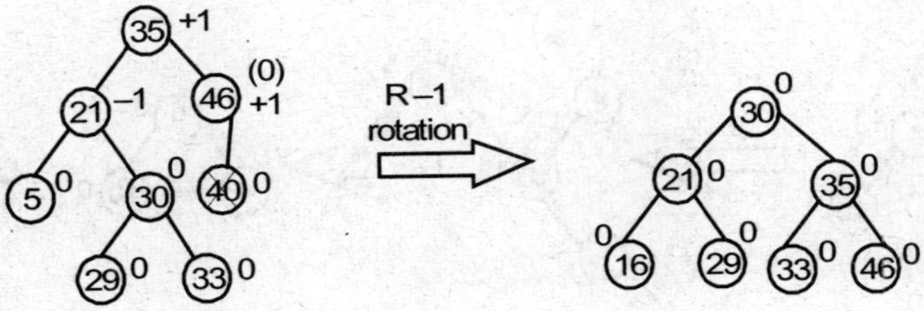

L0 Rotation

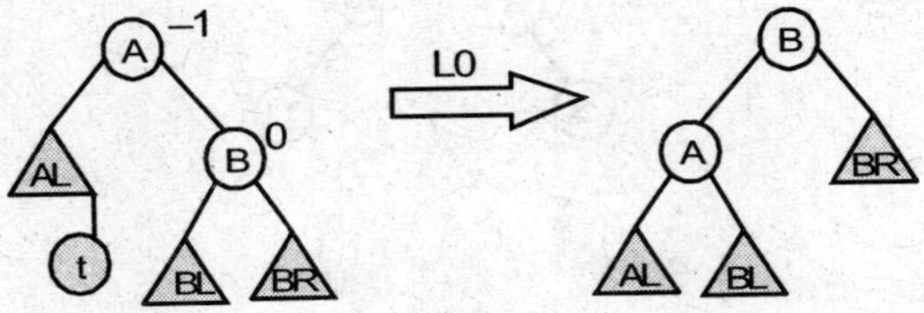

L1 Rotation

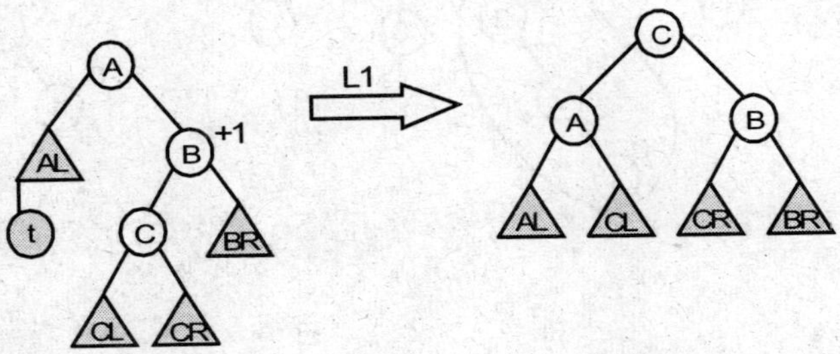

L–1 Rotation

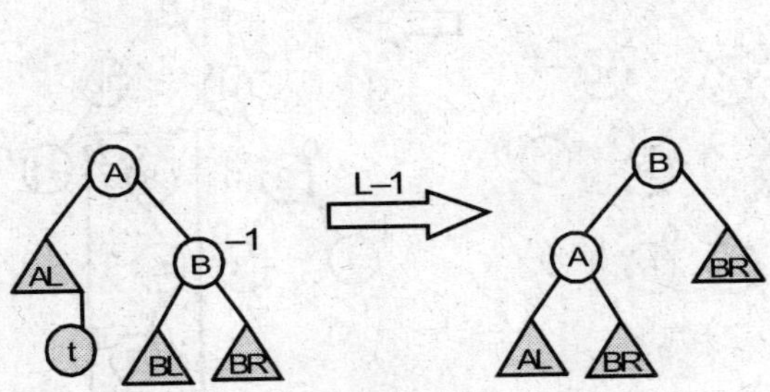

Example

4, 10, 9, 3, 11, 8, 2, 1, 5, 7, 6

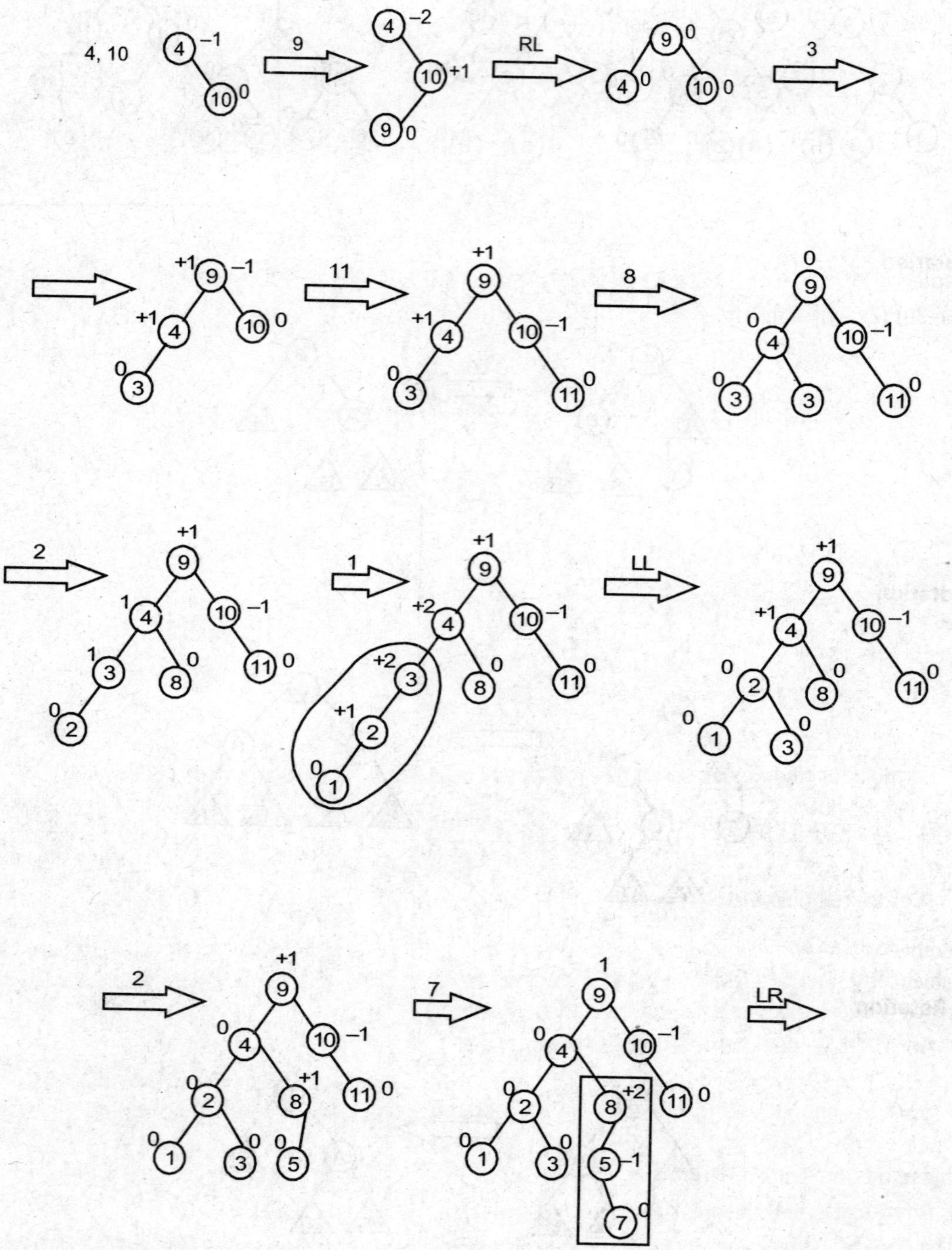

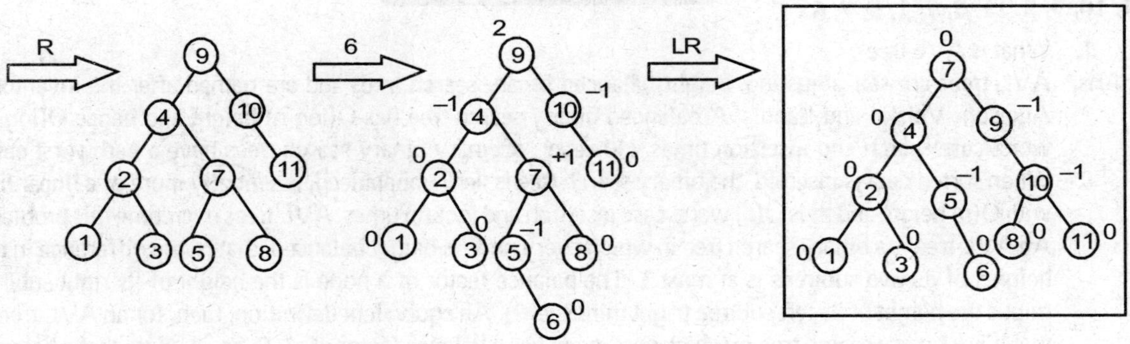

Example

$(u-3b)\ (2x-y)^5 + (e-f)^2$

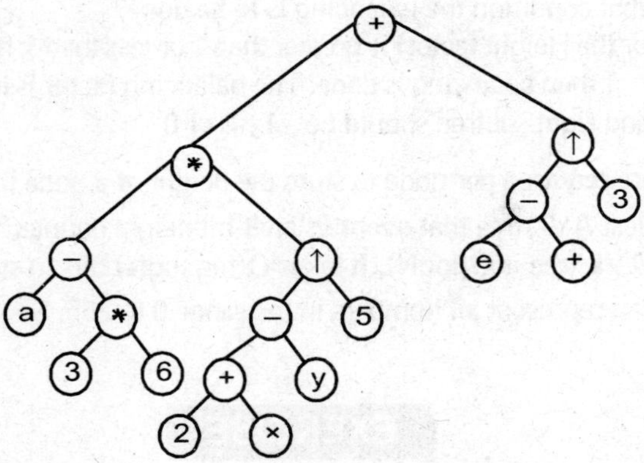

Formula for finding number of possible binary trees given N number of nodes.

$$= \frac{(2n)!}{n! \times (n+1)!}$$

13.4 Comparison to other structures

Both AVL trees and red-black trees are self-balancing binary search trees, so they are very similar mathematically. The operations to balance the trees are different, but both occur in constant time. The real difference between the two is the limiting height. For a tree of size n:

- An AVL tree's height is strictly less than:

$$\log_\phi(n+2) - 1 = \frac{\log_2(n+2)}{\log_2(\phi)} - 1 = \log_\phi(2)\ \log_2(n+2) - 1 \approx 1.44 \log_2(n+2) - 1$$

where ϕ is the Golden Ratio.

- A red-black tree's height is at most $2\log_2(n+1)$

The AVL tree is more rigidly balanced than Red-Black trees, leading to slower insertion and removal but faster retrieval.

Solved Questions

1. What is AVL tree?

Ans. AVL trees are self-adjusting, height-balanced binary search trees and are named after the inventors: Adelson- Velskii and Landis. A balanced binary search tree has O(log n) height and hence O(log n) worst case search and insertion times. However, ordinary binary search trees have a bad worst case. When sorted data is inserted, the binary search tree is very unbalanced, essentially more of a linear list, with O(n) height and thus O(n) worst case insertion and lookup times. AVL trees overcome this problem. An AVL tree is a binary search tree in which every node is height balanced, that is, the difference in the heights of its two subtrees is at most 1. The balance factor of a node is the height of its right subtree minus the height of its left subtree (right minus left!). An equivalent definition, then, for an AVL tree is that it is a binary search tree in which each node has a balance factor of -1, 0, or +1. Note that a balance factor of -1 means that the subtree is left-heavy, and a balance factor of +1 means that the subtree is right-heavy. Each node is associated with a Balancing factor.

Balance factor of each node = height of right subtree at that node - height of left subtree at that node.

2. In an AVL tree, at what condition the balancing is to be done?

Ans. If the pivotal value (or the Height factor) is greater than 1 or less than 1.If the balance factor of any node is other than 0 or 1 or -1 then balancing is done. The balancing factor is height. The difference in height of the right subtree and right subtree should be +1 ,-1 or 0

3. (a) How many bits are required per node to store the height of a node in an N-node AVL tree?

(b) What is the smallest AVL tree that overows an 8-bit height counter?

Ans. (a) The depth of an AVL tree is O(logN). It takes O(log logN) bits to store a number of size O(logN).

(b) With 8 bits one can represent all numbers in the range 0 to 255. So the answer is the smallest AVL tree with height 256.

EXERCISE

1. Perform the following sequence of an operation is a initially empty tree and draw the tree after each operation.
   (a) Insert keys: 0, 2, 4, 6, 8, 10, 12, 14, 16, 18.
   (b) Search for less. 1, 3, 5, 8, 9, 12, 13, 15, 17, 19.
   (c) Delete less. 0, 2, 9, 6, 8, 11, 12, 14, 16.
2. If we maintain a reference to the position of the left -most internal node of an AVL tree, then operation first can be performed in 0(1) time.

   Describe how the implementation of the other dictionary methods needs to be modified to maintain a reference to the left-most position.
3. Create an AVL tree freom a given set of value, 1, +1, B, j, A, E, C, F, D, K, G, L.

CHAPTER 14

B-TREE

14.1 INTRODUCTION

In computer science, a -tree is a tree data structure that keeps data sorted and allows searches, sequential access, insertions, and deletions in logarithmic amortized time. The B-tree is a generalization of a binary search tree in that a node can have more than two children. Unlike self-balancing binary search trees, the B-tree is optimized for systems that read and write large blocks of data. It is commonly used in databases and filesystems.

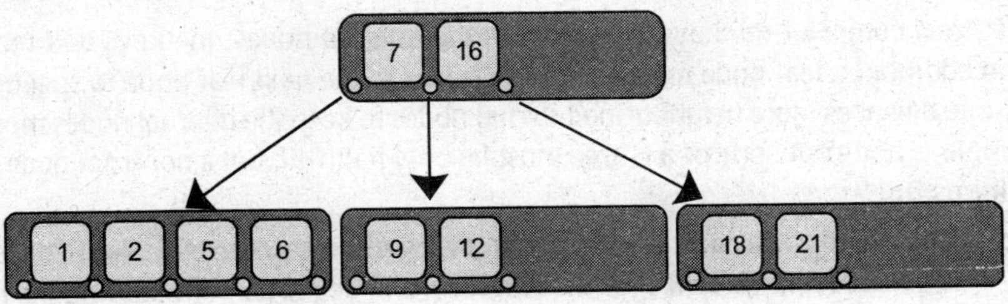

Fig. 14.1 A B-tree of order 2

In B-trees, internal (non-leaf) nodes can have a variable number of child nodes within some pre-defined range. When data is inserted or removed from a node, its number of child nodes changes. In order to maintain the pre-defined range, internal nodes may be joined or split. Because a range of child nodes is permitted, B-trees do not need re-balancing as frequently as other self-balancing search trees, but may waste some space, since nodes are not entirely full. The lower and upper bounds on the number of child nodes are typically fixed for a particular implementation. For example, in a 2-3 B-tree (often simply referred to as a 2-3 tree each internal node may have only 2 or 3 child nodes.

Each internal node of a B-tree will contain a number of keys. Usually, the number of keys is chosen to vary between d and 2d. In practice, the keys take up the most space in a node. The factor of 2 will guarantee that nodes can be split or combined. If an internal node has 2d keys, then adding a key to that node can be accomplished by splitting the 2d key node into two d key nodes and adding the key to the parent node. Each split node has the required minimum number of keys. Similarly, if an internal node and its neighbor each have d keys, then a key may be deleted from the internal node by combining with its neighbor. Deleting the key would make the internal node have d–1 keys joining the neighbor would add d keys plus one more key brought down from the neighbor's parent. The result is an entirely full node of 2d keys.

The number of branches (or child nodes) from a node will be one more than the number of keys stored in the node. In a 2-3 B-tree, the internal nodes will store either one key (with two child nodes) or two keys (with three child nodes). A B-tree is sometimes described with the parameters 1) (2 1) or simply with the highest branching order, (2 1).

A B-tree is kept balanced by requiring that all leaf nodes are at the same depth. This depth will increase slowly as elements are added to the tree, but an increase in the overall depth is infrequent, and results in all leaf nodes being one more node further away from the root.

B-trees have substantial advantages over alternative implementations when node access times far exceed access times within nodes. This usually occurs when the nodes are in secondary storage such as disk drives. By maximizing the number of child nodes within each internal node, the height of the tree decreases and the number of expensive node accesses is reduced. In addition, rebalancing the tree occurs less often. The maximum number of child nodes depends on the information that must be stored for each child node and the size of a full disk block or an analogous size in secondary storage. While 2-3 B-trees are easier to explain, practical B-trees using secondary storage want a large number of child nodes to improve performance.

14.2 VARIANTS

The term B-tree may refer to a specific design or it may refer to a general class of designs. In the narrow sense, a B-tree stores keys in its internal nodes but need not store those keys in the records at the leaves. The general class includes variations such as the B⁺-tree and the B*-tree.

- In the B⁺-tree, copies of the keys are stored in the internal nodes; the keys and records are stored in leaves; in addition, a leaf node may include a pointer to the next leaf node to speed sequential access. The B* -tree balances more neighboring internal nodes to keep the internal nodes more densely packed. For example, a non-root node of a B-tree must be only half full, but a non-root node of a B* -tree must be two-thirds full.
- Counted B-trees store, with each pointer within the tree, the number of nodes in the subtree below that pointer. This allows rapid searches for the Nth record in key order, or counting the number of records between any two records, and various other related operations.

14.3 THE DATABASE PROBLEM

14.3.1 Time to search a sorted file

Usually, sorting and searching algorithms have been characterized by the number of comparison operations that must be performed using order notation. A binary search of a sorted table with N records, for example, can be done in $O(\log_2 N)$ comparisons. If the table had 1,000,000 records, then a specific record could be located with about 20 comparisons: $\log_2 1{,}000{,}000 = 19.931....$

Large databases have historically been kept on disk drives. The time to read a record on a disk drive can dominate the time needed to compare keys once the record is available. The time to read a record from a disk drive involves a seek time and a rotational delay. The seek time may be 0 to 20 or more milliseconds, and the rotational delay averages about half the rotation period. For a 7200 RPM drive, the rotation period is 8.33 milliseconds. For a drive such as the Seagate ST3500320NS, the track-to-track seek time is 0.8 milliseconds and the average reading seek time is 8.5 milliseconds. For simplicity, assume reading from disk takes about 10 milliseconds.

Naively, then, the time to locate one record out of a million would take 20 disk reads times 10 milliseconds per disk read, which is 0.2 second.

The time won't be that bad because individual records are grouped together in a disk block. A disk block might be 16 kilobytes. If each record is 160 bytes, then 100 records could be stored in each block. The disk read time above was actually for an entire block. Once the disk head is in position, one or more disk blocks can be read with little delay. With 100 records per block, the last 6 or so comparisons don't need to do any disk reads the comparisons are all within the last disk block read.

To speed the search further, the first 13 to 14 comparisons (which each required a disk access) must bep sped up.

14.3.2 An index speeds the search

A significant improvement can be made with an index. In the example above, initial disk reads narrowed the search range by a factor of two. That can be improved substantially by creating an auxiliary index that contains the first record in each disk block (sometimes called a sparse index). This auxiliary index would be 1% of the size of the original database, but it can be searched more quickly. Finding an entry in the auxiliary index would tell us which block to search in the main database; after searching the auxiliary index, we would have to search only that one block of the main database—at a cost of one more disk read. The index would hold 10,000 entries, so it would take at most 14 comparisons. Like the main database, the last 6 or so comparisons in the aux index would be on the same disk block. The index could be searched in about 8 disk reads, and the desired record could be accessed in 9 disk reads.

The trick of creating an auxiliary index can be repeated to make an auxiliary index to the auxiliary index. That would make an aux-aux index that would need only 100 entries and would fit in one disk block.

Instead of reading 14 disk blocks to find the desired record, we only need to read 3 blocks. Reading and searching the first (and only) block of the aux-aux index identifies the relevant block in aux-index. Reading and searching that aux-index block identifies the relevant block in the main database. Instead of 150 milliseconds, we need only 30 milliseconds to get the record.

The auxiliary indices have turned the search problem from a binary search requiring roughly log2N disk reads to one requiring only $\log_b N$ disk reads where b is the blocking factor (the number of entries per block: b = 100 entries per block; logb1,000,000 = 3 reads).

In practice, if the main database is being frequently searched, the aux-aux index and much of the aux index may reside in a disk cache, so they would not incur a disk read.

14.3.3 Insertions and deletions cause trouble

If the database does not change, then compiling the index is simple to do, and the index need never be changed. If there are changes, then managing the database and its index becomes more complicated.

Deleting records from a database doesn't cause much trouble. The index can stay the same, and the record can just be marked as deleted. The database stays in sorted order. If there are a lot of deletions, then the searching and storage become less efficient.

Insertions are a disaster in a sorted sequential file because room for the inserted record must be made. Inserting a record before the first record in the file requires shifting all of the records down one. Such an operation is just too expensive to be practical.

A trick is to leave some space lying around to be used for insertions. Instead of densely storing all the records in a block, the block can have some free space to allow for subsequent insertions. Those records would be marked as if they were "deleted" records.

Now, both insertions and deletions are fast as long as space is available on a block. If an insertion won't fit on the block, then some free space on some nearby block must be found and the auxiliary indices adjusted. The hope is enough space is nearby that a lot of blocks do not need to be reorganized. Alternatively, some out-of-sequence disk blocks may be used.

14.3.4 The B-tree uses all those ideas

The B-tree uses all the above ideas. It keeps the records in sorted order so they may be sequentially traversed. It uses a hierarchical index to minimize the number of disk reads. The index is elegantly adjusted with a recursive algorithm. The B-tree uses partially full blocks to speed insertions and deletions. In addition a B-tree minimizes waste by making sure the interior nodes are at least 1/2 full. A B-tree can handle an arbitrary number of insertions and deletions.

14.4 DEFINITION

A B-tree of order m (the maximum number of children for each node) is a tree which satisfies the following properties:

1. Every node has at most m children.
2. Every node (except root) has at least $^{m}/2$ children.
3. The root has at least two children if it is not a leaf node.
4. All leaves appear in the same level, and carry information.
5. A non-leaf node with k children contains k–1 keys.

Each internal node's elements act as separation values which divide its subtrees. For example, if an internal node has three child nodes (or subtrees) then it must have two separation values or elements a_1 and a_2. All values in the leftmost subtree will be less than a_1, all values in the middle subtree will be between a_1 and a_2, and all values in the rightmost subtree will be greater than a_2.

Internal nodes in a B-tree - nodes which are not leaf nodes - are usually represented as an ordered set of elements and child pointers. Every internal node contains a maximum of U children and - other than the root - a minimum of L children. For all internal nodes other than the root, the number of elements is one less than the number of child pointers; the number of elements is between L – 1 and U–1. The number U must be either 2L or 2L–1; thus each internal node is at least half full. This relationship between U and L implies that two half-full nodes can be joined to make a legal node, and one full node can be split into two legal nodes (if there is room to push one element up into the parent). These properties make it possible to delete and insert new values into a B-tree and adjust the tree to preserve the B-tree properties.

Leaf nodes have the same restriction on the number of elements, but have no children, and no child pointers.

The root node still has the upper limit on the number of children, but has no lower limit. For example, when there are fewer than L – 1 elements in the entire tree, the root will be the only node in the tree, and it will have no children at all.

A B-tree of depth n + 1 can hold about U times as many items as a B-tree of depth n, but the cost of search, insert, and delete operations grows with the depth of the tree. As with any balanced tree, the cost grows much more slowly than the number of elements.

Some balanced trees store values only at the leaf nodes, and so have different kinds of nodes for leaf nodes and internal nodes. B-trees keep values in every node in the tree, and may use the same structure for all nodes. However, since leaf nodes never have children, a specialized structure for leaf nodes in B-trees will improve performance.

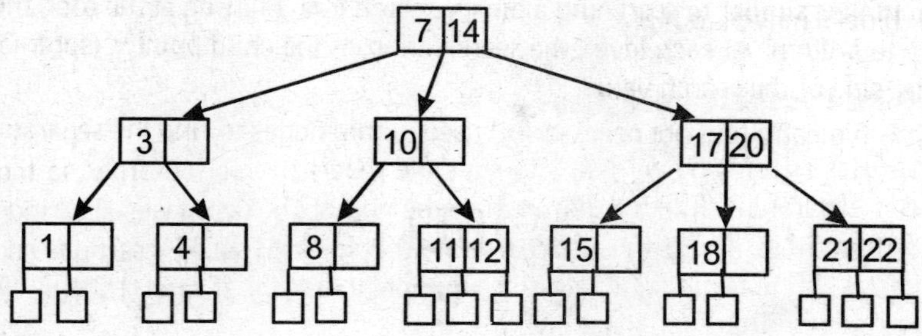

Fig.14.2 A B-tree of order 3.

14.4.1 Theorem

The minimum number of keys in a B-tree of order M ³ 2 and height h ³ 0 is n_h = 2 ém/2ù^h –l.

Extbf Proof Clearly, a B-tree of height zero contains at least one node. Consider a B-tree order M and height h > 0. By Definition⌋, each internal node (except the root) has at least |M/2| sub trees. This implies the minimum number of keys contained in an internal node is $\lceil M/2 \rceil - 1$.

The minimum number of keys a level zero is 1; at level one, $2(\lceil M/2 \rceil - 1)$; at level two, $2\lceil M/2 \rceil(\lceil M/2 \rceil - 1)$; at level three, $2\lceil M/2 \rceil^2(\lceil M/2 \rceil - 1)$; and so on.

Therefore the minimum number of keys in a B-tree of height h > 0 is given by the summation

$$n_h = 1 + 2(\lceil M/2 \rceil - 1)\sum_{i=0}^{h-1} \lceil M/2 \rceil^i$$

$$= 1 + 2(\lceil M/2 \rceil - 1)\left(\frac{\lceil M/2 \rceil^h - 1}{\lceil M/2 \rceil - 1}\right)$$

$$= 2\lceil M/2 \rceil^h - 1.$$

A corollary of Theorem is that the height, h, of a B-tree containing n keys is given by

$$h \le \log_{\lceil M/2 \rceil}((n + 1)/2)$$

Thus, we have shown that a B-tree satisfies the first criterion of a good balance condition — the height of B-tree with n internal nodes is O(logn). What remains to be shown is that the balance condition can be efficiently maintained during insertion and withdrawal operations. To see that it can, we need to look at an implementation.

14.5 BEST CASE AND WORST CASE HEIGHTS

The best case height of a B-Tree is:

$$\log_m n$$

The worst case height of a B-Tree is:

$$\log_{m/2} n$$

where m is the maximum number of children a node can have.

14.6 ALGORITHMS

Warning: the discussion below uses "element", "value", "key", "separator", and "separation value" to mean essentially the same thing. The terms are not clearly defined. There are some subtle issues at the root and leaves.

Search: Searching is similar to searching a binary search tree. Starting at the root, the tree is recursively traversed from top to bottom. At each level, the search chooses the child pointer (subtree) whose separation values are on either side of the search value.

Binary search is typically (but not necessarily) used within nodes to find the separation values and child tree of interest.

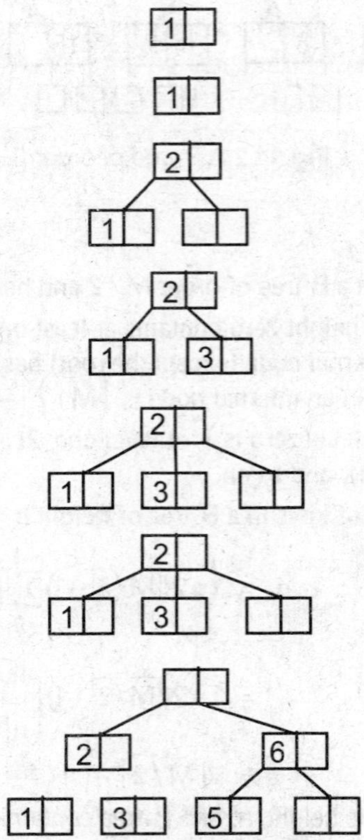

Fig. 14.3. A B Tree insertion example with each iteration.

All insertions start at a leaf node. To insert a new element

Search the tree to find the leaf node where the new element should be added. Insert the new element into that node with the following steps:

1. If the node contains fewer than the maximum legal number of elements, then there is room for the new element. Insert the new element in the node, keeping the node's elements ordered.
2. Otherwise the node is full, so evenly split it into two nodes.
   1. A single median is chosen from among the leaf's elements and the new element.
   2. Values less than the median are put in the new left node and values greater than the median are put in the new right node, with the median acting as a separation value.
   3. Insert the separation value in the node's parent, which may cause it to be split, and so on. If the node has no parent (i.e., the node was the root), create a new root above this node (increasing the height of the tree).

If the splitting goes all the way up to the root, it creates a new root with a single separator value and two children, which is why the lower bound on the size of internal nodes does not apply to the root. The maximum number of elements per node is U – 1. When a node is split, one element moves to the parent, but one element is added. So, it must be possible to divide the maximum number U – 1 of elements into two legal nodes. If this number is odd, then U = 2L and one of the new nodes contains (U – 2)/2 = L – 1 elements, and hence is a legal node, and the other contains one more element, and hence it is legal too. If U–l is even, then U = 2L–1, so there are 2L–2 elements in the node. Half of this number is L–1, which is the minimum number of elements allowed per node.

An improved algorithm supports a single pass down the tree from the root to the node where the insertion will take place, splitting any full nodes encountered on the way. This prevents the need to recall the parent nodes into memory, which may be expensive if the nodes are on secondary storage. However, to use this improved algorithm, we must be able to send one element to the parent and split the remaining U—2 elements into two legal nodes, without adding a new element. This requires U=2L rather than U- 2L-\, which accounts for why some textbooks impose this requirement in defining B-trees.

14.7 INSERTING ITEMS INTO A B-TREE

The algorithm for insertion into a B-Tree begins as do all the other search tree insertion algorithms: To insert item x, we begin at the root and conduct a search for it. Assuming the item is not already in the tree, the unsuccessful search will terminate at a leaf node. This is the point in the tree at which the x is inserted.

If the leaf node has fewer than M–1 keys in it, we simply insert the item in the leaf node and we are done. For example, consider a leaf node with n<M subtrees and n–1 keys of the form

$$T = \{T_0, k, k_2, T_2, ..., k_{n-1} T_{n-1}\}$$

For every new key inserted in the node, a new subtree is required too. In this case because T is a leaf, all its subtrees are empty trees. Therefore, when we insert item x, we really insert the pair of items (x, θ) . Suppose the key to be inserted falls between k_i and k_{i+1}, i.e., $k_i < x < k_{i+1}$. When we insert the pair (x, θ) into T we get the new leaf T given by

$$T' = \{T_0, k_1, T_1, k_2, T_2, ..., k_i, T_i, x, \theta, k_{i+1}, T_{i+1}, ..., k_{n-1}, T_{n-1}\}$$

What happens when the leaf is full? That is, suppose we wish to insert the pair, (x, θ) into a node T which already has M–1 keys. Inserting the pair in its correct position gives a result of the form

$$T' = \{T_0, k_1, T_1, k_2, T_2, ..., k_M, T_M\}$$

However, this is not a valid node in a B-tree of order M because it has M+l subtrees and M keys. The solution is to split node T in half as follows

$$T'_L = \{T_0, k_1, T_1, ..., k_{\lceil M/2 \rceil - 1}, T_{\lceil M/2 \rceil - 1}\}$$

$$T'_R = \{T_{\lceil M/2 \rceil}, k_{\lceil M/2 \rceil + 1}, T_{\lceil M/2 \rceil + 1}, ..., k_M, T_M\}$$

Note, T'_L is a valid B-tree node because it contains $\lceil M/2 \rceil$ subtrees and $\lceil M/2 \rceil - 1$keys. Similarly, T'_R is a valid B-tree node because it contains $\lceil (M+1)/2 \rceil$ subtrees and $\lceil (M+1)/2 \rceil$ –1 keys. Note that there is still a key left over, namely $k_{\lceil M/2 \rceil}$.

There are now two cases to consider--either T is the root or it is not. Suppose T is not the root. Where we once had the single node T, we now have the two nodes, T'_L and T'_R, and the left-over key, $k_{\lceil M/2 \rceil}$. This situation is resolved as follows: First T'_L, replaces T in the parent of T. Next, we take the pair ($k_{\lceil M/2 \rceil}$ T'_R) and recursively insert it in the parent of T.

Figure ⌋ illustrates this case for a B-tree of order three. Inserting the key 6 in the tree causes the leaf node to overflow. The leaf is split in two. The left half contains key 5; and the right, key 7; and key 6 is left over. The two halves are re-attached to the parent in the appropriate place with the left-over key between them.

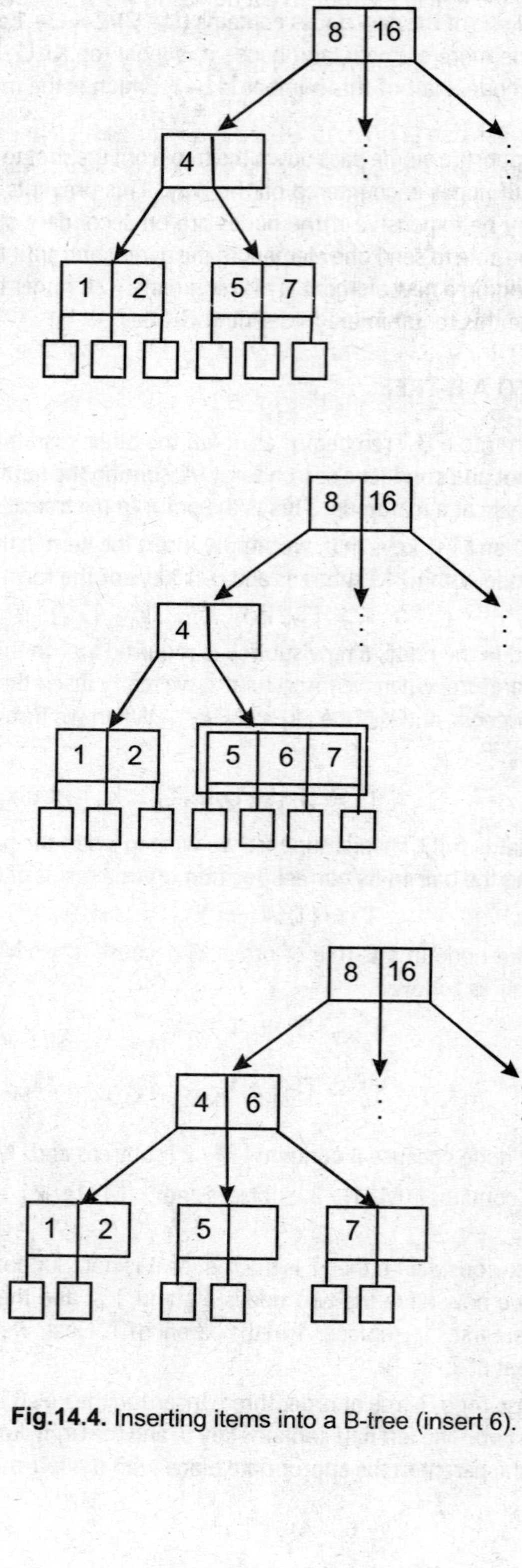

Fig.14.4. Inserting items into a B-tree (insert 6).

If the parent node fills up, then it too is split and the two new nodes are inserted in the grandparent. This process may continue all the way up the tree to the root. What do we do when the root fills up? When the root fills, it is also split. However, since there is no parent into which to insert the two new children, a new root is inserted above the old root. The new root will contain exactly two subtrees and one key, as allowed by Definition].

Figure] illustrates this case for a B-tree of order three. Inserting the key 3 in the tree causes the leaf node to overflow. Splitting the leaf and reattaching it causes the parent to overflow. Similarly, splitting the parent and reattaching it causes the grandparent to overflow but the grandparent is the root. The root is split and a new root is added above it.

14.8 DELETION FROM B-TREE

There are two popular strategies for deletion from a B-Tree.

- locate and delete the item, then restructure the tree to regain its invariants

  or

- do a single pass down the tree, but before entering (visiting) a node, restructure the tree so that once the key to be deleted is encountered, it can be deleted without triggering the need for any further restructuring

The algorithm below uses the former strategy.

There are two special cases to consider when deleting an element:

1. the element in an internal node may be a separator for its child nodes
2. deleting an element may put its node under the minimum number of elements and children.

Each of these cases will be dealt with in order.

14.8.1 Deletion from a leaf node

- Search for the value to delete.
- If the value is in a leaf node, it can simply be deleted from the node,
- If underflow happens, check siblings to either transfer a key or fuse the siblings together.
- if deletion happened from right child retrieve the max value of left child if there is no underflow in left child
- in vice-versa situation retrieve the min element from right

14.8.2 Deletion from an internal node

Each element in an internal node acts as a separation value for two subtrees, and when such an element is deleted, two cases arise. In the first case, both of the two child nodes to the left and right of the deleted element have the minimum number of elements, namely L–1. They can then be joined into a single node with 2L–2 elements, a number which does not exceed U–1 and so is a legal node. Unless it is known that this particular B-tree does not contain duplicate data, we must then also (recursively) delete the element in question from the new node.

In the second case, one of the two child nodes contains more than the minimum number of elements. Then a new separator for those subtrees must be found. Note that the largest element in the left subtree is still less than the separator. Likewise, the smallest element in the right subtree is the smallest element which is still greater than the separator. Both of those elements are in leaf nodes, and either can be the new separator for the two subtrees.

- If the value is in an internal node, choose a new separator (either the largest element in the left subtree or the smallest element in the right subtree), remove it from the leaf node it is in, and replace the element to be deleted with the new separator.
- This has deleted an element from a leaf node, and so is now equivalent to the previous case.

14.8.3 Rebalancing after deletion

If deleting an element from a leaf node has brought it under the minimum size, some elements must be redistributed to bring all nodes up to the minimum. In some cases the rearrangement will move the deficiency to the parent, and the redistribution must be applied iteratively up the tree, perhaps even to the root. Since the minimum element count doesn't apply to the root, making the root be the only deficient node is not a problem. The algorithm to rebalance the tree is as follows:

- If the right sibling has more than the minimum number of elements
  - o Add the separator to the end of the deficient node.
  - o Replace the separator in the parent with the first element of the right sibling.
  - o Append the first child of the right sibling as the last child of the deficient node
- Otherwise, if the left sibling has more than the minimum number of elements.
  - o Add the separator to the start of the deficient node.
  - o Replace the separator in the parent with the last element of the left sibling.
  - o Insert the last child of the left sibling as the first child of the deficient node
- If both immediate siblings have only the minimum number of elements
  - o Create a new node with all the elements from the deficient node, all the elements from one of its siblings, and the separator in the parent between the two combined sibling nodes.
  - o Remove the separator from the parent, and replace the two children it separated with the combined node.
  - o If that brings the number of elements in the parent under the minimum, repeat these steps with that deficient node, unless it is the root, since the root is permitted to be deficient.

The only other case to account for is when the root has no elements and one child. In this case it is sufficient to replace it with its only child.

The algorithm for removing items from a B-tree is similar to the algorithm for removing item from an AVL tree. That is, once the item to be removed has be found, it is pushed down the tree to a leaf node where it can be easily deleted. When an item is deleted from a node it is possible that the number of keys remaining is less than $\lceil M/2 \rceil - 1$. In this case, balancing is necessary.

The algorithm of balancing after deletion is like the balancing after insertion in that it progresses from the leaf node up the tree toward the root. Given a node T which has $\lceil M/2 \rceil - 2$ keys, there are four cases to consider.

In the first case, T is the root. If no keys remain, T becomes the empty tree. Otherwise, no balancing is needed because the root is permitted to have as few as two subtrees and one key. For the remaining cases T is not the root.

In the second case T has $\lceil M/2 \rceil - 2$ keys and it also has a sibling immediately on the left with at least $\lceil M/2 \rceil$ keys. The tree can be balanced by doing an LL rotation as shown in Figure J. Notice that after the rotation, both siblings have at least $\lceil M/2 \rceil - 1$ keys. Furthermore, the heights of the siblings remain unchanged. Therefore, the resulting tree is a valid B-tree.

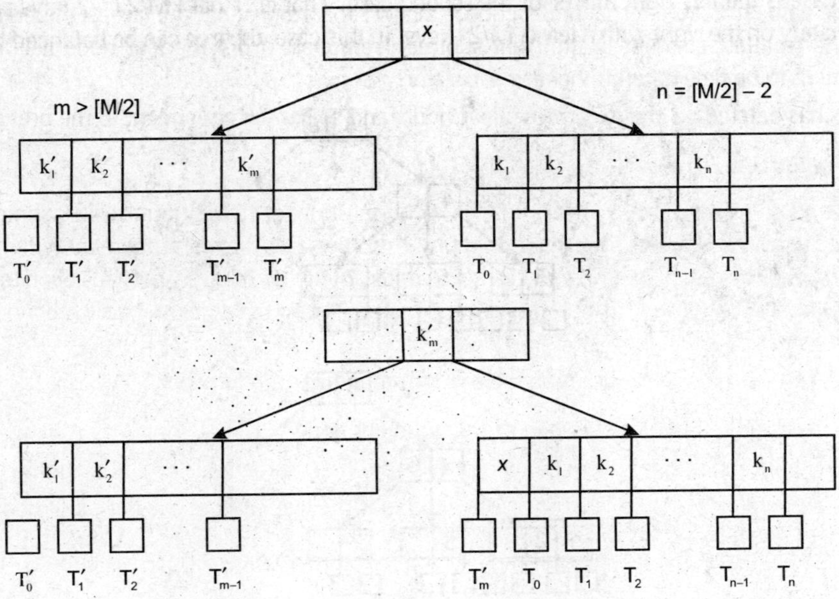

Fig.14.5. LL rotation in a B-tree.

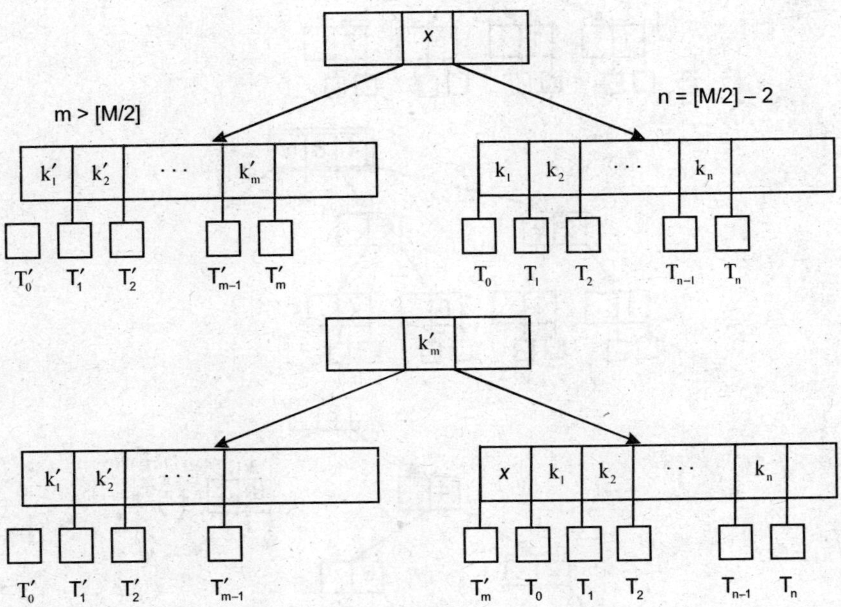

Fig.14.6. Merging nodes in a B-tree.

The third case is the left-right mirror of the second case. That is, T has $\lceil M/2 \rceil - 2$ keys and it also has a sibling immediately on the right with a least $\lceil M/2 \rceil$ keys. In this case, the tree can be balanced by doing an RR rotation .

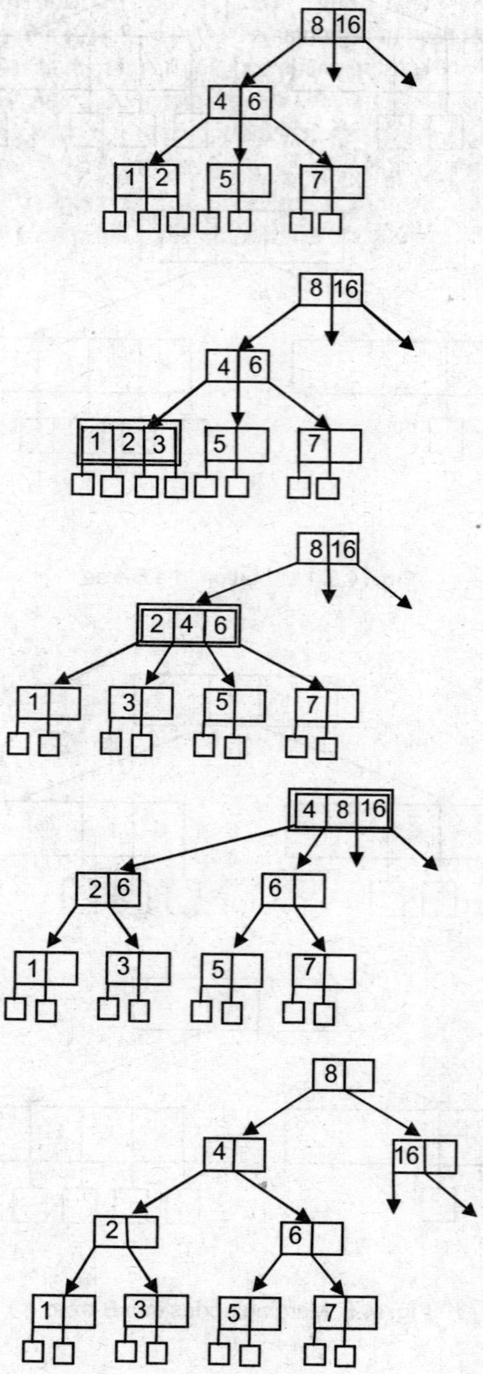

Fig.14.7. Inserting items into a B-tree (insert 3).

In the fourth and final case, T has $\lceil M/2 \rceil$ –2 keys, and its immediate sibling(s) have $\lceil M/2 \rceil$ –1 keys. In this case, the sibling(s) cannot give-up a key in a rotation because they already have the minimum number of keys. The solution is to merge T with one of its siblings as shown in Figure ⌋,

The merged node contains $\lceil M/2 \rceil$ –2 keys from T, $\lceil M/2 \rceil$ –1 keys from the sibling, and one key from the parent (the key x in Figure ⌋). The resulting node contains 2 $\lceil M/2 \rceil$ –2 keys altogether, which is M-2 if Mis even and M–1 if Mis odd. Either way, the resulting node contains no more than M-l keys and is a valid B-tree node. Notice that in this case a key has been removed from the parent of T. Therefore, it may be necessary to balance the parent. Balancing the parent may necessitate balancing the grandparent, and so on, up the tree to the root.

Notice that the height of the B-tree only increases when the root node splits. Furthermore, when the root node splits, the two halves are both attached under the new root. Therefore, the external nodes all remain at the same depth, as required by Definition ⌋.

14.9 RUNNING TIME ANALYSIS

The running time of the downward pass of the insertion algorithm is identical to that of an unsuccessful search (assuming the item to be inserted is not already in the tree). That is, for a B-tree of height h, the worst-case running time of the downward pass is

$$(h + l)(\lceil \log_2(M - 1) \rceil + 2)\, T\langle \text{compare} \rangle + O(h \log M).$$

The second pass of the insertion algorithm does the insertion and balances the tree if necessary. In the worst case, all of the nodes in the insertion path up to the root need to be balanced. Each time the insertPair method is invoked, it calls f indindex which has running time $(\lceil \log 2\ (M–1) \rceil + 2T\langle \text{compare} \rangle + O(hM)$. in the worst case. The additional time required to balance a node is O(M). Therefore, the worst-case running time of the upward pass is

$$(h+1)\ (\lceil \log_2 (M–1) \rceil +2)\ T\ \langle \text{compare} \rangle + O(hM).$$

$$(\lceil \log_2 (M–1) \rceil +2T\langle \text{compare} \rangle + O(hM).$$

Therefore, the total running time for insertion is

$$2\ (h + 1)\ (\lceil \log_2 (M–1) \rceil +2)T\ \langle \text{compare} \rangle + O(hM).$$

According to Theorem ⌋, the height of a B-tree is $h \le \log_{\lceil M-1 \rceil} ((n + 1.2)$, where n is the number of keys in the B-tree. If we assume that two keys can be compared in constant time, i.e., T $\langle$compare$\rangle$ = O(1) then the running time for insertion in a B-tree is simply O (M log n).

Solved Questions

1. Suppose that you have an application in which you want to use B-trees. Suppose that the computer you will be using has disk blocks holding 4096 bytes, the key is 4 bytes long, each child pointer (which is a disk block id) is 4 bytes, the parent is 4 bytes long and the data record reference (which is a disk block id along with a offset within the block) is 8 bytes. You have an application in which you want to store 1,000,000 items in your B-tree. What value would you select for t? What is the maximum number of disk pages that will be brought into main memory during a search? Remember that the root is kept in main memory at all times.

Ans. We want to select t so that a full node uses as much of a disk block as possible. In a full node there are 2t– 1 keys (4 bytes each), 2t– 1 data record references (8 bytes each), 2t child pointers (4 bytes each), a parent pointer (4 bytes), the number of keys (4 bytes) and the leaf bit (which we'll go ahead and assume takes 4 bytes though 1 bit would do). Hence we want to pick t as large as we can so that $12(2t-1)+4(2t)+12 = 32t \leq 4096$. Solving for t yields that we need t = 128. In class, we argued that the number of disk pages that must be read (d-1 using the notation from class) is at most $\log t(n + 1)/2$. Since $\log 128(n + 1)/2 = \log 128 \approx 2.7$ and the number of levels below the root must be an integer, at most 2 disk pages will need to be brought into main memory during a search.

Previous Year University Question

1. Show the result of inserting the following items in an initially empty B – tree of order 5.

   25, 31, 38, 76, 5, 60, 38, 8, 30, 15, 35, 17, 23, 53, 27, 43, 65, 48. [GBTU]

Exercises

1. For each of the following key sequences determine the binary search tree obtained when the keys are inserted one-by-one in the order given into an initially empty tree:
   1. 1,2,3,4,5,6,7.
   2. 4,2,1,3,6,5,7.
   3. 1,6,7,2,4,3,5.
2. For each of the binary search trees obtained in Exercise -J determine the tree obtained when the root is withdrawn.
3. Derive an expression for the total space needed to represent a tree of n internal nodes using each of the following classes:
   1. BinarySearchTree
   2. AVLTree,
   3. MWayTree
   4. BTree

   Hint: For the MWay Tree and BTree assume that the tree contains are k keys, where $k \geq n$
5. To delete a non-leaf node from a binary search tree, we swap it either with the smallest key its right subtree or with the largest key in its left subtree and then recursively delete it from the subtree. In a tree of n nodes, what its the maximum number of swaps needed to delete a key?
6. Devise an algorithm to compute the internal path length of a tree. What is the running time of your algorithm?
7. Devise an algorithm to compute the external path length of a tree. What is the running time of your algorithm?
8. Suppose that you are given a sorted sequence of n keys, $k_0 \leq k_1 \leq ... \leq k_{n-1}$ inserted into a binary search tree.
   1. What is the minimum height of a binary tree that contains n nodes.
   2. Devise an algorithm to insert the given keys into a binary search tree so that the height of the resulting tree is minimized.
   3. What is the running time of your algorithm?
9. Devise an algorithm to construct an AVL tree of a given height h that contains the minimum number of nodes. The tree should contain the keys 1, 2, 3, ..., N_h,

10. Consider what happens when we insert the keys 1.2.3,...,$2^{h+l} - 1$ one-by-one in the order given into an initially empty AVL tree for $h \geq 0$. Prove that the result is always a perfect tree of height h.
11. Devise an algorithm to select the kth key in a binary search tree. For example, given a tree with n nodes, k=0 selects the smallest key, k=n–1 selects the largest key, and k = [n/2] – 1 selects the median key.
12. Devise an algorithm to test whether a given binary search tree is AVL balanced. What is the running time of your algorithm?
13. Devise an algorithm that takes two values, a and b such that $a \leq b$, and which visits all the keys x in a binary search tree such that $a \leq x \leq b$. The running time of your algorithm should be O(N + log n), where N is the number of keys visited and n is the number of keys in the tree.
14. Devise an algorithm to merge the contents of two binary search trees into one. What is the running time of your algorithm?
15. Prove that a complete binary tree is AVL balanced.
16. For each of the following key sequences determine the 3-way search tree obtained when the keys are inserted one-by-one in the order given into an initially empty tree:
    1. 0,1,2,3,4,5,6,7,8,9.
    2. 3, 1,4,5,9,2,6,8,7,0.
    3. 2,7,1,8,4,5,9,0,3,6.

CHAPTER

15

BINOMIAL TREE

15.1 INTRODUCTION

A binomial tree is a general tree with a very special shape:

Definition (Binomial Tree) Thebinomial tree of order $k \geq 0$ with root R is the tree B_k defined as follows

1. If $k = 0$, $B_k = B_0 = \{R\}$.i.e., the binomial trees of order zero consists of a single node, R.
2. If $k > 0, B_k = \{R_1, B_0, B_1, ..., B_{k-}\}$i.e.) the binomial trees of order $k > 0$ comprises the root R, and k binomial subtrees, B_0, B_1 B_{k-1}.

Fig. 15.1 shows the first five binomial trees, B_0, B_4. It follows directly from Definition. that the root of B_k, the binomial tree of order k, has degree k. Since k may arbitrarily large, so too can the degree of the root. Furthermore, the root of a binomial tree has the largest fanout of any of the nodes in that tree.

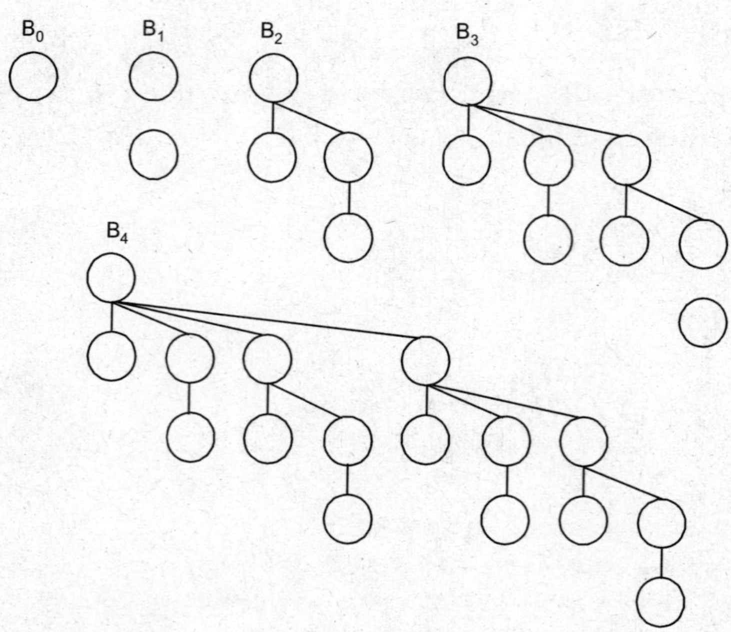

Fig.15.1 Binomial Trees B_0, B_1, ...B_4

The number of nodes in a binomial tree of order k is a function of k:

Theorem 1:The binomial tree of order k, B_k, contains 2^k nodes.

Proof (By induction). Let n_k be the number of nodes in B_k a binomial tree of order k.

Base Case By definition, B_0 consists a single node. Therefore $n_0 = 1 = 2^0$.

Inductive Hypothesis Assume that $n_k = 2^k$ for k = 0,1, 2,..., 1, for some 1 > 0. Consider the binomial tree of order 1 + 1:

$$B_{1+1} = \{R, B_0, B_1, B_2, ..., B_l\}.$$

Therefore the number of nodes in B_{1+L} is given by

$$n_1 + 1 = 1 + \sum_{i=0}^{1} n_i$$

$$= 1 + \sum_{i=0}^{1} 2^i$$

$$= 1 + \frac{2^{1+1} - 1}{2 - 1}$$

$$= 2^{1+1}.$$

Therefore, by induction on 1, $n_k = 2^k$ for all $k \geq 0$.

It follows from Theorem that binomial trees only come in sizes that are a power of two. i.e., $n_k \in \{1, 2, 4, 8, 16, ...\}$. Furthermore, for a given power of two, there is exactly one shape of binomial tree.

Theorem 2:The height of B_k, the binomial tree of order k, is k.

Proof (By induction). Let h_k be the height of B_k, a binomial tree of order k.

Base Case By definition, B_0 consists a single node. Therefore $h_0 = 0$.

Inductive Hypothesis Assume that $h_k = k$ for k = 0,1, 2,..., 1, for some $1 \geq 0$. Consider the binomial tree of order I + 1:

$$B_{1+1} = \{R, B_0, B_1, B_2, ..., B_1\}.$$

Therefore the height B_{1+1} is given by

$$h_{1+1} = 1 + \max_{0 \leq i \leq 1}$$

$$= 1 + \max_{0 \leq i \leq 1}$$

$$= 1 + 1.$$

Therefore, by induction on 1, $h_k = k$ for all $k \geq 0$.

Theorem 2 tells us that the height of a binomial tree of order k is k and Theorem 1 tells us that the number of nodes is $n_k = 2^k$. Therefore, the height of B_k is exactly O(log n)

Fig. 15.2 shows that there are two ways to think about the construction of binomial trees. The first way follows that binomial B_k consists of a root node to which the k binomial trees B_0, B_1,..., B_{k-1} are attached as shown in Fig.15.2 (a).

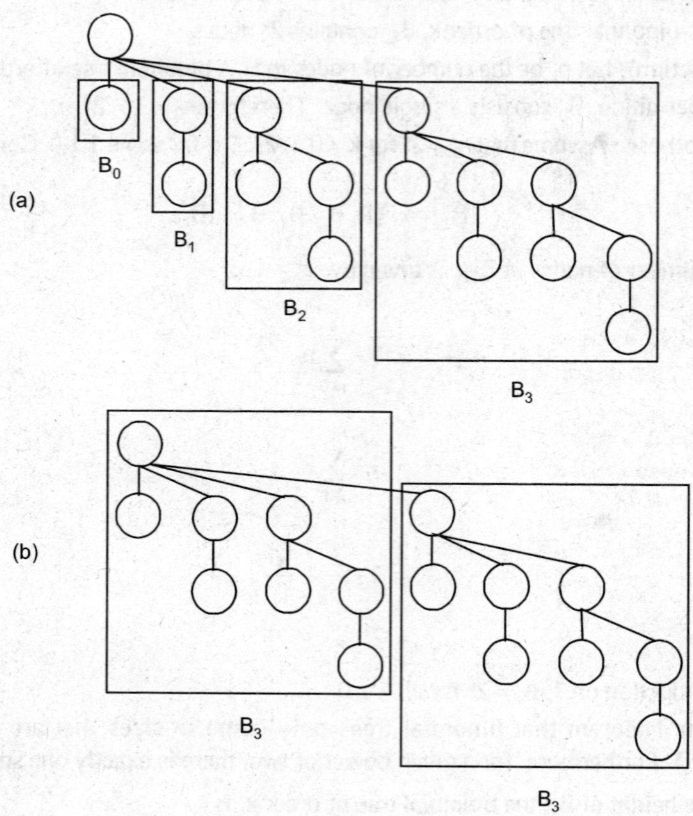

Fig. 15.2 Two Views of Binomial Tree B_4

Alternatively, we can think of B_k as being comprised of two binomial trees of order k–1. For example, Fig.15.2 (b) shows that B_4 is made up of two instances of B_3. In general, suppose we have two trees of order k – l, say B^1_{k-1} and B^2_{k-1} where $B^1_{k-1} = \{R^1, B^1_0, B^1_1, B^1_2, \ldots, B^1_{k-2}\}$. Then we can construct a binomial tree of order k by combining the trees to get

Why do we call B_k a binomial tree? It is because the number of nodes at a given depth in the tree is determined by the binomial coefficient. And the binomial coefficient derives its name from the binomial theorem. And the binomial theorem tells us how to compute the nth power of a binomial. And a binomial is an expression which consists of two terms, such as x + y. That is why it is called a binomial tree!

Theorem (Binomial Theorem) 3:The nth power of the binomial x + y for $n \geq 0$ is given by

$$(x + y)^n = \sum_{i=0}^{n} \binom{n}{i} x^i y^{n-1}$$

where $\binom{n}{1} = \dfrac{n!}{n(n-1)!}$ is called the binomial coefficient.

The following theorem gives the expression for the number of nodes at a given depth in a binomial tree:

Theorem 4: The number of nodes at level 1 in B_k, the binomial tree of order k, where $0 \leq 1 \leq k$, is given by the binomial coefficient $\binom{k}{1}$.

Proof (By induction): Let n_k (l) be the number of nodes at level 1 in B_k, a binomial tree of order k.

Base Case Since B_0 contains a single node, there is only one level in the tree,

l = 0, and exactly one node at that level. Therefore, $n_0(0) = 1 = \binom{0}{0}$

Inductive Hypothesis Assume that $n_k(1) = \binom{k}{1}$. for k = 0,1, 2,..., h, for some $h \geq 0$. The binomial tree of order h + 1 is composed of two binomial trees of height h, one attached under the root of the other. Hence, the number of nodes at level 1 in B_{h+l} is equal to the number of nodes at level 1 in B_h plus the number of nodes at level 1 – 1 in B_h:

$$n_{h+1}(1) = n_h(l) + n_h(l - l)$$

$$= \binom{h}{1} + \binom{h}{1-1}$$

$$= \frac{h!}{(h-1)!1!} + \frac{h!}{(h-(1-1))!(1-1)!}$$

$$= \frac{h!(h+1-1)+h!1}{(h+1-1)!1!}$$

$$= \frac{(h+1)!}{(h+1-1)!1!}$$

$$= \binom{h+1}{1}$$

Therefore by induction on h, $n_k(1) = \binom{k}{1}$

15.2 BINOMIAL HEAP

In computer science, a binomial heap is a heap similar to a binary heap but also supports quickly merging two heaps. This is achieved by using a special tree structure. It is important as an implementation of the mergeable heapabstract data type (also called meldable heap), which is a priority queue supporting merge operation.

15.2.1 Binomial tree

A binomial heap is implemented as a collection of binomial trees (compare with a binary heap, which has a shape of a single binary tree). A binomial tree is defined recursively:

- A binomial tree of order 0 is a single node.
- A binomial tree of order k has a root node whose children are roots of binomial trees of orders k – 1, k – 2, ..., 2, 1, 0 (in this order).

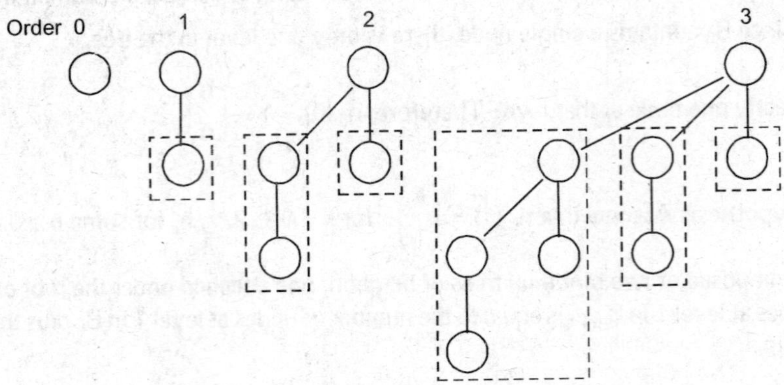

Fig.15.3 Binomial trees of order 0 to 3: Each tree has a root node with subtrees of all lower ordered binomial trees, which have been highlighted. For example, the order 3 binomial tree is connected to an order 2, 1, and 0 (highlighted as blue, green and red respectively) / binomial tree

A binomial tree of order k has 2^k nodes, height k.

Because of its unique structure, a binomial tree of order k can be constructed from two trees of order k–1 trivially by attaching one of them as the leftmost child of the other one. This feature is central to the merge operation of a binomial heap, which is its major advantage over other conventional heaps.

The name comes from the shape: a binomial tree of order n has $\binom{n}{d}$ nodes at depth d.

15.2.2 Structure of a binomial heap

A binomial heap is implemented as a set of binomial trees that satisfy the binomial heap properties:

- Each binomial tree in a heap obeys the minimum-heap property: the key of a node is greater than or equal to the key of its parent.
- There can only be either one or zero binomial trees for each order, including zero order.

The first property ensures that the root of each binomial tree contains the smallest key in the tree, which applies to the entire heap.

The second property implies that a binomial heap with n nodes consists of at most log n + 1 binomial trees. In fact, the number and orders of these trees are uniquely determined by the number of nodes n: each binomial tree corresponds to one digit in the binary representation of number n. For example number 13 is 1101 in binary, $2^3 + 2^2 + 2^0$, and thus a binomial heap with 13 nodes will consist of three binomial trees of orders 3, 2, and 0 (see figure below).

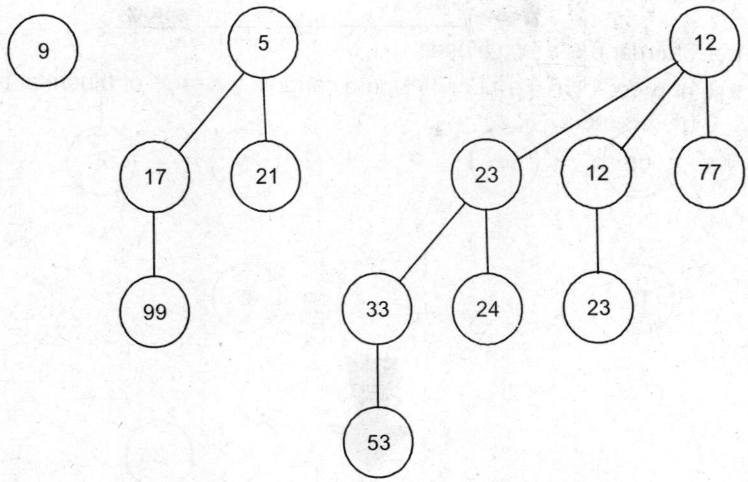

Fig.15.4 Example of a binomial heap containing 13 nodes with distinct J keys. The heap consists of three binomial trees with orders 0, 2, and 3. J

15.3 IMPLEMENTATION

Because no operation requires random access to the root nodes of the binomial trees, the roots of the binomial trees can be stored in a linked list, ordered by increasing order of the tree.

15.3.1 Merge

As mentioned above, the simplest and most important operation is the merging of two binomial trees of the same order within two binomial heaps. Due to the structure of binomial trees, they can be merged trivially. As their root node is the smallest element within the tree, by comparing the two keys, the smaller of them is the minimum key, and becomes the new root node. Then the other tree become a subtree of the combined tree. This operation is basic to the complete merging of two binomial heaps.

```
function merge Tree (p, q)
    if p. root <= q.root
        return p. add Sub Tree (q)
else
    return q. add Sub Tree (p)
```

The operation of merging two heaps is perhaps the most interesting and can be used as a subroutine in most other operations. The lists of roots of both heaps are traversed simultaneously, similarly as in the merge algorithm.

If only one of the heaps contains a tree of order j, this tree is moved to the merged heap. If both heaps contain a tree of order j, the two trees are merged to one tree of order j + 1 so that the minimum-heap property is satisfied. Note that it may later be necessary to merge this tree with some other tree of order j + 1 present in one of the heaps. In the course of the algorithm, we need to examine at most three trees of any order (two from the two heaps we merge and one composed of two smaller trees).

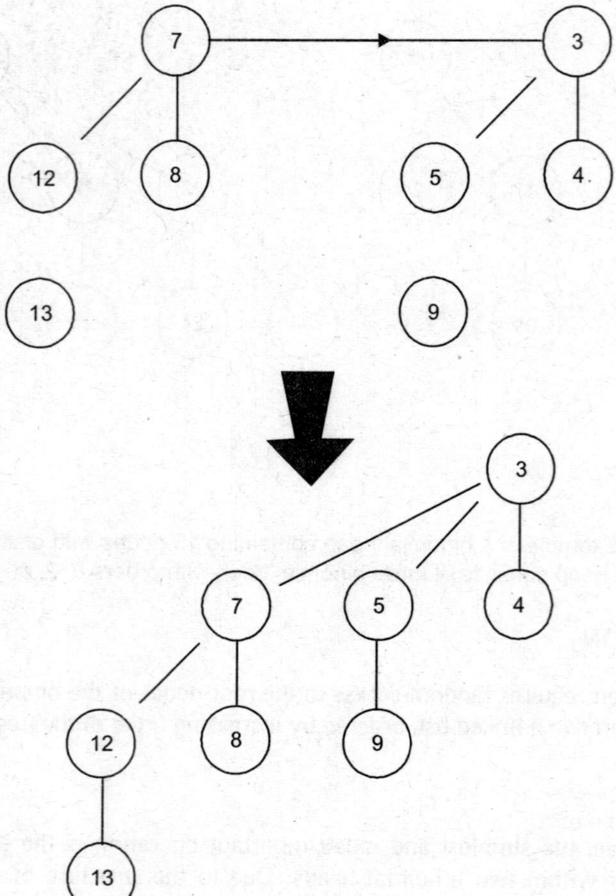

Fig.15.5 To merge two binomial trees of the same order, first compare the root key. Since 7 > 3, the black tree on the left(with root node 7) is attached to the grey tree on the right (with root node 3) as a subtree. The result is a tree of order 3.

Because each binomial tree in a binomial heap corresponds to a bit in the binary representation of its size, there is an analogy between the merging of two heaps and the binary addition of the sizes of the two heaps, from right-to-left. Whenever a carry occurs during addition, this corresponds to a merging of two binomial trees during the merge.

Each tree has order at most log n and therefore the running time is O (log n).

```
function merge(p, q)
    whilenot ( p.end() and q.end() )
        tree = mergeTree(p.currentTree(), q.currentTree())
        ifnot heap.currentTree().empty()
            tree = mergeTree(tree, heap.currentTree())
            heap.addTree(tree)
        else
            heap. addTree(tree)
        heap.next() p.next() q.next()
```

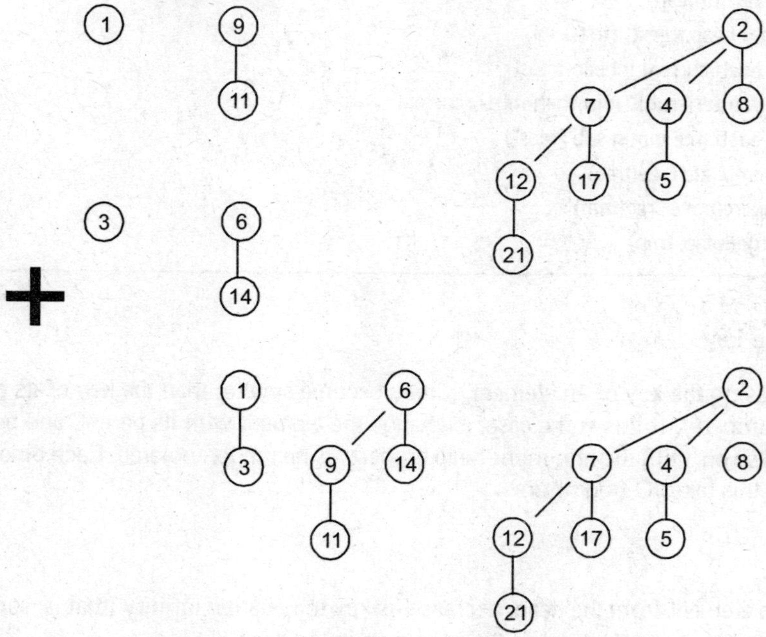

Fig.15.6 This shows the merger of two binomial heaps. This is accomplished by merging two binomial trees of the same order one by one. If the resulting merged tree has the same order as one binomial tree I in one of the two heaps, then those two are merged again

15.3.2 Insert

Inserting a new element to a heap can be done by simply creating a new heap containing only this element and then merging it with the original heap. Due to the merge, insert takes O (log n) time,however it has an amortized time of O (1) (i.e. constant).

15.3.3 Find minimum

To find the minimum element of the heap, find the minimum among the roots of the binomial trees. This can again be done easily in O(log n) time, as there are just O (log n) trees and hence roots to examine.

By using a pointer to the binomial tree that contains the minimum element, the time for this operation can be reduced to O (1). The pointer must be updated when performing any operation other than Find minimum. This can be done in O (log n) without raising the running time of any operation.

15.3.4 Delete minimum

To delete the minimum element from the heap, first find this element, remove it from its binomial tree, and obtain a list of its subtrees. Then transform this list of subtrees into a separate binomial heap by reordering them from smallest to largest order. Then merge this heap with the original heap. Since each tree has at most log n children, creating this new heap is O (log n). Merging heaps is O (log n), so the entire delete minimum operation is O (log n).

```
function deleteMin(heap)
        min = heap.trees().first()
        for each current inheap.trees()
            ifcurrent.rooK min then min = current
        for each tree inmin.subTrees()
            tmp.addTree(tree)
        heap .removeTree(min)
        merge(heap, tmp)
```

15.3.5 Decrease key

After decreasing the key of an element, it may become smaller than the key of its parent, violating the minimum-heap property. If this is the case, exchange the element with its parent, and possibly also with its grandparent, and so on, until the minimum-heap property is no longer violated. Each binomial tree has height at most log n, so this takes O (log n) time.

15.3.6 Delete

To delete an element from the heap, decrease its key to negative infinity (that is, some value lower than any element in the heap) and then delete the minimum in the heap.

15.3.7 Performance

All of the following operations work in 0(log n) time on a binomial heap with n elements:

- Insert a new element to the heap
- Find the element with minimum key
- Delete the element with minimum key from the heap
- Decrease key of a given element
- Delete given element from the heap
- Merge two given heaps to one heap

Finding the element with minimum key can also be done in O (1) by using an additional pointer to the minimum.

15.4 FIBONACCI HEAP

In computer science, a Fibonacci heap is a heap data structure consisting of a collection of trees. It has a better amortized running time than a binomial heap. Fibonacci heaps were developed by Michael L. Fredman and Robert E. Tarjan in 1984 and first published in a scientific journal in 1987. The name of Fibonacci heap comes from Fibonacci numbers which are used in the running time analysis.

Operations insert, find minimum, decrease key, and merge (union) work in constant amortized time Operations delete and delete minimum work in O (log n) amortized time. This means that starting from an empty data structure, any sequence of a operations from the first group and b operations from the second group would take O (a + b log n) time. In a binomial heap such a sequence of operations would take O ((a + b)log (n)) time. A Fibonacci heap is thus better than a binomial heap when b is asymptotically smaller than a.

Using Fibonacci heaps for priority queues improves the asymptotic running time of important algorithms, such as Dijkstra's algorithm for computing Shortest paths.

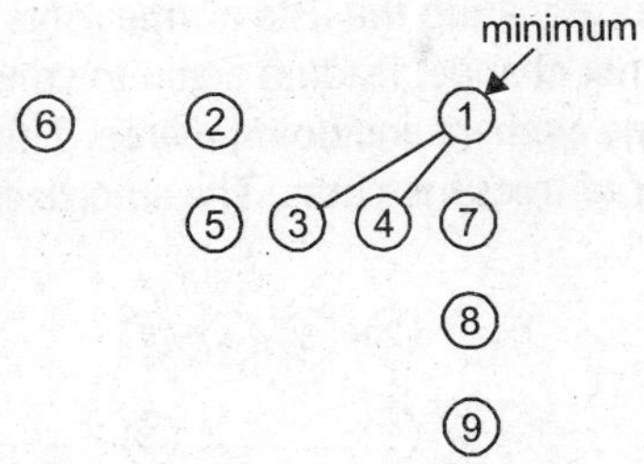

Fig.15.7 Example of a Fibonacci heap. It has three trees of degrees 0, 1 and 3. Three vertices are marked (shown in blue). Therefore the potential of the heap is 9.

A Fibonacci heap is a collection of trees satisfying the minimum-heap property, that is, the key of a child is always greater than or equal to the key of the parent. This implies that the minimum key is always at the root of one of the trees. Compared with binomial heaps, the structure of a Fibonacci heap is more flexible. The trees do not have a prescribed shape and in the extreme case the heap can have every element in a separate tree or a single tree of depth n. This flexibility allows some operations to be executed in a "lazy" manner, postponing the work for later operations. For example merging heaps is done simply by concatenating the two lists of trees, and operation decrease key sometimes cuts a node from its parent and forms a new tree.

However at some point some order needs to be introduced to the heap to achieve the desired running time. In particular, degrees of nodes (here degree means the number of children) are kept quite low: every node has degree at most O (log n) and the size of a subtree rooted in a node of degree k is at least Fk + 2, where Fk is the kthFibonacci number. This is achieved by the rule that we can cut at most one child of each non-root node. When a second child is cut, the node itself needs to be cut from its parent and becomes the root of a new tree (see Proof of degree bounds, below). The number of trees is decreased in the operation delete minimum, where trees are linked together.

As a result of a relaxed structure, some operations can take a long time while others are done very quickly. In the amortized running time analysis we pretend that very fast operations take a little bit longer than they actually do. This additional time is then later subtracted from the actual running time of slow operations. The amount of time saved for later use is measured at any given moment by a potential function. The potential of a Fibonacci heap is given by

Potential = t + 2 m where t is the number of trees in the Fibonacci heap, and m is the number of marked nodes. A node is marked if at least one of its children was cut since this node was made a child of another node (all roots are unmarked).

Thus, the root of each tree in a heap has one unit of time stored. This unit of time can be used later to link this tree with another tree at amortized time 0. Also, each marked node has two units of time stored. One can be used to cut the node from its parent. If this happens, the node becomes a root and the second unit of time will remain stored in it as in any other root.

15.5 IMPLEMENTATION OF OPERATIONS

To allow fast deletion and concatenation, the roots of all trees are linked using a circular, doubly linked list. The children of each node are also linked using such a list. For each node, we maintain its number of children and whether the node is marked. Moreover we maintain a pointer to the root containing the minimum key. Operation find minimum is now trivial because we keep the pointer to the node containing it. It does not change the potential of the heap, therefore both actual and amortized cost is constant. As mentioned above, merge is implemented simply by concatenating the lists of tree roots of the two heaps. This can be done in constant time and the potential does not change, leading again to constant amortized time. Operation insert works by creating a new heap with one element and doing merge. This takes constant time, and the potential increases by one, because the number of trees increases. The amortized cost is thus still constant.

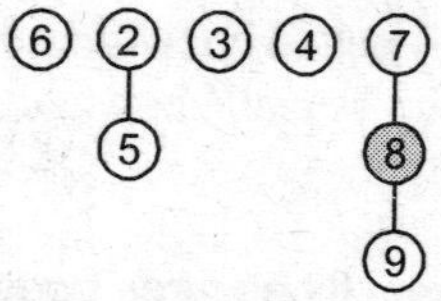

Fig.15.8 Fibonacci heap from Figure 1 after first phase of extract minimum. Node with key 1 (the minimum) was deleted and its children were added as separate trees.

Operation extract minimum (same as delete minimum) operates in three phases. First we take the root containing the minimum element and remove it. Its children will become roots of new trees. If the number of children was d, it takes time O (d) to process all new roots and the potential increases by d – 1. Therefore the amortized running time of this phase is O (d) = O (log n).

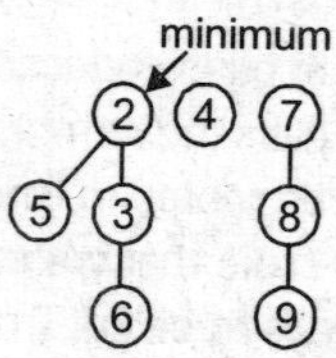

Fig.15.9 Fibonacci heap from Figure 1 after extract minimum is completed. First, nodes 3 and 6 are linked together. Then the result is linked with tree rooted at node 2. Finally, the new minimum is found.

However to complete the extract minimum operation, we need to update the pointer to the root with minimum key. Unfortunately there may be up to n roots we need to check. In the second phase we therefore decrease the number of roots by successively linking together roots of the same degree. When two roots u and v have the same degree, we make one of them a child of the other so that the one with smaller key remains the root. Its degree will increase by one. This is repeated until every root has a different degree. To find trees of the same degree efficiently we use an array of length O (log n) in which we keep a pointer to one root of each degree. When a second root is found of the same degree, the two are linked and the array is updated. The actual running time is O (log n + m) where m is the number of roots at the beginning of the second phase. At the end we will have at most O (log n) roots (because each has a different degree). Therefore the difference in the potential function from before this phase to after O (log n + m) + O (log n) – m = O (log n)

Since we can scale up the units of potential stored at insertion in each node by the constant factor in the O (m) part of the actual cost for this phase.

In the third phase we check each of the remaining roots and find the minimum. This takes O (log n) time and the potential does not change. The overall amortized running time of extract minimum is therefore O (log n).

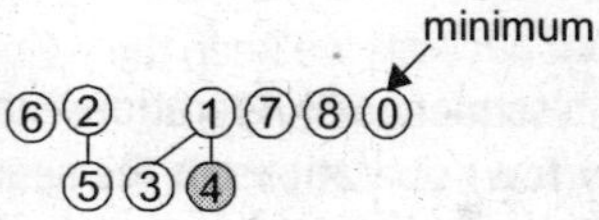

Fig. 15.10 Fibonacci heap from Figure 1 after decreasing key of node 9 to 0. This node as well as its two marked ancestors are cut from the tree rooted at 1 and placed as new roots.

Operation decrease key will take the node, decrease the key and if the heap property becomes violated (the new key is smaller than the key of the parent), the node is cut from its parent. If the parent is not a root, it is marked. If it has been marked already, it is cut as well and its parent is marked. We continue upwards until we reach either the root or an unmarked node. In the process we create some number, say k, of new trees. Each of these new trees except possibly the first one was marked originally but as a root it will become unmarked. One node can become marked. Therefore the potential decreases by at least k – 2. The actual time to perform the cutting was O (k), therefore the amortized running time is constant.

Finally, operation delete can be implemented simply by decreasing the key of the element to be deleted to minus infinity, thus turning it into the minimum of the whole heap. Then we call extract minimum to remove it. The amortized running time of this operation is O (log n).

15.6 PROOF OF DEGREE BOUNDS

The amortized performance of a Fibonacci heap depends on the degree (number of children) of any tree root being O (log n), where n is the size of the heap. Here we show that the size of the (sub)tree rooted at any node x of degree d in the heap must have size at least F_{d+2}, where Fk is the kth Fibonacci number. The degree bound follows from this and the fact (easily proved by induction) that $F_{d+2} \geq \varphi^d$ for all integers $d \geq 0$, where $\varphi = (1+\sqrt{5})/2 = 1.62$. (We then have $n \geq F_{d+2} \geq \varphi^d$, and taking the log to base φ of both sides gives $d \leq \log\varphi^n$ as required).

Consider any node x somewhere in the heap (x need not be the root of one of the main trees). Define size(x) to be the size of the tree rooted at x (the number of descendants of x, including x itself). We prove by induction on the height of x (the length of a longest simple path from x to a descendant leaf), that size (x) $\geq F_{d+2}$, where d is the degree of x.

Base case: If x has height 0, then d = 0, and size(x) = 1 = F_2.

Inductive case: Suppose x has positive height and degree d > 0. Let $y_1, y_2, \ldots, y_d$ be the children of x, indexed in order of the times they were most recently made children of x(y_l being the earliest and y_d the latest), and let $c_1, c_2, \ldots, c_d$ be their respective degrees. We claim that $c_i \geq i - 2$ for each i with $2 \leq i \leq d$: Just before y. was made a child x, $y_1, \ldots, y_{i-1}$ were already children of x, and so x had degree at least i – 1 at that time. Since trees are combined only when the degrees of their roots are equal, it must have been that y_i also had degree at least i – 1 at the time it became a child of x. From that time to the present, y_i can only have lost at most one child (as guaranteed by the marking process), and so its current degree ci is at least i – 2. This proves the claim.

Since the heights of all the y_i are strictly less than that of x, we can apply the inductive hypothesis to them to get size $(y_i) \geq F_{ci+2} \geq F_{ci\,(i-2)+2} = F_i$. The nodes x and y_1 each contribute at least 1 to size(x), and so we have

$$\text{size}(x) \geq \sum_{i=2}^{d} \text{size}(y_1) \geq 2 + \sum_{i=2}^{d} F_i = 1 + \sum_{i=2}^{d} F_i.$$

A routine induction proves that $1 + \sum_{i=0}^{d} F = f_{d+2}$ for any $d \geq 0$, which gives the desired lower bound on size(x).

Worst case

Although the total running time of a sequence of operations starting with an empty structure is bounded by the bounds given above, some (very few) operations in the sequence can take very long to complete (in particular delete and delete minimum have linear running time in the worst case). For this reason Fibonacci heaps and other amortized data structures may not be appropriate for real-time systems.

Solved Questions

1. What is the difference between binary heaps and binomial heaps?

Ans. The key difference between a binary heap and a binomial heap is how the heaps are structured. In a binary heap, the heap is a single tree, which is a complete binary tree. In a binomial heap, the heap is a collection of smaller trees (that is, a forest of trees), each of which is a binomial tree. A complete binary tree can be built to hold any number of elements, but the number of elements in a binomial tree of some order n is always 2^n. Consequently, we only need one complete binary tree to back a binary heap, but we may need multiple binomial trees to back a binomial heap. Interestingly, the orders of the binomial trees used in a binomial heap correspond to the 1 bits set in the binary representation of the number of elements in the forest.

The reason for organizing binomial heaps as they are is that a binomial tree of order n always has exactly 2^n nodes in it. This allows us to make assumptions about the number of elements in the binomial tree without actually having to inspect the structure of that tree. On the other hand, a complete binary tree of some height h may have a variable number of nodes in it depending on how the last row is filled out. The fact that each of the children must have a very precisely-defined structure can also be used to prove that the number of children is at most O(log n), where n is the total number of nodes in the heap, which means that the cost of a delete-min is not too large.

An important detail behind this is that a binomial heap is not any tree that happens to have k children. It's a tree that's rigorously defined as

The binomial tree of order 0 is a single node, and

The binomial tree of order n is a single node with binomial trees of order 0, 1, 2, ..., n - 1 as children.

(Technically, the order 0 special case isn't necessary here). You can see this here:

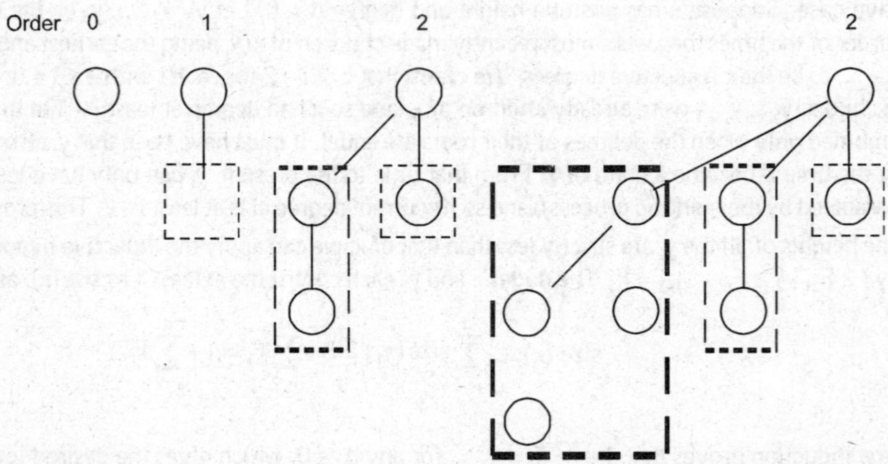

Note that there is exactly one tree of each order, with no flexibility at all in the number or position of the nodes.

However, an important alternative definition is the following:

- The binomial tree of order 0 is a single node, and
- The binomial tree of order n is two binomial trees of order n - 1, with one of the trees made a child of the other.

Using this second definition, it' s a quick induction proof to show that the number of nodes in the tree is 2^n. As a base case, a tree of order 0 has $2^0 = 1$ nodes as required. For the inductive step, if we have two trees of order n – 1, they collectively have $2^{n-1} + 2^{n-1} = 2^n$ nodes as required. Thus the total number of nodes in a binomial tree of order n is exactly 2^n.

The idea for a heap that you' re describing in your final paragraph does not always lead to an efficient runtime. In particular, if you have trees with a huge branching factor and no other structural constraints, then you could in theory build a heap of n nodes consisting of a single node with (n - 1) children. In that case, after deleting the minimum element from the heap, you' d have to look at all n - 1 children to determine which was the new minimum, giving a runtime of O(n). The other structural constraints on trees like complete binary trees, binomial trees, etc. guarantee that this worst-case doesn' t happen.

Previous Year University Question

1. Define Fibonacci heap. Differentiate between Binomial and Fibonacci heap. [GBTU]
2. What are binomial heaps? Explain with example. [KU]

Exercise

1. Write an algorithm to directly insert a node into binomial heap without using Binomial-Heap Union.
2. Explain p pseudo code for Binomial Heal Merge.
3. Prove that binomial tree B_k contains 2^k nodes of which $\binom{k}{i}$ are at depth i, $0 \le i \le k$.
4. Show that if only the mergeable-heap operational are supported, the maximum degree D(n) in an n-node Fiboracci heap is at most $\lceil \lg n \rceil$.

CHAPTER

16

GRAPH

16.1 INTRODUCTION

A graph is an abstract representation of a set of objects where some pairs of the objects are connected by links. The interconnected objects are represented by mathematical abstractions called vertices, and the links that connect some pairs of vertices are called edges. Typically, a graph is depicted in diagrammatic form as a set of dots for the vertices, joined by lines or curves for the edges. Graphs are one of the objects of study in discrete mathematics.

The edges may be directed (asymmetric) or undirected (symmetric). For example, if the vertices represent people at a party, and there is an edge between two people if they shake hands, then this is an undirected graph, because if person A shook hands with person B, then person B also shook hands with person A. On the other hand, if the vertices represent people at a party, and there is an edge from person A to person B when person A knows of person B, then this graph is directed, because knowing of someone is not necessarily a symmetric relation (that is, one person knowing of another person does not necessarily imply the reverse; for example, many fans may know of a celebrity, but the celebrity is unlikely to know of all their fans). This latter type of graph is called a directed graph and the edges are called directed edges or arcs; in contrast, a graph where the edges are not directed is called undirected.

Vertices are also called nodes or points, and edges are also called lines. Graphs are the basic subject studied by graph theory. The word "graph" was first used in this sense by James Joseph Sylvester in 1878.

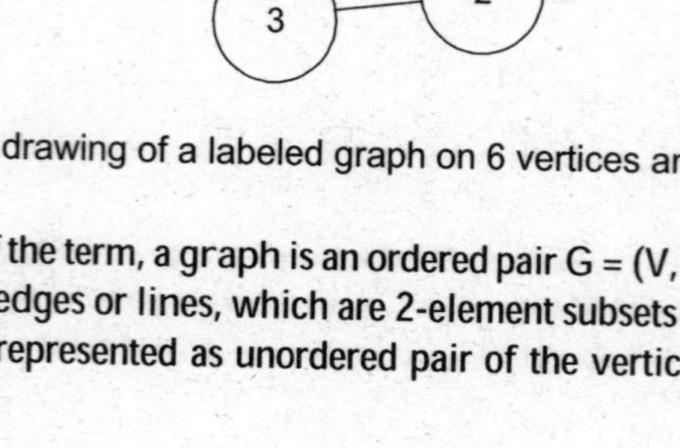

Fig. 16.1 A drawing of a labeled graph on 6 vertices and 7 edges.

In the most common sense of the term, a graph is an ordered pair G = (V, E) comprising a set V of vertices or nodes together with a set E of edges or lines, which are 2-element subsets of V (i.e., an edge is related with two vertices, and the relation is represented as unordered pair of the vertices with respect to the particular edge). To avoid ambiguity, this type of graph may be described precisely as undirected and simple.

Other senses of graph stem from different conceptions of the edge set. In one more generalized notion, E is a set together with a relation of incidence that associates with each edge two vertices. In another generalized notion, E is a multiset of unordered pairs of (not necessarily distinct) vertices. Many authors call this type of object a multigraph or pseudograph.

The vertices belonging to an edge are called the ends, endpoints, or end vertices of the edge. A vertex may exist in a graph and not belong to an edge. V and E are usually taken to be finite, and many of the well-known results are not true (or are rather different) for infinite graphs because many of the arguments fail in the infinite case. The order of a graph is | V | (the number of vertices). A graph's size is | E |, the number of edges. The degree of a vertex is the number of edges that connect to it, where an edge that connects to the vertex at both ends (a loop) is counted twice.

For an edge {u, v}, graph theorists usually use the somewhat shorter notation uv.

16.2 ADJACENCY RELATION

The edges E of an undirected graph G induce a symmetric binary relation ~ on V that is called the adjacency relation of G. Specifically, for each edge {u, v} the vertices u and v are said to be adjacent to one another, which is denoted u ~ v.

16.3 TYPES OF GRAPHS

As stated above, in different contexts it may be useful to define the term graph with different degrees of generality. Whenever it is necessary to draw a strict distinction, the following terms are used. Most commonly, in modern texts in graph theory, unless stated otherwise, graph means "undirected simple finite graph".

16.3.1 Undirected graph

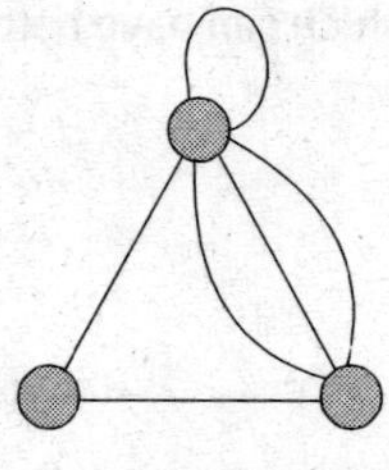

Fig. 16.2 A general example of a graph (actually, a pseudograph) with three vertices and six edges.

A graph in which edges have no orientation, i.e., they are not ordered pairs, but sets {u, v} (or 2-multisets) of vertices.

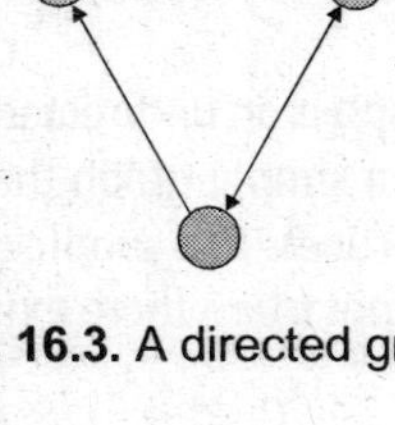

Fig. 16.3. A directed graph.

A directed graph or digraph is an ordered pair D = (,) with

- a set whose elements are called vertices or nodes and
- a set of ordered pairs of vertices, called arcs directed edges or arrows.

An arc a = (x, y) is considered to be directed from x to y y is called the head and x is called the tail of the arc y is said to be a direct successor of x, and x is said to be a direct predecessor of y. If a path leads from x to y, then y is said to be a successor of x and reachable from x, and x is said to be a predecessor of y. The arc (y, x) is called the arc (x, y) inverted.

A directed graph D is called symmetric if, for every arc in D, the corresponding inverted arc also belongs to D. symmetric loop less directed graph D = (,) is equivalent to a simple undirected graph = (,), where the pairs of inverse arcs in correspond 1- to-1 with the edges in thus the edges in G number = A 2, or half the number of arcs in D.

variation on this definition is the oriented graph in which not more than one of (, y) and (y, x) may be arcs.

16.3.3 Mixed graph

A mixed graph G is a graph in which some edges may be directed and some may be undirected. It is written as an ordered triple G = (V, E, A) with V, E, and A has been already defined. Directed and undirected graphs are special cases.

16.3.4 Multigraph

A loop is an edge (directed or undirected) which starts and ends on the same vertex; these may be permitted or not permitted according to the application. In this context, an edge with two different ends is called a link.

The term "multigraph" is generally understood to mean that multiple edges (and sometimes loops) are allowed. Where graphs are defined so as to allow loops and multiple edges, a multigraph is often defined to mean a graph without loops, however, where graphs are defined so as to disallow loops and multiple edges, the term is often defined to mean a "graph" which can have both multipie edges and loops, although many use the term "pseudograph" for this meaning.

16.3.5 Simple graph

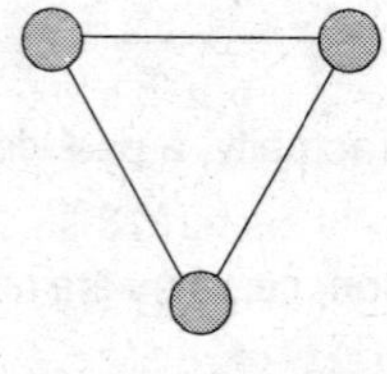

Fig.16.4. A simple graph with three vertices and three edges. Each vertex has degree two, so this is also a regular graph.

As opposed to a multigraph, a simple graph is an undirected graph that has no loops and no more than one edge between any two different vertices. In a simple graph the edges of the graph form a set (rather than a multiset) and each edge is a pair of distinct vertices. In a simple graph with n vertices every vertex has a degree that is less than n (the converse, however, is not true - there exist non-simple graphs with n vertices in which every vertex has a degree smaller than n).

16.3.6 Weighted graph

A graph is a weighted graph if a number (weight) is assigned to each edge. Such weights might represent, for example, costs, lengths or capacities, etc. depending on the problem. The weight of the graph is the sum of the weights given to all edges.

16.3.7 Half-edges, loose edges

In exceptional situations it is even necessary to have edges with only one end, called half-edges, or no ends (loose edges).

16.3.8 Regular graph

A regular graph is a graph where each vertex has the same number of neighbors, i.e., every vertex has the same degree or valency. A regular graph with vertices of degree k is called a k-regular graph or regular graph of degree k.

16.3.9 Complete graph

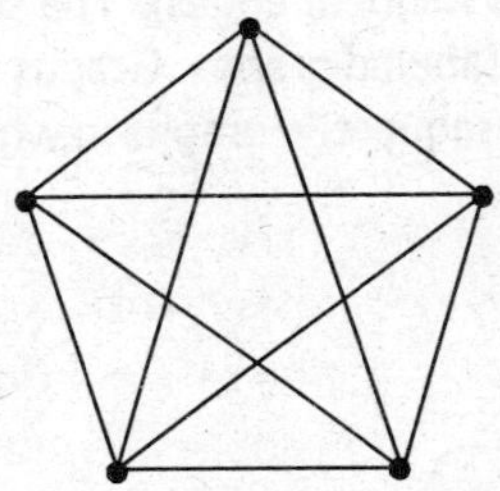

Fig. 16.5. A complete graph with 5 vertices. Each vertex has an edge to every other vertex-Main article: Complete graph

Complete graphs have the feature that each pair of vertices has an edge connecting them.

16.3.10 Finite and infinite graphs

A finite graph is a graph G-(V,E) such that V and E are finite sets. An infinite graph is one with an infinite set of vertices or edges or both. Most commonly in graph theory it is implied that the graphs discussed are finite. If the graphs are infinite, that is usually specifically stated.

16.3.11 Graph classes in terms of connectivity

In an undirected graph G, two vertices u and v are called connected if G contains a path from u to v. Otherwise, they are called disconnected. A graph is called connected if every pair of distinct vertices in the graph is connected; otherwise, it is called disconnected.

A graph is called k-vertex-connected or k-edge-connected if no set of k–1 vertices (respectively, edges) exists that disconnects the graph. A k:-vertex-connected graph is often called simply k-connected.

A directed graph is called weakly connected if replacing all of its directed edges with undirected edges produces a connected (undirected) graph. It is strongly connected or strong if it contains a directed path from u to v and a directed path from v to u for every pair of vertices u, v.

16.4 PROPERTIES OF GRAPHS

Two edges of a graph are called adjacent (sometimes coincident) if they share a common vertex. Two arrows of a directed graph are called consecutive if the head of the first one is at the nock (notch end) of the second one. Similarly, two vertices are called adjacent if they share a common edge (consecutive if they are at the notch and at the head of an arrow), in which case the common edge is said to join the two vertices. An edge and a vertex on that edge are called incident.

The graph with only one vertex and no edges is called the trivial graph. A graph with only vertices and no edges is known as an edgeless graph. The graph with no vertices and no edges is sometimes called the null graph or empty graph, but the terminology is not consistent and not all mathematicians allow this object.

In a weighted graph or digraph, each edge is associated with some value, variously called its cost, weight, length or other term depending on the application; such graphs arise in many contexts, for example in optimal routing problems such as the traveling salesman problem.

Normally, the vertices of a graph, by their nature as elements of a set, are distinguishable. This kind of graph may be called vertex-labeled. However, for many questions it is better to treat vertices as indistinguishable; then the graph may be called unlabeled. (Of course, the vertices may be still distinguishable by the properties of the graph itself, e.g., by the numbers of incident edges). The same remarks apply to edges, so that graphs which have labeled edges are called edge-labeled graphs. Graphs with labels attached to edges or vertices are more generally designated as labeled. Consequently, graphs in which vertices are indistinguishable and edges are indistinguishable are called unlabeled.

Examples

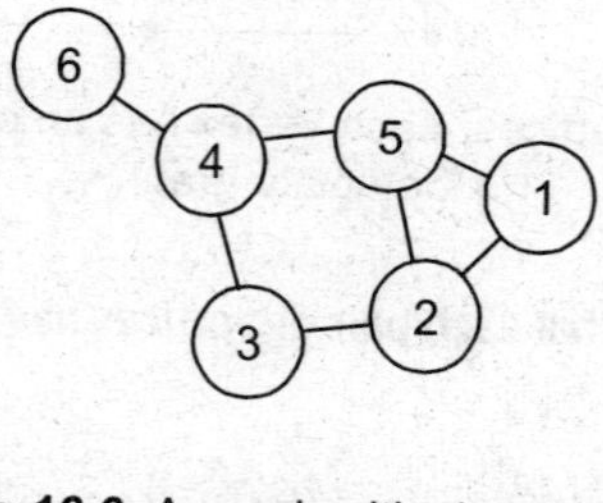

Fig.16.6. A graph with six nodes.

- The diagram at right is a graphic representation of the following graph:

  V= {1, 2, 3, 4, 5, 6}

  E= {{1, 2}, {1, 5}, {2, 3}, {2, 5}, {3, 4}, {4, 5}, {4, 6}}.
- In category theory a small category can be represented by a directed multigraph in which the objects of the category represented as vertices and the morphisms as directed edges. Then, the functors between categories induce some, but not necessarily all, of the digraph morphisms of the graph.
- In computer science, directed graphs are used to represent knowledge (e.g., Conceptual graph), finite state machines, and many other discrete structures.
- A binary relation R on a set X defines a directed graph. An element x of X is a direct predecessor of an element y of X iff xRy.

Solved Questions

1. Let G be a multigraph with V (G) = {v1, v2, , vn}. Prove that the sum of all the entries in the ith row of the adjacency matrix A(G) is the degree of the vertex vi for each i = 1, 2, , n.

Ans. Given i, where $1 \leq i \leq n$, the sum of the entries in the ith row of A(G) is the sum of the numbers of edges joining vi to vj, where j = 1, 2, , n, which is thus the degree of vi in G.

2. Let G be a graph of order 8 and size 15 in which each vertex is of degree 3 or 5. How many vertices of degree 5 does G have?

Ans. Let x and y be the number of vertices in G of degree 3 and 5 respectively. Then $x + y = 8$ and $3x + 5y = 2 \times 15 = 30$. Solving the equations yields (x, y) = (5, 3).

3. Let H be a graph of order 10 such that $3 \leq d(v) \leq 5$ for each vertex v in H. Not every vertex is even. No two odd vertices are of the same degree. What is the size of H?

Ans. Let x, y and z be the number of vertices in H of degree 3,4 and 5 respectively. Since not every vertex is even, $x + z \geq 2$. As no two odd vertices are of the same degree, x = z = 1. Thus, (x, y, z) = (1, 8, 1), and so $e(H) = (3+4 \times 8 + 5)/2 = 20$.

4. Let G be a graph of order 14 and size 30 in which every vertex is of degree 4 or 5. How many vertices of degree 5 does G have?

Ans. Let x and y be the number of vertices in G of degree 4 and 5 respectively. Then $x + y = 14$ and $4x + 5y = 2 \times 30 = 60$. Solving the equations yields (x, y) = (10, 4). Thus, G has 4 vertices of degree 5.

Previous Year University Question

1. What is an Eulerian Walk? Under What conditions, does a multigraph have an Eulerian walk? [Madrass University]
2. Prove or give a counter example : If a graph is bicoherent, then it is biconnected. [Madrass University]
3. Explain Adjacency List and Adjacency Matrix Representation of graph. [MDU]

Exercise

1. Explain the properties of graph.
2. Represent the following graph with
   (a) adjecency list represention
   (b) adjacency matrix representation
   (c) adjaceacy multilist representation

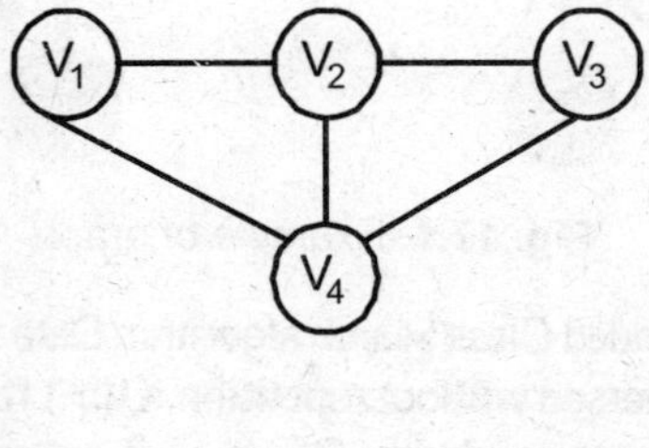

CHAPTER

17

GRAPH TRAVERSAL

17.1 INTRODUCTION

Graph traversal refers to the problem of visiting all the nodes in a graph in a particular manner. Tree traversal is a special case of graph traversal. In contrast to tree traversal, in general graph traversal, each node may have to be visited more than once, and a root-like node that connects to all other nodes might not exist. There are two ways of graph traversal:

1. Depth-first Search

A Depth-first search (DFS) is a technique for traversing a finite undirected graph. DFS visits the child nodes before visiting the sibling nodes, that is, it traverses the depth of the tree before the breadth.

2. Breadth-first Search

A Breadth-first search (BFS) is another technique for traversing a finite undirected graph. BFS visits the sibling nodes before visiting the child nodes.

17.2 DEPTH-FIRST SEARCH

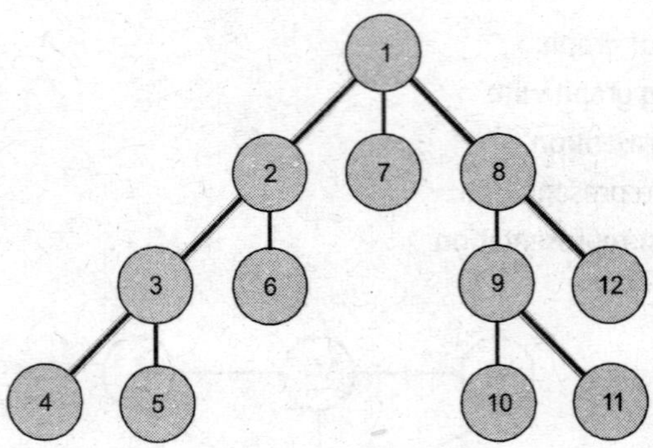

Fig. 17.1. Example of graph

Order in which the nodes are expanded Class Search algorithm Data structure Graph Worst case performance O(| V | + | E |) for explicit graphs traversed without repetition, O(b^d) for implicit graphs with branching factor b searched to depth d Worst case space complexity O(| V |) if entire graph is traversed without repetition, O(longest path length searched) for implicit graphs without elimination of duplicate nodes

Depth-first search (DFS) is an algorithm for traversing or searching a tree, tree structure, or graph. One starts at the root (selecting some node as the root in the graph case) and explores as far as possible along each branch before backtracking.

Formally, DFS is an uninformed search that progresses by expanding the first child node of the search tree that appears and thus going deeper and deeper until a goal node is found, or until it hits a node that has no children. Then the search backtracks, returning to the most recent node it hasn't finished exploring. In a non-recursive implementation, all freshly expanded nodes are added to a stack for exploration.

The time and space analysis of DFS differs according to its application area. In theoretical computer science, DFS is typically used to traverse an entire graph, and takes time $O(|V| + |E|)$, linear in the size of the graph. In these applications it also uses space $O(|V|)$ in the worst case to store the stack of vertices on the current search path as well as the set of already-visited vertices. Thus, in this setting, the time and space bounds are the same as for breadth-first search and the choice of which of these two algorithms to use depends less on their complexity and more on the different properties of the vertex orderings the two algorithms produce.

For applications of DFS to search problems in artificial intelligence, however, the graph to be searched is often either too large to visit in its entirety or even infinite, and DFS may suffer from non-termination when the length of a path in the search tree is infinite. Therefore, the search is only performed to a limited depth, and due to limited memory availability one typically does not use data structures that keep track of the set of all previously visited vertices. In this case, the time is still linear in the number of expanded vertices and edges (although this number is not the same as the size of the entire graph because some vertices may be searched more than once and others not at all) but the space complexity of this variant of DFS is only proportional to the depth limit, much smaller than the space needed for searching to the same depth using breadth-first search. For such applications, DFS also lends itself much better to heuristic methods of choosing a likely-looking branch. When an appropriate depth limit is not known a priori, iterative deepening depth-first search applies DFS repeatedly with a sequence of increasing limits; in the artificial intelligence mode of analysis, with a branching factor greater than one, iterative deepening increases the running time by only a constant factor over the case in which the correct depth limit is known due to the geometric growth of the number of nodes per level.

For the following graph:

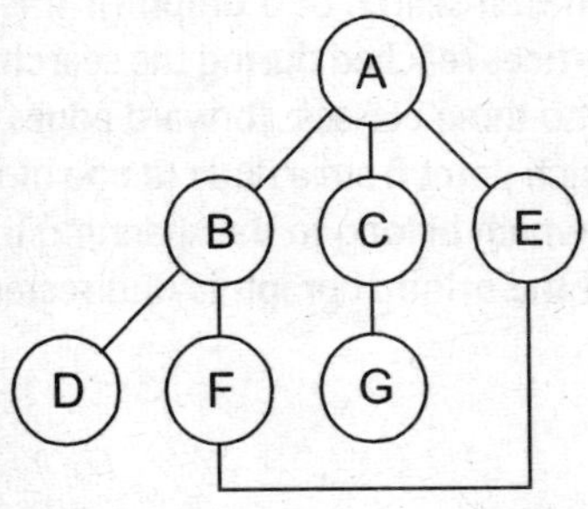

Fig.17.2. a depth-first search starting at A, assuming that the left edges in the shown graph are chosen before right edges, and assuming the search remembers previously-visited nodes and will not repeat them (since this is a small graph), will visit the nodes in the following order: A, B, D, F, E, C, G. The edges traversed in this search form a Tremaux tree, a structure with important applications in graph theory.

Performing the same search without remembering previously visited nodes results in visiting nodes in the order A, B, D, F, E, A, B, D, F, E, etc. forever, caught in the A, B, D, F, E cycle and never reaching C or G.

Iterative deepening prevents this loop and will reach the following nodes on the following depths, assuming it proceeds left-to-right as above:

- 0: A
- 1: A (repeated), B, C, E

(Note that iterative deepening has now seen C, when a conventional depth-first search did not.)

- 2: A, B, D, F, C, G, E, F

(Note that it still sees C, but that it came later. Also note that it sees E via a different path, and loops back to F twice.)

- 3: A, B, D, F, E, C, G, E, F, B

For this graph, as more depth is added, the two cycles "ABFE" and "AEFB" will simply get longer before the algorithm gives up and tries another branch.

17.3 OUTPUT OF A DEPTH-FIRST SEARCH

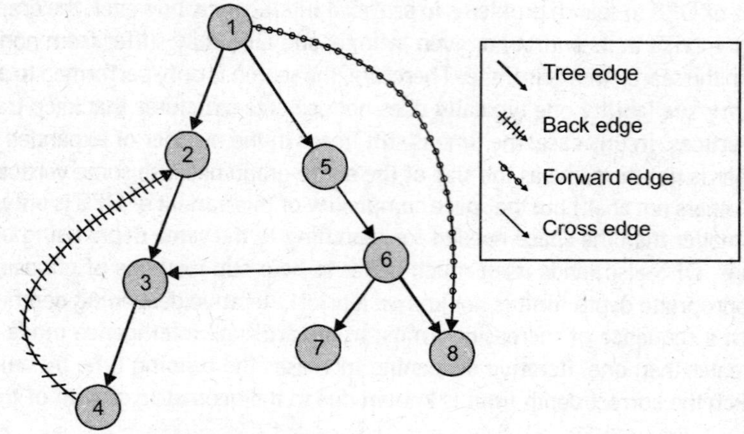

Fig.17.3. The four types of edges defined by a spanning tree

The most natural result of a depth first search of a graph (if it is considered as a function rather than a procedure) is a spanning tree of the vertices reached during the search. Based on this spanning tree, the edges of the original graph can be divided into three classes: forward edges, which point from a node of the tree to one of its descendants, back edges, which point from a node to one of its ancestors, and cross edges, which do neither. Sometimes tree edges, edges which belong to the spanning tree itself, are classified separately from forward edges. It can be shown that if the original graph is undirected then all of its edges are tree edges or back edges.

17.3.1 ALGORITHM

In DFS, each vertex has three possible colors representing its state:

- white: vertex is unvisited;
- gray: vertex is in progress;
- black: DFS has finished processing the vertex.

NB. For most algorithms boolean classification unvisited / visited is quite enough, but we show general case here.

Initially all vertices are white (unvisited). DFS starts in arbitrary vertex and runs as follows:

1. Mark vertex u as gray (visited).
2. For each edge (u, v), where u is white, run depth-first search for u recursively.
3. Mark vertex u as black and backtrack to the parent.

Example: Traverse a graph shown below, using DFS. Start from a vertex with number 1.

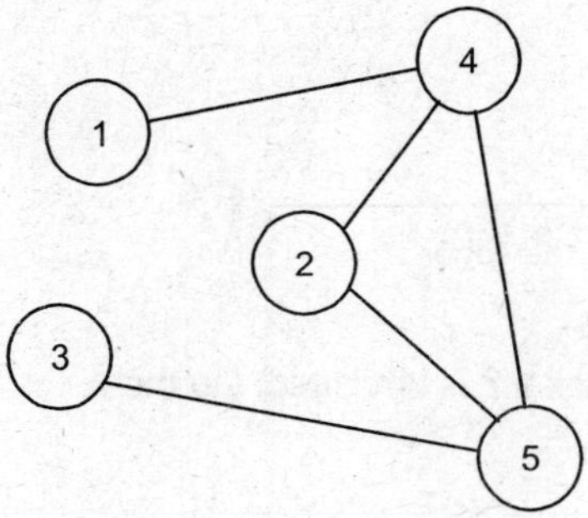

Source graph.

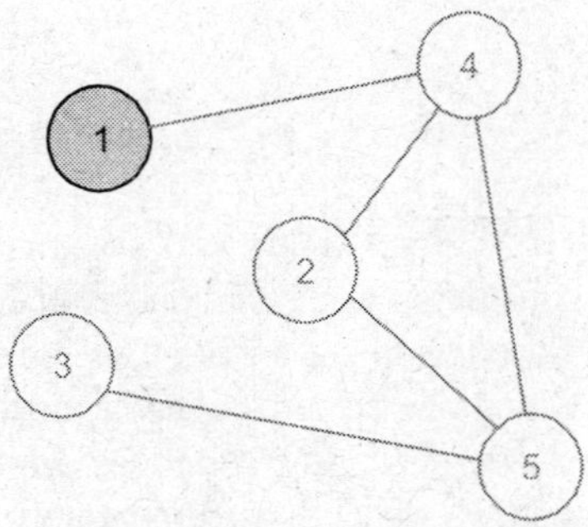

Mark a vertiex 1 as gray.

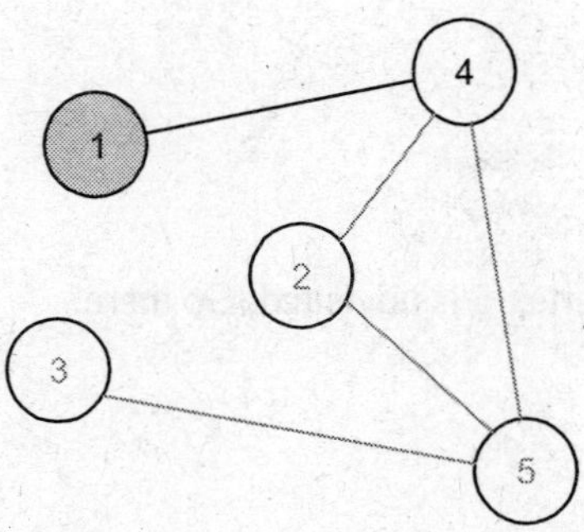

There is an edge (1, 4) and a vertex 4 is unvisited. Go there.

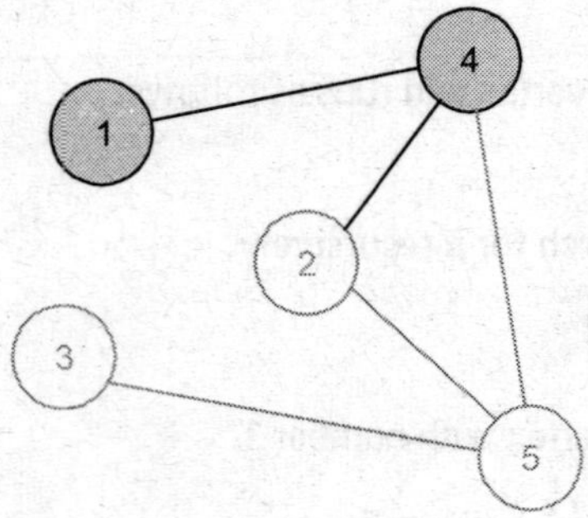

Mark the vertex 4 as gray.

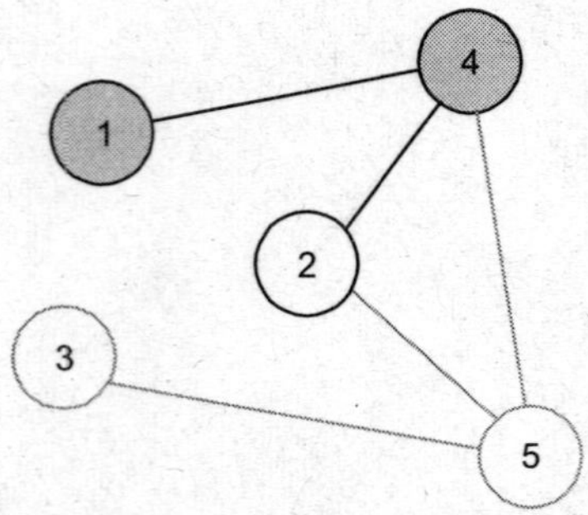

There is an edge (4, 2) and vertex a 2 is unvisited. Go there.

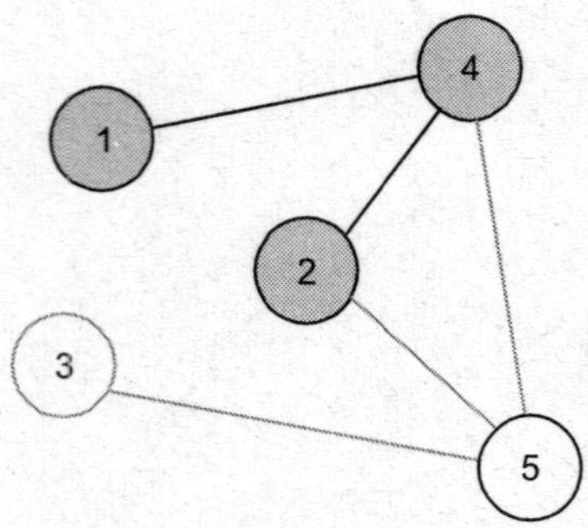

Mark the vertex 2 as gray.

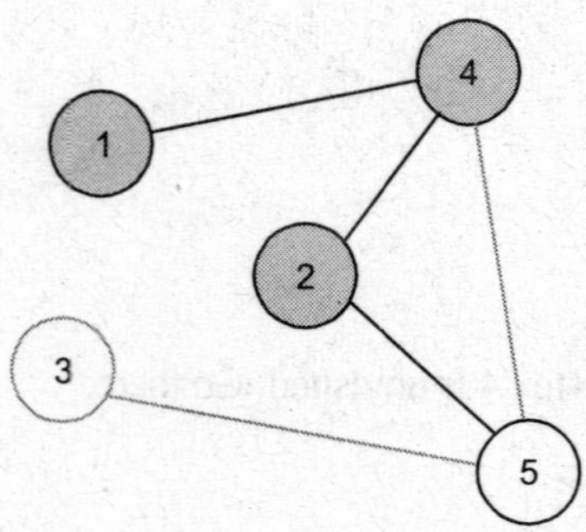

There is an edge (2, 5) and a vertex 5 is unvisited. Go there.

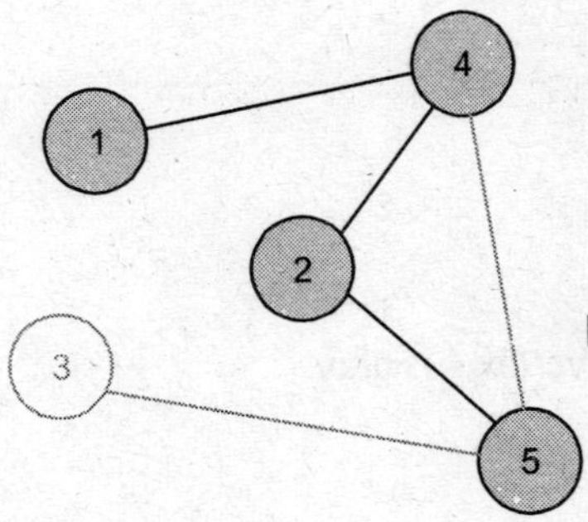

Mark the vertex 5 as gray.

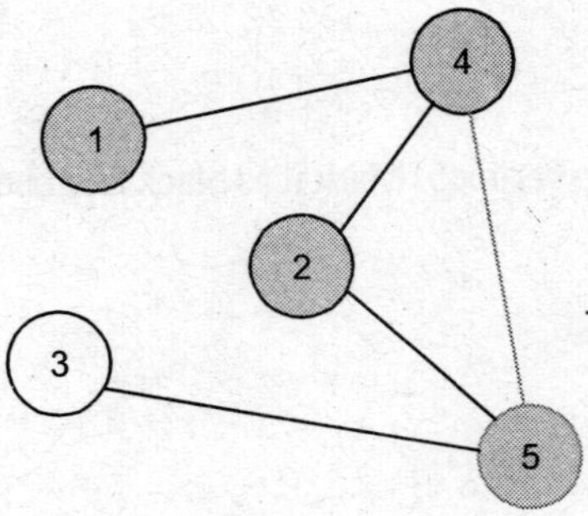

There is an edge (5, 3) and a vertex 3 is unvisited. Go there.

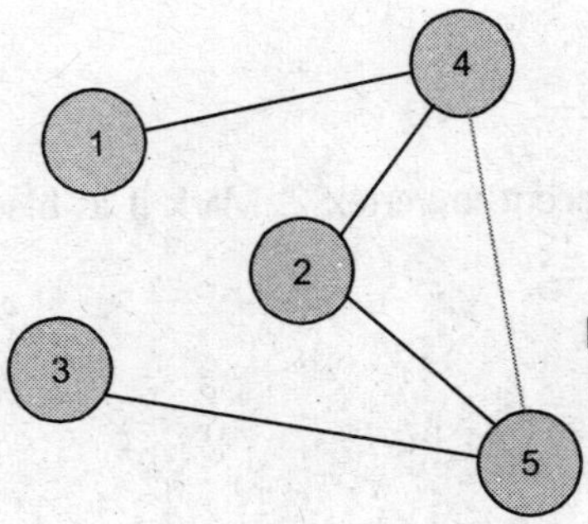

Mark the vertex 3 as gray.

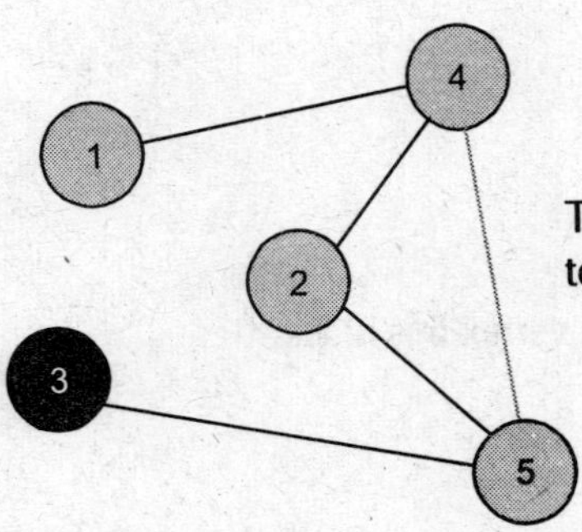

There are no ways to go from the vertex 3. Mark it as black and backtrack to the vertex 5.

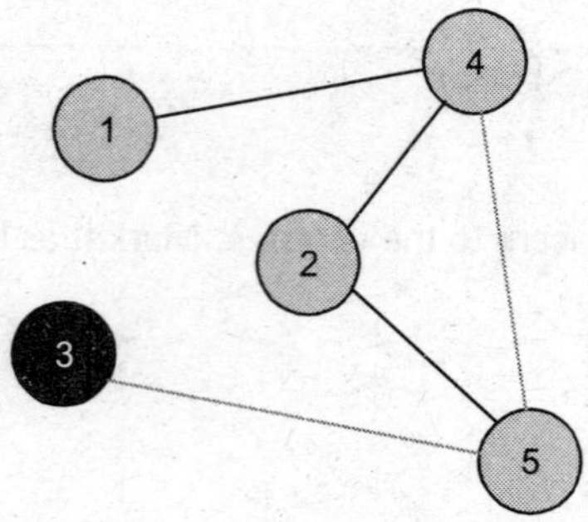

There is an edge (5, 4), but the vertex 4 is gray.

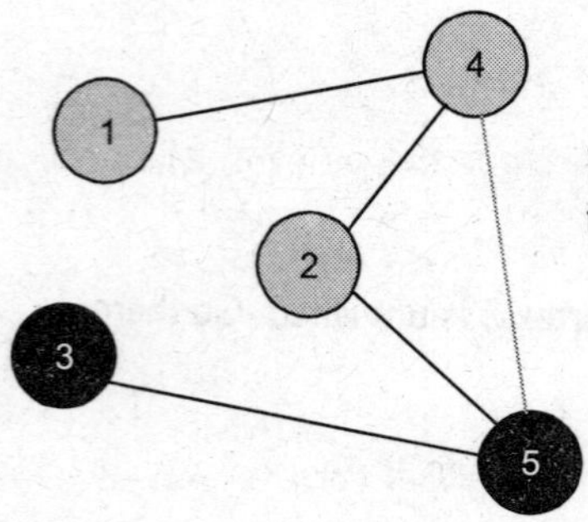

There are no ways to go from the vertex 5. Mark it as black and backtrack to the vertex 2.

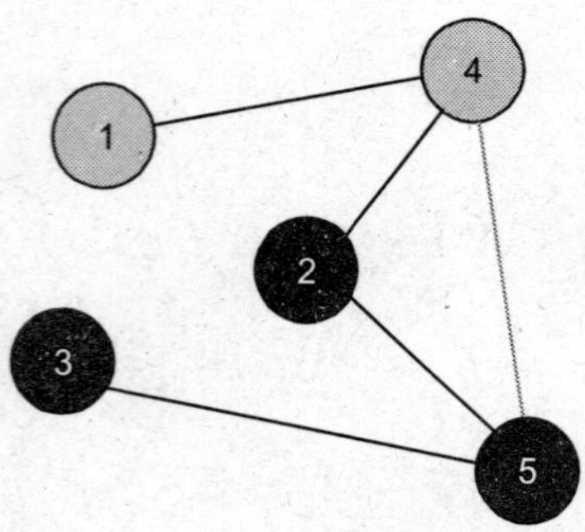

There are no more edges, adjacent to vertex 2. Mark it as black and backtrack to the vertex 4.

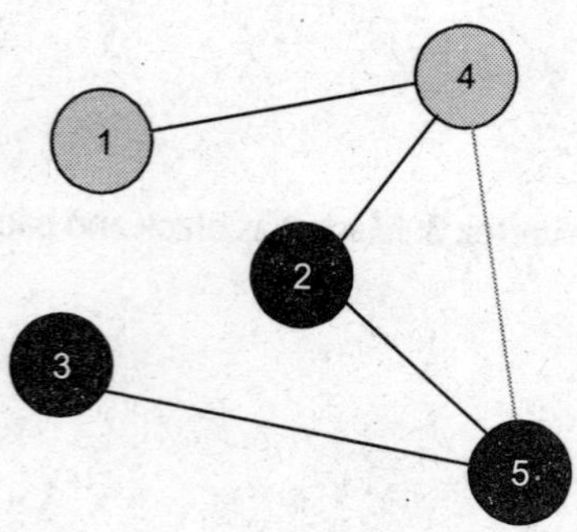

There is an edge (4, 5), but the vertex 5 is black.

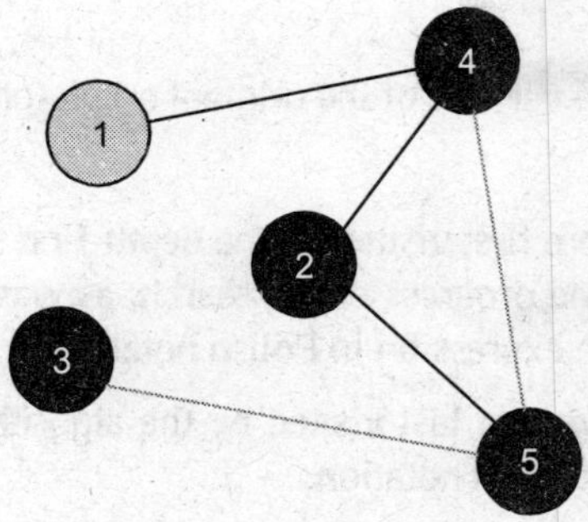

There are no more edges, adjacent to the vertex 4. Mark it as black and backtrack to the vertex 1.

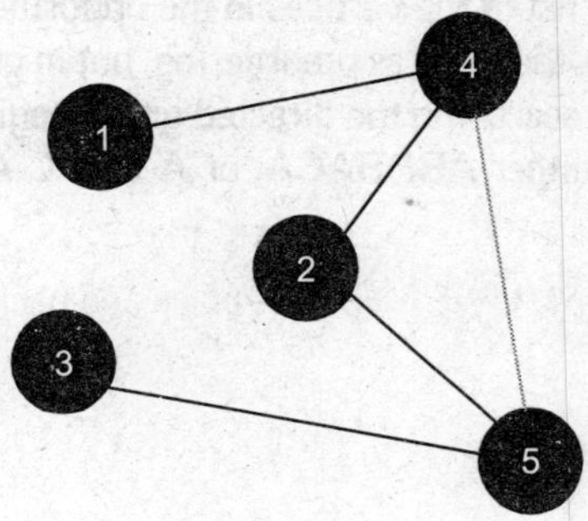

There are no more edges, adjacent to the vertex 1. Mark it as black. DFS is over.

As you can see from the example, DFS doesn't go through all edges. The vertices and edges, which depth-first search has visited is a tree. This tree contains all vertices of the graph (if it is connected) and is called graph spanning tree. This tree exactly corresponds to the recursive calls of DFS.

If a graph is disconnected, DFS won't visit all of its vertices.

DFS(G)

1. Initially color all vertex u ∈ ε v[G], to white
2. Time<-0
   For each vertex u ∈V[G]
   Do if colo [u] = WHITE
   Then DFS_VISIT (u)

```
DFS_VISIT (U)
Color (u) <- gray
Time <-Time +1
D[u] <- Time
For each v ∈ Adg (u)
   Do if color [v] = WHITE
      Then π [v] <- u
   DFS_VISIT (v)
      Color [u] <- BLACK
      Time <-Time +1
      F[u] <- Time
```

17.4 VERTEX ORDERINGS

It is also possible to use the depth-first search to linearly order the vertices of the original graph (or tree). There are three common ways of doing this:

- A preordering is a list of the vertices in the order that they were first visited by the depth-first search algorithm. This is a compact and natural way of describing the progress of the search, as was done earlier in this article. A preordering of an expression tree is the expression in Polish notation.
- A postordering is a list of the vertices in the order that they were last visited by the algorithm. A postordering of an expression tree is the expression in reverse Polish notation.
- A reverse postordering is the reverse of a postordering, i.e. a list of the vertices in the opposite order of their last visit. When searching a tree, reverse postordering is the same as preordering, but in general they are different when searching a graph. For example, when searching the directed graph beginning at node A, one visits the nodes in sequence, to produce lists either ABDBACA, or A C D C A B A (depending upon the algorithm chooses to visit B or C first).

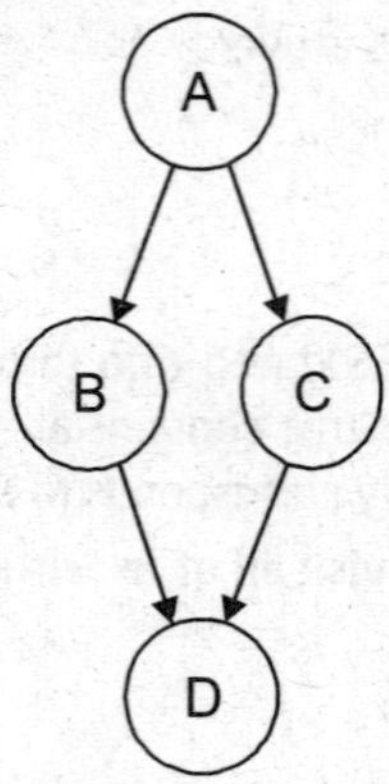

Fig.17.4. Directed graph.

Note that repeat visits in the form of backtracking to a node, to check if it has still unvisited neighbours, are included here (even if it is found to have none). Thus the possible preorderings are A B D C and A C D B (order by node's leftmost occurrence in above list), while the possible reverse postorderings are A C B D and A B C D (order by node's rightmost occurrence in above list). Reverse postordering produces a topological sorting of any directed acyclic graph. This ordering is also useful in control flow analysis as it often represents a natural linearization of the control flow. The graph above might represent the flow of control in a code fragment like and it is natural to consider this code in the order A B C D or A C B D, but not natural to use the order A B D C or A C D B.

```
if  (A) then {
  B
} else {
  C
}
D
```

17.4.1 Applications

Algorithms that use depth-first search as a building block include:

- Finding connected components.
- Topological sorting.
- Finding 2-(edge or vertex)-connected components.
- Finding strongly connected components.
- Planarity Testing
- Solving puzzles' with only one solution, such as mazes. (DFS can be adapted to find all solutions to a maze by only including nodes on the current path in the visited set.)
- bi connectivity.

17.5 Breadth-first search

In graph theory, breadth-first search (BFS) is a graph search algorithm that begins at the root node and explores all the neighboring nodes. Then for each of those nearest nodes, it explores their unexplored neighbor nodes, and so on, until it finds the goal.

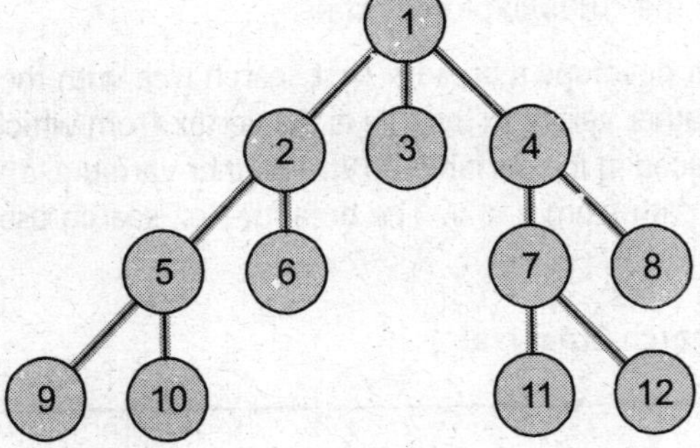

Fig. 17.5. Graph example

Order in which the nodes are expanded

Class	Search algorithm
Data structure	Graph
Worst case performance	$O(\|V\|+\|E\|) = O(b^d)$
Worst case space	$O(\|V\|+\|E\|) =$
Complexity	$O(b^d)$

17.5.1 How it works

BFS is an uninformed search method that aims to expand and examine all nodes of a graph or combination of sequences by systematically searching through every solution. In other words, it exhaustively searches the entire graph or sequence without considering the goal until it finds it. It does not use a heuristic algorithm.

From the standpoint of the algorithm, all child nodes obtained by expanding a node are added to a FIFO (i.e., First In, First Out) queue. In typical implementations, nodes that have not yet been examined for their neighbors are placed in some container (such as a queue or linked list) called "open" and then once examined are placed in the container "closed".

Breadth-first search starts at a given vertex s, which is at level 0. In the first stage, we visit all the vertices that are at the distance of one edge away. When we visit there, we paint as "visited," the vertices adjacent to the start vertex s - these vertices are placed into level 1. In the second stage, we visit all the new vertices we can reach at the distance of two edges away from the source vertex s. These new vertices, which are adjacent to level 1 vertices and not previously assigned to a level, are placed into level 2, and so on. The BFS traversal terminates when every vertex has been visited.

To keep track of progress, breadth-first-search colors each vertex. Each vertex of the graph is in one of three states:

1. Undiscovered;
2. Discovered but not fully explored; and
3. Fully explored.

The state of a vertex, u, is stored in a color variable as follows:

1. color[u] = White - for the "undiscovered" state,
2. color [u] = Gray - for the "discovered but not fully explored" state, and
3. color [u] = Black - for the "fully explored" state.

The BFS(G, s) algorithm develops a breadth-first search tree with the source vertex, s, as its root. The parent or predecessor of any other vertex in the tree is the vertex from which it was first discovered. For each vertex, v, the parent of v is placed in the variable 7r[v]. Another variable, d[v], computed by BFS contains the number of tree edges on the path from s to v. The breadth-first search uses a FIFO queue, Q, to store gray vertices.

Algorithm: Breadth-First Search Traversal

```
BFS(V,E,s)"
    for each u in V – {s}          // for each vertex u in V[G] except s.
        do color[u] ← WHITE
            d[u] ← infinity
            π[u] ← NIL
    color[s] ← GRAY                // Source vertex discovered
    d[s] ← 0                       // initialize
    π[s] ← NIL                     // initialize
    Q←{}                           // Clear queue Q
    ENQUEUE(Q, s)
    while Q is non-empty J
        do u ← DEQUEUE(Q)                     // That is, u = head[Q]
            for each v adjacent to u          // for loop for every node along with edge.
                do if color[v] ←WHITE         // if color is white you've never seen it before
                    then color[v] ← GRAY
                        d[v] ← d[u] + l
                        π[v] ← u
                        ENQUEUE(Q, v)
            DEQUEUE(Q)
    color [u] ← BLACK
```

Example: The following figure illustrates the progress of breadth-first search on the undirected sample graph.

a. After initialization (paint every vertex white, set d[u] to infinity for each vertex u, and set the parent of every vertex to be NIL), the source vertex is discovered in line 5. Lines 8-9 initialize Q to contain just the source vertex s.

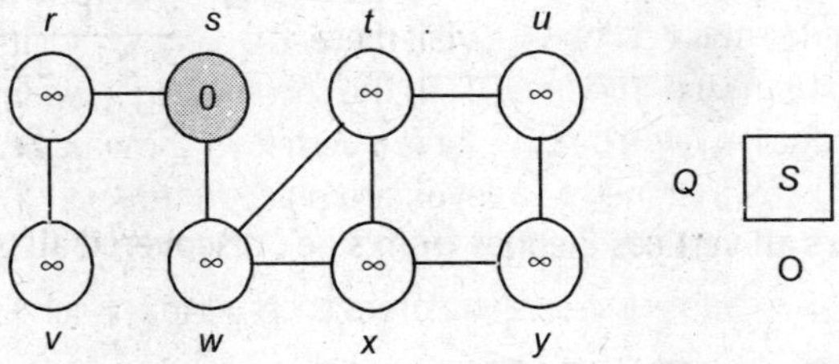

b. The algorithm discovers all vertices 1 edge from s i.e., discovered all vertices (w and r) at level 1.

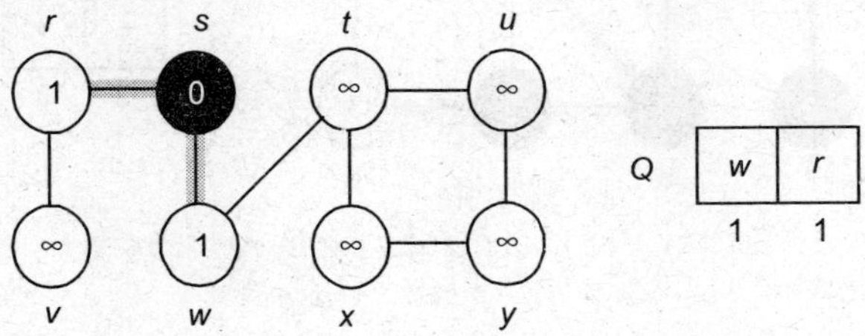

c.

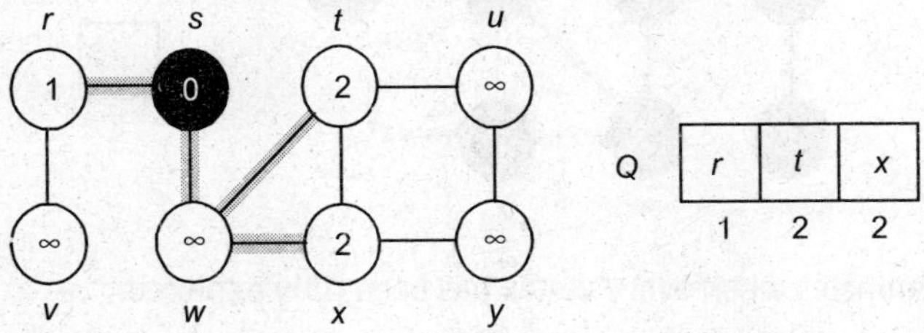

d. The algorithm discovers all vertices 2 edges from s i.e., discovered all vertices (t, x, and v) at level 2.

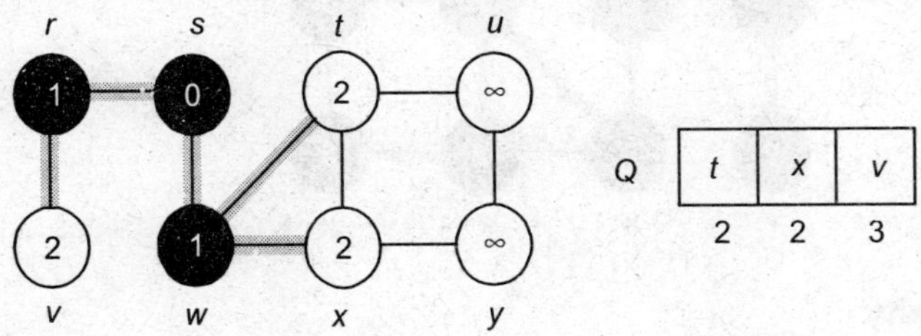

e.

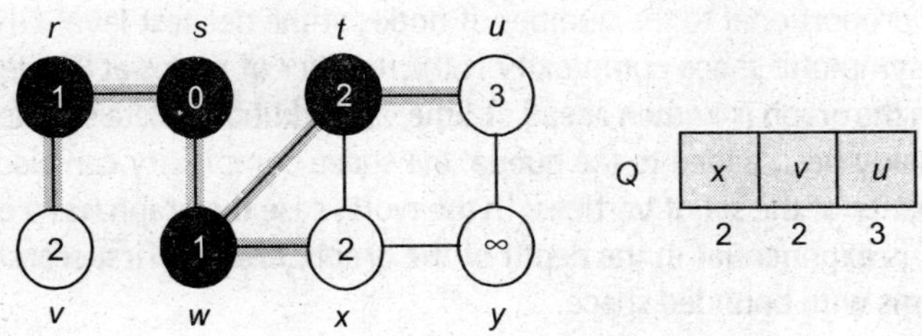

f.

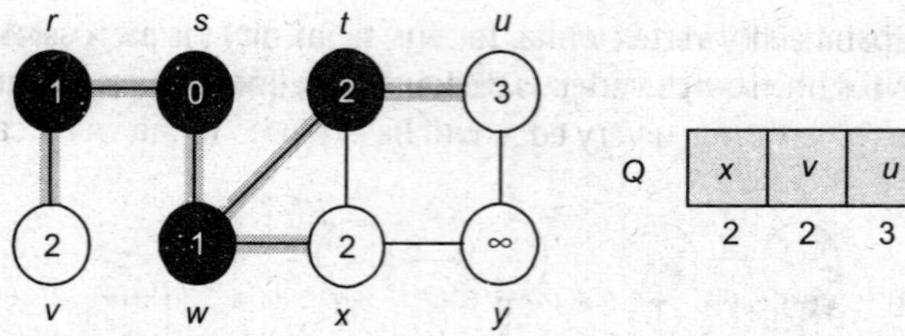

g. **The algorithm discovers all vertices 3 edges from s i.e., discovered all vertices (u and y) at level 3.**

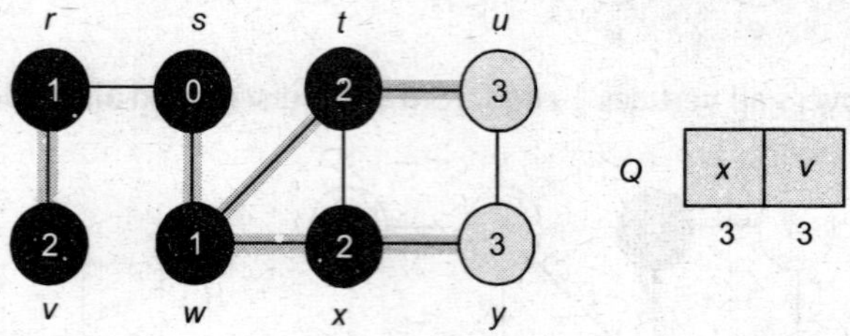

h.

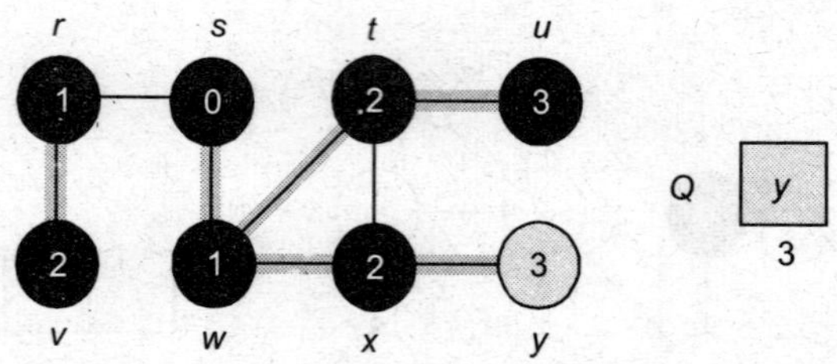

i. **The algorithm terminates when every vertex has been fully explored.**

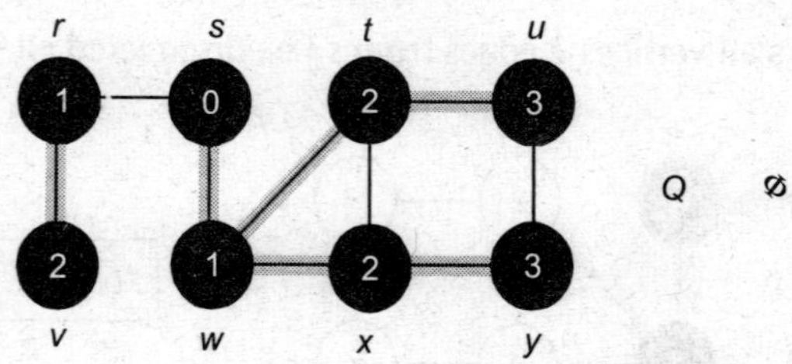

17.5.2 Space complexity

Since all of the nodes of a level must be saved until their child nodes in the next level have been generated, the space complexity is proportional to the number of nodes at the deepest level.Given a branching, factor b and graph depth d the asymptotic space complexity is the number of nodes at the deepest level, $O(b^d)$. When the number of vertices in the graph is known ahead of time, and additional data structures are used to determine which vertices have already been added to the queue, the space complexity can also be expressed as $O(|V|)$ where $|V|$ is the, cardinality of the set of vertices. In the worst case the graph has a depth of 1 and all vertices must be stored. Since it is exponential in the depth of the graph, breadth-first search is often impractical for large problems on systems with bounded space.

17.5.3 Time complexity

Since in the worst case breadth-first search has to consider all paths to all possible nodes the time complexity of breadth-first search is $1 + b + b^2 + b^3 + ... + b^d$ which is $O(b^d)$. The time complexity can also be expressed as $O(|E| + |V|)$ since every vertex and every edge will be explored in the worst case.

17.5.4 Completeness

Breadth-first search is complete. This means that if there is a solution, breadth-first search will find it regardless of the kind of graph. However, if the graph is infinite and there is no solution breadth-first search will diverge.

17.5.5 Proof of completeness

If the shallowest goal node is at some finite depth say d, breadth-first search will eventually find it after expanding all shallower nodes (provided that the branching factor b is finite).

17.5.6 Optimality

For unit-step-cost, breadth-first search is optimal. In general breadth-first search is not optimal since it always returns the result with the fewest edges between the start node and the goal node. If the graph is a weighted graph, and therefore has costs associated with each step, a goal next to the start does not have to be the cheapest goal available. This problem is solved by improving breadth-first search to uniform-cost search which considers the path costs. Nevertheless, if the graph is not weighted, and therefore all step costs are equal, breadth-first search will find the nearest and the best solution.

17.5.7 Bias towards nodes of high degree

It has been empirically observed (and analytically shown for random graphs) that incomplete breadth-first search is biased to wards node s of high degree. This makes a breadth-first search sample of a graph very dificult to interpret. For example, a breadth-first sample of 1 million nodes in Facebook (less than 1% of the entire graph) overestimates the average node degree by 240%

17.6 APPLICATIONS

Breadth-first search can be used to solve many problems in graph theory, for example:

- Finding all nodes within one connected component
- Copying Collection, Cheney's algorithm
- Finding the shortest path between two nodes u and v
- Testing a graph for bipartiteness
- (Reverse) Cuthill-McKee mesh numbering
- Ford-Fulkerson method for computing the maximum flow in a flow network.
- Serialization/Deserialization of a binary tree vs serialization in sorted order, allows the tree to be re constructed in an efficient manner.

Solved Questions

1. What is the difference between BFS and DFS?

Sol. BFS: This can be throught of as being like Dijkstra's algorithm for shortest paths, but with every edge having the same length. However it is a lot simpler and doesn't need any data structures. We just keep a tree (the breadth first search tree), a list of nodes to be added to the tree, and markings (Boolean variables) on the vertices to tell whether they are in the tree or list. Depth first search is another way of traversing graphs, which is closely related to preorder traversal of a tree. Recall that preorder traversal simply visits each node before its children. It is most easy to program as a recursive routine.

2. What is Breadth First Search?

Sol. Breadth-first search is a search algorithm which explores a graph by expanding the most promising node chosen according to a specified rule.

Efficient selection of the current best candidate for extension is typically implemented using a priority queue.

3. What is the difference between DFS and BFS.

Sol. DFS (Depth First Search) and BFS (Breadth First Search) are search algorithms used for graphs and trees. When you have an ordered tree or graph, like a BST, it's quite easy to search the data structure to find the node that you want. But, when given an unordered tree or graph, the BFS and DFS search algorithms can come in handy to find what you're looking for. The decision to choose one over the other should be based on the type of data that one is dealing with.

In a breadth first search, you start at the root node, and then scan each node in the first level starting from the leftmost node, moving towards the right. Then you continue scanning the second level (starting from the left) and the third level, and so on until you've scanned all the nodes, or until you find the actual node that you were searching for. In a BFS, when traversing one level, we need some way of knowing which nodes to traverse once we get to the next level. The way this is done is by storing the pointers to a level's child nodes while searching that level. The pointers are stored in FIFO (First-In-First-Out) queue. This, in turn, means that BFS uses a large amount of memory because we have to store the pointers.

Previous Year University Question

1. Write BFS and DFS algorithms. Explain their working with suitable examples. [OU]
2. What is Multistage graph problem? Write equations for forward approach and backward approach. [GU]

Exercise

1. For a graph given below, obtain the BFS and DFS. Start from V_1

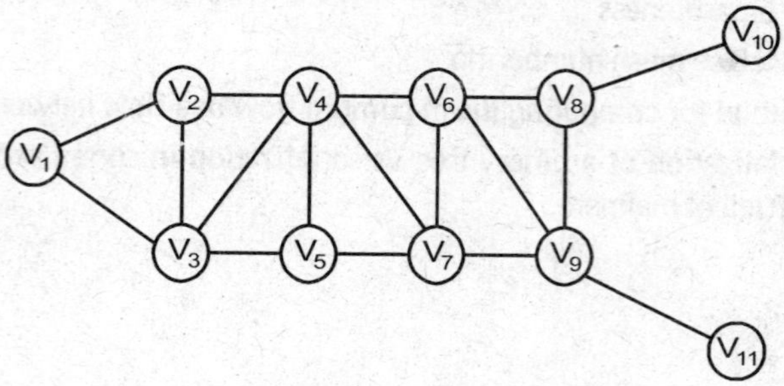

2. Prove that the algorithm for finding cycle in a graph using BFS, complixity is O(n).
3. Write an alongrithm to find bridges is a graph.
4. Prove that if graph is connected undirected graph then no of edge of graph can be in to different biconnected components.
5. Let is be a simple connected graph with n vertices and m edges. Explain why

$$O(\log (n^2)) = O(2\log n) = (\log n).$$

6. Implement DFS algorithm using stack.

CHAPTER 18

DIRECTED ACYCLIC GRAPHS

18.1 INTRODUCTION

A directed acyclic graph (DAG), is a directed graph with no directed cycles. That is, it is formed by a collection of vertices and directed edges, each edge connecting one vertex to another, such that there is no way to start at start at start at some vertex v and follows a sequence of edges that eventually loops back to v again.

DAGs may be used to model several different kinds of structure in mathematics and computer science. A collection of tasks that must be ordered into a sequence, subject to constraints that certain tasks must be performed earlier than other, may be represented as a DAG with a vertex for each task and an edge for each constraints, algorithms too topological ordering may be used to generate a valid sequence. DAGs may also be used to model processes in which information flows in a consistent direction through a network of processor. The reachability relation is a DAG forms a partial orders, and any finite partial order may be represented by a DAG using reachability. Additionally, DAGs may be used as a space-efficient representation of a collection of sequences with overlapping subsequences.

The corresponding concept for undirected graph is a forest, an undirected graph without cycles. Choosing an orientation for a forest produces a special kind of directed acyclic graph called a polytree. However there are many other kinds of directed acyclic graph that are not formed by orienting the edges of an undirected acyclic graphs. For this reason it may be more accurate to call directed acyclic graphs acyclic directed graphs or acyclic diagrphs.

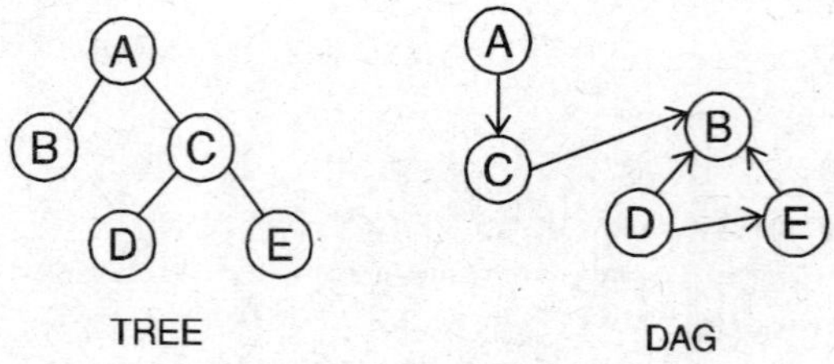

Fig. 18.1 Example of DAG.

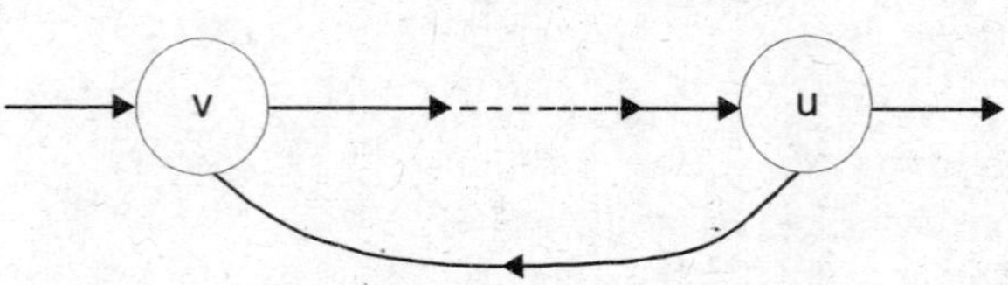

Fig.18.2. A cycle in a digraph

18.2 TEST FOR ACYCLICITY

Result: A digraph is acyclic if and only if its first search does not have back arcs.

Proof: First we prove that

backarc ⇒ cycle.

Let (u ⇒ w) be a backarc. This means that w is an ancestor of v. Thus (w,..., v, w) will be a cycle in the digraph.

Next we show that

cycle ⇒backarc.

Suppose G is cyclic. Consider a cycle and let v be the vertex with the lowest dfnumber on the cycle. See Fig. 18.2 because v is on a cycle, there is a vertex u such that (u ⇒ v) is an edge. Since v has the lowest number among all vertices on the cycle, u must be an descendant of v.

- it can not be a tree arc since dfnumber(v) ≤ dfnumber(u)
- it can not be a forward arc for the same reason
- it can not be a cross arc since v and u are on the same cycle.

Note that the above test for acyclicity has worst case complexity O (e).

18.3 SHORTEST PATHS PROBLEM

Given : A digraph G = (V, E) in which each arc has a non-negative cost and one vertex is designated as the source.

Problem: To determine the cost of the shortest path from the source to every other vertex in V (where the length of a path is just the sum of the costs of the arcs on the path).

18.4 SINGLE SOURCE SHORTEST PATHS PROBLEM

Dijkstra's Algorithm

Dijkstra's algorithm concived by Dutch computer scienist edsger Dijkstra in 1956 and published in 199, is a graph search algorithm that and alone the single - source shortest path problem for a graph with nonnegative edge path costs, producing a shortest path tree. This algorithm is used in routing and as a subroutine in order graph algorithms.

For a given source vertex (node) in the graph, the algorithm finds the path with lowest cost (i.e the shoetest path) between-that vertex and every other vertex. It can also be used for finding costs of shortest paths from a single vertex to a single destination vertex by stoping the algorithm once the shortest path to the destination vertex has been determined. For example, if the vertices of the graph represent cities and edge path cost represent driving distances between pairs of cities connected by a direct road, Dijkstra's algorithm can be used to find the shortest route between one city and all other cities. As a result, the shortlest path first is widely used in network routing protocols, most notably OSPF (open shortest path first).

Dijkstra original algorithm does not use a min-priority queue and runs in $O(|V|^2)$. The common implementation based on a min-priority queue implemented by a Fibonacci heap and running in $O(|\varepsilon| + |V| \log |V|)$. This is asymptotically the fastest known single source shortest path algorithm for arbitrary directed graph with unbounded nonnegative weights.

Let the mode at which use are staring be called the intial node. Let the distance of node be the distance from the initial node to y. Dijkstra's algorithm will try to improve them step by step.

1. Assegn to every node a distance value set it Zero for our initial node and to intinity for all other nodes.
2. Mark all nodes as unvisited. Set intetial node as current
3. For currect node, consider all its unvisited neighbors and calculate their tentative distance. For example, it current node (A) has distance of 6 and an edge connecting it with another node (B) is 2, the distance to B through. A will be 6 + 2 = 8. If distance is less than the previously recorded distance, overwirte the distance.
4. When we are done considering all neighbors of the currect node, mart it as visited. A visited node will not be checked ever again: its distance recorded now id final and minimal.
5. If all nodes have been visited, finish. Otherviews set the unvisited node with the smallest distance as the next "Currect node" and continue from step 3.

```
DIJKSTRA (G, w, s)

INITIALIZE SINGLE-SOURCE (G, s)
S ← { }     // S will ultimately contains vertices of final shortest-path weights from s
Initialize priority queue Q i.e., Q ← V[G]
  while priority queue Q is not empty do
      u ← EXTRACT_MIN(Q)     // Pull out new vertex
      S ← S È{u}
      // Perform relaxation for each vertex v adjacent to u
        for each vertex v in Adj [u] do
            Relax (u, v, w)
```

Like Prim's algorithm, Dijkstra's algorithm runs in O (| E | lg | V |) time.

Example: Step by Step operation of Dijkstra algorithm.

Step 1 Given initial graph G = (V, E). All nodes nodes have infinite cost except the source node, s, which has 0 cost.

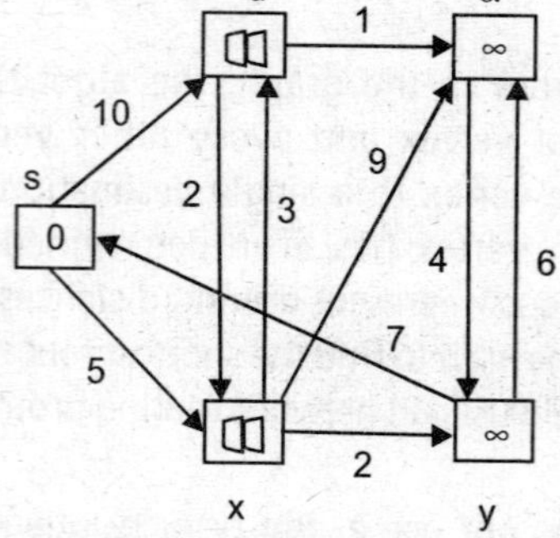

Step 2 First we choose the node, which is closest to the source node, s. We initialize d[s] to 0. Add it to S. Relax all nodes adjacent to source, s. Update predecessor (see red arrow in diagram below) for all nodes updated.

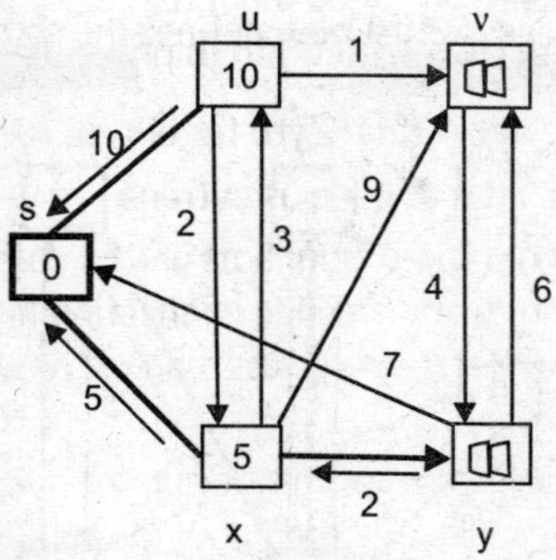

Step 3 Choose the closest node, x. Relax all nodes adjacent to node x. Update predecessors for nodes u, v and y (again notice red arrows in diagram below).

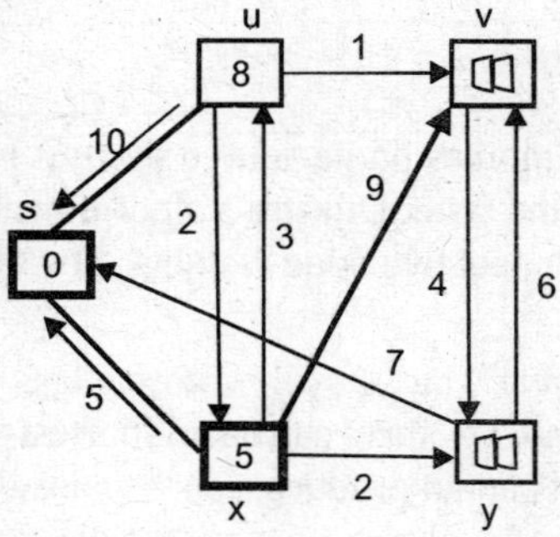

Step 4 Now, node y is the closest node, so add it to S. Relax node v and adjust its predecessor (red arrows remember!).

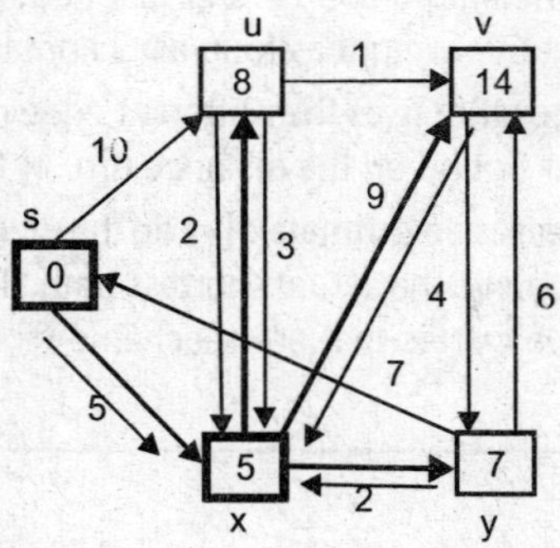

Step 5 Now we have node u that is closest. Choose this node and adjust its neighbor node v.

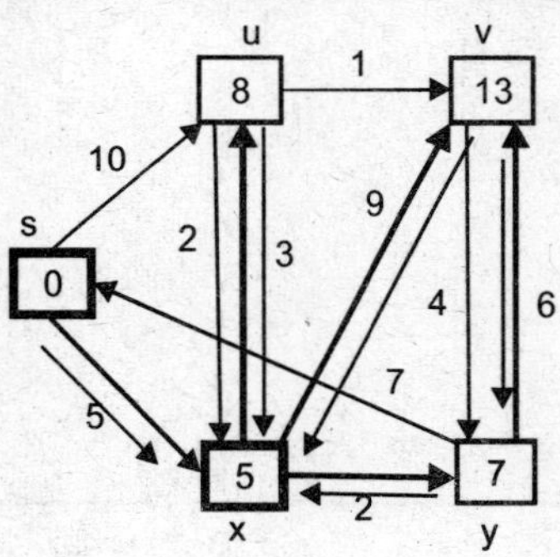

Step 6 Finally, add node v. The predecessor list now defines the shortest path from each node to the source node, s.

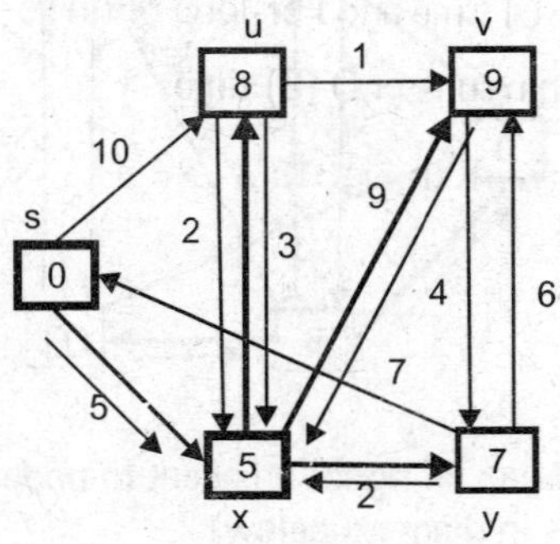

18.5 BELLMAN-FORD ALGORITHM

The Bellman-Ford algorithm computes jingle-source shortest paths in a weighted digraph. For graghs with only non-negative edge weights, the faster Dijkstra's algorithm also solves the problem. Thus, Bellman-Ford is used primarily for graphs with negative edge weights. The algorithm is named after its developers, Richard Bellman and Lester Ford. Jr.

If a graph contains a "negative cycle", i.e., a cycle whose edges sum to a negative value, then walks of arbitrarily low weight can be constructed, i.e., there can be no shortest path. Bellman-ForcTcan detect negative cycles and report their existence, but it cannot produce a correct answer if a negative cycle is reachable from the source.

Let G be a graph containing a negative cycle. One NP-Complete variant of the shortest-path problem asks for the shortest path in G (containing a negative cycle) such that no edge is repeated. this variant of'

Bellman-Ford algorithm solves the single-source shortest-path problem in the general case in which edges of a given digraph can have negative weight as long as G contains no negative cycles.

This algorithm, like Dijkstra's algorithm uses the notion of edge relaxation but does not use with greedy method. Again, it uses d[u] as an upper bound on the distance d[u, v] from u to v.

The algorithm progressively decreases an estimate d[v] on the weight of the shortest path from the source vertex s to each vertex v in V until it achieve the actual shortest-path. The algorithm returns Boolean TRUE if the given digraph contains no negative cycles that are reachable from source vertex s otherwise it returns Boolean FALSE.

```
BELLMAN-FORD (G, w, s)
```

```
1. INITIALIZE-SINGLE-SOURCE (G, s)
2. for each vertex i = 1 to V[G] - 1 do
3.     for each edge (u, v) in E[G] do
4.         RELAX (u, v, w)
5. For each edge (u, v) in E[G] do
6.     if d[u] + w(u, v) < d[v] then
7.         return FALSE
8. return TRUE
```

18.5.1 Analysis

- The initialization in line 1 takes $\Theta(v)$ time
- For loop of lines 2–4 takes O(E) time and For-loop of line 5–7 takes O(E) time.

Thus, the Bellman-Ford algorithm runs in O (E) time.

18.5.2 Example: Consider the digraph in Fig. 18.3

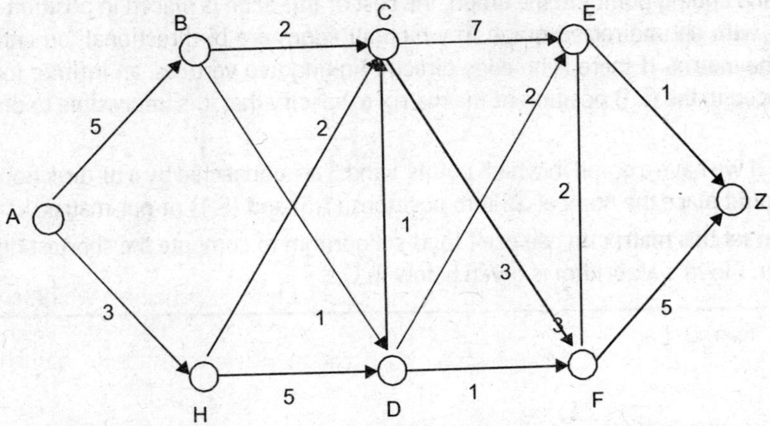

Fig.18.3. An example digraph to illustrate dynamic programming

Step 1. J(Z) = 0

Step 2. E is the only vertex such that J(J) is known $\forall$ I > j such that C(E, J) $\neq$ 0

$$J(E) = C(E, Z) + J(Z) = 1$$

Step 3. Selects F

$$J(F) = \min \begin{cases} C(F, Z) + J(Z) = 5 \\ C(F, E) + J(E) = 3 \end{cases}$$

$$= \min(5, 3) = 3$$

This yields the optimal path F $\rightarrow$ E $\rightarrow$ Z.

Step 4. Select C.

$$J(C) = \min \begin{cases} C(C, E) + J(E) = 8 \\ C(C, F) + J(F) = 6 \end{cases}$$

$$= \min(8, 6) = 6$$

This yields the optimal path C $\rightarrow$ F $\rightarrow$ E $\rightarrow$ Z.

Step 5.

Select D

$$J(D) = \min \begin{cases} C(D, C) + J(C) = 7 \\ C(D, E) + J(E) = 3 = 3 \\ C(D, F) + J(F) = 4 \end{cases}$$

This yields the optimal path D $\rightarrow$ E $\rightarrow$ Z.

⋮

Eventually, we get all the optimal paths and all the optimal costs.

18.6 ALL PAIRS SHORTEST PATHS PROBLEM: FLOYD'S ALGORITHM

This algorithm is designed to find the least-expensive paths between all the vertices in a graph. It does this by operating on a matrix representing the costs of edges between vertices.

Before we invoke Floyd's algorithm we must build a matrix, usually in a two-dimensional array. If there are n vertices in our graph, our matrix will be n × n. Each row in the matrix represents a "starting" vertex in the graph while each column in the matrix represents an "ending" point in the graph. If there is an edge between a starting point i and ending point j in the graph, the cost of this edge is placed in position (i, j) of the matrix. If we are dealing with an undirected graph in which all edges are bi-directional, an entry is also made in position (j, i) of the matrix. If there is no edge directly linking two vertices, an infinite (or, in practice, very large) value is placed in the (i, j) position of the matrix to specify that it is impossible to directly move from i to j.

For example, if we have a graph in which points 1 and 5 are connected by a bi-directional edge with a cost of 22 units, we would place the number 22 into positions (1,5) and (5,1) of our matrix.

Once we have set this matrix up, we use Floyd's algorithm to compute the shortest distance between all points in the graph. Floyd's algorithm is given below in C:

```
int floyds (int *matrix) {
  int k, i, j ;

  for (k = 1; k <= n; k++)
    for (i = 1; i <= n; i + +)
      for (j = 1; j <= n;j++)
        if (matrix[i][j] > (matrix [i] [k] + matrix[k][j]))
          matrix [i, j] = matrix [i] [k] + matrix [k] [j];
}
```

When this routine finishes the entries in all positions of the matrix represent the lowest-cost traversal between the row-vertex and column-vertex.

Floyd's algorithm works by looking for all non-direct paths between two vertices that have a less-expensive total cost than the best way yet found to move between said vertices. If such a path is found, it becomes the value against which future indirect paths between these vertices are tested. In the end, each element of the matrix represents the lowest-cost traversal between the vertices it's row and column represent. Remember that if the graph is directed, so is the answer in (i, j) of the matrix; moreover, (i, j) may not be equal to (j,i) in a di-graph.

n^3 time. In the next section we will discuss an alternative to Floyd's algorithm called Dijkstra's algorithm. It is important to note, however, that for dense graphs (i.e. graphs with many edges) Floyd's algorithm is as good as or better than Dijkstra's algorithm.

The algorithm works by updating two matrices, namely D_k and Q_k, n times for a n - node network. The matrix D_k, in any iteration k, gives the value of the shortest distance (time) between all pairs of nodes (i, j) as obtained till the kth iteration. The matrix Q_k has q_{ij}^{k} as its elements. The value of q_{ij}^{k} gives the immediate predecessor node from node i to node j on the shortest path as determined by the kth iteration. D_0 an Q_0 give the starting matrices and D_n and Q_n give the final matrices for an n-node system. The first task is to determine D_0 and Q_0. D_0 is taken up first. The element d_{ij} of matrix D_0 are defined as follows:

If a link (branch) exists between nodes i and j the length of the shortest path between these nodes equals length l (i, j) of branch (i, j) which connects them. Should there be several branches between nodes i and node j, the length of the shortest path d_{ij}^0 must equal the length of the shortest branch, i.e.:

$$d_{ij}^0 = \min[l_1(i,j), l_2(i,j), ..., l_m(i,m)]$$

whre m is the number of branches between node i and node j.

It is clear that $d_{ij}^0 = 0$ when i = j. In the case when there is no direct link between node i and node j, we have no information at the beginning concerning the length of the shortest path between these two nodes so we treat them as though they were infinitely far from each other, that is,

$$d_{ij}^0 = \infty$$

Elements q_{0j}^0 of the predecessor matrix Q_0 are defined as follows:

First, we assume that $q_{0j}^0 = i$, for $i \neq j$, i.e. that for every pair of nodes (i, j) for $i \neq j$, the immediate predecessor of node j on the shortest path leading from node i to node j is actually node i. After defining D_0 and Q_0 the following steps are used repeatedly to determine D_n and Qn.

Step 1: Let k = 1

Step 2: We calculate elements d_{ij}^k of the shortest path length matrix found after the k-th passage through algorithm D_k using the following equation:

$$d_{ij}^k = \min\lfloor d_{ij}^{k-1}, d_{ik}^{k-1} + d_{kj}^{k-1} \rfloor$$

Step 3: Elements q_{ij}^k of predecessor matrix Q_k found after the k-th passage through the algorithm are calculated as follows:

$$q_{ij}^k = \frac{d_{ij}^{k-1}, \text{for } d_{ik}^{k-1} \neq d_{kj}^{k-1}}{q_{ij}^{k-1}, \text{otherwise}}$$

Step 4: If k = n, the algorithm is finished. If k < n, increase A: by 1, i.e. K = k+1 and return to step 2.

Let us now look at the algorithm in a little more detail. In step 2, each time we go through the algorithms we are checking as to whether a shorter path exists between node i and j other than the path we already know about which was established during one of the earlier passages through the algorithm. If we establish that $d_{ij}^{k-1} \neq d_{ij}^{k-1}$, i.e. if we establish during the k -th passage through the algorithm that the length of the shortest path d_{kj}^k between nodes i and j is less than the length of the shortest path d_{ij}^{k-1} known previous to the k-th passage, we have to change the immediate predecessor node to node j. Since the length of the new shortest path is:

$$d_{ij}^k = d_{ik}^{k-1} + d_{k,j}^{k-1}$$

it is clear that in this case node k is the new immediate predecessor node to j, and therefore:

$$q_{ij}^k = q_{kj}^{k-1}$$

This is actually done in the third algorithmic step. It is also clear that the immediate predecessor node to node j does not change if, at the end of step 2, we have established that no other new, shorter path exists. This means that:

$$q_{ij}^{k} = q_{kh}^{k-1} \text{ for } d_{kj}^{k} = d_{kj}^{k-1}$$

When we go through the algorithm n times (n is the number of nodes in the transportation network), elements d_{ij}^{n} of final matrix D_n will constitute the shortest path going from node i to node j.

Example: Determine the shortest paths between all pairs of nodes on transportation network shown in Figure Fig. 4.

Branch lengths are shown on the figure.

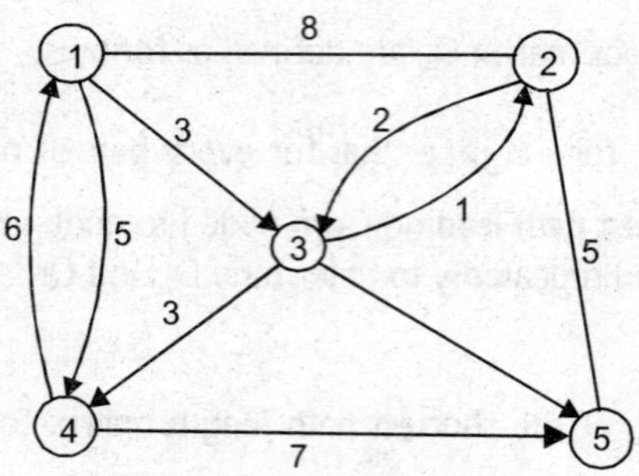

Fig. 18.4 Transportation network for studying Floyd's algorithm.

Starting matrix D_0 is as follows:

$$D_0 = \begin{array}{c} \\ 1 \\ 2 \\ 3 \\ 4 \\ 5 \end{array} \begin{array}{c} \begin{matrix} 1 & 2 & 3 & 4 & 5 \end{matrix} \\ \begin{bmatrix} 0 & 8 & 3 & 5 & \infty \\ 8 & 0 & 2 & \infty & 5 \\ \infty & 1 & 0 & 3 & 4 \\ 6 & \infty & \infty & 0 & 7 \\ \infty & 5 & \infty & \infty & 0 \end{bmatrix} \end{array}$$

All elements along the main diagonal of matrix D_0 equal zero since by definition $d_{ij}^{0} = 0$ for $i = j$ .We note element $d_{1,2}^{0}$ of matrix D_0. This element equals 8 since the length of the branch connecting nodes 1 and 2 is 8. Element $d_{3,1}^{0}$ equals infinity since the network has no branch which is oriented from node 3 to node 1. Element $d_{5,1}^{0}$ of matrix D_0 equals infinity as well since there is direct branch linking nodes 5 and 1. Starting matrix Q_0 is as follows:

$$Q_0 = \begin{array}{c} \\ 1 \\ 2 \\ 3 \\ 4 \\ 5 \end{array} \begin{array}{c} \begin{matrix} 1 & 2 & 3 & 4 & 5 \end{matrix} \\ \begin{bmatrix} - & 1 & 1 & 1 & 1 \\ 2 & - & 2 & 2 & 2 \\ 3 & 3 & - & 3 & 3 \\ 4 & 4 & 4 & - & 4 \\ 5 & 5 & 5 & 5 & - \end{bmatrix} \end{array}$$

First we note that node i is the immediate predecessor of node j on the shortest path leading from node i to node j (for $i \neq j$). For this reason we have, for example:

$$q^0_{2,1} = q^0_{2,3} = q^0_{2,4} = q^0_{2,5} = 2$$

We now go to the first algorithmic step. Let k = 1. As an illustration of Step 2 we calculate the elements of the first three rows of matrix D_1. Calculations for other rows are left as an exercise.

$$d^1_{1,2} = \min\left[d^0_{1,2}; d^0_{1,1} + d^0_{1,2}\right] = \min[8; 0 \div 8] = 8$$

$$d^1_{1,3} = \min\left[d^0_{1,3}; d^0_{1,1} + d^0_{1,3}\right] = \min[3; 0 \div 8] = 3$$

$$d^1_{1,4} = \min\left[d^0_{1,4}; d^0_{1,1} + d^0_{1,4}\right] = \min[5; 0 \div 5] = 5$$

$$d^1_{1,5} = \min\left[d^0_{1,5}; d^0_{1,1} + d^0_{1,5}\right] = \min[\infty; 0 \div \infty] = \infty$$

$$d^1_{2,1} = \min\left[d^0_{2,1}; d^0_{2,1} + d^0_{1,1}\right] = \min[8; 8 \div 8] = 8$$

$$d^1_{2,3} = \min\left[d^0_{2,3}; d^0_{2,1} + d^0_{1,3}\right] = \min[2; 8 \div 3] = 2$$

$$d^1_{2,4} = \min\left[d^0_{2,4}; d^0_{2,1} + d^0_{1,4}\right] = \min[\infty; 8 \div 3] = 13$$

$$d^1_{2,5} = \min\left[d^0_{2,5}; d^0_{2,1} + d^0_{1,5}\right] = \min[5; 8 \div \infty] = 5$$

$$d^1_{3,1} = \min\left[d^0_{3,1}; d^0_{3,1} + d^0_{1,1}\right] = \min[\infty; \infty \div \infty] = \infty$$

$$d^1_{3,2} = \min\left[d^0_{3,2}; d^0_{3,1} + d^0_{1,2}\right] = \min[1; \infty \div 8] = 1$$

$$d^1_{3,4} = \min\left[d^0_{3,4}; d^0_{3,1} + d^0_{1,4}\right] = \min[3; \infty \div 5] = 3$$

$$d^1_{3,5} = \min\left[d^0_{3,5}; d^0_{3,1} + d^0_{1,5}\right] = \min[4; \infty \div \infty] = 4$$

Matrix D_1 is as follows:

$$D_1 = \begin{array}{c} \\ 1 \\ 2 \\ 3 \\ 4 \\ 5 \end{array} \begin{array}{c} \begin{array}{ccccc} 1 & 2 & 3 & 4 & 5 \end{array} \\ \begin{bmatrix} 0 & 8 & 3 & 5 & \infty \\ 8 & 0 & 2 & \textcircled{13} & 5 \\ \infty & 1 & 0 & 3 & 4 \\ 6 & \textcircled{14} & 9 & 0 & 7 \\ \infty & 5 & \infty & \infty & 0 \end{bmatrix} \end{array}$$

Matrix elements which changed values compared to the values they had in matrix D_o are circled.

So, for example, the shortest distance between nodes 2 and 4 is 13 after the first algorithic step. In starting matrix D_o this distance was ∞. Since

$$d^1_{2,4} = d^1_{2,4} + d^0_{2,1} + d^0_{1,4} = 13 < \infty d^0_{2,4}$$

then node 1 is the new immediate predecessor of node 4 on the shortest path from node 2 to node 4. After passing through the algorithm the first time, Q_1 looks like this:

$$Q_1 = \begin{array}{c} \\ 1 \\ 2 \\ 3 \\ 4 \\ 5 \end{array} \begin{array}{c} \begin{array}{ccccc} 1 & 2 & 3 & 4 & 5 \end{array} \\ \begin{bmatrix} - & 1 & 1 & 1 & 1 \\ 2 & - & 2 & 1 & 2 \\ 3 & 3 & - & 3 & 3 \\ 4 & 1 & 1 & - & 4 \\ 5 & 5 & 5 & 5 & - \end{bmatrix} \end{array}$$

After the second, third, fourth and fifth passages through the algorithm, matrices D_2, Q_2, D_3, Q_3, D_4, Q_4 and D_5, Q_5 are as follows:

$$D_2 = \begin{array}{c} \\ 1 \\ 2 \\ 3 \\ 4 \\ 5 \end{array} \begin{array}{c} \begin{array}{ccccc} 1 & 2 & 3 & 4 & 5 \end{array} \\ \begin{bmatrix} 0 & 8 & 3 & 5 & 13 \\ 8 & 0 & 2 & 13 & 5 \\ 9 & 1 & 0 & 3 & 4 \\ 6 & 14 & 9 & 0 & 7 \\ 13 & 5 & 7 & 18 & 0 \end{bmatrix} \end{array} \quad Q_2 = \begin{array}{c} \\ 1 \\ 2 \\ 3 \\ 4 \\ 5 \end{array} \begin{array}{c} \begin{array}{ccccc} 1 & 2 & 3 & 4 & 5 \end{array} \\ \begin{bmatrix} - & 1 & 1 & 1 & 2 \\ 2 & -2 & 1 & 2 & 2 \\ 2 & 3 & - & 3 & 3 \\ 4 & 1 & 1 & - & 4 \\ 2 & 5 & 2 & 1 & - \end{bmatrix} \end{array}$$

$$D_3 = \begin{array}{c} \\ 1 \\ 2 \\ 3 \\ 4 \\ 5 \end{array} \begin{array}{c} \begin{array}{ccccc} 1 & 2 & 3 & 4 & 5 \end{array} \\ \begin{bmatrix} 0 & 4 & 3 & 5 & 7 \\ 8 & 0 & 2 & 5 & 5 \\ 9 & 1 & 0 & 3 & 4 \\ 6 & 10 & 9 & 0 & 7 \\ 13 & 5 & 7 & 10 & 0 \end{bmatrix} \end{array} \quad Q_3 = \begin{array}{c} \\ 1 \\ 2 \\ 3 \\ 4 \\ 5 \end{array} \begin{array}{c} \begin{array}{ccccc} 1 & 2 & 3 & 4 & 5 \end{array} \\ \begin{bmatrix} - & 3 & 1 & 1 & 3 \\ 2 & - & 2 & 3 & 2 \\ 2 & 3 & - & 3 & 3 \\ 4 & 3 & 1 & - & 4 \\ 2 & 5 & 2 & 3 & - \end{bmatrix} \end{array}$$

$$D_4 = \begin{array}{c} \\ 1 \\ 2 \\ 3 \\ 4 \\ 5 \end{array} \begin{array}{c} \begin{array}{ccccc} 1 & 2 & 3 & 4 & 5 \end{array} \\ \begin{bmatrix} 0 & 4 & 3 & 5 & 7 \\ 8 & 0 & 2 & 5 & 5 \\ 9 & 1 & 0 & 3 & 4 \\ 6 & 10 & 9 & 0 & 7 \\ 13 & 5 & 7 & 10 & 0 \end{bmatrix} \end{array} \quad Q_4 = \begin{array}{c} \\ 1 \\ 2 \\ 3 \\ 4 \\ 5 \end{array} \begin{array}{c} \begin{array}{ccccc} 1 & 2 & 3 & 4 & 5 \end{array} \\ \begin{bmatrix} - & 3 & 1 & 1 & 3 \\ 2 & - & 2 & 3 & 2 \\ 2 & 3 & - & 3 & 3 \\ 4 & 3 & 1 & - & 4 \\ 2 & 5 & 2 & 3 & - \end{bmatrix} \end{array}$$

$$D_5 = \begin{array}{c} \\ 1 \\ 2 \\ 3 \\ 4 \\ 5 \end{array} \begin{array}{c} \begin{array}{ccccc} 1 & 2 & 3 & 4 & 5 \end{array} \\ \begin{bmatrix} 0 & 4 & 3 & 5 & 7 \\ 8 & 0 & 2 & 5 & 5 \\ 9 & 1 & 0 & 3 & 4 \\ 6 & 10 & 9 & 0 & 7 \\ 13 & 5 & 7 & 10 & 0 \end{bmatrix} \end{array} \quad Q_5 = \begin{array}{c} \\ 1 \\ 2 \\ 3 \\ 4 \\ 5 \end{array} \begin{array}{c} \begin{array}{ccccc} 1 & 2 & 3 & 4 & 5 \end{array} \\ \begin{bmatrix} - & 3 & 1 & 1 & 3 \\ 2 & - & 2 & 3 & 2 \\ 2 & 3 & - & 3 & 3 \\ 4 & 3 & 1 & - & 4 \\ 2 & 5 & 2 & 3 & - \end{bmatrix} \end{array}$$

Matrices D_5 and Q_5 furnish us with complete information on the lengths of the shortest paths and the nodes on those paths between all pairs of nodes in the transportation network. For example the shortest paths from, node 5 to node 4 has a length of 10. Also by studying the Q_5 matrix one can obtain the shortest paths from, node 5 to node 4. As per Q_5, the immediate predecessor node to node 5 for the shortest path from 5 to 4 is $q^5_{5A} = 3$. Hence 3 to 4 forms the final link on the shortest path from J to 4. Next the predecessor node to node 3 on the shortest path from 5 to 3 is $q^5_{52} = 2$ Hence 2 to 3 to 4 forms a part of the shortest path from 5 to 4. Proceeding similarly, we see, $q^5_{52} = 5$. Hence 5 to 2 to 3 to 4 is the shortest path.

18.7 TOPOLOGICAL SORT

A topological sort or topological ordering of a directed graph is a linear ordering of its vertices such that, for every edge uv, u comes before v in the ordering. For instance, the vertices of the graph may represent tasks to be performed, and the edges may represent constraints that one task must be performed before another; in this application, a topological ordering is just a valid sequence for the tasks. A topological ordering is possible if and only if the graph has no directed cycles, that is, if it is a directed acyclic graph (DAG). Any DAG has at least one topological ordering, and algorithms are known for constructing a topological ordering of any DAG in linear time.

The canonical application of topological sorting (topological order) is in scheduling a sequence of jobs or tasks; topological sorting algorithms were first studied in the early 1960s in the context of the PERT technique for scheduling in project management The jobs are represented by vertices, and there is an edge from x to y if job x must be completed before job y can be started (for example, when washing clothes, the washing machine must finish before we put the clothes to dry). Then, a topological sort gives an order in which to perform the jobs.

In computer science, applications of this type arise in instruction scheduling, ordering of formula cell evaluation when recomputing formula values in spreadsheets, logic synthesis, determining the order of compilation tasks to perform in makefiles, and resolving symbol dependenciesjn linkers.

The graph shown to the left has many valid topological sorts, including:

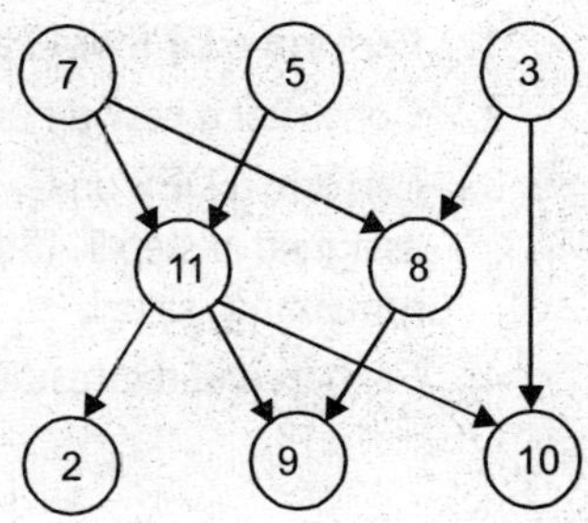

- 7, 5, 3, 11, 8, 2, 9, 10 (visual left-to-right, top-to-bottom)
- 3, 5, 7, 8, 11, 2, 9, 10 (smallest-numbered available vertex first)
- 3,7,8,5,11,10,2,9
- 5, 7, 3, 8, 11, 10, 9, 2 (least number of edges first)
- 7, 5, 11, 3, 10, 8, 9, 2 (largest-numbered available vertex first)
- 7,5,11,2,3,8,9,10

```
L ← Empty list that will contain the sorted elements
S ← Set of all nodes with no incoming edges
while S is non-empty do
    remove a node n from S
    insert n into L
    for each node m with an edge e from n to m do
        remove edge e from the graph
```

```
            if m has no other incoming edges then
                insert m into S
if graph has edges then
    output error message (graph has at least one cycle)
else
    output message (proposed topologically sorted order: L)
```

18.8 STRONG COMPONENTS

A strongly connected component of a digraph is a maximal set of vertices in which there is a path from any one vertex to any other vertex in the set.

A Digraph G — Strong Components of G

Fig.18.5. Strong components of a digraph

Let G = (V, E) be a digraph. We can partition V into equivalence classes V_i, $1 \leq i \leq r_1$, such that vertices v and w are equivalent if there is a path from v to w and a path from w to v.

Let E_i, $1 \leq i \leq r$, be the set of arcs with head and tail both in V_i. Then the graphs (V_i, E_i) are called the strong components of G. A digraph with only one strong component is said to be strongly connected. Depth-first-search can be used to efficiently determine the strong components of a digraph. Kosaraju's (1978) algorithm for finding strong components in a graph:

1. Perform a DFS of G and number the vertices in order of completion of the recursive calls.
2. Construct a new directed graph G_r by reversing the direction of every arc in G.
3. Perform a DFS on G_r starting the search from the highest numbered vertex according to the numbering assigned at step 1. If the DFS does not reach all vertices, start the next DFS from the highest numbered remaining vertex.
4. Each tree in the resulting spanning forest is a strong component of G.

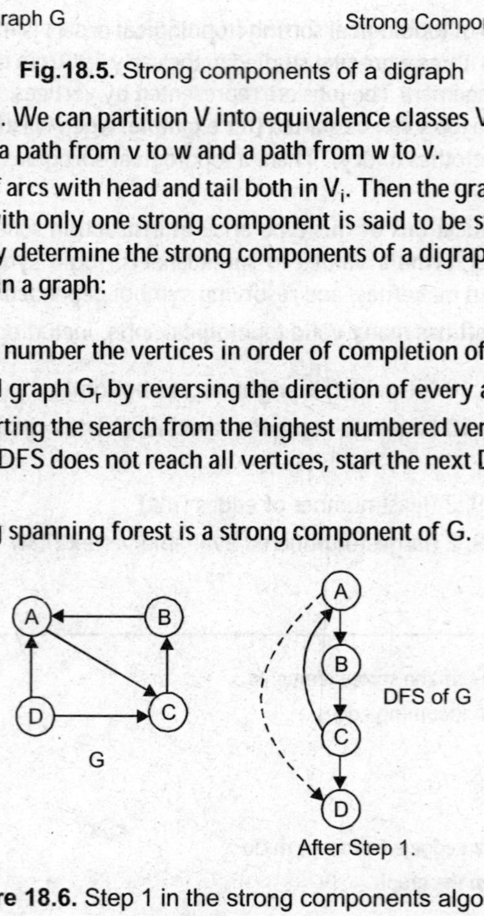

G — After Step 1.

Figure 18.6. Step 1 in the strong components algorithm

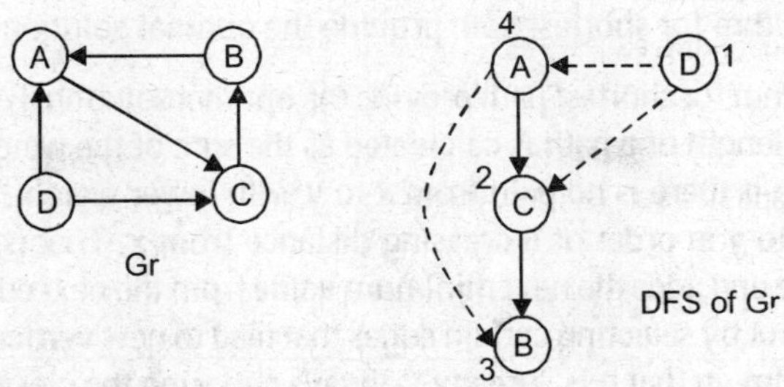

Fig. 18.7. Step 3 in the strong components algorithm

Solved Questions

1. Write an algorithm to find the shortest path in Graphs ?

Ans. The Floyd–Warshall algorithm compares all possible paths through the graph between each pair of vertices. Assume edge Cost(i, j) returns the cost of the edge from i to j (infinity if there is none), n is the number of vertices, and edge Cost(i, i) = 0.

```
Algorithm
int path[][]; // a 2-D matrix.
// At each step, path[i][j] is the (cost of the) shortest path
// from i to j using intermediate vertices (1..k-1).
// Each path[i][j] is initialized to edgeCost (i,j)
// or ∞ if there is no edge between i and j.
procedure FloydWarshall ()
for k in 1..n
for each pair (i,j) in {1,..,n}x{1,..,n}
path[i][j] = min ( path[i][j], path[i][k]+path[k][j] );
```

2. Write a single source shortest path algorithm and its time complexity?

Ans. Dijkstra's algorithm solves the single-source shortest-path problem when all edges have non-negative weights. It is a greedy algorithm and similar to Prim's algorithm. Algorithm starts at the source vertex, s, it grows a tree, T, that ultimately spans all vertices reachable from S. Vertices are added to T in order of distance i.e., first S, then the vertex closest to S, then the next closest, and so on. Following implementation assumes that graph G is represented by adjacency lists.

```
DIJKSTRA (G, w, s)
INITIALIZE SINGLE-SOURCE (G, s)
S ← { }   // S will ultimately contains vertices of final shortest-path weights from s
Initialize priority queue Q i.e., Q ← V[G]
while priority queue Q is not empty do
u ← EXTRACT_MIN(Q)   // Pull out new vertex
S ← S È {u}"
// Perform relaxation for each vertex v adjacent to u
for each vertex v in Adj[u] do
Relax (u, v, w)
```

Analysis

Like Prim's algorithm, Dijkstra's algorithm runs in O(|E|lg|V|) time.

3. Does dijkstra's algorithm for shortest path provide the optimal solution ?

Ans. Yes, dijkstra's algorithm for shortest path provide the optimal solution.To find the shortest path between points, the weight or length of a path is calculated as the sum of the weights of the edges in the path. A path is a shortest path is there is no path from x to y with lower weight. Dijkstra's algorithm finds the shortest path from x to y in order of increasing distance from x. That is, it chooses the first minimum edge, stores this value and adds the next minimum value from the next edge it selects. It starts out at one vertex and branches out by selecting certain edges that lead to new vertices. It is similar to the minimum spanning tree algorithm, in that it is "greedy", always choosing the closest edge in hopes of an optimal solution.

Previous Year University Question

1. What are single source shortest paths? Write down Dikekstra's algorithm for it. [GBTU]
2. Describe Flayod warshells algorithms for finding all pairs shortest path algorithm. [KU]
3. Give an algorithm that determines weather or not a given undirected graph G = (V,E) contains a cycle. Your algorithm should run in O(V) time. [GBTU]
4. For the graph (weighted, directed)

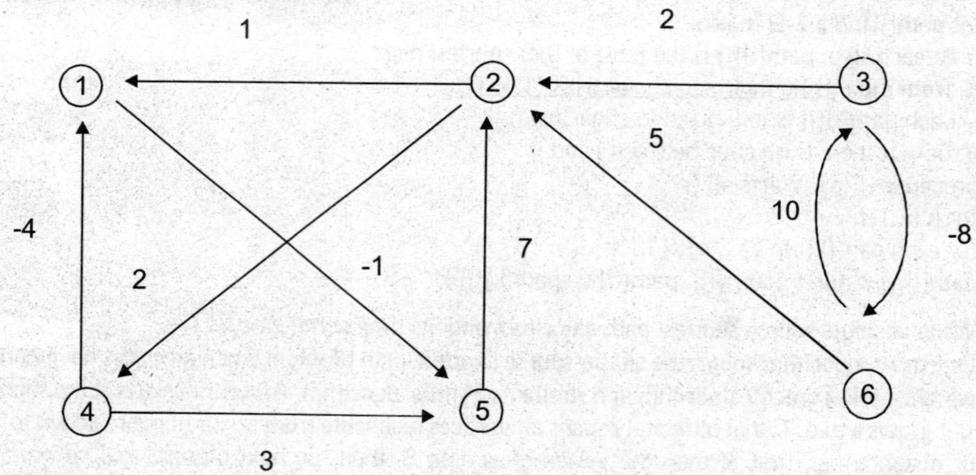

Apply floyd – warshall Algorithm for constructing shortest path. Show the Matrix $D^{(k)}$ that results each iterations. [GBTU]

5. Use Dijkstra's algorithm to find single source shortest path algorithm for the following graph taking vertex s as a source.

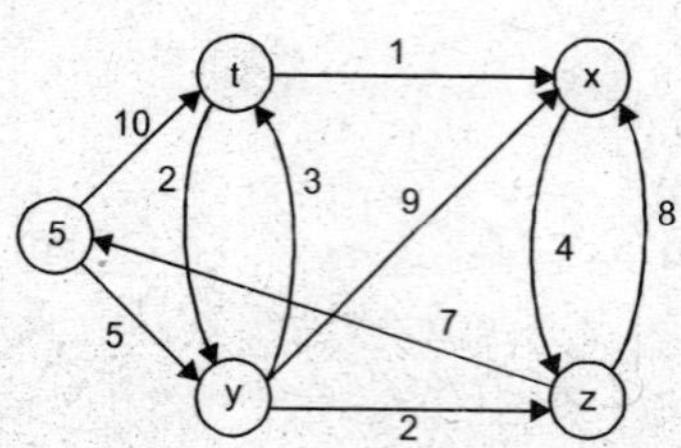

[MDU]

EXERCISE

1. Give a simple example of a directed graph with negative-weight edges for which Dijkstra's algorithm produces incorrect answers. Why doesn't the proof of Dijkstra's algorithm go through when negative-weight edges are allowed? 2.
2. Give an example of a four node directed graph with some negative-weight edges for which Dijkstra's algorithm produces incorrect answers. Also, give an example of a four node directed graph with some negative-weight edges for which Dijkstra's algorithm always produces correct answers. In either case, justify your answer. 3.
3. Explain how to modify Dijkstra's algorithm so that if there is more than one minimum path from source to a destination vertex, then a path with the fewest number of edges is chosen. 4.
4. Suppose that in implementing Dijkstra's shortest path algorithm, one uses an AVL tree rather than a partially ordered tree for representing the dynamic set of non-special Vertices. What will be the worst case complexity of the algorithm if an adjacency list representation is used for the digraph? Would you still prefer the partially ordered tree implementation?
5. We are given a directed graph G = (V, E) on which each edge (u, v) ε E has an associated value r(u, v), which is a real number in the range $0 \leq r(u, v) \leq 1$ that represents the reliability of a communication channel from vertex u to vertex v. We interpret r(u, v)as the probability that the channel from u to v will not fail, and we assume that these probabilities are independent. Give an efficient algorithm to find the most reliable path between two vertices.
6. Write a program to find the longest path in a directed acyclic graph. What is the complexity of the algorithm?
7. Describe a mathematical model for the following scheduling problem: Given tasks $T_1, T_2, \ldots, T_n$, which require time $t_1, h, \ldots, t_n$ to complete, and a set of constraints, each of the form Tj must be completed prior to the start of T_i, find the minimum time necessary to complete all the tasks assuming unlimited number of processors to be available.
8. In a depth-first search of a directed graph G = (V, E), define d (v) as the timestamp when v is visited for the first time and f (v)the timestamp when the search finishes examining the adjacency list of v. Show that an edge (u, v) ε E is
   (a) a tree edge or forward edge if and only if $d[u] < d[v] < f[v] < f[u]$.
   (b) a back edge if and only if $d[v] < d[u] < f[u] < f[v]$.
   (c) a cross edge if and only if $d[v] < f[v] < d[u] < f[u]$.
9. An Euler Tour of a connected, directed graph G = (V, E) is a cycle that traverses each edge of G exactly once, although it may visit a vertex more than once.
   (a) Show that G has an Euler tour if and only if indegree (v) = outdegree(v) ∀ v ε V.
   (b) Describe an O(e) algorithm to find an Euler tour of G if one exists, where e is the number of edges.
10. Design an efficient algorithm to determine whether a given DAG is a tree.
11. Let G = (V, E) be a digraph. Define a relation R on V such that uRv if and only if u and v lie on a common (not necessarily simple) cycle. Prove that is an equivalence relation on V.

CHAPTER

19

UNDIRECTED GRAPHS

19.1 INTRODUCTION

An undirected graphs is a graph is which the nodes are corrected by undirected areas. An undirected arc is an edge that has no arrow. Both ends of an undirected arc are equivalent an edge is an undirected graph as a set rather than an ordered pair.

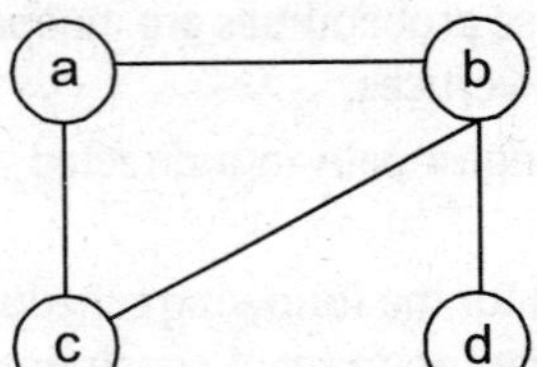

Fig. 19.1 An Undirected Graph.

19.1.1 Definition

An undrected graph is an ordered pair

G = {V, E} with the following properties:

1. The first component, V is a finite, non-empty set. The elements of V are called the vertices of G.
2. The second component, E, is a finite set of sets. Each element of E is a set that is compried of exactly two (distinct) vertices. The elements of E are called the edges of G.

For example, consider the undirected graph G = {V, E}

comprised of four vertices and four edges:

V = {a, b, c, d}

E = {{a, b}, {a, c}, {b, c} { b, d}}

The graph G can be represented graphically as shown in Fig. 19.1 The vertices are represented by approprintely labeled circles, and the edges are represented by lines that are connect. associated vertices.

Note that because an edge in an undirected graph is a set {a, b} ≡ {b, a} and since E is also a set, it cannot contain more then one instance of a given edge. Another consciquence of defination is that there cannot be edge from a node to itself in an undirected graph because an edge is a set of size two and a set cannot contain duplicate.

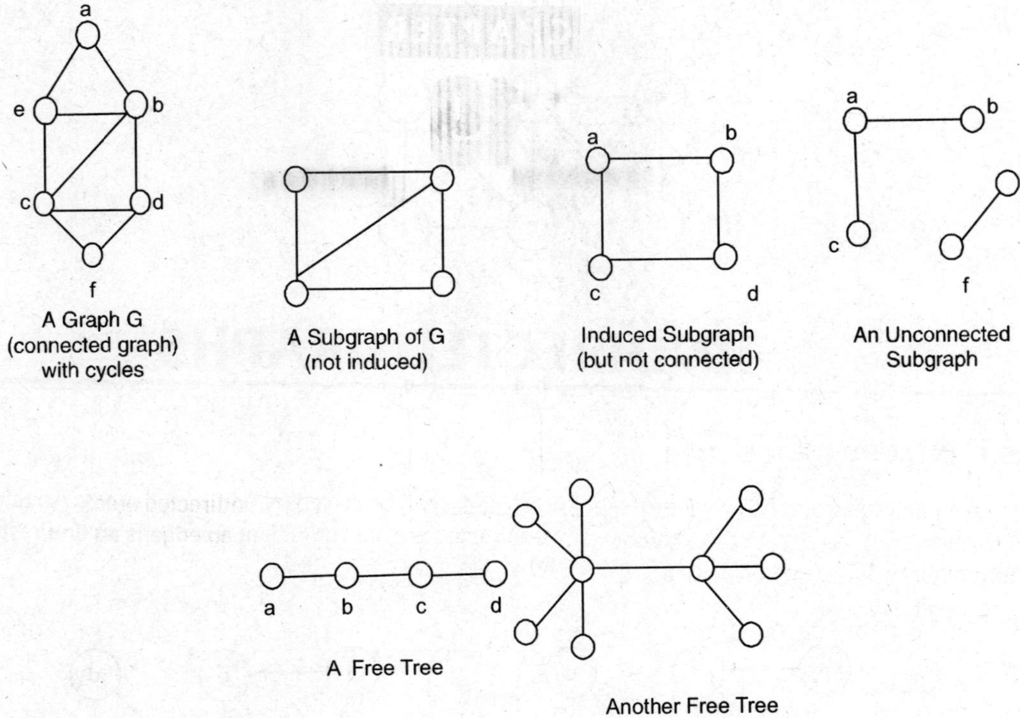

Fig. 19.2 Exaples of undirected graphs

19.2 MINIMUM-COST SPANNING TREES

In this section we consider undirected graphs and their subgraphs. A subgraph of a graph $G = (\nu, \varepsilon)$ is any graph $G' = (\nu', \varepsilon')$ such that $G' = (\nu', \varepsilon')$ and $\nu' \subseteq \nu$ and $\varepsilon' \subseteq \varepsilon$. In particular, we consider connected undirected graphs and their minimal subgraphs . The minimal subgraph of a connected graph is called a spanning tree:

19.2.1 Definition (Spanning Tree)

Consider a connected, undirected graph $G = (\nu, \varepsilon)$. A spanning tree of G is a subgraph of G, say $T = (\nu', \varepsilon')$, with the following properties:

1. $\nu' = \nu$.
2. T is connected.
3. T is acyclic.

Fig. 19.3 shows an undirected graph, G_{13}, together with three of its spanning trees. A spanning tree is called a tree because every acyclic undirected graph can be viewed as a general, unordered tree. Because the edges are undirected, any vertex may be chosen to serve as the root of the tree. For example, the spanning tree of G_{13} given in Figure 19.3 (c) can be viewed as the general, unordered tree G_{13} given in Figure 19.3 (c) can be viewed as the general unordered tree

$$\{b, \{a\}, \{c\}, \{e, \{d\}, \{f\}\}\}.$$

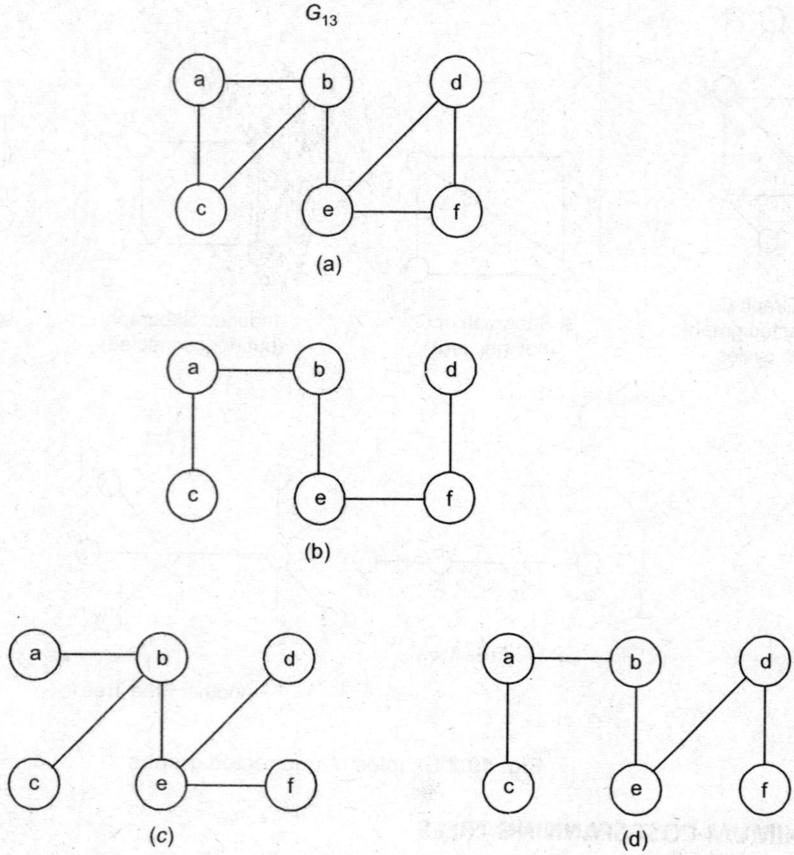

Fig. 19.3 An undirected graph and three spanning trees.

According to Definition , a spanning tree is connected. Therefore, as long as the tree contains more than one vertex, there can be no vertex with degree zero. Furthermore, the following theorem guarantees that there is always at least one vertex with degree one:

Theorem: Consider a connected, undirected graph $G = (\nu, \varepsilon)$, where $|\nu| > 1$. Let $T = (\nu, \varepsilon')$ be a spanning tree of G. The spanning tree T contains at least one vertex of degree one.

Proof: (By contradiction). Assume that there is no vertex in T of degree one. That is, all the vertices in T have degree two or greater. Then by following edges into and out of vertices we can construct a path that is cyclic. But a spanning tree is acycli--a contradiction. Therefore, a spanning tree always contains at least one vertex of degree one.

According to Definition, the edge set of a spanning tree is a subset of the edges in the spanned graph. How many edges must a spanning tree have? The following theorem answers the question:

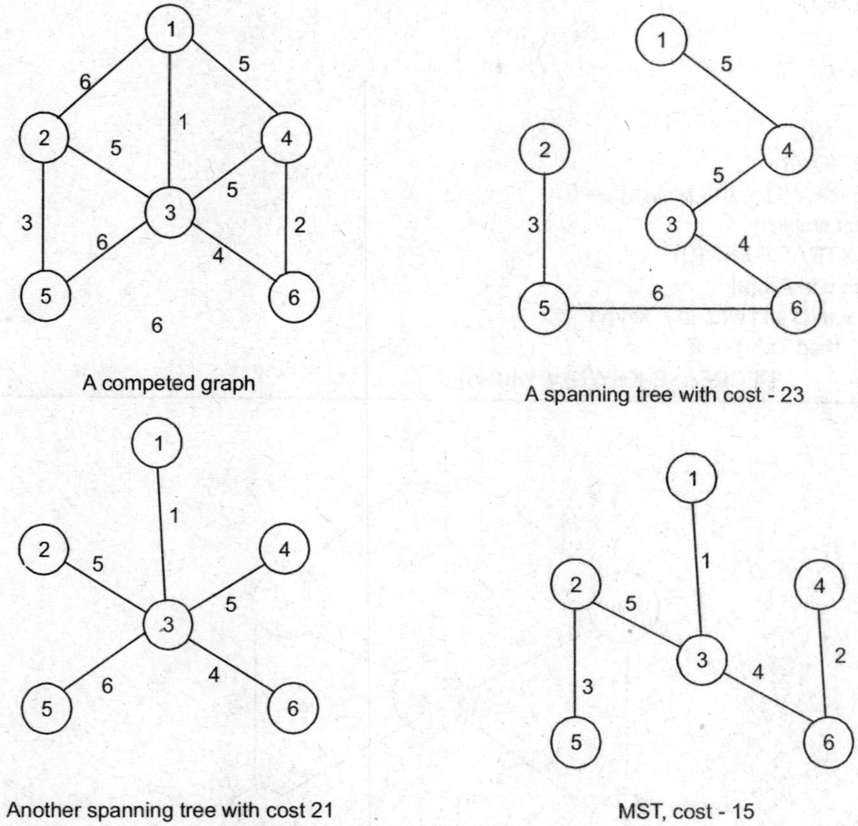

Fig. 19.4 Spanning trees in a connected graph

19.3 PRIM'S ALGORITHM

Prim's algorithm is a greedy algorithm that finds a minimum spanning tree for a connected weighted undirected graph. This means it finds a subset of the edges that forms a tree that includes every vertex, where the total weight of all the edges in the tree is minimized.

The only spanning tree of the empty graph (with an empty vertex set) is again the empty graph. The following description assumes that this special case is handled separately. The algorithm continuously increases the size of a tree, one. edge at a time, starting with a tree consisting of a single vertex, until it spans all vertices.

- Input: A non-empty connected weighted graph with vertices V and edges E (the weights can be negative).
- Initialize: V_{new} = {x}, where x is an arbitrary node (starting point) from V, E_{new} = {}
- Repeat until V_{new} = V:
  - o Choose an edge (u, v) with minimal weight such that u is in V_{new} and v is not (if there are multiple edges with the same weight, any of them may be picked)
  - o Add v to V_{new}, and u, v) to E_{new}
- Output: V_{new} and E_{new} describe a minimal spanning tree

```
PRIM (V, E, w, r)
Q ← {}
for each u in V
  do key[u] ← ∞
     π [u] ← NIL
     INSERT(Q, u)
DECREASE-KEY(Q, r, 0)// kcey[r ] ← 0
while Q is not empty
  do u ← EXTRACT-MIN(Q)
     for each v in Adj[u]
       do if v in Q and w(u, v) < key[v]
            then 7π[v] ← u
                 DECREASE-KEY(Q, v, w(u, v))
```

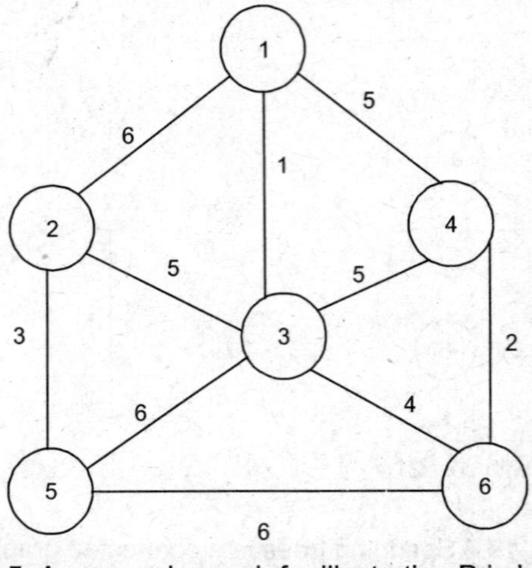

Figure 19.5. An example graph for illustrating Prim's algorithm

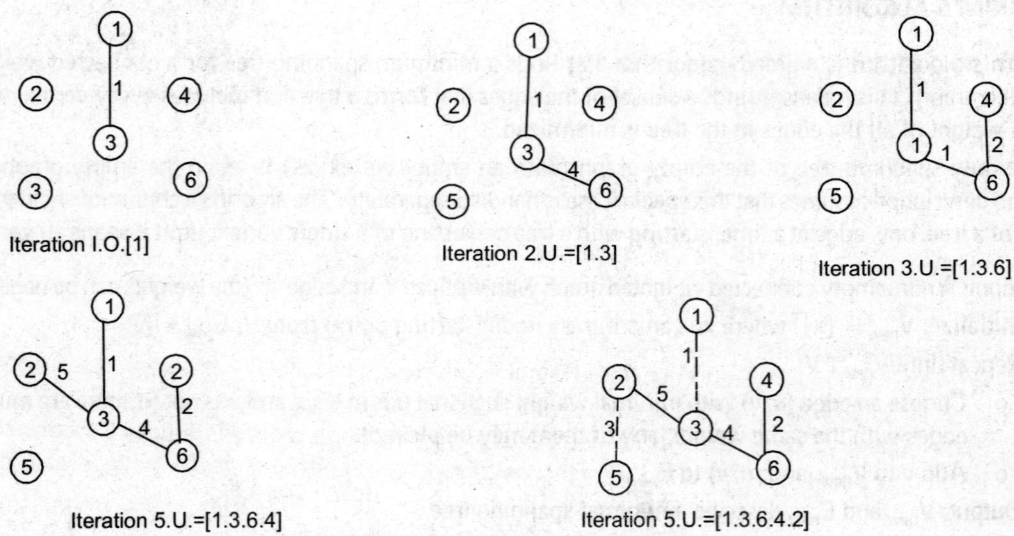

Figure 19.6. Illustration of Prim's algorithm

At each step, we can scan lowcost to find the vertex in V- U that is closest to U. Then we update lowcost and closest taking into account the new addition to U.

Complexity: $O(n^2)$

Example: Consider the digraph shown in Fig. 19.6.

Step 1

U = {1} V – U = {2, 3, 4, 5, 6}

Closet		lowcost
V–U	U	
2	1	6
3	1	1
4	1	5
5	1	∞
6	1	∞

Select vertex 3 to include in U

Step 2

U = {1, 3} V – U = {2, 4, 5, 6}

Closet		lowcost
V–U	U	
2	3	5
4	1	5
5	3	6
6	3	4

Now select vertex 6

Step 3

U = {1, 3, 6} V–U = {2,4,5,6}

Closest		lowcost
V–U	U	
2	3	5
4	6	2
5	3	6

Now select vertex 4, and so on

A simple implementation using an adjacency matrix graph representation and searching an array of weights to find the minimum weight edge to add requires $O(V^2)$ running time. Using a simple binary heap data structure and an adjacency list representation, Prim's algorithm can be shown to run in times O (E log V) where E is the number of edges and V is the number of vertices. Using a more sophisticated Fibonacci heap, this can be brought down to O(E + V log V), which is asymptotically faster when the graph is dense enough that E is Ω(V).

19.4 KRUSKAL'S ALGORITHM

Kruskal's algorithm is an algorithm in graph theory that finds a minimum spanning tree for a connected weighted graph. This means it finds a subset of the edges that forms a tree that includes every vertex, where the total weight of all the edges in the tree is minimized. If the graph is not connected, then it finds a minimum spanning forest (a minimum spanning tree for each connected component). Kruskal's algorithm is an example of a greedy algorithm.

Algorithm:

- create a forest F (a set of trees), where each vertex in the graph is a separate tree
- create a set S containing all the edges in the graph
- while S is nonempty and F is not yet spanning
  - o remove an edge with minimum weight from S
  - o if that edge connects two different trees, then add it to the forest, combining two trees into a single tree
  - o otherwise discard that edge.

At the termination of the algorithm, the forest has only one component and forms a minimum spanning tree of the graph.

Start with an empty set A, and select at every stage the shortest edge that has not been chosen or rejected, regardless of where this edge is situated in the graph.

```
KRUSKAL(V, E, w)
A ← { } Set A will ultimatery contains the eages of the MST
for each vertex v in V
  do MAKE-SET(v)
sort E into nondecreasing order by weight w
for each  u, v) taken from the sorted list
  do if FIND-SET(u) = FIND-SET(v)
     then A ← A {(u, v)}
          UNION (u, v)
return A
```

Illustrative Examples

Lets run through the following graph quickly to see how Kruskal's algorithm works on it:

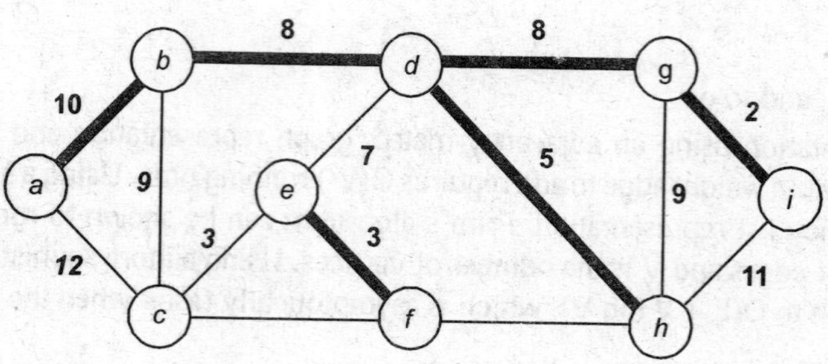

We get the shaded edges shown in the above figure.

Edge (c, f): safe
Edge (g, i): safe
Edge (e, f): safe
Edge (c, e): reject
Edge (d, h): safe
Edge (f, h): safe
Edge (e, d): reject
Edge (b, d): safe
Edge (d, g): safe
Edge (b, c): reject
Edge (g, h): reject
Edge (a, b): safe

At this point, we have only one component, so all other edges will be rejected. [We could add a test to the main loop of KRUSKAL to stop once |V| – 1 edges have been added to A.]

Note Carefully: Suppose we had examined (c, e) before (e, f). Then would have found (c, e) safe and would have rejected (e, f).

Example (CLRS) Step-by-Step Operation of Kurskal's Algorithm.

Step 1. In the graph, the Edge(g, h) is shortest. Either vertex g or vertex h could be representative. Lets choose vertex g arbitrarily.

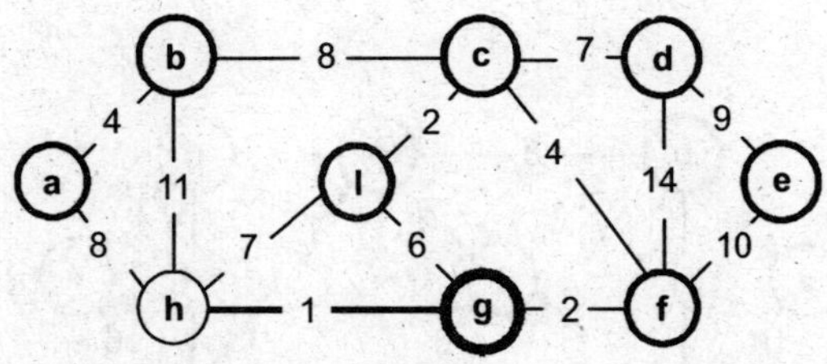

Step 2. The edge (c, i) creates the second tree. Choose vertex c as representative for second tree.

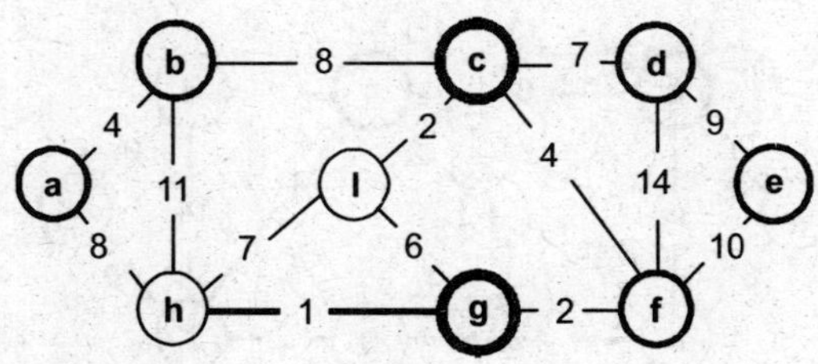

Step 3. Edge (g, f) is the next shortest edge. Add this edge and choose vertex g as representative.

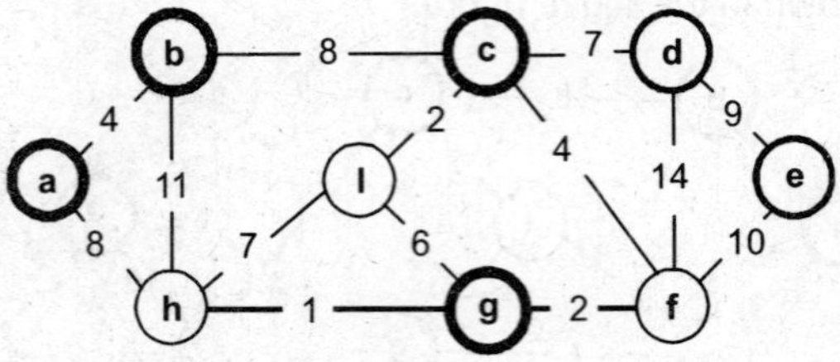

Step 4. Edge (a, b) creates a third tree.

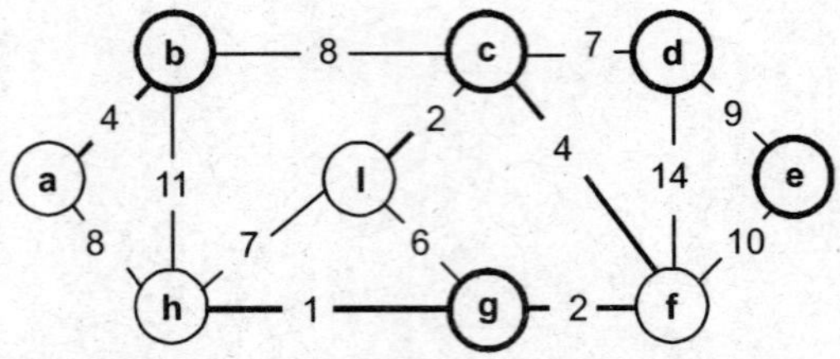

Step 5. Add edge (c, f) and merge two trees. Vertex c is chosen as the representative.

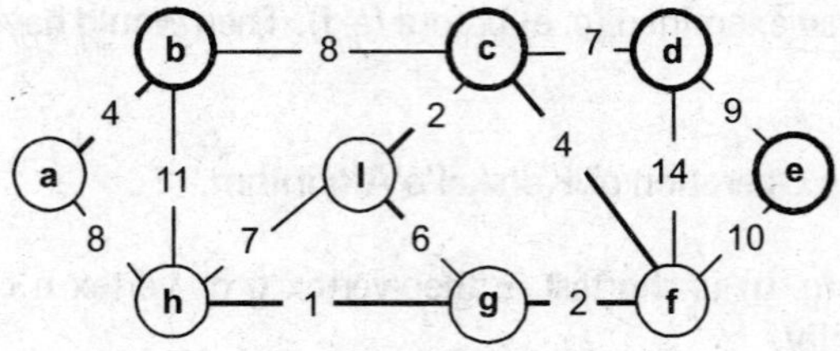

Step 6. Edge (g, i) is the next next cheapest, but if we add this edge a cycle would be created. Vertex c is the representative of both.

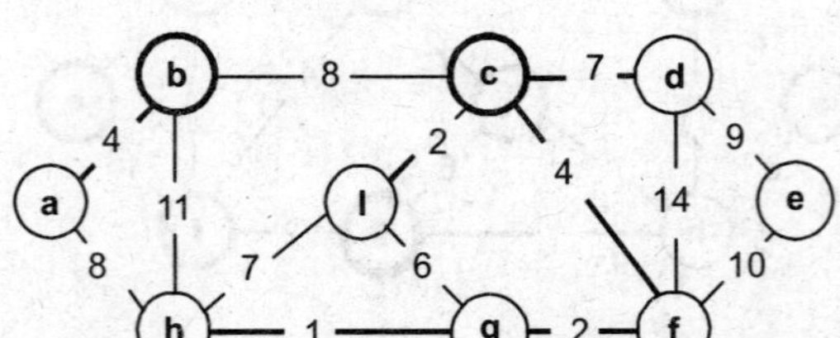

Step 7. Instead, add edge (c, d).

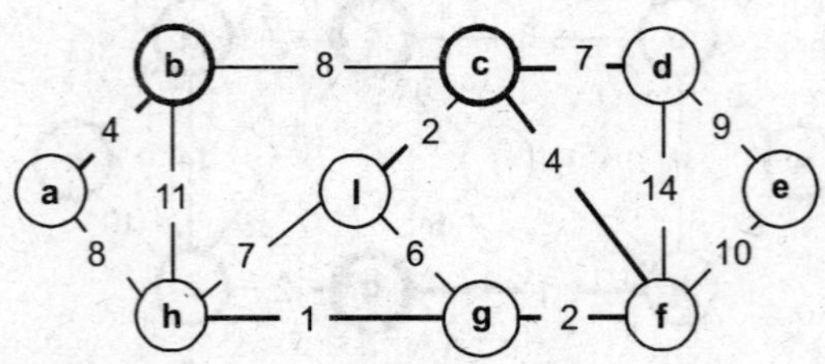

Step 8. If we add edge (h, i), edge (h, i) would make a cycle.

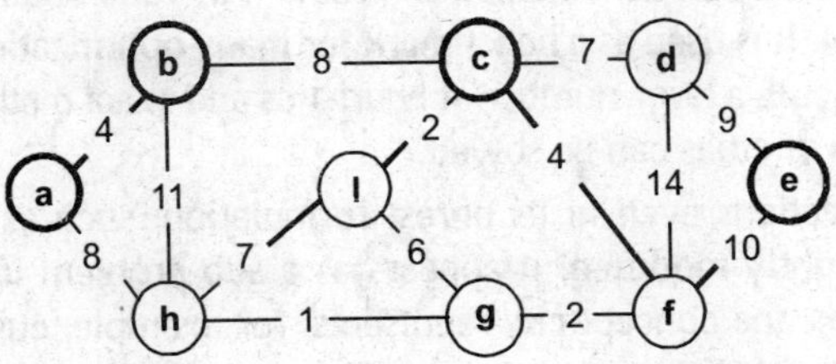

Step 9. Instead of adding edge (h, i) add edge (a, h).

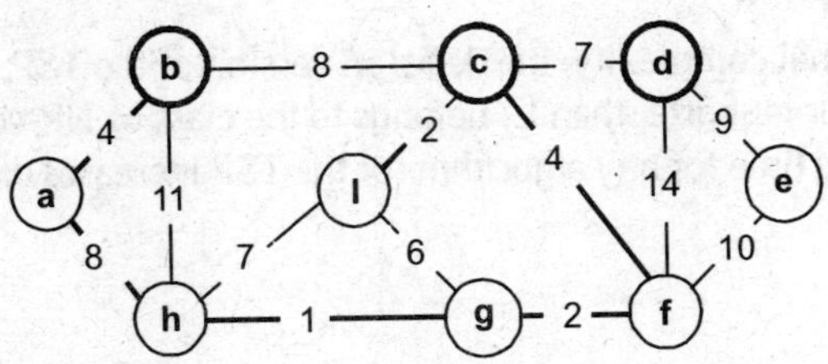

Step 10. Again, if we add edge (b, c), it would create a cycle. Add edge (d, e) instead to complete the spanning tree. In this spanning tree all trees joined and vertex c is a sole representative.

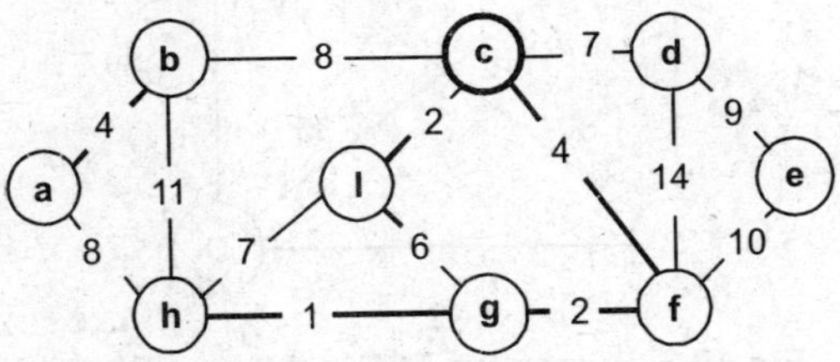

Analysis

Where E is the number of edges in the graph and V is the number of vertices, Kruskal's algorithm can be shown to run in Q(E log E)time. or equivalently, O(E log V) time, all with simple data structures. These running times are equivalent because:

- E is at most V^2 and $\log V^2$ = 21ogV is O(log V).
- If we ignore isolated vertices, which will each be their own component of the minimum spanning forest, $V \leq E + 1$, so log V is O (log E).

We can achieve this bound as follows: first sort the edges by weight using a comparison sort in O (E log E) time; this allows the step "remove an edge with minimum weight from S" to operate in constant time. Next, we use a disjoint-set data structure (Union&Find) to keep track of which vertices are in which components. We need to perform O(E) operations, two 'find' operations and possibly one union for each edge. Even a simple disjoint-set data structure such as disjoint-set forests with union by rank can perform O(E) operations in O(E log V) time. Thus the total time is O(E log E) = O(E log V).

19.5 TRAVELING SALESMAN PROBLEM

The Travelling Salesman Problem (TSP) is an NP-hard problem in combinatorial optimization studied in operations research and theoretical computer science. Given a list of cities and their pairwise distances, the task is to find a shortest possible tour that visits each city exactly once.

The problem was first formulated as a mathematical problem in 1930 and is one of the most intensively studied problems in optimization. It is used as a benchmark for many optimization methods. Even though the problem is computationally difficult, a large number of heuristics and exact methods are known, so that some instances with tens of thousands of cities can be solved.

The TSP has several applications even in its purest formulation, such as planning, logistics. and the manufacture of microchips. Slightly modified, it appears as a sub-problem in many areas, such as DNA sequencing. In these applications, the concept city represents, for example, customers, soldering points, or DNA fragments, and the concept distance represents travelling times or cost, or a similarity measure between DNA fragments. In many applications, additional constraints such as limited resources or time windows make the problem considerably harder.

In the theory of computational complexity, the decision version of the TSP (where, given a length L, the task is to decide whether any tour is shorter than L) belongs to the class of NP-complete problems. Thus, it is likely that the worst case running time for any algorithm for the TSP increases exponentially with the number of cities.

19.5.1 As a graph problem

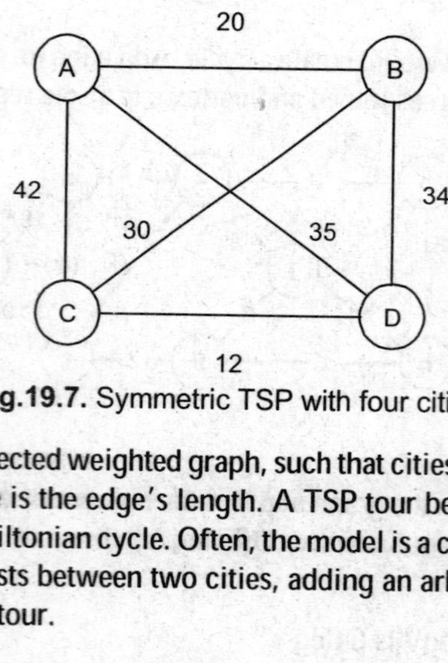

Fig.19.7. Symmetric TSP with four cities

TSP can be modeled as an undirected weighted graph, such that cities are the graph's vertices paths are the graph's edges, and a path's distance is the edge's length. A TSP tour becomes a Hamiltonian cycle. and the optimal TSP tour is the shortest Hamiltonian cycle. Often, the model is a complete graph (i.e., an edge connects each pair of vertices), If no path exists between two cities, adding an arbitrarily long edge will complete the graph without affecting the optimal tour.

19.5.2 Asymmetric and symmetric

In the symmetric TS , the distance between two cities is the same in each opposite direction, forming an undirected graph. This symmetry halves the number of possible solutions. In the asymmetric TS , paths may not exist in both directions or the distances might be different, forming a directed graph. Traffic cnllisions one-way streets, and airfares for cities with different departure and arrival fees are examples of how this symmetry could break down.

19.5.3 With metric distances

In the metric TS , also known as delta-TS or Δ-TSP, the intercity distances satisfy the triangle inequality. This can be understood as "no shortcuts", in the sense that the direct connection from A to B is never longer than the detour via C:

$$C_{ij} \le C_{ik} + C_{kj}$$

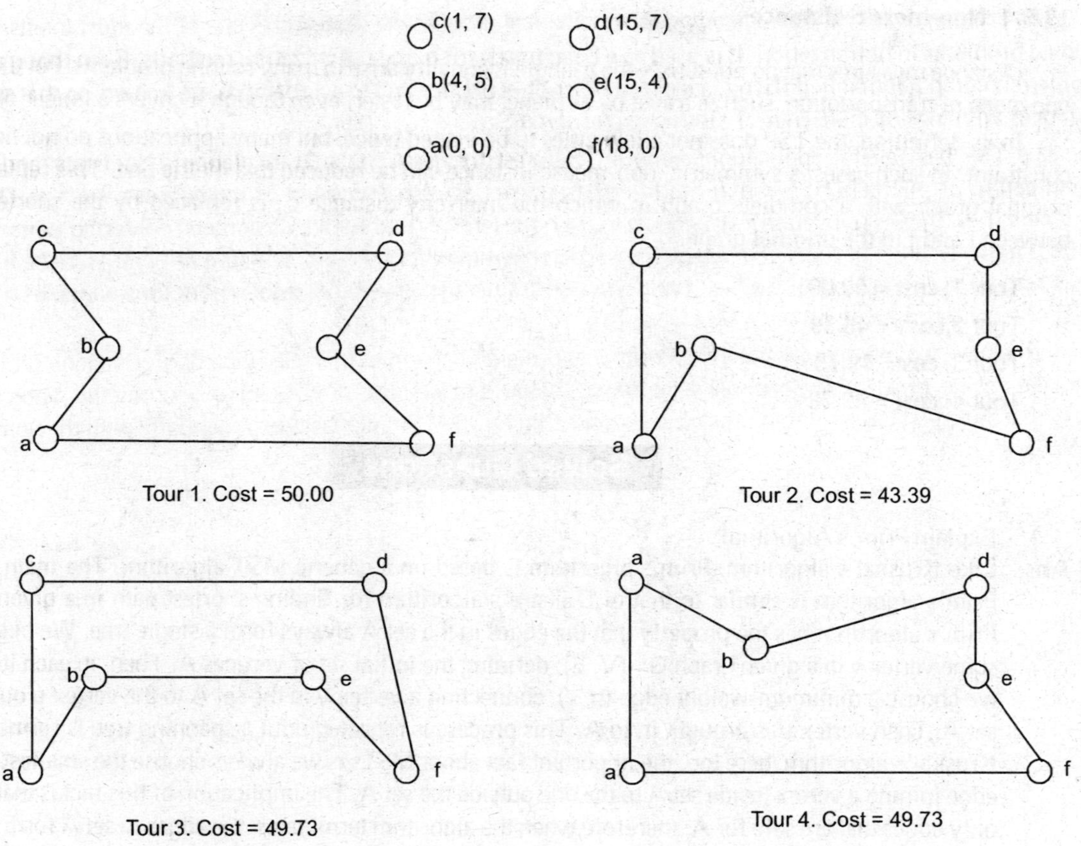

Figure 19.8 A six-city TSP and some tours

These edge lengths define a metric on the set of vertices. When the cities are viewed as points in the plane, many natural distance-functions are metrics.

- In the Euclidean TSP the distance between two cities is the Euclidean distance between the corresponding points.
- In the Rectilinear TSP the distance between two cities is the sum of the differences of their x- and y-coordinates. This metric is often called the Manhattan distance or city-block metric.
- in the maximum metric, the distance between two points is the maximum of the differences of their x- and y-coordinates.

The last two metrics appear for example in routing a machine that drills a given set of holes in a printed circuit board. The Manhattan metric corresponds to a machine that adjusts first one co-ordinate, and then the other, so the time to move to a new point is the sum of both movements. The maximum metric corresponds to a machine that adjusts both co-ordinates simultaneously, so the time to move to a new point is the slower of the two movements.

Despite the simplification over the general case, the metric TSP problem with an arbitrary metric is still NP-complete.

19.5.4 Non-metric distances

Distance measures that do not satisfy the triangle inequality arise in many routing problems. For example one mode of transportation, such as travel by airplane, may be faster, even though it covers a longer distance.

In its definition, the TSP does not allow cities to be visited twice, but many applications do not need this constraint. In such cases, a symmetric, non-metric instance can be reduced to a metric one. This replaces the original graph with a complete graph in which the inter-city distance c_{ij} is replaced by the shortest path between i and j in the original graph.

Tour 1. cost = 50.00

Tour 2,cosV= 48.39

Tour 3, cost= 49.73

Tour 4. cost = 49.78

Solved Questions

1. Explain Prim's Algorithm.

Ans. Like Kruskal's algorithm, Prim's algorithm is based on a generic MST algorithm. The main idea of Prim's algorithm is similar to that of Dijkstra's algorithm for finding shortest path in a given graph. Prim's algorithm has the property that the edges in the set A always form a single tree. We begin with some vertex v in a given graph G =(V, E), defining the initial set of vertices A. Then, in each iteration, we choose a minimum-weight edge (u, v), connecting a vertex v in the set A to the vertex u outside of set A. Then vertex u is brought in to A. This process is repeated until a spanning tree is formed. Like Kruskal's algorithm, here too, the important fact about MSTs is we always choose the smallest-weight edge joining a vertex inside set A to the one outside the set A. The implication of this fact is that it adds only edges that are safe for A; therefore when the algorithm terminates, the edges in set A form a MST.

```
MST_PRIM (G, w, v)
Q ← V[G]
for each u in Q do
   key [u] ← ∞
key [r] ← 0
π[r] ← NIl
while queue is not empty do
   u ← EXTRACT_MIN (Q)
   for each v in Adj[u] do
      if v is in Q and w(u, v) < key [v]
         then π[v] ← w(u, v)
            key [v] ← w(u, v)
```

2. Does the minimum spanning tree of a graph give the shortest distance between any 2 specified nodes?

Ans. No. Minimal spanning tree assures that the total weight of the tree is kept at its minimum. But it doesn't mean that the distance between any two nodes involved in the minimum-spanning tree is minimum.

Previous Year University Question

1. What is minimum spanning tree ? Write Prim's algorithm for finding minimum spanning tree. [OU]
2. Jot down four vertices A,B,C and D and construct all possible spanning trees. [Madrass University]
3. Write Prims algorithm for finding minimum spanning tree.Analyse its time complexity. Compare it with Krushkal's algorithm. [KU]
4. Find the minimum cost spanning tree of the given graph using prim's algorithm. [GBTU]

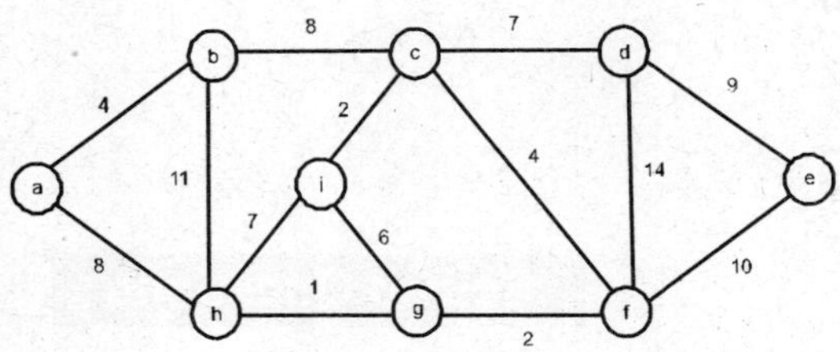

5. With the help of a suitable example, explain Kruskal's algorithm for determining the minimal spanning tree. [Madrass University]
6. Write prim's algorithms to find minimum spanning tree of the graph with an example. [MDU]
7. Write any one algorithm to find minimum spanning tree of the graph. Take suitable example to explain it. [MDU]
8. Write and explain krushkal's algorithm to find the minimum spalling tree from a graph with example and derive its time complexity. [MDU]

Exercise

1. Consider an undirected graph G = (V, E), with n vertices. Show how a one dimensional
2. array of length $\frac{n(n-1)}{2}$ can be used to represent G.

   Give an algorithm that determines whether or not a given undirected graph G = (V, E) contains a cycle. The algorithm should run in O(| V |) time independent of | E |.
3. Design an algorithm to enumerate all simple cycles of a graph. How many such cycles can there be? What is the time complexity of the algorithm?
4. Let (u, v) be a minimum-weight edge in a graph G. Show that (u, v) belongs to some minimum spanning tree of G.
5. Let e be maximum-weight edge on some cycle of G = (V, E). Prove that there is a minimum spanning tree of G′ = (V, E - {e}) that is also a minimum spanning tree of G.
6. For an undirected graph G with n vertices and e edges, show that $\sum_{1}^{n} = 1\, d_i = 2e$ where d_i is the degree of vertex i (number of edges incident on vertex i).
7. The diameter of a tree T= (V, E) is defined by $\max_{u,v\in V} \delta(u,v)$ where $\delta(u, v)$ is the shortest-path distance from vertex u to vertex v. Give an efficient algorithm to compute the diameter of a tree, and analyze the running time of the algorithm.

8. An Eulerian walk in an undirected graph is a path that starts and ends at the same vertex, traversing every edge in the graph exactly once. Prove that in order for such a path to exist, all nodes must have even degree.
9. Two binary trees T_1 and T_2 are said to be isomorphic if T_1 can be transformed into T_2 by swapping left and right children of (some of the) nodes in T_1. Design an efficient algorithm to decide id two given trees are isomorphic. What is the time complexity of your algorithm?

CHAPTER

20

DYNAMIC PROGRAMMING

20.1 INTRODUCTION

Dynamic programming is a method for solving complex problems by breaking them down into simpler subproblems. It is applicable to problems exhibiting the properties of overlapping subproblems which are only slightly smaller and optimal substructure When applicable, the method takes far less time than naive methods.

The key idea behind dynamic programming is quite simple. In general, to solve a given problem, we need to solve different parts of the problem (subproblems), then combine the solutions of the subproblems to reach an overall solution. Often, many of these subproblems are really the same. The dynamic programming approach seeks to solve each subproblem only once, thus saving a lot of computation. This is especially useful when the number of repeating subproblems is exponentially large.

Top-down dynamic programming simply means storing the results of certain calculations, which are later used again since the completed calculation is a sub-problem of a larger calculation. Bottom-up dynamic programming involves formulating a complex calculation as a recursive series of simpler calculations.

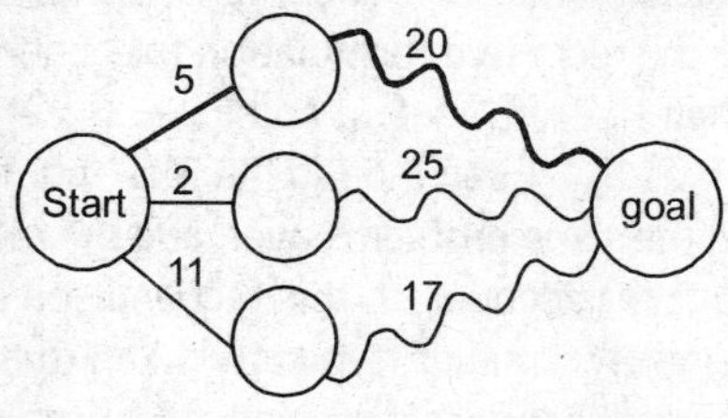

Fig. 20.1. Finding the shortest path in a graph using optimal substructure; a straight line indicates a single edge; a wavy line indicates a shortest path between the two vertices it connects (other nodes on these paths are not shown); the bold line is the overall shortest path from start to goal.

Dynamic programming is both a mathematical optimization method and a computer programming method. In both contexts it refers to simplifying a complicated problem by breaking it down into simpler subproblems in a recursive manner. While some decision problems cannot be taken apart this way, decisions that span several points in time do often break apart recursively; Bellman called this the "Principle of Optimality". Likewise, in computer science, a problem which can be broken down recursively is said to have optimal substructure.

If subproblems can be nested recursively inside larger problems, so that dynamic programming methods are applicable, then there is a relation between the value of the larger problem and the values of the subproblems In the optimization literature this relationship is called the Bellman equation.

20.2 DYNAMIC PROGRAMMING IN MATHEMATICAL OPTIMIZATION

In terms of mathematical optimization, dynamic programming usually refers to simplifying a decision by breaking it down into a sequence of decision steps over time. This is done by defining a sequence of value functions V_1, V_2, ... V_n, with an argument y representing the state of the system at times i from 1 to n. The definition of $V_n(y)$ is the value obtained in state y at the last time n. The values V_{i-1} at earlier times i=n−1, (n − 2),...,2, 1 can be found by working backwards, using a recursive relationship called the Bellman equation. For i = 2,...n, V_{i-1} at any state y is calculated from V_i by maximizing a simple function (usually the sum) of the gain from decision i−1 and the function V_i at the new state of the system if this decision is made. Since V has already been calculated for the needed states, the above operation yields V_{i-1} for those states. Finally, V_1 at the initial state of the system is the value of the optimal solution. The optimal values of the decision variables can be recovered, one by one, by tracking back the calculations already performed.

20.3 DYNAMIC PROGRAMMING IN COMPUTER PROGRAMMING

There are two key attributes that a problem must have in order for dynamic programming to be applicable: optimal substructure and overlapping subproblems which are only slightly smaller. When the overlapping problems are, say, half the size of the original problem the strategy is called "divide and conquer" rather than "dynamic programming". This is why mergesort, quicksort, and finding all matches of a regular expression are not classified as dynamic programming problems.

Optimal substructure means that the solution to a given optimization problem can be obtained by the combination of optimal solutions to its subproblems. Consequently, the first step towards devising a dynamic programming solution is to check whether the problem exhibits such optimal substructure. Such optimal substructures are usually described by means of recursion. For example, given a graph G = (V, E), the shortest path p from a vertex u to a vertex v exhibits optimal substructure: take any intermediate vertex w on this shortest path p. If p is truly the shortest path, then the path p_1 from u to w and p_2 from w to v are indeed the shortest paths between the corresponding vertices Hence, one can easily formulate the solution for findingshortest paths in a recursive manner, which is what the Bellman-Ford algorithm does.

Overlapping subproblems means that the space of subproblems must be small, that is, any recursive algorithm solving the problem should solve the same subproblems over and over, rather than generating new subproblems. For example, consider the recursive formulation for generating the Fibonacci series: $F_i = F_{i-1} + F_{i-2}$, with base case $F_1 = F_2 = 1$. Then $F_{43} = F_{42} + F_{41}$, and $F_{42} = F_{41} + F_{40}$. Now F_{41} is being solved in the recursive subtrees of both F_{43} as well as F_{42}. Even though the total number of subproblems is actually small (only 43 of them), we end up solving the same problems over and over if we adopt a naive recursive solution such as this. Dynamic programming takes account of this fact and solves each subproblem only once. Note that the subproblems must be only slightly smaller (typically taken to mean a constant additive factor) than the larger problem; when they are a multiplicative factor smaller the problem is no longer classified as dynamic programming.

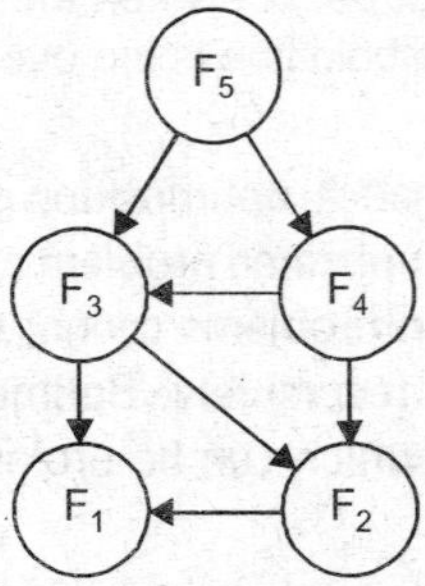

Fig. 20.2. The subproblem graph for the Fibonacci sequence. The fact that it is not a tree indicates overlapping subproblems.

This can be achieved in either of two ways:

1. Top-down approach: This is the direct fall-out of the recursive formulation of any problem. If the solution to any problem can be formulated recursively using the solution to its subproblems, and if its subproblems are overlapping, then one can easily memoize or store the solutions to the subproblems in a table. Whenever we attempt to solve a new subproblem, we first check the table to see if it is already solved. If a solution has been recorded, we can use it directly, otherwise we solve the subproblem and add its solution to the table.
2. Bottom-up approach: This is the more interesting case. Once we formulate the solution to a problem recursively as in terms of its subproblems, we can try reformulating the problem in a bottom-up fashion: try solving the subproblems first and use their solutions to build-on and arrive at solutions to bigger subproblems. This is also usually done in a tabular form by iteratively generating solutions to bigger and bigger subproblems by using the solutions to small subproblems. For example, if we already know the values of F_{41} and F40, we can directly calculate the value of F_{42}.

Some programming languages can automatically memoize the result of a function call with a particular set of arguments, in order to speed up call-by-name evaluation (this mechanism is referred to as call-by-need). Some languages make it possible portably (e.g. Scheme, Common Lisp or Perl), some need special extensions (e.g. C++,). Some languages have automatic memoization built in, such as tabled Prolog. In any case, this is only possible for a referentially transparent function.

20.4 OPTIMAL CONSUMPTION AND SAVING

A mathematical optimization problem that is often used in teaching dynamic programming to economists (because it can be solved by hand) concerns a consumer who lives over the periods t = 0, l,2,...,T and must decide how much to consume and how much to save in each period.

Let c_t be consumption in period t, and assume consumption yields utility $u(c_t) = \ln(c_t)$ as long as the consumer lives. Assume the consumer is impatient, so that he discounts future utility by a factor b each period, where $0 < b < 1$. Let k_t be capital in period t. Assume initial capital is a given amount $k_0 > 0$, and suppose that this period's capital and consumption determine next period's capital as $k_{t+1} = Ak_t^\alpha - c_t$, where A is a positive constant and $0 < a < 1$.

Assume capital cannot be negative. Then the consumer's decision problem can be written as follows:

$$\max \sum_{t=0}^{T} b^t \ln(c_t) \text{ subject to } k_{t+1} = Ak_t^\alpha - c_t \geq 0 \text{ for all } t = 0, 1, 2 \ldots T.$$

Written this way, the problem looks complicated, because it involves solving for all the choice variables $c_0, c_1, c_2, \ldots, c_T$ and $k_1, k_2, k_3, \ldots, k_{T+1}$ simultaneously. (Note that k_0 is not a choice variable—the consumer's initial capital is taken as given.)

The dynamic programming approach to solving this problem involves breaking it apart into a sequence of smaller decisions. To do so, we define a sequence of value functions $V_t(k)$, for t = 0,1,2,...,T,T + 1 which represent the value of having any amount of capital k at each time t. Note that $V_{T+1}(k) = 0$, that is, there is (by assumption) no utility from having capital after death.

The value of any quantity of capital at any previous time can be calculated by backward induction using the Bellman equation. In this problem, for each t = 0,1,2,..., T, the Bellman equation is

$$V_t(k_t) = \max(\ln(c_t) + bV_{t+1}(k_t + 1)) \text{ subject } k_{t+1} = Ak_t^\alpha - c_t \geq 0$$

This problem is much simpler than the one we wrote down before, because it involves only two decision variables, c_t and k_{t+1}. Intuitively, instead of choosing his whole lifetime plan at birth, the consumer can take things one step at a time. At time t, his current capital k, is given, and he only needs to choose current consumption c_t and saving k_{t+1}.

To actually solve this problem, we work backwards. For simplicity, the current level of capital is denoted as k. V_{T+1} (k) is already known, so using the Bellman equation once we can calculate $V_T(k)$, and so on until we get to $V_0(k)$,which is the value of the initial decision problem for the whole lifetime. In other words, once we know $V_{T-j+1}(k)$, we can calculate V_{T-j} (k), which is the maximum of $\ln(c_{T-j}) + bV_{T-j+1}(Ak^a - c_{T-j})$, where c_{T-j} is the choice variable and $Ak^\alpha - C_{T-j} \geq 0$.

Working backwards, it can be shown that the value function at time t = T–j is

$$V_{T-j}(k) = \alpha \sum_{i=0}^{j} a^i b^i \ln k + v_{T-j}$$

where each v_{T-j} is a constant, and the optimal amount to consume at time t = T–j is

$$C_{T-j}(k) = \frac{1}{\sum_{i=0}^{j} a^i b^i} Ak^a$$

which can be simplified to

$$c_T(k) = Ak^a, \quad c_{T-1}(k) = \frac{Ak^a}{1+ab}, \text{ and } c_{T-2}(k) = \frac{Ak^a}{1+ab+a^2b^2},$$

We see that it is optimal to consume a larger fraction of current wealth as one gets older, finally consuming all remaining wealth in period T, the last period of life.

20.5 FIBONACCI SEQUENCE

Here is a naive implementation of a function finding the nth member of the Fibonacci sequence, based directly on the mathematical definition:

```
function fib(n)
    if n = 0 return 0
    if n = 1 return 1
    return fib(n – 1) + fib (n – 2)
```

Notice that if we call, say, fib(5), we produce a call tree that calls the function on the same value many different times:

```
1. fib(5)
2. fib(4) + fib(3)
3. (fib(3) + fib(2)) + (fib(2) + fib(l))
4. ((fib (2) + fib(l)) + (fib(l) + fib(O))) + ((fib(l) + fib(O)) + fib(l) )
5. (((fib(l) + fib(0)) + fib(l)) + (fib(l) + fib(0))) + ((fib(l) +fib(0)) + fib(l) )
```

In particular, fib(2) was calculated three times from scratch. In larger examples, many more values of fib, or subproblems, are recalculated, leading to an exponential time algorithm.

Now, suppose we have a simple map object, m, which maps each value of fib that has already been calculated to its result, and we modify our function to use it and update it. The resulting function requires only Q(n) time instead of exponential time:

```
var m : = map (0 → 0, 1 → 1)
function fib(n)
    if map m does not contain key n
        m[n] := fib(n - 1) + fib(n - 2)
    return m[n]
```

This technique of saving values that have already been calculated is galled memoization: this is the top-down approach, since we first break the problem into subproblems and then calculate and store values.

In the bottom-up approach we calculate the smaller values of fib first, then build larger values from them. This method also uses O (n) time since it contains a loop that repeats n – 1 times, however it only takes constant (O (I)) space, in contrast to the top-down approach which requires O (n) space to store the map.

```
function fib(n)
  var previousFib := 0, currentFib := 1
  if n = 0
      return 0
  else if n = 1
      return 1
  repeat n - 1 times
        var newFib := previousFib + currentFib
        previousFib := currentFib
        currentFib := newFib
  return currentFib
```

In both these examples, we only calculate fib(2) one time, and then use it to calculate both fib(4) and fib(3), instead of computing it every time either of them is evaluated. (Note the calculation of the Fibonacci sequence is used to demonstrate dynamic programming. An O(1) formula exists from which an arbitrary term can be calculated, which is more efficient than any dynamic programming technique.)

20.6 A TYPE OF BALANCED 0-1 MATRIX

Consider the problem of assigning values, either zero or one, to the positions of an n × n matrix, n even, so that each row and each column contains exactly n/2 zeros and n/2 ones. For example, when n = 4, four possible solutions are

$$\begin{bmatrix} 0 & 1 & 0 & 1 \\ 1 & 0 & 1 & 0 \\ 0 & 1 & 0 & 1 \\ 1 & 0 & 1 & 0 \end{bmatrix} \text{and} \begin{bmatrix} 0 & 0 & 1 & 1 \\ 0 & 0 & 1 & 1 \\ 1 & 1 & 0 & 0 \\ 1 & 1 & 0 & 0 \end{bmatrix} \text{and} \begin{bmatrix} 1 & 1 & 0 & 0 \\ 0 & 0 & 1 & 1 \\ 1 & 1 & 0 & 0 \\ 0 & 0 & 1 & 1 \end{bmatrix} \text{and} \begin{bmatrix} 1 & 0 & 0 & 1 \\ 0 & 1 & 1 & 0 \\ 0 & 1 & 1 & 0 \\ 1 & 0 & 0 & 1 \end{bmatrix}$$

We ask how many different assignments there are for a given n. There are at least three possible approaches: brute force, backtracking, and dynamic programming. Brute force consists of checking all assignments of zeros and ones and counting those that have balanced rows and columns (n / 2 zeros and n / 2 ones). As there are $\binom{n}{n/2}^n$ possible assignments, this strategy is not practical except maybe up to n = 6. Backtracking for this problem consists of choosing some order of the matrix elements and recursively placing ones or zeros, while checking that in every row and column the number of elements that have not been assigned plus the number of ones or zeros are both at least n / 2. While more sophisticated than brute force, this approach will visit every solution once, making it impractical for n larger than six, since the number of solutions is already 116963796250 for n = 8. Dynamic programming makes it possible to count the number of solutions without visiting them all.

We consider k × n boards, where $1 \le k \le n$, whose k rows contain n / 2 zeros and n/ 2 ones. The function f to which memoization is applied maps vectors of n pairs of integers to the number of admissible boards (solutions). There is one pair for each column and its two components indicate respectively the number of ones and zeros that have yet to be placed in that column. We seek the value of f (n/2, n/2), (n/2, n/2,),... (n/2, n/2,) (n arguments or one vector of n elements). The process of subproblem creation involves iterating over every one of $\binom{n}{n/2}$ possible assignments for the top row of the board, and going through every column, subtracting one from the appropriate element of the pair for that column, depending on whether the assignment for the top row contained a zero or a one at that position. If any one of the results is negative, then the assignment is invalid and does not contribute to the set of solutions (recursion stops). Otherwise, we have an assignment for the top row of the k × n board and recursively compute the number of solutions to the remaining (k – 1) × n board, adding the numbers of solutions for every admissible assignment of the top row and returning the sum, which is being memoized. The base case is the trivial subproblem, which occurs for a 1 × n board. The number of solutions for this board is either zero or one, depending on whether the vector is a permutation of n / 2 (0, 1) and n / 2 (1, 0) pairs or not.

For example, in the two boards shown above the sequences of vectors would be

((2, 2)	(2, 2)	(2, 2)	(2, 2))	((2, 2)	(2, 2)	(2, 2)	(2, 2))	k = 4
0	1	0	1	0	0	1	1	
((1, 2)	(2, 1)	(1, 2)	(2, 1))	((1, 2)	(1, 2)	(2, 1)	(2, 1})	k = 3
1	0	1	0	0	0	1	1	
((1, 1)	(1, 1)	(1, 1)	(1, 1))	((0, 2)	(0, 2)	(2, 0)	(2, 0))	k = 2
0	1	0	1	1	1	0	0	
((0, 1)	(1, 0)	(0, 1)	(1, 0))	((0, 1)	(0, 1)	(1, 0)	(1, 0))	k = 1
1	0	1	0	1	1	0	0	
((0, 0)	(0, 0)	(0, 0)	(0, 0))	((0, 0)	(0, 0)	(0, 0)	(0, 0))	

The number of solutions (sequence A058527 in OEIS) is
1, 2, 90, 297200, 116963796250, 6736218287430460752....

20.7 CHECKERBOARD

Consider a checkerboard with n × n squares and a cost-function c (i, j) which returns a cost associated with square i, j (i being the row, j being the column). For instance (on a 5 × 5 checkerboard),

5	6	7	4	7	8
4	7	6	1	1	4
3	3	5	7	8	2
2	–	6	7	0	–
1	–	–	*5*	–	–
	1	2	3	4	5

Thus c (I, 3) = 5

Let us say you had a checker that could start at any square on the first rank (i.e., row) and you wanted to know the shortest path (sum of the costs of the visited squares are at a minimum) to get to the last rank, assuming the checker could move only diagonally left forward, diagonally right forward, or straight forward. That is, a checker on (1,3) can move to (2,2), (2,3) or (2,4).

5					
4					
3					
2		×	×	×	
1			0		
	1	2	3	4	5

This problem exhibits optimal substructure. That is, the solution to the entire problem relies on solutions to subproblems. Let us define a function q(i,j) as

q(i, j) = the minimum cost to reach square (i, j)

If we can find the values of this function for all the squares at rank n, we pick the minimum and follow that path backwards to get the shortest path. Note that q(i, j) is equal to the minimum cost to get to any of the three squares below it (since those are the only squares that can reach it) plus c(i, j). For instance:

5					
4			A		
3		B	C	D	
2					
1					
	1	2	3	4	5

q(A) = min(q(B),q(C),q(D)) + c (A)

Now, let us define q(i,j) in somewhat more general terms:

$$q(i,j) = \begin{cases} \infty & j < 1 \text{ or } j > n \\ c(i,j) & i = n \\ \min(q(i-1,j-1), q(i-1,j), q(i-1,j+1) + c(i,j) & \text{otherwise.} \end{cases}$$

The first line of this equation is there to make the recursive property simpler (when dealing with the edges, so we need only one recursion). The second line says what happens in the last rank, to provide a base case. The third line, the recursion, is the important part. It is similar to the A,B,C,D example. From this definition we can make a straightforward recursive code for q(i,j). In the following pseudocode, n is the size of the board, c(i, j) is the cost-function, and min() returns the minimum of a number of values:

```
function minCost(i, j)
    if j < 1 or j > n
        return infinity
    else if i = n
        return c(i, j)
    else
        return min ( minCost(i+1, j-1), minCost(i+1, j), minCost(i+1, j+1) ) + c(i, j)
```

It should be noted that this function only computes the path-cost, not the actual path. We will get to the path soon. This, like the Fibonacci-numbers example, is horribly slow since it spends mountains of time recomputing the same shortest paths over and over. However, we can compute it much faster in a bottom-up fashion if we store path-costs in a two-dimensional array q[i, j] rather than using a function. This avoids recomputation; before computing the cost of a path, we check the array q[i, j] to see if the path cost is already there.

We also need to know what the actual shortest path is. To do this, we use another array p[i, j], a predecessor array. This array implicitly stores the path to any square s by storing the previous node on the shortest path to s, i.e. the predecessor. To reconstruct the path, we lookup the predecessor of s, then the predecessor of that square, then the predecessor of that square, and so on, until we reach the starting square. Consider the following code:

```
Function computeShortestPathArrays()
    for x from 1 to n
        q[l, x] := c(1, x)
    for y from 1 to n
        q[y, 0] := infinity
        q[y, n + 1] := infinity
    for y from 2 to n
        for x from 1 to n
            m := min(q[y–l, x–1], q[y–l, x], q[y–l, x+1])
            q[y, x] := m + c(y, x)
            if m = q[y–1, x–1]
                p[y, x] := –1
            else if m = q[y–l, x]
                p[y, x] := 0
            else
                p[y, x] := 1
```

Now the rest is a simple matter of finding the minimum and printing it.

```
    function computeShortestPath()
    computeShortestPathArrays()
    minIndex := 1
    min := q[n, 1]
    for i from 2 to n
        if q[n, i] < min
            minIndex := i
            min := q[n, i]
    printPath(n, minIndex)
function printPath(y, x)
    Print(x)
    Print("<-")
    if y = 2
        Print(x + p[y, x])
    else
        printPath(y-1, x + p[y, x])
```

20.8 SEQUENCE ALIGNMENT

In genetics, sequence alignment is an important application where dynamic programming is essential. Typically, the problem consists of transforming one sequence into another using edit operations that replace, insert, or remove an element. Each operation has an associated cost, and the goal is to find the sequence of edits with the lowest total cost.

The problem can be stated naturally as a recursion, a sequence A is optimally edited into a sequence B by either:

1. inserting the first character of B, and performing an optimal alignment of A and the tail of B
2. deleting the first character of A, and performing the optimal alignment of the tail of A and B
3. replacing the first character of A with the first character of B, and performing optimal alignments of the tails of A and B.

The partial alignments can be tabulated in a matrix, where cell (i,j) contains the cost of the optimal alignment of A[l..i] to B[l..j]. The cost in cell (i,j) can be calculated by adding the cost of the relevant operations to the cost of its neighboring cells, and selecting the optimum.

20.9 THE KNAPSACK PROBLEM.

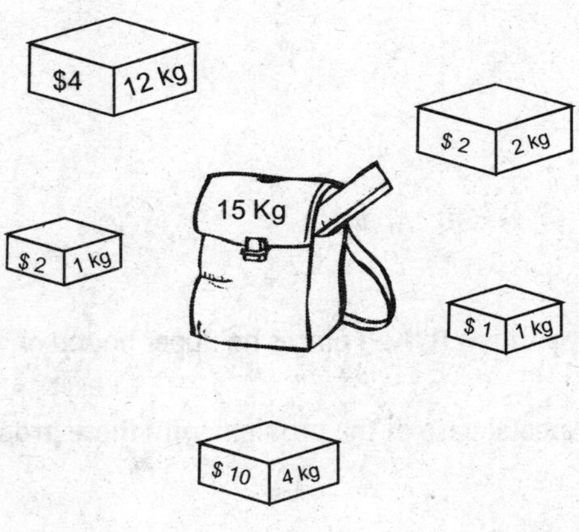

Fig.20.3. Example of a one-dimensional (constraint) knapsack problem: which boxes should be chosen to maximize the amount of money while still keeping the overall weight under or equal to 15 kg? A multiple constrained problem could consider both the weight and volume of the boxes. Modeling the shapes and sizes would instead constitute a packing problem. (Solution: if any number of each box is available, then three yellow boxes and three grey boxes; if only the shown boxes are available, then all but the green box.)

The knapsack problem or rucksack problem is a problem in combinatorial optimization: Given a set of items, each with a weight and a value, determine the number of each item to include in a collection so that the total weight is less than or equal to a given limit and the total value is as large as possible. It derives its name from the problem faced by someone who is constrained by a fixed-size knapsack and must fill it with the most useful items. The problem often arises in resource allocation with financial constraints. A similar problem also appears in combinatorics, complexity theory, cryptography and applied mathematics. The decision problem form of the knapsack problem is the question "can a value of at least V be achieved without exceeding the weight W?"

20.9.1 Definition

In the following, we have n kinds of items, 1 through n. Each kind of item i has a value v_i and a weight w_i We usually assume that all values and weights are nonnegative. To simplify there presentation, we can alsc assume that the items are listed in increasing order of weight. The maximum weight that we can carry in the bag is W.

The most common formulation of the problem is the 0-1 knapsack problem, which restricts the number x_i of copies of each kind of item to zero or one. Mathematically the 0-1-knapsack problem can be formulatec as:

- Maximize $\sum_{i=1}^{n} v_i x_i$
- Subject to $\sum_{i=1}^{n} w_i x_i \leq W, \quad x_i \in \{0,1\}$

The bounded knapsack problem restricts the number x_i of copies of each kind of item to a maximum integer value c_i. Mathematically the bounded knapsack problem can be formulated as:

- Maximize $\sum_{i=1}^{n} v_i x_i$
- Subject to $\sum_{i=1}^{n} w_i x_i \leq W, \quad x_i \in \{0,1,\ldots,c_i\}$

The unbounded knapsack problem (UKP) places no upper bound on the number of copies of each kind of item.

Of particular interest is the special case of the problem with these properties:

- it is a decision problem,
- it is a 0 – 1 problem,
- for each kind of item, the weight equals the value: $w_i = v_i$.

Notice that in this special case, the problem is equivalent to this: given a set of nonnegative integers, does any subset of it add up to exactly W? Or, if negative weights are allowed and W is chosen to be zero, the problem is: given a set of integers, does any subset add up to exactly 0? This special case is called the subset sum problem. In the field of cryptography the term knapsack problem is often used to refer specifically to the subset sum problem.

If multiple knapsacks are allowed, the problem is better thought of as the bin packing problem.

20.9.2 Computational complexity

The knapsack problem is interesting from the perspective of computer science because

- there is a pseudo-polynomial time algorithm using dynamic programming
- there is a fully polynomial-time approximation scheme, which uses the pseudo-polynomial time algorithm as a subroutine

- the problem is NP-complete to solve exactly, thus it is expected that no algorithm can be both correct and fast (polynomial-time) on all cases
- many cases that arise in practice, and "random instances" from some distributions, can nonetheless be solved exactly.

The subset sum version of the knapsack problem is commonly known as one of Karp' s 21 NP-complete problems.

There have been attempts to use subset sum as the basis for public key cryptography systems, such as the Merkle-Hellman knapsack cryptosystem. These attempts typically used some group other than the integers. Merkle-Hellman and several similar algorithms were later broken, because the particular subset sum problems they produced were in fact solvable by polynomial-time algorithms.

One theme in research literature is to identify what the "hard" instances of the knapsack problem look like, or viewed another way, to identify what properties of instances in practice might make them more amenable than their worst-case NP-complete behaviour suggests.

Several algorithms are freely available to solve knapsack problems, based on dynamic programming approach, branch and bound approach or hybridizations of both approaches.

20.10 DYNAMIC PROGRAMMING SOLUTION OF KNAPSACK PROBLEM

Unbounded knapsack problem

If all weights ($w_1, \ldots, w_n$, W) are nonnegative integers, the knapsack problem can be solved in pseudo-polynomial time using dynamic programming. The following describes a dynamic programming solution for the unbounded knapsack problem.

To simplify things, assume all weights are strictly positive ($w_i > 0$). We wish to maximize total value subject to the constraint that total weight is less than or equal to W. Then for each $w \leq W$, define m [w] to be the maximum value that can be attained with total weight less than or equal to w. m[W] then is the solution to the problem.

Observe that m[w] has the following properties:

- m[0] = 0 (the sum of zero items, i.e., the summation of the empty set)
- $m[w] = \max(m[w - 1], \max_{w_i \leq w} (v_i + m[w - w_i])$

where v_i is the value of the i-th kind of item.

Here the maximum of the empty set is taken to be zero. Tabulating the results from m [0] up through m [W] gives the solution. Since the calculation of each m [w] involves examining n items, and there are W values of m [w] to calculate, the running time of the dynamic programming solution is O(nW). Dividing w_1, w_2, ..., wn, W by their greatest common divisor is an obvious way to improve the running time.

The O(nW) complexity does not contradict the fact that the knapsack problem is NP-complete, since W, unlike n, is not polynomial in the length of the input to the problem. The length of the W input to the problem is proportional to the number of bits in W, log W, not to W itself.

20.10.1 0-1 knapsack problem

A similar dynamic programming solution for the 0–1 knapsack problem also runs in pseudo-polynomial time. As above, assume $w_1, w_2, \ldots, w_n$, are strictly positive integers. Define m[i,w] to be the maximum value that can be attained with weight less than or equal to w using items up to i.

We can define m[i,w] recursively as follows:

- m[0, w] = 0
- m[i, 0] = 0
- m[i, w] = m [i– 1, w] if w_i > w (the new item is more than the current weight limit)
- m[i, w] = max(m[i – 1, w], m[i –1,w– w_i] +) if $w_i \le$ w.

The solution can then be found by calculating m[n,W]. To do this efficiently we can use a table to store previous computations. This solution will therefore run in O (nW) time and O (nW) space.

Let 11 = 20 kg , V1 =160 ; 12=30 kg , V2 =180 ; 13=10 kg , V3 =200 ; W = 50 kg.

m[i,w]=max(m[i-I,w],m[i-I,W-wi]+vi) and wi<=W

m[i,w]=m[i-I,w] if wi>W

where m[i,w] to be the maximum value that can be attained with weight less than or equal to w using items up to i.

m[3,50]=max(m[2,50],m[2,40]+200)

m[2,50]=max(m[I,50],m[I,20]+180)

m[I,50]=160.

m[I,20]=160.

=> m[2,50]=340 ... (1)

m[2,40]=max(m[I,40],m[I,10]+180)

m[I,40]=160.

m[I,10]=m[0,10]=>0.

m[2,40]=180 ... (2)

from Equ. (1)&(2)...

m[3,50]=380. (Answer)

20.11 THE TRAVELING SALESPERSON PROBLEM

We have seen that we can solve one type of integer programming (the knapsack problem) with dynamic programming. Let's try another.

The traveling salesperson problem is to visit a number of cities in the minimum distance. For instance, a politician begins in Delhi and has to visit Mumbai, Kolkata, and Chennai before returning to New York. How can she minimize the distance traveled? The distances are as in Table 20.1.

	New York	Miami	Dallas	Chicago
1. Delhi	—	1334	1559	809
2. Mumbai	1334	—	1343	1307
3. Kolkata	1559	1343	—	921
4. Chennai	809	1397	921	—

Table 20.1. TSP example problem.

The real problem in solving this is to define the stages, states, and decisions. One natural choice is to let stage t represent visiting t cities, and let the decision be where to go next. That leaves us with states. Imagine we chose the city we are in to be the state. We could not make the decision where to go next, for we do not know where we have gone before. Instead, the state has to include information about all the cities visited, plus the city we ended up in. So a state is represented by a pair (i,S) where S is the set of t cities already visited and i is the last city visited (so i must be in S). This turns out to be enough to get a recursion.

The stage 3 calculations are

- $f_3(\{2_1 3,4\}) = 1334$
- $f_3(3,\{2,3,4\}) = 1559$
- $f_3(4,\{2,3,4J) = 809$.

For other stages, the recursion is

$$f_t(i, S) = \min_{j \neq 1 \text{ and } j \notin s} \{c_{ij} + f_{t+1}(j, S \cup j)\}.$$

You can continue with these calculations. One important aspect of this problem is the so called curse of dimensionality. The state space here is so large that it becomes impossible to solve even moderate size problems. For instance, suppose there are 20 cities. The number of states in the 10th stage is more than a million. For 30 cities, the number of states in the 15th stage is more than a billion. And for 100 cities, the number of states at the 50th stage is more than 5,000,000,000,000,000,000,000,000,000,000. This is not the sort of problem that will go away as computers get better.

Longest Common subsequence

In the longest common subsequence, we are given two sequence $X = < x_1, x_2, \ldots x_m >$ and $y = < y_1, y_2, \ldots y_n >$ and wish to find a maximum-length common subnsequence of x and y.

In LCS problem, we are given two chracter strings, x and y, of length n and m, respectively and are asked to find a longest string S that is a subsequence of both x and y. Since x and y are character strings, we have a natrual set of indices with which to define subproblem-indices into string x and y. let us define subproblem therefore as that of computing the length of the longest common subsequence of x [0-- i] and y [0... j], denoted $L[i,j]$.

This definition allow us to rewrite $L[i,j]$ in terms of optimal subproblem solutin So, we consider the following two cases.

Case 1: x [1] = y [j]

Let C = X [i] = y [j] that is a longest common subsequence of X [0.. i] and y [0 .. j] ends with C. To prove this, let use suppose that it is not true. There has to be some longest common subsequence x $[x_i]$ x $[i_2]$ -- $[x_{ik}]$ = y $[j_k]$ = C, then we get the same sequece by setting $i_K = i$ and $j_K = j$. Altenately, if Y $[j_k] \neq C$, then we can get an even longer common subsequence by adding C to the end. Thus a LCS of

x[0.. i] and y [0...j] ends with C = x [i] = y [j].

Therefore we set

$$L[i,j] = L[i-1, j-1] + 1 \text{ If } x[i] = y[j] \qquad \ldots \text{(i)}$$

Case 2: x [i] $\neq$ y [j]

In this case, we cannot have a common subsequence that includes both X [i] and y [j]. That is, a common subsequence can end with X[i], y [j] or neither,but not both.

Therefore, we set

$$L[i,j] = \max\{L[i-l,j], L[i,j-1]\} \text{ if } x[i] \neq y[j] \qquad \ldots \text{(ii)}$$

In order to make equations (1) and (2) make sense in the boundary cases when i = 0 or j = 0 or j = 0, we define L [i, –1] = 0 for i = – 1, 0, 1,..., n – 1 and L [–1, j] = 0 for j = – 1, 0, 1, 0, 1, ..., m – 1

LCS Alogrithm

```
LCS – LENGTH (x, y)
    m ← length [x]
    n ← length [y]
      for i ← 1 to m
          do c [i, 0] ← 0
      for    j ← 0 to n
        C [0, j] ← 0
      for i ← 1 to m
  do for j ← 1 to 1 to n
        do if xi = yi
  then c [i, j]) ← c [i – 1, j – 1] + 1
        b[i, j ] ← " ↖ "
  else  if c [i – 1, j] ≥ c [i, j – 1]
           then c [i, j] ← c [i – 1, j]
               b [i, j] ← " ↑ "
  else      c [i, j] ← c [i, j – 1]
               b [i, j] ← " ← "
return c and b
```

Example

x = < A, B, C, B, D, A , B >

y = < B, D, C, A, B, A >

	0	1	2	3	4	5	6
	y_i	B	D	C	A	B	A
0 x_i	0	0	0	0	0	0	0
1 A	(0)	↑ 0	↑ 0	↑ 0	↖ 1	←1	↖ 1
2 B	0	↖ (1)	← (1)	←1	↑ 1	↖ 2	←2
3 C	0	↑ 1	↑ 1	↖ (2)	← (2)	↑ 2	↑ 2
4 B	0	↖ 1	↑ 1	↑ 2	↑ 2	↖ (3)	←3
5 D	0	↑ 1	↑ 2	↑ 2	↑ 2	↑ (3)	↑ 3
6 A	0	^ 1	↑ 2	↑ 2	↖ 3	↑ 3	↖ (4)
7 B	0	↖ 1	↑ 2	↑ 2	↑ 3	↖ 4	↑ (4)

Optimal binary search trees

Optimal binary search tree is a tree with lowest expected search time. Suppose that we are designing a program to translate tent from English to spanish. for each occurace of each english word in the text, we need to look up its spanish equivalent. one way to perform these look up operations is to build a binary search tree with n English words as key and spanish equivalent as satelite data. Because we will search the tree for each individual word in the tent, we want the total time spent searching to be as low as possible. we could ensure an O(longn) search time per occurrence by using a red block tree or any other balanced binary search tree.

In optimal binary search tree. We ar given a sequence K = < K_1, K_2, ... K_n > of n distinct keys in sorted order (so that $K_1 < K_2 <..... K_n$), and we wish to build a binary search tree from these keys. for each key K_i, we have a probability p_i that a search will be for k_i. some searches may be for values no K, and so we also have n +1 "dummy keys" d_0 d_1, d_2 ... d_n representing values no in K Thus, do represents all values less than K_1, dn represents all values greater than K_n, and for i = 1, 2,..., n – 1, the dummy key d_i represents all values between k_i and $k_i + 1$. For each dummy key d_i, we have a probability q_i that a search will correspond to d_i.

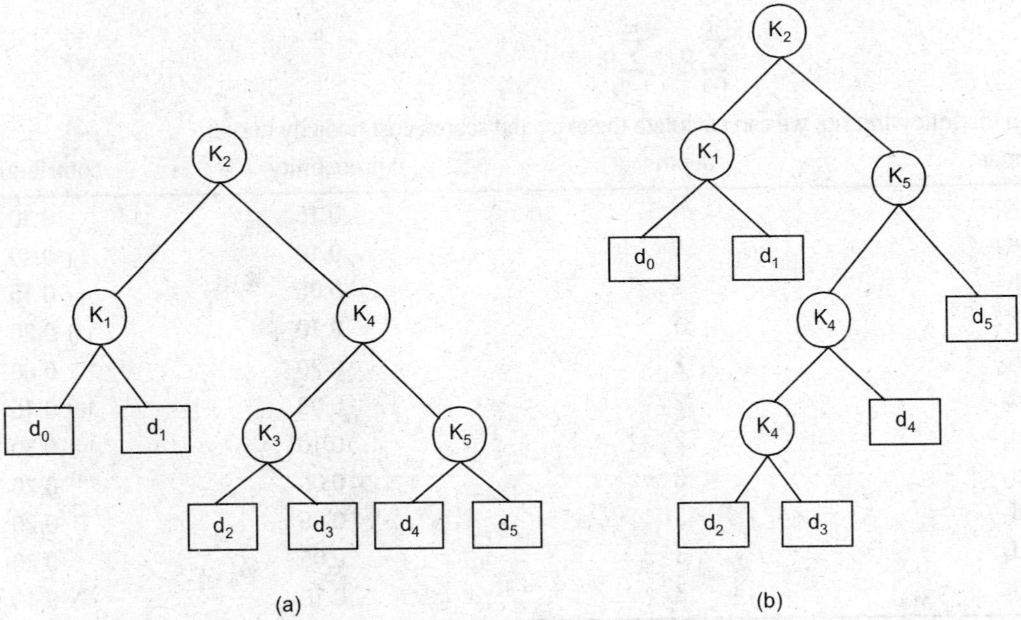

Fig. 20.4. two binary search tree for a set of n = 5 keys with the following probabilities

i	0	1	2	3	4	5
p_i		0.15	0.05	0.05	0.10	0.20
q_i	0.05	0.10	0.05	0.05	0.05	0.10

(a) A binary search tree with expected search cost 2.80

(b) A binary search tree with expected search cost 2.75. This tree is optimal.

In the above fig, it shows two binary search trees for a set of n = 5 keys. Each key ki is either successful 1 finding some kdy ki) or unsuccessful (finding some dummy key d_i) and so we have

$$\sum_{i=1}^{n} P_i + \sum_{i=0}^{n} q_i = 1$$

Because we have probabilities of search for each key and each dummy key, we can determine the expected cost of a search in a given binary tree T. Let us assume that the actual cost of a search is the number of nodes examined i.e. the dept of the node found by the search in T, plus 1, Then then the expected cost of search in T is.

$$E\text{ [Search cost in T]} = \sum_{i=1}^{n} (\text{dept}_T(Ki)+1).P_i + \sum_{i=0}^{n} (\text{depth}_T(d_i)+1).q_i$$

$$= 1 + \sum_{i=1}^{n} \text{depth}_T(Ki)\ pi + \sum_{i=0}^{n} \text{depth}_T(d_i)\ q_i$$

where depth_T denotes a node's depth in the tree T. The last equality follows from the equation

$$\sum_{i=1}^{n} p_i + \sum_{i=0}^{n} q_i = 1$$

In the following fig, we can calculate the expected search cost node by node.

node	depth	probability	contribution
K_1	1	0.15	0.30
K_2	0	0.10	0.10
K_3	2	0.05	0.15
K_4	1	0.10	0.20
K_5	2	0.20	0.60
d_0	2	0.05	0.15
d_1	2	0.10	0.30
d_2	3	0.05	0.20
d_3	3	0.05	0.20
d_4	3	0.05	0.20
d_5	3	0.10	0.40
Total			2.80

For a given set of probilities, our goal is to constructed a binary search tree whose expected search cost is smallest. We call such a tree an optimal binary search tree.

Example: Let n = 4 and (a_1, a_2, a_3, a_4) = (do, if, int, while).

Let P (1: 4) = (3, 3, 1, 1) and q (0:4) = (2, 3, 1, 1, 1). The p's and q's have been multiplied by 16 for convenience. Initially, we have

$w(i,i) = q(i), C(i,i) = 0$ and $r(i,i) = 0, 0 \le i \le 4.$

observation $w(i,j) = p(j) + q(j) + w(i,j-1)$, we get

$$w(0,1) = P(1) + q(1) + w(0,0) = 8$$

$$c(0,1) = w(0,1) + \min\{c(0,0) + C(1,1)\} = 8$$

r (0, 1) = 1

w (1, 2) = p (2) + q (2) + w (1, 1) = 7

c (1, 2) = $w(1,2)+\min\{C(1,1)+C(2,2)\}=7$

r (0, 2) = 2

w (2, 3) = $p(3)+q(3)+w(2,2)=3$

c (2, 3) = $w(2,3)+\min\{c(2,2)+c(3,3)\}=3$

r (2, 3) = 3

w (3, 4) = p (4)+ q(4) + w (3, 3) = 3

c (3, 4) = w (3, 4) + min {c (3, 3) + (4, 3)} = 3

r (3. 4) = 4

knowing w (i, i + 1) and c (i, i +1), $0 \le i < 4$, we can computing w (i, i + 2), and r (i, i + 2) $0 \le i < 3$. This process can be repeated until w (0, 4), c (0, 4) and r (0, 4) are obtained. The table shows the results of this computation. The box in row i and column j shows the values of w (j, j + i), C (j, j + i) and r (j, j + i) respectively the computation is carried out by row from row 0 to row 4. From the table we see that C (0,4) = 32 is the minimum cost of a binary search tree for (a_1, a_2, a_3, a_4). The root of tree $t0_4$ is a_2. Hence, the left subtree is $t0_4$ is a_2. Hence, the left subtree is $t0_1$ and the right sub tree t_{24}. tree $t0_1$ has root a_1 and subtree too and t_{11}.

Tree t_{24} has root a_3; its left subtree is t_{22} and its right subtree t_{34}. Thus, with the data in the table it is possible to reconstruct to_4.

	0	1	2	3	4
0	$w_{00}=2$ $c_{00}=0$ $r_{00}=0$	$w_{11}=3$ $c_{11}=0$ $r_{11}=0$	$w_{22}=1$ $c_{22}=0$ $r_{22}=0$	$w_{33}=1$ $c_{33}=0$ $r_{33}=0$	$w_{44}=1$ $c_{44}=0$ $r_{44}=0$
1	$w_{01}=8$ $c_{01}=8$ $r_{02}=1$	$w_{12}=7$ $c_{12}=7$ $r_{12}=2$	$w_{23}=3$ $c_{23}=3$ $r_{23}=3$	$w_{34}=3$ $c_{34}=3$ $r_{34}=4$	
2	$w_{02}=12$ $c_{02}=19$ $r_{02}=1$	$w_{13}=9$ $c_{13}=12$ $r_{13}=2$	$w_{24}=5$ $c_{24}=8$ $r_{24}=3$		
3	$w_{03}=16$ $c_{04}=32$ $r_{04}=2$	$w_{14}=11$ $c_{14}=19$ $r_{14}=2$			
4	$w_{04}=16$ $c_{04}=32$ $r_{04}=2$				

Fig compuation of c (0, 4), w (0, 4) and r (0, 4) and r (0, 4)

The above example illustratrates how to determine the c's and r's and r's and also how to reconstruct $t0_n$ knowing the r's'. let us examine the complexity of this procedure to evaluate the c's and r's evaluation described in the above example requires to compute c (i, j) for (j – i) = 1, 2, ..., n in that order. when j – 1 = m, there are n – m + 1 c (i, j)'s to compute. The compuation of each of these c (i, j)'s requires us to find the minimum of m qualities. Hence, each such c(i, j) can be computed in time 0(m). The total time for all c (i, j)'s with j – 1 = m is therefore 0 (nm – m^2). The total time to evaluate all the c (i, j)'s and r (i, j)'s is

Therefore.

$$\sum_{1 \le m \le n} (nm - m^2) \;=\; n^3)$$

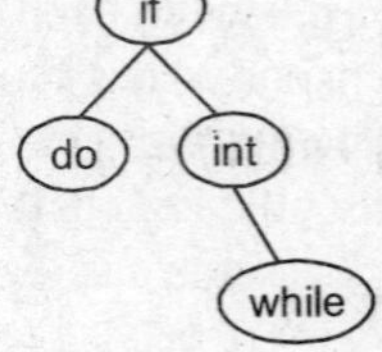

Fig. 20.5 Optimal search tree for example.

```
OBST (p, q, n)
for i ← 0 to n – 1 do
w[i,i] ← q[i]; r[i,i] ← 0; c[i,i] ← 0;
w[i,i+1] ← q[i]+q[i+1]+P[i+1];
r[i,i+1] ← i+1;
  c[i,i+1] ← q[i]+q[i+1] ← P[i+1];
w[n,n] ← q[n]; r[n,n] ← 0; c[n,n] ← 0.0;
for m ← 2 to n do || find optimal trees with m nodes.
   for i ← 0 to n – m do
      j ← i + m;
   w[i,j] ← w[i,j–1]+P[j]+q[j];
   k ← find (c,r,i,j);
 c[i,j] ← w[i,j]+c[i,k–1]+c[k,j];
    r[i,j] ← k;
 c[0,n], w[0,n], r[0,n]);
```

```
Algorithm find (c, r, i, j)
     min ← ∞ ;
for m ← r[i,j–1] to r[i+1,j] do
if (c[i,m–1]+c[m,j]) < min then
 min ← C[i,m–1]+c(n,j); 1 ← m;
     return 1;
This finds a minimum – cost
binary search tree.
```

Solved Questions

1. What is Knapsack problem?

Ans. The knapsack problem or rucksack problem is a problem in combinatorial optimization: Given a set of items, each with a weight and a value, determine the count of each item to include in a collection so that the total weight is less than or equal to a given limit and the total value is as large as possible. It derives its name from the problem faced by someone who is constrained by a fixed-size knapsack and must fill it with the most useful items. In the following, we have n kinds of items, 1 through n. Each kind of item i has a value v_i and a weight w_i. We usually assume that all values and weights are nonnegative. To simplify the representation, we can also assume that the items are listed in increasing order of weight. The maximum weight that we can carry in the bag is W. The most common formulation of the problem is the 0-1 knapsack problem, which restricts the number x_i of copies of each kind of item to zero or one. Mathematically the 0-1-knapsack problem can be formulated as:

- maximize $\sum_{i=1}^{n} vixi$
- subject to $\sum_{i=1}^{n} wixi \leq W,\ xi \in \{0,1\}$

The bounded knapsack problem restricts the number x_i of copies of each kind of item to a maximum integer value c_i. Mathematically the bounded knapsack problem can be formulated as:

- maximize $\sum_{i=1}^{n} vixi \leq W,$
- subject to $\sum_{i=1}^{n} wixi \leq W,\ xi \in \{0,1\ldots,\ c_i\}$

The unbounded knapsack problem (UKP) places no upper bound on the number of copies of each kind of item.

Of particular interest is the special case of the problem with these properties:
- it is a decision problem,
- it is a 0-1 problem,
- for each kind of item, the weight equals the value: $w_i = v_i$.

2. What is the dynamic programmic solution to Knapsack problem?

Ans. If all weights (w_1,...., wn, W) are nonnegative integers, the knapsack problem can be solved in pseudo-polynomial time using dynamic programming. The following describes a dynamic programming solution for the unbounded knapsack problem.

To simplify things, assume all weights are strictly positive ($w_i > 0$). We wish to maximize total value subject to the constraint that total weight is less than or equal to W. Then for each $w \leq W$, define m[w] to be the maximum value that can be attained with total weight less than or equal to w. m[W] then is the solution to the problem.

Observe that m[w] has the following properties:

- m[0] = 0(the sum of zero items, i.e., the summation of the empty set)

- $m[w] = \max_{w_i \leq w} (v_i + m[w - w_i])$

where v_i is the value of the i-th kind of item.

0-1 knapsack problem

A similar dynamic programming solution for the 0-1 knapsack problem also runs in pseudo-polynomial time. As above, assume $w_1, w_2, \ldots, w_n$, W are strictly positive integers. Define m[i,w] to be the max mum value that can be attained with weight less than or equal to w using items up to i.

We can define m[i,w] recursively as follows:

- $m[0, w] = 0$
- $m[i, 0] = 0$
- $m[i, w] = m[i - 1, w]$ if $w_i > w$ (the new item is more than the current weight limit)
- m[i, w] = max(m[i m[i, w] = m[i – 1, w], m[i – 1, w – w_i] + v_i)if $w_i \leq w$.

3. What is the difference between divide and conquer and dynamic programming?

Ans. Both solve problem by dividing prob into sub-problems

(1) But in Dynamic programming the sub problems are not independent where as in divide and conquer the sub problems are independent of each other

(2) Dynamic programming solves the sub problem only once and then stores it in table whereas divide and conquer does more work on the sub problems and hence has more time consumption.

4. What are elements of dynamic programming?

Ans. Elements of Dynamic Programming

- Optimal sub-structure (Principle of Optimality) an optimal solution to the problem contains within it optimal solutions to sub-problems.
- Overlapping subproblems there exist some places where we solve the same subproblem more than once.

Previous Year University Question

1. Draw the portion of the state tree generated by LCBB for the following Knapsack instance n=5,(p1,p2...p5=(10,15,6,8,4),(W1,W2,...W5)=(4,6,3,4,2), m=12. [OU]
2. What is "Dyanamic Programming"? Explain (with the help of an example) how an optimal binary search tree can be constructed using the technique of dyanamic programming. Derive the formulae used. [CU]
3. Explain (with the help of an example) how the travelling salesman problem can be solved using the technique of dynamic programming. [OU]
4. Obtain the dynamic programming algorithm for the 0/1 knapsack problem of n instances. Assume suitable data for n instances knapsack. [GBTU]
5. Explain dynamic programming. Apply it on Matrix Chain multiplication problem. [GBTU]
6. With reference to the knapsack problem, state the condition under which it is clearly optimal to pack all the objects in the knapsack. [Madrass University]

7. Design a dynamic programming algorithm to find an optimal binary search tree for a set of keys with given probabilities of access. [Madrass University]
8. What is dynamic programming? Explain its use in problem solving. [KU]
9. Explain dynamic programming method to solve a problem. Use the same method to solve the travelling saleman problem with given distance matrix:

$$\begin{bmatrix} 0 & 5 & 10 & 15 \\ 3 & 0 & 6 & 8 \\ 4 & 12 & 0 & 11 \\ 7 & 7 & 8 & 0 \end{bmatrix}$$

[MDU]

10. Discuss the dynamic programming techniques. Also explain the main difference between greedy and dynamic programming with the help of example. [MDU]
11. State 0/1 knapsack problem. Apply dynamic programming technique to solve this problem. [MDU]
12. Describe dynamic programming method with a suitable example. [MDU]
13. Explain Huffman codes and Optimal Binary Search Tree. [MDU]
14. Write an algorithm to find an Optimal Binary Search tree using dynamic programming. [OU]
15. What do you understand by Optimal Binary search tree? Justify significanceof OBST with the help of suitable example. [MDU]
16. Write algorithm for optimal binary search tree. [OU]

Exercise

1. Given for types of items with the following respective weights and values.

   $T = < T_1, T_2, T_3, T_4 >$

   $W_i = (1, 4, 5, 6)$

   $Vi = (4, 5, 6, 4)$

   and the propack capacity W = 6. Find optional solution.
2. Find all possible solution for the
   (a) 4 × 4 chessboard, 4 queen problem.
3. Find the longest common subsequence from the given two sequence of character.
   (a) P = (ABC DBC DCDD)
       Q (BCDCD)
   (b) P = (1001011101101)
       Q = (10101)

CHAPTER

21

GREEDY ALGORITHM

21.1 INTRODUCTION

A greedy algorithm is any algorithm that follows the problem solving metaheuristic of making the locally optimal choice at each stage with the hope of finding the global optimum.

For example, applying the greedy strategy to the traveling salesman problem yields the following algorithm: "At each stage visit the unvisited city nearest to the current city". In general, greedy algorithms are used for optimization problems.

In general, greedy algorithms have five pillars:

1. A candidate set, from which a solution is created
2. A selection function, which chooses the best candidate to be added to the solution
3. A feasibility function, that is used to determine if a candidate can be used to contribute to a solution
4. An objective function, which assigns a value to a solution, or a partial solution, and
5. A solution function, which will indicate when we have discovered a complete solution

Greedy algorithms produce good solutions on some mathematical problems, but not on others. Most problems for which they work well have two properties:

21.1.1 Greedy choice property

We can make whatever choice seems best at the moment and then solve the subproblems that arise later. The choice made by a greedy algorithm may depend on choices made so far but not on future choices or all the solutions to the subproblem. It iteratively makes one greedy choice after another, reducing each given problem into a smaller one. In other words, a greedy algorithm never reconsiders its choices. This is the main difference from dynamic programming, which is exhaustive and is guaranteed to find the solution. After every stage, dynamic programming makes decisions based on all the decisions made in the previous stage, and may reconsider the previous stage's algorithmic path to solution.

21.1.2 Optimal substructure

"A problem exhibits optimal substructure if an optimal solution to the problem contains optimal solutions to the sub-problems."

21.1.3 Cases of failure

For many other problems, greedy algorithms fail to produce the optimal solution, and may even produce the unique worst possible solution. One example is the traveling salesman problem mentioned above: for each number of cities there is an assignment of distances between the cities for which the nearest neighbor heuristic produces the unique worst possible tour.

Imagine the coin example with only 25-cent, 10-cent, and 4-cent coins. The greedy algorithm would not be able to make change for 41 cents, since after committing to use one 25-cent coin and one 10-cent coin it would be impossible to use 4-cent coins for the balance of 6 cent. Whereas a person or a more sophisticated algorithm could make change for 41 cents change with one 25-cent coin and four 4-cent coins.

21.2 APPLICATIONS

Greedy algorithms mostly (but not always) fail to find the globally optimal solution, because they usually do not operate exhaustively on all the data. They can make commitments to certain choices too early which prevent them from finding the best overall solution later. For example, all known greedy coloring algorithms for the graph coloring problem and all other NP-complete problems do not consistently find optimum solutions. Nevertheless, they are useful because they are quick to think up and often give good approximations to the optimum.

If a greedy algorithm can be proven to yield the global optimum for a given problem class, it typically becomes the method of choice because it is faster than other optimisation methods like dynamic programming. Examples of such greedy algorithms are Kruskal's algorithm and Prim's algorithm for finding minimum spanning trees, Dijkstra's algorithm for finding single-source shortest paths, and the algorithm for finding optimum Huffman trees.

The theory of matroids, and the more general theory of greedoids, provide whole classes of such algorithms.

Greedy algorithms appear in network routing as well. Using greedy routing, a message is forwarded to the neighboring node which is "closest" to the destination. The notion of a node's location (and hence "closeness") may be determined by its physical location, as in geographic routing used by ad-hoc networks. Location may also be an entirely artificial construct as in small world routing and distributed hash table.

21.2.1 Examples

- In the Macintosh computer game Crystal Quest the objective is to collect crystals, in a fashion similar to the travelling salesman problem. The game has a demo mode, where the game uses a greedy algorithm to go to every crystal. The artificial intelligence does not account for obstacles, so the demo mode often ends quickly.
- The Matching pursuit is an example of greedy algorithm applied on signal approximation.

21.3 GREEDY APPROACH

Greedy Algorithm works by making the decision that seems most promising at any moment; it never reconsiders this decision, whatever situation may arise later.

As an example consider the problem of "Making Change".

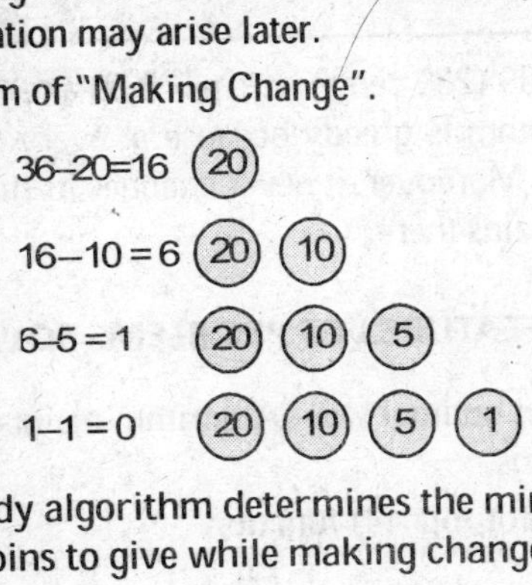

Fig. 21.1. The greedy algorithm determines the minimum number of coins to give while making change

These are the steps a human would take to emulate a greedy algorithm to represent 36 cents using only coins with values {1, 5, 10, 20}. The coin of the highest value, less than the remaining change owed, is the local optimum. (Note that in general the change-making problem requires dynamic programming or integer programming to find an optimal solution; US and other currencies are special cases where the greedy strategy works.)

Coins available are:

- dollars (100 cents)
- quarters (25 cents)
- dimes (10 cents)
- nickels (5 cents)
- pennies (1 cent)

Problem Make a change of a given amount using the smallest possible number of coins.

21.3.1 Informal Algorithm

- Start with nothing.
- at every stage without passing the given amount.

o add the largest to the coins already chosen.

21.3.2 Formal Algorithm

Make change for n units using the least possible number of coins.

```
MAKE-CHANGE (n)
    C ←{100, 25, 10, 5, 1}     // constant.
    Sol ← {};                  // set that will hold the solution set.
    Sum ← 0 sum of item in solution set
    WHILE sum not = n
        x = largest item in set C such that sum + x ≤ n
        IF no such item THEN
            RETURN "No Solution"
        S ← S {value of x}
            sum <— sum + x
        RETURN S
```

Example: Make a change for 2.89 (289 cents) here n = 2.89 and the solution contains 2 dollars, 3 quarters, 1 dime and 4 pennies. The algorithm is greedy because at every stage it chooses the largest coin without worrying about the consequences. Moreover, it never changes its mind in the sense that once a coin has been included in the solution set, it remains there.

21.4 CHARACTERISTICS AND FEATURES OF PROBLEMS SOLVED BY GREEDY ALGORITHMS

To construct the solution in an optimal way. Algorithm maintains two sets. One contains chosen items and the other contains rejected items.

The greedy algorithm consists of four (4) function.

1. A function that checks whether chosen set of items provide a solution.
2. A function that checks the feasibility of a set.
3. The selection function tells which of the candidates is the most promising.
4. An objective function, which does not appear explicitly, gives the value of a solution.

21.4.1 Structure Greedy Algorithm

- Initially the set of chosen items is empty i.e., solution set.
- At each step
  - o item will be added in a solution set by using selection function.
  - o IF the set would no longer be feasible
    reject items under consideration (and is never consider again).
  - o ELSE IF set is still feasible THEN
    add the current item.

21.4.2 Definitions of feasibility

A feasible set (of candidates) is promising if it can be extended to produce not merely a solution, but an optimal solution to the problem. In particular, the empty set is always promising why? (because an optimal solution always exists)

Unlike Dynamic Programming, which solves the subproblems bottom-up, a greedy strategy usually progresses in a top-down fashion, making one greedy choice after another, reducing each problem to a smaller one.

Greedy-Choice Property

The "greedy-choice property" and "optimal substructure" are two ingredients in the problem that lend to a greedy strategy.

Greedy-Choice Property says that a globally optimal solution can be arrived at by making a locally optimal choice.

21.5 KNAPSACK PROBLEM

Statement A thief robbing a store and can carry a maximal weight of w into their knapsack. There are n items and i^{th} item weigh w_i and is worth v_i dollars. What items should thief take?

There are two versions of problem

I. Fractional knapsack problem

The setup is same, but the thief can take fractions of items, meaning that the items can be broken into smaller pieces so that thief may decide to carry only a fraction of x, of item i, where 0 **xi,**1.

Exhibit greedy choice property.

Greedy algorithm exists.

Exhibit optimal substructure property.

Which algorithm exist. ??

II 0-1 knapsack problem

The setup is the same, but the items may not be broken into smaller pieces, so thief may decide either to take an item or to leave it (binary choice), but may not take a fraction of an item.

Exhibit No greedy choice property.

No greedy algorithm exists.

Exhibit optimal substructure property.

Only dynamic programming algorithm exists.

21.5.1 Greedy Solution to the Fractional Knapsack Problem

There are n items in a store. For i =1,2, . . . , n, item i has weight $w_i > 0$ and worth $v_i > 0$. Thief can carry a maximum weight of W pounds in a knapsack. In this version of a problem the items can be broken into smaller piece, so the thief may decide to carry only a fraction x_t of object i, where $0 \leq x_s < 1$. Item i contributes $x_i w_i$, to the total weight in the knapsack, and $x_i v_i$ to the value of the load.

In Symbol, the fraction knapsack problem can be stated as follows. maximize ${}^nS_{i=1}\, x_i v_i$ subject to constraint ${}^nS_{i=1}\, x_i w_i \leq W$

It is clear that an optimal solution must fill the knapsack exactly, for otherwise we could add a fraction of one of the remaining objects and increase the value of the load. Thus in an optimal solution ${}^nS_{i=1}\, x_i w_i = W$

```
  reedy-fractional-knapsack (w, v, W)
FO. i =1 to n
    do x[i] =0
weight = 0
while weight < W
  do i = best remaining item
      IF weight + w[i] ≤ W
          then x[i] = 1
              weight = weight + w[i]
          else
              x[i] = (w – weight) / w[i]
weight = W
return x
```

21.5.2 Analysis

If the items are already sorted into decreasing order of v_i / w_i, then the while-loop takes a time in O(n) Therefore, the total time including the sort is in O(n log n). If we keep the items in heap with largest v_i/W_i at the root. Then

- creating the heap takes O(n) time
- while-loop now takes O(log n) time (since heap property must be restored after the removal of root)

Although this data structure does not alter the worst-case, it may be faster if only a small number of items are need to fill the knapsack.

One variant of the 0-1 knapsack problem is when order of items are sorted by increasing weight is the same as their order when sorted by decreasing value.

Example 1: n knnprock problem n = 3, m = 20

(P_1, P_2, P_3) = (2 , 2 , 1) and (w_1, w_2, w_3) = (1 , 1 j, 10)

Solution.

	(x_1, x_2, x_3)	$\Sigma w_i x_i$	$\Sigma p_i x_i$
1.	$\left(\frac{1}{2},\frac{1}{3},\frac{1}{4}\right)$	16.5	24.25
2.	$\left(1,\frac{2}{15},0\right)$	20	28.2
3.	$\left(0,1,\frac{1}{2}\right)$	20	31
4.	$\left(0,1,\frac{1}{2}\right)$	20	31.5

Solution 4 yields maximum profit.

Example 2: For n = 7, m = 15, $(P_1, \ldots P_7)$ = (10, 5, 15, 7, 6, 18, 3) $(w_1 \ldots w_7)$ = (2, 3 , 5, 7, 1, 4, 1)

Solution.

	$x, x_2, x_3, x_5, x_6, x_7,$	$\Sigma w_i x_i$	$\Sigma p_i x_i$
1.	(1, 1, 0, 1, 1, 0, 1)	14	31
2.	(1, 0, 1, 0, 1, 1, 0)	13	52
3.	(1, 1, 1, 0, 1, 1, 0)	15	54
4.	(1, 1, 1, 0, 0, 0, 1)	15	51

Solution 3 give optimal solution

The optimal solution to this problem is to sort by the value of the item in decreasing order. Then pick up the most valuable item which also has a least weight. First, if its weight is less than the total weight that can be carried. Then deduct the total weight that can be carried by the weight of the item just pick. The second item to pick is the most valuable item among those remaining. Keep follow the same strategy until thief cannot carry more item (due to weight).

Proof: One way to proof the correctness of the above algorithm is to prove the greedy choice property and optimal substructure property. It consist of two steps. First, prove that there exists an optimal solution begins with the greedy choice given above. The second part prove that if A is an optimal solution to the original problem S, then A – a is also an optimal solution to the problem S – s where a is the item thief picked as in the greedy choice and S – s is the subproblem after the first greedy choice has been made. The second part is easy to prove since the more valuable items have less weight. Note that if V'/ W', is not it can replace any other because W'< W, but it increases the value because V' > V.

Theorem: The fractional knapsack problem has the greedy-choice property.

Proof: Let the ratio v'/w' is maximal. This supposition implies that v'/w' ≥ v/w for any pair (v, w), so v' v / w > v for any (v, w). Now Suppose a solution does not contain the full w' weight of the best ratio. Then by replacing an amount of any other w with more w' will improve the value.

21.6 AN ACTIVITY SELECTION PROBLEM

An activity-selection is the problem of scheduling a resource among several competing activity.

Problem Statement

Given a set S of n activities with and start time, S_t and f_i, finish time of an ith activity. Find the maximum size set of mutually compatible activities.

Compatible Activities

Activities i and j are compatible if the half-open internal $[s_i, f_i)$ and $[s_j, f_j)$ do not overlap, that is, i and j are compatible if $s_i \geq f_j$ and $S_j \geq f_i$

Greedy Algorithm for Selection Problem

I. Sort the input activities by increasing finishing time.
$F_i \leq f_2 \leq ... \leq f_n$

II. Call GREEDY-ACTIVITY-SELECTOR (s, f)

```
1. n = length [s]
2. A={i}
3. j = 1
4. for i = 2 to n
5.     do if Si ≥ fj
6.          then A=AU{i}
7.               j=i
8. return set A
```

Operation of the algorithm

Example 3: Let 11 activities are given S = {p, q, r, s, t, u, v, w, x, y, z} start and finished times for proposed activities are (1,), (3,), (0,), ,), (3,), ,), (, 10), (, 11), (, 12), (2, 13) and (12, 1).

A = {p} Initialization at line 2

A = {p, s} line 6 - 1st iteration of FO - loop

A = {p, s, w} line 6 -2nd iteration of FO - loop A = {p, s, w, z} line 6 - 3rd iteration of FO -loop

Out of the FO -loop and eturn A = {p, s, w, z}

Example 4: Given 10 activities along with their start and finish time.

S = < A_1, A_2, A_3, A_4, A_5, A_6, A_7, A_8, A_9, A_{10} >

S_i = < 1, 2, 3, 4, 5, 6, 7, 8, 9,10 >

f_i = < 5, 3, 4, 6, 7, 8, 9,10 >

Solution:

Activity	A_2	A_2	A_3	A_4	A_5	A_6	A_7	A_8	A_9	A_{10}
Start	2	3	1	4	5	6	8	7	9	10
Finish	3	4	5	6	7	8	10	11	12	13

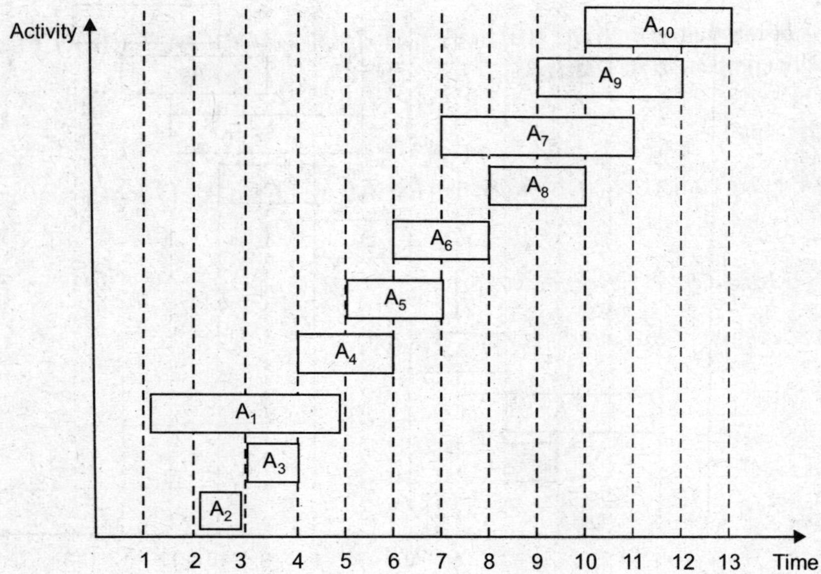

Now schedule A_2

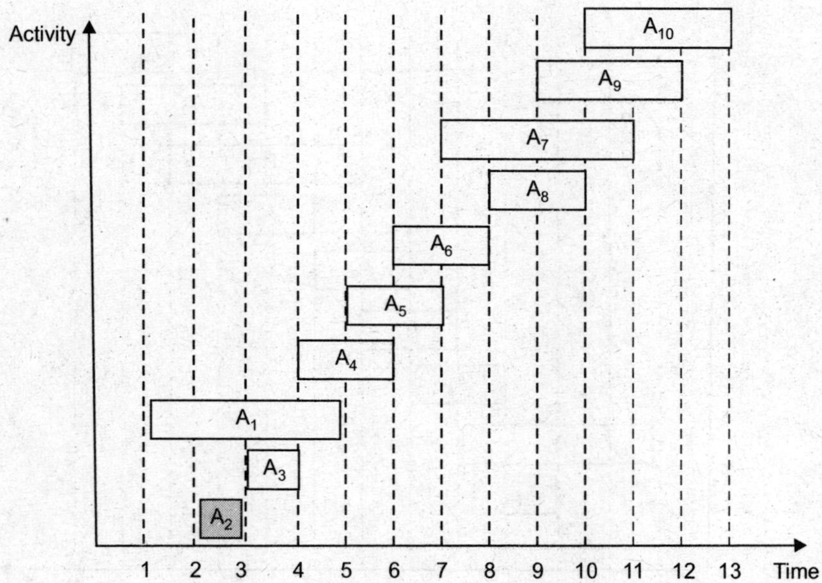

Next A_3 as A_2 and A_3 are non-interfering.

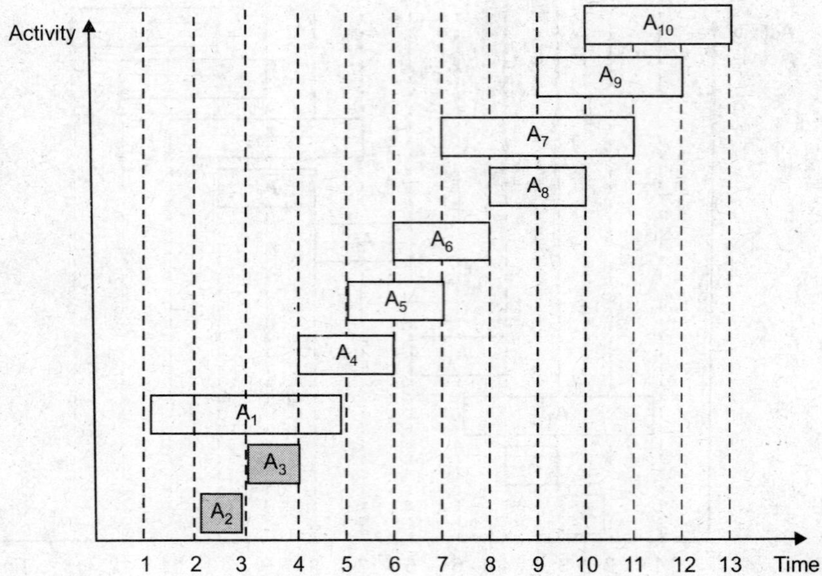

Skip. A_1, as it is interfering

Next, schedule A_4, as A_2, A_3 and A_4 all non-intefering

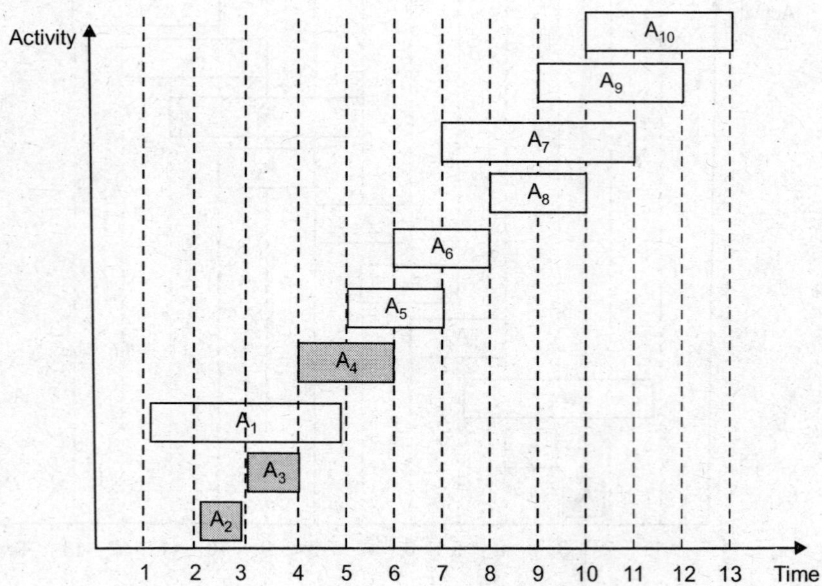

Skip. A_5 as they are interfering

Next: schedule A_6, as A_2, A_3, A_4, A_5 and are non-interfering

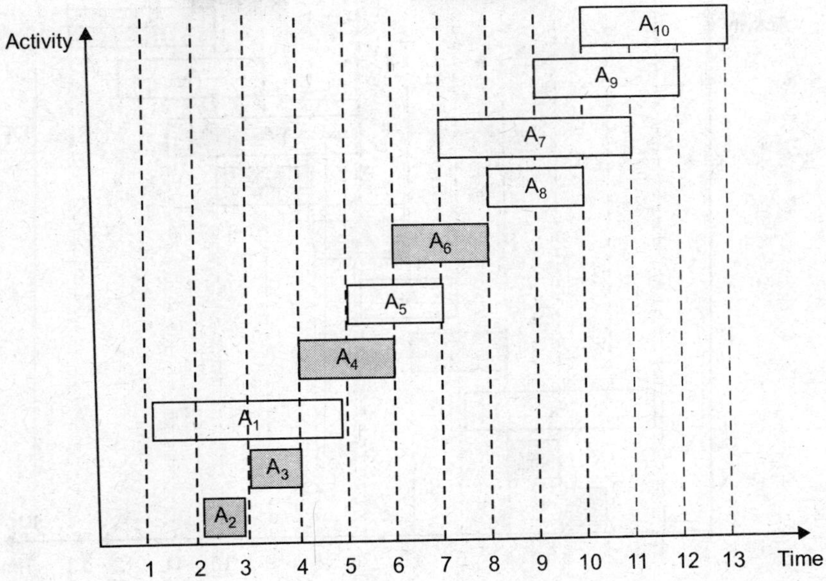

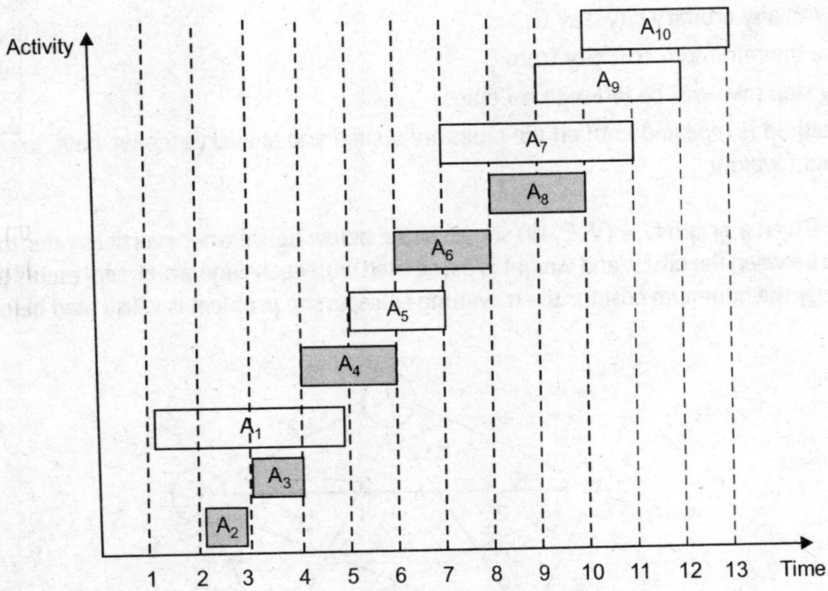

Skip. A_7, A_9 as they are interfering

Next schedule A_{10}, as A_2, A_3, A_4, A_5, A_6, A_8, and A_{10}, are non-interfering

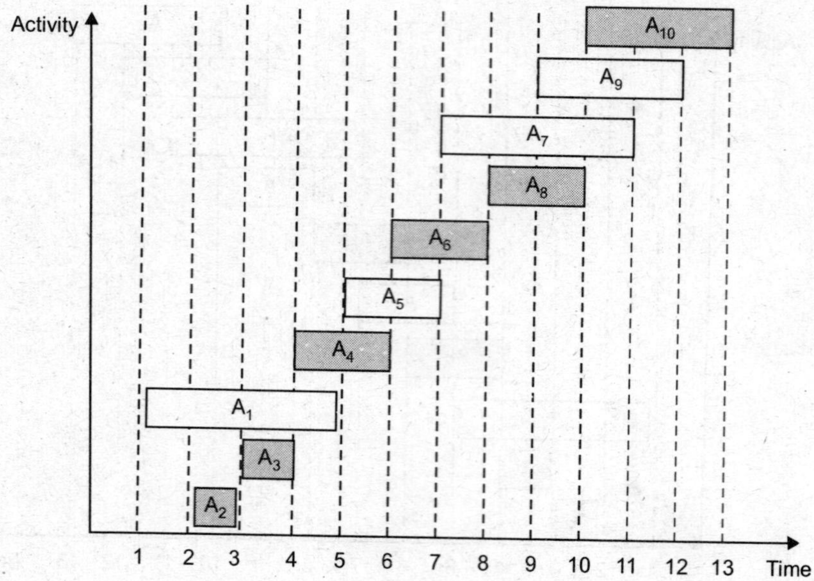

Final Activity schedule: <A_2, A_3, A_4, A_5, A_8, A_{10}, >

Greedy Starting for travelling salesman problem

- Start with any arbitary city, say C_1.
- Choose the minimum cost city from C_1.
- At any step i we will be left with n-i cities.
- The method is repeated until all the cities are visited and at every step we have to select the city with minimum weight.

Example 5: Given a graph G = (V, E, W) shown in the below figure where vertices refer to cities, edge refer to connection between the cities, and weight is associated with each edge which represents the cost. Using the Greedy startegy the minimum cost for the travelling salesperson problem is illustrated below.

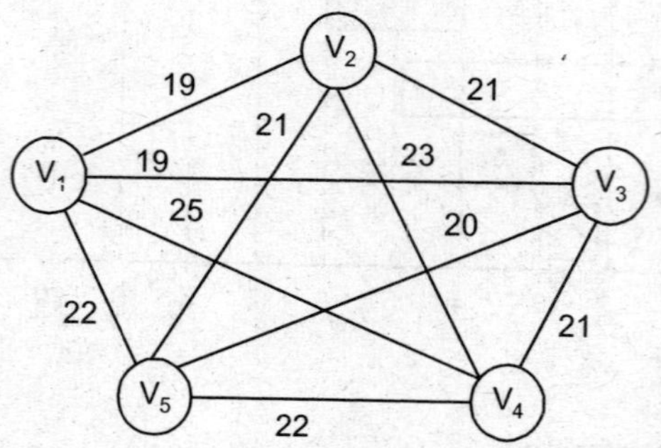

Fig. 21.2. Graph G. Vertices refer to cities, edges refer to links b/w cities and weights refer to cost of the links.

Solution. The cost adjacency matrix of graph G

$$\text{cost ij} = \begin{array}{c} \\ \textcircled{V_1} \\ V_2 \\ V_3 \\ V_4 \\ V_5 \end{array} \begin{array}{c} \begin{matrix} V_1 & V_2 & V_3 & V_4 & V_5 \end{matrix} \\ \begin{bmatrix} 0 & 20 & 19 & 25 & 22 \\ 20 & 0 & 21 & 23 & 21 \\ 19 & 21 & 0 & 21 & 20 \\ 25 & 23 & 21 & 0 & 22 \\ 22 & 21 & 20 & 22 & 0 \end{bmatrix} \end{array}$$

The tour starts from city V_1, mark V_1, and select the minimum cost city reachable from city V_1

$$\begin{array}{c} \\ \textcircled{V_1} \\ V_2 \\ V_3 \\ V_4 \\ V_5 \end{array} \begin{array}{c} \begin{matrix} V_1 & V_2 & V_3 & V_4 & V_5 \end{matrix} \\ \begin{bmatrix} 0 & 20 & \textcircled{19} & 25 & 22 \\ 20 & 0 & 21 & 23 & 21 \\ 19 & 21 & 0 & 21 & 20 \\ 25 & 23 & 21 & 0 & 22 \\ 22 & 21 & 20 & 22 & 0 \end{bmatrix} \end{array}$$

Mark city V_3 and select minimum cost city reachable from city V_3

$$\begin{array}{c} \\ \textcircled{V_1} \\ V_2 \\ \textcircled{V_3} \\ V_4 \\ V_5 \end{array} \begin{array}{c} \begin{matrix} V_1 & V_2 & V_3 & V_4 & V_5 \end{matrix} \\ \begin{bmatrix} 0 & 20 & \textcircled{19} & 25 & 22 \\ 20 & 0 & 21 & 23 & 21 \\ 19 & 21 & 0 & 21 & \textcircled{20} \\ 25 & 23 & 21 & 0 & 22 \\ 22 & 21 & 20 & 22 & 0 \end{bmatrix} \end{array}$$

Mark city V_5 and slect minimum cost city reachable from city. V_5.

$$\begin{array}{c} \\ \textcircled{V_1} \\ V_2 \\ \textcircled{V_3} \\ V_4 \\ \textcircled{V_5} \end{array} \begin{array}{c} \begin{matrix} V_1 & V_2 & V_3 & V_4 & V_5 \end{matrix} \\ \begin{bmatrix} 0 & 20 & \textcircled{19} & 25 & 22 \\ 20 & 0 & 21 & 23 & 21 \\ 19 & 21 & 0 & 21 & \textcircled{20} \\ 25 & 23 & 21 & 0 & 22 \\ 22 & \textcircled{21} & 20 & 22 & 0 \end{bmatrix} \end{array}$$

Mark city V_2 and select minimum cost city reachable from city V_2.

$$\begin{array}{c} \\ \textcircled{V_1} \\ \textcircled{V_2} \\ \textcircled{V_3} \\ V_4 \\ \textcircled{V_5} \end{array} \begin{array}{c} \begin{array}{ccccc} V_1 & V_2 & V_3 & V_4 & V_5 \end{array} \\ \begin{bmatrix} 0 & 20 & \textcircled{19} & 25 & 22 \\ 20 & 0 & 21 & \textcircled{23} & 21 \\ 19 & 21 & 0 & 21 & \textcircled{20} \\ 25 & 23 & 21 & 0 & 22 \\ 22 & \textcircled{21} & 20 & 22 & 0 \end{bmatrix} \end{array}$$

Mark city V_4 and select minimum cost city reachable from city

$$\begin{array}{c} \\ \textcircled{V_1} \\ \textcircled{V_2} \\ \textcircled{V_3} \\ \textcircled{V_4} \\ \textcircled{V_5} \end{array} \begin{array}{c} \begin{array}{ccccc} V_1 & V_2 & V_3 & V_4 & V_5 \end{array} \\ \begin{bmatrix} 0 & 20 & \textcircled{19} & 25 & 22 \\ 20 & 0 & 21 & \textcircled{23} & 21 \\ 19 & 21 & 0 & 21 & \textcircled{20} \\ \textcircled{25} & 23 & 21 & 0 & 22 \\ 22 & \textcircled{21} & 20 & 22 & 0 \end{bmatrix} \end{array}$$

Using the greedy startegy we get the following four of total cost

V_1 19 V_3 20 V_5 21 V_2 23 V_4 25 V_1 = 108

The solution to the travelling salesperson problem according to greedy startegy is shown in figure.

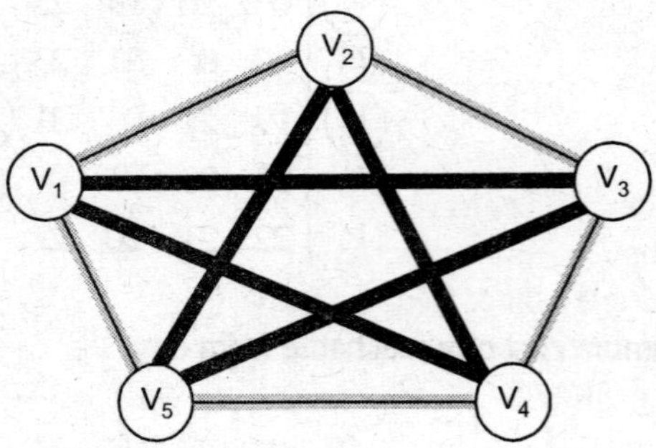

Fig. 21.3. Graph G, Solution to travelling sales person problem according to greedy startegy

21.7 LECTURE HALL PROBLEM

As an example consider the example. Given a set of activities to among lecture halls. Schedule all the activities using minimal lecture halls.

In order to determine which activity should use which lecture hall, the algorithm uses the GREEDY-ACTIVITY-SELECTOR to calculate the activities in the first lecture hall. If there are some activities yet to be scheduled, a new lecture hall is selected and GREEDY-ACTIVITY-SELECTOR is called again. This continues until all activities have been scheduled.

```
LECTURE-HALL-ASSIGNMENT (s, f)
n = length [s]
for i = 1 to n
      do HALL [i] = NIL
k=1
while (Not empty (s))
      do HALL [k] = GREEDY-ACTIVITY-SELECTOR (s, t, n)
            k = k + 1
return HALL
```

Following changes can be made in the GREEDY-ACTIVITY-SELECTOR (s, f, n)

```
j = first (s)
A = i
for i =j + 1 to n
      do if s(i) not= "-"
            then if
```

```
GREED-ACTIVITY-SELECTOR (s, f, n)

j = first (s)
A = i =j + 1 to n
      if s(i] not = "-" then
            if S[i] >[j]
              then A =AU{i}
                        s[i] = "-"
                              j = i
return A
```

Correctness

The algorithm can be shown to be correct and optimal. As a contradiction, assume the number of lecture halls are not optimal, that is, the algorithm allocates more hall than necessary. Therefore, there exists a set of activities B which have been wrongly allocated. An activity b belonging to B which has been allocated to hall H[i] should have optimally been allocated to H[k]. This implies that the activities for lecture hall H[k] have not been allocated optimally, as the GREED-ACTIVITY-SELECTOR produces the optimal set of activities for a particular lecture hall.

Analysis

In the worst case, the number of lecture halls require is n. GREED-ACTIVITY-SELECTOR runs in $\theta(n)$. The running time of this algorithm is $O(n^2)$.

Two important Observations

- Choosing the activity of least duration will not always produce an optimal solution. For example, we have a set of activities {(3, 5), (6, 8), (1, 4), (4, 7), (7, 10)}. Here, either (3, 5) or (6, 8) will be picked first, which will be picked first, which will prevent the optimal solution of {(1, 4), (4, 7), (7, 10)} from being found.

- Choosing the activity with the least overlap will not always produce solution. For example, we have a set of activities {(0, 4), (4, 6), (6, 10), (0, 1), (1, 5), (5, 9), (9, 10), (0, 3), (0, 2), (7, 10), (8, 10)}. Here the one with the least overlap with other activities is (4, 6), so it will be picked first. But that would prevent the optimal solution of {(0, 1), (1, 5), (5, 9), (9, 10)} from being found.

21.8 HUFFMAN CODES

Huffman code is a technique for compressing data. Huffman' s greedy algorithm look at the occurrence of each character and it as a binary string in an optimal way.V_1

Example 6

Suppose we have a data consists of 100,000 characters that we want to compress. The characters in the data occur with following frequencies.

	a	b	c	. d	e	f
Frequence	45,000	13,000	12,000	16,000	9.000	5,000

Consider the problem of designing a "binary character code" in which each character is represented by a unique binary string.

FIXED LENGTH CODE

In fixed length code, needs 3 bits to represent six(6) characters.

	a	b	c	d	e	f
Frequency	45,000	13,000	12,000	12,000	9,000	5,000
Fixed Length code	000	001	010	011	100	101

This method require 3000,000 bits to code the entire file.

How do we get 3000,000?

- Total number of characters are 45,000 + 13,000 + 12,000 + 16,000 + 9,000 + 5,000 = 1000,000.
- Add each character is assigned 3-bit codeword => 3 * 1000,000 = 3000,000 bits.

Conclusion

Fixed-length code requires 300,000 bits while variable code requires 224,000 bits.

=> Saving of approximately 25%.

Prefix Codes

In which no codeword is a prefix of other codeword. The reason prefix codes are desirable is that they simply encoding (compression) and decoding.

Can we do better?

A variable-length code can do better by giving frequent characters short codewords and infrequent characters long codewords.

	a	b	c	d	e	f
Frequency	45,000	13,000	12,000	12,000	9,000	5,000
Fixed Length code	0	101	100	111	1101	1100

Character 'a' are 45,000

each character 'a' assigned 1 bit codeword.

1 * 45,000 = 45,000 bits.

Characters (b, c, d) are 13,000 + 12,000 + 16,000 = 41,000

each character assigned 3 bit codeword

3 * 41,000 = 123,000 bits

Characters (e, f) are 9,000 + 5,000 = 14,000

each character assigned 4 bit codeword.

4 * 14,000 = 56,000 bits.

Implies that the total bits are: 45,000 + 123,000 + 56,000 = 224,000 bits

Encoding: Concatenate the codewords representing each characters of the file.

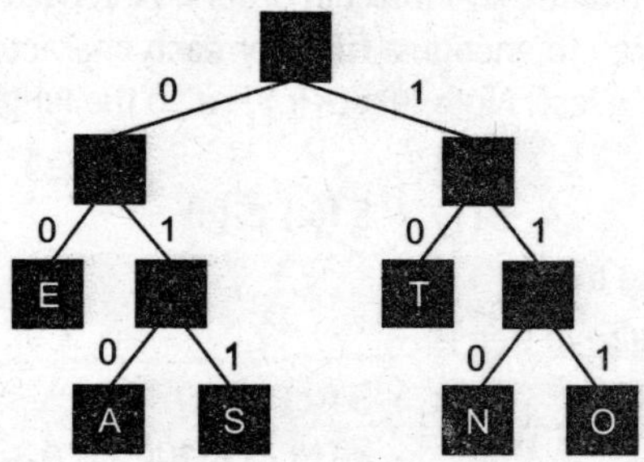

String	Encoding
TEA	10 00 010
SEA	01100 010
TEN	10 00 110

Example 7: From variable-length codes table, we code the3-character file abc as:

a b c

0 101 100

⇒ 0.101.100 = 0101100

Decoding

Since no codeword is a prefix of other, the codeword that begins an encoded file is unambiguous.

To decode (Translate back to the original character), remove it from the encode file and repeatedly parse.

For example in "variable-length codeword" table, the string 001011101 parse uniquely as 0.0.101.1101, which is decode to aabe.

The representation of " decoding process" is binary tree, whose leaves are characters. We interpret the binary codeword for a character as path from the root to that character, where 0 means "go to the left child" and 1 means "go to the right child". Note that an optimal code for a file is always represented by a full (complete) binary tree.

Theorem: A Binary tree that is not full cannot correspond to an optimal prefix code.

Proof: Let T be a binary tree corresponds to prefix code such that T is not full. Then there must exist an internal node, say x, such that x has only one child, y. Construct another binary tree, T, which has save leaves as T and have same depth as T except for the leaves which are in the sub tree rooted at y in T. These leaves will have depth in T, which implies T cannot correspond to an optimal prefix code. To obtain T, simply merge x and y into a single node, z is a child of parent of x (if a parent exists) and z is a parent to any children of y. Then T has the desired properties: it corresponds to a code on the same alphabet as the code which are obtained, in the subtree rooted at y in T have depth in T strictly less (by one) than their depth in T. This completes the proof.

	a	b	c	d	e	f
Frequency	45,000	13,000	12,000	12,000	9,000	5,000
Fixed Length code	000	001	010	011	100	101
Variabl-length code	0	101	100	111	1101	1100

From now on consider only full binary tree

If C is the alphabet from which characters are drawn, then the tree for an optimal prefix code has exactly |c| leaves (one for each letter) and exactly |c|-l internal orders. Given a tree T corresponding to the prefix code, compute the number of bits required to encode a file. For each character c in C, let f(c) be the frequency of c and let $d_T(c)$ denote the depth of c's leaf. Note that $d_T(c)$ is also the length of codeword. The number of bits to encode a file is

$$B(T) = S f(c) d_T(c)$$

which define as the cost of the tree T.

For example, the cost of the above tree is

$$\begin{aligned} B(T) &= S f(c) d_T(c) \\ &= 45*1+13*3 + 12*3 + 16*3 + 9*4+5*4 \\ &= 224 \end{aligned}$$

Therefore, the cost of the tree corresponding to the optimal prefix code is 224 (224*1000 = 224000).

CONSTRUCTING A HUFFMAN CODE

A greedy algorithm that constructs an optimal prefix code called a Huffman code. The algorithm builds the tree T corresponding to the optimal code in a bottom-up manner. It begins with a set of |c| leaves and perform |c|-l "merging" operations to create the final tree.

```
Data Structure used: Priority queue = Q
Huffman (c)
n = |c|
Q = c
for i =1 to n-1
  do z = Allocate-Node ()
     x = left[z] = EXTRACT_MIN(Q)
     y = right[z] = EXTRACT_MIN(Q)
     f[z] = f [x] + f [y]
     INSERT (Q, z)
return EXTRACT_MIN(Q)
```

Analysis

- Q implemented as a binary heap.
- line 2 can be performed by using BUILD-HEAP in O(n) time.
- FOR loop executed |n| – 1 times and since each heap operation requires O(lg n) time.
  => the FOR loop contributes (|n| – 1) O(lg n)
  => O(n lg n)
- Thus the total running time of Huffman on the set of n characters is O(nlgn).

Operation of the Algorithm

An optimal Huffman code for the following set of frequencies

a:l b:l c:2 d:3 e:5 g:13 h:2

Note that the frequencies are based on Fibonacci numbers.

Since there are letters in the alphabet, the initial queue size is n = 8, and 7 merge steps are required to build the tree. The final tree represents the optimal prefix code.

The codeword for a letter is the sequence of the edge labels on the path from the root to the letter. Thus, the optimal Huffman code is as follows:

h : 1
g : 1 0
f : 1 1 0
e : 1 1 1 0
d : 1 1 1 1 0
c : 1 1 1 1 1 0
b : 1 1 1 1 1 1 0
a : 1 1 1 1 1 1 1

As we can see the tree is one long limb with leaves n=hanging off. This is true for Fibonacci weights in general, because the Fibonacci the recurrence is

$F_{i+1} + F_i + F_{i-1}$ implies that $\Sigma_i F_i = F_{i+2} - 1$.

To prove this, write F_j as $F_{j+1} - F_{j-1}$ and sum from 0 to i, that is, $F_{-1} = 0$.

Correctness of Huffman Code Algorithm

Proof Idea

Step 1: Show that this problem satisfies the greedy choice property, that is, if a greedy choice is made by Huffman's algorithm, an optimal solution remains possible.

Step 2: Show that this problem has an optimal substructure property, that is, an optimal solution to Huffman's algorithm contains optimal solution to subproblems.

Step 3: Conclude correctness of Huffman's algorithm using step 1 and step 2.

Lemma - Greedy Choice Property Let c be an alphabet in which each character c has frequency f[c]. Let x and y be two characters in C having the lowest frequencies. Then there exists an optimal prefix code for C in which the codewords for x and y have the same length and differ only in the last bit.

Proof Idea: Take the tree T representing optimal prefix code and transform T into a tree T representing another optimal prefix code such that the x characters X and y appear as sibling leaves of maximum depth in T'. If we can do this, then their code words will have same length and differ only in the last bit.

Proof: Let characters b and c are sibling leaves of maximum depth in tree T. Without loss of generality assume that f [b] ≥ f [c] and f [x] ≤ f [y]. Since f [x] and f [y] are lowest leaf frequencies in order and f [b] and f [c] are arbitrary frequencies in order. We have f [x] ≤ f [b] and f [y] ≤ f [c]. As shown in the above figure, exchange the positions of leaves to get first T′ and then T″. By formula, $B(t) = \Sigma_{c \text{ in } C} f(C)d_T(C)$, the difference in cost between T and T′ is

$$\begin{aligned} B(T) - B(T) &= f[x]d_T(x) + f(b)d_T(b) - [f[x]d_T(x) + f[b]\, d_T(b)] \\ &= (f[b] - f[x])\,(d_T(b) - d_T(x)) \\ &= (\text{non-negative})(\text{non-negative}) \\ &\geq 0 \end{aligned}$$

Two Important Points

The reason f [b] – f [x] is non-negative because x is a minimum frequency leaf in tree T and the reason $d_T(b) - d_T(X)$ is non-negative that b is a leaf of maximum depth in T.

Similarly, exchanging y and c does not increase the cost which implies that B (T) – B (T) ≥ 0. This fact in turn implies that B (T′) = B(T ′), and since T is optimal by supposition, which implies B(T′), = B(T). Therefore, T″ is optimal in which x and y are sibling leaves of maximum depth, from which greedy choice property follows. This complete the proof

Lemma - Optimal Substructure Property

Let T be a full binary tree representing an optimal prefix code over an alphabet C, where frequency f [c] is define for each character c belongs to set C. Consider any two characters x and y that appear as sibling leaves in the tree T and let z be their parent. Then, considering character z with frequency f [z] = f [x] + f [y], tree T = T – {x, y} represents an optimal code for the alphabet C′ = C – {x, y}U{z}.

Proof: We show that the cost B(T) of tree T can be expressed in terms of the cost B(T′). By considering the component costs in equation, $B(T) = \Sigma f(c)d_T(c)$, we show that the cost B (T) of tree T can be expressed in terms of the cost B (T′) of the tree T′. For each C belongs to C – {x, y}, we have $d_T(c) = d_T(c)$

$$\begin{aligned} \Sigma cin_C\ f[c]d_T(c) &= S_{cinC-\{x,y\}}\, f[c]\, d_{T'}(c) \\ &= f[x](d_{T'}(z) + 1 + f[y]\,(d_{T'}(z) + 1) \\ &= (f[x] + f[y])\, d_{T'}(z) + f[x] + f[y] \end{aligned}$$

And $$B(T) = B(T') + f(x) + f(y)$$

if T′ is non-optimal prefix code for C′, then there exists a T″ whose leaves are the characters belongs to C such that B(T″) < B(T′). Now, if x and y are added to T′ as a children of Z, then we get a prefix code for alphabet C with cost B (T″) + f [x] + f [y] < B(T), Contradicting the optimality of T. Which implies that, tree T′ must be optimal for the alphabet C.

Theorem: Procedure HUFFMAN produces an optimal prefix code.

Proof: Let S be the set of integers n ≥ 2 for which the Huffman procedure produces a tree of representing optimal prefix code for frequency f and alphabet C with | c | = n. If C = {x, y}, then Huffman produces one of the following optimal trees.

This clearly shows 2 is a member of S. Next assume that n belongs to S and show that (n +1) also belong to S. Let C is an alphabet with | c | = n + 1. By lemma 'greedy choice property', there exists an optimal code tree T for alphabet C. Without loss of generality, if x and y are characters with minimal frequencies then a. x and y are at maximal depth in tree T and b. and y have a common parent z. Suppose that T = T - {x, y} and C = C – {x, y}U{z} then by lemma-optimal substructure property (step 2), tree T′ is an optimal code tree for | C| Since | C′ | = n and n belongs to S, the Huffman code procedure produces an optimal code tree T* for C. Now let T** be the tree obtained from T* by attaching x and y as leaves to z. Without loss of generality, T** is the tree constructed for C by the Huffman procedure. Now suppose Huffman selects a and b from alphabet C in first step so that f [a] not equal f [x] and f [b] = f [y]. Then tree C constructed by Huffman can be altered as in proof of lemma-greedy-choice-property to give equivalent tree with a and y siblings with maximum depth. Since T′ and T* are both optimal for C′, implies that B(T) = B(T*) and also B (T**) = B(T) why? because

$$\begin{aligned} B(T^{**}) &= B(T^*) - f[z]d_T{}^*(z) + [f[x] + f[y]]\,(d_T{}^*(z) + 1)] \\ &= B(T^*) + f[x] + f[y] \end{aligned}$$

Since tree T is optimal for alphabet C, so is T**. And T** is the tree constructed by the Huffman code. And this completes the proof.

Theorem: The total cost of a tree for a code can be computed as the sum, over all internal nodes, of the combined frequencies of the two children of the node.

Proof: Let tree be a full binary tree with n leaves. Apply induction hypothesis on the number of leaves in T. When n = 2 (the case n = l is trivially true), there are two leaves x and y (say) with the same parent z, then the cost of T is

$$\begin{aligned} B(T) &= f(x)d_T(x) + f[y]d_T(y) \\ &= f[x] + f[y] \qquad \text{since } d_T(x) = d_T(y) = 1 \\ &= f[\text{child}_1 \text{ of } z] + f[\text{child}_2 \text{ of } z] \end{aligned}$$

Thus, the statement of theorem is true. Now suppose n > 2 and also suppose that theorem is true for trees on n – 1 leaves.

Let c_1 and c_2 are two sibling leaves in T such that they have the same parent p. Letting T′ be the tree obtained by deleting c_1 and c_2, we know by induction that

$$\begin{aligned} B(T) &= \Sigma_{\text{leaves } 1' \text{ in } T'}\, f[1']\, d_T(1') \\ &= \Sigma_{\text{internal nodes } i' \text{ in } T'}\, f[\text{child}_1 \text{of } i'] + f[\text{child}_2 \text{ of } 1'] \end{aligned}$$

Using this information, calculates the cost of T.

$$\begin{aligned} B(T) &= \Sigma_{\text{leaves } 1' \text{ in } T}\, f[l]d_T(l) \\ &= \Sigma_{1 \text{not}=c_1,c_2}\, f[l]d_T(l) + f[c_l]\, d_T(c_1) - 1) + f[c_2]\, d_T(c_2) - 1) + \\ &\qquad f[c_1] + f[c_2] \\ &= \Sigma_{\text{leaves } 1' \text{ in } T'}\, f[l]d_{T'}(l) + f[C_1] + f[C_2] \\ &= \Sigma_{\text{internal nodes } i' \text{ in } T'}\, f[\text{child}_1 \text{ of } i'] + f[\text{child}_2 \text{ of } i'] + f[d] + f[c_2] \\ &= \Sigma_{\text{internal nodes } i \text{ in } T}\, f[\text{child}_1 \text{of } i] + f[\text{child}_1 \text{ of } i] \end{aligned}$$

Thus the statement is true. And this completes the proof.

The question is whether Huffman's algorithm can be generalize to handle ternary codewords, that is codewords using the symbols 0, 1 and 2. Restate the question, whether or not some generalized version of Huffman's algorithm yields optimal ternary codes? Basically, the algorithm is similar to the binary code example given in the CLR-text book. That is, pick up three nodes (not two) which have the least frequency and form a new node with frequency equal to the summation of these three frequencies. Then repeat the procedure. However, when the number of nodes is an even number, a full ternary tree is not possible. So take care of this by inserting a null node with zero frequency.

Correctness

Proof is immediate from the greedy choice property and an optimal substructure property. In other words, the proof is similar to the correctness proof of Huffman's algorithm.

21.9 SPANNING TREES

A spanning tree of a graph is any tree that includes every vertex in the graph. Little more formally, a spanning tree of a graph G is a subgraph of G that is a tree and contains all the vertices of G. An edge of a spanning tree is called a branch; an edge in the graph that is not in the spanning tree is called a chord. We construct spanning tree whenever we want to find a simple, cheap and yet efficient way to connect a set of terminals (computers, cites, factories, etc.). Spanning trees are important because of following reasons.

- Spanning trees construct a sparse sub graph that tells a lot about the original graph.
- Spanning trees a very important in designing efficient routing algorithms.
- Some hard problems (e.g., Steiner tree problem and traveling salesman problem) can be solved approximately by using spanning trees.
- Spanning trees have wide applications in many areas, such as network design, etc.

Greedy Spanning Tree Algorithm

One of the most elegant spanning tree algorithm that I know of is as follows:

- Examine the edges in graph in any arbitrary sequence.
- Decide whether each edge will be included in the spanning tree.

Note that each time a step of the algorithm is performed, one edge is examined. If there is only a finite number of edges in the graph, the algorithm must halt after a finite number of steps. Thus, the time complexity of this algorithm is clearly O(n), where n is the number of edges in the graph.

Some important facts about spanning trees are as follows:

- Any two vertices in a tree are connected by a unique path.
- Let T be a spanning tree of a graph G, and let e be an edge of G not in T. The T+e contains a unique cycle.

Lemma The number of spanning trees in the complete graph K_n is n^{n-2}.

Greediness It is easy to see that this algorithm has the property that each edge is examined at most once. Algorithms, like this one, which examine each entity at most once and decide its fate once and for all during that examination are called greedy algorithms. The obvious advantage of greedy approach is that we do not have to spend time reexamining entities.

Consider the problem of finding a spanning tree with the smallest possible weight or the largest possible weight, respectively called a minimum spanning tree and a maximum spanning tree. It is easy to see that if a graph possesses a spanning tree, it must have a minimum spanning tree and also a maximum spanning tree. These spanning trees can be constructed by performing the spanning tree algorithm (e.g., above mentioned algorithm) with an appropriate ordering of the edges.

Minimum Spanning Tree Algorithm

Perform the spanning tree algorithm (above) by examining the edges is order of non decreasing weight (smallest first, largest last). If two or more edges have the same weight, order them arbitrarily.

Minimum Spanning Trees

A minimum spanning tree (MST) of a weighted graph G is a spanning tree of G whose edges sum is minimum weight. In other words, a MST is a tree formed from a subset of the edges in a given undirected graph, with two properties:

- it spans the graph, i.e., it includes every vertex of the graph.
- it is a minimum, i.e., the total weight of all the edges is as low as possible.

Let G = (V, E) be a connected, undirected graph where V is a set of vertices (nodes) and E is the set of edges. Each edge has a given non negative length.

Problem: Find a subset T of the edges of G such that all the vertices remain connected when only the edges T are used, and the sum of the lengths of the edges in T is as small as possible.

Let G′ = (V, T) be the partial graph formed by the vertices of G and the edges in T. [Note: A connected graph with n vertices must have at least n–1 edges AND more that n–1 edges implies at least one cycle]. So n–1 is the minimum number of edges in the T. Hence if G′ is connected and T has more that n–1 edges, we can remove at least one of these edges without disconnecting (choose an edge that is part of cycle). This will decrease the total length of edges in T.

G′ = (V, T) where T is a subset of E. Since connected graph of n nodes must have n-1 edges otherwise there exist at least one cycle. Hence if G′ is connected and T has more that n-1 edges. Implies that it contains at least one cycle. Remove edge from T without disconnecting the G″ (i.e., remove the edge that is part of the cycle). This will decrease the total length of the edges in T. Therefore, the new solution is preferable to the old one.

Thus, T with n vertices and more edges can be an optimal solution. It follow T must have n-1 edges and since G′ is connected it must be a tree. The G′ is called Minimum Spanning Tree (MST).

Solved Questions

1. What is a greedy algorithm?

Ans. A greedy algorithm is an algorithm that follows the problem solving heuristic of making the locally optimal choice at each stage with the hope of finding a global optimum. On some problems, a greedy strategy need not produce an optimal solution, but nonetheless a greedy heuristic may yield locally optimal solutions that approximate a global optimal solution.

2. What is difference between dynamic programming and greedy algorithm?

Ans. Dynamic Programming Bottom up (while Greedy is top-down)

- Dynamic programming can be overkill; greedy algorithms tend to be easier to code

3. What is activity selection problem?

Sol. Scheduling a resource among several competing activities

- Definition
  - $S=\{1, 2,\ldots, n\}$ – activities that wish to use a resource and a finish time fi, where si ≤ fi
  - If selected, activity i takes place during the half-open interval [si, fi)
  - Activities i and j are compatible if [si, fi) and [sj, fj) don't overlap
  - The activity-selection problem is to select a maximum-size set of mutually compatible activities

4. Following are 7 activities with their respective deadlines and penalities.

ai 1 2 3 4 5 6 7

di 4 2 4 3 1 4 6

wi 70 60 50 40 30 20 10

Solve using the task scheduling such that penalty is minimized

Ans. The solution to this problem is {a2, a4, a1, a3, a7, a5, a6}

penality, w5 + w6 = 50

5. What is Tower of Hanoi problem?

Ans. The Tower of Hanoi is a mathematical game or puzzle. It consists of three rods, and a number of disks of different sizes which can slide onto any rod. The puzzle starts with the disks in a neat stack in ascending order of size on one rod, the smallest at the top, thus making a conical shape.

The objective of the puzzle is to move the entire stack to another rod, obeying the following rules:

- Only one disk may be moved at a time.
- Each move consists of taking the upper disk from one of the rods and sliding it onto another rod, on top of the other disks that may already be present on that rod.
- No disk may be placed on top of a smaller disk.

The puzzle can be played with any number of disks, although many toy versions have around seven to nine of them. The game seems impossible to many novices, yet is solvable with a simple algorithm. The number of moves required to solve a Tower of Hanoi puzzle is 2^n-1, where n is the number of disks.

Previous Year University Question

1. Explain how the branch and bound technique can be used to solve 0/1 Knapsack problem. [OU]
2. Write control Abstraction for Greedy method. [OU]
3. Define the (Greedy) Knapsack problem. What is the trivial case of the problem? Explain. [OU]
4. Explain how the Greedy Knapsack problem can be solved. Write the algorithm used. [OU]
5. Describe greedy method. Find the optimal solution to the knapsack instance n = 3, W = [100, 14, 10], P = [20, 18, 15] and C = 116 using greedy method. [GBTU]
6. What is greedy algorithm? Write its pseudo code prove that the fractional knapsack problem has a greedy-choice property. [GBTU]
7. State the knapsack problem and explain how it can be solved using a branch and bound algorithm. [Madrass University]

8. Explain the Greedy method and Divide and Conquer strategy to find optimal solution to the problem. To which type of problems they are applied. [MDU]
9. State single source shortest problem. Write an algorithm based on greedy method to obtain solution to shortest path problem. Also discuss how running time is affected by representation of graph. [MDU]
10. Describe the greedy method and Divide and conquer strategy to find optimal solution to the problem. To which type of problems they are applied? [MDU]
11. Explain the greedy approach for algorithm design? Devise a solution for fractional knapsack using greedy approach? Give its time complexity. [MDU]

Exercise

1. Find the optimal schedule for the following jobs with n = 7, profits (p_1 .... P_7) = (3, 6, 21, 19, 1, 6, 31). and deadline (d_1, d_2.... d_7) = (1, 3, 5, 3, 2, 1, 2).
2. Consider the knaprack instance n = 3, (w_1, w_2, w_3) = (2, 4, 5) and (p_1, p_2, p_3) = (1, 5. 7) m = 5. Find optimal solution.
3. For Knapsack instance n = 8, m = 20,

   $$(p_1 \ldots p_8) = (10, 5. 15, 7, 6, 18, 20, 3)$$
   $$(w_1 \ldots w_8) = (2, 3, 5, 7, 14, 2, 1)$$

   Find optimal solution.
4. Obtain a set of optimal Huffman codes for maner (m_1.... m_8) with relative frequencies (q_1.... q_8) = (4, 5, 7, 8, 9, 10, 11, 20).
5. Show how to solve fractional knaprack problem is $\theta(n)$ time.

CHAPTER

22

STRING MATCHING

22.1 INTRODUCTION

String matching consists of finding one or more generally, all of the occurrences of a pattern in a text. Finding a certain pattern in a text is a problem arises in text-editing programs and web "surfing". Here we study various fundamental text processing algorithms for quickly performing string searching and string matching.

22.2 PROBLEM FORMULATION

Given a text array, T [1 . . n], of n character and a pattern array, P [1 .. m], of m characters. The problem is to find an integer s, called valid shift where $0 \leq s < n - m$ and T [s +1 ... s + m] = P[1 . . m]. In other words, to find whether P in T i.e., where P is a substring of T. The elements of P and T are character drawn from some finite alphabet such as {0, 1} or {A, B, ... Z,a,b, . . . ,z}.

Given a string T [1 . . n], the substrings is define as T [i. . j] for some $0 \leq i \leq j \leq n-1$, that is, the string formed by the characters in T from index i to index j, inclusive. This means that a string is a substring of itself (simply take i = 0 and j = m).

The proper substring, of string T [I .. n] is T [i. j] for some 0 < i ** j n –1. That is, we must have either i > 0 or j < m –1.

Using these definition, we can say given any string T [1 .. n], the substrings are

T[i..j] = T [i] T [i+1]T [i + 2]. .. T [j] for some $0 \leq i \leq j \leq n-1$.

And proper substrings are

T [i. .] = T [i] T [i] + 1] T [i + 2] ... T[j] for some 0 < i j n –1.

Note that if i > j, then T [i .. j] is equal to the empty string or null, which has length zero.

Using these notations, we can define of a given string T [1 . . n] as T [0 . . i] for some $0 \leq i \leq n-1$ and suffix of a given string T [i .. n] as T [i. . n –1] for some $0 \leq i \leq n-1$.

For example, given string T [I .. B] is

T:	a	b	c	a	b	a	a	b	c	a	b	a	c

then a proper substring of T is

a	b	a	a

a prefix string of T is

a	b	c

and a suffix string of T is

b	a	c

Suppose we given string w, x, y and z

w :	a	b	c

x :	a	b	c	a

y :	a	b	c	a	b

z :	a	b	c	a	b	a	a	b

Here

x is a substring of z.

y is a substring of z.

Since |x| ≤ | y | therefore, we have

x is a

y :	a	b	c	a

substring of b

y |

x :	a	b	c	a

In this case,

Since | y | ≥ | x |

therefore x is a substring of y

y :	a	b	c	a	b

x :	a	b	c	a

In this case, since

|x| = |w|

therefore, x = y

x = a b c

w = a b c

22.3 NAÏVE STRING MATCHING

The na ve approach simply test all the possible placement of Pattern P[1 . . m] relative to text T [1.. n] Specifically, we try shift s = 0, 1, . . ., n– m, successively and for each shift, s. Compare T [s +1 . . s + m] to P [1. . m]

NAÏVE_STRING_MATCHER (T, P)

```
1.  n ← length [T]
2.  m ← length [P]
3.  for s ← 0 to n – m do
4.      if P [l . . m] = T [s +1 ..s + m]
5.          then return valid shift s
```

The naive string-matching procedure can be interpreted graphically as a sliding a pattern P[1 .. m] over the text T [1 .. n] and noting for which shift all of the characters in the pattern match the corresponding characters in the text.

In other to analysis the time of naive matching, we would like to implement above algorithm to understand the test involves in line 4.

Note that in this implementation, we use notation P[1 .. j] to denote the substring of P from index i to index j.

That is, P[1..j] = P [i] P [i +1] ... P [j].

NAÏVE_STRING_MATCHER (T, P)

```
1.  n ← length [T]
2.  m ← length [P]
3.  for s ← 0 to n–m do
4.      j ← 1
5.      while j ← m and T [s + j ] = P [ j ] do
6.          j ← j + l
7.      If j > m then
8.  return valid shift s
9.  return no valid shift exist    // i.e., there is no substring of T matching P.
```

Referring to implementation of naive matcher, we see that the for-loop in line 3 is executed at most n – m +1 times, and the while-loop in line 5 is executed at most m times. Therefore, the running time of the algorithm is O ((n – m +1)m), which is clearly O (nm). Hence, in the worst case, when the length of the pattern, m are roughly equal, this algorithm runs in the quadratic time.

One worst case is that text, T, has n number of A's and the pattern, P, has (m –1) number of A's followed by a single B.

22.4 KNUTH-MORRIS-PRATT ALGORITHM

Knuth, Morris and Pratt discovered first linear time string-matching algorithm by following a tight analysis of the na'i've algorithm. Knuth-Morris-Pratt algorithm keeps the information that na'fve approach wasted gathered during the scan of the text. By avoiding this waste of information, it achieves a running time of O(n + m), which is optimal in the worst case sense. That is, in the worst case Knuth-Morris-Pratt algorithm we have to examine all the characters in the text and pattern at least once.

22.4.1 The Failure Function

The KMP algorithm preprocess the pattern P by computing a failure function f that indicates the largest possible shift s using previously performed comparisons. Specifically, the failure function f (j) is defined as the length of the longest prefix of P that is a suffix of P [i.. j].

```
KNUTH-MORRIS-PRATT FAILURE (P)

  Input: Pattern with m characters
  Output: Failure function f for P [i. .j]

i ← 1
j ← 0
f(0) ← 0
while i ← m do
  if P [j] = P [i]
     f (i) ← j + 1
       i ← j + l
       j ← j + 1
else if
       j ← f(j – 1)
else
       f(i) ← 0
         i ← i +1
```

Note that the failure function f for P, which maps j to the length of the longest prefix of P that is a suffix of P [l .. j], encodes repeated substrings inside the pattern itself.

As an example, consider the pattern P = a b a c a b. The failure function, f (j), using above algorithm is

j	a 1 2 3 4 5

P(j)	a	b	a	c	a	b
f(j)	0	0	1	0	1	2

By observing the above mapping we can see that the longest prefix of pattern, P, is "a b" which is also a suffix of pattern P.

Consider an attempt to match at position i, that is when the pattern P [0 .. m –1] is aligned with text P [i. . i + m –1].

T :	a	b	a	c	a	a	b	a	c	c

P :	a	b	a	c	a	b	

Assume that the first mismatch occurs between characters T [i + j] and P[j] for 0 < j < m. In the above example, the first mismatch is T [5] = a and P [5] = b.

Then, T [i. . i + j –1] = P[0 .. j –1] = u

That is, T [0 .. 4] = P[0 .. 4] = u, in the example [u = a b a c a] and

T [i +j] ≠ P [j] i.e., T[5] ≠ P [5], In the example [T [5] = a ≠ b = P [5]].

When shifting, it is reasonable to expect that a prefix v of the pattern matches some suffix of the portion u of the text. In our example, u = a b a c a and v = a b a c a, therefore, 'a' a prefix of v matches with 'a' a suffix of u. Let l(i') be the length of the longest string P [0 .. j –1] of pattern that matches with text followed by a character c different from P [j]. Then after a shift, the comparisons can resume between characters T [i + j] and P [l (j)], i.e., T(5) and P(l)

T:	a	b	a	c	a	a	b	a	c	c

P:			a	b	a	c	a	b

Note that no comparison between T [4] and P [l] needed here.

```
KNUTH-MORRIS-PRATT (T, P)

Input: Strings T[0 . . n] and P[0 . . m]
Output: Starting index of substring of T matching P

f ← compute failure function of Pattern P
i ← 0
j ← 0
while i < length[T] do
    if j ← m—1 then
       return i– m+1    // we have a match
    i ← i +1
    j ← j + 1
else if j > 0
     j ← f(j–1)
  else
     i ← i +1
```

22.4.2 Analysis

The running time of Knuth-Morris-Pratt algorithm is proportional to the time needed to read thé characters in text and pattern. In other words, the worst-case running time of the algorithm is O (m + n) and it requires O(m) extra space. It is important to note that these quantities are independent of the size of the underlying alphabet.

22.5 BOYER-MOORE ALGORITHM

The Boyer-Moore algorithm is consider the most efficient string-matching algorithm in usual applications, for example, in text editors and commands substitutions. The reason is that it woks the fastest when the alphabet is moderately sized and the pattern is relatively long.

The algorithm scans the characters of the pattern from right to left beginning with the rightmost character. During the testing of a possible placement of pattern P against text T, a mismatch of text character T [i] = c with the corresponding pattern character P [j] is handled as follows: If c is not contained anywhere in P, then shift the pattern P completely past T [i]. Otherwise, shift P until an occurrence of character c in P gets aligned with T [i].

This technique likely to avoid lots of needless comparisons by significantly shifting pattern relative to text.

22.5.1 Last Function

We define a function last (c) that takes a character c from the alphabet and specifies how far may shift the pattern P if a character equal to c is found in the text that does not match the pattern

$$= \begin{cases} \text{index of the last occurrence} & \text{if c is in P} \\ \text{last of c in pattern P} & \\ -1 & \text{otherwise} \end{cases}$$

For example consider

T:	0	1	2	3	4	5	6	7	8	9
	a	*b*	*a*	*c*	*a*	*a*	*b*	*a*	*c*	*c*

P:	*a*	*b*	*a*	*c*	*a*	*b*
	0	1	2	3	4	5

last(a) is the index of the last (rightmost) occurrence of 'a' in P, which is 4.

last (c) is the index of the last occurrence of c in P, which is 3

'd' does not exist in the pattern there we have last (d) = –1.

c	a	b	c	d
last (c)	4		3	–1

Now, for 'b' notice

T: a b a c a a b a c c

P: a b a c a b

Therefore, last(b) is the index of last occurrence of b in P, which is 5

The complete last (c) function

c	a	b	c	d
last (c)	4	5	3	–1

22.6 BOYER-MOORE ALGORITHM

BOYER_MOOREJVIATCHER (T, P)

Input: Text with n characters and Pattern with m characters
Output: Index of the first substring of T matching P

```
Compute function last
i ← m –1
j ← m –1
Repeat
    If P [ j ] = T [i] then
        if j = 0 then
            return i              // we have a match
else
    i ← i –1
    j ← j – 1
else
    i ← i + m – Min (j, 1 + last [T [i]])
    j ← m – 1
until i > n – 1
Return "no match"
```

22.6.1 Analysis

The computation of the last function takes O (m + | Σ |) time and actual search takes O (mn) time. Therefore the worst case running time of Boyer-Moore algorithm is O (nm + | Σ |). Implies that the worst-case running time is quadratic, in case of n = m, the same as the naive algorithm.

- Boyer-Moore algorithm is extremely fast on large alphabet (relative to the length of the pattern).
- The payoff is not as for binary strings or for very short patterns.
- For binary strings Knuth-Morris-Pratt algorithm is recommended.
- For the very shortest patterns, the naive algorithm may be better.

Solved Questions

1. Given the following 2 strings S and T, find their longest common subsequence.

   S = ABA DC T = BACBAD

Ans. B A C B A D
A 0 1 1 1 1 1
B 1 1 1 2 2 2
A 1 2 2 2 3 3
 1 2 2 2 3 3
D 1 2 2 2 3 4
C 1 2 3 3 3 4

Thus LCS is 4.

2. Compare the running time for Na ve String Matching and Knuth Morris Pratt algorithm for string Matching.

Ans. Running time for Na ve String Matching : O((n-m+1) m)
Running time for KMP Matcher: O((n-m+1) m)

Previous Year University Question

1. Give algorithm for native string matching. [GGSIPU]

Exercise

1. For a given text string
   T = (a a b b a b a b b b a a b a b a b)
   and pattern stray P = (a b b a)
   Find whether P is present is T or not
2. Using Knuth-Morris-Pratt algorithm find pattern P = (10001) is in test
   T = (1011100010110) or not.
3. Using Boyer-Moore algorithm search the pattern P = (100010) is that.
   T = (10101111010010110).

CHAPTER

23

DISJOINT-SET DATA STRUCTRES

23.1 INTRODUCTION

Many times the efficiency of an algorithm depends on the data structures used in the algorithm. A wise choice in the structure you use in solving a problem can reduce the time of execution, the time to implement the algorithm and the amount of memory used. During SRM competitions we are limited to a time limit of 2 seconds and 64 MB of memory, so the right data structure can help you remain in competition. While some Data Structures have been covered before, in this article we'll focus on data structures for dis oint sets.

23.2 PROBLEM

Let's consider the following problem: In a room are N persons, and we will define two persons are friends if they are directly or indirectly friends. If A is a friend with B, and B is a friend with C, then A is a friend of C too. A group of friends is a group of persons where any two persons in the group are friends. Given the list of persons that are directly friends find the number of groups of friends and the number of persons in each group. For example N = 5 and the list of friends is: 1-2, 5-4, and 5-1. Here is the figure of the graph that represents the groups of friends. 1 and 2 are friends, then 5 and 4 are friends, and then 5 and 1 are friends, but 1 is friend with 2 therefore 5 and 2 are friends, etc. In the end there are 2 groups of friends: one group is {1, 2, 4, 5}, the other is {3}.

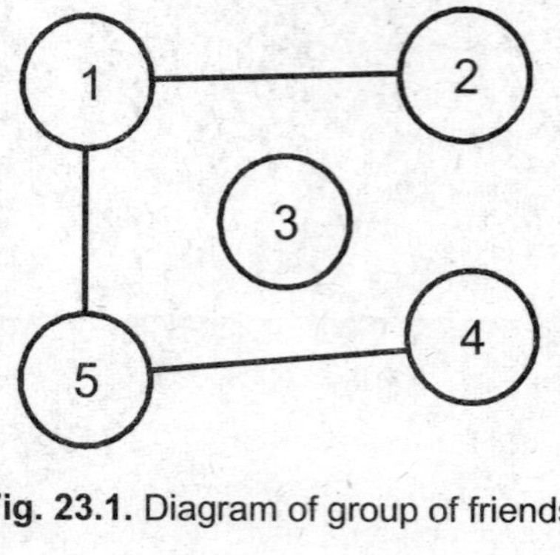

Fig. 23.1. Diagram of group of friends

23.2.1 Solution

This problem can be solved using BFS, but let's see how to solve this kind of problem using data structures for dis oint sets. First of all: a dis oint-set data structure is a structure that maintains a collection S1, S2, S3, ...,

Sn of dynamic dis oint sets. Two sets are dis oint if their intersection is null. For example set {1, 2, 3} and set {1, 5, 6} aren't dis oint because they have in common {1}, but the sets {1, 2, 3} and {5, 6} are dis oint because their intersection is null. In a data structure of dis oint sets every set contains a representative, which is one member of the set.

Let's see how things will work with sets for the example of the problem. The groups will be represented by sets, and the representative of each group is the person with the biggest index. At the beginning there are 5 groups (sets): {1}, {2}, {3}, {4}, {5}. Nobody is anybody's friend and everyone is the representative of his or her own group.

The next step is that 1 and 2 become friends, this means the group containing 1 and the group with 2 will become one group. This will give us these groups: {1,2} , {3}, {4}, {5}, and the representative of the first group will become 2. Next, 5 and 4 become friends. The groups will be {1,2}, {3}, {4, 5}. And in the last step 5 and 1 become friends and the groups will be {1, 2, 4, 5}, {3}. The representative of the first group will be 5 and the representative for second group will be 3. At the end we have 2 sets, the first set with 4 elements and the second with one, and this is the answer for the problem example: 2 groups, 1 group of 4 and one group of one.

Perhaps now you are wondering how you can check if 2 persons are in the same group. This is where the use of the representative elements comes in. Let's say we want to check if 3 and 2 are in the same group, we will know this if the representative of the set that contains 3 is the same as the representative of the set that contains 2. One representative is 5 and the other one is 3 therefore 3 and 2 aren't in same groups of friends.

23.2.2 Some operations

Let's define the following operations:

- CR AT -S T(x) – creates a new set with one element {x}.
- M RG -S TS(x, y) – merge into one set the set that contains element x and the set that contains element y (x and y are in different sets). The original sets will be destroyed.
- FIND-S T(x) – returns the representative or a pointer to the representative of the set that contains element x.

The solution using these operations

Let's see the solution for our problem using these operations:

```
Read N
for   (each person x from 1 to N) CR AT -S T(x)
for   (each pair of friends (x y) ) if (FIND-S T(x) = FIND-S T(y)) M RG -
S TS (x, y)
```

Now if we want to see if 2 persons (x, y) are in same group we check if FIND-S T(x) == FIND-S T (y).

We will analyze the running time of the dis oint-set data structure in terms of N and M, where N is the number of times that CR AT -S T(x) is called and M is the total number of times that CR AT -S T (x), M RG -S TS(x, y) and FIND-S T(x) are called. Since the sets are dis oint, each time M RG -S TS (x, y) is called one set will be created and two will be destroyed, giving us one less set. If there are n sets after n-1 calls of M RG -S TS(x,y) there will remain only one set. That's why the number of M RG -S TS (x,y) calls is less than or equal to the number of CR AT -S T(x) operations.

23.3 IMPLEMENTATION WITH LINKED LISTS

One way to implement disjoint set data structures is to represent each set by a linked list. Each element (object) will be in a linked list and will contain a pointer to the next element in the set and another pointer to the representative of the set. Here is a figure of how the example of the problem will look like after all operations are made. The blue arrows are the pointers to the representatives and the black arrows are the pointers to the next element in the sets. Representing sets with linked lists we will obtain a complexity of O(l) for CREATE-SET(x) and FIND-SET(x). CREATE-SET(x) will just create a new linked list whose only element (object) is x, the operation FIND-SET(x) just returns the pointer to the representative of the set that contains element (object) x.

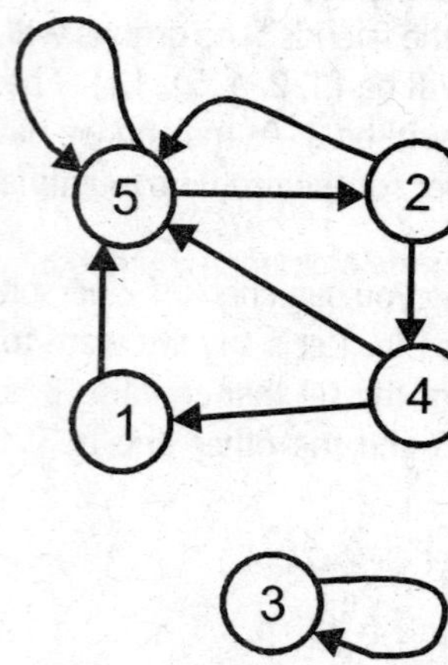

Fig. 23.2. Disjoint set data structures

Now let's see how to implement the MERGE-SETS(x, y) operations. The easy way is to append x's list onto the end of y's list. The representative of the new set is the representative of the original set that contained y. We must update the pointer to the representative for each element (object) originally on x's list, which takes linear time in terms of the length of x's list. It's easy to prove that, in the worst case, the complexity of the algorithm will be 0(M^2) where M is the number of operations MERGE-SETS(x, y). With this implementation the complexity will average O(N) per operation where N represents the number of elements in all sets.

23.4 THE "WEIGHTED UNION HEURISTIC"

Let's see how a heuristic will make the algorithm more efficient. The heuristic is called "a weighted-union heuristic." In this case, let's say that the representative of a set contains information about how many objects (elements) are in that set as well. The optimization is to always append the smaller list onto the longer and, in case of ties, append arbitrarily. This will bring the complexity of the algorithm to O(M + NlogN) where M is the number of operations (FIND-SET, MERGE-SETS, CREATE-SETS) and N is the number of operations CREATE-SETS.

So far we reach an algorithm to solve the problem in O(M + NlogN) where N is the number of persons and M is the number of friendships and a memory of O(N). Still the BFS will solve the problem in O(M + N) and memory of O(N + M). We can see that we have optimized the memory but not the execution time.

23.4.1 Next step: root trees

The next step is to see what we can do for a faster implementation of disjoint set data structures. Let's represent sets by rooted trees, with each node containing one element and each tree representing one set. Each element will point only to its parent and the root of each tree is the representative of that set and its own parent. Let's see, in steps, how the trees will look for the example from the problem above.

Step 1: nobody is anybody friend

We have 5 trees and each tree has a single element, which is the root and the representative of that tree.

Step 2: 1 and 2 are friends, MERGE-SETS(1, 2):

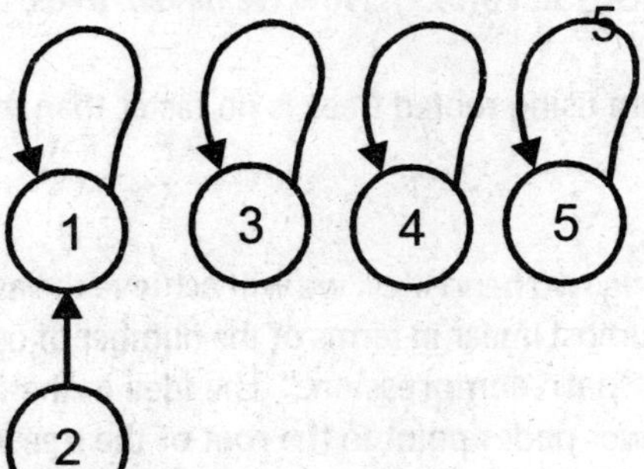

The operation made is MERGE-SETS(1, 2). We have 4 trees one tree contain 2 elements and have the root 1. The other trees have a single element.

Step 3: 5 and 4 are friends, MERGE-SETS(5, 4)

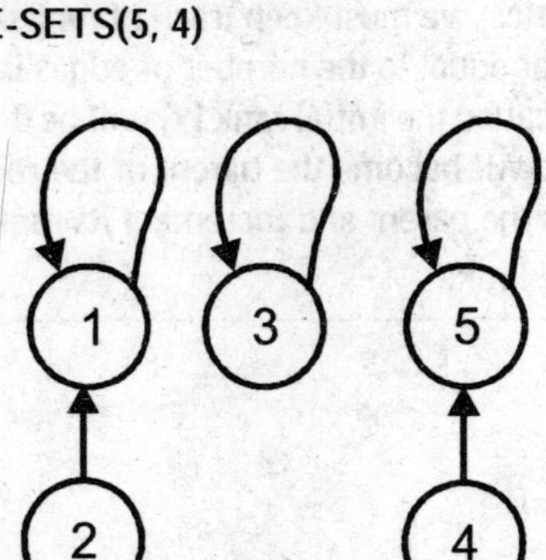

The operation made is MERGE-SETS(5, 4). Now we have 3 trees, 2 trees with 2 elements and one tree with one element.

St p : 5 and 1 are friends, MERGE-SETS(5, 1)

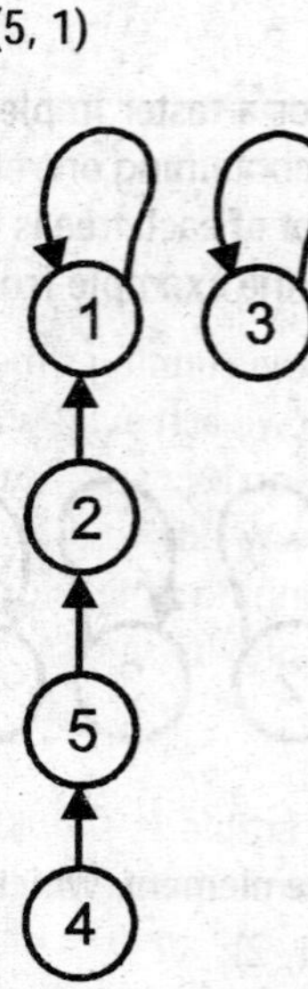

The operation made is MERGE-SETS(5, 1). Now we have 2 trees, one tree has 4 elements and the other one has only one element.

As we see so far the algorithm using rooted trees is no faster than the algorithm using linked lists.

23.5 TWO HEURISTICS

Next we will see how, by using two heuristics, we will achieve the asymptotically fastest disjoint set data structure known so far, which is almost linear in terms of the number of operations made. These two heuristics are called "union by rank" and "path compression." The idea in the first heuristic "union by rank" is to make the root of the tree with fewer nodes point to the root of the tree with more nodes. For each node, we maintain a rank that approximates the logarithm of the sub-tree size and is also an upper bound on the height of the node. When MERGE-SETS(x, y) is called, the root with smaller rank is made to point to the root with larger rank. The idea in the second heuristic "path compression," which is used for operation FIND-SET(x), is to make each node on the find path point directly to the root. This will not change any ranks. To implement a disjoint set forest with these heuristics, we must keep track of ranks. With each node x, we keep the integer value rank [x], which is bigger than or equal to the number of edges in the longest path between node x and a sub-leaf. When CREATE-SET(x) is called the initial rank [x] will be 0. When a MERGE-SETS(x, y) operation is made then the root of higher rank will become the parent of the root of lower rank - or, in case of tie, we arbitrarily choose one of the roots as the parent and increment its rank.

Let's see how the algorithm will look.

```
Let P[x] = the parent of node x.
CREATE-SET(x)
  P [x] = x
  rank [x] = 0
MERGE-SETS (x, y)
  PX = FIND-SET(X)
  PY =FIND-SET(Y)
  If (rank[PX] > rank[PY]) P[PY] = PX
  Else P[PX] = PY
  If (rank[PX] == rank[PY]) rank[PY] = rank[PY] + 1
```

And the last operation looks like:

```
FIND-SET(x)
If (x != P[x]) p[x] = FIND-SET (P[X])
Return P[X]
```

Now let's see how the heuristics helped the running time. If we use only the first heuristic "union by rank" then we will get the same running time we achieved with the weighted union heuristic when we used lists for representation. When we use both "union by rank" and "path compression," the worst running time is O(m a(m,n)), where a(m,n) is the very slowly growing inverse of Ackermann's function. In application a(m,n) <= 4 that's why we can say that the running time is linear in terms of m, in practical situations. (For more details on Ackermann's function or complexity see the references below.)

23.6 BACK TO THE PROBLEM

The problem from the beginning of the article is solvable in O(N + M) and O(N) for memory using disjoint-set data structure. The difference for time execution is not big if the problem is solved with BFS, but we don't need to keep in memory the vertices of the graph. Let's see if the problem was like: In a room are N persons and you had to handle Q queries. A query is of the form "x y 1," meaning that x is friends with y, or "x y 2" meaning that we are asked to output if x and y are in same group of friends at that moment in time. In this case the solution with disjoint-set data structure is the fastest, giving a complexity of O(N + Q).

23.7 CONCLUSIONS

Disjoint-set data structures are a helpful tool for use in different algorithms, or even for solving problems in an SRM. They are efficient and use small amount of memory. They are useful in applications like "Computing the shorelines of a terrain," "Classifying a set of atoms into molecules or fragments," "Connected component labeling in image analysis," and others.

Solved Questions

1. Adapt the aggregate proof to obtain amortized time bounds of O(1) for MAKE-SET and FIND-SET and O(lg n) for UNION using the linked-list representation and the weighted-union heuristic.

Ans. We want to show that we can assign O(1) charges to MAKE-SET and FIND-SET and an O(lg n) charge to UNION such that the charges for a sequence of these operations are enough to cover the cost of the sequence. O(m+n lg n), according to the theorem. When talking about the charge for each kind of operation, it is helpful to also be able to talk about the number of each kind of operation. Consider the usual sequence of m MAKE-SET, UNION, and FIND-SET operations, n of which are MAKE-SET operations, and let l < n be the number of UNION operations. (Recall the discussion in Section 21.1 about there being at most n – 1 UNION operations.) Then there are n MAKE-SET operations, l UNION operations, and m – n – l FIND-SET operations. The theorem didn't separately name the number l of UNIONs; rather, it bounded the number by n. If you go through the proof of the theorem with l UNIONs, you get the time bound O(m – l+l lg l) = O(m+l lg l) for the sequence of operations.
That is, the actual time taken by the sequence of operations is at most c(m +l lg l),
for some constant c.
Thus, we want to assign operation charges such that
(MAKE-SET charge) n
+(FIND-SET charge) (m – n – l)
+(UNION charge) l

$\geq c(m + l \lg l)$,

so that the amortized costs give an upper bound on the actual costs.

The following assignments work, where c is some constant $\geq$ c:

- MAKE-SET: c
- FIND-SET: c
- UNION: c

(lg n + 1)

Substituting into the above sum, we get

c_n + c(m – n – l) + c

(lg n + 1)l = cm + c l lg n

= c(m + l lg n)> c(m + l lg l) .

2. Suggest a simple change to the UNION procedure for the linked-list representation that removes the need to keep the tail pointer to the last object in each list. Whether or not the weighted-union heuristic is used, your change should not change the asymptotic running time of the UNION procedure. (Hint: Rather than appending one list to another, splice them together.)

Ans. Let.s call the two lists A and B, and suppose that the representative of the new list will be the representative of A. Rather than appending B to the end of A, instead splice B into A right after the first element of A. We have to traverse B to update representative pointers anyway, so we can just make the last element of B point to the second element of A.

3. Give a sequence of m MAKE-SET, UNION, and FIND-SET operations, n of which are MAKE-SET operations, that takes Θ(m lg n) time when we use union by rank only.

Ans. You need to and a sequence of m operations on n elements that takes Θ (m lg n) time. Start with n MAKE-SETs to create singleton sets {x1} , {x2} , . . . , {xn}. Next perform the n – 1 UNION operations shown below to create a single set whose tree has depth lg n.

UNION(x1, x2) n/2 of these

UNION(x3, x4)

UNION(x5, x6)

...

UNION(xn – 1, xn)

UNION(x2, x4) n/4 of these

UNION(x6, x8)

UNION(x10, x12)

...

UNION(xn – 2, xn)

UNION(x4, x8) n/8 of these

UNION(x12, x16)

UNION(x20, x24)

...

UNION(xn – 4, xn)

...

UNION(xn/2, xn) 1 of these

Finally, perform m – 2n + 1 FIND-SET operations on the deepest element in the tree. Each of these FIND-SET operations takes Ω (lg n) time. Letting m $\geq$ 3n, we

4. Show that any sequence of m MAKE-SET, FIND-SET, and LINK operations, where all the LINK

operations appear before any of the FIND-SET operations, takes only O(m) time if both path compression and union by rank are used. What happens in the same situation if only the path-compression heuristic is used?

Ans. With the path-compression heuristic, the sequence of m MAKE-SET, FIND-SET, and LINK operations, where all the LINK operations take place before any of the FIND-SET operations, runs in O(m) time. The key observation is that once a node x appears on a find path, x will be either a root or a child of a root at all times thereafter.

We use the accounting method to obtain the O(m) time bound. We charge a MAKE-SET operation two dollars. One dollar pays for the MAKE-SET, and one dollar remains on the node x that is created. The latter pays for the first time that x appears on a find path and is turned into a child of a root. We charge one dollar for a LINK operation. This dollar pays for the actual linking of one node to another.

We charge one dollar for a FIND-SET. This dollar pays for visiting the root and its child, and for the path compression of these two nodes, during the FIND-SET. All other nodes on the find path use their stored dollar to pay for their visitation and path compression. As mentioned, after the FIND-SET, all nodes on the and path become children of a root (except for the root itself), and so whenever they are visited during a subsequent FIND-SET, the FIND-SET operation itself will pay for them. Since we charge each operation either one or two dollars, a sequence of m operations is charged at most 2m dollars, and so the total time is O(m). Observe that nothing in the above argument requires union by rank. Therefore, we get an O(m) time bound regardless of whether we use union by rank.

5. Give a simple proof that operations on a disjoint-set forest with union by rank but without path compression run in O(m lg n) time.

Ans. Clearly, each MAKE-SET and LINK operation takes O(1) time. Because the rank of a node is an upper bound on its height, each find path has length O(lg n), which in turn implies that each FIND-SET takes O(lg n) time. Thus, any sequence of m MAKE-SET, LINK, and FIND-SET operations on n elements takes O(m lg n) time. It is easy to prove an analogue of Lemma 21.7 to show that if we convert a sequence of m_ MAKE-SET, UNION, and FIND-SET operations into a sequence of m MAKE-SET, LINK, and FIND-SET operations that take O(m lg n) time, then the sequence of m_ MAKE-SET, UNION, and FIND-SET operations takes O(m_ lg n) time.

6. Professor Dante reasons that because node ranks increase strictly along a path to the root, node levels must monotonically increase along the path. In other words, if rank(x) > 0 and p[x] is not a root, then level(x) ≤ level(p[x]). Is the professor correct?

Ans. Professor Dante is mistaken. Take the following scenario. Let n = 16, and make 16 separate singleton sets using MAKE-SET. Then do 8 UNION operations to link the sets into 8 pairs, where each pair has a root with rank 0 and a child with rank 1. Now do 4 UNIONs to link pairs of these trees, so that there are 4 trees, each with a root of rank 2, children of the root of ranks 1 and 0, and a node of rank 0 that is the child of the rank-1 node. Now link pairs of these trees together, so that there are two resulting trees, each with a root of rank 3 and each containing a path from a leaf to the root with ranks 0, 1, and 3. Finally, link these two trees together, so that there is a path from a leaf to the root with ranks 0, 1, 3, and 4. Let x and y be the nodes on this path with ranks 1 and 3, respectively. Since A1(1) = 3, level(x) = 1, and since A0(3) = 4, level(y) = 0. Yet y follows x on the find path.

Previous Year University Question

1. What operations are supported on disjoint sets? [GBTU]
2. Write algorithms for Union and find operations for disjoint sets. [MDU]

EXERCISE

1. Find $S_1 \cup S_2$ for following tree

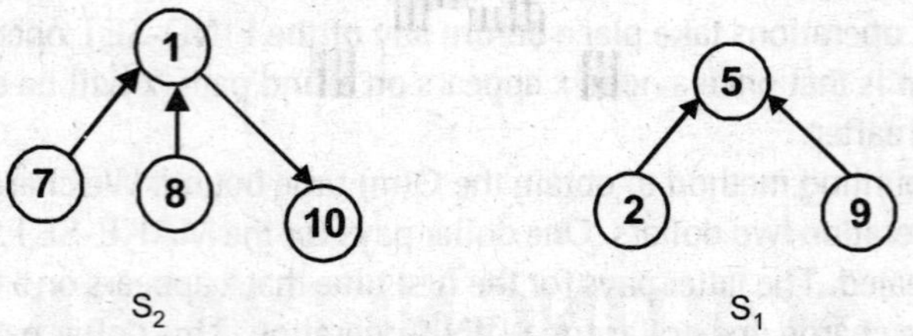

2. Write non recursive version of FIND-SET.

3. Prove for any integer $r \geq 0$, there are atmost $\frac{n}{2r}$ nodes of r.

CHAPTER

24

SORTING NETWORK

24.1 INTRODUCTION

A sortin net ork is an abstract mathematical model of a network of wires and comparator modules that is used to sort a sequence of numbers. Each comparator connects two wires and sort the values by outputting the smaller value to one wire, and the larger to the other. The main difference between sorting networks and comparison sorting algorithms is that the sequence of comparisons is set in advance, regardless of the outcome of previous comparisons. This independence of comparison sequences is useful for parallel execution of the algorithms. Despite the simplicity of the model, sorting network theory is surprisingly deep and complex.

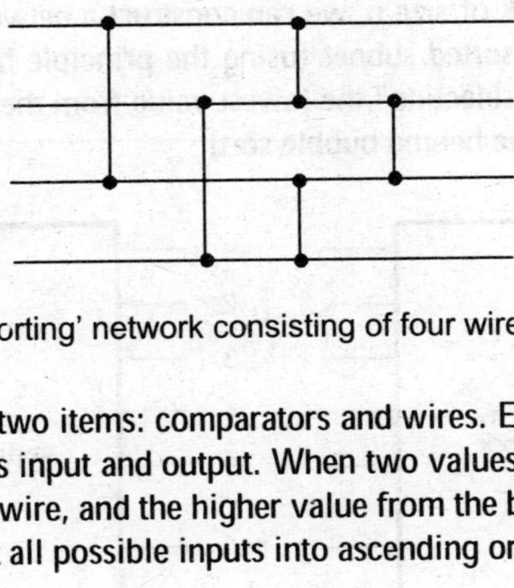

Fig. 24.1. A simple sorting' network consisting of four wires and five connectors

A sorting network consists of two items: comparators and wires. Each wire carries with it a value, and each comparator takes two wires as input and output. When two values enter a comparator, the comparator emits the lower value from the top wire, and the higher value from the bottom wire. A network of wires and comparators that will correctly sort all possible inputs into ascending order is called a sorting network.

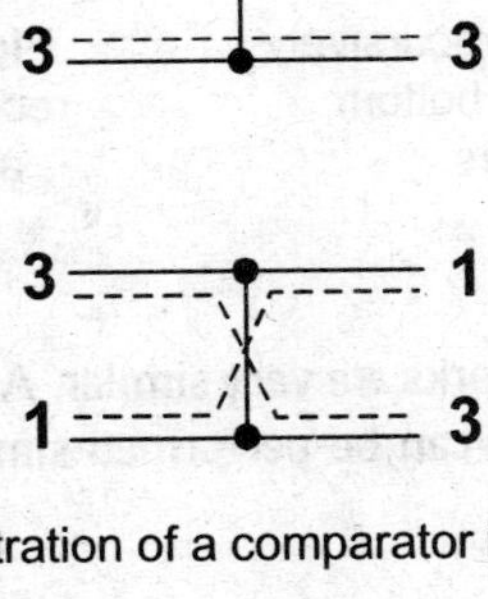

Fig. 24.2. Demonstration of a comparator in a sorting network.

The full operation of a simple sorting network is shown below. It is easy to see why this sorting network will correctly sort the inputs; note that the first four comparators will "sink" the largest value to the bottom and "float" the smallest value to the top. The final comparator simply sorts out the middle two wires.

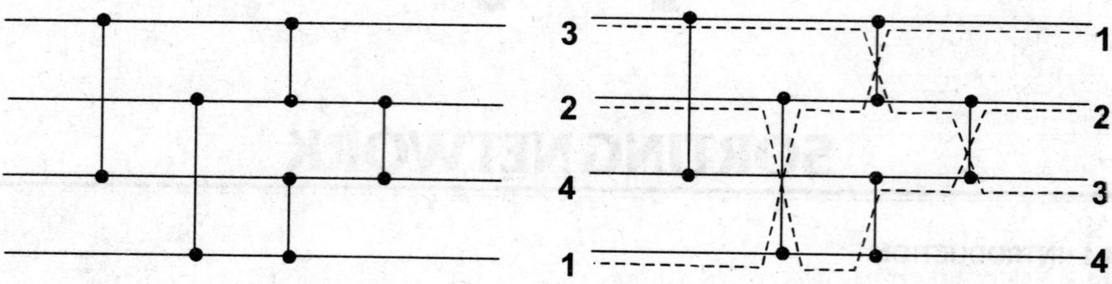

Fig. 24.3. operation of a simple sorting network

24.2 INSERTION AND SELECTION NETWORKS

We can easily construct a network of any size recursively using the principles of insertion and selection. Assuming we have a sorting network of size n, we can construct a network of size n + 1 by "inserting" an additional number into the already sorted subnet (using the principle behind insertion sort). We can also accomplish the same thing by first "selecting" the lowest value from the inputs and then sort the remaining values recursively (using the principle behind bubble sort).

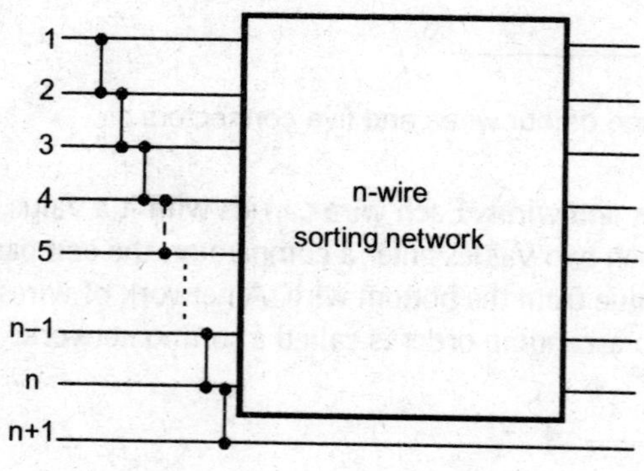

Fig. 24.4. A sorting network constructed recursively that first sinks the largest value to the bottom and then sorts the remaining wires. Based on bubble sort

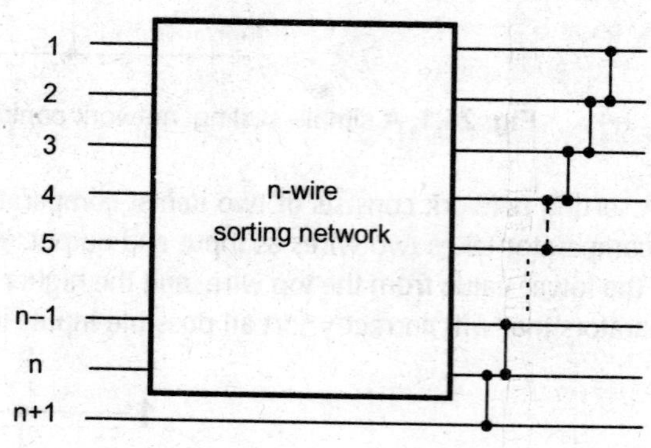

Fig. 24.5. A sorting network constructed recursively that first sorts the first n wires, and then inserts the remaining value. Based on insertion sort

The structure of these two sorting networks are very similar. A construction of the two different variants, which collapses together comparators that can be performed simultaneously shows that, in fact, they are identical.

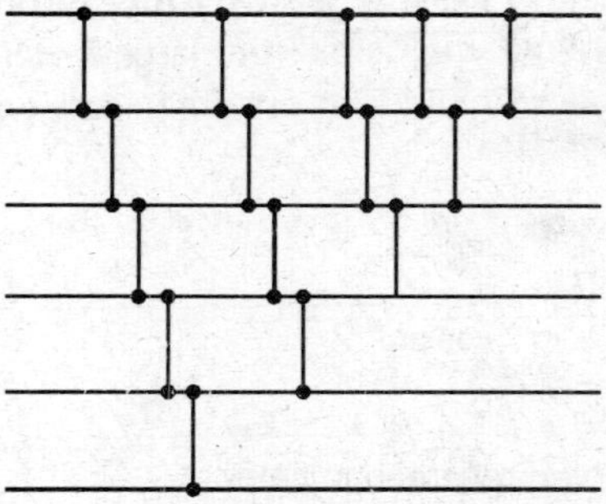

Fig. 24.6. Bubble sorting

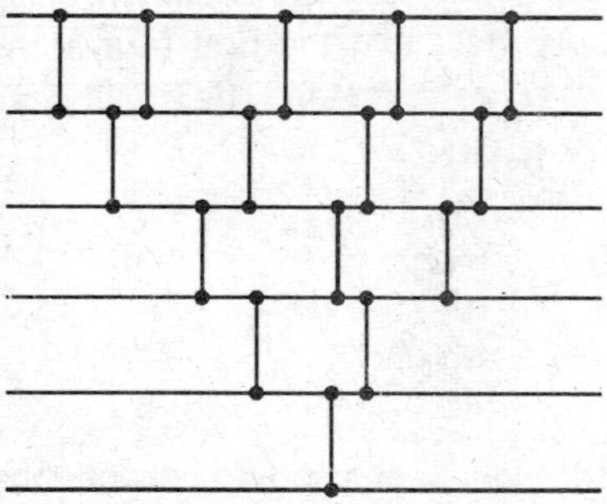

Fig. 24.7. Insertion sorting network

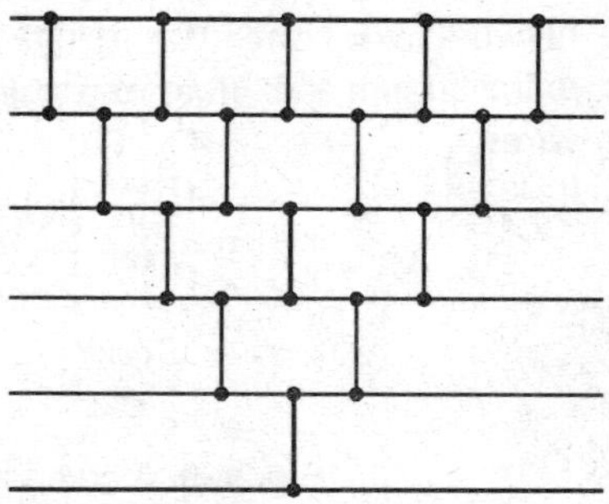

Fig. 24.8. When allowing for parallel comparators, bubble sort and insertion sort are identical

24.3 EFFICIENT NETWORKS

The insertion network has a large depth of O(n) making it impractical. There are simple networks which achieve depth $O((\log n)^2)$ (hence size $O(n (\log n)^2)$), such as Batcher odd-even mergesort, bitonic sort, Shell sort, and the Pairwise sorting network. These networks are often used in practice.

24.4 ZERO-ONE PRINCIPLE

While it is easy to prove the validity of some sorting networks (like the insertion bubble sorter), it is not always so easy. There are n! permutations of numbers in an n-wire network, and to test all of them would take a significant amount of time, especially when they are larger. However, because of the so-called zero-one principle, far fewer trials are in fact needed to test the validity of a sorting network.

The zero-one principle states that a sorting network is valid if it can sort all 2^n sequences of 0s and Is. This not only drastically cuts down on the number of tests needed to ascertain the validity of a network, it is of great use in creating many constructions of sorting networks as well. The principle has been proven by a special case of the Bouricius's Theorem in 1 54 by W. G. Bouricius.

24.5 TOPOLOGY AND RETROGRADE VIEW

In order to reduce the number of test cases needed to assert the validity of an n-input sorting network, we can use topology of the network or retrograde software analysis Through retrograde software analysis, we analyze a network reversed in time starting from the sorted output, then going backward. If we combine the zero-one principle and retrograde analysis, we need only n test cases, in which case we have to follow gradually from 1 to 2 testing paths. If we use topology of a sorting network, we need to check at first about n^2 test cases; basically we try to connect each input with each upper output using the network wiring without ever going back or down, and then we check that paths combined are independent regarding used comparators.

24.6 OPTIMAL SORTING

The efficiency of a sorting network can be measured by its total size (the number of comparators used), or by its depth (the maximum number of comparators along any path from an input to an output). The asymptotically best known sorting network, called AKS network after its discoverers Ajtai, Komlos, and Szemeredi, achieves depth 0(log n)• and-size O(n log n) for n inputs, which is asymptotically optimal. A simplified version of the AKS network was described by Paterson. While an important theoretical discovery, the AKS network has little or no practical application because of the large linear constants hidden by the Big-O notation. These are partly due to a construction of an expander graph. Finding sorting networks with size en log n for small c remains a fundamental open problem.

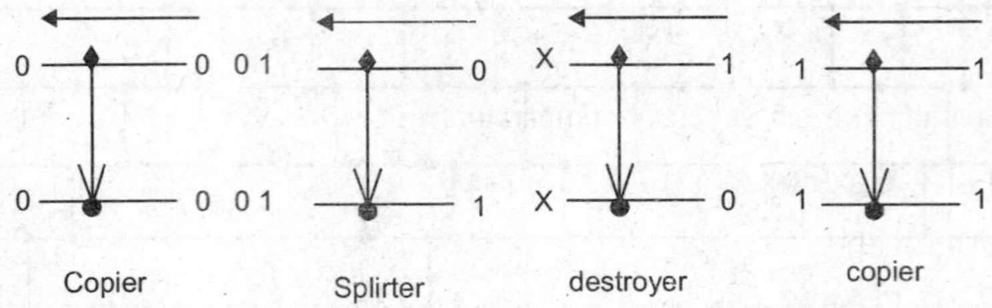

Fig.24.9. A comparator module in a sorting network observed reversed in time

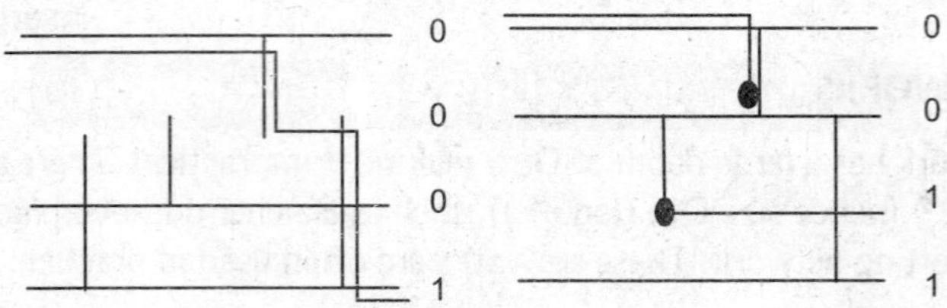

Fig.24.10: Two topological test cases for an assumed invalid 4-input sorting network

Some important progress in designing optimal sorting network is done using genetic algorithm technique as well.

For 1 to 8 inputs optimal sorting networks are known. They have respectively 0, 1,3, 5, 9, 12, 16 and 19 comparators The optimal depths for up to 10 inputs are known and they are respectively 0, 1, 3, 3, 5, 5, 6, 6, 7, 7.

Solved Questions

1. Prove that any sorting network on n inputs has depth at least lg n.

Ans. Consider any input element x. After 1 level of the network, x can be in at most 2 different places, in at most 4 places after 2 levels, and so forth. Thus we need at least lg n depth to be able to move x to the right place, which could be any of the n (= 2lg n) outputs.

2. Prove that the number of comparators in any sorting network is Ω (n lg n).

Ans. Simulation of any sorting network on a serial machine is a comparison sort, hence there are Ω (n lg n) comparisons/comparators. Intuitively, since the depth is Ω (lg n) and we can perform at most n/2 comparisons at each depth of the network, this Ω (n lg n) bound makes sense.

3. We can represent an n-input comparison network with c comparators as a list of c pairs of integers in the range from 1 to n. If two pairs contain an integer in common, the order of the corresponding comparators in the network is determined by the order of the pairs in the list. Given this representation, describe an O(n + c)-time (serial) algorithm for determining the depth of a comparison network.

Ans. We take advantage of the comparators appearing in sorted order within the network in the following pseudocode.

for i ←1 to n

do d[i] ← 0

for each comparator (i, j) in the list of comparators

do d[i] ← d[j] ← max(d[i], d[j]) + 1

return max1d"id"n d[i]

This algorithm implicitly finds the longest path in a dag of the comparators (in which an edge connects each comparator to the comparators that need its outputs).

Even though we don't explicitly construct the dag, the above sort produces a topological sort of the dag. The first for loop takes O (n) time, the second for loop takes O (c) time, and computing the maximum d[i] value in the return statement takes O (n) time, for a total of O(n + c) = O(n + c) time.

Previous Year University Question

1. Explain the bitnic sorting network. [KU]
2. Write short notes on:
   (a) Comparision network
   (b) Merging network [KU]

Exercise

1. How many zero-one bitonic sequences of length n are there?
2. Prove that BITONIC SORTER contain n 1g n comparators
3. Prove zero-one principle for a decision-tree model
4. Prove that any sorting network on n inputs has depth at learnt lg n.
5. Prove that depth of sorter (n) is (lg n) (1g n+ 1)/2
6. Draw a 2n – input merging network for n = 3
7. What is the depth of a 2n - input odd even merging network?

CHAPTER

25

MAXIMUM FLOW

25.1 INTRODUCTION

This article covers a problem that often arises in real life situations and, as expected, in programming contests, with Top Coder being no exception. It is addressed mostly to coders who are not familiar with the subject, but it may prove useful to the more experienced as well. Lots of papers have been written, and there are many algorithms known to solve this problem. While they are not the fastest, the algorithms presented here have the advantage of being simple and efficient, and because of this they are usually preferred during a contest setup. The reader is advised to read the article on graph theory first, as the concepts presented there are needed to understand those presented here.

25.1.1 The Standard Maximum Flow Problem

So, what are we being asked for in a max-flow problem? The simplest form that the statement could take would be something along the lines of: "A list of pipes is given, with different flow-capacities. These pipes are connected at their endpoints. What is the maximum amount of water that you can route from a given starting point to a given ending point?" or equivalently "A company owns a factory located in city X where products are manufactured that need to be transported to the distribution center in city Y. You are given the one-way roads that connect pairs of cities in the country, and the maximum number of trucks that can drive along each road. What is the maximum number of trucks that the company can send to the distribution center?"

A first observation is that it makes no sense to send a truck to any other city than Y, so every truck that enters a city other than Y must also leave it. A second thing to notice is that, because of this, the number of trucks leaving X is equal to the number of trucks arriving in Y.

Suppose have a in which every edge has a certain capacity c associated with it, a starting vertex (the source, X in the example above), and an ending vertex (the sink). We are asked to associate another value f satisfying $f \leq c$ for each edge such that for every vertex other than the source and the sink, the sum of the values associated to the edges that enter it must equal the sum of the values associated to the edges that leave it. We will call f the flow along that edge. Furthermore, we are asked to maximize the sum of the values associated to the arcs leaving the source, which is the total flow in the network.

The image below shows the optimal solution to an instance of this problem, each edge being labeled with the values f/c associated to it.

Now how do we actually solve the problem? First, let us define two basic concepts for understanding flow networks: residual networks and augmenting paths. Consider an arbitrary flow in a network. The residual network has the same vertices as the original network, and one or two edges for each edge in the original. More specifically, if the flow along the edge x-y is less than the capacity there is a forward edge x-y with a

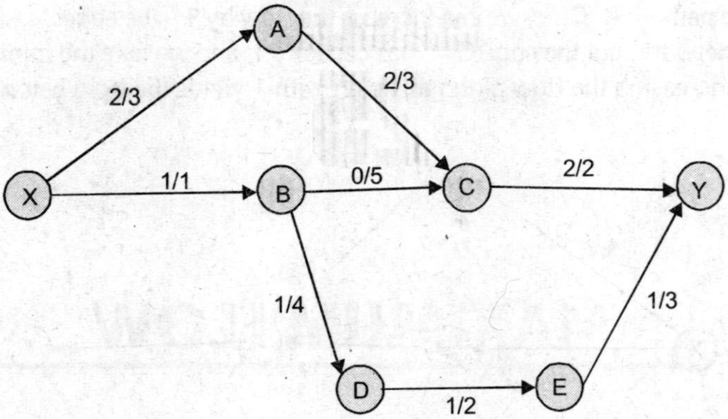

Fig. 25.1a. Maximum Flow in a network

capacity equal to the difference between the capacity and the flow (this is called the residual capacity), and if the flow is positive there is a backward edge y-x with a capacity equal to the flow on x-y. An augmenting path **is simply a path from the source to the sink in the residual network, whose purpose is to increase the flow in the original one. It is important to understand that the edges in this path can point the "wrong way" according to the original network. The path capacity of a path is the minimum capacity of an edge along that path. Let's take the following example:**

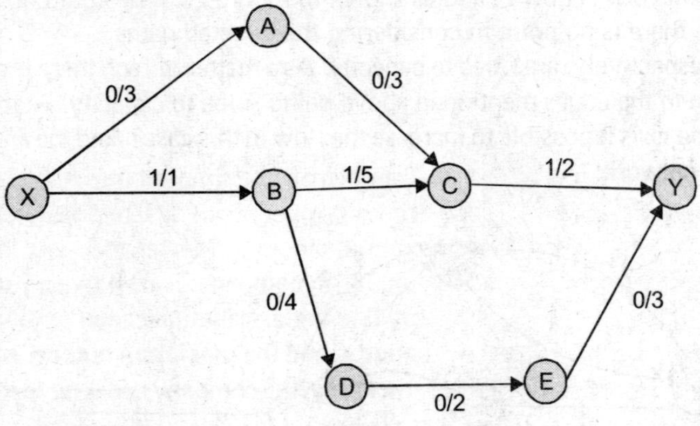

Fig. 25.2a

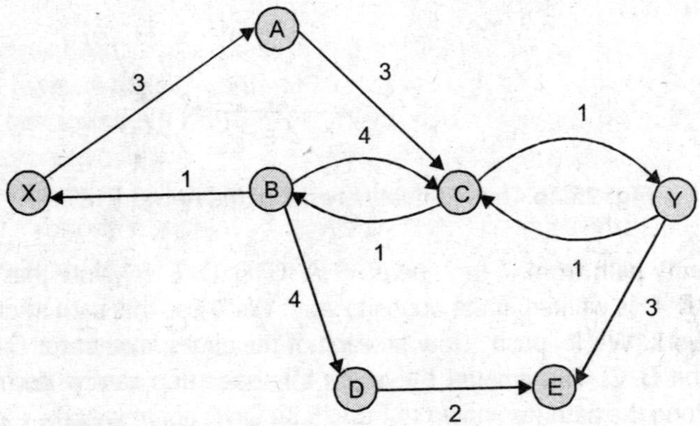

Fig. 25.2b: The residual network of the network in 2a

By considering the path A C , we can increase the flow by 1 – the edges A and AC have capacity of 3, as in the original network, but the edge C has capacity 1, and we take the minimum of these values to get the path capacity. Increasing the flow along this path with 1 yields the flow below:

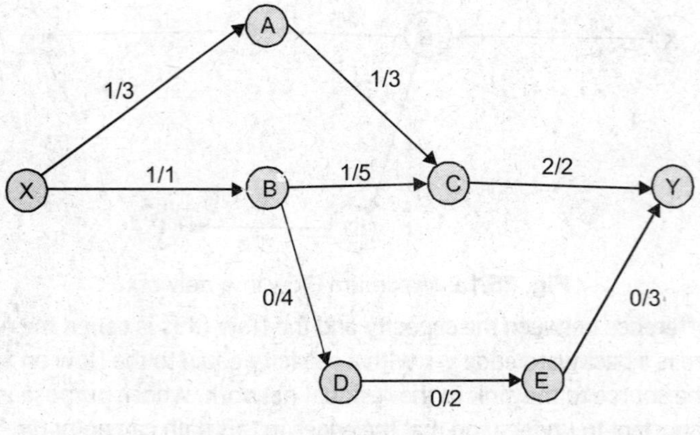

Fig. 25 3a

The value of the current flow is now 2, and as shown in Figure 25.1 we could do better. Şo, let's try to increase the flow. Clearly, there is no point in considering the directed paths A C or B D E as the edges C and B, respectively, are filled to capacity. As a matter of fact, there is no directed path in the network shown above, due to the edges mentioned above being filled to capacity. At this point, the question that naturally comes to mind is: is it possible to increase the flow in this case? And the answer is yes, it is. et's take a look at the residual network:

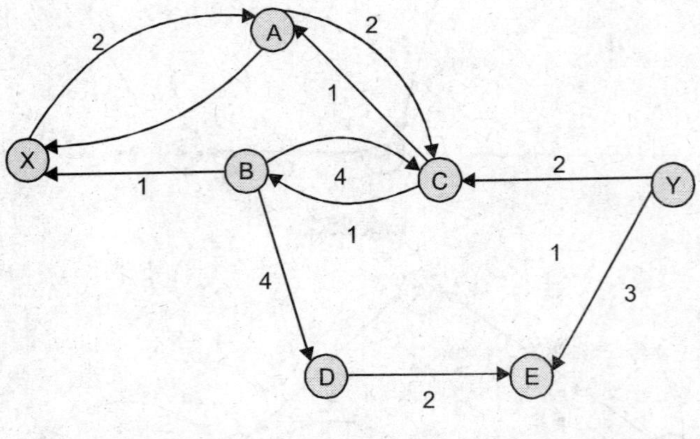

Fig. 25.3b The residual network of the network in 3a

et's consider the only path from to here: A C B D E . Note that this is not a path in the directed graph, because C B is walked in the opposite way. We'll use this path in order to increase the total flow in the original network. We'll "push" flow on each of the edges, except for C B which we will use in order to "cancel" flow on B C. The amount by which this operation can be performed is limited by the capacities of all edges along the path (as shown in Fig. 25.3b Once again we take the minimum, to conclude that this path also has capacity 1. pdating the path in the way described here yields the flow shown in Figure

25.1a We are left with the following residual network where a path between the source and the sink doesn't exist:

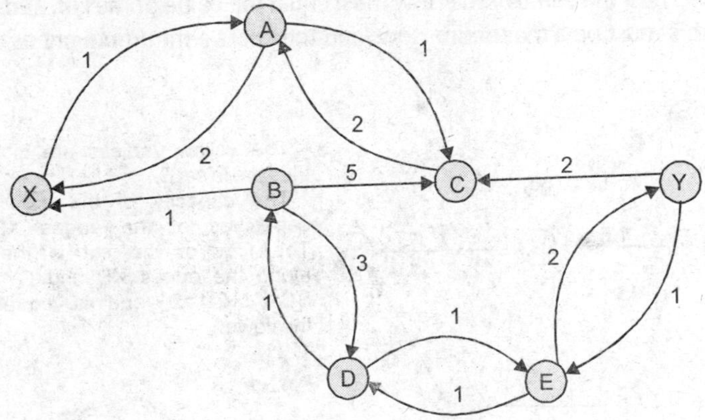

Fig. 25.1b The residual network of the network in 1 a

This example suggests the following algorithm: start with no flow everywhere and increase the total flow in the network while there is an augmenting path from the source to the sink with no full forward edges or empty backward edges - a path in the residual network. The algorithm (known as the Ford-Fulkerson method) is guaranteed to terminate: due to the capacities and flows of the edges being integers and the path-capacity being positive, at each step we get a new flow that is closer to the maximum. As a side note, the algorithm isn't guaranteed to even terminate if the capacities are irrationals.

What about the correctness of this algorithm? It is obvious that in a network in which a maximum flow has been found there is no augmenting path, otherwise we would be able to increase the maximum value of the flow, contradicting our initial assumption. If the converse of this affirmation is true, so that when there is no augmenting path, the value of the flow has reached its maximum, we can breathe a sigh of relief, our algo is correct and computes the maximum flow in a network. This is known as the max-flow min-cut theorem and we shall justify its correctness in a few moments.

A cut in a flow network is simply a partition of the vertices in two sets, let's call them A and B, in such a way that the source vertex is in A and the sink is in B. The capacity of a cut is the sum of the capacities of the edges that go from a vertex in A to a vertex in B. The flow of the cut is the difference of the flows that go from A to B (the sum of the flows along the edges that have the starting point in A and the ending point in B), respectively from B to A, which is exactly the value of the flow in the network, due to the entering flow equals leaving flow -property, which is true for every vertex other than the source and the sink.

Notice that the flow of the cut is less or equal to the capacity of the cut due to the constraint of the flow being less or equal to the capacity of every edge. This implies that the maximum flow is less or equal to every cut of the network. This is where the max-flow min-cut theorem comes in and states that the value of the maximum flow through the network is exactly the value of the minimum cut of the network. et's give an intuitive argument for this fact. We will assume that we are in the situation in which no augmenting path in the network has been found. et's color in yellow, like in the figure above, every vertex that is reachable by a path that starts from the source and consists of non-full forward edges and of non-empty backward edges. Clearly the sink will be colored in blue, since there is no augmenting path from the source to the sink. Now take every edge that has a yellow starting point and a blue ending point. This edge will have the flow equal to the capacity, otherwise we could have added this edge to the path we had at that point and color the ending point in yellow. Note that if we remove these edges there will be no directed path from the source to the sink in the graph. Now consider every edge that has a blue starting point and a yellow ending point. The flow on this edge must be 0 since otherwise we could have added this edge as a backward edge on the current path and color the starting point in yellow. Thus, the value of the flow must equal the value of the cut, and since every flow is less or equal to every cut, this must be a maximum flow, and the cut is a minimum cut as well.

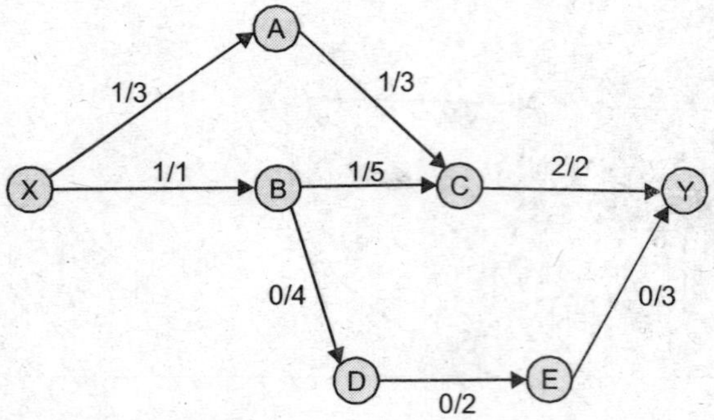

The yellow vertices are in set A and those In blue are in set B.

The capecity of the cut is the sum of the capacities of the edges XB and Cy: 1-2=3. The flow of the cut is the sum of the flow along the edges XB and CY minus the flow on BC: 1+2-1=2, and is equal to the value of the flowe.

Fig. 25.4 Acute in a network

In fact, we have solved another problem that at first glance would appear to have nothing to do with maximum flow in a network, ie. given a weighted directed graph, remove a minimum-weighted set of edges in such a way that a given node is unreachable from another given node. The result is, according to the max-flow min-cut theorem, the maximum flow in the graph, with capacities being the weights given. We are also able to find this set of edges in the way described above: we take every edge with the starting point marked as reachable in the last traversal of the graph and with an unmarked ending point. This edge is a member of the minimum cut.

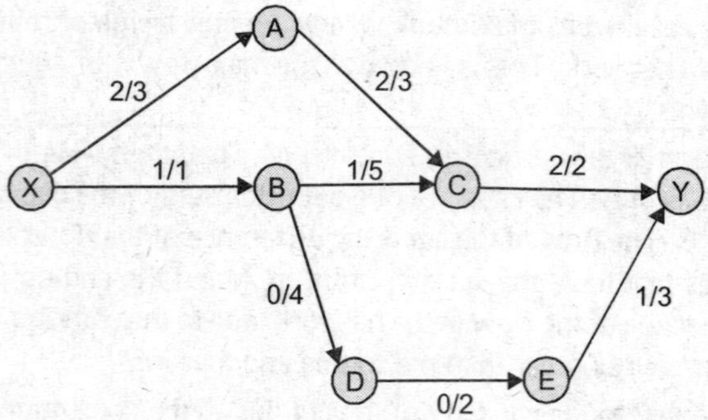

The minimum cut of this network is the sum of the chapatties of XB and CY and equals 3. which is also the value of the maximum flow.

Fig. 25.5

25.2 AUGMENTING-PATH ALGORITHMS

The neat part of the Ford-Fulkerson algorithm described above is that it gets the correct result no matter how we solve (correctly!!) the sub-problem of finding an augmenting path. However, every new path may increase the flow by only 1, hence the number of iterations of the algorithm could be very large if we carelessly choose the augmenting path algorithm to use. The function max flow will look like this, regardless of the actual method we use for finding augmenting paths:

```
max_flow ()
result = 0
  while  (true)
       // the function find_path returns the path capacity of the
  // augmenting path found
    path_capacity = find_path ()
    // no augmenting path found
    if (d = 0) exit while
    else result += path_capacity
end while
return result
```

To keep it simple, we will use a 2-dimensional array for storing the capacities of the residual network that we are left with after each step in the algorithm. Initially the residual network is just the original network. We will not store the flows along the edges explicitly, but it's easy to figure out how to find them upon the termination of the algorithm: for each edge x-y in the original network the flow is given by the capacity of the backward edge y-x in the residual network. Be careful though; if the reversed arc y-x also exists in the original network, this will fail, and it is recommended that the initial capacity of each arc be stored somewhere, and then the flow along the edge is the difference between the initial and the residual capacity.

We now require an implementation for the function find_path. The first approach that comes to mind is to use a depth-first search (DFS), as it probably is the easiest to implement. Unfortunately, its performance is very poor on some networks, and normally is less preferred to the ones discussed next.

The next best thing in the matter of simplicity is a breadth-first search (BFS). Recall that this search usually yields the shortest path in an un-weighted graph. Indeed, this also applies here to get the shortest augmenting path from the source to the sink. In the following pseudocode we will basically: find a shortest path from the source to the sink and compute the minimum capacity of an edge (that could be a forward or a backward edge) along the path - the path capacity. Then, for each edge along the path we reduce its capacity and increase the capacity of the reversed edge with the path capacity.

```
bfs ()
  queue Q
  push source to Q
  mark source as visited
  keep an array from with the semnification: from[x] is the
previous vertex visited in the shortest path from the source to x;
initialize from with -1 (or any other sentinel value)
  while Q is not empty
     where = pop from Q
     for each vertex next adjacent to where
       if next is not visited and capacity[where][next] > 0
         push next to Q
         mark next as visited
```

```
            from [next] = where
            if next = sink
               exit while loop
         end for
      end while
      // we compute the path capacity
      where = sink, path  cap = infinity
      while from[where]    −1
         prev = from[where] // the previous vertex
         path  cap = min(path  cap, capacity[prev][where])
         where = prev
      end while
         // we update the residual network; if no path is found the while
   loop will not be entered
         where = sink
         while from[where]    −1
            prev = from[where]
            capacity[prev][where] −= path  capacity
                  capacity[where][prev] += path  capacity
            where = prev
         end while
         // if no path is found, path  cap is infinity if path  cap = infinity
            return 0
         else return path  cap
```

As we can see, this is pretty easy to implement. As for its performance, it is guaranteed that this takes at most   /   steps, where N is the number of vertices and M is the number of edges in the network. This number may seem very large, but it is over-estimated for most networks. For example, in the network we considered 3 augmenting paths are needed which is significantly less than the upper bound of 28. Due to the O   ) running time of BFS (implemented with adjacency lists) the worst-case running time of the shortest-augmenting path max-flow algorithm is O(   ), but usually the algorithm performs much better than this.

Next we will consider an approach that uses a priority-first search (PFS), that is very similar to the Dijkstra heap method explained here. In this method the augmenting path with a maximum path capacity is preferred. Intuitively this would lead to a faster algorihem, since at each step we increase the flow with the maximum possible amount. However, things are not always so, and the BFS implementation has better running times on some networks. We assign as a priority to each vertex the minimum capacity of a path (in the residual network) from the source to that vertex. We process vertices in a greedy manner, as in Dijkstra's algorithm, in decreasing order of priorities. When we get to the sink, we are done, since a path with a maximum capacity is found. We would like to implement this with a data structure that allows us to efficiently find the vertex with the highest priority and increase the priority of a vertex (when a new better path is found) - this suggests the use of a heap which has a space complexity proportional to the number of vertices. In TopCoder matches we may find it faster and easier to implement this with a priority queue or some other data structure that approximates one, even though the space required might grow to being proportional with the number of edges. This is how the following pseudocode is implemented. We also define a structure node that has the members vertex and priority with the above significance. Another field from is needed to store the previous vertex on the path.

```
pfs()
  priority queue P
  push node(source, infinity, -1) to P
  keep the array from as in bfs()
  // if no augmenting path is found, path cap will remain 0
  path cap = 0
  while P  is not empty
    node aux = pop from P
    where = aux.vertex, cost = aux.priority
    if we already visited where continue
    from[where] = aux.from
    if where = sink
      path cap = cost
      exit while loop
    mark where as visited
    for each vertex next adjacent to where
      if capacity[where][next]   0
        new  cost = min(cost, capacity [where] [next] )
        push node(next, new cost, where) to P
    end for
  end while
  // update the residual network
  where = sink
  while from[where]   -1
    prev = from[where]
    capacity[prev][where] -= path cap
    capacity[where][prev] += path cap
    where = prev
  end while
  return path cap
```

The analysis of its performance is pretty complicated, but it may prove worthwhile to remember that with PFS at most 2   1 U steps are required, where   is the maximum capacity of an edge in the network. As with BFS, this number is a lot larger than the actual number of steps for most networks. Combine this with the O(lg   ) complexity of the search to get the worst-case running time of this algorithm.

Now that we know what these methods are all about, which of them do we choose when we are confronted with a max-flow problem? The PFS approach seems to have a better worst-case performance, but in practice their performance is pretty much the same. So, the method that one is more familiar with may prove more adequate. Personally, I prefer the shortest-path method, as 1 find it easier to implement during a contest and less error prone.

25.3 MAX-FLOW/MIN-CUT RELATED PROBLEMS

How to recognize max-flow problems? Often they are hard to detect and usually boil down to maximizing the movement of something from a location to another. We need to look at the constraints when we think we have a working solution based on maximum flow - they should suggest at least an $O(N^3)$ approach. If the number of locations is large, another algorithm (such as dynamic programming or greedy), is more appropriate.

The problem description might suggest multiple sources and/or sinks. For example, in the sample statement in the beginning of this article, the company might own more than one factory and multiple distribution centers. How can we deal with this? We should try to convert this to a network that has a unique source and sink. In order to accomplish this we will add two "dummy" vertices to our original network - we will refer to them as super-source and super-sink. In addition to this we will add an edge from the super-source to every ordinary source (a factory). As we don't have restrictions on the number of trucks that each factory can send, we should assign to each edge an infinite capacity. Note that if we had such restrictions, we should have assigned to each edge a capacity equal to the number of trucks each factory could send. Likewise, we add an edge from every ordinary sink (distribution centers) to the super-sink with infinite capacity. A maximum flow in this new-built network is the solution to the problem - the sources now become ordinary vertices, and they are subject to the entering-flow equals leaving-flow property. You may want to keep this in your bag of tricks, as it may prove useful to most problems.

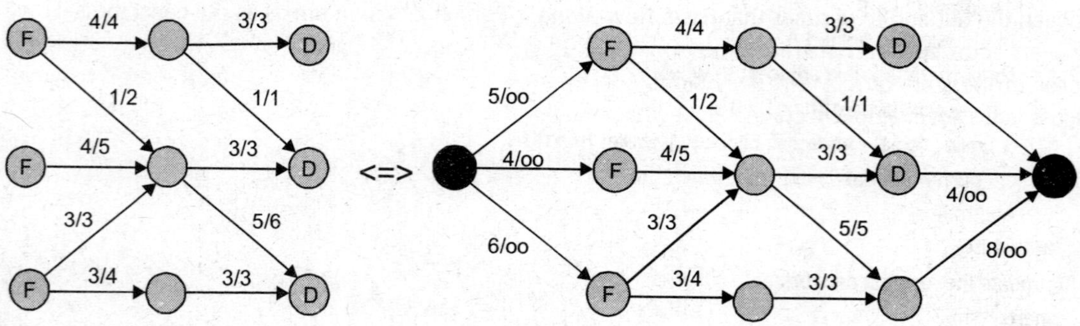

Fig 25. Reduction *of* a multiple-source multiple-Sink-Max max-flow problem

What if we are also given the maximum number of trucks that can drive through each of the cities in the country (other than the cities where the factory and the distribution center are located)? In other words we have to deal with vertex-capacities too. Intuitively, we should be able to reduce this to maximum-flow, but we must find a way to take the capacities from vertices and put them back on edges, where they belong. Another nice trick comes into play. We will build a network that has two times more vertices than the initial one. For each vertex we will have two nodes: an in-vertex and an out-vertex, and we will direct each edge x-y from the out-vertex of x to the in-vertex of y. We can assign them the capacities from the problem statement. Additionally we can add an edge for each vertex from the in to the out-vertex. The capacity this edge will be assigned is obviously the vertex-capacity. Now we just run max-flow on this network and compute the result.

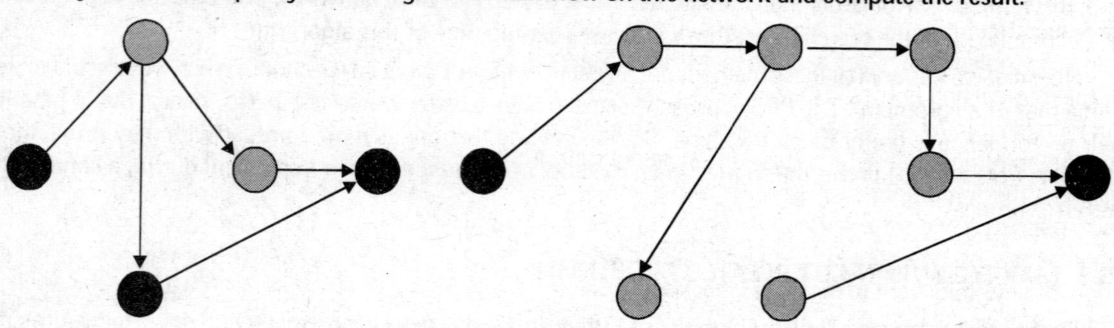

Fig 25.7 Eliminating vertex-capacities

Maximum flow problems may appear out of nowhere. Let's take this problem for instance: "You are given the in and out degrees of the vertices of a directed graph. Your task is to find the edges (assuming that no edge can appear more than once)." First, notice that we can perform this simple test at the beginning. We can compute the number M of edges by summing the out-degrees or the in-degrees of the vertices. If these numbers are not equal, clearly there is no graph that could be built. This doesn't solve our problem, though. There are some greedy approaches that come to mind, but none of them work. We will combine the tricks discussed above to give a max-flow algorithm that solves this problem. First, build a network that has 2 (in/out) vertices for each initial vertex. Now draw an edge from every out vertex to every in vertex. Next, add a super-source and draw an edge from it to every out-vertex. Add a super-sink and draw an edge from every in vertex to it. We now need some capacities for this to be a flow network. It should be pretty obvious what the intent with this approach is, so we will assign the following capacities: for each edge drawn from the super-source we assign a capacity equal to the out-degree of the vertex it points to. As there may be only one arc from a vertex to another, we assign a 1 capacity to each of the edges that go from the outs to the ins. As you can guess, the capacities of the edges that enter the super-sink will be equal to the in-degrees of the vertices. If the maximum flow in this network equals M - the number of edges, we have a solution, and for each edge between the out and in vertices that has a flow along it (which is maximum 1, as the capacity is 1) we can draw an edge between corresponding vertices in our graph. Note that both x-y and y-x edges may appear in the solution. This is very similar to the maximum matching in a bipartite graph that we will discuss later. An example is given below where the out-degrees are (2, 1, 1, 1) and the in-degrees (1, 2, 1, 1).

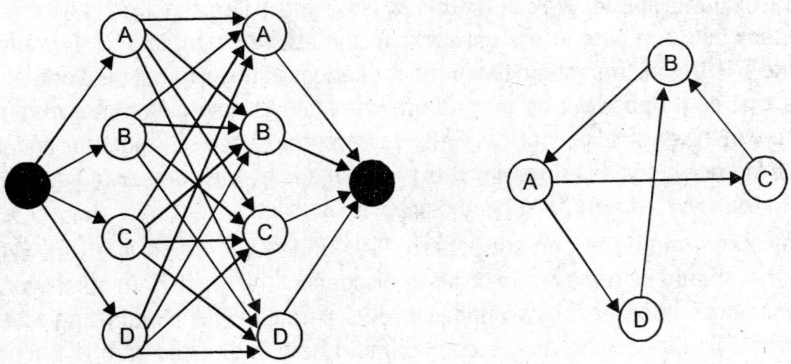

Fig. 25.8

Some other problems may ask to separate two locations minimally. Some of these problems usually can be reduced to minimum-cut in a network. Two examples will be discussed here, but first let's take the standard min-cut problem and make it sound more like a TopCoder problem. We learned earlier how to find the value of the min-cut and how to find an arbitrary min-cut. In addition to this we will now like to have a minimum-cut with the minimum number of edges. An idea would be to try to modify the original network in such a way that the minimum cut here is the minimum cut with the minimum edges in the original one. Notice what happens if we multiply each edge capacity with a constant T. Clearly, the value of the maximum flow is multiplied by T, thus the value of the minimum cut is T times bigger than the original. A minimum cut in the original network is a minimum cut in the modified one as well. Now suppose we add 1 to the capacity of each edge. Is a minimum cut in the original network a minimum cut in this one? The answer is no, as we can see in Figure 8 shown below, if we take T = 2.

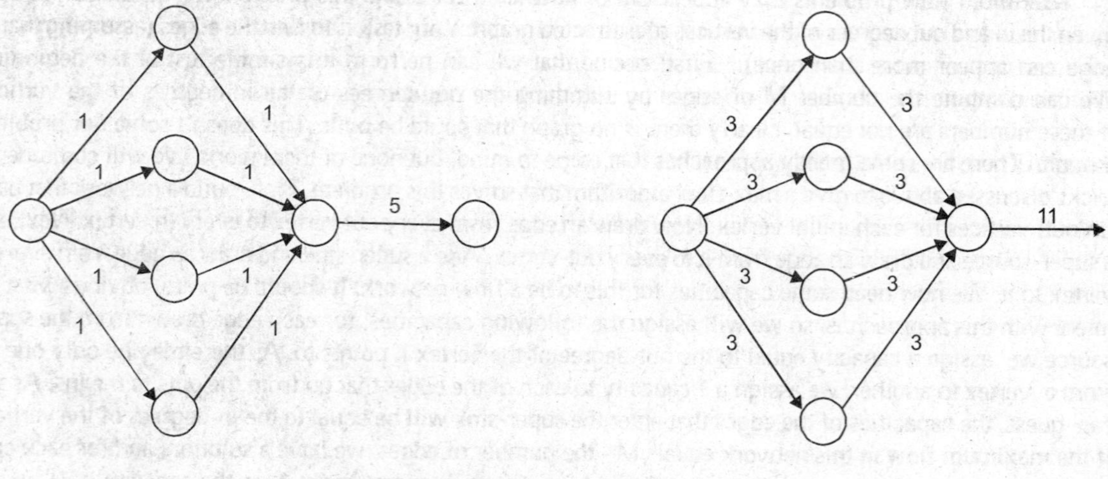

Fig. 25.9 The minimum cut before/after

Why did this happen? Take an arbitrary cut. The value of the cut will be T times the original value of the cut, plus the number of edges in it. Thus, a non-minimum cut in the first place could become minimum if it contains just a few edges. This is because the constant might not have been chosen properly in the beginning, as is the case in the example above. We can fix this by choosing T large enough to neutralize the difference in the number of edges between cuts in the network. In the above example T = 4 would be enough, but to generalize, we take T = 10, one more than the number of edges in the original network, and one more than the number of edges that could possibly be in a minimum-cut. It is now true that a minimum-cut in the new network is minimum in the original network as well. However the converse is not true, and it is to our advantage. Notice how the difference between minimum cuts is now made by the number of edges in the cut. So we just find the min-cut in this new network to solve the problem correctly.

et's illustrate some more the min-cut pattern: "An undirected graph is given. What is the minimum number of edges that should be removed in order to disconnect the graph?" In other words the problem asks us to remove some edges in order for two nodes to be separated. This should ring a bell - a minimum cut approach might work. So far we have only seen maximum flow in directed graphs, but now we are facing an undirected one. This should not be a very big problem though, as we can direct the graph by replacing every (undirected) edge x-y with two arcs: x-y and y-x. In this case the value of the min-cut is the number of edges in it, so we assign a 1 capacity to each of them. We are not asked to separate two given vertices, but rather to disconnect optimally any two vertices, so we must take every pair of vertices and treat them as the source and the sink and keep the best one from these minimum-cuts. An improvement can be made, however. Take one vertex, let's say vertex numbered 1. Because the graph should be disconnected, there must be another vertex unreachable from it. So it suffices to treat vertex 1 as the source and iterate through every other vertex and treat it as the sink.

What if instead of edges we now have to remove a minimum number of vertices to disconnect the graph? Now we are asked for a different min-cut, composed of vertices. We must somehow convert the vertices to edges though. Recall the problem above where we converted vertex-capacities to edge-capacities. The same trick works here. First "un-direct" the graph as in the previous example. Next double the number of vertices and deal edges the same way: an edge x-y is directed from the out-x vertex to in-y. Then convert the vertex to an edge by adding a 1-capacity arc from the in-vertex to the out-vertex. Now for each two vertices we must solve the sub-problem of minimally separating them. So, just like before take each pair of vertices and treat the out-vertex of one of them as the source and the in-vertex of the other one as the sink (this is because the only arc leaving the in-vertex is the one that goes to the out-vertex) and take the lowest value of the maximum flow. This time we can't improve in the quadratic number of steps needed, because the first vertex may be in an optimum solution and by always considering it as the source we lose such a case.

25.4 MAXIMUM BIPARTITE MATCHING

This is one of the most important applications of maximum flow, and a lot of problems can be reduced to it. A matching in a graph is a set of edges such that no vertex is touched by more than one edge. Obviously, a matching with a maximum cardinality is a maximum matching. For a general graph, this is a hard problem to deal with.

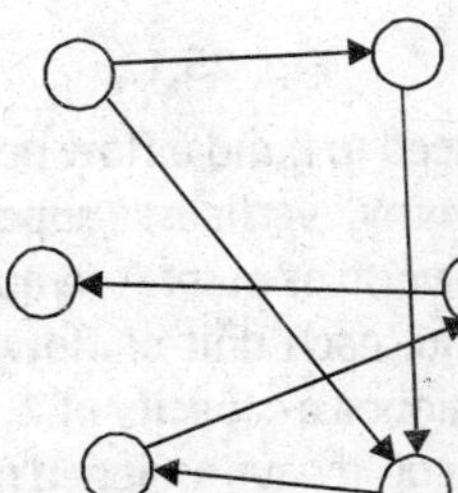

Fig. 25.10

et's direct our attention towards the case where the graph is bipartite - its vertices can be split into two sets such that there is no edge connecting vertices from the same set. In this case, it may sound like this: "Each of your employees can handle a given set of jobs. Assign a job to as many of them as you can."

A bipartite graph can be built in this case: the first set consists of your employees while the second one contains the jobs to be done. There is an edge from an employee to each of the jobs he could be assigned. An example is given below:

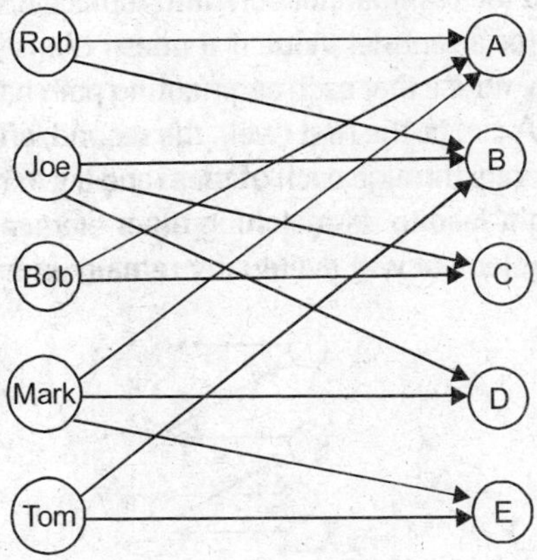

Fig. 25.11

So, oe can do jobs B, C and D while Mark wouldn't mind being assigned jobs A, D or E. This is a happy case in which each of your employees is assigned a job:

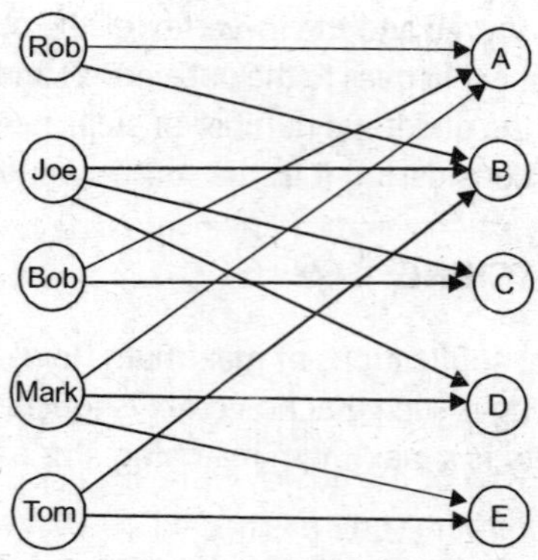

Fig. 25.12

In order to solve the problem we first need to build a flow network. Just as we did in the multiple-source multiple-sink problem we will add two "dummy" vertices: a super-source and a super-sink, and we will draw an edge from the super-source to each of the vertices in set A (employees in the example above) and from each vertex in set B to the super-sink. In the end, each unit of flow will be equivalent to a match between an employee and a job, so each edge will be assigned a capacity of 1. If we would have assigned a capacity larger than 1 to an edge from the super-source, we could have assigned more than one job to an employee. Likewise, if we would have assigned a capacity larger than 1 to an edge going to the super-sink, we could have assigned the same job to more than one employee. The maximum flow in this network will give us the cardinality of the maximum matching. It is easy to find out whether a vertex in set B is matched with a vertex x in set A as well. We look at each edge connecting x to a vertex in set B, and if the flow is positive along one of them, there exists a match. As for the running time, the number of augmenting paths is limited by min(|A|,|B|), where by |X| is denoted the cardinality of set X, making the running time O(N M), where N is the number of vertices, and M the number of edges in the graph.

An implementation point of view is in place. We could implement the maximum bipartite matching just like in the pseudocode given earlier. Usually though, we might want to consider the particularities of the problem before getting to the implementation part, as they can save time or space. In this case, we could drop the 2-dimensional array that stored the residual network and replace it with two one-dimensional arrays: one of them stores the match in set B (or a sentinel value if it doesn't exist) for each element of set A, while the other is the other way around. Also, notice that each augmenting path has capacity 1, as it contributes with just a unit of flow. Each element of set A can be the first (well, the second, after the super-source) in an augmenting path at most once, so we can just iterate through each of them and try to find a match in set B. If an augmenting path exists, we follow it. This might lead to de-matching other elements along the way, but because we are following an augmenting path, no element will eventually remain unmatched in the process.

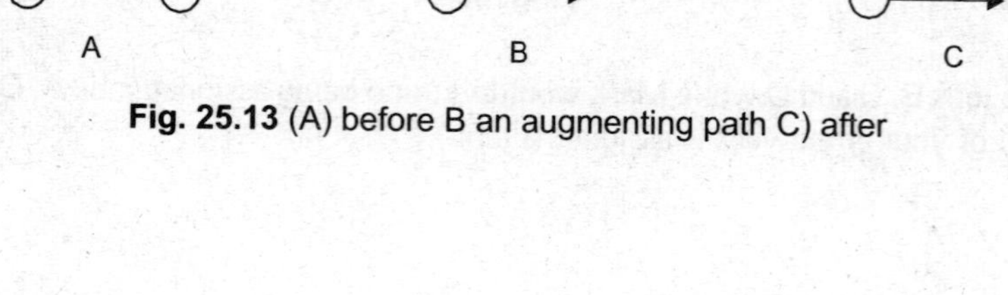

Fig. 25.13 (A) before B an augmenting path C) after

Now let's solve some TopCoder problems

25.5 ROOKATTACK

This problem asks us to place a maximum number of rooks on a row x co chessboard with some squares cut out. The idea behind this might be a little hard to spot, but once this is done, we get into a standard maximum bipartite-matching problem.

Notice that at most one rook can be placed on each row or column. In other words, each row corresponds at most to one column where a rook can be placed. This suggests a bipartite matching where set A is composed of elements corresponding to every row of the board, while set B consists of the columns. For each row add edges to every column if the corresponding square is not cut out of the board. Now we can just run maximum bipartite-matching in this network and compute the result. Since there are at most row co edges, the time complexity of the algorithm is: O(row co)

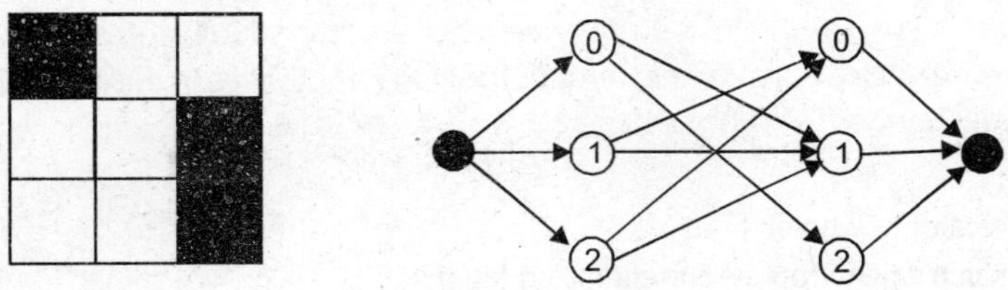

Fig. 25.14 Example 3 and the corresponding network

```
class RookAttack
        // a list of the non-empty squares for each row
    vector 1st [300];
    // in this. arrays we keep matches found to every row and column
    int row match[300], col match[300];
    // we search for an augmenting path starting with row source
    bool find match(int source)
        // from[x] = the row-vertex that precedes x in the path
        int from[300], where, match;
        memset(from, -1, sizeof(from));
        from[source] = source;
        deque q;
        q.push back(source) ;
        bool found path = false;
        while ( found path       q.empty())
            // where = current row-vertex we are in
            where = q.front(); q.pop front();
            // we take every uncut square in the current row
            for (int i = 0; i    1st[where] ,size() ; ++ i)
            match = 1st[where][i];
            // next = the row matched with column    atc
            int next = col match[match];
            if (where  = next)
```

```
            // no row matched with column match thus
we found an augmenting path
            if  (next == –1)     {
              found_path = true;
              break;
            }
            // a check whether we already visited
the row-vertex next
            if  (from[next] == -1)     {
              q.push__back (next) ;
              from[next] = where;
            }
          }
        }
      }
      if  ( !found_path)
        return false;
       while (from[where] != where) {
          // we de-match where from its current match (aux)
and match it with match
            int aux = row_match[where];
            row_match[where] = match;
            col_match[match] = where;
            where = from[where];
            mtch = aux;
        }
        // at this point where = source
        row_match[where] = match;
        col_match[match] = where;
        return true;
      }

        public:
        int howMany(int rows, int cols, vector cutouts)
        {   // build 1st from cutouts; column j should appear in
row's i list if square (i, j) is present on the board

        int ret = 0;
        memset(row^match, -1, sizeof(row_match));
        memset(col_match, -1, sizeof(col_match));
        // we try to find a match for each row
        for (int i = 0; i < rows; ++ i)
           ret += find_match(i);
        return ret;
      }
};
```

Let's take a look at the DFS version, too. We can implement the find_match function like this: for each non-empty square in the current row try to match the row with its corresponding column and call find_match recursively to attempt to find a new match for the current match (if the current match exists - if not, an augmenting path is found) of this column. If one is found, we can perform the desired match. Note that to make this run in time we must not visit the same column (or row) twice. Notice the C++ code below is extremely short:

```
bool find_match(int where) {
    // the previous column was not matched
    if (where == -1)
    return true;
for (int i = 0; i < 1st[where] .size (); ++ i)  {
    int match = 1st[where][i];
    if (visited[match] == false)  {
      visited[match] = true;
      if (find_match(col_match[match])) {
        col_match[match] = where;
        return true;
      }
   }
}
return false;
}
```

This runs in time because the number of augmenting paths is the same for both versions. The only difference is that BFS finds the shortest augmenting-path while DFS finds a longer one. As implementation speed is an important factor in Top Coder matches, in this case it would be a good deal to use the slower, but easier DFS version.

The following version of the problem is left as an exercise for the reader: to try and place as many rooks as possible on the board in such a way that the number of rooks on each row is equal to the number of rooks on each column (it is allowed for two rooks to attack each other).

25.6 GRADUATION

In this problem we are given a set of requirements, each stating that a number of classes should be taken from a given set of classes. Each class may be taken once and fulfills a single requirement. Actually, the last condition is what makes the problem harder, and excludes the idea of a greedy algorithm. We are also given a set of classes already taken. If it weren't for this, to ensure the minimality of the return, the size of the returned string would have been (if a solution existed) the sum of the number of classes for each requirement. Now as many classes as possible must be used from this set.

At first glance, this would have been a typical bipartite-matching problem if every requirement had been fulfilled by taking just a single class. Set A would have consisted of the classes available (all characters with ASCII code in the range 33-126, except for the numeric characters '0'-'9'), while the set of requirements would have played the role of set B. This can be taken care of easily. Each requirement will contribute to set

B with a number of elements equal to the number of classes that must be taken in order to fulfill it - in other words, split each requirement into several requirements. At this point, a bipartite-matching algorithm can be used, but care should be allotted to the order in which we iterate through the set of classes and match a class with a requirement.

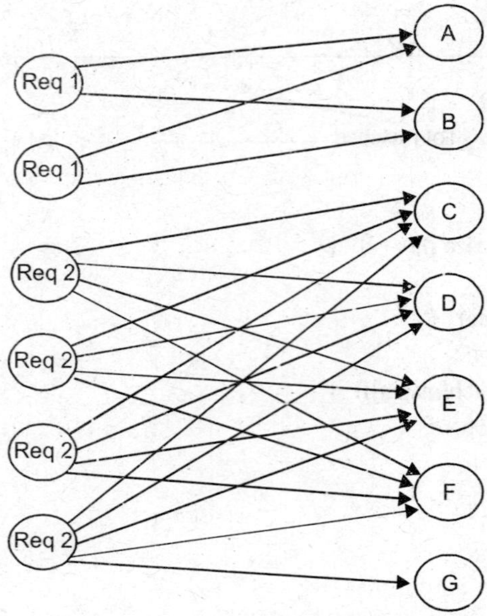

Fig 25.15 Example 4 from the problem statement

It is important to understand that any order to iterate through set A can be considered when solving the standard bipartite-matching problem. For example, it doesn't matter what element from set A we choose to be the first one to be matched. Consider the solution found by the algorithm containing this element x from A, matched with an element y from B. Also, we should consider any optimal solution. Clearly, in the optimal, y must be matched with an element z from A, otherwise we can add the pair x to the matching, contradicting the fact that the solution is optimal. Then, we can just exchange z with x to come with a solution of the same cardinality, which completes the proof.

That being said, to gain as much as possible from the classes already taken we first must match each of these with a requirement. If, after completing this step, all requirements are fulfilled, we just need to return the empty string, as there is no need for taking more classes. Now we have to deal with the requirement that the return must be the first in lexicographic order. It should be obvious now that the other classes must be considered in increasing order. If a match is found for a class, that class is added to the return value. In the end, if not every requirement is fulfilled, we don't have a solution. The implementation is left as an exercise for the reader.

As a final note, it is possible to speed things up a bit. To achieve this, we will drop the idea of splitting each requirement. Instead we will modify the capacities of the edges connecting those with the super-sink. They will now be equal to the number of classes to be taken for each requirement. Then we can just go on with the same approach as above.

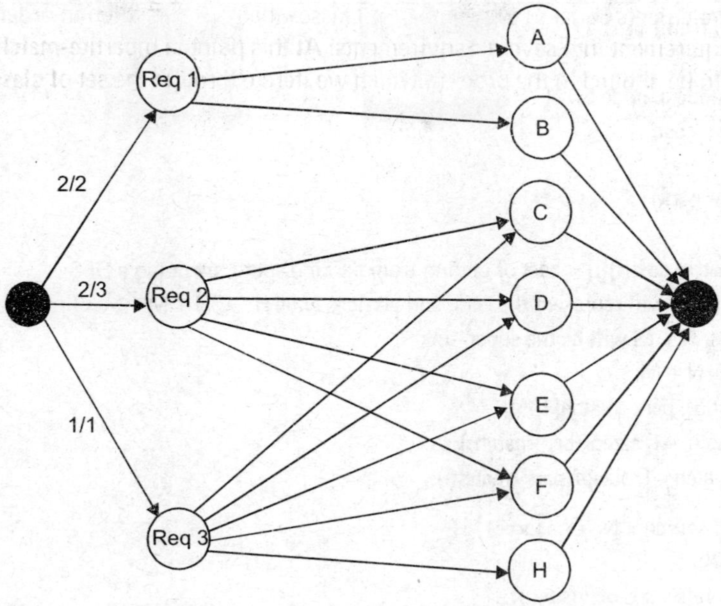

Fig 25.16 Example 4 (ram the problem statement

25.7 PARKING

In this problem we have to match each of the cars with a parking spot. Additionally the time it takes for all cars to find a parking spot must be minimized. Once again we build a bipartite graph: set A is the set that consists of the cars and set B contains the parking spots. Each edge connecting elements from different sets has as the cost (and not the capacity) the time required for the car to get to the parking spot. If the spot is unreachable, we can assign it an infinite cost (or remove it). These costs are determined by running breadth-first search.

For solving it, assume that the expected result is less than or equal to a constant D. Then, there exists a matching in which each edge connecting a car and a parking spot has the cost less than or equal to D. Thus, removing edges with cost greater than D will have no effect on the solution. This suggests a binary search on D, removing all edges with cost greater than D, and then performing a maximum bipartite-matching algorithm. If a matching exists in which every car can drive to a parking spot, we can decrease D otherwise we must increase it.

However, there is a faster and more elegant solution using a priority-first search. Instead of keeping D fixed as above, we could try to successively increase D whenever we find that it is too low. We will start with D = 0. Then we iterate through each of the cars and try to find an augmenting path in which no edge has a cost larger than D. If none exists, we increase D until one path exists. Obviously, we will increase it with the smallest possible amount. In order to achieve this, we will search for the augmenting path with the smallest cost - the cost of the path is the maximum cost of an edge on that path. This can be done with a priority-first search similar to the PFS augmenting-path algorithm presented in the first section of the article.

```
struct node
  int where, cost, from;
  node(int  where, int  cost, int  from): where( where),
```

```
    cost(_cost), from(_from) {};
    };
     bool operator < (node a, node b)   {
        return a.cost > b.cost;
    }
    int minTime(vector park)
    {
      // build a cost matrix cost[i][j] = cost of getting from parking spot j, by doing a BFS
    // vertices 0,1, ..., N - 1 will represent the cars, and vertices N, N+l, ..., N + M - 1 will represent
    // the parking spots; N + M will be the super-sink
       int D = 0, sink = N + M;
       int car_match[105], park_match[105];
       memset(car_match, -1, sizeof(car_match)) ;
       memset(park_match, -1, sizeof(park_match));

    for (int source = 0; source < N; ++ source)    {
       bool visited[210];
       memset(visited, false, sizeof(visited));
       int from[210];
       memset(from, -1, sizeof(from));
       priority__queue pq;
       pq.push(node(source, 0, -1));
       while (!pq.empty())    {
          int est = pq.top().cost, where = pq.top().  where,
  _from = pq.top().from;
           pq.pop () ;
           if (visited[where]) continue;
           visited[where] = true;
           from [where] = __from;
           // if where is a car try all M parking spots
           if  (where < N)    {
             for  (int i =' 0; i < M; ++ i) {
                  // if the edge doesn't exist or this car
   is already matched with this parking spot
                    if (cost[where] [i] == infinity ||
   car_match[where] == i) continue;
                 int ncst = max(est, cost[where][i]);
                 // the i-th parking spot is N + i
                 pq.push(node(N + i, nest, where));
             }
           }
           else  {
             //  if this parking spot is unmatched we found
   the augmenting path with minimum cost
```

```
        if  (park_match[where – N] == –1)    {
            from[sink] = where;
            // if D needs to be increased, increase it
            D = max(D, est);
            break;
        }
      // otherwise we follow the backward edge
      int next = park_match[where - N] ;
      int nest = max(est, cost[next][where]);
      pq.push(node(next, nest, where) );
    }
  }
  int where = from[sink];
  // if no augmenting path is found we have no solution
  if  (where == -1)
     return -1;
  //   follow the augmenting path
  while (from[where] > -1)  {
  int prev = from[where];
  //  if where is a parking spot the edge (prev, where)
  is a forward edge and the match must be updated
  if  (where >= N) {
     car_match [prev] = where;
     park_match [where - N] = prev;
   }
   where = prev;
  }
 }
 return D;
}
```

Solved Questions

1. Professor Adam has two children who, unfortunately, dislike each other. The problem is so severe that not only do they refuse to walk to school together, but in fact each one refuses to walk on any block that the other child has stepped on that day. The children have no problem with their paths crossing at a corner. Fortunately both the professor' s house and the school are on corners, but beyond that he is not sure if it is going to be possible to send both of his children to the same school. The professor has a map of his town. Show how to formulate the problem of determining if both his children can go to the same school as a maximum-flow problem.

Ans. Create a vertex for each corner, and if there is a street between corners u and v, create directed edges (u, v) and (v, u). Set the capacity of each edge to 1. Let the source be corner on which the professor.s house sits, and let the sink be the corner on which the school is located. We wish to Þnd a ßow of value 2 that also has the property that (,) is an integer for all vertices and . Such a ow represents two edge-disjoint paths from the house to the school.

2. Prove that for any pair of vertices and and any capacity and flow functions c and , we have c (,) + c (,) = c(,) + c(,).

Ans. c (,) + c (,) = c(,) – (,) + c(,) – (,)

(by de nition)

= c(,) + c(,)

(by skew symmetry: (,) = – (,))

3. Suppose that a flow network = (,) has symmetric edges, that is, (,) if and only if (,) . Show that the Edmonds-Karp algorithm terminates after at most /4 iterations.

(int For any edge (,), consider how both δ(s, u) and δ(v, t) change between times at which (u, v) is critical.)

Ans. From the time (u, v) is a critical edge until it is again a critical edge, δ(s, u) increases by at least 2, as shown in Theorem 26.9. Similarly, you can show that δ(v, t) also increases by at least 2. Thus the length of the augmenting path s _ u → v _ t increases by at least 4 between times (u, v) is critical. Since the length of an augmenting path cannot exceed|V|–1, (u, v) can be critical < |V| /4 times.

Edmonds-Karp terminates when there are no more augmenting paths, so it must terminate when there are no more critical edges, which takes at most (# edges) (max # times each edge critical) < |E f | (|V| / 4) iterations. In general, |E f | ≤ |E|, so the number of iterations is at most (actually, fewer than) |E| |V| / 2. But if we assume that G always has edges in both directions (i.e., (u, v) ∈E if and only if (v, u) ∈E), then |E f | d ≤ |E|, and the number of iterations is at most |E| |V| /4.

4. Prove that the generic push-relabel algorithm spends a total of only O(V E) time in performing all the O(V2) relabel operations.

Ans: Each time we call RELABEL(u), we examine all edges (u, v) ∈ Ef . Since the number of relabel operations is at most 2|V| –1 per vertex, edge (u, v) will be examined during relabel operations at most 4|V| – 2 = O(V) times (at most 2 |V| –1 times during calls to RELABEL(u) and at most 2|V| –1 times during calls to RELABEL(v)). Summing up over all the possible residual edges, of which there are at most 2|E| = O(E), we see that the total time spent relabeling vertices is O(V E).

Previous Year University Question

1. What are flow networks? Explain their use in brief. [KU]

Exercise

1. Prove that if (u, v) ∉ E and (v, u) ∉ E then f (u, v) = + (v, u) = 0.
2. For any vertex v other then source or sink show that total flow learning v must be equal.
3. State maximum flow problem us learning programming problem.

CHAPTER

26

AMORTIZED ANALYSIS

26.1 INTRODUCTION

In an amortized analysis, the time required to perform a sequence of data structure operations is average over all operation performed. Amortized analysis can be used to show that average cost of an operation is small, if one average over a sequence of operations, even though a single operation might be expensive. Unlike the average probability distribution function, the amortized analysis guarantees the 'average' performance of each operation in the worst case.

There are three most common techniques used in amortized analysis. The main difference is the way the cost is assign.

1. A : Computes an upper bound T(n) on the total cost of a sequence of n operations.
2. A n n : Overcharge some operations early in the sequence. This 'overcharge' is used later in the sequence for pay operation that charges less than they actually cost.
3. n : Maintain the credit as the potential energy to pay for future operations.

Aggregate Method

26.2 AGGREGATE METHOD CHARACTERISTICS

- It computes the worst case time (n) for a sequence of n operations.
- The amortized cost is (n)/n per operation.
- It gives the average performance of each operation in the worst case.
- This method is less precise than other methods, as all operations are assigned the same cost.

26.2.1 Application 1: Stack operations

In the following pseudocode, the operation STACK-EMPTY returns TRUE if there are no object currently on the stack, and FALSE otherwise.

```
MULTIPOP(s, k)
    while (.NOT. STACK-EMPTY(s) and k    0)
        do pop(s)
            k = k-l
```

Analysis

Worst-case cost for MULTIPOP is O(n). There are n successive calls to MULTIPOP would cost $O(n^2)$. We get unfair cost $O(n^2)$ because each item can be poped only once for each time it is pushed. In a sequence of n mixed operations the most times multipop can be called n/2.Since the cost of push and pop is 0(1), the cost of n stack operations is O(n). Therefore, amortized cost of an operation is the average: O(n)In O(1).

26.2.2 Application 2: Binary Counter

We use an array A[0 . . l] of bits, where length [A] , as the counter. A binary number x that is stored in the counter has its lowest-order bit in A[0] and its highest-order bit is A[-1], so that $^{k-1}S_{i=0}\, 2^i A[i]$. Initially, x = 0, and thus A[i] = 0 for i = 0, 1, . . ., 1. To add 1 (modulus 2) to the value in the counter, use the following pseudocode.

```
                    (A
    i    0
    while i < length [A] and A[i] = 1
        do A[i]    0
              i = i +1
    if i < length [A]
      then A[i]    1
```

A single execution of INCREMENT takes O( ) in worst case when Arrays contains all 's. Thus, a sequence of n INCREMENT operation on an initially zero counter takes (n) in the worst case. This bound is correct but not tight.

26.3 AMORTIZED ANALYSIS

We can tighten the analysis to get a worst-case cost for a sequence of an INCREMENT' S by observing that not all bits flip each time INCREMENT is called.

Bit A[0] is changed ceiling n times (every time)
Bit A[0] is changed ceiling $[n/2^1]$ times (every other time)
Bit A[0] is changed ceiling $[n/2^2]$ times (every other time)
Bit A[0] is changed ceiling $[n/2^i]$ times.

In general, for i = 0, 1,.. ., lg n, bit A[i] flips $n/2^i$ times in a sequence of n INCREMENT operations on an initially zero counter. For i > $\lfloor \lg(n) \rfloor$ bit A i never flips at all. The total number of flips in a sequence is thus floor(log) $_{i=0}\, n/2^i < n\, ^{\infty}S_{i=0}\, 1/2^i = 2n$

Therefore, the worst-case time for a sequence of n INCREMENT operation on an initially zero counter is therefore O(n), so the amortized cost of each operation is O(n)In = O(1).

26.4 ACCOUNTING METHOD

In this method, we assign changes to different operations, with some operations charged more or less than they actually cost. In other words, we assign artificial charges to different operations. Any overcharge for an operation on an item is stored (in an bank account) reserved for that item. Later, a different operation on that item can pay for its cost with the credit for that item. The balanced in the (bank) account is not allowed to become negative. The sum of the amortized cost for any sequence of operations is an upper bound for the actual total cost of these operations. The amortized cost of each operation must be chosen wisely in order to pay for each operation at or before the cost is incurred.

26.4.1 APPLICATION 1: STACK OPERATION

Recall the actual costs of stack operations were:

PUSH (s, x)	1
POP (s)	1
MULTIPOP (s,)	min (,s)

The amortized cost assignments are

PUSH	2
POP	0
MULTIPOP	0

Observe that the amortized cost of each operation is O(1). We must show that one can pay for any sequence of stack operations by charging the amortized costs.

The two units costs collected for each PUSH is used as follows:

- 1 unit is used to pay the cost of the PUSH.
- 1 unit is collected in advanced to pay for a potential future POP.

Therefore, for any sequence for n PUSH, POP, and MULTIPOP operations, the amortized cost is an

i $^{j=1}$ $_i$ 3 - iactual

= 3i - ($2^{floor(lg\ )+1}$ + i -floor(lgz) - 2)

If i = 2 , where ≥ 0, then

C_i 3i (2 1 i 2)

2

If i 2 , where ≥ 0 and 1 ≤ ≤ 2 , then

C_i = 3i- (2 1 i – 2)

2 2

This is an upperbound on the total actual cost. Since the total amortized cost is O(n) so is the total cost. As an example, consider a sequence of n operations is performed on a data structure. The ith operation costs i if i is an exact power of 2, and 1 otherwise. The accounting method of amortized analysis determine the amortized cost per operation as follows:

Let amortized cost per operation be 3, then the credit C, after the ith operation is: Since 1 and 1, so credit C_i always greater than zero. Hence, the total amortized cost n, that is O(n) is an upper bound on the total actual cost. Therefore, the amortized cost of each operation is O(n)/n = O(1).

Another example, consider a sequence of stack operations on a stack whose size never exceeds . After every operations, a copy of the entire stack is made. We must show that the cost of n stack operations, including copying the stack, is O(n) by assigning suitable amortized costs to the various stack operations.

There are, of course, many ways to assign amortized cost to stack operations. One way is:

PUSH	4,
POP	0,
MULTIPOP	0,
STACK-COPY	0.

Every time we PUSH, we pay a dollar (unit) to perform the actual operation and store 1 dollar (put in the bank). That leaves us with 2 dollars, which is placed on x (say) element. When we POP x element off the stack, one of two dollar is used to pay POP operation and the other one (dollar) is again put into a bank account. The money in the bank is used to pay for the STACK-COPY operation. Since after dollars in the bank and the stack size is never exceeds , there is enough dollars (units) in the bank (storage) to pay for the STACK-COPY operations. The cost of n stack operations, including copy the stack is therefore O(n). operations, there are atleast

26.4.2 Application 2: Binary Counter

We observed in the method, the running time of INCREMENT operation on binary counter is proportion to the number of bits flipped. We shall use this running time as our cost here.

For amortized analysis, charge an amortized cost of 2 dollars to set a bit to 1. When a bit is set, use 1 dollar out of 2 dollars already charged to pay the actual setting of the bit, and place the other dollar on the bit as credit so that when we reset a bit to zero, we need not charge anything.

The amortized cost of psuedocode INCREMENT can now be evaluated:

```
(A
```

```
1. i = 0
2. while i < length[A] and A[i] = 1
3.         do A[i]   0
4.              i   i 1
5. if i< length[A]
6.         then A[i]   1
```

Within the while loop, the cost of resetting the bits is paid for by the dollars on the bits that are reset. At most one bit is set, in line 6 above, and therefore the amortized cost of an INCREMENT operation is at most 2 dollars (units). Thus, for n INCREMENT operation, the total amortized cost is O(n), which bounds the total actual cost.

Consider a Variant

Let us implement a binary counter as a bit vector so that any sequence of n INCREMENT and RESET operations takes O(n) time on an initially zero counter,. The goal here is not only to increment a counter but also to read it to zero, that is, make all bits in the binary counter to zero. The new field , max[A], holds the index of the high-order in A. Initially, set max[A] to -1. Now, update max[A] appropriately when the counter is incremented (or reset). By contrast the cost of RESET, we can limit it to an amount that can be covered from earlier INCREMENT'S.

(A

```
1. i =1
2. while i < length [A] and A[i] = 1
3.     do A[i]    0
4.          i = i +1
5. if i < length[A]
6.     then A[i] = I
.      if i > max[A]
8.         then max[A] = i
9.         else max[A] = -1
```

```
(A

For i = 0 to max[A]
    do A[i] = 0
max[A] = -1
```

For the counter we assume that it cost 1 dollar to flip a bit. In addition to that we assume that we need 1 dollar to update max[A]. Setting and Resetting of bits work exactly as the binary counter: Pay 1 dollar to set bit to 1 and placed another 1 dollar on the same bit as credit. So, that the credit on each bit will pay to reset the bit during incrementing. In addition, use 1 dollar to update max[A] and if max[A] increases place 1 dollar as a credit on a new high-order 1. (If max[A] does not increase we just waste that one dollar). Since RESET manipulates bits at some time before the high-order 1 got up to max[A], every bit seen by RESET has one dollar credit on it. So, the zeroing of bits by RESET can be completely paid for by the credit stored on the bits. We just need one dollar to pay for resetting max [A].

Thus, charging 4 dollars for each INCREMENT and 1 dollar for each RESET is sufficient, so the sequence of n INCREMENT and RESET operations take (n) amortized time.

26.5 POTENTIAL METHOD

This method stores pre-payments as potential or potential energy that can be released to pay for future operations. The stored potential is associated with the entire data structure rather than specific objects within the data structure.

Notation

- D_0 is the initial data structure (e.g., stack)
- D_i is the data structure after the ith operation.
- c_i is the actual cost of the ith operation.
- The potential function ψ maps each D_i to its potential value $\psi(D_i)$

The amortized cost $\hat{c}_i$ of the ith operation w.r.t potential function ψ is defined by

$$\hat{c}_i = c_i + \psi(D_i) - \psi(D_i\ \ ), \qquad \dots (1)$$

The amortized cost of each operation is therefore

$\hat{c}_i$ = [Actual operation cost] + [change in potential].

By the eq.I, the total amortized cost of the n operation is

$$\sum_{i=1}^{n} \hat{}_i = \sum_{i=1}^{n} (c_i + \psi)(_i) - \psi(_{i-1}))$$
$$= \sum_{i=1}^{n} c_i + \sum_{i=1}^{n} \psi(_i) - \sum_{i=1}^{n} \psi(_{i-1})$$
$$= \sum_{i=1}^{n} c_i + \psi(_1) - \psi(_2) + \ldots + \psi(_{n-1}) + \psi(_n) - \{\psi(_0) + \psi(_1) + \ldots + \psi(_{n-1})$$
$$= \sum_{i=1}^{n} c_i + \psi(_n) - \psi(_0) \quad \ldots (2)$$

If we define a potential function ψ so that $\psi(_n) \geq \; _0)$, then the total amortized cost $\sum_{i=1}^{n} \hat{c}_i$ is an upper bound on the total actual cost.

As an example consider a sequence of n operations performed on a data structure. The ith operation costs i if i is an exact power of 2 and 1 otherwise. The potential method of amortized determines the amortized cost per operation as follows:

Let $\quad \psi(_i) \quad 2i - 2^{\lfloor lgi+1 \rfloor} + 1$, then

$\psi(_0) = 0$. Since $2^{\lfloor lgi+1 \rfloor} \geq 2i$ where $i > 0$,

Therefore, $\quad \psi(D_i) \geq 0 = \psi(D_0)$

If i = 2k where ≥ 0 then

$$2^{\lfloor lgi+1 \rfloor} = 2^{K+1} \quad 2i$$
$$2^{\lfloor lgi \rfloor} \quad 2 \quad i$$

$\Rightarrow$
$$c_i = c_i + \psi(D_i) - \psi(D_{i-1})$$
$$= i + (2i - 2i + I) - \{2(i-I) - i+I\}$$
$$= 2$$

If $\quad i = 2 \quad$ where ≥ 0 and $1 \leq j * 2$

then $\quad 2^{\lfloor lgi+1 \rfloor} = 2^{[lgi]}$

$\Rightarrow \quad c_i \quad c_i \quad \psi(D_i) - \psi(D_{i-1}) = 3$

Because $\quad \sum_{i=1}^{n} c_i = \sum_{i=1}^{n} c_i + \psi(_n) - \psi(D0)$

and $\psi(D_i) \geq (_0)$, so, the total amortized cost of n operation is an upper bound on the total actual cost. Therefore, the total amortized cost of a sequence of n operation is O(n) and the amortized cost per operation is O(n)/n O(1).

26.5.1 Application 1- Stack Operations

Define the potential function ψ on a stack to be the number of objects in the stack. For empty stack $_0$, we have $(_0) = 0$. Since the number of objects in the stack can not be negative, the stack $_i$ after the ith operation has nonnegative potential, and thus

$$\psi(D_i) \geq 0 = \psi(D_0).$$

Therefore, the total amortized cost of n operations w.r.t. function ψ represents an upper bound on the actual cost.

Amortized costs of stack operations are

If the ith operation on a stack containing s object is a PUSH operation, then the potential difference is

$$\psi(_i) - \psi(D_{i-1}) = (s + 1) - s = 1$$

In simple words, if i^{th} is PUSH then $(i-1)^{th}$ must be one less. By equation , the amortized cost of this PUSH operation is

$$\Rightarrow \quad \hat{c}i = ci + \psi(D_i) - \psi(D_{i-1}) = 1 + 1 = 2$$

If the ith operation on the stack is MULTIPOP(S,) and ′ = min(,s) objects are popped off the stack. The actual cost of the operation is ′, and the potential difference is

$$\psi(D_i) - \psi(D_{i-1}) = -{}'$$

why this is negative? Because we are taking off item from the stack. Thus, the amortized cost of the MULTIPOP operation is

$$\Rightarrow \quad \hat{c}_i = c_i + \psi(D_i) - \psi(D_{i-1}) = {}' - {}' = 0$$

Similarly, the amortized cost of a POP operation is 0.

Analysis

Since amortized cost of each of the three operations is O(1), therefore, the total amortized cost of n operations is O(n). The total amortized cost of n operations is an upper bound on the total actual cost.

Lemma: If data structure is Binary heap: Show that a potential function is O(nlgn) such that the amortized cost of EXTRACT-MIN is constant.

Proof: We know that the amortized cost $\hat{}_i$ of operation i is defined as

$$\hat{c}_i = c_i + \psi(D_i) - \psi(D_{i-1})$$

For the heap operations, this gives us

$$c_1 \lg n = c_2 \lg(n + c_3) + \psi(D_i) - \psi(D_{i-1}) \text{ (Insert)} \quad \text{... (1)}$$

$$c_4 = c_5 \lg(n + c_6) + \psi(D_i) - \psi(D_{i-1}) \text{ (EXTRACT-MIN)} \quad \text{... (2)}$$

Consider the potential function $\psi(D) = \lg(n!)$, where n is the number of items in . From equation (1), we have

$$\Rightarrow \quad (c_1 - c_2)\lg(n + c_3) = \lg(n!) - \lg((n-1)!) = \lg n.$$

This clearly holds if $c_1 = c_2$ and $c_3 = 0$.

From equation (2), we have

$$\Rightarrow \quad c_4 - c_5 \lg(n + c_6) = \lg(n!) - \lg((n+l)!) = -\lg(n+l).$$

This clearly holds if $c_4 = 0$ and $c_4 = c_6 = 1$.

Remember that stirlings function tells that $\lg(n!) = \theta(\theta \lg n)$, so

$$\Rightarrow \quad \psi(D) = \theta(n \lg n)$$

And this completes the proof.

26.5.2 Application 2: Binary Counter

Define the potential of the counter after i^{th} INCREMENT operation to be bi, the number of 1's in the counter after i^{th} operation.

Let i^{th} INCREMENT operation resets t_i bits. This implies that actual cost = atmost $(t_i + 1)$. Why? Because in addition to resetting t_i it also sets at most one bit to 1.

Therefore, the number of 1's in the counter after the ith operation is therefore $b_i * b_{i-1} - t_{i+1,}$ and the potential difference is

$\psi(D_i) - \psi(D_{i-1}) \leq (b_{i-1} - t_i + 1) - b_{i-1} = 1 - t_i$

Putting this value in equation (1), we get

$\Rightarrow \quad \hat{c}_i = c_i + \psi(D_i) - \psi(D_{i-1})$

$\Rightarrow \quad (t_i + 1) + (1 - t_i)$

$\Rightarrow \quad = 2$

If counter starts at zero, then $\psi(\ _0) = 0$. Since $\psi(D_i) \geq 0$ for all i, the total amortized cost of a sequence of n INCREMENT operation is an upper bound on the total actual cost, and so the worst-case cost of n INCREMENT operations is O(n).

If counter does not start at zero, then the initial number are 1's (= $\ _0$).

After 'n' INCREMENT operations the number of 1's = b_n, where $0 \leq \ _0, b_n \leq$.

Since $\quad {}^n\Sigma_{i=1} \hat{c}_i = (c_i + \psi(\ _i) + \psi(\ _{i-1}))$

$\Rightarrow \quad {}^n\Sigma_{i=1} \hat{c}_i = {}^n\Sigma_{i=1} c_i + {}^n\Sigma_{i=1} \psi(\ _i) + {}^n\Sigma_{i=1} \psi(\ _{i-1})$

$\Rightarrow \quad {}^n\Sigma_{i=1} \hat{c}_i = {}^n\Sigma_{i=1} c_i + \psi(\ _n) - \psi(\ _0)$

$\Rightarrow \quad {}^n\Sigma_{i=1} c_i = {}^n\Sigma_{i=1} + \psi(\ _0) - \psi(\ _n)$

We have $\hat{c}_i \leq 2$ for all $1 \leq i < n$. Since $\psi(D_i) = \ _0$ and $\psi(\ _n) = b$, the total cost of n INCREMENT operation is

Since $\quad {}^n\Sigma_{i=1} c_i = {}^n\Sigma_{i=1} \hat{c}_1 + \psi(\ _n) - \psi(\ _0)$

$\Rightarrow \quad \leq {}^n\Sigma_{i=1} 2 - \ _n + \ _0$ why because $c_i < 2$

$\Rightarrow \quad 2\, {}^n\Sigma_{i=1} 2 - \ _n \ _0$

$\Rightarrow \quad = 2n - \ n +$

Note that since $\ _0 \leq$, if we execute at least n $\Omega.(\ )$ INCREMENT Operations, the total actual cost is O(n), no matter what initial value of counter is.

Implementation of a queue with two stacks, such that the amortized cost of each ENQUEUE and each DEQUEUE Operation is 0(1). ENQUEUE pushes an object onto the first stack. DEQUEUE pops off an object from second stack if it is not empty. If second stack is empty, DEQUEUE transfers all objects from the first stack to the second stack to the second stack and then pops off the first object. The goal is to show that this implementation has an O(1) amortized cost for each ENQUEUE and DEQUEUE operation. Suppose $\ _i$ denotes the state of the stacks after i^{th} operation. Define $\psi(D_i)$ to be the number of elements in the first stack. Clearly, $\psi(\ _0) = 0$ and $\psi(D_i) \geq \psi(\ _0)$ for all i. If the ith operation is an ENQUEUE operation, then $\psi(D_i) - \psi(D_{i-1}) = 1$

Since the actual cost of an ENQUEUE operation is 1, the amortized cost of an ENQUEUE operation is 2. If the $_i{}^{th}$ operation is a DEQUEUE, then there are two case to consider.

s : When the second stack is not empty.

In this case we have $\psi(D_i) - \psi(D_{i-1}) = 0$ and the actual cost of the DEQUEUE operation is 1.

s : When the second stack is empty.

In this case, we have $\psi(D_i) - \psi(D_{i-1}) = -\psi(D_{i-1})$ and the actual cost of the DEQUEUE operation is $\psi(D_i\ ) + 1$.

In either case, the amortize cost of the DEQUEUE operation is 1. It follows that each operation has O(1) amortized cost

26.5.3 Dynamic Table

If the allocated space for the table is not enough, we must copy the table into larger size table. Similarly, if large number of members erased from the table, it is good idea to reallocate the table with a smaller size. Using amortized analysis we shall show that the amortized cost of insertion and deletion is constant and unused space in a dynamic table never exceeds a constant fraction of the total space.

Assume that the dynamic table supports following two operations:

TABLE-INSERT

This operation add an item in the table by copying into the unused single slot. The cost of insertion is

TABLE-DELETE

This operation removes an item from the table by freeing a slot. The cost of deletion is 1.

Load Factor

The number of items stored in the table, n, divided by the size of the table, m, is defined as the load factor and denoted as $(\alpha) = m/n$

The load factor of the empty table (size m = 0) is 1.

A table is full when there exists no used slots. That is, the number of items stored in the table equals the number of available slots (m = n). In this case

Load factor $\Rightarrow T(a) = nlm = 1$

Proposed Algorithm

1. Initialize table size to m =1.
2. Keep inserting elements as long as size of the table less than number of items i.e., n < m.
3. enerate a new table of size 2m and set m <-- 2m.
4. Copy items (by using elementary insertion) from the old table into the new one.
5. OTO step 2.

Analysis

If n elementary insert operations are performed in line 4, the worst-case cost of an operation is O(n), which leads to an upper bound of $O(n^2)$ on the total running time for n operations.

Aggregate Analysis

The ith insert operation causes an expansion only when i - 1 an exact power of 2. Let c_i be the cost of the ith insert operation. Then

$C_i = i$ if i - 1 is an exact power of 2

1 Otherwise

As an example, consider the following illustration.

	A	
n	m	1
1	1	1+1
2	2	1+2
3	4	1
4	4	1+4
5	8	1
6	8	1
7	8	1
8	8	1
9	16	1+8
10	16	1

The total cost of n insert operations is therefore

$$^n\Sigma_{i=1} c^i \leq {}^{\text{floor (gn)}} \Sigma_{j=0} 2j$$
$$= n + [2^{\text{floor (1gn| +1}} -1]/[2-1] \quad \text{since } {}^n\Sigma_{k=0} x^k = [x^{n+1} -1]/[x-1]$$
$$= n + 2^{1gn} . 2-1$$
$$= n + 2n - 1$$
$$= 3n-l$$
$$< 3n$$

Therefore, the amortized cost of a single operation is

$$= \frac{\text{Totalcost}}{\text{Number of operations}}$$
$$= 3n/n$$
$$= 3$$

Asymptotically, the cost of dynamic table is O(l) which is the same as that of table of fixed size.

Accounting Method

Here we guess charges to 3$. Intuitively, each item pays for 3 elementary operations.

1. 1$ for inserting immediate item.
2. 1$ for moving item (re-insert) when the table is expanded.
3. 1$ for moving another item (re-insert) has already been moved once when that table is expanded.

Solved Questions

1. What if when we resize we just increase the size by 1. Is that a good idea?

Ans. Not really. If our n operations consist of n pushes then even just considering the array-resizing cost we will incur a total cost of at least 1 + 2 + 3 + 4 + . . . + (n –1) = n(n –1)/2. That' s an amortized cost of (n –1)/2 per operation just in resizing.

2. What if instead we decide to double the size of the array when we resize?

Ans. This is much better. Now, in any sequence of n operations, the total cost for resizing is 1 + 2 + 4 + 8 + . . . + 2i for some 2i < n (if all operations are pushes then 2i will be the largest power of 2 less than n). This sum is at most 2n – 1. Adding in the additional cost of n for inserting/removing, we get a total cost < 3n, and so our amortized cost per operation is < 3.

Exercise

1. If the set of stack operations included a MULTIPUSH operation, which pushes k items onto the stack would the O(1) bound on the amortized cost of stack operation continue to hold?
2. What is the total cost of execiting n of stack operations PUSH, POP and MULTIPOP
3. Show that the amortized cost of each ENQUEUE and DEQUE UE operation on stack is O(1).

CHAPTER

27

APPROXIMATE ALGORITHMS

27.1 INTRODUCTION

An approximate algorithm is a way of dealing with NP-completeness for optimization problem. This technique does not guarantee the best solution. The goal of an approximation algorithm is to come as close as possible to the optimum value in a reasonable amount of time which is at most polynomial time.

Suppose we have some optimization problem instance i, which has a large number of feasible solutions. Also let c(i) be the cost of solution produced by approximate algorithm and c*(i) be the cost of optimal solution. For minimization problem, we are interested in finding a solution of a given instance /' in the set of feasible solutions, such that c(i)/c*(i) be as small as possible. On the other hand, for maximization problem, we are interested in finding a solution in the feasible solution set such that c*(i)/c(i) be as small as possible.

We say that an approximation algorithm for the given problem instance i, has a ratio bound of p(n) if for any input of sign n, the cost c of the solution produced by the approximation algorithm is within a factor of p(n) of the cost c* of an optimal solution. That is max(c(i)/c* (i)/c(i)) $\leq$ p(n)

This definition applies for both minimization and maximization problems.

Note that p(n) is always greater than or equal to 1. If solution produced by approximation algorithm is true optimal solution then clearly we have p(n) = 1.

For a minimization problem, $0 < c^*(i) \leq c(i)$, and the ratio c(i)/c*(i) gives the factor by which the cost of the approximate solution is larger than the cost of an optimal solution. Similarly, for a maximization problem, $0 < c(i) \leq c^*(i)$, and the ratio c*(i)Ic(i) gives the factor by which the cost of an optimal solution is larger than the cost of the approximate solution.

27.2 RELATIVE ERROR

We define the relative error of the approximate algorithm for any input size as

mod[c(i)– c*(i)/ c*(i)]

We say that an approximate algorithm has a relative bound of ε(n) if

mod[c(i) – c *(i)/c*(i)] $\leq \varepsilon$(n)

27.3 VERTEX COVER

Definition: A vertex-cover of an undirected graph G=(V, E) is a subset of V' subset of V such that if edge (u, v) is an edge of G then either u in V or v in V' (or both).

Problem: Find a vertex-cover of maximum size in a given undirected graph.

This optimal vertex-cover is the optimization version of an NP-complete problem but it is not too hard to find a vertex-cover that is near optimal.

APPRO - ERTE CO ER(: ra h)

1. c ← {}
2. ← [ ]
3. while ′ is not empty do
4. Let (,) be an arbitrary edge of ′
5. c ← c U { , }
6. Remove from every edge incident on either or
7. return c

Example

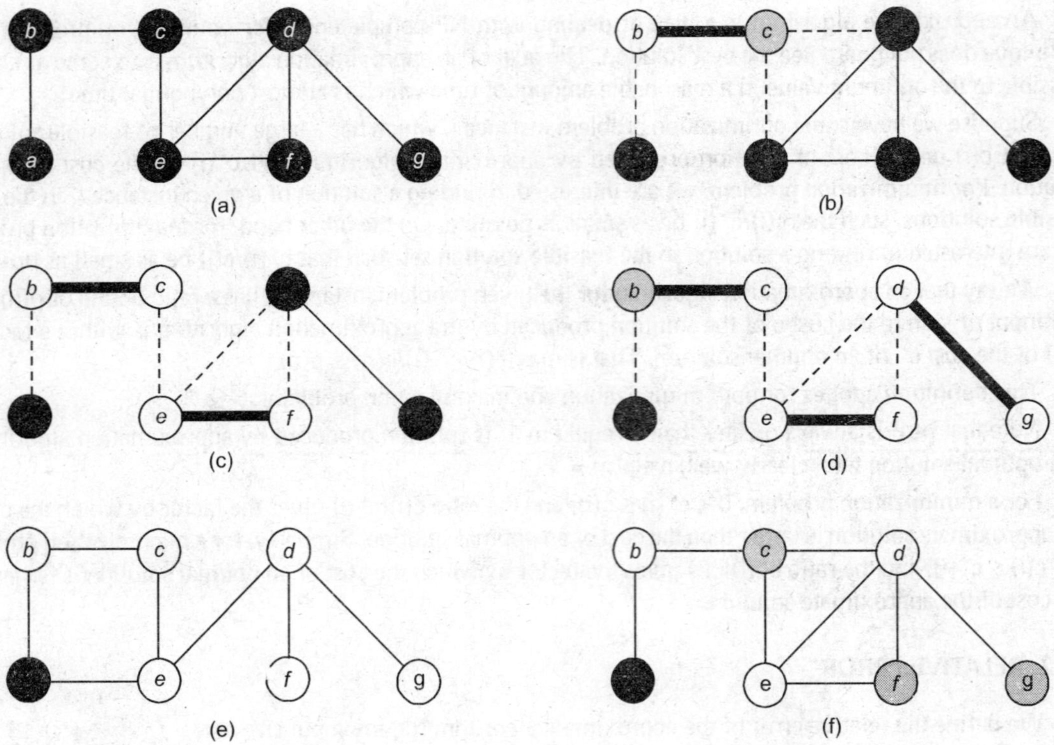

Fig 27.1 Example of Approx Vertex cover

27.3.1 Analysis

It is easy to see that the running time of this algorithm is O(+), using adjacency list to represent .

Theore : A O - T -CO is a l n mial-tim 2-a ximat alg it m i. ., t alg it m as a ati n b n 2.

oal: Since this a minimization problem, we are interested in smallest possible c/c*. Specifically we want to show c/c ≤ 2 = (n). In other words, we want to show that APPROX- ERTEX-CO ER algorithm returns a vertex-cover that is atmost twice the size of an optimal cover.

Proof: Let the set c and c* be the sets output by APPROX- ERTEX-CO ER and OPTIMAL- ERTEX-CO ER respectively. Also, let A be the set of edges selected by line 4.

Because, we have added both vertices, we get c = 2/A but OPTIMAL- ERTEX-CO ER would have add one of two.

⇒ clc ≤ (n) = 2

Formally, since no two edge in A are covered by the same vertex from c* (since, once an edge is picked in line 4, all other edges that are incident on its endpoints are deleted from in line 6) and we the lower bound:

|c* ≥ A ... (1)

On the size of an OPTIMAL- ERTEX-CO ER.

In line 4, we picked both en points yielding an upper bound on the size of ertex-Cover.

|c ≤ 2| A|

Since, upper bound is an exact in this case, we have

|c = 2| A| ... (2)

Take |c|/2 = | A| and put it in equation (1)

|c*| ≥ | c |/2

| c*|/| c | ≥ 1/2

| c* |/| c | ≤ 2 = (n)

proving the theorem.

27.4 TRAVELLING SALESMAN PROBLEM

Pro le : Given a complete undirected graph =(,) that has nonnegative integer cost c(, v) associated with each edge (,) in E, the problem is to find a hamiltonian cycle (tour) of with minimum cost.

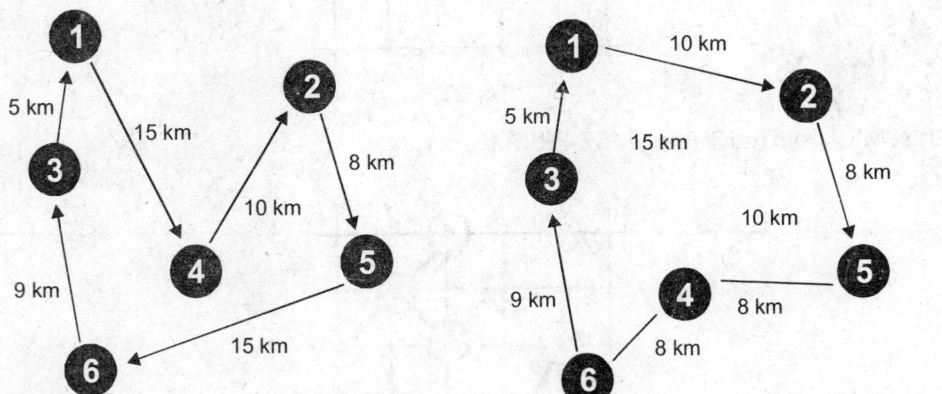

Fig 27.2 A salespersons starts from the city 1 and has to visit six cities (1 through 6) and must come back to the starting city i.e., 1. The first route (left side) 1→ 4 → 2 → 5 → 6 → 3 → 1 with the total length of 62 km, is a relevant selection but is not the best solution. The second route (right side) 1→ 2 → 5 → 4 → 6 → 3 → 1 represents the must better solution as the total distance, 48 km, is less than for the first route.

Suppose c(A) denoted the total cost of the edges in the subset A subset of E i.e.,

$$c(A) = \Sigma u,v \text{ in } A\ c(u,v)$$

Moreover, the cost function satisfies the triangle inequality. That is, for all vertices u, v, w in V, w have $c(u, w) \leq c(u, v) + c(v, w)$.

Note that the TSP problem is NP-complete even if we require that the cost function satisfies the triangle inequality. This means that it is unlikely that we can find a polynomial-time algorithm for TSP.

27.4.2 TSP with the Triangle-Inequality

When the cost function satisfies the triangle inequality, we can design an approximate algorithm for TSP that returns a tour whose cost is not more than twice the cost of an optimal tour.

27.4.3 Outline of an APPROX-TSP-TOUR

First, compute a MST (minimum spanning tree) whose weight is a lower bound on the length of an optimal TSP tour. Then, use MST to build a tour whose cost is no more than twice that of MST's weight as long as the cost function satisfies triangle inequality.

27.4.4 Operation of APPROX-TSP-TOUR

Let root r be a in following given set of points (graph).

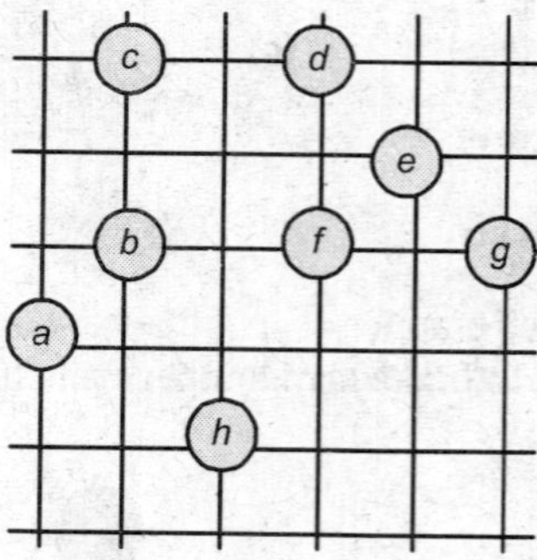

Fig. 27.3

Construct MST from root a using MST-PRIM (G, c, r).

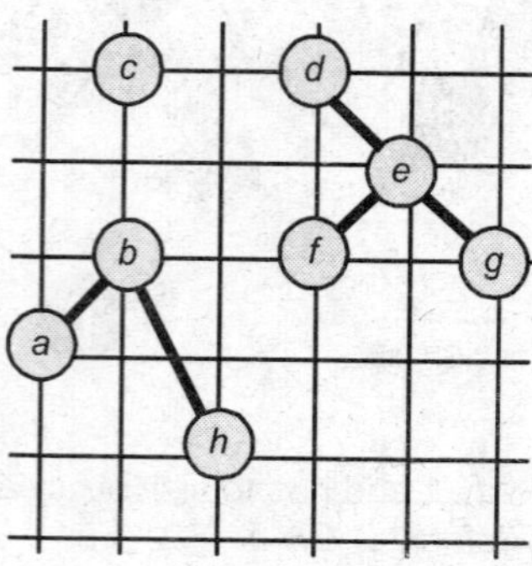

Fig. 27.4

List vertices visited in preorder walk. L = {a, b, c, h, d, e, f, g}

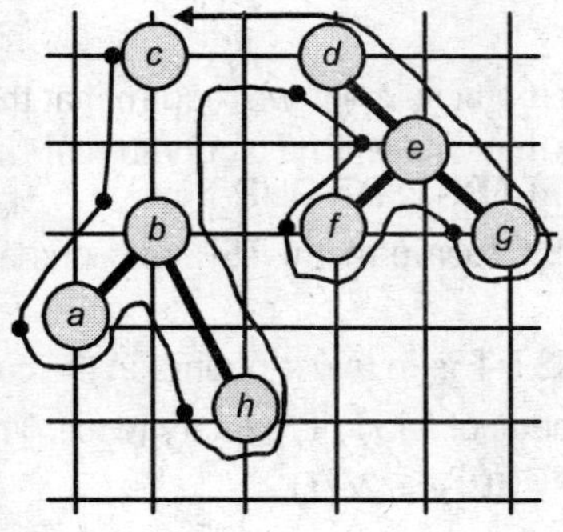

Fig. 27.5

Return Hamiltonian cycle.

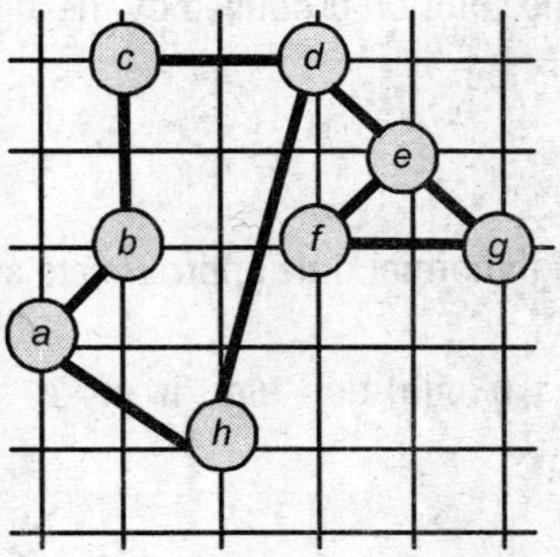

Fig. 27.6

Optimal TSP tour for a given problem (graph) would be

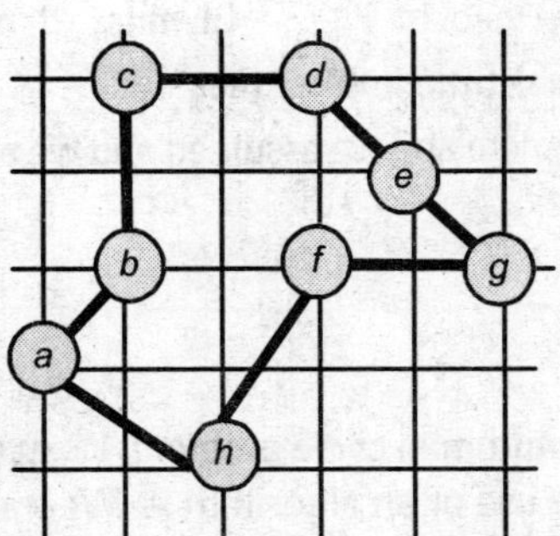

Fig. 27.7

which is about 23 shorter.

Theore : A O -TS -TO is a l n mial-tim 2-a ximati n alg it m TS it t iangl in alit .

Proof:

1. We have already shown that APPROX-TSP-TOUR-time.
2. Let * denote the optimal tour. Observe that a TSP with one edge removed is a spanning tree (not necessarily MST).

It implies that the weight of the MST T is in lower bound on the cost of an optimal tour. c(T) = c (*)

A Full walk, W, traverse every edge of MST, T, exactly twice. That is,

$$c( ) = 2c(T)$$

which means

$$c( ) \leq 2c(*)$$

and we have

$$c( )/c(*) \leq (n) = 2$$

That is, the cost of walk, c( ), of the solution produced by the algorithm is within a factor of (n)=2 of the cost c(*) of an optimal solution.

27.5 THE GENERAL TSP

Without the triangle inequality, a polynomial time approximate algorithm with constant approximation ratio not exist unless = .

Theore : if ≠ , t is n l n mial-tim alg it m it a ximati n ati ≥ 1 g n al TS .

Proof:

Suppose to the contrary that there exists a polynomial-time algorithm A for ≥ l.

Now, use algorithm A to solve instance of HAM-CYCLE problem in polynomial-time. Since HAM-CYCLE problem is NP-complete then by theorem

l an -c m l t bl m is l n mial-tim s l abl , t n = . i al ntl , i an bl m in is n t l n mial-tim s l abl t an n -c m l t bl m is l n mial s l abl .

Solving HAM-CYCLE in polynomial-time implies that = .

Since the HAM-CYCLE is NP-complete and we assumed and we assumed that ≠ , a contradiction is arise.

27.6 REDUCTION

Let = (,) be an instance of Hamiltonian cycle problem. We want to determine efficiently whether contains a Hamiltonian cycle by making use of an algorithm A. We transform into an instance of the TSP problem as follows:

Consider a complete graph ′ =(, ′) where E′ = {(, v): , v in and ≠ }. Assign an integer cost to each edge in ′ as follows:

c(,) = 1 if (,) in

| |+1 otherwise

Because algorithm A is guaranteed to return a tour of cost no more than times the cost of an optimal tour, if graph contains a Hamiltonian cycle, then A must return it. If has no Hamiltonian cycle, then A returns a tour of cost more than | |. Therefore, we can use algorithm A to solve Hamiltonian cycle problem in polynomial time and this is impossible unless = .

Solved Questions

1. Which formula is the best approximation for the depth of a heap with n nodes?

Ans. c. log (base 2) of n

Previous Year University Question

1. What is Directed Hamiltonian Cycle? Prove that CNF - Satisfiability reduces to Directed Hamiltonian Cycle. O
2. What is a Hamlitonian Cycle ? Give an example. O
3. With reference to the travelling salesman problem, is the cost matrix always symmetric? ustify your answer. a ass ni sit
4. Define approximation algorithms. What is approximation ratio? Approximate the Travelling Salesman problem with triangle inequality. T

Exercise

1. For which graph Approve-vectex-cover always yields a suboptimal solution?
2. Write an algorithm to find optimal vertex cover for a tree in linear time.
3. Show that any plannar graph can be paintal using of most four colours.
4. Give an algorithm for the TSP which find a solution within a factor of S/L.

CHAPTER

28

NP-COMPLETENESS

28.1 IMPORTANCE OF NP-COMPLETENESS

Most algorithms we have studied so far have polynomial-time running times. According to Cormen, Leiserson, and Rivest, polynomial-time algorithms can be considered tractable for the following reasons.

(1) Although a problem which has a running time of say $O(n^{20})$ or $O(n^{100})$ can be called intractable, there are very few practical problems with such orders of polynomial complexity.

(2) For reasonable models of computation, a problem that can be solved in polynomial time in one model can also be solved in polynomial time on another.

(3) The class of polynomial-time solvable problems has nice closure properties (since polynomials are closed under addition, multiplication, etc.)

The class of NP-complete (Non-deterministic polynomial time complete) problems is a very important and interesting class of problems in Computer Science. The interest surrounding this class of problems can be attributed to the following reasons.

(1) No polynomial-time algorithm has yet been discovered for any NP-complete problem at the same time no NP-complete problem has been shown to have a super polynomial-time (for example exponential time) lower bound.

(2) If a polynomial-time algorithm is discovered for even one NP-complete problem, then all NP-complete problems will be solvable in polynomial-time.

It is believed (but so far no proof is available) that NP-complete problems do not have polynomial-time algorithms and therefore are intractable. The basis for this belief is the second fact above, namely that if any single NP-complete problem can be solved in polynomial time, then every NP-complete problem has a polynomial-time algorithm. Given the wide range of NP-complete problems that have been discovered to date, it will be sensational if all of them could be solved in polynomial time.

It is important to know the rudiments of NP-completeness for anyone to design "sound" algorithms for problems. If one can establish a problem as NP-complete, there is strong reason to believe that it is intractable. We would then do better by trying to design a good approximation algorithm rather than searching endlessly seeking an exact solution. An example of this is the TSP (Traveling Salesman Problem), which has been shown to be intractable. A practical strategy to solve TSP therefore would be to design a good approximation algorithm. This is what we did in Chapter ., where we used a variation of ruskal's minimal spanning tree algorithm to approximately solve the TSP. Another important reason to have good familiarity with NP-completeness is many natural interesting and innocuous-looking problems that on the surface seem no harder than sorting or searching, are in fact NP-complete.

28.2 OPTIMIZATION PROBLEMS AND DECISION PROBLEMS

NP-completeness has been studied in the framework of decision problems. Most problems are not decision problems, but optimization problems (where some value needs to be minimized or maximized). In order to apply the theory of NP-completeness to optimization problems, we must recast them as decision problems. We provide an example of how an optimization problem can be transformed into a decision problem.

Example: Consider the problem SHORTEST-PATH that finds a shortest path between two given vertices in an unweighted, undirected graph G = (V, E). An instance of SHORTEST-PATH consists of a particular graph and two vertices of that graph. A solution is a sequence of vertices in the graph, with perhaps an empty sequence denoting that no path exists. Thus the problem SHORTEST-PATH is a relation that associates each instance of a graph and two vertices with a solution (namely a shortest path in this case). Note that a given instance may have no solution, exactly one solution, or multiple solutions.

A decision problem PATH related to the SHORTEST-PATH problem above is : Given a

graph G = (V, E), two vertices $u, v \in V$, and a non-negative integer , does a path exist in G between u and v whose length is at most ?

Note that the decision problem PATH is one way of casting the original optimization problem as a decision problem. We have done this by imposing a bound on the value to be optimized. This is a popular way of transforming an optimization problem into a decision problem.

If an optimization problem is easy then its related decision problem is easy as well. Similarly, if we can provide evidence that a decision problem is hard, we also provide evidence that its related optimization problem is hard.

28.3 EXAMPLES OF SOME INTRACTABLE PROBLEMS

(a) Traveling Salesman Problem

A Hamiltonian cycle in an undirected graph is a simple cycle that passes through every vertex exactly once.

Optimization Problem: Given a complete, weighted graph, find a minimum-weight Hamiltonian Cycle.

Decision Problem: Given a complete, weighted graph and an integer , does there exist a Hamiltonian cycle with total weight at most .

(b) Subset Sum

The input is a positive integer C and n objects whose sizes are positive integers s_1, s_2, , sn.

Optimization Problem: Among all subsets of objects with sum at most C, what is the largest subset sum?

Decision Problem: Is there a subset of objects whose sizes add up to exactly C?

(c) Knapsack Problem

This is a generalization of the subset sum problem. Consider a knapsack of capacity C where C is a positive integer and n objects with positive integer sizes $s_1, s_2, \ldots, s_n$ and positive integer profits $p_1, p_2, \ldots, p_n$.

Optimization Problem: Find the largest total profit of any subset of the objects that fits in the knapsack.

Decision Problem: Given , is there a subset of the objects that fits in the knapsack and has total profit at least ?

(d) Bin Packing

Suppose we have unlimited number of bins each of unit capacity and n objects with sizes $s_1, s_2, \ldots, s_n$ where the sizes s_i (i = 1,..., n) are rational numbers in the range $< si \leq 1$

Optimization Problem: Determine the smallest number of bins into which the objects can be packed and find an optimal packing. Decision Problem: Given an integer k, do the objects fit in k bins?

(e) Job Shop Scheduling

Suppose there are n jobs, $J_1, J_2, \ldots, J_n$ to be processed one at a time in non-preemptive fashion. Let the processing time be $t_1, t_2, \ldots, t_n$ and the due dates be $d_1, d_2, \ldots, d_n$. A schedule for the jobs is a permutation π of 1, 2,..., n. Job J_i (i = 1,..., n) will incur a penalty of p_i (i = 1,..., n) if it misses the due-date in the given schedule π. If processed within the due-date, the penalty is taken as zero. The processing times, due-dates, and penalties are all positive integers. The penalty of a schedule is the sum of penalties incurred by jobs processed according to that schedule.

Optimization Problem: Determine the minimum possible penalty for a schedule and find an (optimal) schedule that achieves the minimum penalty.

Decision Problem: Given a non-negative integer k, does there exist a schedule with penalty at most K?

28.4 SATISFIABILITY

A propositional variable is one that can be assigned the value true or false. A literal is a propositional variable or its negation. A clause is a sequence of literals separated by the logical OR operator. A propositional formula is said to be in conjunctive normal form (CNF) if it consists of a sequence of clauses separated by the logical AND operator. For example,

$$(p \vee q \vee s \wedge \bar{q} \vee r) \wedge \bar{p} \vee \bar{g} \vee r \vee \bar{s})$$

A truth assignment for a set of propositional variables is an assignment of true or false value to each propositional variable. A truth assignment is said to satisfy a formula if it makes the value of the formula true.

3-SAT (Decision Problem): Given a CNF formula in which each clause is permitted to contain at most three literals, is there a truth assignment to its variables that satisfies it?

28.5 THE CLASSES P AND NP

An algorithm is said to be polynomially bounded if its worst-case complexity is bounded by a polynomial function of the input size. A problem is said to be polynomially bounded if there is a polynomially bounded algorithm for it.

P is the class of all decision problems that are polynomially bounded. The implication is that a decision problem X ∈ P can be solved in polynomial time on a deterministic computation model (such as a deterministic Turing machine).

NP represents the class of decision problems which can be solved in polynomial time by a non-deterministic model of computation. That is, a decision problem X ∈ NP can be solved in polynomial-time on a non-deterministic computation model (such as a non-deterministic Turing machine). A non-deterministic model can make the right guesses on every move and race towards the solution much faster than a deterministic model.

A deterministic machine, at each point in time, executes an instruction. Depending on the outcome of executing the instruction, it then executes some next instruction, which is unique. A non-deterministic machine on the other hand has a choice of next steps. It is free to choose any that it wishes. For example, it can always choose a next step that leads to the best solution for the problem. A non-deterministic machine thus has the power of extremely good, optimal guessing.

As an example, let us consider the decision version of TSP: Given a complete, weighted graph and an integer k, does there exist a Hamiltonian cycle with total weight at most k?

A smart non-deterministic algorithm for the above problem starts with a vertex, guesses the correct edge to choose, proceeds to the next vertex, guesses the correct edge to choose there, etc. and in polynomial time discovers a Hamiltonian cycle of least cost and provides an answer to the above problem. This is the power of non-determinism. A deterministic algorithm here will have no choice but take super-polynomial time to answer the above question.

Another way of viewing the above is that given a candidate Hamiltonian cycle (call it certificate), one can verify in polynomial time whether the answer to the above question is

YES or NO. Thus to check if a problem is in NP, it is enough to prove in polynomial time that any YES instance is correct. We do not have to worry about NO instances since the program always makes the right choice.

It is easy to show that P $\subseteq$. NP. However, it is unknown whether P = NP. In fact, this question is perhaps the most celebrated of all open problems in Computer Science.

28.6 NP-COMPLETE PROBLEMS

The definition of NP-completeness is based on reducibility of problems. Suppose we wish to solve a problem X and we already have an algorithm for solving another problem Y. Suppose we have a function T that takes an input x for X and produces T(x), an input for Y such that the correct answer for X on x is yes if and only if the correct answer for Y on T(x) is yes. Then by composing T and the algorithm for y, we have an algorithm for X.

- If the function T itself can be computed in polynomially bounded time, we say X is polynomial y reducible to Y and we write $X \leq_p Y$.
- If X is polynomially reducible to Y, then the implication is that Y is at least as hard to solve as X. i.e. X is no harder to solve than Y.
- It is easy to see that
- $X \leq Y$ and $Y \in P$ implies $X \in P$.

28.7 NP-HARDNESS AND NP-COMPLETENESS

A decision problem Y is said to be NP-hard if $X \leq_p Y \; \forall X \in NP$. An NP-hard problem Y is said to be NP-complete if $Y \in NP$. NPC is the standard notation for the class of all NP-complete problems.

Informally, an NP-hard problem is a problem that is at least as hard as any problem in NP. If, further, the problem also belongs to NP, it would become NP-complete. It can be easily proved that if any NP-complete problem is in P, then NP = P. Similarly, if any problem in NP is not polynomial-time solvable, then no NP-complete problem will be polynomial-time solvable. Thus NP-completeness is at the crux of deciding whether or not NP = P. Using the above definition of NP-completeness to show that a given decision problem, say Y, is NP-complete will call for proving polynomial reducibility of each problem in NP to the problem Y. This is impractical since the class NP already has a large number of member problems and will continuously grow as researchers discover new members of NP. A much more practical way of proving NP-completeness of a decision problem Y is to discover a problem

$X \in NPC$ such that $Y \leq_p X$. Since X is NP-complete and $\leq$ p is a transitive relationship, the above would mean that $Z \leq Y \; \forall Z \in NP$. Furthermore if Y** NP, then Y is NP-complete. The above is the standard technique used for showing the NP-hardness or NP-completeness of a givən decision problem. For example, all the decision problems given in Section 10.2 can be shown to be NP-complete by the above technique. An interesting question is: how was the first member of NPC found? Stephen Cook showed the NP-completeness of the problem 3-SAT by directly proving that X ≤ C p3-SAT ∀ X ∈ NP. If a problem is NP-complete, it does not mean that all hopes are lost. If the actual input sizes are small, an algorithm with, say, exponential running time may be acceptable. On the other hand, it may still be possible to obtain near-optimal solutions in polynomial-time. Such an algorithm that returns near-optimal solutions (in polynomial time) is called an approximation algorithm. Using Kruskal's algorithm to obtain a suboptimal solution to the TSP is an example of this.

28.8 ADVERSARY ARGUMENT

Linear Reduction

A problem X, reduces to another problem, Y, if we can efficiently transform instances of the problem X into instances of the problem B in such a way that solving the transformed instances yields the solution to the original instance.

Formal Definitions

The problem A is linearly reducible to perform B, Denoted $A < {}^1B$, if the existence an algorithm for B that runs in a time O(t(n)) for any function t(n) implies that there exists an algorithm for A that also runs in a time O(t(n)).

If $A \leq {}^1B$ and $B \leq {}^1A$ then A and B are linearly equivalent and denoted $A == {}^1B$.

Also, the linear reduction are transitive:

if $A \leq {}^1B$ and $B \leq {}^1C$, then $A \leq {}^1C$.

Linear equivalence are transitive reflexive and symmetric. (Hence, equivalent.)

28.9 NP-COMPLETENESS AND REDUCTION

There are many problems for which no polynomial-time algorithms ins known. Some of these problems are traveling salesperson, optimal graph coloring, the knapsack problem, Hamiltonian cycles, integer programming, finding the longest simple path in a graph, and satisfying a Boolean formula.

These problems belongs to an interesting class of problems, called the NP-Complete" problems, whose status is unknown. The NP-Complete problems are tractable i.e., require a superpolynomial time. The reason is that a polynomial time algorithm to solve any one of the NP-Complete problems would automatically provide us with polynomial-time algorithms for all of them.

The basic idea is that there may be problems that are hard to solve, but the validity of any purported solution can be verified easily.

Consider the problem "Hamiltonian Cycle". Hence an undirected graph, the problem is to find a path that starts from some node, visits each node once and only once, and returns to the starting node. If such cyc e exists, we say that the graph is Hamiltonian. This problem is hard. However, it is easy to verify whether a "given" sequence of nodes defines a Hamiltonian cycle.

28.10 POLYNOMIAL-TIME ALGORITHM

1. Algorithms with worst case running time of $O(n^k)$, where k is a constant, are called tractable others are called intractable or super-polynomial.
2. Formally, an algorithm is polynomial-time algorithm if there exists a polynomial p(n) such that the algorithm can solve any instance of size n in a time O(p(n)).
3. Problem requiring $\Omega(n^{35})$ time to solve are essentially intractable for large n. Most known polynom al time algorithm run in time $O(n^k)$ for fairly low value of k.

The advantages in considering the class of polynomial-time algorithms is that all reasonable deterministic single processor model of computation can be simulated on each other with at most a polynomial slow-down.

28.11 DECISION PROBLEM

For these problems, the answer is either yes or no or equivalently either true or false.

For example, the problem "Find a Hamiltonian cycle in graph G" is not a decision problem, but "Is graph G Hamiltonian?" is a decision problem.

The theory of NP-Completeness is concerned with the notion of polynomially varifiable properties. Intuitively, a decision problem X is polynomial-time verifiable if someone could show that x in X whenever this is so. Given this example (i.e., x in X), one should be able to verify in polynomial-time (efficiently or easily) that indeed x in X. However, if in fact x not in X, then one should not be falsely show that x in X.

28.11.1 Example: Hamiltonian Cycle

This problem is difficult but it is easily verifiable: If one produces a Hamiltonian cycle, we can easily verify that it is correct. On other hand, nothing one could show to us would convince us that the graph is Hamiltonian if it is not.

Consider a decision problem X. Let the set Q be the proof space of X. A proof system for X is a set F of pairs <x, q>. For any x in X there must exist at least one q in Q such that <x, q> in F; on the other hand no such q must exist when x in X. Therefore, it suffices to such that for some q in Q such that <x, q> in F to convince that x in X.

Formally, F is a subset of X × Q such that

(For all x in X) (There exists q in Q) [<x, q > in F]

Any q such < x, q> in F is called a proof or a certified that x in X.

Note that

(For all x not in X) (For all q in Q) [<x, q > not in F] is implicit in the requirement that F must be a subset of X × Q.

For example, if X is the set of all Hamiltonian graphs, let Q be a set of sequences of graph nodes and define <G, δ) in F if and only if the sequence of nodes δ specifies a Hamiltonian cycle in graph G.

The class NP correspond to the decision problems that have an efficient proof system, which means that each yes-instance must have at least one certificate whose validity can be verified quickly.

Definition

NP is the class of decision problems X that admit a proof system F subset X × Q such that there exists a polynomial p (n) and a polynomial-time algorithm A such that

- For all x in X there exists a q in Q such that <x, q> in F and moreover the size of q is at most p(n), where n is the size of x.
- For all pairs <x, q>, algorithm A can verify whether or not <x, q> in F. In other words, F in P.

The Hamiltonian graph example files this definition. A Hamiltonian cycle in a graph, if it exists, takes less space to describe than the graph itself, and it can be verified in linear time whether a sequence of nodes defines a Hamiltonian cycle.

28.12 OPTIMIZATION PROBLEM

The problems in which some value must be minimized or maximized. Optimization problems can recast in terms of a decision problem by placing a bound on value to be optimized. For example, in recasting the shortest-path problem as the decision.

28.12.1 Polynomial Reduction

Definition

Let A and B two problems. We say that A is polynomially turing reducible to B if there exists an algorithm for sorting A in a time that would be polynomial if we could solve arbitrary instance of problem B at unit cost. This is denoted $A_T = <^P B$.

Note that if $A_T = <^P B$ and $B_T = <^P A$ then $A == {}^P B_T$ and is called polynomially turing equivalent and polynomial reductions are transitive if $A_T = <^P B$ and $B_T = <^P A$ then $A_T = <^P C$.

As an example, prove the polynomial equivalence of two versions of the Hamiltonian problem.

Let

HAM == the problem of finding a Hamiltonian cycle in the graph if one exists and HAMD == the problem of deciding whether or not a graph is Hamiltonian.

We allow an algorithm for HAM to return an arbitrary answer when presented with non-Hamiltonian graph.

The following theorem say that it is not significant harder to find a Hamiltonian cycle than to decide if a graph is Hamiltonian

Theorem: HAM $== {}^P HAMD_T$

Proof:

1. HAMD $< {}^P HAMD_T$ direction
   Consider the following algorithm

```
HamD (G:graph)
    δ ← Ham (G)
    if δ defines a Hamiltonian Cycle
HamD (G: graph)
  δ ← Ham(G)
  if δ defines a Hamiltonian Cycle in G
     then return true
     else return false
```

This algorithm solves HAMD correctly provided algorithm Ham solves problem HAM correctly: by definition of HAM, algorithm Ham must return a Hamiltonian cycle in G provided one exists, in which case HamD correctly return true. Conversely, if the graph is not Hamiltonian, the output 8 returned by Ham cannot be a Hamiltonian cycle, and thus HamD will correctly return false.

If we count the call on Ham at a unit cost then algorithm HamD clearly takes polynomial time.

HAMD $\leq {}^P HAMD_T$ direction

We are to find a Hamiltonian cycle assuming we know how to decide if such cycle exist. The idea is to remove each edge in turn and see whether the graph skill be Hamiltonian. We keep the edge if its removed would make the graph non-Hamiltonian; otherwise remove it

The resulting graph will still be Hamiltonian because we never make a change that would destroy this property. Moreover, the graph contains only the edges necessary to define a Hamiltonian cycle. Therefore, it suffices to follow the edges of the final graph to obtained a Hamiltonian cycle in the original graph.

Here is a greedy algorithm

```
Ham (G = (V, E))
    if HamD(G) = false
        then return "No Solution"
    For each e in E
        do if HamD(<V, A\{e}>)
            then E ← E \{e}
```

δ ← Sequence of nodes obtained by following the unique cycle remaining in G.

If we count each call on HamD at unit cost then clearly Ham takes polynomial time.

28.13 ABSTRACT PROBLEM

We define a n abstract problem Q to be a binary relation on a set I of problem instances and a set of problem solutions.

For example, An instance of SHORTEST-PATH is a triple consisting of a graph and given two vertices, < G, U, V>. A solution is a sequence of vertices in the graph including empty sequence (no path).

1. SHORTEST-PATH: Find a shortest path between two given vertices in an unweight and undirected graph G = (V, E).

In case of decision problem, we can view an abstract decision problem as a function that maps the instance set, I, to the solution set {0, 1}

$f: I \rightarrow \{0, 1\}$

$f: I \rightarrow$ solution $\{0, 1\}$

For example, a decision problem PATH related to this shortest-path problem is, "Given a graph G = (V, E), two vertices u, v in V, and a nonnegative integer k, does a path exist in G between u and v whose length is at most k?

28.14 ENCODINGS

An encoding of a set S of abstract objects is a mapping 'e' from S to the set of binary strings

$e : s \rightarrow$ binary string

For example, encoding of natural number N = {0, 1, 2, 3, 4, ... } as the string {0, 1, 10, 11, 100,... }. Using this encoding e (4) = 100. In the ASCII code e(A) = 100 0001.

Concrete Problem

A problem whose set of instances is the set of binary strings.

28.15 POLYNOMIAL-TIME COMPUTABLE FUNCTION

A function f : {0, 1} →* {0, 1} is polynomial-time computable function if there exists a polynomial time algorithm A that given any input x in {0, 1}*, produces f(x) as output.

The two codings e_1 and e_2 are polynomially related for some set of problem instances I, if there exists two polynomial-time computable function f_{12} and f_{21} such that for any i in I, we have $f_{12}(e_1(i)) = e_2(i)$ and $f_{21}(e_2(i)) = e_1(i)$. That is the encoding $e_2(i)$ can be computed from encoding $e_1()$ by a polynomial-time algorithm, and vice versa.

Lemma: Let Q be an abstract decision problem on an instance set I, and let e_1 and e_2 be polynomially related encoding on I. Then, $e_1(Q)$ in P if and on if $e_2(Q)$ in P.

Proof: Let $e_1(Q)$ can be solved in $O(n^k)$ time

Suppose, for instance i, encoding can be computed from encoding $e_1(i)$ in $O(n^e)$ where $n = |e_2(i)|$

To solve problem $e_2(Q)$ on input $e_2(i)$.

first compute $e_1(i)$

Conversion takes $O(n^e)$ and

therefore, $|e_1(i)| = O(n^e)$.

run algorithm for $e_1(Q)$ on $e_1(i)$

Solving the problem on $e_1(i)$

takes $O[|e_1(i)|^k] = O(n^{ck})$.

Since both c and k are constant therefore $O(n^{ck})$ is polynomial.

And since, the argument in the other is symmetric, this completes the proof.

28.16 FORMAL LANGUAGE

An alphabet S is a finite set of symbols.

A language over S is a subset of the set of all strings of symbols from S.

E is the empty language.

S* is the language consisting of all strings of symbols from S.

Operations on Languages

Interconnection: L_1 Cap L_2

Union: L_1 Cup L_2

Complement: I = –1

Concatenation of L_1 and L_2: L = {x_1x_2: x_1 in L_1 and x_2 in L_2}

Closure or Kleene star of L

L^* = {e} Cup L Cup L^2 Cup L^3 Cup . . .

L^* = L^0 Cup L^1 Cup L^2 Cup . . . Cup L^n

where L^n is L concatenated n times with itself.

From the language theory, perspective, the set of instances for any decision problem Q is the set S^*, where S = {0, 1}.

Since decision problem Q is entirely characterized by those instances of problem that produce a 1 (true) answer, Q can be viewed as a language L over S = {0, 1}, where

L = {x in S^x : Q(x)=1}

For example,

1. The decision problem PATH has the following corresponding language.

PATH = {(G, u, v, k) : G = (V, E) is an undirected graph, u, v in V, k >= 0 is an integer, and there exists a path from u to v in G whose length is atmost k}.

The formal-language expresses the relation between decision problems and algorithms that solve them.

An algorithm A accepts a string x in {0, 1}* if, given input x, the algorithm outputs A(x) = 1.

The language accepted by an algorithm A is the set L = {x in{0,l}^{x} : A(x) =1}, i.e., the set of strings that the algorithm accepta.

An algorithm A rejects a string x if A (x) = 0.

The language L is decided by an algorithm A if every binary string is either accepted or rejected by the algorithm.

A language L is accepted in polynomial time by an algorithm A if for any length-n string x in L, the algorithm accepts x in time for some constant k.

A language L is decided in polynomial time by an algorithm A if for any length-n string x in {0, 1}*, the algorithm decides x $O(n^k)$ time for constant k.

Key Points

To accept a language in polynomial time, an algorithm A consider only strings in L i.e., x in L.

To decide a language in polynomial time, an algorithm A must consider all string in {0, 1}*.

For example, the language PATH, as define above, can be accepted in polynomial time. One polynomial-time accepting algorithm would be

Compute the distance d from u to v using a breadth first search.

Compare: If d ≤ k

then return true {and halt}.

else {keep computing}

An algorithm accepts a strings belonging to PATH in polynomial time. But algorithm is unable to reject a string that does not belong to PATH.

KEY POINT

In order to decide an algorithm must explicitly reject (returns 0 or False) in addition accept (return 1 or True).

28.17 COMPLEXITY CLASS P

Recall P is the set of all decision problem that are solvable in polynomial time.

An algorithm definition by using language theory:

P ={L: L Subset {0,1}* and there exists an algorithm A that decides L in polynomial time}.

Theorem: P = {L: L is accepted by a polynomial-time algorithm}

Proof: The set of language decided by a polynomial-time algorithm is a subset of those accept by a polynomial algorithm.

Only show that if L is accepted by polynomial-time algorithm, it is also decided by a polynomial-time algorithm.

Let L be a language accepted by some polynomial-time algorithm, say A.

Use a "simulation" argument to constant another polynomial-time algorithm A" that decides L.

Because A accept L in $O(n^k)$ time for some constant k, there also exists a constant c such that A accepts L in at most $T = cn^k$ steps.

For input string x, the algorithm A′ simulates the action of A for time T. At the end of time T, algorithm A′ inspects the behavior of A.

If A has accepted x, then A′ accepts x by outputting a 1.

If A has not accepted x, then A′ rejects x by outputting a 0.

The overhead of A′ does not increase the running time by more than a polynomial factor, and thus A′ is a polynomial-time algorithm that decides L.

Note: Algorithm A′ is a polynomial-time algorithm since A is polynomial-time algorithm.

28.17.1 Problems

- 36.1-1 Let us define the optimization problem LONGEST-PATH-LENG as the relation that associates each instance of an undirected graph and the two vertices u and v. The decision problem LONGEST-PATH is define as

LONGEST-PATH =

{<G, u, v, k>: G = (V, E) is an undirected graph, u, v in V, k>=0 is an integer, and there exists a simple path from u to v whose length is at least k}

Our goal is to proof that the optimization problem LONGEST-PATH-LENGTH can be solved in polynomial-time if and only if Longest-Path in P.

Forward direction: If LONGEST-PATH-LENGTH can be solved in polynomial-time then following is a polynomial-time algorithm for LONGEST-PATH.

```
1. INPUT: G, u, v, k.
2. RUN the LONGEST-PATH-LENGTH on G, u, v.
3. Suppose x be the result.
4. If x ≥ k.
5.     then return True.
6.     else return False
```

Clearly this algorithm requires polynomial time provided we count the call on LONGEST-PATH-LENGTH at unit cost and LONGEST-PATH is in P.

Backward Direction: Suppose LONGEST-PATH can be solved in polynomial-time, then following is a polynomial-time algorithm for LONGEST-PATH-LENGTH:

```
1. INPUT: G, u, v
2. FOR k = n-l to 0
      do RUN LONGEST-PATH on G, u, v, k
         IF result of LONGEST-PATH is TRUE
            THEN return k
             ELSE return arbitrary answer.
```

Clearly this requires only polynomial time, and LONGEST-PATH-LENGTH is in P.
This completes the proof.

Problem: Find the longest simple cycle in an undirected graph

To define this problem formally, one could phrase as an "abstract problem", which is a kind of relation:

LONGEST-SIMPLE-PATH = {<G, k>: G =(V, E) is an undirected graph, c is one of the longest simple cycle in G where length is k}.

A closely related decision problem is "Given an undirected graph G = (V, E), and an integer k, does G have a simple cycle of length at least k?

Note that since this is a decision problem, it must give a yes-or-no answer.

The language corresponding to the decision problem is :

SIMPLE-Cycle = {(G, k) is an undirected graph, K>= is an integer, and there exists a simple cycle in G whose length is at least k}.

In the Encodings

A formal encoding of directed graphs as binary strings using adjacency matrix representation.

To encode this type of graph as a bit string, list the bits in the matrix, in left-to-right, top-to-bottom order.

0	1	0	0	1
1	0	1	1	1
0	1	0	1	0
0	1	1	0	1
1	1	1	1	0

This matrix-representation of graph could be encoded as:

0 1 0 0 1 1 0 1 1 1 0 1 0 1 0 0 110111010

Since we know the matrix is square, we can create it by counting the bits in the input, taking the square root, and writing the bits in the matrix in same order. The representation uses order. The representation uses $|V|^2$ bits.

A formal encoding of directed graph as binary string using adjacency-list representation.

This is little more complicated. The simplest thing we could do is to just write an ASCII file, with the nth line of file being the vertex number, followed by the numbers of all the vertices connected to this vertex.

For example, elementary graph algorithms could be written as:

1	2	5		
1	1	5	3	4
1	2	4		
1	2	5	3	
1	4	1	2	

Clearly, an ASCII text file can be represented as a string of bits; that is how one could save some bits by writing the numbers in binary. At any rate, the number of words of memory required for the adjacency-list representation wiil be O(|V| + |E|). Each vertex number will be between 1 and |V|, and so will require Theta (lg|V|) bits to store. So, the total number of bits needed will be O((|V| + |E|) lg|V|)

Now the question is "are these two representations are polynomially related?" To show that these representations are polynomially related, one can how that one representation can be transform into other representation in a polynomial-time.

To Convert the matrix to the adjacency list:

Repeat for every row
    Scan through the row from left-to-right.
    Add the column number to the list

To Convert the adjacency list to matrix:

Start with a matrix M of all 0's.

Let i be a counter of what line you are at. In that line:
    if hit the number j
        then put a 1 at M[i,j]

Suppose that a language L can accept any string x^{is} in L in polynomial time, but that the algorithm that does this runs in superpolynomial time if string x is not in L. Now the question is whether or not a language L cab be decided in polynomial-time. Let n be the size of the input, and assume that we are given some algorithm A and a polynomial p(n) meeting the following conditions:

If a string x is in L, then algorithm A halts and answer yes in no more than p(n) steps.

If the string x is not in L, then we know that string x is in L. If algorithm A answers NO, or has not yet stopped running (does not halt), then we know that string x is not in L.

Therefore, answer to the above question is yes, language L can be decided in polynomial time.

To say same thing in slightly different words we can say that to "accept" a language an algorithm (Turing Machine) halts on all x in L, but may not halt on x not in L. If on 'yes' instance the algorithm always halts in time less that c^{nk} where c and k are constants, then another algorithm can be designed to stop it self after c^{nk} steps, and thus decide the language.

Show that the class P is closed under union, intersection, concatenation, complement, and Kleene star. Put it another way, if L_1, L_2 are in P then L_1 U L_2 is in P, etc. Let L_1, L_2 be in P and A], A_2 be algorithms which decide L_1, L_2 within polynomial time. Then all new algorithm A_3 (below) can be constructed in polynomial time.

L_1 Union L_2 = {x: (x is in L_1) or (x is in L_2) }

```
Algorithm A3 (x)
```

```
IF (A,(x) = I orA2(x)=I)
    THEN return 1;
    ELSE return 0

L1 + L2 = {xy: (x is in L1) and (y is in L2) }

Algorithm A3(z)
(let |z| = n and z = Z]Z2 ... zn)
FOR i = o to n
   do IF (A;(z1 . . . Zi) = 1 and
        A2(zi+1 . . . zn)= 1)
        THEN return 1
return 0
```

28.18 POLYNOMIAL-TIME VERIFICATION

Suppose we are given the instance <G, u, v, k> of the decision problem PATH and a path p from u to v. We can easily check (or verify) that indeed p belongs to PATH (in polynomial-time). The p can be view as a "certificate" or "proof.

Hamiltonian Cycle

A hamiltonian cycle of an undirected graph G = (V, E) is a simple cycle that contains each vertex in V. A hamiltonian graph is a graph with a hamiltonian cycle.

Decision problem Version.

Does a graph G have a hamiltonian cycle?

In formal language:

HAM-CYCLE = {<G> : G is a hamiltonian graph}.

Decide the language HAM-CYCLE?

Brute Force Algorithm

Check all permutations of the vertices of G to see if given instance <G> is a hamiltonian path.

Analysis

If n vertices in the graph, then there are n! permutation and n! is *($2^{nl/2}$). And **. is not $O(n^k)$. Thus, this naive algorithm does run in polynomial time and in fact, no polynomial time algorithm is known (i.e., this problem is NP-complete).

Verification Algorithm

It is a two argument algorithm A(x, y), where x is an input string giving problem instance and y is a binary string giving a proposal solution and called certificate or proof.

A(x, y) = 1, if y is a solution

= 0, otherwise.

An algorithm A verifies an input string x if there exists a certificate y such that A(x, y) = 1.

The formal language verified by a verification algorithm A is

L = {x is in {0, 1}*: there exists y is in {0, 1} such that A(x, y) = 1}

Intuitively, an algorithm A(x, y) verifies a language L is for any string x in L, there is a certificate y that algorithm A(x, y) can use to prove that x belongs to L.

28.19 THE COMPLEXITY CLASS NP

The class of languages (i.e.,) decision problems) that can be verified by polynomial-time algorithm.

Formally, a language L belongs to NP if and only if there exists a two-input polynomial-time algorithm A and constant c such that

L = {x belongs to {x, 1}*: there exists a certificate (proof) y with | y | = $O(|x|^c)$ such that A(x, y) = 1)

We say that algorithm A (x, y) verifies language L in polynomial time.

Lemma: P subset NP

Proof: There is a polynomial-time algorithm B that decides L.

Define A(x, y) = B(x) for any x belongs to {0, 1} * and for any certificate y. Algorithm A (x, y) ignores y and accepts those x belongs to L.

Note that we only need to show that a certificate exists; we don't need to verify a particular certificate.

Complexity class co-NP

This is the set of languages L such that L belongs to NP. It is unknown whether NP = Co-NP.

28.20 REDUCIBILITY

Intuitively, a problem A can be reduced to another problem B if any instance of A can be "rephrased" as an instance of B, the solution to the instance of B provides a solution to the instance of A. A language Li is polynomial-time reducible to another language L_2, denoted $L \leq_p L_2$ if there exists a polynomial-time computable function f:{0, 1}* → {0, 1}* such that for all x belongs to {0, 1}*, x belongs to L_1 if and only if f (x) belongs to L_2. We call the function f the reduction function, and a polynomial-time algorithm F that computes a reduction function f.

Solved Questions

1. Is the traveling salesman (optimization version) NP Complete?

Ans. The best way to understand this is probably to read the discussions below, but in short, while your reasoning is generally correct, your (and my - AC) definition of NP-Complete (NP-C) was wrong. NP-C is defined in terms of decision problems. In the case of the Travelling Salesman Problem (TSP) the decision problem is "does a route exist of length less than k?". You can see that it is trivial to check this, given a path, in polynomial time (just measure the length of the path).

It is true that validating the solution for this decision problem is weaker than finding a minimal path, but finding the path remains as hard (even if the final answer is less aesthetically rewarding). This is by design (on reflection it makes a lot of sense -therwise we would often have the problem that verification is equivalent to the problem itself, as you were thinking in this case).

So, given this corrected definition of NP-C, the TSP is NP-C.

2. What are P, NP, NP-complete, and NP-hard?

Ans. There are two classes of problems, P, and NP (there are many, many more, but we will ignore the rest here). These stand for "Polynomial" and "Non-deterministic Polynomial".

Assuming knowledge of big-O notation, we'll move on from there. Request an explanation and you shall have it.

Problems in P are solvable by a polynomial-time algorithm (runs in $O(f(n))$, where f is polynomial). This includes things like sorting and triangulation.

Problems in NP are checkable by a polynomial-time algorithm, but not necessarily solvable. Generally, we mean NP minus P, when we say NP (so they are only checkable). This means that, given the solution to an instance of the problem, we can verify that it is the correct solution in polynomial time, but that we couldn't have come up with it on our own, in polynomial time. An easy example of this is subset sum: given a set of numbers, does there exist a subset whose sum is zero? It turns out that this is not solvable in polynomial time, but given the answer, we can easily check that it is right (the decision problem is a little harder to see, but assume you are given the actual subset).

Now, we have to discuss NP-Complete and NP-Hard, which requires a discussion of reducibility. Reducibility is the notion that, given an instance of some hard problem, we can quickly construct an instance of some other problem, whose answer would help us solve the first problem.

The typical logic is this: you claim to have a fast algorithm to, say, solve subset sum. I create a machine that, in polynomial time, takes a traveling salesman problem instance, and creates from it, an instance of subset sum. If you can give my machine the answer to that question, it will, again in polynomial time, change that back into the answer for my original traveling salesman problem. Therefore, if your subset sum algorithm is really polynomial, then I have just added some extra bits to it and created a polynomial time algorithm for solving traveling salesman problems. If I can create such a machine, then it creates a notion of reducibility, that is, traveling salesman is reducible to subset sum, which indicates that subset sum is at least as hard as traveling salesman. Intuitively, one might imagine that with all the universal truth out there, one could say that traveling salesman has no polynomial-time solution. In that case, the above would be a proof by contradiction, that subset sum also has no polynomial time solution.

Now, we can pretty easily state what NP-Complete and NP-Hard are:

If two problems can be reduced to each-other, they are in some sense, "equivalent". All problems in NP that are so equivalent, are called NP-Complete.

If there is an NP-Complete problem that can be reduced to some problem H, then H is NP-Hard. This means that, in some sense, H is at least as hard as all the NP-Complete problems, but note that there does not need to be a reduction from H to any NP-Complete problem, so H might be harder than all the NP problems.

One proves that a problem is NP-Hard by taking an existing NP-Complete problem (3-SAT and Traveling Salesman are my favorites, since they work well for geometry), and using it to generate input to your problem, such that an answer to your problem is equivalent to solving the NP-Complete problem you chose.

3. What is an NP-complete problem?

Ans. NP stands for Non-deterministic Polynomial time.

This means that the problem can be solved in Polynomial time using a Non-deterministic Turing machine (like a regular Turing machine but also including a non-deterministic "choice" function). Basically, a solution has to be testable in poly time. If that's the case, and a known NP problem can be solved using the given problem with modified input (an NP problem can be reduced to the given problem) then the problem is NP complete.

The main thing to take away from an NP-complete problem is that it cannot be solved in polynomial time in any known way. NP-Hard/NP-Complete is a way of showing that certain classes of problems are not solvable in realistic time.

Edit: As others have noted, there are often approximation solutions for NP-Complete problems. In this case, the approximation solution usually gives a approximation bound using special notation which tells us how close the approximation is.

Previous Year University Question

1. Explain NP-completeness theory. [OU]
2. Explain P, NP and NP complete. [GGSIPU]
3. Show relationship between P, NP, NP-complete, NP-Hard problems. [OU]
4. Show that CNF-satisfiability is reducable to Clique decision problem. [OU]
5. Distinguish between NP-hard and NP-complete problems giving one example for each. [OU]
6. Explain the "satisfiability problem". [OU]

7. **Explain the clique decision problem.** **[OU]**
8. **Discuss the relationship between the class P. NP, NP-complete and NP-Hard problems with suitable example of each class.** **[GBTU]**
9. **Write short note on**
   (i) Cook's Theorem
   (ii) NP Hard and NP Complete Problem
   (iii) Prove that travelling salesman problem is NP hard
   (iv) Satisfiability **[MDU]**

Exercises

1. **Show that an algorithm that makes at most a constant number of calls to polynomial-time subroutines runs in polynomial time, but that a polynomial number of calls to polynomial-time subroutines may result in an exponential-time algorithm.**
2. **A Hamiltonian path in a graph is a simple path that visits every vertex exactly once. Show that the decision problem of determining whether or not there is a Hamiltonian path from a given vertex u to another given vertex v belongs to NP**
3. **Show that the $\leq$ relation is a transitive relation on the set of problems.**
4. **Given an undirected graph, the Hamiltonian cycle problem determines whether a graph has a Hamiltonian cycle. Given that the Hamiltonian cycle problem for undirected graphs is NP-Complete, what can you say about the Hamiltonian cycle problem for directed graphs? Provide reasons for your answer.**

CHAPTER

29

MATRIX OPERATIONS

29.1 INTRODUCTION

The rules for addition, substraction, multiplications and divisions between matrices are as follows. Let first assume that matrix A and are used to construct matrix . It must follows that for

Addition: A $_{ij}$ = ay by

Substraction: = A $_{ij}$ = ay by

ultiplication: Z = A* , if columns in A = rows in B; $_{ij} = a_{i1} * b_{ij} + a_{i2} * b_{2j} + a_{i3} * b_{3j} + \ldots a_{im} * b_{nj}$

The rules for multiplication and division o a matri by a scalar (a real number) are simpler. If matrix Z is constructed by multiplying all elements of matrix A by a scalar c, hen its elements are $_{ij} = c*a_{ij}$. In an analogous manner, dividing matrix A by c gives $_{ij} = (l/c)*a_{ij}$.

All these operations are illustrated in Figure 1. Let's revisit these one by one.

If $A = \begin{bmatrix} 3 & 6 \\ 5 & 8 \\ 2 & 9 \end{bmatrix}$ $\begin{bmatrix} -6 & 1 \\ 0 & 9 \\ 8 & 3 \end{bmatrix}$ then A $\begin{bmatrix} -3 & 7 \\ 5 & 17 \\ 5 & 12 \end{bmatrix}$ then A $\begin{bmatrix} 9 & 5 \\ 5 & -1 \\ -10 & 6 \end{bmatrix}$

if c 2 then $cA = \begin{bmatrix} 6 & 12 \\ 10 & 16 \\ -4 & 18 \end{bmatrix}$ then $A\,c = \begin{bmatrix} 1.5 & 3 \\ 2.5 & 4 \\ -1 & 4.5 \end{bmatrix}$

if $A = \begin{bmatrix} 4 & 1 & 9 \\ 6 & 2 & 8 \\ 11 & 10 & 12 \end{bmatrix}$ $\begin{bmatrix} 2 & 9 \\ 5 & 12 \\ 8 & 10 \end{bmatrix}$ then A* $= \begin{bmatrix} 85 & 138 \\ 86 & 158 \\ 69 & 149 \\ 168 & 339 \end{bmatrix}$

Fig. 29.1: Some matrix operations.

29.2 ADDITION AND SUBSTRACTION OF MATRICES

To add or substract matrices these must be of identical order. This just means that the matrices involved must have the same number of rows and columns. If they don't have the same number of rows and columns we cannot add or substract these.

The expression

$$Z_{ij} = a_{ij} + b_{ij}$$

means "to element in row i, column j of matrix A add element in row i, column j of matrix . If we do this with each element of A and B we end with matrix . An example is given in Figure 2.

$$\mathbf{A}=\begin{bmatrix}3 & 6\\5 & 8\\-2 & 9\end{bmatrix}\mathbf{B}=\begin{bmatrix}-6 & 1\\0 & 9\\8 & 3\end{bmatrix}\mathbf{Z}=\mathbf{A}+\mathbf{B}=\begin{bmatrix}-3 & 7\\5 & 17\\6 & 12\end{bmatrix}$$

$$Z_{ij} = a_{ij} + b_{ij}$$

$z_{11} = 3 + -6 = -3$	$z_{12} = 6 + 1 = 7$
$z_{21} = 5 + 0 = 5$	$z_{22} = 8 + 9 = 17$
$z_{31} = -2 + 8 = 6$	$z_{32} = 9 + 3 = 12$

Fig 29.2: Addition operation

Substraction is performed in analogous manner. The expression

$$z_{ij} = a_{ij} - by$$

means "to element in row i, column j of matrix A deduct element in row i, column j of matrix B". If we do this with each element of A and B we end with matrix Z. See Figure 3.

$$\mathbf{A}=\begin{bmatrix}3 & 6\\5 & 8\\-2 & 9\end{bmatrix}\mathbf{B}=\begin{bmatrix}-6 & 1\\0 & 9\\8 & 3\end{bmatrix}\mathbf{Z}=\mathbf{A}\ \ \mathbf{B}=\begin{bmatrix}9 & 5\\5 & -1\\-10 & 6\end{bmatrix}$$

$$z_{ij} = a_{ij} - b_{ij}$$

$z_{11} = 3 - (-6) = 9$	$z_{12} = 6 - 1 = 5$
$z_{21} = 5 - 0 = 5$	$z_{22} = 8 - 9 = -1$
$z_{31} = -2 - 8 = -6$	$z_{32} = 9 - 3 = 6$

Fig 29.3: Substraction operation.

29.3 MULTIPLICATION OF MATRICES

Consider two matrices A and B with the following characteristics: the number of columns in A equals the number of rows in B. These are conformable with respect to one another, and they can be multiplied together to form a new matrix Z.

The expression

$$z_{ij} = a_{ij} * b_{1j} + a_{i2} * b_{2j} + a_{3j} * b_{3j} + \ldots a_{im} * b_{nj}$$

means "add the products obtained by multiplying elements in each i row of matrix A by elements in each j column of matrix B". Figure 4 illustrates what we mean by this statement.

$$A=\begin{bmatrix}4 & 1 & 9\\ 6 & 2 & 8\\ 7 & 3 & 5\\ 11 & 10 & 12\end{bmatrix} \quad B=\begin{bmatrix}2 & 9\\ 5 & 12\\ 8 & 10\end{bmatrix} \quad Z=A*B=\begin{bmatrix}85 & 138\\ 86 & 158\\ 69 & 149\\ 168 & 339\end{bmatrix}$$

$$z_{ij} = a_{i1} * b_{1j} + b_{2j} + a_{i3} + ... a_{im} * b_{nj}$$

$z_{11} = 4*2 + 1*5 + 9*8 = 85$ $z_{21} = 4*9 + 1*12 + 9*10 = 138$

$z_{21} = 6*2 + 2*5 + 8*8 = 86$ $z_{22} = 6*9+ 2*12+ 8*10 = 158$

$z_{31} =7*2 + 3*5+5*8 = 69$ $z_{32} = 7*9 + 3*12 + 5*10 = 149$

$z_{41} = 11*2+ 10*5 + 12*8= 168$ $z_{42}= 11*9 + 10*12 + 12*10 = 339$

Fig 29.4. Multiplication operation

Matrix multiplication has a catch as we mentioned before. The order in which we multiply terms does matter. The reason for this is that we need to multiply row elements by column elements and one by one. Therefore A*B and B*A can produce different results. We say "can produce" because there exist special cases in which the operation is conmutative (order does not matter).

29.4 MULTIPLICATION AND DIVISION OF MATRICES BY A SCALAR

The rules for multiplication and division of a matrix by a scalar are similar. Since multiplying a number x by 1/c is the same as dividing x by c, lets consider these operations at once. If all elements of matrix A are multiplied by a scalar c to construct matrix Z, hence $z_{ij} = c*a_{ij}$. Similarly dividing matrix A by c gives $z_{ij} = (l/c)*a_{ij}$. The expression $z_{ij} = c*a_{ij}$ means "multiply each element in row i column j times c", and the expression $z_{ij} = l/c*a_{ij} = a_{ij}/c$ means "divide each element in row i column j by c". These two operations are shown in Figure 5, where c = 2.

$$A = \begin{bmatrix}3 & 6\\ 5 & 8\\ -2 & 9\end{bmatrix} \quad Z= CA = \begin{bmatrix}6 & 12\\ 10 & 16\\ -4 & 18\end{bmatrix} \quad Z = \frac{A}{C} = \begin{bmatrix}1.5 & 3\\ 2.5 & 4\\ -1 & 4.5\end{bmatrix}$$

$$z_{ij} = c*aij \qquad z_{ij} = \frac{a_{ij}}{c}$$

if   c = 2   if   c = 2

$z_{11} = 2*3 = 6$ $z_{12} = 2*6 = 12$ $z_{11} = 3/2 = 1.5$ $z_{12} = 6/2 = 3$

$z_{21} = 2*5 = 10$ $z_{22} = 2*8 = 16$ $z_{21}= 5/2 = 2.5$ $z_{22} = 8/2 = 4$

$z_{31} = 2*(-2) = -4$ $z_{32} = 2*9 = 18$ $z_{31} = -2/2 = -1$ $z_{32} = 9/2 = 4.5$

Fig 29.5 Multiplication and division of a matrix by a scalar

Figure 6 shows that a scalar matrix is obtained when an identity matrix is multiplied by a scalar. As we will see in Part 3 of this tutorial, deducting a scalar matrix from a regular matrix is an important operation.

$$I = \begin{bmatrix} 1 & 0 & 0 \\ 0 & 1 & 0 \\ 0 & 0 & 1 \end{bmatrix} = c*1 = \begin{bmatrix} c & 0 & 0 \\ 0 & c & 0 \\ 0 & 0 & c \end{bmatrix}$$

Identitymatrix   Scalar matrix

Fig 29.6 Scalar matrix obtained by multiplying an identity matrix by a scalar.

29.5 ORTHOGONAL MATRICES

A regular matrix (one whose determinant is not equal to zero) M is said to be orthogonal if when multiplied by its transpose the identity matrix I is obtained; i.e., $M*M^T = I$. Orthogonal matrices have interesting properties. If M is orthogonal:

1. its transpose and inverse are identical: $M^T = M^{-1}$
2. when multiplied by its transpose the product is commutative: $M*M^T = M^T*M$.
3. its transpose is also an orthogonal matrix.
4. when multipled by an orthogonal matrix the product is an orthogonal matrix.
5. its determinant is +/– 1. The reverse is not necessarily true; i.e., not all matrices whose determinant is +/– 1 are orthogonal.
6. the sum of the square of the elements in a given row or column is equal to 1.
7. when multiplied, the corresponding elements in two rows or columns-i.e., dot product- is equal to zero.

Conversely, a square matrix (one with same number of rows and columns) is orthogonal if the following conditions both exist:

1. the sum of the square of the elements in every row or column is equal to 1.
2. the sum of the products of corresponding elements in every pair of rows or columns -i.e., dot products- is equal to zero.

As we can see, it is quite easy to determine if a regular or square matrix is orthogonal. Just look for any of these properties.

29.6 TRANSPOSE AND INVERSE PROPERTIES

The following transpose properties are observed in matrices

$$(ABC)^T = C^T B^T A^T$$
$$(ABC^T)^T = (C^T)^T B^T A^T = C B^T A^T$$

The following inverse properties are observed in matrices

$$(ABC)^{-1} = C^{-1} B^{-1} A^{-1}$$
$$(ABC^{-1})^{-1} = (C^{-1})^{-1} B^{-1} = C B^{-1} A^{-1}$$
$$A^{-1} A = A A^{-1} = I = 1$$

Since matrix division is not defined, it is impossible to divide a matrix expression by a given matrix. However, the desired effect is achieved by multiplying the expression by the inverse of the given matrix (2).

29.7 DETERMINANTS

Although the following is an incomplete definition, a determinant (det) can be described as a function that associates a scalar to a square matrix. This can assume any real value including zero. A matrix with a nonzero determinant is an invertible matrix (we can calculate its inverse matrix). If the determinat is zero (det = 0) is called a non-invertible matrix. Don't worry about matrix inversions, yet.

To indicate that we are referring to determinant A and not to matrix A we surround the symbol A by pipes ("|"). The symbolic definition of a determinant for a matrix A is shown in Figure 7 and for m = n = 2 and m = n = 3

$$|A| = \Sigma(-1)^{V} a_{1i} * a_{2j} * a_{3j} ... a_{nt}$$

for n = 2 $\quad n! = 2*1 = 2$ terms

$$|A| = a_{11}{}^{*} - a_{12}{}^{*} a_{21}$$

for = 3 $\quad n!3*2*1 = 6$ terms

$$|A| = a11*a22*a33 + a12*a23*a31 + a13*a21*a32 - a12*a21*a33 - a13*a22*a31 - a11*a23*a32$$

Fig. 29.7 Some determinants.

In the figure, the second subscripts are all distinct, the number of terms is n! and v is the number of inversions of the second subscripts. Thus, the determinant of a matrix of order n=2 has two terms and 1 negative sign and the determinant of a matrix of order n =3 has 6 terms and 3 negative signs. Sample calculations are given in Figure 8.

$$A = \begin{bmatrix} 13 & 5 \\ 2 & 4 \end{bmatrix}$$

m = n = 2 square matrix

$$|A| = a_{11}{}^{*} a_{22} - a_{12}{}^{*} a_{21}$$

$$|A| = 13*4 - 2*5 = 52 - 10$$

$$|A| = 42$$

$$A = \begin{bmatrix} 12 & 6 & -9 \\ 3 & 18 & 15 \\ 4 & 11 & 5 \end{bmatrix} \text{m = n = 3 square matrix}$$

$$|A| = a11*a22*a33*a12*a23*a13*a21*a32 - a12*a21*a33*a13*a22*a31*a11*a23*a32*$$

$$|A| = 12*8*5 + 6*15*4 + (-9)*3*11 - (-9)*8*8 - 12*15*11 - 6*3*5$$

$$|A| = -1239$$

Fig 29.8: Sample calculations of determinants

There are other methods for solving determinants (triangularization, reduction methods, etc). For large matrices there are plenty of software solutions to choose from.

If the determinant of a square matrix is not zero, its matrix is described as a regular matrix. If the determinant is zero, its matrix is described as a singular matrix. The problem of transforming a regular matrix into a singular matrix is referred to as the éigenvalue problem.

29.8. STRASSEN ALGORITHM

In the mathematical discipline of linear algebra, the Strassen algorithm, named after Volker Strassen, is an algorithm used for matrix multiplication. It is faster than the standard matrix multiplication algorithm, but would be slower than the fastest known algorithm for extremely large matrices, and is useful in practice for large matrices.

29.8.1. Algorithm

Let A, B be two square matrices over a ring R. We want to calculate the matrix product C as C = AB

$A, B, C \in R^{2^n \times 2^n}$

If the matrices A, B are not of type $2^n \times 2^n$ we fill the missing rows and columns with zeros. We partition A. B and C into equally sized block matrices

$$A = \begin{bmatrix} A_{1,1} & A_{1,2} \\ A_{2,1} & A_{2,2} \end{bmatrix}, B = \begin{bmatrix} B_{1,1} & B_{1,2} \\ B_{2,1} & B_{2,2} \end{bmatrix}, C = \begin{bmatrix} C_{1,1} & C_{1,2} \\ C_{2,1} & C_{2,2} \end{bmatrix}$$

with

$$A_{i,j}, B_{i,j}, C_{i,j} \in R^{n-1} \times 2^{n-1}$$

then

$$C_{1,1} = A_{1,1} + B_{1,1} + A_{1,2} B_{2,1}$$
$$C_{1,2} = A_{1,1} + B_{1,2} + A_{1,2} B_{2,2}$$
$$C_{2,2} = A_{2,1} + B_{1,2} + A_{2,2} B_{2,2}$$

With this construction we have not reduced the number of multiplications. We still need 8 multiplications to calculate the $C_{i,j}$ matrices, the same number of multiplications we need when using standard matrix multiplication.

Now comes the important part. We define new matrices

$$M_1 := (A_{1,1} + A_{2,2})(B_{1,1} + B_{2,2})$$
$$M_2 := (A_{2,1} + A_{2,2})B_{1,1}$$
$$M_3 := A_{1,1}(B_{1,1} - B_{2,2})$$
$$M_4 := A_{1,1}(B_{2,1} - B_{1,1})$$
$$M_5 := (A_{1,1} + A_{1,2})B_{2,2}$$
$$M_6 := (A_{2,1} - A_{1,1})(B_{1,1} + B_{1,2})$$
$$M_7 := (A_{1,2} - A_{2,2})(B_{2,1} + B_{2,2})$$

which are then used to express the $C_{i,j}$ in terms of M_k Because of our definition of the M_k we can eliminate one matrix multiplication and reduce the number of multiplications to 7 (one multiplication for each M_k) and express the $C_{i,j}$ as

$$C_{1,1} = M_1 + M_4 - M_5 + M_7$$

$$C_{1,2} = M_3 + M_5$$
$$C_{2,1} = M_2 + M_4$$
$$C_{2,2} = M_1 - M_2 + M_3 + M_6$$

We iterate this division process n times until the submatrices degenerate into numbers (elements of the ring R).

Practical implementations of Strassen's algorithm switch to standard methods of matrix multiplication for small enough submatrices, for which those algorithms are more efficient. The particular crossover point for which Strassen's algorithm is more efficient depends on the specific implementation and hardware.

29.8.2 Asymptotic complexity

The standard matrix multiplication takes approximately $2N^3$ (where $N = 2^n$) arithmetic operations (additions and multiplications); the asymptotic complexity is $O(N^3)$.

The number of additions and multiplications required in the Strassen algorithm can be calculated as follows: let f (n) be the number of operations for a $2^n \times 2^n$ matrix. Then by recursive application of the Strassen algorithm, we see that $f(n) = 7f(n-1) + l4^n$, for some constant l that depends on the number of additions performed at each application of the algorithm. Hence $f(n) = (7 + o(l))^n$, i.e., the asymptotic complexity for multiplying matrices of size $N = 2^n$ using the Strassen algorithm is

$$O([7 + o(l)]^n) = O(N^{\log_2 7+0(1)}) \approx O(N^{2.807}) \approx O(N^{2.807})$$

The reduction in the number of arithmetic operations however comes at the price of a some what reduced numerical stability.

29.9 Matrix chain multiplication

Matrix chain multiplication is an optimization problem that can be solved using dynamic programming. Given a sequence of matrices, we want to find the most efficient way to multiply these matrices together. The problem is not actually to perform the multiplications, but merely to decide in which order to perform the multiplications.

We have many options because matrix multiplication is associative. In other words, no matter how we parenthesize the product, the result will be the same. For example, if we had four matrices A, B, C, and D, we would have:

$$(ABC)D = (AB)(CD) = A(BCD) = A(BC)D = ...$$

However, the order in which we parenthesize the product affects the number of simple arithmetic operations needed to compute the product, or the efficiency. For example, suppose A is a 10×30 matrix, B is a 30×5 matrix, and C is a 5×60 matrix. Then,

$$(AB)C = (10\times30\times5) + (10\times5\times60) = 1500 + 3000 = 4500 \text{ operations}$$
$$A(BC) = (30\times5\times60) + (10\times30\times60) = 9000 + 18000 = 27000 \text{ operations.}$$

Clearly the first method is the more efficient. Now that we have identified the problem, how do we determine the optimal parenthesization of a product of n matrices? We could go through each possible parenthesization (brute force), but this would require time 0(2"), which is very slow and impractical for large n. The solution, as we will see, is to break up the problem into a set of related subproblems. By solving subproblems one time and reusing these solutions many times, we can drastically reduce the time required. This is known as dynamic programming.

29.9.1. A Dynamic Programming Algorithm

To begin, let's assume that all we really want to know is the minimum cost, or minimum number of arithmetic operations, needed to multiply out the matrices. If we're only multiplying two matrices, there's only one way to multiply them, so the minimum cost is the cost of doing this. In general, we can find the minimum cost using the following recursive algorithm:

- Take the sequence of matrices and separate it into two subsequences.
- Find the minimum cost of multiplying out each subsequence.
- Add these costs together, and add in the cost of multiplying the two result matrices.
- Do this for each possible position at which the sequence of matrices can be split, and take the minimum over all of them.

For example, if we have four matrices ABCD, we compute the cost required to find each of (A)(BCD), (AB)(CD), and (ABC)(D), making recursive calls to find the minimum cost to compute ABC, AB, CD, and BCD. We then choose the best one. Better still, this yields not only the minimum cost, but also demonstrates the best way of doing the multiplication: just group it the way that yields the lowest total cost, and do the same for each factor.

Unfortunately, if we implement this algorithm we discover that it's just as slow as the naive way of trying all permutations! What went wrong? The answer is that we're doing a lot of redundant work. For example, above we made a recursive call to find the best cost for computing both ABC and AB. But finding the best cost for computing ABC also requires finding the best cost for AB. As the recursion grows deeper, more and more of this type of unnecessary repetition occurs.

One simple solution is called memoization: each time we compute the minimum cost needed to multiply out a specific subsequence, we save it. If we are ever asked to compute it again, we simply give the saved answer, and do not recompute it. Since there are about $n^2/2$ different subsequences, where n is the number of matrices, the space required to do this is reasonable. It can be shown that this simple trick brings the runtime down to $0(n^3)$ from 0(2"), which is more than efficient enough for real applications. This is top-down dynamic programming.

Pseudocode:

```
Matrix-Chain-Order(int p[])
{
    n = p.length - 1;
    for  (i = 1; i <= n; i++)
        m[i,i] = 0;
  for (L=2; L<=n; L++) { // L is chain length
      for (i=l; i<=n-L+l; i++)  {
          j = i+L-1;
          m[i,j] = MAXINT;
          for (k=i; k<=j-l; k++)    {
              q = m[i,k] + m[k+l,j] + p [i-1]*p[k]*p[j];//Matrix Ai has
the dimension  p[i-l] x p[i].
              if  (q < m[i,j]) {
                  m[i,j] = q;
                  s[i,j ] = k;
              }
          }
      }
  }
}
```

- Note : The first index for p is 0 and the first index for m and s is 1

Another solution is to anticipate which costs we will need and precompute them. It works like this:

- For each k from 2 to n, the number of matrices:
    - o Compute the minimum costs of each subsequence of length k, using the costs already computed.

When we're done, we have the minimum cost for the full sequence. Although it also requires $O(n^3)$ time, this approach has the practical advantages that it requires no recursion, no testing if a value has already been computed, and we can save space by throwing away some of the subresults that are no longer needed. This is bottom-up dynamic programming: a second way by which this problem can be solved.

Solved Questions

1. Explain Strassen's Matrix Multiplication.

Ans. It uses only 7 scalar multiplications to multiply two 2x2 matrices. It divides each of A,B and C matrices into four n/2 x n/2 matrices and rewriting equation C=AB as:

$$\begin{pmatrix} r & s \\ t & u \end{pmatrix} = \begin{pmatrix} a & b \\ c & d \end{pmatrix} \begin{pmatrix} e & f \\ g & h \end{pmatrix}$$

r =P5+P4-P2+P6

s=P1+P2

t=P3+P4

u=P5+P1-P3-P7

Where:

P1=a(f-h)

P2=(a+b)h

P3=(c+d)e

P4=d(g-e)

P5=(a+d)(e+h)

P6=(b-d)(g+h)

P7=(a-c)(e+f)

2. What is the time complexity for matrix multiplication and Strassen's Matrix Multiplication?

Ans. Matrix Multiplication=$\Theta(n^3)$

Strassen's Matrix Multiplication: $\Theta(n^{2.81})$

3. What is Matrix Chain Multiplication Problem?

Ans. Suppose we have a sequence or chain $A_1, A_2, \ldots, A_n$ of n matrices to be multiplied. There are many possible ways (parenthesizations) to compute the product

Example: consider the chain $A_1, A_2, A_3, A_4$of 4 matrices

Let us compute the product $A_1A_2A_3A_4$

There are 5 possible ways:

$(A_1 (A_2 (A_3 A_4)))$

$(A_1 ((A_2 A_3) A_4))$

$((A_1 A_2)(A_3 A_4))$

$((A_1 (A_2 A_3)) A_4)$

$(((A_1 A_2) A_3) A_4)$

Matrix-chain multiplication problem states that given a chain $A_1, A_2, \ldots, A_n$ of n matrices, where for i=1, 2, …, n, matrix Ai has dimension $p_{i-1} \times p_i$. Parenthesize the product $A_1, A_2, \ldots, A_n$ such that the total number of scalar multiplications is minimized.

Previous Year University Question

1. Write Strassen's Matrix multiplication algorithm. Determine the time complexity. [OU09]
2. Use strassen's algorithm to compute the product of two given matrices:

$$\begin{bmatrix} 1 & 3 \\ 5 & 7 \end{bmatrix} \text{ and } \begin{bmatrix} 8 & 4 \\ 6 & 2 \end{bmatrix}$$ [GBTU]

3. Explain Strassen's matrix multiplication with suitable example. [MDU]

Exercise

1. Prove that $(x\ y)^T = Y^T\ X^T$
2. Prove that if X and Y are inverse of Z then X = Y.
3. Prove that for any two matrices X and Y. rank (X, Y) $\leq$ min (rank (X), rank (Y)).
4. Use strarren's algorithm to compute the matrix product

$$\begin{pmatrix} 1 & 4 \\ 8 & 9 \end{pmatrix}\begin{pmatrix} 5 & 6 \\ 2 & 4 \end{pmatrix}$$

5. What is the largest x such that if you can multiply 3 × 3 matrix using x multiplication then you can multiply n × n matrix in time O (n^{lg} 7)?

CHAPTER 30

BACKTRACKING

30.1 INTRODUCTION

Backtracking is a general algorithm for finding all (or some) solutions to some computational problem, that incrementally builds candidates to the solutions, and abandons each partial candidate c ("backtracks") as soon as it determines that c cannot possibly be completed to a valid solution.

The classic textbook example of the use of backtracking is the eight queens puzzle, that asks for all arrangements of eight queens on a standard chessboard so that no queen attacks any other. In the common backtracking approach, the partial candidates are arrangements of k queens in the first k rows of the board, all in different rows and columns. Any partial solution that contains two mutually attacking queens can be abandoned, since it cannot possibly be completed to a valid solution. Backtracking can be applied only for problems which admit the concept of a "partial candidate solution" and a relatively quick test of whether it can possibly be completed to a valid solution. It is useless, for example, for locating a given value in an unordered table. When it is applicable, however, backtracking is often much faster than brute force enumeration of all complete candidates, since it can eliminate a large number of candidates with a single test.

Backtracking is an important tool for solving constraint satisfaction problems, such as crosswords, verbal arithmetic, Sudoku, and many other puzzles. It is often the most convenient (if not the most efficient technique for parsing, for the knapsack problem and other combinatorial optimization problems. It is also the basis of the so-called logic programming languages such as Icon, Planner and Prolog. Backtracking is also utilized in the (diff) difference engine for the MediaWiki software.

Backtracking depends on user-given "black box procedures" that define the problem to be solved, the nature of the partial candidates, and how they are extended into complete candidates. It is therefore a metaheuristic rather than a specific algorithm — although, unlike many other meta-heuristics, it is guaranteed to find all solutions to a finite problem in a bounded amount of time. The term "backtrack" was coined by American mathematician D. H. Lehmer in the 1950s. The pioneer string-processing language SNOBOL (1962) may have been the first to provide a built-in general backtracking facility.

30.2. Pseudocode

In order to apply backtracking to a specific class of problems, one must provide the data P for the particular instance of theproblem that is to be solved, and six procedural parameters. root, reject, accept, first, next, and output. These procedures should take the instance data P as a parameter and should do the following:

1. root("P"): return the partial candidate at the root of the search tree.
2. reject(P,c): return true only if the partial candidate c is not worth completing.
3. accept(P,c): return true if c is a solution of P, and false otherwise.

4. first(,c) generate the first extension of candidate c.
5. next(,s) generate the next alternative extension of a candidate, after the extension s.
6. output(,c) use the solution c of , as appropriate to the application.

The backtracking algorithm reduces then to the call bt(root( )), where bt is the following recursive procedure:

```
procedure bt(c)
    if reject(P, c)    then return
    if accept(P,c)     then output (P, c)
    s ← then first (P, c)
  hile s ≠ Λ do
bt (s)
s ← next (P, s)
```

30.3. USAGE CONSIDERATIONS

The reject procedure should be a boolean-valued function that returns true only if it is certain that no possible extension of c is a valid solution for . If the procedure cannot reach a definite conclusion, it should return false. An incorrect true result may cause the bt procedure to miss some valid solutions. The procedure may assume that reject(,t) returned false for every ancestor t of c in the search tree. On the other hand, the efficiency of the backtracking algorithm depends on reject returning true for candidates that are as close to the root as possible. If reject always returns false, the algorithm will still find all solutions, but it will be equivalent to a brute-force search.

The accept procedure should return true if c is a complete and valid solution for the problem instance , and false otherwise. It may assume that the partial candidate c and all its ancestors in the tree have passed the reject test. Note that the general pseudo-code above does not assume that the valid solutions are always leaves of the potential search tree. In other words, it admits the possibility that a valid solution for can be further extended to yield other valid solutions.

The first and next procedures are used by the backtracking algorithm to enumerate the children of a node c of the tree, that is, the candidates that differ from c by a single extension step. The call first(,c) should yield the first child of c, in some order; and the call next(,s) should return the next sibling of node s, in that order. Both functions should return a distinctive "null" candidate, denoted here by Λ', if the requested child does not exist.

Together, the root, first, and next functions define the set of partial candidates and the potential search tree. They should be chosen so that every solution of occurs somewhere in the tree, and no partial candidate occurs more than once. Moreover, they should admit an efficient and effective reject predicate.

30.4. EARLY STOPPING VARIANTS

The pseudo-code above will call output for every candidate that is a solution to the given instance . The algorithm is easily modified to stop after finding the first solution, or a specified number of solutions; or after testing a specified number of partial candidates, or after spending a given amount of CPU time.

30.5 THE N-QUEENS PROBLEM

Fig. 30.1 N Queens Problem

What is the maximum number of queens that can be placed on an ^{nXn}chessboard such that no two attack one another? The answer is "queens, which gives eight queens for the usual 8x8Aboard The number of different ways the "queens can be placed on an nxn chessboard so that no two queens may attack each other for the first few "are 1, 0, 0, 2, 10, 4, 40, 92, ... The number of rotationally and reflectively distinct solutions are 1, 0, 0, 1,2, 1, 6, 12, 46, 92, ... The 12 distinct solutions for n = 8are illustrated above, and the remaining 80 are generated by rotation and reflection

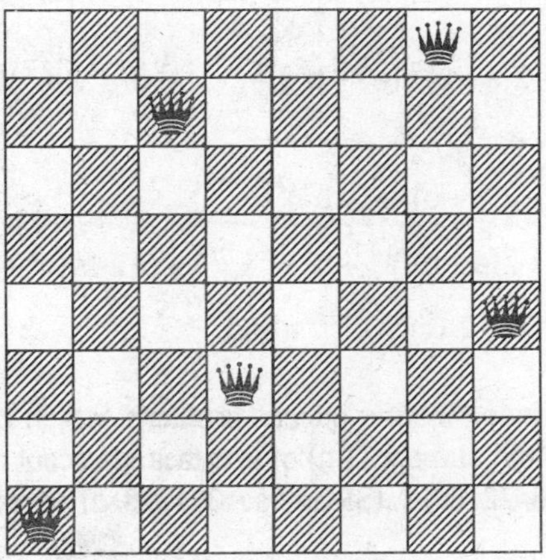

Fig. 30.2 N Queens Problem for $n = 8$

The minimum number of queens needed to occupy or attack all squares of an 8x8 board is 5 Dudeney gave the following results for the number of distinct arrangements x-"(A- "'of fe queens attacking or occupying every square of an nxn board for which every queen is attacked ("protected") by at least one other, with the n= 8value given by Steinhaus The 4860 solutions in the n = 5 case may be obtained from 638 fundamental arrangements by rotation and reflection.

k queens	$n \times n$	$N_P(k, n)$
3	4	3
3	5	37
3	6	1
4	7	5
5	8	4860

Dudeney also gave the following results for the number of distinct arrangements n_u (k, n) of k queens attacking or occupying every square of an $n \times n$ board for which no two queens attack one another (they are "not protected").

queens	$n \times n$	$N_P(k, n)$
1	2	1
1	3	1
3	4	2
3	5	2
3	6	17
4	7	1
4	8	91

Vardi generalizes the problem from a square chessboard to one with the topology of the torus. The number of solutions for n queens with n odd are 1, 0, 10, 28, 0, 88, ... Vardi also considers the toroidal "semiqueens" problem, in which a semiqueen can move like a rook or bishop, but only on positive broken diagonals. The number of solutions to this problem for n queens with n odd are 1, 3, 15, 133, 2025, 37851, ... and 0 for even n.

Velucchi gives the solution to the question, "How many different arrangements of k queens are possible on an order n chessboard?" as l/8th of the coefficient of $a^k\, b^{k^2-k}$ in the polynomial

$$p(a, b, n) = \begin{cases} (a+b)^2 + 2(a+b)^n (a^2+b^2)^{(n^2-2)/2} + 3(a^2+b^2)^{n^2/2} + 2(a^4+b^4)^{n^2/4} \\ \text{n even} \\ (a+b)^{n^2} + 2(a+b)(a^4+b^4)^{(n^2-1)/4} \\ (a+b)^{n^2} + 2(a+b)(a^4+b^4)^{(n^2-1)/4} + (a+b)(a^2+b^2)^{(n^2-1)/2} \\ +4(a+b)^n (a^2+b^2)^{(n^2-n)/2} \text{ n odd} \end{cases} \quad \dots (1)$$

Velucchi also considers the nondominating queens problem, which consists of placing "queens on an order "chessboard to leave a maximum number U(n) of unattacked vacant cells. The first few values are 0, 0, 0, 1, 3, 5, 7, 11, 18, 22, 30, 36, 47, 56, 72, 82, ... (Sloane's A001366). The results can be generalized to k queens on an $n \times n$ board.

30.6 15 PUZZLE

1	2	3	4
5	6	7	8
9	10	11	12
13	14	15	

Fig. 30.3. 15 Puzzle Problem

The "15 puzzle" is a sliding square puzzle commonly (but incorrectly) attributed to Sam Loyd. However, research by Slocum and Sonneveld has revealed that Sam Loyd did not invent the 15 puzzle and had nothing to do with promoting or popularizing it. The puzzle craze that was created by the 15 puzzle began in January 1880 in the United States and in April in Europe and ended by July 1880. Loyd first claimed in 1891 that he invented the puzzle, and he continued until his death a 20 year campaign to falsely take credit for the puzzle. The actual inventor was Noyes Chapman, the Postmaster of Canastota, New York, and he applied for a patent in March 1880.

The 15 puzzle consists of 15 squares numbered from 1 to 15 that are placed in a 4×4 box leaving one position out of the 16 empty. The goal is to reposition the squares from a given arbitrary starting arrangement by sliding them one at a time into the configuration shown above. For some initial arrangements, this rearrangement is possible, but for others, it is not.

To address the solubility of a given initial arrangement, proceed as follows. If the square containing the number ^{i}appears "before" (reading the squares in the box from left to right and top to bottom) "numbers that are less than i, then call it an inversion of order^{n}, and denote it n_i. Then define

$$N \equiv \sum_{i=1}^{15} n_i = \sum_{i=1}^{15} n_i$$

where the sum need run only from 2 to 15 rather than 1 to 15 since there are no numbers less than 1 (so n_1 must equal 0). Stated more simply,.N=i (p) is the number of permutation inversions in the list of numbers. Also define to be the row number of the empty square.

2	1	3	4
5	6	7	8
9	10	11	12
13	14	15	

Fig. 30.4. 15 Puzzle Problem Example

Then if N + e is even, the position is possible, otherwise it is not. In other words, if the permutation symbol $(-1)^{i(p)}$of the list is + 1, the position is possible, whereas if the signature is –1, it is not. This can be formally proved using alternating groups. For example, in the arrangement shown above,$n_2 = 1$(2 precedes 1) and all other $n_i = 0$ so N = I and the puzzle cannot be solved.

13	10	11	6
5	7	4	8
1	12	14	9
3	15	2	

Fig. 30.5. 15 Puzzle Problem Example

Similarly, in the above random arrangement of squares, the inversion counts are 12, 9, 9, 5, 4, 4, 3, 3, 0, 3, 3, 2, 1, 1, and 0, giving an inversion sum of 59. Since this number is odd, the above arrangement of the puzzle cannot be solved.

While odd permutations of the puzzle are impossible to solve all even permutations are solvable Despite the assertion of Herstein and Kaplansky that "no really easy proof seems to be known," Archer presented a simple proof. A more general result due to Wilson showed that for any connected graph on "nodes, with the exception of cycle graphs C_n and the thetaO graph, either exactly half or all of the ^{M}-possible labelings are obtainable by sliding labels, depending on whether the graph is bipartite has six inequivalent labelings, while C_n has $(n-2)!$ inequivalent labeling.

Reversing the order of the "8 Puzzle" made on a 3×3 board can be proved to require at least 26 moves, although the best solution requires 30 moves 'The number of distinct solutions in 28, 30, 32,... moves are 0, 10, 112, 512, ... giving 634 solutions better than the 36-move solution given by Dudeney

The maximum number of moves required to solve the n×n generalization of the 15 puzzle for n =1, 2, ... are 0,6, 31,80,...

Solved Questions

1. What is the best case search for a ascending sorted solution?

Ans. $\Omega(n)$.

2. What is descending sorted solution?

Ans. $\Omega(n)$.

3. What is the worst case?

Ans. Recall that a complete tree of height h has $2^{h+1}-1$ nodes, the decision tree for sorting n items has height n. Brute force search of the complete space, $\Theta(2^{n+1})$.

4. Which node(s) does the algorithm back-up to after printing node k?

Ans. All the way to node a.

5. Trace and generate the call tree for the first 4 print executions. Initial call is: preOrderBT(X[])

Ans:

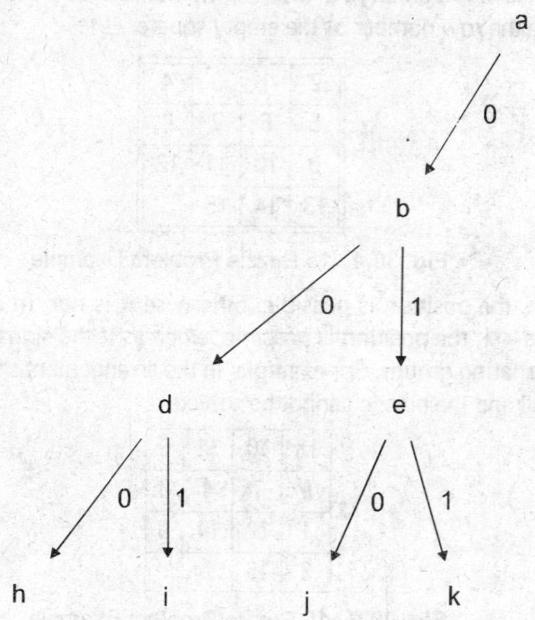

```
DFSbtChange( X[1..i], change )
-- pre: X[1..i] specifies first i components of a solution
-- post: Solution X[1..i]
1. if change = 0 then print X[1..i]
2. else
3. for each x ∈ {25, 10, 5, 1} do
4. if change - x >= 0 then
5. X[i+1] ← x
6. DFSbtChange( X[1..i+1], change - x )
```

6. Give the first solution found for DFSbtChange(X[1..i], 11).

Ans.

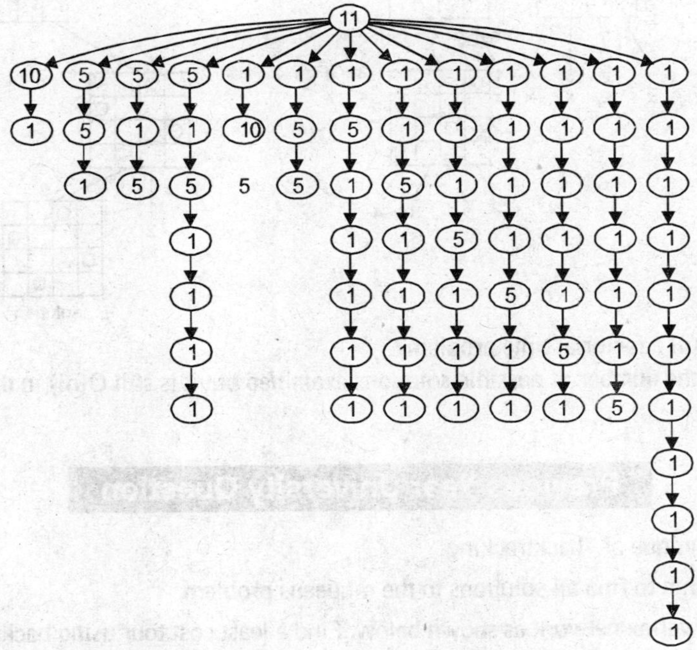

7. Can a Queen be placed anywhere above in row 3 without conflicting?

Ans. No

8. What is the next partial solution after 8?

Ans. Continue to find the next solution.

9. Why not use an arbitrary initial lower bounds of <0+0+0+0> = cost 0?

Ans. Would increase the number of possible solutions explored. Assume all assignments to person a have been made.

The costs of person a would be: a1=9+0+0+0=9, a2=2, a3=3, and a4=8. Exploring a2, would assign b with costs of a2+b1=2+6+0+0=8, a2+b3=2+3=5, a2+b4=2+7=9.

The best lower bound is now a3=3 when, using a more accurate initial lower bound it was 16, we never had to explore assignments other than a2.

10. **Are there any other partial solutions from 6?**

Ans. No, only state 7.

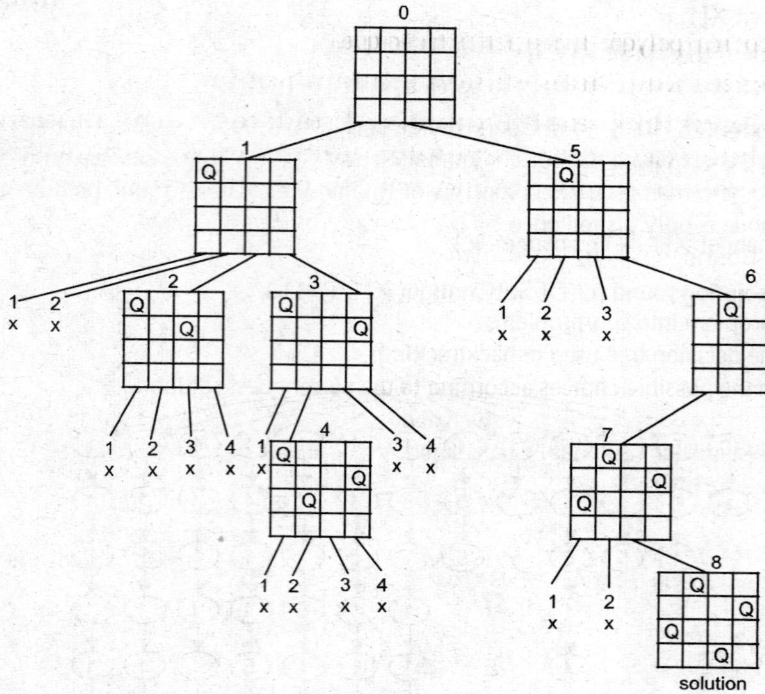

11. **Is assignment still a factorial time problem?**

Ans. We can reduce the number of possible solutions examined but it is still O(n!) in the worst case.

Previous Year University Question

1. Explain the technique of "backtracking. [OU10]
2. Write an algorithm to find all solutions to the n-queens problem. [OU10]
3. Consider a four vertex network as shown below. Find a least cost tour using backtracking method. [GBTU]

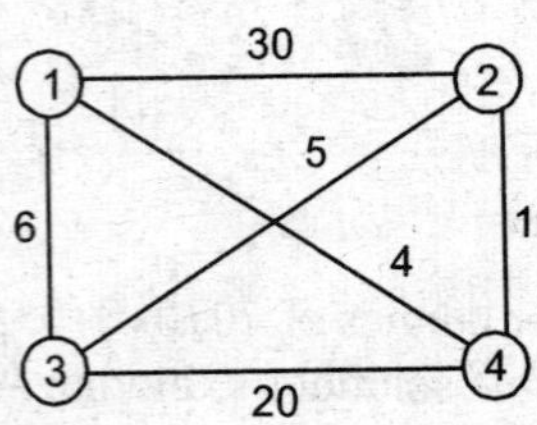

4. What is the sum of subset problem? Let w = {5,7,10,12,15,18,20} and m = 35.
5. Find all possible subsets of w that sum to m using recursive backtracking algorithm for it. Draw the portion of state space tree that is generated. [GBTU]

6. Why are backtracking algorithms called method of last resort? [Madrass University]
7. How many solutions are there to the eight queens problem? How many distinct solutions are there if we do not distinguish solutions that can be transferred into one another by rotations and reflections? [Madrass University]
8. Explain the optimal polygon triangulation technique. [KU]
9. Explain Branch and bound streategy to solve a particular problem. [MDU]

Ans. Branch-and-Bound: Branch-and-Bound divide a problem to be solved into a number of sub-problems, similar to the strategy backtracking. The animation uses the travelling-salesman problem as an example. The travelling-salesman problem comprises of finding the cheapest round path on a weighted graph where each node is only visited once.

Branch-and-Bound:

Basic Idea:

(i) Split the problem into sub-problems.

(Similar to the decision tree used in backtracking)

(ii) Constrain the possible choices according to the current best solution.

For example: If the current costs at a given node exceed the current minimum costs (for minimization) the rest of the sequence need not be calculated.

Travelling-Salesman Problem:

Bounsd = 28

Current costs = 28

Cheapest current round trip : A-D-E-B-C-A

	A	B	C	D	E
A	–	20	30	10	11
B	15	–	16	4	2
C	3	5	–	2	4
D	19	6	18	–	3
E	16	4	7	16	–

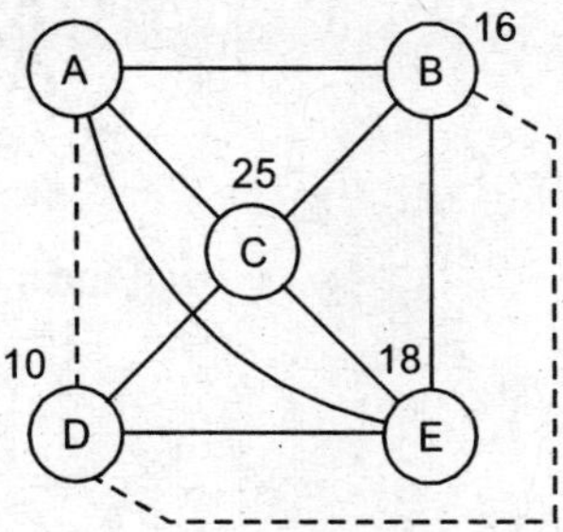

Bound = 28

Current cost = 31 more expensive than cheapest trip

Cheapest curent round trip : A-D-E-B-C-A

10. Discuss Branch and Bound streatigy by solving Travelling Salesman problem for any graph and analyse the time complexity for the same. [MDU]
11. Differentiate between Backtracking and Branch and Bound method. [MDU]
12. Give an algorithm for graph colouring using Backtracking and analyse the time complexity of the same. [MDU]

13. Explain Dynamic Programming method to solve a problem and use the same method to solve the following Travelling salesperson Problem with given distance matrix:

$$\begin{bmatrix} 0 & 5 & 10 & 15 \\ 3 & 0 & 6 & 8 \\ 4 & 12 & 0 & 11 \\ 7 & 7 & 8 & 0 \end{bmatrix}$$

[MDU]

14. What is 0/1 Knapsack problem? Solve this problem using Branch and Bound method taking suitable example. [MDU]
15. What do you understand by Backtracking? Discuss. [MDU]
16. Write backtracking algorithm to find the chromatic number of a given graph. [MDU]
17. Find all Hamiltionian cycles in the following graph using backtracking. [MDU]

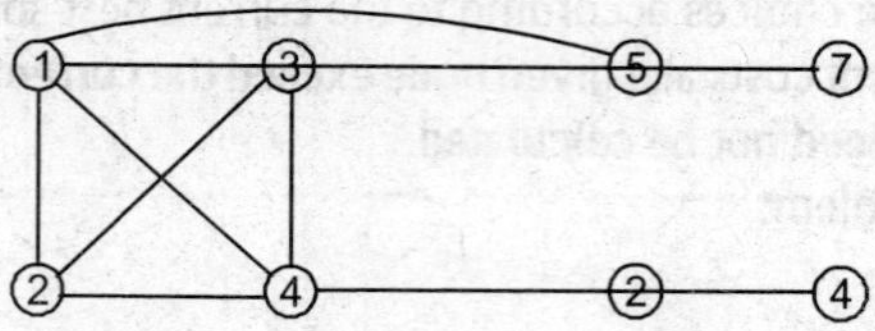

Exercise

1. Run the n-queen's problem for n = 8, 9, 11.
2. Prove $\sum_{i=1}^{16}$ less (i) + x is even in 15-puzzle problem.
3. Prove that running true of n-queen's algorithm is O (p (n!). where P (n) is polynomial is D.

Model Questions

1. Differentiate between Binary and Binary Search Tree.
2. Is 2n+1= O(2n)?
3. What is the worst case running time of Quick Sort?
4. What is the worst case running time of algorithm to delete each element from the linked list?
5. Which is more efficient of BFS and DFS?
6. What are maximum and minimum number of elements in a heap of height h?
7. Where in a heap might the smallest element reside?
8. Differentiate between NP Hard and NP Complete .
9. What is time complexity ?
10. What is space complexity?
11. Give brief concept of Divide and conquer.
12. Write an algorithm to sort an array containing 0's and 1's with complexity of order of n .
13. What is recursion?What are its drawbacks?
14. The order of complexity of Binary Search in Best case is -----in the average case is -------in the worst case is ________
15. If W= MNOP,list all substrings of W.
16. Define the term Divide and Conquer.
17. How does heap Sort work?
18. Explain the backtracking Problem with 4 Queens on a 4 4 chess board.
19. Define non deterministic algorithm.
20. Write an algorithm that will traverse a binary tree level by level. That is root is visited first then the intermediate children of root then grand children of root and so on.
21. What are the advantages of dynamic programming over greedy method?
22. What are the various techniques for design of various algorithms?
23. How the time and space complexities measured for an algorithm?
24. What is the order of Bubble Sort?
25. What are the conditions under which backtracking can be used?
26. What is Optimal Merge Pattern Problem?
27. What is algorithm for in order traversal?

28. What is solution space in Backtracking Techniques ?
29. How will Merge Sort sort the 6 numbers:
    40, 10, 20 , 18, 16,62. by divide and conquer technique.
30. What is Binary Search Tree?
31. What are various steps used in design of an algorithms?Give an example of algorithm which is infinite in nature.
32. What is the order of the computation for the following loop.
    for(i=1,i<n,i+1)
    for(=1, <n, +1)
33. Give the definition for 0/1 knapsack problem.
34. What are the various set operations possible?
35. What is algorithm of Pre Order Traversal.
36. What is NP Hard Problem?
37. What is Ordering Paradigm?
38. Differentiate between full and complete Binary Tree.
39. Write an algorithm for insertion sort. Also give its computing time.
40. What is lower bound?
41. What are explicit and implicit constraints?
42. What is algebraic simplification?
43. How will u represent a polynomial using dense representation strategy.
44. Differentiate between Deterministic and Non Deterministic algorithms.
45. What is Criterion Function ?
46. Define the Principal of Optimality.
47. What are Decision Problems?
48. What is Interpolation of polynomial?
49. Describe an algorithm to insert and delete edges in the ad acency list representation for an undirected graph .Remember that the edge (i,) appears on the ad acency list for both vertex i and
50. Give an algorithm to count number of leaf nodes in a Binary Tree t and what is its computing time
51. Explain basic concepts of NP hard and NP Complete problems.
52. Explain the use of asymptotic notations in the analysis of algorithms
53. What type of operations can be performed on string's .Explain at least 2 operations on strings with algorithms.
54. Write short notes on the following:
    (a) Dynamic Programming
    (b) Branch and Bound
55. What do you mean by Time and space complexity. Among Quick Sort,Insertion Sort ,Heap Sort, Which algorithm is best to sort the data and why?
56. What are the disadvantages of Binary Search algorithm .What will be the order of complexity of a Binary Search in the unsuccessful case
57. Here are 16 integers:
    22 36 6 79 26 45 75 13 31 62 27 76 33 16 62 47 .Sort them using a Quick Sort ,Insertion Sort Heap

Sort,Bin Sort,treating them as a pair of digits in a range of 0-9.

58. Let G be a connected and undirected graph .Write an algorithm to find out minimum number of edges to be added to G so that G becomes disconnected .Your algorithm should output such a set of edges. What are time and space requirements of your algorithm.
59. Explain Merge Sort
60. What is time and space complexity of "Insertion Sort"?Explain.
61. Write an string processing algorithm to identify whether a particular sequence of character is in string or not.
62. What are the various methods or techniques in which various algorithms can be expressed?
63. What is criterion function in backtracking?What is solution space for backtracking problem? Explain by taking sum of subset as a problem
64. What is LC Search. How does it help in finding a solution for Branch and Bound Algorithm.
65. Explain algorithm for evaluating a polynomial in coefficient exponent form.
66. What is 8 Queens problem?How does backtracking helps in solving it.
67. What is Greedy Method ?Write an algorithm for knapsack problem using Greedy Method.
68. What is Optimal Merge Pattern problem. Merge the files (X1,X2....X5)of length 20,30,10,5,30 respectively. Also represent the merge pattern using Binary Tree.
69. Define Principal of Optimality. Explain 0/1 knapsack problem using Dynamic Programming.
70. What is evaluation and interpolation of Polynomials. Explain by giving a suitable example
71. Justify the statement "An optimization problem can be solved in the polynomial time if and only if the corresponding decision problem can."
72. Explain the Big Oh notation used in the analysis of algorithm
73. What is the computing time for the following statement

```
{
for i=1to m do
for i=1 to n do
c[i, ]:= a[i, ]+ b[i, ];
}
```

74. Write an algorithm to delete an element from a linked list .Also mention the worst case running time for this operation.
75. Explain the connected and Biconnected components in Graphs.
76. Explain the tree traversal techniques.
77. Using suitable example explain straightforward evaluation of polynomials
78. Give brief concept of Algebraic Simplification and algebraic transformation
79. Explain the various path traversal techniques with example.
80. Define Algorithm and also explain the different criterion that all algorithms must satisfy.
81. Explain how to validate and analyze the algorithm .
82. Using the recursive algorithm ,explain how the tower of Hanoi problem can be solved. What will be time and space complexity for the algorithms.
83. Algorithm sum(a,n)

```
{
s=0.0;
```

```
for i=1 to n do
s=s+a[i];
return s ;
}
```

84. Explain why we use a asymptotic notation .Also define the following notations
Big Oh Omega Theta
85. Explain an algorithm to insert 5 elements in stack and in a Queue.
86. Explain the different terminologies for tree and graph
87. Explain what do you mean by algebraic problem .Discuss various techniques for algebraic problems.
88. Define Prim's and Kruskal Algorithms
89. Explain Traveling Salesperson Problem
90. What do you mean by dynamic programming .Explain All pairs Shortest Path problem with example
91. Solve 4 Queens Problem using Backtracking
92. What is dynamic Programming. What is Multi Stage Graph Problem
93. What do you mean by sorting .What are various sorting Techniques .Explain any 2.
94. Solve 0/1 knapsack Problem using Greedy Method.
95. Solve 0/1 knapsack Problem using Dynamic Programming.
96. Explain evaluation and interpolation with example.
97. What is NP Hard and NP Complete ?Explain with example.
98. Differentiate between Deterministic and Non Deterministic Algorithms.
99. Explain the algorithm for Quick Sort .On what input does Quick Sort exhibit its worst case behavior
100. What is Multi Stage Graph Problem? How does dynamic problem help in solving it
101. Write short notes on
    (a) Approximation Algorithms
    (b) Combinatorial Algorithms
102. Write an algorithm to find nth minimum and maximum element using divide and conquer strategy
103. What is Traveling Salesperson Problem?.Find the solution of the following Traveling Salesperson Problem? Find the solution of the following salesman problem
104. Calcu late the number of swaps to sort the following data using bubble sort 5, 3, 2, 0, -4, -10, 15, 1
105. Give pictorial representation of each pass.
106. What is criterion function and solution space of Backtracking? Explain and solve four Queen's problem using Backtracking
107. Explain in detail various Set algorithms
108. What is Greedy method? Give general algorithm for it. State and write Knapsack problem using Greedy Method
109. Give State space representation for 4 Queen's problem. Number the nodes as in
    (i) DFS
    (ii) BFS
    (iii) D Search
110. Solve 15 Puzzle Problem using Branch and Bound .Initial arrangement of tiles is given below
111. Prove using the formal definition of Big O,(you need to give a ,c,,n0)

$5n-3=O(n)$

$2n^2+3n+20=O(n^2)$

112. Prove using definition of Omega(you need to give a ,c,,n0)

$3n-10=Omega(n)$

$n^2-5n-20=Omega(n^2)$

113. By taking suitable example explain how the sum of Subset problem can be solved by using Backtracking algorithm design technique.
114. Explain the following algorithm design techniques ;
    (a) Backtracking
    (b) Branch and Bound
    (c) Dynamic Programming
    (d) Divide and Conquer
115. Write and explain the algorithms for Disjoint Set Union if we are given two sets Si and Sj
116. Define Knapsack problem. Solve the following using Knapsack Problem

n=3,m=20

(P1,P2,P3)=(24,25,15)

(W1,W2,W3)=(18,15,10)

117. Define Job Sequencing with Deadlines .Solve the following problem using Job Sequencing with Deadlines:

n=4,(P1,P2,P3,P4)=(100,10,15,27)

(D1,D2,D3,D4)=(2,1,2,1)

118. Define Optimal Storage on Tapes. Solve the following using this technique: n=3, (L1,L2,L3)=(5,10,3)
119. Define Optimal Merge Pattern .Find Optimal Merge pattern for 10 files whose lengths are 28,32,12,5,84,53,91,35,3,11
120. Obtain a set of Optimal Huffman Codes for the messages(M1........M7)with relative frequencies (q1....q7)=(4,5,7,8,10,12,20).Draw the decode tree for this set of codes.
121. Define the Traveling Salesperson Problem .Solve problem using TSP where the edge lengths are given as:

0	10	15	20
5	0	9	10
6	13	0	12
8	8	9	0

122. What do you mean by deterministic and Non Deterministic Algorithms. Differentiate between them. Write example for each of them.
123. Define NP Hard and NP Complete .Represent the relation between them. Prove that P is a subset of NP.
124. What is Clique Decision Problem. Show that clique optimization reduces to clique decision problem.
125. What are approximation Algorithms. Define absolute approximation and Eapproximation with example.
126. What is Algorithm .Write the various performance analysis techniques of Algorithm. Discuss advantages and disadvantages of each
127. What is data structure ?Explain various data structures with examples

128. Write algorithm for Quick Sort using divide and Conquer .
129. What is Divide and Conquer algorithm. Use this algorithm to find maximum and minimum from a given array
130. Write an algorithm for Merge Sort using Divide and Conquer.
131. What do you mean by dynamic programming. Explain multistage Graphs using dynamic Programming
132. What are Strings. What are various String Algorithms. Explain any two of them.
133. Explain 0/1 knapsack problem using any two techniques you know
134. Explain asymptotic notations .Also explain the following notations:
    (a) Big O
    (b) Omega
    (c) Theta
135. What do you mean by complexity of an algorithm .Define time and space complexity with examples
136. Explain various traversal techniques for trees
137. Explain various traversal techniques for graphs
138. What is Backtracking. Explain various problems solved by backtracking
139. What is Backtracking. Solve 8 Queens problem by backtracking
140. Explain various search techniques for trees
141. Explain various search techniques for graphs
142. How sum of subset problem is solved by Backtracking
143. What is graph coloring. Explain it with example .Show that a graph is 4 color able
144. What do you mean by Branch and Bound. Solve 15-puzzle problem
145. Define the following
    (i) LC Search
    (ii) FIFO Branch and Bound
    (iii) LC branch and Bound
146. Define Principle of Optimality .Explain how does it holds on the following problems:
    (i) knapsack
    (ii) Optimal Merge Pattern
    (iii) Shortest Path

(Please Write your Exam Roll No. immediately) **Exam. Roll No. ....**

END-TERM EXAMINATION

Third Semester [MCA] - DECEMBER 2005

Paper Code: MCA 205 **Subject: Design and Analysis of Algorithm**

Time: 3 Hours **(Batch-2004)** **Maximum Marks: 60**

Note: Attempt five questions in all, including Q. 1 which is compulsory.

Q1. (a) Given three functions ($n!$, n^n and 2^{2n}), which has the largest growth rate and which the smallest?

(b) Is merge sort a stable sorting algorithm? Justify your answer. (2)

(c) What is the similarity and difference of dynamic programming and divide-and-conquer? (2)

(d) Will either Kruskal's or Prim's algorithm work correctly on graphs that have negative edge weights? (1)

(e) When a problem is said to be polynomially reducible? (1)

(f) What is an optimal binary search tree? (1)

(g) What is a Huffman tree? (1.5)

(h) What are the time complexities of Quick Sort? (1.5)

Q2. (a) Explain the various asymptotic notations used to analyze an algorithm. (5)

(b) Solve the recurrence relation for the no. of key comparisons made by merge sort in the worst case. (You may assume that $n = 2^k$). (4)

(c) Define Master Theorem. (3)

Q3. (a) Design a (n^2) algorithm for finding an optimal binary search tree. (6)

(b) Consider the problem of scheduling n obs of known duration's t_1, t_2, .. t_n for execution by a single processor. The obs can be executed in any order, one ob at a time. You want to find a schedule that minimizes the total time spent by all the obs in the system. Design a Greedy algorithm for this problem. (The time spent by one ob is the sum of waiting time and execution time). (6)

Q4. Apply Kruskal's algorithm to find a minimum spanning tree of the following graph. (5)

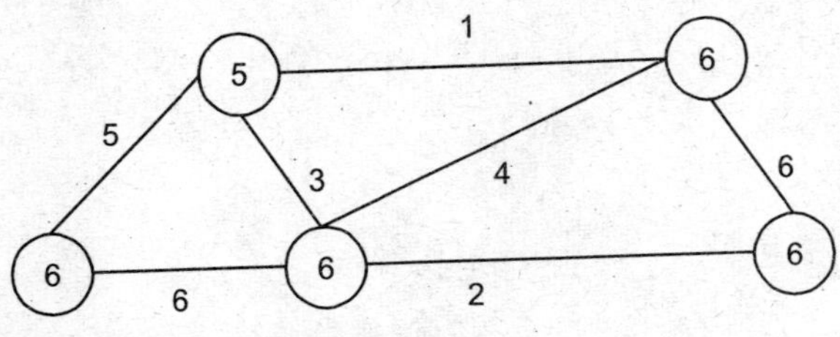

(b) Prove the correctness of Kruskal's algorithm. (5)

(c) Define dis oint subsets. (2)

Q5. (a) Give an O (V+E)-time algorithm to compute the component graph of a directed graph G = (V, E). Make sure that there is at most one edge between two vertices in the component graph your algorithm produces. (6)

(b) Let $Ax \leq b$ be a system of m difference constraints in n unknowns. Show that the Bellman-Ford algorithm, when run on the corresponding constraints graph, maximizes $\sum_{i=1} x_i$ subject to $Ax \leq b$ and $x_i \leq 0$ for all x_i (6)

Q6. (a) Explain Rabin-Karp algorithm for string matching. What is its worst case running time? (6)

(b) What do you mean by string-matching automata? Write a pseudo code to compute the transaction function δ from a given pattern P [1.....m]. (6)

Q7. (a) Show that the class P, viewed as a set of languages, is closed under union, intersection, concatenation, complement. (6)

(b) A clique in an undirected graph G= (V, E) is a subset $V' \subseteq V$ of vertices, each pair of which is connected by an edge in E. The size of a clique is the no. of vertices it contains. The clique problem is the optimization problem of finding a clique of maximum size in a graph. Prove that the clique problem is NP-complete. (6)

Q8. Write notes on following:- (12)

(i) Strassen's algorithm for Matrix Multiplication

(ii) The Knuth-Morris-Pratt algorithm.

(iii) Strongly connected components.

(Please Write your Exam Roll No. immediately) **Exam. Roll No. ....**

END-TERM EXAMINATION

DECEMBER 2006

Paper Code: MCA 205 **Subject: Design and Analysis of Algorithm**

Time: 3 Hours **Maximum Marks: 60**

Note: Attempt all question as directed. All questions have internal choice.

Q1. Attempt any four parts:- (3 × 4=12)

(a) Solve the recurrence relation by iteration $T(n) = T(n-1) + n^4$.

(b) Show that the solution of $T(n) = T(\lceil n/2 \rceil) + 1$ is $0(\log n)$.

(c) Apply quick sort algorithm on the following list 10, 2, 12, 7, 4, 6, 9, 5, 1, 3, 11, 0.

(d) Show that the merge sort algorithm follows divide and conquer paradigm.

(e) Write an algorithm for linear search and find its complexity.

(f) What is stable algorithm?

Q2. Attempt any three parts:- (4 × 3 =12)

(a) Find the longest common subsequence of

Author-affil refers to the affiliation of author

X = <A, B, C, D, A, B>

Y = <B, D, C, A, B, A>

(b) Construct the Huffman codes for first eight Fibonacci number.

(c) Compare dynamic programming and divide and conquer paradigm.

(d) Let n = 5, $(P_1, P_2, \ldots\ldots\ldots, P_5) = (20, 15, 10, 5, 1)$ and $(d_1\text{-}d_5) = (2, 2, 1, 3, 3)$. Find the optimal schedule.

(e) Write three operations and their implementation on disjoint sets.

(f) What is optimal binary search tree?

Q3. Attempt any two parts :- (6 × 2 =12)

(a) Suppose the dimensions of matrices A, B, C, D are 20 x 2, 2 x 15, 15 x 40 and 40 x 4 respectively. What will be the optimum number of scalar multiplications?

(b) Write Dijkstra algorithm to solve single source shortest path problem and analyze its time-complexity.

(c) How the Bellman-ford algorithm is used to detect the presence of negative edge cycle in the given graph?

Q4. Attempt any two parts :- (6 × 2 =12)

(a) Write PRIM's algorithm for finding out minimum spanning tree and derive its complexity.

(b) Use Floyd –Warshall's algorithm to find the shortest path between all pair of vertices in the graph?

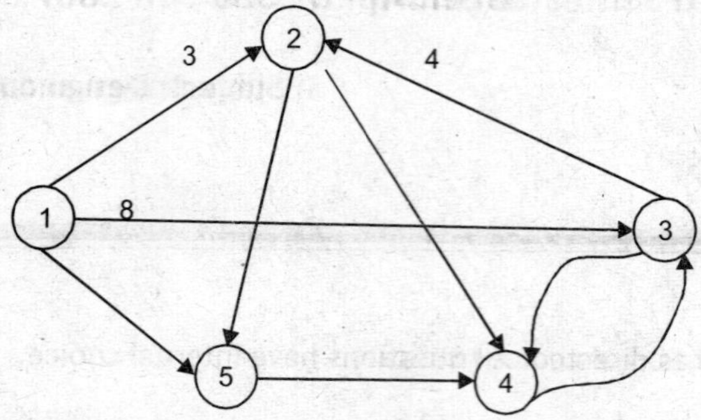

(c) Give the Knuth-Morris-Pratt algorithm for pattern matching. Discuss its performance and failure functions.

Q5.Attempt any two parts :- (6 x 2 =12)

(a) Discuss the Strassen's algorithm for matrix manipulation. Show that two n × n matrices can be in θ ($n^{\log_2 7}$) time..

(b) Prove that satisfiability of Boolean formula in 3-conjunctive normal form (3-CNF) is NP-Complete.

(c) Analyze the time complexity of Rabin-Karp algorithm.

(Please Write your Exam Roll No. immediately) Exam. Roll No. ....

END-TERM EXAMINATION

Third Semester [MCA] - DECEMBER 2007

Paper Code: MCA 205 **Subject: Design and Analysis of Algorithm**

Time: 3 Hours **Maximum Marks: 60**

Note: Attempt all questions. Internal choice I indicated.

Q1. (i) Discuss time complexity of quick sort.

(ii) Define dynamic programming.

(iii) I merge sort a stable sorting algorithm? Justify your answer.

(iv) Define optional binary search tree.

(v) What o you mean by Huffman codes?

(vi) What is string matching?

(vii) When a problem is said to be polynomially reducible? Discuss briefly.

(viii) What do you mean by recurrences?

(ix) Define spanning tree.

(x) What is divide-and –conquer problem?

Q2 (a) Develop and describe an algorithm for quick sort.

(b) What is merge sort? How is it useful and? Explain briefly.

OR

Explain the following briefly:

(i) Data structures for disjoint sets

(ii) Strassen's algorithm for Matrix Multiplications

Q3. Differentiate between simple programming and dynamic programming in detail with their Relative merits, demerits, use and applications through suitable examples.

OR

Describe the following briefly:

(i) Greedy algorithms

(ii) Matrix Chain Multiplication

UNIT-II

Q4. Describe Kruskal's algorithm to find a minimum spanning tree of a graph and also prove its Correctness.

OR

Explain the following briefly:

(i) Prim's algorithm for finding minimum cost spanning trees

(ii) Floyed-Warshall algorithm for all pair shortest paths

UNIT-IV

Q5. What is finite automata? How string matching can be implemented through it? Explain in detail with examples.

OR

Write short notes on the following:

(i) Knuth-Morris Pratt algorithm

(ii) NP-Complete problem

(Please Write your Exam Roll No. immediately) **Exam. Roll No. ....**

END-TERM EXAMINATION

Third Semester [MCA] - DECEMBER 2008

Paper Code: MCA 205 **Subject: Design and Analysis of Algorithm**
Paper Id-44205 **(Batch-2004)**
Time: 3 Hours **Maximum Marks: 60**

Note: Q.1 Is compulsory. Attempt any four questions from the rest

Q1. Different between complexity of an algorithm and that of a problem. (3)

(b) Show that linear search is of order O(n) (4)

(c) Dijkshra's algorithm to find shortest path between a pair of nodes in a graph is a greedy algorithm Justify the statement (3)

(d) Illustrate with an example that quick short is as good as bubble sort in some situation (3)

(e) Draw a finite automata that find matching (first occurrences) of the substring 'abbac' over Σ {a, bc,d,e,} over (4)

(f) Create a binary surch tree for the element (10,6 18,8,16 20 4) (3)

Q2. (a) Prove that a sorting algorithm cannot be faster than O(n logn). (5)

(b) Show that finding minimum and maximum in a list of n items can be accomplished using $\frac{3n}{2}-2$ comparisons. (5)

Q3. (a) What is separate chaining? Show that average searching time for successful search using separate chaining is $1+\frac{\alpha}{2}$ where a is load factor in hashing. (5)

(b) The general form of the master theorem is given as T(n) = aT(n/b+ f(n) Explain the meaning of term n, a, b and f(n). Solve the equation for the case when a = b and f(n) = kn. (5)

Q4 (a) Construct on optimal binary search tree for the following items having corresponding proobailitics gives in the table below. (6)

Items	1	2	3	4	5
Prob	0.24	0.22	0.23	0.3	0.01

(b) Find time complexity of the following program segments: (4)

```
abs (int n)
    {
    If (n=1) return –1:
    If (n = =1)return 1:
    else return (n+abc(n–1)):
    }
```

Q5. Write code to topologically sort a directed graph by repeatedly finding a vertex of in- degree 0 and deleting it from the graph. Make sure your algorithm runs in at most $\theta(n^2)$ time. (6)

(b) Give a big-oh upper bound on the running time of the far-loop that includes Function f(n) whose big-oh upper bound is O(f(n)) (4)

for (int i=1: 1<=n: i++)

f(n):

Q6. (a) Show that recurrence equitation $a_n = a_{n/2} + 1$: $a_1 = 1$ corresponds to binary search. Solve the recurrence equation to prove that it is $O(\text{long}_2 n)$. (4)

(b) Write algorithm to determine whether an undirected graph is biconnected or not. Explain the term 'articulation point' (6)

Q7. Write short notes on any two of the following:- (2×5=10)

(a) NP-hard complexity class

(b) Order Statistics

(Please Write your Exam Roll No. immediately) **Exam. Roll No. ....**

END-TERM EXAMINATION

Third Semester [MCA] - DECEMBER 2009

Paper Code: MCA 205 **Subject: Design and Analysis of Algorithm**

Time: 3 Hours **Maximum Marks: 60**

Note: Q1 which is compulsory. Attempt one question from each Unit.

Q1. (a) Differentiate between quick sort and mergesort algorithms. (2)

(b) Find the maximum and minimum element in an array with minimum complexity. (3)

(c) Differentiate between Divide and Conquer and Dynamic programming. (2)

(d) Give algorithm for native string matching. (2)

(e) Find complexity of $\sum_{i=1}^{n} i^3$. . (2)

(f) Explain P, NP and NP complete. (3)

(g) Find strongly connected components for the following figure: (2)

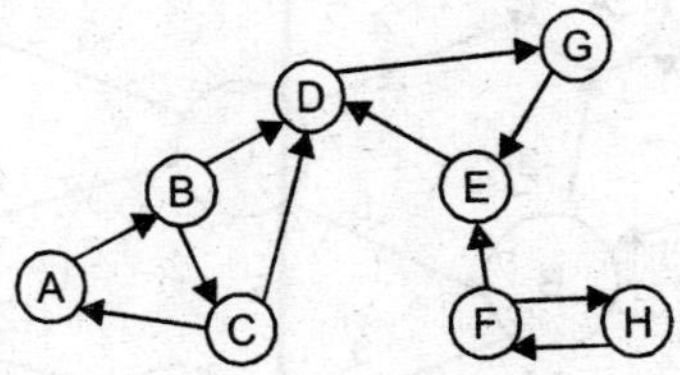

(h) Find spanning tree for the following figure:- (2)

(i) Solve using Strassen's Matrix multiplication method. (2)

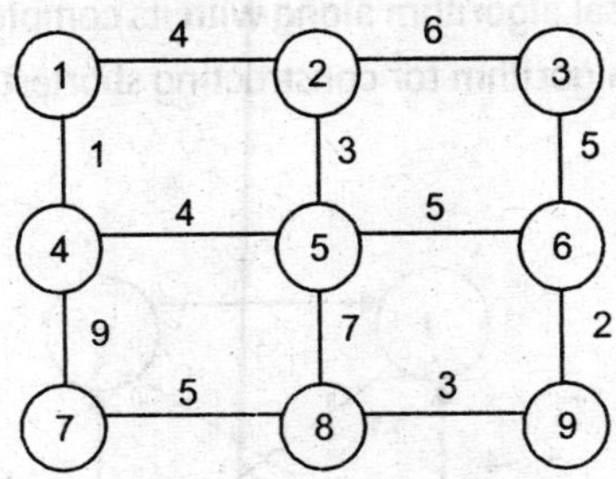

$$\begin{pmatrix} 1 \\ 3 \end{pmatrix} * \begin{pmatrix} 2 & 1 \\ 1 & 2 \end{pmatrix}$$

UNIT-I

Q.2. (a) Solve $T(n) = 2T(n/4) + \sqrt{n}$ for $T(1) = 1$. (4)

(b) Show how to multiply the complex numbers (a+bi) and (c+di) using only three real multiplications. (6)

Q.3 (a) Solve $T(n) = T(n/2) + T(n/4) + T(n/8) + n$ for $T(1) = 1$. (5)

(b) Give algorithm with complexity for selection in expected linear time. (5)

UNIT-II

Q.4 (a) Explain Matrix Chain Multiplication using dynamic programming. (5)

(b) Find the Huffman code for (5)

Variables	A	B	C	D	E	F	G	H
Frequencies	0.25	0.25	0.14	0.14	0.055	0.055	0.055	0.055

Q.5 (a) Find the LCS of ABCDABCD and BCDADCB. (5)

(b) Give the iterative algorithm with complexity for Activity Selection Problem. (5)

UNIT-III

Q6 (a) Find the shortest path from S to F for the following figure: (5)

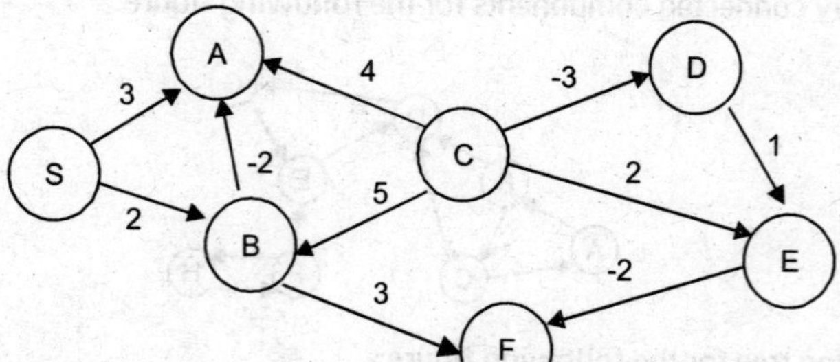

(b) Give Breath first traversal algorithm along with its complexity. (5)

Q.7 (a) Apply Floyd Warshall algorithm for constructing shortest path for the Following figure, showing the matrix. (5)

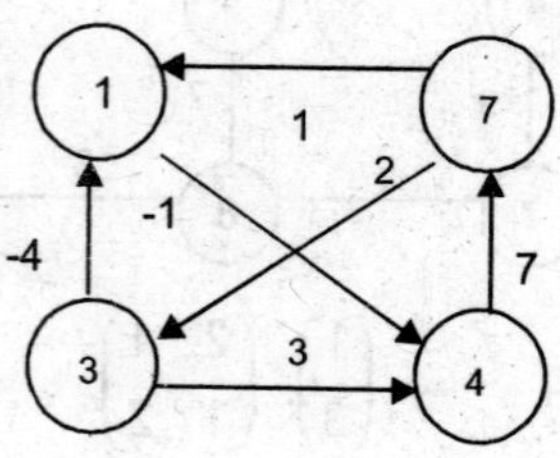

(b) Give Dijkastra algorithm along with its complexity. (5)

UNIT-IV

Q.8 (a) Construct the string matching automation for the pattern P=ababcab and Illustrate its operation on the text string T=aaababababcababccab. (5)

(b) Prove that vertex cover problem is NP-complete. (5)

Q9 (a) Compute the prefix function (KMP method) for the pattern ababbabbabbababbabb when the alphabet is $\Sigma=\{a,b\}$. (5)

(b) Prove that 3-satisfiability is NP-complete. (5)

(Please Write your Exam Roll No. immediately) **Exam. Roll No. ....**

END-TERM EXAMINATION

IV Semester [B.Tech.] - February 2012

Paper Code: ETCS 204 **Subject: Algorithms Analysis and Design**

Time: 3 Hours **Maximum Marks: 30**

Note: Q1 which is compulsory & any two more questions from remaining.

Q1. (a) What is the worst case complexity of selection sort & how it is different from the worst case complexity of insertion sort. (2)

(b) Distinguish between Big O notation & small o notation. (2)

(c) If $f(n) = a_0 + a_1 n + a_2 n^2 + ... + a_{m-1} n^{m-1} + a_m n^m$ then prove that $f(n) = O(n^m)$. (2)

(d) Prove that $(n+a)^b = O(n^b)$ for any real constants a & b, where b > 0. (2)

(e) Prove that $Log\ n! = O\,(n \log n)$ (2)

Q.2. (a) How Strassen's Matrix Multiplication has improved the complexity of Matrix Multiplication? What are the disadvantages of Strassen's algorithm? (4)

(b) Write down quick sort algorithm & find out the worst case time complexity of Quick Sort. (6)

Q.3. (a) Write the algorithm for finding longest common subsequence. (4)

(b) Compute the optimal parenthesization for matrix multiplication operation for the matrix chain $P_{3*_I} Q_{5*4} R_{4*5} S_{5*3}$. (6)

Q.4. Solve the following recurrences

(a) $T(n) = 3T(n/4) + n \log n$ use Master's Method. (2.5)

(b) $T(n) = T(n/4) + T(n/8) + T(n/16)$ use Recursion Tree Method. (2.5)

(c) $T(n) = 2T(\sqrt{n}) + 1$ (2.5)

(d) Devise an algorithm which can simultaneously obtain min & max element from the given set of elements. (2.5)